To my father and mother, who lived through it.

Contents

Acknowledgements

I am deeply grateful to those who have made it possible for me to extend my research to the private collections of documents cited in this book; notably to Mrs Stephen Lloyd for permission to see her father's diaries and letters; also to Lady White and Mr Tristan Jones, Lord Caldecote, Lady Vansittart, Captain S. W. Roskill, Dr Brian Bond and Pall Mall Press (Diary of Major-General Pownall), and the Syndics of the Cambridge University Library. I acknowledge my debt to the Comptroller of the Stationery Office for permission to quote from the state papers deposited in the Public Records Office.

My particular gratitude is due to Professor Martin Wight, Professor F. S. Northedge, Dr Klaus Hildebrand, and Mr Christopher Thorne who read part or all of the manuscript and made many helpful criticisms and suggestions. The opinions advanced below are, however, my own.

I acknowledge my debt to the following publishers and authors in quoting from works of which they hold the copyright: Butterworth and Co Ltd for *Step by Step* by Sir Winston Churchill; Cassell and Co Ltd for *Memoirs* by the Earl of Woolton and *Munich 1938* by Keith Robbins; Cassell and Houghton Mifflin Co for *Facing the Dictators* by the Earl of Avon; William Collins Sons and Co for the *Diplomatic Diaries of Oliver Harvey* edited by John Harvey and *Nine Troubled Years* by Viscount Templewood; Collins and Dodd Mead and Co for *Fullness of Days* by the Earl of Halifax; Constable and Co Ltd for *The Ironside Diaries 1937–40* edited by R. Macleod and D. Kelly; Victor Gollancz Ltd for *Vansittart in Office* by Ian Colvin; Hamish Hamilton for *The Life of Halifax* by the Earl of Birkenhead; Rupert Hart-Davis Ltd for *Old Men Forget* by Alfred Duff Cooper; Hutchinson Ltd for *Geoffrey Dawson and Our Times* by J. E. Wrench; Macmillan and Co Ltd and Macmillan Inc for *The Life of Neville Chamberlain* by Sir Keith Feiling, *Lord Lothian* by J. R. M. Butler and *Munich, Prologue to Tragedy* by Sir John Wheeler-Bennett; Macmillan and Co Ltd and Harper and Row for *Tides of Fortune* by Sir Harold Macmillan; Oxford University

Press and Harvard University Press for *American Appeasement 1933–8* by Arnold Offner; Royal Institute of International Affairs and Fertig, Howard Inc for *The Speeches of Adolf Hitler 1922–39* edited by N. H. Baynes; Royal Institute of International Affairs and Harper and Row for *The Challenge to Isolation 1937–40* by W. L. Langer and S. E. Gleason; George Weidenfeld and Nicolson Ltd and Houghton Mifflin Co for *The Appeasers* by Martin Gilbert and Richard Gott; Ziff Davis Publishing Co for *Triumph of Reason* by Pierre Cot; F. S. Northedge for his article in *International Affairs*, January 1970.

Finally, I should like to thank Mr Andrew Hardman for his helpful assistance; the staff of the Public Record Office for their courtesy and help; and Mrs R. G. Coffin, who, as usual, managed to reduce an untidy manuscript to order.

List of Abbreviations

CID	Committee of Imperial Defence
DBFP	*Documents on British Foreign Policy*
DGFP	*Documents on German Foreign Policy*
DPRC	Defence Policy and Requirements Committee
DRC	Defence Requirements Committee
FPC	Foreign Policy Committee
FRUS	*Foreign Relations of the United States*
SDP	Sudeten German Party (Sudeten deutsche Partei)

Introduction

So long as a balance of power exists in the world, British foreign policy in 1937–9 will be a matter of controversy. Appeasement, as defined by the Chamberlain Government in 1938, has usually been taken as the nadir of British weakness, yet it has also been seen as an inevitable consequence of the British predicament, a realistic attempt to hold the dictators at bay in Europe. So much has been written since 1938 that the subject has acquired a specialised historiography of its own. Knowledge of Czech, Polish, Italian and Yugoslav sources has become, for the historian of international affairs, a necessary supplement to the better-known British, German and American documents. Some apology should therefore be given for a book which not only adds to the number, but concentrates almost entirely on one single aspect of the story.

The questions from which this book grew originated in an earlier study of British policy in the period 1933–6.[1] A coherent policy towards Germany had emerged, between the failure of the League of Nations' Disarmament Conference in 1934 and the end of 1936, which can best be described as the search for an Anglo-German détente backed by the use of an efficient bomber air force as a deterrent, in the modern sense. After the retirement of Ramsay MacDonald in 1935 and the succession of Stanley Baldwin as Prime Minister, this policy extended broadly through the Government's policy-making machine – Cabinet, Foreign Office, military advisers and civilian departments – and it fitted adequately the strategic and diplomatic commitments to France and Belgium under the 1925 Locarno Pact. At the same time, it represented as direct an involvement in the problem of European security as the Dominions of the Commonwealth could accept.

Foreign policy in other tense areas of the world had been accommodated to the prior aim of such a détente ever since the highly important report of the Defence Requirements Committee in 1934 had pinpointed Germany as the ultimate threat to Britain's security. Thus there had been attempts to come to terms with Japan in the Far East, or to work out a policy of containment with the United States; some of the strategic problems of the Middle East, especially the Suez Canal, had been settled by the 1936 Treaty with Egypt; and the Government of India Act in 1935 appeared to have safeguarded the future of India as the first non-white Dominion. To some extent also, the Baldwin Government had bolstered up its policy towards Germany by a search for allies within Europe – by the creation of the Stresa Front in April 1935 and by overtures to Russia in the same year.

Neville Chamberlain's foreign policy, after he became Prime Minister in 1937, appears from a study of the Cabinet archives to have been a much more radical departure from this earlier tradition than has usually been described. To begin with, although he had been Chancellor of the Exchequer for the previous five years, he imposed a ready-made comprehensive policy which had scarcely altered since he had first attacked the Baldwin line in 1934. His sense of urgency combined with his masterful running of a largely subservient Cabinet to produce an almost unique situation in modern British government in which both Foreign Office and military advisers were subordinated to a process of decision-making by a small inner group. At the same time, Treasury criteria and a system of rationing were imposed on the rearmament programme. The deterrent was abandoned in favour of a defensive strategy intended only to repel a direct German attack on Britain. The fighter strength of the air force was built up at the expense of the bomber strike force, in order to meet the much-feared 'knock-out blow', and the Army's Field Force, promised for the defence of north-east France and Belgium, was pared down into insignificance.

The logical consequence was a curious blend of withdrawal from Europe and heightened sensitivity to possible causes of European war. The onus was laid on the Foreign Office to come to terms with less urgent threats in the world – Italy or Japan. As Lord Halifax, Foreign Secretary after February 1938, said: 'Diplomacy must bear the burden of diminishing Britain's enemies.'[2] Thereafter the Government hoped to be free to make more positive overtures to Germany to appease her grievances and reach a settlement on the basis not of fear by deterrence but of mutual interests and separate spheres of influence. Britain pledged herself to the unilateral settlement of the trouble centres of middle Europe – as defined by Germany: Austria, Czechoslovakia, Danzig. As a by-product, the entente with France was allowed to cool.

A much fuller explanation of this transformation is needed in order to understand how, after only fourteen months of Chamberlain's premiership, the British found themselves represented at the Munich Conference in September 1938. Equally, an appreciation of the underlying continuities within British policy is needed to explain the bizarre circumstances in which Britain sought first to undermine the security of Czechoslovakia and then to prop up that of the ramshackle territory of Poland.

The question of British motivation has been dealt with many times before, at great length, and in Britain by two separate schools of historians, one emphasising Hitler's long-term plan for world domination, the other concentrating on the pragmatic nature of German policy, the limits of Hitler's power and the ineptitude of Western diplomacy.[3] The nub of debate lies both in the evaluation of Hitler's intentions – whether he determined on war as an instrument of policy, or whether he took advantage of the opportunities offered by Western leaders and blundered into the conflict of 1939 – and in the intention behind policy formation in Britain and France. So much polemic literature has been produced that the public image of 'appeasement' is rooted in popular mythology as a symbol of feeble abrogation of power. With a few notable exceptions, the limits of British power, the constrictions imposed by military weakness, overseas commitments, the policy of the Dominions and the isolationism of the United States have not been taken fully into account. The opening of the British archives to 1939 under the thirty-year rule now makes possible a fuller analysis of how the Chamberlain Government understood the international situation and what they tried to do. Given the detailed studies of German foreign policy, available in recent years, the two can be set side by side and tentative conclusions can be drawn about the likelihood of success, either for the Cabinet's policy or, hypothetically, for the alternatives which were rejected.

What follows is intended only as a preliminary comment on British policy in the light of the new documents available

about the process of policy formation itself. The published
Documents on British Foreign Policy (London, HMSO) show
the diplomatic machine at work, the inflow of information, and
the transmission of the decisions of the Government. But they
do not usually give the memoranda which would show how
policy was made in the Foreign Office; and, more important,
they are not evaluated. In the whole government machine, the
Foreign Office is only a part. Powerful though the Foreign
Secretary has always been, he is not the only arbiter in foreign
affairs, and the balance between him and the Prime Minister
and Cabinet shifted many times in the inter-war years. To decide
the importance of any messages from an embassy or foreign
mission, we need to know whether they reached the Cabinet in
the form in which they were written, or whether they were
transmitted by the Foreign Secretary as part of a general
survey. To take a specific example: where the reports from
Sir Nevile Henderson, Ambassador in Berlin, concerning Hitler's
preparations for war against Czechoslovakia in September 1938
conflicted with those of the Military Attaché, Colonel Mason
MacFarlane, whose were presented most directly to the Cabinet?
Of the messages sent out instructing action: did they originate
in the Cabinet, an inner group, in discussions between Prime
Minister and Foreign Secretary, or on the initiative of the
Foreign Office itself? All the diplomatic sources must be read
with some idea in mind of the style of the Government and
the details of how fundamental decisions were made.

The second weakness of the published sources is that they are
largely diplomatic. The history of strategic planning has been
kept separate – with unfortunate effects, for the two are insepar-
able. The major review of defence policy and preparations
begun during the spring of 1937, when Chamberlain took over
this responsibility from Baldwin, had repercussions on British
freedom of action in international affairs down to the time
defence was again reviewed in March 1939. The form of defence
expenditure and the balance between the three Services
influenced not only the type of foreign policy which was
regarded as possible but it suggested, even dictated, what was
desirable.

The opening of the Cabinet minutes and the sometimes more
important minutes of Cabinet committees, such as the Foreign
Policy Committee or the Committee on Czechoslovakia, as well

as the Committee of Imperial Defence, provides few revelations in the obvious sense, but enables the historian to see the total nature of British policy and to judge it on a broader basis. The planning of an initiative like the overture to Mussolini late in 1937 was made with the defence situation in mind, not merely in the Mediterranean but in the Far East; and it took account of the Service estimates, the maintenance of a policy of balanced budgets, and the likely response of trade unions to demands for transfer of skilled labour. When judging one policy against another, the historian must know which courses were not open at all, either because of the cost to the economy or the adverse weight of public opinion.

Policy can only be based on information. The Cabinets of the 1930s were short of intelligence about the political state of Germany and the Cabinet papers reveal how, partly empirically and partly by what can only be described as intuition, the Government made up its mind on such crucial questions as the balance between moderates and extremists among the German leaders, or the likelihood of a German response to overtures promising colonies or the transfer of the Sudeten German areas of Czechoslovakia. Likewise, they suggest how information was evaluated and what type of presentation was most likely to influence different ministers.

In addition, the Cabinet papers emphasise obscure but important factors. The attitude of the Dominions towards new British commitments in Europe was made harshly clear at the Imperial Conference in 1937. Thereafter the opinions of Canada, South Africa and, to a lesser extent, Australia were cast against any extra involvement which might weaken the ability of the mother country to defend the Atlantic and the Pacific. Fear of the break-up of the Empire was not the least of the pressures narrowing the Government's freedom of action, up to and including September 1939.

In the absence of the French diplomatic documents it has always been hard to assess the British relationship with the second partner in the Munich settlement. The Cabinet papers show only too clearly the British attitude and, though one-sided, they explain much of what appeared to British observers, then and later, to be mere vacillation on the part of France's political leaders.

But the greatest value of the Government archives is that

they reveal the mechanism of policy-formation as it was under Baldwin and as it became under Chamberlain. It becomes easier to understand the complexity of the process when the different advice fed into it from many sources inside government can be evaluated, when the flavour of personalities, the hierarchy of ministers and the existence of an opposition within the Cabinet can be described. In particular, the strange position taken by the Foreign Secretaries, Eden and Halifax, becomes clearer and the influence, if any, of pressure groups outside the curtilage of Whitehall can be assessed. Taken together with the number of private collections of documents now available, a reasonably coherent description of policy-formation is possible – a working model which is generally valid for the period, and which can be tested empirically by the behaviour of the Government during the six months after Munich.

Of the private collections used here, Chamberlain's manuscript diary and his letters to his two sisters, Ida and Hilda, which he wrote in longhand almost every week of his political life, are the most important. They were utilised only with extreme discretion by his two biographers, Sir Keith Feiling and Iain Macleod. The papers of Sir Samuel Hoare and Sir Robert Vansittart, and Sir Thomas Inskip's manuscript diary, though not so definitive as the official papers, are less inhibited and make plain the influence and interaction of personalities – showing how far the Chamberlain Government broke with the existing traditions of British policy during 1937, and also, despite well-known exceptions, how greatly this was based on consensus within the Cabinet.

This study is orientated from the point of view of the Cabinet and is therefore deliberately selective in its inquiry into the immense archives of the Foreign Office. A limited number of examples have been used to show the divisions among officials, the effect these had within the Office on the general evolution of policy towards Germany, and what was the impact on successive Foreign Secretaries of multiple conclusions drawn from the same information. An attempt has been made to suggest what overall influence the Office retained in the later period of the Chamberlain system, and also the balance which the Cabinet held between the advice of diplomats and the military experts. The regular reports and minutes of the Committee of Imperial Defence and especially the Chiefs of Staff sub-committee show what questions the Cabinet asked, and what underlying strategic assumptions were shared by all. It is less easy to chart the accuracy or effectiveness of information passed into the machine by the Secret Service, whose archives have not been opened up, although some of their memoranda were occasionally included in Foreign Office summaries for the Cabinet.

In this type of inquiry some sources are of limited value. Because of their attitude to public opinion and because, in the nature of their plans, it was inexpedient for ministers to say in public what they were attempting to do in private, *Hansard* and press reports of public speeches are better sources of information about the critics of the Government than of the real nature of Government policy. Peripheral sources, such as the papers of Lord Lothian, Gilbert Murray, Lord Cecil of Chelwood or George Lansbury, tend to show the advice showered on ministers rather than the advice they actually sought. Like the notables outside the Government, most backbench MPs, the Parliamentary Opposition and the Press appear to have made little impact on decisions during the Chamberlain Government. Estimates made from Cabinet discussion and Foreign Office memoranda may be one-sided, but they suggest that, whereas the influence of prominent members of the Conservative Party was substantial, that of others grew less the further they stood from political power. Chamberlain's Cabinet was more sensitive to the political realities of the party system than to pressure groups beyond the House of Commons. In any case, although public opinion was often spoken of by ministers, the thing they believed it to be bore little relation to reality, quite apart from the fact that on the personality of the Prime Minister whose supremacy in these matters was almost undisputed, public opinion, however defined, made little impression.

Cabinet minuting can err. It is usually prepared and carefully tailored, not for the future, but for the next meeting which has to work on distinct decisions made the week before. Sometimes the process of smoothing down acerbities of discussion can be seen in private diaries. There was no Thomas Jones writing his diary in 1938, and Sir Maurice Hankey, who also kept a private record, retired several months before Munich. Inskip's diary covers too short a period to act as a firm check. But in the case of Cabinet committees and most Cabinet meetings, ministers' discussion is given at length and it is hard to read all their debates over three years without discovering the balance between them, the social composition of the Cabinet, the preponderance of the Prime Minister, his relations with his Foreign Secretaries, and the reasons for the choice of an inner group.

Having confined the book to the study of the process of government, and relied most heavily on Government archives, there is a danger that the conclusion might be one which the Government itself would have wished to perpetuate. I have tried to avoid the temptation of saying that because there were very good reasons for not taking action other than what was done the Government was necessarily correct.

A definitive study of policy formation would have to utilise the methods of operational research as well as the definitions of social anthropology. However, a plain historical analysis may be of value in deciding whether appeasement* was the product of rational deliberation or panic-stricken awareness of Britain's weakness; whether it was shaped or not by the coercion of allies and the response, or lack of response, from France, the Dominions and the United States; whether it was the result of inter-departmental argument, and, if so, how far Foreign Office, Treasury or armed Services respectively were responsible; whether credible alternatives existed and were discussed, and why they were rejected. An attempt to answer these questions may illustrate Britain's peculiar position in the world in the late 1930s – a nation still expected to exercise power in defence of global interests within a system which could scarcely work without the co-operation of America and Russia, where, by her own involvement and past history, Britain nevertheless became the principal opponent of the European dictatorships; whose Government tried for three years to find an alternative to war and failed.

KEITH MIDDLEMAS
University of Sussex, 1971

* Throughout, the word 'appeasement' is taken to mean the policy of meeting German demands and grievances without asking for firm reciprocal advantages; asking instead only for future 'mutual understanding'. The offer of a colonial settlement which was made in March 1938, and the policy towards Czechoslovakia, which culminated at Munich, both fall into this category; the 1935 negotiations for a Western air pact, and the Anglo-German Naval Treaty, which bound Germany down to a fixed ratio of warships, do not.

1 Britain and Germany in the 1930s

A nation on the long path of adjustment between holding the balance of world power in its own interests and the attempt to preserve what it still holds against other greater powers must pay peculiar attention to the creation of its foreign policy. One must be evolved which takes precisely into account the balance between power and aims, because diplomacy alone is unavailing if it is not backed by military or economic strength. The intangible factor of moral or traditional influence is not renewable.

A clear formulation of global policy was hard to make at any moment between 1918 and 1939, because of Britain's mixture of inherited assumptions from the nineteenth century and twentieth-century difficulties. Nevertheless, because of the fact that her resources and influence were declining in relation to Germany, the United States, Russia and Japan, and because of her economic dependence on overseas trade, Britain had a stake in the continued preservation of the existing order greater than that of any other major power. This generalisation had a sharp relevance in any comparison between the 1930s and the pre-1914 world. The National Government, after its formation in 1931, was continually preoccupied with the thinness of the veneer of British prosperity. The advocacy of rearmament was always opposed by arguments about the maintenance of Britain's economic position. Having seen the effects of the Depression, the German inflation of the 1920s, and the chaotic aftermath of the First World War, Ministers were hypersensitive to what was at risk if stability were lost.

Dependence on the maintenance and steady growth of the international economy extended beyond the mere numerical calculation of imports and exports. Britain lived by trade and had not been a self-supporting economy since the early nineteenth century but, even more, she depended on a stable international situation, exchange rates and the responsible financial policies of other nations. Between the end of the First

World War and the restoration of the Gold Standard in 1925, it had been a cardinal aim of British policy to restore economic security to Europe; to stabilise the fluctuating exchanges, to settle inter-allied debts and to place reparations on a level which would permit the financial resurrection of Central Europe.

Admittedly, after the panic of 1931 and in response to the Depression, it was Britain who first abandoned the Gold Standard and by the policy of protection followed the United States' lead in the economic *sauve qui peut* which followed. But the fact that world trade then fell by one third from its high peak of 1928 was taken to emphasise the precarious nature of the terms for British survival. War, as 1914–18 had shown, was the greatest disaster which could happen to a trading nation. Markets had been lost or taken by others, vast debts had piled up internally and abroad, overseas investments had been liquidated, patterns of trade and the balance of payments had been distorted. At home, industry had been converted to a war economy, an enormous loss in terms of peace-time aims; resources, both in men and material, had been squandered; and a whole social revolution had occurred which, to Conservative politicians in the 1930s, seemed to have been the major source of many of the inter-war discontents. Among the far-sighted at home and in the United States and in some parts of the Empire, such as India, there was speculation as to whether Britain could in any recognisable form survive the impact of another world war.

The central principle of British policy was to avoid any disruption of the existing order. To prevent shifts in the balance among great powers and to reconcile local difficulties and tensions was the constant aim of the Foreign Office. If peace anywhere were threatened, Britain could not ignore it. Possession of an empire made for strategic weakness rather than strength as a third force counterbalancing Germany and the United States. The Dominions were never united in an imperial foreign policy and were only rarely sympathetic to the European involvement of Britain, yet they represented liabilities which had to be defended. Since none of the widely separated Dominions could have stood up to aggression by a major power, imperial defence was more of a burden than a reassurance. Britain, therefore, became the broker of international affairs, prime advocate of the view of the League of Nations once

expressed by Lloyd George as 'machinery capable of readjusting
and correcting possible mistakes',[1] chief instrument for rewriting the provisions of the Versailles settlement, and downgrading
the burden of reparations payments. Revision of the latter by
agreement in 1924, 1929 and 1932 was regarded by both
Labour and Conservative governments as a triumph of inter-war
diplomacy. Indeed, in the words of a Foreign Office memorandum of 1935, 'from the earliest years following the war, it was
our policy to eliminate those parts of the Peace Settlement
which, as practical people, we knew to be untenable and
indefensible'.[2] What was to be feared was violent change, the
forcing of frontiers, conquest, whether this was Turkey's growth
in the Middle East, the Italian seizure of Corfu, the Japanese
invasion of Manchuria or the remilitarisation of the Rhineland.
There was what F. S. Northedge calls 'a basic Conservatism in
regard to the prevailing international order, appropriate to a
wealthy contented Power, with a larger stake in the external
world than it was in fact able to defend, and apprehensive as
to the effect on its accumulated interests of violence or revolutionary change almost anywhere'.[3]

Steadily, after the Locarno Pact and the halcyon period of
1925–9, British foreign policy came to resemble the act of a
man juggling too many plates in the air, worn down by the
strain of balancing inadequate resources against successive commitments, in crises too frequent to allow time to recover poise.
What was intended to be a policy of détente leading to the
mutual tolerance of the European great powers became a frustrating exercise in reconciliation whose failure led to what the
British Government of 1937–9 called 'appeasement'.

The task of diplomacy might have been easier if the main
threat had not come from Nazi Germany. Against the expansionist vigour of Japan, Britain tried to enlist the resources of
the United States; against Italy's adventures in Abyssinia and
Spain there was at least the moral force of the League of
Nations; westward aggression by Russia would have found all
Europe on the side of collective security. Germany's expansion
in central and south-eastern Europe, however, posed a peculiarly difficult set of questions for Britain, not only in relation to
unwelcome possible allies like Russia, but to her involvement in
Europe at all. The policy of reconciliation required a British
interest in areas of Eastern Europe where it had, traditionally,

rarely existed; yet such was the direction of Germany's foreign policy by 1937 that success came to depend largely on Britain's acquiescence in German hegemony and her consequent abandonment of interest in Europe altogether. Given Hitler's drive for *Weltmacht,* this dilemma could not be avoided, even by 'appeasement'.

In the making of foreign policy, these very general factors were complicated by the conscious and unconscious assumptions of ministers, Members of Parliament, civil servants, military advisers and the mass of journalists, intellectuals, party activists and so on, who made up the political élite. The interaction of different groups, as well as the formulation of abstract quantities like 'public opinion', was governed at least partly by ideas about the state of the economy, the nature of war, Britain's great-power status, and the responsibility of politicians to a democratic electorate.

Economic policy provided a permanent, almost unchangeable, element in the making of foreign policy after the Depression of 1929–33. In spite of the success which the Government was quick to claim for the introduction of protection and the lowering of interest rates, they believed, unjustifiably, that the boom which grew in 1933–5 and restored Britain to recovery almost before any other industrial nation was fragile. To a large extent, both the boom and the other major factor of the 1930s, the steady fall in the price of primary products (and hence in the cost of living), grew irrespective of government action. Yet Neville Chamberlain, as Chancellor of the Exchequer from 1931–7, continued to balance his budgets as if Britain had not gone off the Gold Standard, and economic policy was tailored to fit an international confidence whose relevance had vanished with the crisis of 1931. Planned expansion, whether in the depressed areas or in relation to industrial reconstruction and rearmament, was rigidly controlled.

Britain's inward-looking tendencies were reinforced by the effects of the measures taken to fight the world depression. Protection, devaluation, abandonment of the Gold Standard, the attempt to create an Imperial economic bloc at the Ottawa Conference in 1932, and the growing reliance on the sterling area, were all isolationist and in the minds of British politicians they combined to restrict the resources available for the scale

of armaments appropriate to the international situation, if they
did not actually make them appear otiose.

At the same time, the belief that prosperity was just around
the corner, which existed very strongly as the domestic boom
grew, encouraged the attitude that it was dangerous and futile
to rock the boat. Sound preoccupation with economic strength
as the fourth arm of war was frequently projected, without
full evaluation, into arguments against conversion to a 'war
economy' on the pattern Germany was believed to have followed
after 1935. In spite of its beneficial effects on the permanent
unemployment problem, many economists condemned rearmament as a distortion of the market economy.

Nostalgia for the late 1920s, when the Service budgets reached
their lowest annual figure and when the Ten Year Rule* had
been set on a sliding scale, crossed party lines, giving encouragement equally to the claims of pacifists and successive Chancellors
of the Exchequer. To the political dangers of an arms race,
economists added the spectre of rival blocs entrenched behind
strategic and tariff barriers, trading on terms which owed
nothing to the smooth working of the pre-war international
economy.

Nevertheless, few of those who acknowledged her diminishing power were able to conceive of Britain as withdrawing into
isolationism in the manner of the United States after 1918.
During the 1930s, nearly everyone of influence in the decision-
making hierarchy had been born before the Boer War. The
anxieties of their youth had concerned the future of the Empire,
or the industrial efficiency of Britain in relation to Germany
and the United States. However disquieting, these were the
problems of a great power with no intention of abandoning its
world-wide interests. For ten years after Versailles, British
governments refused to acknowledge that the pre-1914 situation
could not be restored. Thus men in their fifties and sixties had
then only the years after 1929 to conform to a world in which
Britain was short both of allies and resources. Their slow
readjustment delayed continuously the formulation of a policy
of economic or strategic alliances more suited to the 1930s.

Attitudes towards war were founded in less rational calcula-

---

* The assumption made by the Treasury and Committee of Imperial Defence in
forward contingency planning and the drafting of estimates for the armed services
that no war against a major power was to be expected for ten years.

tions. War has been defined as both the failure and the extension of diplomacy. In the interwar years, the latter was thought blasphemy. After 1918, to plan another war seemed inconceivable. To men in the 1930s it was as terrible a prospect as thermo-nuclear war is today. It was the age of the bomber, when Baldwin's elliptical warning, 'the bomber will always get through', was taken too literally; when, after the summer manoeuvres of 1934, Churchill could describe London as 'the greatest target in the world ... a valuable fat cow, tied up to attract the beasts of prey'. Guernica became the example of what could be achieved by precision bombing raids and there was then no experience to show how fast fighters, yet unbuilt, could decimate bomber squadrons before they approached. Expert calculations made by the Air Ministry in 1936 suggested that London might suffer half a million casualties in the first three months of war.

War was regarded as an absolute evil. Baldwin called it 'the most fearful terror and prostitution of man's knowledge that ever was known'.[4] The very fact that a world war had never been threatened in the first ten years after Versailles gave illusory weight – in some minds – to the concept of collective security and by contrast darkened the already sombre warnings of British statesmen about its effects if war did break out. The British Government did not risk a war of any sort in the years between the Chanak incident of 1922 and March 1939, nor did British ministers imagine that others would do so, except in the most urgent and extreme national interests. They assumed that even opposed nations had the same fundamental interest in peace, and proceeded to negotiate with them on that basis. On this, if nothing else, Baldwin and Chamberlain, the Conservative leaders after 1931, gave a common lead: 'There may be Governments deliberately planning the future, leading reluctant or unsuspecting peoples into the shambles. It sometimes looks as if it is so. I confess that in my own political experience I have not encountered Governments possessed of all these malevolent qualities.'*

Finally, it seemed to Conservative politicians especially that, as a result of the social upheaval of the First World War,

---

* Baldwin's speech to the Peace Society, 31 Oct 1935; also 'I do not believe that such a Government in any way exists among civilized peoples' (Neville Chamberlain, *In Search of Peace* (edited speeches) (London 1939) p. 50).

foreign policy, like the more arcane subject of monetary policy, had been brought down to the democratic arena. Extension of the franchise, increasing readership of an expanding mass daily press, and the contentiousness shown in matters of foreign and imperial policy by the Labour Party and the trade unions, made politicians conscious that 'public opinion' had added a new dimension to diplomacy. The change can be seen in the growth of the activities of the Union of Democratic Control and the Independent Labour Party during the First World War, the work of two Labour Governments afterwards, and the success of working-class eruptions into foreign policy, such as trade-union intervention against the supply of arms to Poland in 1920. The extent to which Governments accepted that it had occurred can be seen in the late 1930s. It would have astonished Lord Curzon or Lord Salisbury that in 1938 the Cabinet should decide not to ask the TUC for co-operation in making skilled labour available in the aircraft factories by dilution elsewhere for fear that the Council might demand, as a condition, that the Government should lay the whole Czechoslovak problem before the League of Nations.[5]

Foreign policy was affected not only by Government attitudes to public opinion – especially to the results of by-elections – but also by the one-sided positions taken up on specific issues, by pressure groups aiming to convert the electorate as a whole. Intense preoccupation with Italian aggression in Abyssinia and the civil war in Spain contrasted with the generally tolerant attitude towards Germany's military reoccupation of the Rhineland in 1936, a far greater threat to European security than either of the others. The widespread acceptance of the legitimacy of German revisionist claims against the Treaty of Versailles has often been described.[6] It helps to explain why, even as late as 1938, Czechoslovakia could be pilloried for her alleged mal-treatment of the Sudeten German minority, in order to justify German demands for partition of the only tolerably democratic state in central Europe.

Wide misconceptions about the sources of Britain's influence in international affairs grew out of such attitudes. The theory that the building-up of armaments had been an autonomous cause of the 1914 war was widely accepted. Even during the election of 1935, which was based on a rearmament programme, the Prime Minister could say as part of his argument to the

Peace Society, 'I give you my word that there will be no great armaments.'[7] No reductions in British defence budgets won such universal agreement as those imposed by Churchill as Chancellor of the Exchequer between 1925 and 1929. In the absence of overt threats, standing armies appeared to be unnecessary. In the wealth of pacts, agreements, and declarations, signatures held the weight, not force of arms. The League of Nations possessed no common international force; the Locarno Pact had no proper military machinery. It is true that in April 1936, after the German reoccupation of the Rhineland, staff talks between Britain and France were held, but they soon lapsed. Arms limitation, the chief and easiest approach to disarmament, frequently ran counter to Britain's long-term interests: the limit of fifty cruisers, voluntarily accepted at the London Naval Conference in 1930, became an onerous strategic burden within five years. Between 1933 and 1935, rearmament and the creation of an air deterrent as the best means to strengthen Britain's external policies had to take place away from the public, in the shadows.

It was, after all, too easy to ask: what were these arms for? Lloyd George's liking for unprepared conferences had temporarily weakened faith in top-level diplomacy after 1920, yet the inter-war years were still a period in which diplomats and politicians held supreme faith in the power of negotiation. Trust in fundamentally similar interests in peace, international trade and security buoyed up belief in the possibility of compromise. Sympathy for German revisionism as a means to strengthen the economic and political framework of Europe was as evident at the time of the reoccupation of the Rhineland as it had been in the early 1920s. Neville Chamberlain held only to a rather more extreme degree the general view that international problems could be solved if only those responsible could get round a table and do a deal. Indeed, to take the opposite view is to abrogate foreign policy altogether. The world economic crisis after 1929, with its revelation of the fragility of the structure, increased faith that other nations would not rock the boat. The illusion lay in a misunderstanding about the nature of national strength. Influence exists in so far as others believe in it. The exercise of influence without strength is bluff – and again and again, when they believed war was at

stake, British Governments of the 1930s revealed themselves
unwilling or unable to bluff.

In their attitude towards the threat from Nazi Germany,
British decision-makers hovered uneasily between the doctrine
of the free hand and the historic principle of the balance of
power in Europe. In the first place, they held that Britain
should never, by making treaties, place the vital freedom to
declare war or to avoid it, in the hands of any other nation
or group of nations. What had been a guiding principle during
the nineteenth century was expressed clearly in the words of a
Foreign Office memorandum written in April 1926:   *Lasted to 1938*

> Our sole object is to keep what we have and live in peace. Many
> foreign countries are playing for a definite stake and their policy
> is shaped accordingly. It is not so in our case. To the casual
> observer our foreign policy may appear to lack consistency and
> continuity, but both are there. We keep our hands free in order
> to throw our weight into the scale and on behalf of peace.[8]

In pursuit of this aim, for twenty years after the end of the
First World War, Britain at first refused to guarantee French
security against the fear of a resurgent Germany, and then
refused to take on more than the guarantee of the Western
frontier laid down in the Locarno Pact. When the danger that
Britain might be involved in a general war because of France's
security arrangements with Eastern Europe (notably with
Czechoslovakia) became obvious in 1938, the Chamberlain
Government studiously avoided any pledge of intervention. As
late as December 1938, after that promise had been forced out
of them by the Munich crisis, Sir Alexander Cadogan, Permanent Under-Secretary at the Foreign Office, was telling the
Foreign Policy Committee of the Cabinet that there should be
no repetition of the situation in which Britain and France had
been faced 'with the alternatives of fighting without any hope
of saving Czechoslovakia, or of defaulting on the guarantee'.[9]

The Dominions, who had opposed the Locarno Pact, and
who continued generally in the 1930s to object to any further
British commitment in Europe which would lessen the capacity
of the mother country to defend them, objected especially to
a commitment to France covering German aggression against
Czechoslovakia, and this pressure on London was used by the

British Government at will, to justify its profoundly mistrustful attitude towards Continental involvement.

At another level, however, adherence to the balance-of-power principle proved stronger. The domination of Europe by a single power had been held contrary to Britain's interests since the sixteenth century and in the inter-war years, at certain moments, the British Government admitted that there was a deeper layer of meaning to the entente with France than they were prepared to acknowledge in public.* In 1934, a commitment to go to war in defence of Holland was accepted privately by the National Government as a corollary of Locarno.† Defence of Belgium was only partly abrogated after her withdrawal from the Locarno obligations in 1937. Even when it had almost withdrawn the undertaking of an expeditionary force to aid France under Locarno, the Chamberlain Cabinet reluctantly accepted that in the last resort it was an overriding British interest not to see France defeated by Germany. Hitler might sweep eastwards almost at will in 1938, but the balance of power in western Europe should not, in the last resort, be overthrown.

This assumption was decisive for Anglo-German relations in the 1930s. Hitler's policy (see Chapter 5) was not initially directed against Britain, who was to be allowed her own sphere of influence, but against France and Russia. If Britain held to the defence of France, with all her entangling commitments in Eastern Europe, conflict became inevitable. Very few members of the Government thought this through to its conclusion before 1937, but in that year the Chiefs of Staff reported: 'If France becomes involved by decisions in which we should have no part, we are in danger of being drawn into a general European war, even though at that moment it might be highly dangerous for us.'[10] The underlying principle, hedged about though it

---

* For example, the unwillingness of Bonar Law in January 1923 to push France too far, despite her occupation of the Ruhr; the détente begun by Baldwin and Poincaré in October 1923; the work of Austen Chamberlain towards Locarno in 1925; the partnership with France in making the Stresa Front; and the acknowledgement of a British defence obligation in northwest Europe, between 1934–7.
† Cabinet Disarmament Committee debates on European Security, Mar-Apr 1934. (CAB 27/506.) There was also no question of waiting until Belgium fell to a German attack—Baldwin's dictum, 'We should be involved long before such an event happened: in fact, he thought that as soon as France became implicated we should inevitably become implicated too', was accepted without challenge, as the logical interpretation of the Locarno Pact (19 Apr 1934).

was with qualifications and restrictions, was never actually denied and the Chiefs of Staff enunciated it shortly before the fall of Austria. If France was 'in great danger . . . we cannot afford to allow [her] to be overrun and aerodromes established on French soil. Over the centuries the British people have fought to prevent the Low Countries falling to the possession of a hostile power.'[11]

The question at issue in 1938 was how to prevent this happening as a result of what the British Government regarded as side-issues – the fates of Austria and Czechoslovakia.

In spite of their reluctance to accept specific commitments, inter-war Governments had taken on certain long-term obligations, but by 1937, when Chamberlain became Prime Minister, the most substantial of these had become untenable and there had grown up instead a series of temporary expedients designed to preserve the status quo. It was too late for all but the most sanguine to hope for the resuscitation of the League: Britain's wholehearted allegiance had been in doubt long before the extent of her practical responsibilities under the Covenant had become clear in 1935, when the chief burden of imposing sanctions against Italy during the Abyssinian crisis fell on the British Navy. Even a decade earlier, only the Western European obligations had been enshrined in the Locarno Pact, and these limited duties were shown to be beyond Britain's capacity, when she proved impotent to aid France in preventing the German reoccupation of the Rhineland in 1936. In both cases the British Government gained the maximum unpopularity with their potential friends for the least possible benefit. By 1937 the only provisions of the Covenant or the Peace Treaty which excited much support in Britain were those which provided for her own safety against external threats.

The provisions of Locarno, the only European security agreement signed by Britain in the inter-war years, had, likewise, been undermined. The Pact provided for mutual guarantees between Britain, France, Belgium, Germany and Italy, individually and collectively to secure the 1918 western frontier of Germany, and the demilitarisation of the Rhineland. This was the most that could be offered to France by Austen Chamberlain and Baldwin, against the opposition of the Labour Party, much of the Conservative Party and most of the Dominions. There was no support for a guarantee of Germany's eastern frontier, and instead France chose to extend her long search for security there, by pacts with Poland and Czechoslovakia, and by the creation of the Little Entente (Czechoslovakia, Rumania and Yugoslavia). The list of loopholes in the Locarno Pact under which action could be avoided was considerable (Britain was not bound to involve herself alone in any Franco-German dispute unless the offence were 'flagrant' and 'unprovoked') and the real limitation of Britain's commitment was admitted by its author, Austen Chamberlain – it could not, he said in 1925, be 'more narrowly circumscribed to the conditions under which we have an actual vital national interest'.[12]

Nothing was done to make Locarno credible by regular staff talks with France even when it became clear after 1933 that Germany was the only likely aggressor on the Rhine frontier. Instead, the search for security continued through limitation of armaments, and the less binding agreement made between Britain, France and Italy at Stresa in April 1935. The reaffirmation of Locarno made at that time was clearly directed against Germany and in the circumstances probably did more harm than good to the Pact itself. Nevertheless it represented the high point of solidarity before the signature of the Franco-Soviet Pact and the Anglo-German Naval Agreement – and the Abyssinian war – split the three members of the Front apart. The German reoccupation of the Rhineland in March 1936, coming as it did at the nadir of Anglo-French relations when Italy was wholly estranged by sanctions, was not resisted and although, when Britain, Belgium and France met in London afterwards to address themselves to Germany, they spoke of themselves as the Locarno Powers, they were reduced in effect to the pre-1914 entente.

Britain's commitments thereafter were even more limited. The staff talks which followed in April 1936 were strenuously opposed in the House of Commons and were allowed to lapse. Belgium began to withdraw from what was left of Locarno and was formally released in April 1937. Britain and France renewed their pledges, but the British Government began to reduce the size of the Expeditionary Force promised for the defence of north-west Europe. Within a year its duties had been redefined in an imperial rather than European sense:

first, home defence; second, defence of overseas territories; third, defence of treaty obligations; fourth and last, the help of France.

The links of Imperial defence provided an ill-defined network of obligation and security. The Dominions and Britain were well aware of their mutual interdependence, but this lay between each Dominion and Britain, not between the Dominions as a whole. After the Imperial Conference of 1923, when hopes of a common economic policy based on protection were destroyed by the loss of the general election in Britain, any serious chance of a common foreign policy between them, founded on strategic and economic interests, evaporated. The fears and aims of Australia and New Zealand dictated one attitude, while those of Canada, South Africa, and later India enforced others. New Zealand, for example, being a member of the League Council, was most keenly in favour of sanctions against Italy in 1935–6; Australia and South Africa opposed them. These centrifugal tendencies were barely held in check by the continued work of the Committee of Imperial Defence Secretariat, the Dominions Office and the liaison between the High Commissioners in London and the Imperial Government. After the Defence Requirements Committee Report of 1934 (see below, page 33) had defined Germany as the long-term threat to Britain, Sir Maurice Hankey, Secretary of the Committee of Imperial Defence, had to visit Australia to reassure her Government that the apparent downgrading of the Japanese danger had not undone Britain's commitments in the Pacific. Canada refused to act as a reserve producer of aircraft for British use in 1936, and South Africa showed herself favourable to Germany on almost every issue in the 1930s, except the return of Germany's former African colonies.

Fear of the consequences if Britain should become too weak led the Dominions to make larger claims than equity warranted. Instead of the structure of defence being regarded as a permanent integrated alliance, with the unified advisory centre in London, it rested in practice very largely on the British Navy, reinforced by the overseas defence squadrons of the Air Force.*

---

* In addition, the type of warfare for which Britain had prepared materially affected the design of British weapons and scale of equipment; the most notable example being the development of light tanks for use in overseas theatres of war, in preference to heavy ones for a European situation.

After the Imperial Conference of 1926, the Dominions accepted an Admiralty scheme for three categories of a theoretical Empire navy, comprising the main fleet, the (cruiser-based) defence of communications, and local defence, but they made little serious effort to fulfil the responsibilities even of the third category. Australia and New Zealand had as much reason as Britain, therefore, to complain that, at the London Naval Conference of 1930, at the insistence of the United States, the nominal strength of cruisers was cut from 70 to 50, totals which included the Dominion navies. A permanent weakness was established in the face of Japanese naval expansion which was never restored either by the accelerated defence-programme for Singapore after 1932, or by increases in Far East aircraft strength. But no corresponding effort came from Canada or South Africa, and the Imperial Conference of 1937 revealed separatist, exclusive fears and ambitions which added substantially to the difficulties of the British Government.

Far from reviving the understanding that, in a major world crisis, the Dominions would respond to the defence of the United Kingdom, this Conference emphasized the concessions which Britain would have to make in order to preserve the appearance of a unified strategy. In an agenda which the secretariat was hard put to minute for a unanimous final communiqué, Britain's involvement in European politics aroused intense controversy. The British desired some statement of Imperial solidarity with which to face the combination of Germany, Japan and Italy, but MacKenzie King, Prime Minister of Canada, offered nothing: 'There was in Canada a great dread lest the country should be committed at the Imperial Conference to some obligation arising out of the European situation.'[13] He did not want a resolution which would create difficulties at home among the isolationists or the French separatists of Quebec. Hertzog, Prime Minister of South Africa, agreed and added, gratuitously but far-sightedly, that he could not guarantee his country's support if Britain became involved in war with Germany over Czechoslovakia.

More serious was the Dominions' rejection of the League of Nations, because lip-service to the Covenant had been the only common factor in the dissolving fabric of imperial policy since 1926.[14] MacKenzie King 'did not want to base Canadian policy on the League. If the Covenant remained as at present, that meant supporting collective security, which he did not believe in.'[15] Hertzog 'could not agree in advance to principles which might conceivably run counter to the country's interests'. It was true that New Zealand, a member of the League Council and the most consistent supporter of Britain, objected, and that her Prime Minister, Savage, succeeded in getting a commitment to the Covenant inserted as a footnote in the final report. But the result of the final debate on Imperial Defence was highly unsatisfactory for the British Government. The Dominion Prime Ministers had been told of Britain's military weakness, of the hopes that an armaments industry might be created in Australia and Canada (as Hankey and Baldwin had urged since 1934) and of the need for increased naval contributions. Instead of responding, MacKenzie King made it clear that Canada was not, and had no intention of being, represented on the Committee of Imperial Defence in London. He and Hertzog wished to omit all references to Imperial Defence from the final report. The demand of Savage and Lyons, Prime Minister of Australia, that it should be made clear they felt otherwise and wished to state so publicly, turned the drafting into an exercise of higher casuistry, and Lyons' appeal for a Pacific Security Pact went unheeded.

The lack of cohesion, separatism, the fear that Canada, so closely linked economically with the United States, and divided racially,* might lapse into complete neutrality, and that pro-German sympathies within South Africa might render her as divided in support for Britain as in 1914, were all heightened by the Conference. British statesmen might legitimately have argued that, if the institution which they were attempting to preserve seemed likely to fragment, they would be better to delay, waiting for a great issue to unite it, before setting it in the European balance.

Negative though the influence of the Dominions was, in the two years before the outbreak of war it represented a major external handicap on any policy designed to strengthen European security against Hitler. In their own understandable interests, half of the participants at the Imperial Conference were behind the doctrine of appeasement.[16] Yet the Dominions relied heavily on British sources – Foreign Office, CID,

* MacKenzie King frequently cited as his justification the attitude of Quebec and its outspoken French-Canadian Prime Minister.

B

Dominions Office – for their assessments of the European situation and it is at least partly true to say that the British themselves had conditioned this response. Nowhere among the political élite in Britain was there a desire to rip away the mystique which surrounded the Commonwealth, nor were there demands for an assessment of what the association really meant in terms of profit and loss. The most criticism made was that the Dominions should take a greater share of the defence burden. Even this was not pressed home during the 1930s.

It would have been understandable if, after 1937, the National Government had looked for support for its European policy from the former allies of 1918, France and the United States, but it did not. Briefly, after the German reoccupation of the Rhineland, relations between Paris and London improved, but this was only a temporary reversal of trends dating back at least to 1934. France's system of alliances in Eastern Europe was weakening, while her political and social state deteriorated, justifying the worst fears of Neville Chamberlain who had expressed shocked dismay at the immorality and instability of the system ever since the Stavisky scandal in 1934.[17] France's economic depression deepened at the time it began to lift in Britain and the United States; and in the general apathy of public opinion towards foreign affairs which followed the brief vigour of the Doumergue–Barthou Government, the bourgeois core of the French right became fiercely anti-Communist and correspondingly inert towards Germany's expansion. The election of May 1936 gave a narrow majority for a left-wing coalition and the new Prime Minister, Léon Blum, formed the Popular Front. His attempt to introduce an equivalent of the New Deal produced a wave of immense strikes, a fall in the franc and the vicious political in-fighting of right and left which, inflamed by the Spanish Civil War and further disfigured by the scurrilous press-campaigns of papers like *Gringoire*, introduced what is still known in France as *la mauvaise période*.

None of this was welcome to the British Government, who had been forced to confess their military inability to help prevent the reoccupation of the Rhineland.[18] Britain entered a more rapid phase of rearmament in 1936–7, following the decisions taken in 1934; but France, who still had the largest army in Europe, began to decline in relation to Germany at a rate which, faithfully reported by the Service attachés in Paris, frightened the British Government into just the isolationism which the Baldwin Government, in spite of the Rhineland disaster, had managed to avoid in 1936. Not only was the vaunted French air force becoming obsolete in the face of new German and British models, but the monthly rate of production of fighters fell very low in the second half of 1936 and that of bombers was reduced almost to zero.[19] As Sir Robert Vansittart, Permanent Under-Secretary of the Foreign Office, minuted in November 1937: 'It looks as if most of the French equipment is out of date. This, coupled with their decline in productivity, is exceedingly serious and may have still more serious consequences.'[20] The French Army was the only substantial Continental defence of the remains of Locarno, but the old strategic certainties were being eroded. Belgium's withdrawal from Locarno deprived France of the ability to invade the Ruhr and vitiated the defence of the territory north of the Maginot Line, unless Britain chose to fill it. Even the French Army became suspect. As General Mittelhauser was to admit later:

From 1936 onwards the Supreme War Council discussed the importance of the use of tanks and airplanes but without arriving at any agreement. In 1938 the Germans already had two armoured divisions completely organised and prepared to take the field, while we had not been able to organise even one at the beginning of the war.[21]

France's support could appear a liability to a Prime Minister less convinced than Baldwin of the necessity of the entente with France. But if Britain disengaged herself from Europe was there hope to be found in the United States? Was there any shadow of the *Pax Anglo-Saxonica* which Lord Lothian, among others, had foreseen in 1934?

The extremely narrow limits of power of either the State Department or the President to associate the United States with even the shadow of a European policy were shown in January 1935 when, in spite of their combined efforts, a move to apply for membership of the World Court was defeated, largely because of public opposition whipped up by the alliance between the newspaper magnate, Randolph Hearst, the demagogue Detroit priest Father Coughlin, and Senator Huey Long. The World Court was a body independent even of the League of Nations, and Roosevelt was fresh from an overwhelming Congressional election victory, yet the isolationism of the mass of the American public was thought to be too strong.

The United States made no response to Germany's 1935 announcement of her air force programme and conscription; American private oil companies did more to break sanctions by building up Italy's oil supplies than any others; and in February 1936, against the wishes of Secretary of State, Cordell Hull, the Neutrality Act was extended so that it became impossible for the United States to supply arms even to members of the League acting in concert against an aggressor. At the time of the occupation of the Rhineland the German Ambassador, Hans Luther, reported that the State Department 'felt that the German step was to have been expected; that it is indeed understandable since, after all, it is German territory which is involved and that it promises a pacification of the European atmosphere'.[22] Even in commercial affairs affecting American interests, the Government proved reluctant to impose countervailing duties under existing legislation, against subsidised German exports.[23] Finally, in spite of Roosevelt's overwhelming success in the presidential election in November 1936, which could surely have given him some freedom of action, American policy towards the Spanish Government in the civil war remained one of the most unbending neutrality.

Until at least the beginning of 1937 there appeared to be no hope for Britain that the United States would take a helpful line against Japanese aggression in China, or towards Germany, or even by amending the neutrality legislation. It is doubtful indeed if the American Government had a distinct European policy at all. At a press conference held after the announcement of German rearmament in March 1935, Secretary Hull was reduced to telling journalists that America followed European events carefully, and that her 'moral influence always encouraged European people to live up to their treaties'.[24] More frankly, President Roosevelt wrote to William Dodd, American Ambassador in Berlin, on 16 April: 'I feel very helpless to render any particular service to immediate or permanent peace at this time.'[25]

A slight change began in December 1936 with an increase in Latin American solidarity expressed, indirectly against Germany, at the Buenos Aires Conference, and with the overture made to Chamberlain by Roosevelt in February 1937. Yet, on that occasion, Sir Ronald Lindsay, British Ambassador in Washington, was careful to advise Chamberlain and Eden, the Foreign Secretary, to be cautious in their reply. The British duly blamed Germany in forthright terms and suggested to Roosevelt that help in the Far East and amendment of the neutrality legislation would be the best his Government could do. Nothing happened until 1 June 1937 when an evasive answer was given by Hull and his Under-Secretary, Sumner Welles.

The unsatisfactory sequel is described in Chapter 4. Nothing, at the time Neville Chamberlain became Prime Minister, contradicted the British view that American policy was halting and confused. For a generation, the political élite had accepted American isolationism as a fact of world diplomacy.[26] Even those committed to involving the United States in Europe, like Sir Samuel Hoare, could write in retrospect: 'Rightly or wrongly we were deeply suspicious, not indeed of American good intentions, but of American readiness to follow up inspiring words with any practical action.'[27] Such attitudes were not changed by the slight shift in the cold wind from the West, and they were indeed sometimes welcome to members of the élite who saw in a form of Atlanticism a way out, for Britain also, from European entanglements and dilemmas.

Towards Russia, whose status as a major power was accepted by Conservative Governments only with the greatest reluctance, British policy was ambivalent and undecided. There was, first, the sheer ignorance of Russian motivation which seemed to arise from a vast but obscure dynamism bearing little relation to the normal canons of foreign policy of great powers; and secondly there was the ideological dilemma which had made it far easier for Labour Governments, in 1923-4 and 1929-31, than Conservatives to initiate negotiations with Russia – though not necessarily to find any more sympathetic response – and which opposed all Soviet overtures in the later 1930s with a prior assumption of mistrust.

The rise of the Nazi power was a more immediate threat to Soviet Russia than to the West because of the clear indications in *Mein Kampf* that an eastward expansion was planned, and because of the fundamental ideological conflict between communism and fascism. For the first time in her short revolutionary history, Russia needed Western allies and the signing of the Four Power Pact (between Britain, France, Italy and Germany) in

1933 emphasised the fact, by apparently excluding Russia from a Western grouping. After intense diplomatic effort, and taking advantage of offers from Poland, France and Italy, Russia helped create a new security arrangement in Eastern Europe and became a member of the League. The proposed Eastern Locarno pact of 1934 offered hopes of neutralisation of the German threat, but when that failed it was replaced by the Franco-Soviet Pact of May 1935 and the consequent Treaty with Czechoslovakia (contingent on Czechoslovakia's 1925 Locarno agreement with France).

Britain passed through a short period of amity with Russia early in 1935, at the time of Eden's visit to Moscow and the Stresa Front, but the Anglo-German Naval Treaty offended Russia as bitterly as it did France, and the failure to check the occupation of the Rhineland aroused Soviet suspicions of the weakness of both Western powers. Through 1936, fed by the internal conflicts of French politics, the British attitude towards the civil war in Spain, and the line-up of Italy and Germany in the anti-Comintern Pact, fear spread in Russia that the Western powers would come to terms with Germany at her expense and permit an attack on Poland, Czechoslovakia and the Ukraine.

The relationship between revulsion against the capitalist states of the West and the Stalinist terror of 1936–8, the treason trials and purges of the high command, cannot be assessed, but what was known in Britain at the time offered evidence that Russia was unsound and undesirable as an ally of any sort. Between the denunciations by Maxim Litvinov, Soviet envoy at Geneva, for Britain's alleged pro-fascist sympathies with Franco, and the reports of Lord Chilston, British Ambassador in Moscow, that the purge of the Red Army had rendered Russia powerless to fight an offensive war,* the British Government made up its mind against co-operation with Russia, long before the Czechoslovak crisis began.

They may have been right to think that Russian external attitudes were only facets of an internal situation which they

---

* It is probably a fair comment on the quality of information from Russia to quote a letter from Chamberlain in Oct 1937 saying that Chilston was complaining that no Russians came to see him. 'As a result he gets no information and the condition of the country is a mystery to him. He never sees Stalin, nor does any one of his colleagues . . .' (Chamberlain letters, 9 Oct 1937). Ignorance so complete does not seem to have disturbed either the Foreign Office or the Prime Minister.

could not understand. Russia's consistent actions in the Czechoslovak crisis of 1938, when ironically she seemed to be the last
loyal member of the League, may have been merely another
aspect of her duplicity. On the other hand, in her approaches
to Russia, Britain treated this nominally friendly power in a way
vastly inferior to Germany. During the round of visits made by
Simon, the Foreign Secretary, and Eden, in March 1935, it was
the latter, the junior minister, who went to Moscow, while both
went to Berlin; and this sort of behaviour, as Churchill believed,
may well have encouraged the Russians to withdraw from the
West. In the absence of a credible Soviet historiography there
can be no certain answer. The main criticism to be made is
that the British Government dismissed what was, potentially,
the second greatest industrial and military power in Europe
without analytical justification. Russian protestations may have
been as misleading as American, but they deserved equal consideration. In regard to Eastern policy, the politicians – rather
than the Foreign Office* – committed the fundamental error of
rejecting a potential ally for the sole reason that they did not feel
in sympathy with her.

To the extent that the external circumstances of the British
predicament in 1937 tended to encourage the new Cabinet to
adopt a policy independent of France, Russia and the United
States, defence of British interests had to be conducted alone.
Obligations in other parts of the world substantially increased
this burden. In the treaty ports, foreign concessions and commercial investments in China and South-East Asia, above all at
Hong Kong and Singapore, lay a substantial part of Britain's
total overseas investment. In Shanghai alone, her assets were
valued at £64 million at the time of the crisis with Japan in
1932. The head of the Foreign Office, Sir Robert Vansittart,
wrote then, 'If Japan continues unchecked . . . our position and
vast interests in the Far East will never recover',[28] and after the
Chiefs of Staff request for abolition of the Ten Year Rule in
1932, revision of the defences of Singapore and Hong Kong
had formed the first halting essay in rearmament. In spite of
the change, however, Vansittart was not being unduly alarmist

---

* Vansittart, at least, continually urged the Chamberlain Government not to
exclude Russia (Memoranda of 25 July, 13 and 20 Sept, 7 Dec 1938 – Vansittart
Papers).

when he added: 'we must be done for in the Far East unless the United States are eventually prepared to use force'. The plain truth was that Britain had no adequate Far Eastern naval deterrent. Japanese ambition appeared to be sated by the conquest of Manchuria, but the establishment there of a closed economy and the attempt to set up a puppet regime in northern China showed that the danger to Western commercial interests was only dormant.

The Defence Requirements Committee Report of 1934, while recognising that Germany was the ultimate threat, envisaged Japan as the more immediate, and British policy during the next two years wobbled between the Treasury view of 'making eyes at Japan' and that of the majority of the Cabinet who were uneasy about alienating the United States. Reconciliation proved impossible to achieve: Japan withdrew from all naval negotiations in 1936 and began to build up a massive battle fleet. In China itself, diplomatic efforts to combat Japanese expansion had some success. A mission headed by Sir Frederick Leith-Ross, the Government's Chief Economic Adviser, was sent in 1935 to offer practical help in the form of currency stabilisation and an international loan. Leith-Ross failed, however, to persuade Japan to co-operate with the West, and to restore the concert of the Nine-Power Treaty of 1922 – the last occasion on which the policies of Britain, the United States and Japan had been ostensibly in harmony.

The extent of British influence in the Far East was strictly limited by Japan's own aggressive intentions in China. The signature of the anti-Comintern Pact with Germany was ominous, although directed primarily against Russia, but the ambivalence of Japanese policy, as the balance of power between militarists and moderates shifted backwards and forwards in Tokyo, reinforced the DRC prediction that the problem of the Far East would decline relatively in gravity. Early in 1937 tension relaxed, partly because of the strain imposed on the Japanese economy by an attempt to undermine that of China and to undersell Britain in Asian markets. In China itself the Nationalists and Communists combined under the leadership of Chiang Kai-shek and Japan's puppet regime in the north disintegrated.

Britain's Far Eastern policy, however, depended equally on the United States. Whether they chose to warn Japan against aggression in China, or attempted to reconcile the existence of their interests with moderate opinion in Tokyo, the British had to be sure that the United States would not be outraged by either course. Cordell Hull, the United States Secretary of State, refused co-operation of any sort in the scheme proposed at the Imperial Conference in May 1937 by Lyons, Prime Minister of Australia, for a non-aggression pact in the Far East which should tie Japan down to respecting British possessions and the integrity of Australia and New Zealand; and stigmatised it as another British plot to drag the United States into 'entangling alliances'. British policy was forced to conform to a most unsatisfactory mould – too weak to check Japan, too committed to withdraw her over-stretched defences. In the years after the Shanghai crisis of 1932, the Government was unable to neutralise the Far Eastern threat, or to make by agreement with Japan the sort of strategic economies which would have eased rearmament in the European sphere. Any overtures to Germany had to be made with this permanent lesion in mind.

In the Middle East, the burden was less. The defence of Egypt was regarded in the Foreign Office as late as 1926 as the fourth most important objective of foreign policy after securing the Covenant, the Versailles Treaty and the Washington Treaties of 1922.[29] By 1937 these three had diminished in value but the route to India and the Far East still lay, for practical purposes, through the Suez Canal and represented a primary lifeline of Imperial defence. The gravity of the Italian threat from Libya in the sanctions campaign of 1935–6 menaced Cairo and the Canal; Italy's well-equipped torpedo-bombers might be launched against the Mediterranean fleet, Malta and Alexandria; and four capital ships might be lost, whose primary function was the defence of the Far East, and India, against Japan.

The Egyptian question was finally resolved by improving relations with Turkey and by the signature of a Treaty with Egypt in July 1936, which separated Britain's security interests in the Canal from her former territorial claims. A year earlier, the Government of India Act had at last been passed, foreshadowing India's future as a dominion and briefly patching over the political discontents and the communal hatreds of Hindus and Moslems. But the worst area of the Middle East was Palestine, which contained the potential time-bomb of the

Jewish national home, with all that the issue meant for neighbouring Arab states and Britain's dependence on the oil of the Middle East. During 1938, a full-scale Arab rebellion broke out, to the unrestrained delight of Germany and Italy who tried to foment a wider war.[30] A substantial part of Britain's army was pinned down in Palestine up to the outbreak of war in September 1939. Nor did defence of the Canal end with the Egyptian Treaty: beyond lay the problems of security of the Sudan and East Africa. Germany laid claim to the former colony of Tanganyika, which was regarded as a vital strategic interest and was not at first included in the various schemes by which central Africa became the quarry for territory to satisfy German ambitions in 1937. The defence of the east African seaboard was so sketchy that, in spite of the facilities offered by the Simonstown naval base, the Overseas Defence Committee of the CID spent part of the summer of 1937 trying to involve the South African Government as well.

These expedients indicated the precarious limits of Britain's strategic power at the beginning of 1937. But they were expedients designed to hold the status quo or to modify it in Britain's interest, leaving the Government free to concentrate what little strength it had elsewhere. At the centre, a dual policy was evolved. Britain set out to improve relations with Germany whilst hedging her bets elsewhere in the world.

The development of rearmament as a definite policy of deterrence occurred between 1932, when the shock of the Japanese attack on Shanghai inspired the Service Chiefs to demand the abolition of the Ten Year Rule, and the succession of Neville Chamberlain in 1937. The first stage began with the abandonment of the Rule in March 1932 when a new impetus was given to anti-aircraft development at home and the defences of Singapore. No significant increase in expenditure was permitted at this time, and although the military advisers pressed continuously for the worst deficiencies at least to be made up, the search for disarmament continued during 1933 through the mechanism of the League of Nations. Nevertheless progress was made in political education towards rearmament – signified, to the public, in the speeches of Baldwin, Lord President of the Council, who defined Britain's goal, in March 1933, as parity with Germany – air parity in the positive sense that, if other nations would not disarm, Britain must rearm to meet them. A year later, in the House of Commons on 8 March 1934, he extended the claim : 'In air strength and air power, this country shall no longer be in a position inferior to any country within striking distance of our shores.'[31]

Meanwhile, the Defence Requirements Committee of the CID, with Hankey as chairman, had been set up to study how to repair the deficiencies and the undeniable inability of the Services to perform their obligations. Their first report, produced on 29 February 1934, was a document of great significance, because it defined the enemy against whom Britain should rearm. Japan (the danger which had called the Committee into being) was the most immediate but was declining in gravity. Germany was the real threat: 'We take Germany as the ultimate potential enemy against whom our long-range defensive policy must be directed.'[32]

Positive proposals backed up the DRC's strategic arguments: the deficiencies of the Navy should be repaired, enough to be able to 'show a tooth' against Japan in the Pacific; in the air, the aim of the original fifty-two squadrons scheme of 1923 should be completed, plus the first stage of the home-defence scheme – an immediate increase of forty squadrons, with twenty-five to follow later; and the Army should receive a regular Field Force of five divisions capable of operating in a European theatre of war within a month. Finally, the Committee warned against the danger of a war on two or more fronts. At that stage Italy did not appear to be a major threat, although they warned that it might take four years of the rearmament campaign before Britain was fitted to meet her.

The cost of implementing the Report threw the Cabinet into a major political crisis during April and May 1934.[33] The chief opposition to the £76 million scheme came from the Treasury and the Chancellor of the Exchequer, Neville Chamberlain, who wished to cut back the Field Force, the capital expansion of the Navy and the proposal to build up an air force bomber counter-strike, in favour of a plan of air defence at home, limited liability in Europe and an overture to Japan. Reductions totalling £20 million were demanded. In the end, owing largely to the resistance put up by Baldwin, the original total and the balance between the Services remained much as it had been laid down by the DRC: that is, sufficient (hopefully) to hold the status quo in the Pacific and to meet Germany on equal terms. Within the air programme, however, the majority of the new squadrons (33 out of $41\frac{1}{2}$) were transferred to home defence – the first overt sign of the new policy. To compensate for this paring-down of Far East squadrons the first stage of the Singapore base was accelerated. At the same time, the role of the Army in Europe was defined: the defence of the Low Countries and north-west France against German aggression was to be regarded as a vital interest. The five-division field-force was established, at least on paper. The extra concentration on the Air Force was not intended to prejudice the Navy and Army, whose minimum requirements were reserved, but to act as a deterrent to Germany,* and within the air programme bombers were given higher priority. For the next three years this general theory remained untouched, though not unquestioned.

The next stage of rearmament saw the formulation of strategy based on the political decisions of 1934. The Defence Policy and Requirements Committee was set up in July 1935: 'To keep the defensive situation as a whole constantly in review, so as to ensure that our defensive arrangements and our foreign policy are in line, and to advise the Cabinet and the CID in the light of the international and financial situation as to any necessary changes in policy, or in the defence proposals.'[34]

Acceleration of the original programme was further stimulated by the DRC's second report in July 1935. Already the Air Force target, defined by the Air Parity Sub-Committee in May, had become that of numerical parity with Germany. By the end of July, an extra 1,500 machines with full reserves had been approved for construction. The Navy won the modernisation of four capital ships, the first move towards a two-power standard,† plus further anti-aircraft defences for the fleet; while the Army, later in 1935, was given £$9\frac{1}{2}$ million more for the Field Force, spread over four years. Finally, Lord Weir‡ was

---

* A fuller description of the evolution of the deterrent theory will be found in Middlemas and Barnes, *Baldwin*, chs 27 and 28. One quotation may be given here, that of the Secretary for Air Cunliffe-Lister – this was, he said 'a deterrent to Germany, not to pursue an air race'. (17 July 1934, CAB 23/79.)

† That is, a navy capable of meeting the fleets of two other major powers.

‡ Industrialist and expert in matters of production, frequently consulted by Governments during the inter-war years; sometime President of the Employers' Confederation.

brought in to advise on production difficulties in the air programme; and some provision was made for the machine-tool industry.

But the limitations which Chamberlain had obtruded in 1934* became more serious as rearmament moved from repairing deficiencies into the stage of expansion. Even Baldwin had admitted the cogency of financial considerations so long as the balance between the Services was regulated by the military experts rather than by the Treasury.[35] After the summer of 1935 difficulties developed in geometrical progression: to the rivalry of the Services and the perennial struggle for funds were added the sharply rising cost of technological advances in research and development, shortages of skilled labour, lack of productive capacity, and, to a serious degree, the competing claims of economic stability and social welfare. The election of November 1935 gave the Government a mandate for qualified rearmament but the gain in public opinion was not reflected in easement of the complicated industrial handicaps.

After a third report of the DRC in January 1936, the problems intensified. The Air Force Scheme F (see below, page 220), which the Committee endorsed, provided for an increase in front-line strength of 234 machines and reserves up to full war strength of 225 per cent. Eight thousand new machines were to be ordered between 1936 and 1939, largely of the latest types, Hampdens, Wellingtons, Hurricanes, Spitfires and Blenheims. This was the period when the greatest risks were taken, when the bombers Battle, Hampden and Wellington were ordered in bulk, before the prototypes had been tested, and when the Bristol Beaufort was ordered straight off the drawing-board. The new naval programme allowed for capital-ship replacement at last and for cruiser construction up to a new total of seventy, for Imperial defence. Only the Army lagged behind, a state of affairs at least partly due to the inefficient direction of the War Office, but also to an increasing degree of doubt about its role in relation to Europe.

The complicated difficulties of organising production and labour were outlined succinctly by Lord Weir to the Defence

* 'In particular the Chancellor of the Exchequer does not bind himself, or his successors, to find the additional sums mentioned in the report within five years, nor in the particular year to which they are allotted.' (18 July 1934, CAB 23/79.)

Policy and Requirements Committee on 13 January 1936, to the dismay of the Service ministers, and the argument about the permanent balance between rearmament – which until then had been essentially an *ad hoc* creation – and the civilian economy, was raised in full. Some of the bottlenecks in production and the supply of labour were resolved after the appointment of Sir Thomas Inskip as Minister for Co-ordination of Defence in March 1936, but argument over the wider issues did not diminish. The new post was a compromise between a full Ministry of Defence and the existing structure of the CID, and it failed in its major objective. Inskip became neither a deputy Prime Minister, as was originally intended, nor a presumptive Minister of Defence, but rather a technician, smoothing out inter-service rivalries. The Defence White Paper of 1936 admitted that some of these underlying difficulties existed, but papered them over for the public. There was to be no interference with the 'course of normal trade'[36] a rule which belied the atmosphere of urgency given by the increased estimates for construction; and this impression was not entirely countered by the innovation of a reserve of industrial supply, beyond the normal range of government and private arms manufacture. Encouraged by the relatively quiet atmosphere of the Far East towards the end of 1936, the Treasury, and Chamberlain in particular, returned to the earlier scheme of limited liability which involved a new approach to Germany and Italy and a cutting-back of the Field Force and the bomber counter-strike in favour of fighter defence.

The debates in the Cabinet in the spring of 1937 changed character rapidly as Chamberlain began to take over responsibility for defence, well in advance of his actual succession as Prime Minister. The Defence White Paper of 1936 had implied that the Field Force was to continue on the 1934 strength of five divisions, but the poor performance of the War Office, particularly of Duff Cooper, the Secretary of State, in the Cabinet and the continued success of the Air Minister, Lord Swinton, in building up the Air Force deterrent, permanently altered the political balance between the two services. In December 1936, in an attempt to offset their disadvantage, the War Office put in a claim for a substantial Field Force, not merely of five divisions fully equipped for immediate overseas service, but of four Territorial Army divisions, to be ready within four months of the outbreak of war. Immediately the Air Ministry replied with a demand for full numerical equality with Germany by 1939.

Chamberlain, Chancellor and prospective Prime Minister, responded as he had done in 1934. Rearmament, he told the Cabinet on 6 February 1937, could no longer be financed out of revenue: he would have to ask for legislation to enable the Treasury to raise a defence loan; and, in the face of further increases, he as Chancellor 'would have soon to propose a fixed limit for the Services'.[37] That spring was bedevilled by other issues, chiefly arguments over control of the Fleet Air Arm, which created difficult problems for Lords Swinton and Weir, and weakened both in the face of Chamberlain's rising power, but while Baldwin was still Prime Minister a profound change in strategic policy had begun which involved the air deterrent as well as the Field Force.

The carefully contrived balance between the Services evolved in 1934–5 had been intended to provide resources for diplomacy to avoid the sombre effect of the warnings of the Defence Requirements Committee against a war on two or more fronts. Enough had been provided, the Government thought, to maintain the commitments of Imperial defence and the obligations and interests in the Far East. In Europe there was some hope, by the end of 1936, that the Air Force would reach a position near enough to parity with Germany to constitute a deterrent in its own right, by threatening to pulverise the industrial heart of Germany; that the Navy would remain strong enough on the ratio of the Anglo-German Naval Treaty to fulfil its role in blockade; and that the Field Force would be sufficient aid to France and Belgium to resist German aggression by land. But the malign force of foreign affairs did not permit Baldwin's Government to take much advantage of their effort.

The chief aim of British foreign policy in Europe, after the failure of the protracted League of Nations' Disarmament Conference in 1934, can best be described as the search for a détente with Germany. Mussolini's Abyssinian war introduced a confusing and ultimately fatal element, but relations with

Italy, like those with Japan, were handled fitfully in comparison to the threat from Nazi expansion. British policy towards Germany in the three years after 1934 ran at a number of different levels and the story is too complicated to outline except in very general terms.[38] Acceptance of the DRC report signified the end of the National Government's hopes – of MacDonald and Simon in particular – that the Hitler regime could be reconciled in terms of an understanding based on disarmament. Slowly the memory of the various schemes presented at the Disarmament Conference and the pacts discussed during 1933–4 was expunged and replaced by the realisation that Germany, having walked out of the Conference and the League in October 1933, would neither return nor cease to rearm.

Thereafter, the Government reverted to a policy of firmness, based on the rearmament programme and the air deterrent, combined with overtures to Germany which owed their substance to Locarno, rather than the League. Since the murder of Dollfuss, the Austrian Prime Minister, occurred in a Nazi-inspired *putsch* in July 1934, the change of strategy came not before time, but it created a dilemma which rearmament alone could not resolve: the middle way,* between a policy of firm alliances with France and Italy against Germany (which was in defiance of what British public opinion was believed to want), and one of indifference to European interests, was extremely hard to find unless Britain acquiesced in France's own search for alliances in Eastern Europe – a course which raised in Germany the spectre of 'encirclement'. For two years the British Government tried to ride both horses at once, with deleterious effects on France, Russia and the United States; and the détente with Germany was not achieved.

France's own search for an Eastern Locarno, adding Poland and Russia to the three countries of the Little Entente – the strategy of Louis Barthou, Foreign Minister in the Doumergue Government – was agreed to by the British in July 1934, on the understanding that the Pact should include Germany, and

---

* Once defined by Vansittart, looking back, in Dec 1936 as 'a comprehensive European settlement, and when that failed . . . a Five Power Summit . . . confined to settlements first in Western and Central Europe, without the complication of any further agreement in Eastern Europe' (31 Dec 1936, C8998/8998/18 (FO 371/19949).)

the Government recommended it to the ambassadors in Rome, Berlin and Warsaw. For three months that summer it seemed as though the concert of Europe might be revived, and the Eastern Pact linked with the existing Locarno arrangements and the League. Italy offered some support and, more important, moved troops, apparently to safeguard Austrian independence, when Dollfuss was killed. But the plan broke on the absolute unwillingness of Nazi Germany to be bound down – nominally on her claim for 'full equality of status' which France denied – and on the perennial mistrust between Poland and Russia. The assassination of Barthou on 9 October, in Marseilles, with King Alexander of Yugoslavia, buried the whole scheme.

In 1935, as Germany moved steadily into the period of 'secret preparations for aggression'[39], a second attempt at détente was made. Pierre Laval, the French Foreign Minister, and Mussolini made an agreement in January 1935 which prepared the way for an accord between the four Locarno powers, Italy, France, Belgium and Britain, to begin a new round of direct negotiation with Germany. By the Anglo-French declaration of 4 February 1935 Germany was invited to join the Eastern Locarno and to subscribe to a Western Air Pact. The negotiations led directly to the Stresa Front in April, in which the two, together with Italy, agreed to work for both objectives and to uphold Austrian independence. Germany saw herself denounced and isolated; but the effect was very shortly undermined by the divergent national policies of all three components of the Front.

Germany had only undertaken to 'examine' the Anglo-French invitation. The British Defence White Paper of March 1935, with its announcement of military increases and a clear warning directed at Germany's illegal rearmament, gave Hitler the opportunity to postpone the projected visit of Simon and Eden. When the two ministers finally reached Berlin, Hitler made his well-known boast that Germany had already reached parity with Britain in the air. Publicly he announced the existence of the German air force, introduced conscription, and laid claim to the need for a standing army of thirty-six divisions.

The Franco-Soviet Pact which was signed on 2 May, though an obvious consequence of the failure to create an Eastern Locarno, was most unwelcome in Britain, and France herself reacted even more violently against the Anglo-German Naval Agreement* which was announced six weeks later. Since it seemed to restrict an arms race only in the Service which concerned Britain as an Imperial power, France regarded it as a piece of shameless self-interest, destructive of Versailles, and took very little part in the London Naval Conference later in the year. Mistrust, dating back to the 1920s, spread like dry rot in the Stresa Front, even before the Italian invasion of Abyssinia, Laval's pro-Italian policy and the disaster which followed the Hoare–Laval Pact, reduced it to dust.

Germany made the Abyssinian crisis the excuse for avoiding consideration of the Air Pact, as Hitler admitted openly to Sir Eric Phipps, the British Ambassador in Berlin, in January 1936,[40] and with the Eastern Locarno it disappeared hastily from the European canvas. Taking full advantage of the disunity of the Western powers, the involvement of Italy in Africa, and on the spurious pretext of the French ratification of the Franco-Soviet Pact, Germany then denounced the Locarno Treaty and reoccupied the Rhineland in March 1936, in total defiance of the Treaty of Versailles. Mutual distrust, military unpreparedness in France and Britain and the pro-German inclination of British public opinion ensured that no action was taken. The subterranean stage of German recovery was complete.

The remaining Locarno powers met in London, reaffirmed their allegiance to the Pact on 19 March and denounced the German action. Subsequently, Britain directed a series of questions to Hitler, seeking to probe the wide assurances of future good behaviour which he had offered at the time of the occupation, and to tie him down now that the principal cause of animus against Versailles had been summarily disposed of. The questionnaire was evaded and during the summer of 1936 German motivation became even more obscure to British eyes.

A sequence of overtures from Berlin, the visit to London of von Neurath, the Foreign Minister, in January and Hitler's statement that 'the notion of hostility between France and

---

* In order to secure a pause in German naval construction, and to set a fixed limit which Germany could pass only at the price of a public declaration of aggressive ambition, the British signed an agreement with Germany on 18 June 1935 which limited German naval strength to 35 per cent of that of the British Empire. Germany reserved the right to build submarines up to parity strength.

Germany was absurd . . . our people are in no way hereditary enemies'[41] seemed to substantiate optimism about a détente later in 1936; and certainly influential formers of opinion, like Field-Marshal Smuts and Geoffrey Dawson, the editor of *The Times,* were prepared to take them seriously. It would be, Dawson said, 'sheer folly to refuse to get the utmost out of the professions which accompanied [the occupation] whether they are sincere or not'.[42] The direct approach, suggesting a visit to Hitler, which was made to Baldwin in May, offered confirmation of a hope which the Cabinet and Foreign Office were painfully anxious to accept.* But Baldwin refused, judging that the German move was intended to widen the split created between France and Britain by the Abyssinian crisis. Some members of the Cabinet believed that a détente might have been obtained with Germany in the second half of 1936 but it became clear that the price would be the loss of whatever friendship with France remained. The hopeful omens had been falsified too often in the previous three years for anything but the most cautious distrust of German offers.

Vansittart defined the foreign policy of the last year of the Baldwin Government as 'cunctation'. The complexities of the rearmament programme and the growing conflict between maintenance of air parity with Germany and the risk of distorting the economy, emphasised the need to come to terms while Britain was still in a position to exercise power. Separatist tendencies among the remaining Locarno powers were only too clearly advertised in October 1936, when Belgium began to slip away from her obligations, exposing the north-west frontier of France, undefended by the Maginot Line. The Spanish Civil War and intervention by Italy and Germany revealed the danger at France's rear. While it was not surprising that the Popular Front Government of Léon Blum found the old entente increasingly attractive, anti-French feeling grew in Britain, particularly in the section of the Cabinet which looked to Chamberlain as Baldwin's successor, and who took their arguments from the growing obsolescence of the French air force and the unstable and socialist character of her internal politics.

Yet the temptation to make a deal with Germany at the expense of France was resisted. Nothing so strong as an

---

* The separate Foreign Office overtures are described later, p.111.

alliance with France was even suggested in London, but the promises of a Field Force and air and naval co-operation in case of German aggression remained. On 20 November 1936, Eden, in a speech at Leamington which was widely accepted as summing up British policy, laid down, in words not greatly different from those of the Foreign Office memorandum of 1926 quoted earlier, the cases for which Britain would go to war: for her own defence and that of any part of the Commonwealth; in aid of France and Belgium 'against unprovoked aggression in accordance with our existing obligations'; if a new Western European Pact *were* made, in defence of Germany under the same conditions; and in pursuit of the treaties of alliance with Iraq and Egypt. These were all the 'definite obligations'. Beyond that, Britain might declare war in aid of a victim of aggression 'where, in our judgment, it would be proper under the provisions of the Covenant to do so'. This doctrine would have been acceptable equally to Austen Chamberlain or to most later Foreign Secretaries, 'for nations cannot be expected to incur automatic military obligations save for areas where their vital interests are concerned'.[43] It remained the standard definition of British policy through most of 1937.[44]

So long as non-intervention in Spain was imposed without too obvious infringements, so long as Germany remained less committed, politically and militarily, than Italy in the Civil War, some chance of a détente remained. The Eden–Baldwin policy of keeping Germany guessing ensured that nothing irrevocable was done between 1935 and the end of 1936, while Britain grew steadily in military strength. In the first Cabinet meeting of 1937 Eden said that British policy must be 'to try and restrain the Nazi party ... this could best be achieved by our present policy of being firm, but always ready to talk'.[45] As late as March 1937, Oliver Harvey* sent a memorandum to his chief suggesting that

> We none of us believe that Germany is quite certain yet what she wants ... on the other hand, we know what we want—peace and no aggression—and we should not ignore the psychological effect of our determination backed by strength on an undecided Germany, conscious of obvious economic and strategic weakness.[46]

But this line could not be pursued for much longer without

---

* Eden's Private Secretary and closest adviser in the Foreign Office.

making irreversible judgements. The year 1937 was to reveal that Germany would permit overtures from Britain only if the entente with France were extinguishcd. This was unacceptable. As Harvey emphasised, Eden's policy was based on widening the 'peace front' with France, the United States and Russia. German rearmament was still ahead of Britain, however: 'cunctation' would have run into severe difficulties even if it had not come to appear as supine delay to the new Prime Minister, who desired a policy of rapid agreement with Germany, and who had far less understanding of, or affection for, the entente with France. Already, at the Cabinet meeting on 13 January, the Lord Privy Seal, Lord Halifax, was complaining of the fact that Eden corresponded freely with Delbos, the French Foreign Minister, but not with von Neurath, his German counterpart.

There is no reason to suppose that the abandonment of the dual policy which had been evolved in the previous four years was inevitable, but by the spring of 1937 it was necessary to review it both in military and diplomatic terms. Limited success like non-intervention in Spain, which may have prevented more general war, was not enough to outweigh the fact that Germany was no nearer a détente than in 1934, in spite of British rearmament. In some ways the relative position was much worse. Moreover the deterrent itself had run into technical difficulties, shortages of skilled labour and the rival demands of Navy and Army. A great argument about the balance between rearmament and welfare, and what was the normal order of priorities for an industrial trading nation, could no longer be postponed. Meanwhile, as Germany built faster than Britain, demands for action before she became too powerful or intransigent could be heard from erstwhile supporters of the Eden–Baldwin line, like Fisher, Hankey, Weir, Halifax and Sir Samuel Hoare (for example, the FO proposals (pp. 110–11)).

Swept away by this wave, the 'cunctation' policy was abandoned during 1937, yet the value of delaying tactics towards Germany had not been positively disproved. There was an alternative to the course which Chamberlain actually chose, and the fact that it was postponed until the creation of a firm military alliance with France in March 1939 does not mean that it would have been less effective if it had been prolonged through 1937–8.

2 Chamberlain's Way

In March 1937, at President Roosevelt's instigation, Henry Morgenthau, United States Secretary of the Treasury, wrote to Neville Chamberlain suggesting an Anglo-American attempt to lower tension in Europe. In his reply, Chamberlain placed the blame for the growth of tension firmly on Germany, and advised the American Government in words which scarcely admit a charge of weakness:

[Germany] is not likely to agree to any disarmament which would defeat her purpose. The only consideration which would influence her to a contrary decision would be the conviction that her efforts to secure superiority of force were doomed to failure by reason of the superior force which would meet her if she attempted aggression....[1]

It is significant that Morgenthau should have written to Chamberlain while still Chancellor of the Exchequer. His succession to Baldwin had not been assured until after the Abdication of Edward viii in December 1936, in spite of the fact that he was senior minister and had been heir presumptive for five years. Rather like Eden, waiting uneasily after 1951 for Churchill to retire, Chamberlain had borne loyally the doubt and frustration about the date. Baldwin would have retired at the end of 1936 if it had not been for the Abdication[2] but it was not until his last year of office that he was convinced Chamberlain should follow him. Chamberlain could write, as late as December 1935, 'I believe Baldwin will stay on for the duration and by the next election I shall be 70 and shan't care much, I dare say, for the strenuous life of leader, even if someone else hasn't overtaken me before then.'[3] But by March 1937 he had taken over in the supremely important areas of defence and foreign policy, and, as his diary shows, he was busy Cabinet-making.

Certain well-developed factors in Chamberlain's character were to be of marked importance in his handling of foreign affairs and relationships with foreign heads of state. His first biographer, Sir Keith Feiling, did justice to his private virtues, his happy family life, sense of humour and perceptive interest in music and the arts. In many ways he was unusually at peace with himself and the surroundings from which he drew strength. He was meticulous in his family piety, in his regular letters to his wife and his sisters, Ida and Hilda, and in setting out, for them at least, the springs of his political activity. He respected the memory of his father Joseph almost to the point of idolatry, and there was more than mere hyperbole in his speech on the introduction of the Import Duties Act in 1932, the climax, so he styled, it, of his father's Tariff Campaign twenty-nine years before.

I believe he would have found consolation for the bitterness of his disappointment, if he could have foreseen that these proposals, which are the direct and legitimate descendants of his own conception, would be laid before the House of Commons, which he loved, in the presence of one and by the lips of the other of the two immediate successors of his name and blood.[4]

For Sir Austen, his half-brother, the great Foreign Secretary, he had similar feelings : Eden was wrong to think him hurt, when at a dinner party shortly before he became Prime Minister, Austen banteringly dismissed his analysis of the Austrian problem with the comment, 'Neville, you must remember you don't know anything about foreign affairs.'[5] When Austen died, Neville wrote with a depth of feeling rarely admitted, even in his private correspondence, 'From my earliest days I have looked up to Austen with perhaps much more deference, as well as affection, than is usually the case where the difference of years was so small. He was a rare good brother to me and the only one I had.'[6]

Birmingham was still the political suburb of the Chamberlain family in the 1930s, the base from which he drew his political strength, more than Austen, whose prescriptive right to high office was scarcely challenged in the inter-war years. When the city lauded him as Prime Minister in 1937, he wrote: 'It reminded me of the old days when the people used to run after father's carriage . . . it does warm one's heart to feel that these people have given one their confidence so freely.'[7] Yet, outside the world he knew, he was a stranger cautiously probing the unknown through mists of shyness. He had few political friends, and he confided in hardly any of the civil servants who served him well; and whose loyalty and skill he nevertheless acknowledged. The fact that he respected very few men, other than those whose insight and weight of logic rivalled his own, is only a partial explanation of his austere and rather forbidding façade. No one with his intensity of family feeling could be called lonely, but he was solitary to a marked degree. He was ill at ease even among his Tory colleagues in the clubbable atmosphere of the House of Commons smoking-room and excessively harsh towards the Labour opposition through lack of human understanding. Self-sufficiency served him in place of public praise, if his private letters and notes are to be believed. His friends had to be not only his equals, but to share the same, or similar, background and temperament. He was conscious that the Press and public found him unattractive and he accepted the unpopularity which frequently descends on Chancellors of the Exchequer with a wry form of resignation, sometimes pleasantly humble but often edging on self-righteousness. Fishing was his favourite sport: one at which a man is his own measure and critic, which calls pre-eminently for patience, skill and tenacity, and where problems can be posed unequivocally, and finally solved.

Sir Horace Wilson, who knew him better than most, wrote*

He never gave half the time to cultivate the acquaintance of members of the Opposition, or even the rank and file of his own party. He was shy and reserved : [remember] his passion for work. P.M.'s have to deal with policy and administration, personnel. He read papers assiduously, generally from beginning to end, and seemed never to tire, whatever the hour. After the usual harassing day he would start on tightly packed boxes of papers at 11 p.m. or later, and not go to bed until he had finished them. These seemed more important than becoming 'friends' with possible opponents or critics. Vain efforts to get him to attend the Derby, Wimbledon, Lords. 'It would be humbug and I won't be party to it.'

Solitariness encouraged the characteristics of his later years: the sense of duty, conceived of as a personal mission, and an almost demonic urge to solve problems, either in his own

---

* In a memorandum in the Thomas Jones papers with the heading 'This is either a memorandum by Sir H.W. or my summary of such a memorandum. T.J. 18.11.51.' Future references to this memorandum are given as 'Wilson Memorandum'.

department or those of other ministers, regardless of public applause or his colleagues' feelings. This latter urge lent a grim enjoyment to his duty, as he admitted in a characteristic comment: 'the amount of work you have to do largely depends on what you make for yourself. Unhappily it is part of my nature that I cannot contemplate any problem without trying to find a solution for it.'[8] In the autumn of 1936, moved by rereading his brother's published letters, he reflected on the characteristics which he had inherited. 'There are very few brief moments when I can't bear to talk or think of the politics that have become my main purpose in life. Indeed, my fear is always lest this prime interest should obliterate my other interests in art or music or books or flowers or natural history.'[9]

His approach to foreign affairs was by no means the myopic view from the Birmingham town hall with which Lloyd George, among many detractors, liked to amuse himself.* The horror of war which he shared with most of his contemporaries was based not only on the revulsion against the use of war as an instrument of policy, but on a much deeper belief in rationality as the foundation of all human behaviour. Every aspect of his personality, his religion, as well as his feeling for music, testified to a love of order. About war he wrote with unconcealed hatred and disgust. War 'wins nothing, cures nothing, ends nothing'. 'When I think . . . of the 7 million young men who were cut off in their prime, the 13 million who were maimed and mutilated, the misery and the suffering of the mothers and the fathers . . . in war there are no winners, but all are losers.'[10]

When the Abyssinian crisis was building up and Mussolini riding high, he wrote: 'It does seem barbarous that in these days it should still be in the power of one man, for the whim or to pursue his personal influence, to throw away the lives of thousands of Italians.'[11] And in a speech at Birmingham in April 1938 after the fall of Austria he expounded his belief most fully:

We pass no judgment here upon the political system of other countries, but neither Fascism nor Communism is in harmony with

---

* Although it has been well said of him: 'the world he understood was a world of businessmen where contracts were secret and enforceable without violence and difficulties could be ironed out round the conference table; and where the keenest rivals could, by hard bargaining, reach mutually profitable agreements'. (W. L. McElwee, *Britain's Locust Years* (London 1962) p. 257.)

our temper and creed . . . and yet, do not forget that we are all members of the human race and subject to the like passions and affections and fears and desires. There *must* be something in common between us, if only we can find it, and perhaps by our very aloofness from the rest of Europe, we may have some special part to play as conciliator and mediator.[12]

To carry out this far from ignoble creed, Chamberlain shaped himself for the highest office in a way surprising in a Chancellor of the Exchequer, whose past history might be held to have befitted him much more to solve domestic problems of the country's economy. It is true that he was spoken of as a potential successor to Simon at the Foreign Office in December 1933[13] but he refused to let his name be considered. The opportunity came again a year later and was again rejected – 'there are some very important things to do at the F.O. but I would rather have someone else to do them – if he would do them. How I should hate the social side of it and the constant visits to Geneva.'[14] Moreover, 'I should hardly have time to feel my feet before the election would be on us and I very much mistrust P. Cunliffe-Lister's judgment at the Exchequer.'[15] He might also have become Minister for Co-ordination of Defence but for his hesitation at leaving the Treasury in what he believed to be weaker or unorthodox hands. The post went instead to Inskip, at the time, curiously enough, spoken of as potential rival successor as Prime Minister;[16] but Chamberlain's experience and seniority could never be ignored.

It has sometimes been asserted that his foreign policy in 1937–9 was the outcome of the situation which he found when he became Prime Minister in May 1937. This is based partly on the misapprehension that his interest in defence and rearmament in 1934–7 sprang primarily from his concern about finance and partly because he appeared to have had no experience nor close involvement in foreign affairs. Certainly the amount of time taken up by the Chancellor during foreign-policy debates in Cabinet before 1934 was relatively small, but the entries in his diary and his letters are full of a lively interest in the subject, especially after his first experience of an international conference at Lausanne in July 1932 where the subject of reparations was raised for the last time.

Until then his experience had been limited, like most other ministers, to the Foreign Office papers circulated to the Cabinet.

While Austen was Foreign Secretary, Neville scarcely dared to intervene. But the evolution of the Tariff policy by his committee during the period in opposition from 1929-31, and the negotiations with the Dominions which led up to the Economic Conference at Ottawa in 1932, widened his horizons remarkably. At Lausanne where he met his European contemporaries, von Neurath, von Papen, Herriot, he learned lessons which were to be curiously well remembered in the future.* Afterwards, he summed up his impressions, which are of considerable interest as pointers to the future:

This has been an education to me in the ways of the foreigner. He simply can't contemplate getting down to business without long preliminary sparring and skirmishing. To disclose at an early stage what you really want and how far you really mean to go is, to his mind, to lay yourself at your opponent's mercy and it seems inconceivable to him that anyone should be so foolish. When therefore we, in our impatient blundering way, blurt out our intentions without any prologue, the foreigner can't believe that we could be so simple. He says, of course les Anglais must begin like that. But what is his game? What is he concealing and how far is he prepared to come away from the position he has taken up?

He showed little respect for the Italians or Belgians and noted sardonically: 'The French talk at interminable length on generalities, they protest their loyalty, their frankness and their disinterestedness. Meanwhile, they send out an army of agents who nose around and try and find out what the other fellow means to do and where is his last ditch.'[17]

He kept up acquaintance with foreign and other statesmen through occasional friendly conversations with Beck, Prime Minister of Poland, Flandin, Tyrell, the Ambassador in Paris and some of the Dominion statesmen† but his main field of force lay within the Cabinet. Even before the strategic debates

---

* Of von Papen he wrote—'I can quite understand the blunders he made during the war, now I see how he behaves here' (letter of 4 July 1932). Seven years later, in September 1939, when Papen made an absurd overture to Britain through the British Minister at Ankara, Chamberlain told the Cabinet that 'he regarded Herr von Papen as most hysterical and unreliable. He had seen a great deal of him during the Lausanne Conference.' (CAB 23/99.)

† 'As a rule the Dominion statesmen are not impressive, but I must say I took very much to [Menzies] and was glad to find him a strong imperialist.' (Chamberlain letters, 1 Apr 1935.)

of April–May 1934, he involved himself in the Far East question by insisting on an embargo on arms supply to China and Japan and was surprised at the hostile reaction of the latter.[18] He opposed the British Disarmament Convention in November 1933, because of the offence he thought it would give to France and Italy, and he tried to persuade the Cabinet to 'recognise the reasonableness of the two main German objections and declare that the Conference must be adjourned while we and Italy explored the possibility of the situation in Berlin and Paris'.[19] In the last months of 1933, according to his diary, he was taking a 'very active part' in foreign affairs and he had already come to despise the Foreign Secretary, Sir John Simon, for his 'pitiable part' – 'he seems temperamentally unable to make up his mind to action when a difficult situation arises'.[20]

Chamberlain's activities reached far beyond the normal pre-occupations of the Treasury, and his incursions into foreign policy and strategy were resented even then. The scheme which he worked out for limited liability in Europe – for a series of mutual guarantees between the European states 'under which, on breach of the convention, each of the other signatories undertakes to put a limited specified force at the disposal of a joint body ... it would, in fact, be an international police force, not to replace but to aid the aggrieved party'[21] – though ingenious, was opposed by the Foreign Office and Chiefs of Staff because of the economies it would have demanded in the DRC pro-gramme and because of the need for Britain to come to terms with Japan over the balance of power in the Far East.

Chamberlain lost all round in 1934 but he believed that he had made his point:

> I could not expect to change the long held opinions of the Services and Foreign Office in a few words single-handed. But I have made them all think more seriously about the subject than they have ever done before and my retirement is only tem-porary.... For the old aphorism 'force is no remedy' I would substitute 'the fear of force is the only remedy' ... and so I have practically taken charge now of the defence requirements of the country.[22]

He was being unduly optimistic. Only on the theme of the air deterrent – 'we shall be more likely to deter Germany from mad-dogging if we have an Air Force which, in case of need, could bomb the Ruhr from Belgium'[23] – where his views coincided with those of Baldwin, were they acceptable. Rather wearily, he wrote at the end of the year, when naval conversations with Japan and the United States were about to start: 'I wish I were in at the conversations but of course I have no status there and could only pull strings. I hope the puppets will make the gestures I want.'[24]

As his eminence within the Cabinet grew, however, Chamberlain established a prerogative to speak on foreign policy[25] so that in March 1935 he could say: 'As you will see I have become a sort of acting P.M. – only without the actual power of the P.M. I have to say "Have you thought?" or "What would you say?" when it would be quicker to say "This is what you must do".'[26]

He would have liked to have gone with MacDonald and Simon to Stresa 'but that, of course, is impossible'.[27] The continuity of his views showed in his approval of the Anglo-German Naval Treaty, and he understood quickly the implications of Mussolini's designs on Abyssinia. One of his suggestions at least is of interest as a foretaste of his approach to later, somewhat similar, questions of aggression. 'It was not her colonial aspirations, but her proposal to achieve them by war, that we objected to.'[28]

Hoare succeeded the discredited Simon in June 1935, and although Chamberlain would have preferred Eden he was soon endorsing Hoare's firm speech at Geneva, in September, on sanctions against Italy. But in the next nine months Chamberlain swung finally against the League as a power in international affairs. Even in August 1935 he had replaced it, in his own mind, by what he called 'a reconstructed League to deal with European affairs. . . . What I shall work for is a Britain strong enough to make it impossible for her wishes to be flouted again, as Mussolini has flouted them now.'[29]

The occupation of the Rhineland confirmed his belief that the League was futile. He concurred in the declaration of the Locarno powers on 19 March 1936 and in the questionnaire directed to Hitler, but he was already looking ahead: 'If we could get this trouble behind us and start Europe on a new basis, we should I believe see a rapid expansion, for the undertone is firm and enterprise is just waiting for the restoration of confidence to go ahead.'[30] Meanwhile, 'the League had failed to stop the [Abyssinian] war or to protect the victims and had thereby demonstrated the failure of collective security as now understood'.[31] Over Italian aggression it had 'conspicuously failed to do more than exacerbate feelings all round and will be charged, not without justification, with having encouraged Abyssinia to commit suicide'.[32]

These conclusions led to his most dramatic incursion, as Chancellor, into foreign affairs – the unauthorised speech to the 1900 Club in June, in which he called the continuance of sanctions 'the very mid-summer of madness'. He asked, 'Is it not apparent that the policy of sanctions involves, I do not say war, but a risk of war?'[33] and he advocated in their place regional security pacts almost indistinguishable from the unfashionable alliances of the pre-war era. Coming as it did just when the Cabinet had been considering what was the right moment to withdraw, the Chancellor's public démarche prevented them from gaining any tactical advantage. But he took a high line, in private; and it is clear that it had not been an unintentional gaffe:

I did it deliberately because I felt that the party and the country needed a lead, and an indication that the Government was not wavering and drifting without a policy . . . I did not consult Anthony Eden [the Foreign Secretary] because he would have been bound to beg me not to say what I proposed.[34]

By 1936 the position denied him two years before had been won. As Baldwin's heir presumptive, he was listened to in spheres far beyond the normal activity of Chancellor. And his European policy, as it can be deduced from his letters, diaries and speeches at the time, was devoted primarily to re-establishing good relations with Germany. He was scarcely sympathetic towards Fascism – he had called Hitler's regime 'the bully of Europe' and blamed 'her own selfish aggrandizement and pride'[35] for the murder of Dollfuss – but because Germany was the most powerful unfriendly nation in Europe he believed, logically, that in her feeble state Britain must come to terms. He did not expect to be able to choose Britain's allies simply because he liked them. Since at least the beginning of 1935 he had been in favour of firm settlement and had suggested to Simon that the way to talk to Hitler was to say that there were only two ways of getting security and peace. One: Regional pacts on Locarno lines. Two: Alliances and a balance of power. We wanted the first but could not get it without him and if he would not play we should be forced into Two.[36]

When still Chancellor in early 1937 he had a conversation with Nevile Henderson, before the latter went as Ambassador to Germany, and urged him 'to take the line of co-operation with Germany, if possible. N.C. felt it was not the business of this country to interfere with forms of Government which other countries chose to have.'[37]

'If only,' he told Ivan Maisky, the Soviet Ambassador, in July 1937, 'we could sit down at a table with the Germans and run through all their complaints and claims with a pencil, this would greatly relieve all tension',[38] and in some of his letters he expressed his more precise plans for such questions as the return of former colonies.

It is really impossible to declare that in no circumstances and at no time would we ever consider the surrender of our mandate over any territory which we hold now.... I don't believe myself that we could purchase peace in a lasting settlement by handing over Tanganyika to the Germans, but if I did I would not hesitate for a moment to do so. It would be of no more value to them than it is to us.[39]

Italy was of less importance. He accepted the priorities of the DRC Report even though he disagreed with its recommendations. He had none of the respect for the strength of Mussolini's dictatorship, which he unwillingly conceded to Hitler. He commended Eden's diplomatic work during the early stages of the Abyssinian crisis, in 1935, but there is no evidence before 1937 of the urgency which later drove him to seek a closer understanding with Italy as a precondition of the overtures to Berlin.

It was not the Chancellor's prerogative to draft memoranda on foreign affairs for the Cabinet, but his estimate of the relative usefulness to Britain of France, Russia and the United States was already well developed. According to Maisky he had said that he regarded Russia as Britain's enemy[40] – unreliable evidence perhaps, but partly confirmed by his remarks about the Soviet Union during the Czechoslovak crisis. He certainly did not regard the Soviet military machine as a spent force after the purges of 1936, as many less critical minds did.

There is no doubt that Russia has made herself a formidable military power and though I cannot believe that she would be foolish enough to invade Germany or Manchukuo, she would inflict some very nasty wounds on anyone who came within reach of her claws. The German–Japanese agreement is really an admission of nervousness in both.[41]

But this awareness expressed itself, as it had done sometimes with his predecessor,* in a willing fatalism about the likelihood of conflict between the fascist and communist ideologies and a complete indifference to the security arrangements of Eastern Europe.[42]

Chamberlain had shown himself intolerant towards the United States at the time of the World Economic Conference of 1933 and he blamed President Roosevelt bitterly for refusing to stabilise the dollar;[43] thereafter he remained permanently suspicious of American motives and particularly sceptical about any firm connection between the protestations of the State Department and action. His lack of illusion was confirmed by the behaviour of American private industry, in particular of the oil companies, in defying the President and flooding Italy with exports when the League was attempting to impose sanctions. He detested the isolationism and anti-British tone of much of the American press† and blamed the United States Government for the failure to reach a naval agreement with Japan in 1934–5. By 1937 his mistrust was combined with a certain patronising optimism. He favoured trade agreements with the United States and Canada, so he wrote, 'because I reckoned it would help to educate American opinion to act more and more

---

* Baldwin to Churchill: 'If there is any fighting to be done, I should like to see the Bolsheviks and the Nazis doing it.' (CAB 21/438, 29 July 1936).

† 29 Jan 1933: 'Once more one is forced to the conclusion that we have the misfortune to be dealing with a nation of cads.' Later, on 10 Nov 1934: 'It is perhaps fortunate that the British public is kept in complete ignorance of the way we are represented to the other "English speaking" people. . . . One's motives are impugned, one's methods are denounced and no American would read these accounts without thanking God that he had a 100% honest-to-God he-man American to hold up his end against those smiling, treacherous, false Britons who were always betraying him behind his back to the common enemy. There is a calm assumption throughout that Great Britain has nothing else to do but serve American interests. . . .' (Diary entries).

with us and because I felt sure it would frighten the totalitarians. Coming at this moment it looks just like an answer to the Berlin, Rome, Tokyo Axis.'* But his opinion, from which he rarely wavered, was put most clearly in a letter of August 1937, after the outbreak of the Sino-Japanese war. 'The Americans have a long way to go before they become helpful partners in world affairs. I have tried to get them to come in in China and Japan but they were too frightened of their own people – though I believe if they had been willing to play, there was enough chance of stopping hostilities.'[44]

The insular orientation of his foreign policy included an indifference to earlier commitments to France, in particular towards the understanding that Britain would provide a field force for the defence of north-western Europe, which offended against all his strategic assumptions. Chamberlain did not share Halifax's open contempt for French politicians (see below, page 190), but he tended to emphasise the instability and corruptness of French politics and it was characteristic that, when the Chautemps ministry fell for the second time early in 1938, he should tell an American friend: 'France's weakness is a public danger, just when she ought to be a source of strength and confidence, and as a friend she has two faults which destroy half her value. She never can keep a secret for more than half an hour, nor a Government for more than nine months.'[45]

Chamberlain's experience of the actual workings of the Foreign Office was limited and what was lacking was amply made up by mistrust. His interventions in the four years before he became Prime Minister tended to come when crises or debates had already begun, and his relative ignorance of the sources and continuity of problems encouraged both intolerance and over-optimism. 'It is curious,' he wrote in 1934, while reading the third volume of J. L. Garvin's life of his father, 'that I too should be trying to bring about an understanding with another country, on almost identical grounds and contending all the time with the lethargy of the Foreign Office.'[46] In the last year of the Baldwin Government, he began to suspect the existence of an irresponsible Foreign Office mentality, unrelated to the practical realities of the economic and strategic

---

* Feiling, *Neville Chamberlain*, p. 308, Nov 1937. The trade agreements were eventually signed in Nov 1938.

C

position, and manoeuvring a lightweight Foreign Secretary.*
He turned, therefore, towards an entirely distinct thesis, elements
of which he outlined to the Cabinet when explaining his National
Defence Contribution in April 1937. Not only were diplomacy,
defence and economic strength part of a single question; they
had to be presented as such. Thus the sharp shock of the new
tax – which he had to withdraw later at the request of the
Conservative Party Finance Committee – was intended to spell
out the cost, obligations and responsibility of defence. The
electorate must realise that they could not have rearmament
without paying for it.

All the elements of danger are here . . . and I can see that we
might easily run—in no time—into a series of crippling strikes,
ruining our programme, a sharp steepening of costs due to wage
increases, leading to the loss of our export trade, a feverish and
artificial boom, followed by a disastrous slump, and finally the
defeat of the Government and the advent of an ignorant and
unprepared and heavily pledged opposition, to handle a crisis as
severe as that of 1931.[47]

The debates of the second half of 1936 were concerned with
defence rather than diplomacy, and because the result underwrote the foreign policy of 1937 Chamberlain's attitude was of
great importance. He did not wish, as he often emphasised,
to choose the cheapest method of defence rather than the best,
but he overlaid all argument with the fiat that the Chancellor
must emphasise the over-all effect of military demands on the
domestic economy and social programmes of the Government.
It was true, as he said in May 1935, that he had 'insisted on
the need for such a recasting of our Air Programme as would
show its truly formidable character and thus act as a
deterrent',[48] but, unlike the Chiefs of Staff and the Prime
Minister, he had always believed diplomatic action could
reduce the need for a great navy and a Continental army. 'I
have been greatly alarmed,' he added, 'at some of the proposals [in the second Defence Requirements Committee report]
which appear to me panicky and wasteful.' Later, in 1936:
'I do not believe that [war] is imminent. By careful diplomacy

* Hankey also believed this. Describing Eden's resignation, he said: 'He allowed
himself to be swayed too much by a lot of sloppy people at the F.O.,' and affirmed
that Baldwin had blamed himself for not 'straightening up' the Office before he
retired. (Hankey: correspondence with his son, 1 Mar 1938. Hankey papers.)

I believe we can stave it off, perhaps indefinitely, but if we were now to follow Winston [Churchill]'s advice and sacrifice our commerce to the manufacture of arms, we should inflict a sudden injury upon our trade, from which it would take generations to recover.'[49]

Insistence on economic stability was a theme which would recur regularly through 1937. Some time before, he defined his role as arbiter, as he saw it, between the conflicting demands:

When the country learns what we have spent on armaments over and above the estimates, it is going to get a shock and it will be a very good thing because it may help to prepare them for worse—much worse—to come. Oh dear, oh dear, who would be a Chancellor of the Exchequer in such times?... I suppose the answer is that I know no one that I would trust to hold the balance between rigid orthodoxy and a fatal disregard of sound principles and the rights of posterity.[50]

The correlation of sound principles and unyielding orthodoxy is too obvious a generation later.

What emerged most clearly before he became Prime Minister was strong distaste for the concept of an Expeditionary Force for use on the Continent. 'I believe our resources will be more profitably employed in the air and on the sea', he wrote early in 1936, 'than in building up great armies'; and much of his work over the next twelve months was dedicated to pruning the claims of the War Office for a fully equipped Field Force with Territorial Army reserves.[51] In spite of his categoric opposition to a Regular Army larger than five divisions, or to any role other than anti-aircraft defence for the Territorial Army,[52] he was unable to undo the promises to defend northwest Europe, so long as Baldwin held effective power. But as the Cabinet debate on the role of the Army rumbled uneasily into February 1937 he was able to write:

I have at last got a decision about the Army and it practically gives me all I want. The Regular Army is to be armed *cap a pié* with the most modern equipment, to be ready to go anywhere at any time. But we are not committed to sending it anywhere, anywhen. The Territorials are to be given similar equipment, but only in sufficient quantity as to enable them to train.... The War Office have renounced all ideas of a continental Army on the scale of 1914–18.[53]

External circumstances had changed but Chamberlain had won the battle he had lost in 1934.

The consequences of his first major victory over the Service ministers followed rapidly, as the defence review of April 1937 (see below, page 116) unravelled many of the Baldwin Government's strategic assumptions. But these changes, which would have affected fundamentally the conduct of British diplomacy quite apart from the new direction given to the foreign policy of the Cabinet, were not unwelcome to the majority of his colleagues, even to Eden who welcomed the end of what, after the end of 1936, had become something of an interregnum. In spite of Chamberlain's avowal to Nancy Astor that he meant to be his own Foreign Secretary[54] there was no substantial discord between the two men before the middle of 1937.

It may have been true, as Jones suspected, that 'his team is not a very loyal one to him personally' but there were no grounds for anyone who had been a member of the Cabinet in the previous four years for agreeing with Jones that 'he is still rather a dark horse, especially in foreign affairs'.[55] Chamberlain's policy had been expressed time and again, for those who had watched him closely. It was noted even by perceptive members of the Opposition: Hugh Dalton, after a talk with Oliver Harvey in March 1937, 'expressed anxiety lest Chamberlain, when he became P.M., would favour the idea of direct Anglo-German agreement'.[56] Yet the Foreign Office failed to see it. Harvey reassured Dalton: 'on the contrary, he fully shared A. E. [Eden]'s views on foreign policy ...'. Eden himself suspected nothing,[57] and no one seems to have forecast the vigour with which Chamberlain would seize the freedom of action his new office gave him, and which he took for granted the Foreign Office would concede. As he confided to his sister Hilda: 'I believe the double policy of rearmament and better relations with Germany and Italy will carry us safely through the danger period, if only the Foreign Office will play up.'[58]

3 Power and Influence

Like a bulldozer sweeping away the ruins of a decayed mansion, Neville Chamberlain destroyed the foreign policy of his predecessor and cleared the site ready to set up his own. He did not alter the structure of policy-making in Whitehall, but instead, where necessary, superimposed his own means and men. It is a central theme of this study that the impact of the new Prime Minister's ready-made strategy in 1937 was directly responsible for the policy which the Cabinet followed down to March 1939 and that other agencies – Foreign Office civil servants, backbench MPs, party headquarters and the Press – played subsidiary parts. On their own, despite the attention which has been paid to them by historians, none of the other 'appeasers' could have subordinated the part played in peace-making by the Foreign Office, Chiefs of Staff and the Foreign Secretary himself. But these changes did not occur at once, and the process must be described as it affected the different levels in Whitehall and beyond, in order to evaluate the influence of each.

The new Prime Minister's style and methods contrasted sharply with those of Baldwin. As his first biographer wrote, 'masterful, confident and ruled by an instinct for order, he would give a lead and perhaps impart an edge on every question'.[1] Where Baldwin had been slow to dictate to or override his colleagues, allowing them a wide freedom under a permissive style of leadership, Chamberlain imposed speed, acuteness, impatience. He demanded precision and relevance in argument, and was intolerant of those who did not, or could not, share his mastery of business methods. He despised those who thought first 'not is this right, but how will this affect the House of Commons or my constituents? My method is to try and make up my own mind first on the proper course, and then try and put others through the same course of reasoning.'[2] He allowed little credit to those who reached the same end by other, less analytical means.

The effect of his personality on the Cabinet was striking. Hoare wrote later: 'Chamberlain seemed at once to crystallise all the fluid forces in the Cabinet. His clear-cut mind and concrete outlook had an astringent effect upon opinions and preferences that had hitherto been only sentiments and impressions. As soon as he succeeded Baldwin, I became increasingly conscious of two distinct points of view in the Cabinet.'[3]

In spite of the growth of faction, however, Chamberlain was never subject to the attacks on his leadership from within the Cabinet and the Conservative Party which had entangled Baldwin in 1930 and 1936. Attacks from his colleagues did not unduly worry him for there was no obvious successor and no aspiring second in command, as he had been for Baldwin. The complete failure of those who tried to run Eden as an alternative Prime Minister, after his resignation, revealed as much about Chamberlain's political power as it did about Eden's character. Nor did the opposition in the House of Commons, where the Labour Party responded to Chamberlain's barely disguised contempt with a bitterness not seen since the early 1920s, deter him, in spite of the indirect warnings he received.[4]

Opposition was treated firmly, and with a mild surprise. Instead of glossing over fundamental differences, as Baldwin had sometimes done, when Churchill was Chancellor of the Exchequer in 1925, or with MacDonald in 1933–4, Chamberlain tended to draw them out. It became more dangerous to be a heretic within the group like Eden than an infidel like Churchill outside. Arguments were pursued to their logical conclusion and had to end, ultimately, in acquiescence or resignation. Chamberlain's own command of logic made the latter choice hard even in Eden's case, and one result of the new Prime Minister's style was the growth of a form of mutual accommodation among the majority which could be called timeserving if it had not been so patently honest. The frantic attempts of nearly all ministers to smooth over Eden's scruples and preserve Cabinet unity, and the closing of ranks after Chamberlain's first visit to Hitler in September 1938, are good examples of their inability to face the implications of disunity.

The second result was to enhance Chamberlain's tendency to work with an inner group, excluding the full Cabinet from the central decisions on foreign policy. In times of strong disagreement this is often a feature of the Cabinet system – witness the development of the atom bomb by the Attlee Government or the conduct of the Suez affair in 1956 – but Chamberlain translated it into a principle of government; just as Lloyd George had used the War Cabinet because he thought it a more efficient way of transacting business. Thus as early as December 1934, as part of an anti-Simon manoeuvre, Chamberlain was advocating 'a committee of selected members who would make an inner Cabinet'.[5] The Foreign Policy Committee, which was set up in April 1936 to discuss revision of the League of Nations and to plan future foreign policy, was in part his idea and he used it enthusiastically as an institution for forward planning as soon as he came to power. In his diary for 5 May 1937, he mentioned specifically 'My purpose [is] to have a sort of Inner Cabinet on policy'.

The freedom of Cabinet discussion on foreign policy, even when the decisions had already been made elsewhere, remains a surprising feature of the administration (in contrast with the practice of many earlier Prime Ministers and at least two who followed him).[6] Chamberlain's belief in the cathartic power of logic and his awareness of his own political strength both permitted and encouraged frankness, so long as it was followed by conversion. Some meetings appear to have resembled Buchmanite rallies, with ministers publicly acknowledging their errors. At the same time, opposition outside and the undoubted loyalty and admiration* of his colleagues intensified in him a feeling of dedication and struggle against great odds, and isolation from opinions beyond his own narrow circle. All four of the inner Cabinet of 1938 – Chamberlain, Halifax, Simon and Hoare – were more remote from public or party opinion, and made more of a virtue of it, than a later generation can easily understand.

Prime Minister and Foreign Secretary together have a peculiar responsibility for the conduct of foreign policy and, although formally responsible to the Cabinet, it is perfectly normal for them to treat the full body of ministers in a purely consultative way. Within Chamberlain's experience, both Curzon and Austen Chamberlain had taken for granted the support of Bonar Law and Baldwin and the acquiescence of their Cabinets in what

---

* The clearest, if somewhat ludicrous expression of love for Chamberlain is to be found in *Chips, the Diaries of Sir Henry Channon*, ed. R. V. Rhodes James (London 1967).

they did. In Eden, however, Chamberlain imagined he had found a Balfour to his Salisbury and he had pressed his claims rather than those of Hoare in 1935.* Eden responded: 'Before Chamberlain became Prime Minister, I would think it true that he and I were closer to each other than to any other member of the Government, exchanging opinions on many Cabinet matters without any disagreement.'[7]

The relationship which Chamberlain envisaged when he took over the Government, however, owed much more to the example of Lloyd George and Curzon. His annoyance at a passage in a speech of Eden's on Germany in January 1937 – 'Anthony did not get my comments . . . I was very sorry as up to then he had done well . . .' – was only a straw in the wind, but on 1 August, after his forecast of progress for the 'double policy . . . if only the F.O. will play up', Chamberlain showed where he intended Eden's place to be: 'I see indications that the F.O. are inclined to be jealous but though it is natural that they should be annoyed at press headlines about the "Chamberlain touch" instead of the "Eden touch" there is no desire on my part to take credit away from the Foreign Secretary and I shall try now to put him in the foreground again.'[8]

Eden's position came to depend on his fulfilling a series of requirements which became increasingly irksome and antipathetic, quite apart from the deep-rooted division on policy towards the dictator countries. With his successor, Lord Halifax, there were no ideological or temperamental differences. Chamberlain was one of the very few in political life who called Halifax Edward, and he seems quite early to have inherited the same friendship and respect which Halifax had given to Baldwin. Their backgrounds were wholly different – Chamberlain's rich industrial upbringing, heavily tinged with politics and the Unitarian tradition, contrasted at every point with that of the leisured, aristocratic high churchman, with his passion for hunting and his great estates on the Yorkshire wolds. Perhaps their very incompatibility heightened the qualities which they shared – self-containment, the assurance of profound conviction tempered only by inner standards, and large unconcern

---

* As early as Mar 1933, Chamberlain commented: 'That young man is coming along rapidly; not only can he make a good speech but he has a good head and what advice he gives is listened to by the Cabinet' (Letters, 25 Mar 1933, also letters, 22 June 1935).

for the opinions of the world. Their closest bond was an almost complete agreement about the direction of Britain's foreign policy. Long before Eden's resignation, in the spring of 1937, Chamberlain had offered Halifax the Lord Presidency of the Council, a post ideally suited to a roving commission in foreign affairs. After making Simon Chancellor, Halifax's was the second Cabinet appointment; Chamberlain felt strongly enough about it to exclude Lord Runciman even at the price of his resignation.[9]

The fitness to be Foreign Secretary of a man who had had a wholly undistinguished career at the Board of Education, as Minister of Agriculture, and as Secretary for War was not in doubt to his colleagues who had marvelled at his work for India as Viceroy from 1926–31. As Hoare wrote later: 'might he not have the same success in Europe that he had won in Asia?'[10] The inspired unorthodoxy of his meeting with Gandhi might be repeated with Hitler and Mussolini. And Halifax had a second important qualification: he wished strongly to take part in foreign affairs.*

How sympathetic he was towards the policy of a détente with Germany and disengagement from France was perhaps not clear at first to his colleagues. The officials of the Foreign Office noted the same characteristics he had shown in other ministries: 'He said he was very lazy and disliked work,' Harvey, now his Private Secretary, wrote. 'Could he hunt on Saturdays? I said there was a lot of work but much of it could be done at home or in the train and we agreed that he needn't see as much as A.E. used to do.'[11] Such remoteness was not necessarily a disadvantage. As Harvey acknowledged, Eden had tried to cover too much paper work, like MacDonald before him. But if Halifax were moulding his style on that of Austen Chamberlain, he lacked the master's intellectual equipment just as he lacked Eden's long acquaintance with foreign diplomats and the essential minutiae of day-to-day diplomacy. Lack of perception was to have serious consequences during his first visit to Germany in November 1937.

It was not until March 1938 that Halifax's contempt for, and dislike of, the French became a major factor in policy-

---

* 'I was untrammelled by any immediate administrative duty and therefore able to do any other work with which the Prime Minister might wish me to help. In this way I came to be a good deal associated with what Eden was doing at the Foreign Office . . .' (Lord Halifax, *Fullness of Days* (London 1957) p. 183).

making, but he did not hide his feelings about Germany. He had a curiously dispassionate, almost etymological interest in the dictators and their followers, which bordered on moral blindness: he could write, for example, of Goering –

> I was immensely entertained at meeting the man. One remembered all the time that he had been concerned with the 'clean-up' in Berlin on June 30 1934 and I wondered how many people he had been responsible for getting killed. ... A modern Robin Hood: producing on me a composite impression of film-star, gangster, great land-owner interested in his property, Prime Minister, Party manager, head gamekeeper at Chatsworth.[12]

After serving with him only for a fortnight, Harvey evinced surprise 'that H. with all his High Church principles is not more shocked at Hitler's proceedings – but he is always trying to understand Germans. He easily blinds himself to unpleasant facts and is ingenious and even jesuitical in rounding awkward corners in his mind.'[13] The possibility that Halifax might be raised to such a level of outrage that he would cross even Chamberlain never showed in his early days as Foreign Secretary.

The other members of the inner group were Simon and Inskip. (Hoare replaced Inskip when the Inner Cabinet was formalised in August 1938.) Whatever feelings Chamberlain had had about Simon as Foreign Secretary, he chose him for his first Cabinet appointment, as Chancellor of the Exchequer 'because we had worked so happily and effectively together'.[14] He was amply rewarded: Simon's budgetary policy followed his own traditions as he had built them up since 1931. Simon insisted, in identical terms, on the underlying importance of financial stability in relation to rearmament – a principle tailored neatly for economy. They were at one on the introduction of rationing for the armed-service estimates, which was imposed in February 1938.

Chamberlain had stood by Hoare almost to the end when, in the extraordinary revolt of December 1935, the rest of the Cabinet had demanded and forced the resignation of the Foreign Secretary who had signed the Hoare–Laval Pact. Nevertheless Hoare's obvious hawking after high office in the next two years had made him grievously unpopular, particularly with Halifax, and Chamberlain distrusted what he regarded as an absurd ambition to follow him as leader of the

Conservative Party. 'Our people,' he wrote, 'would not have him,'[15] but he respected his ability sufficiently to give him the Home Office, in preference to his own protégé, Kingsley Wood. Hoare had no political base within the National Government and his standing, rather like his opinions, fluctuated according to the circumstances of the day. On the other hand, he had had widely useful experience at the Air Ministry and Admiralty and he was a shrewd observer of politics – *Nine Troubled Years* is still the best account of the Munich crisis written by a participant.

The Inner Cabinet comprised three past or present Foreign Secretaries, of whom Simon and Hoare were of notable intellectual calibre. But both were notorious sycophants of the Prime Minister, and Halifax never carried disagreement into opposition until the last stage of the Munich crisis. Inskip on the other hand was less amenable. His work as Co-ordinator had been very largely administrative: he had never become deputy Prime Minister, as originally intended, nor had he risen above the level of an arbitrator easing competing Service claims. Chamberlain found him useful during 1937 as a functionary to impose the new strategy, which culminated in the rationed budget; but the exercise proved self-defeating for Inskip's own place.

Chamberlain made only a few cautious changes in his Government in June 1937. He brought in Lord Dunglass – 'my new and excellent Private Secretary' – but he was reluctant even to promote his close associate, Kingsley Wood, though he had forced him on Baldwin in 1933[16] and though Wood's views on Germany were strikingly similar to his own. Perhaps he was kept in reserve, like R. A. Butler, appointed as Halifax's junior minister after Eden resigned, or Lord Runciman, the National Liberal who, after a painful series of recriminations at not being offered a place among the inner council, withdrew, saying more gracefully, 'that if there was at any time any work to be done in which he could help, he would be glad to do it'.[17] The mission which he led to Prague, sixteen months later, was mid-way between a consolation prize and a test of fitness for future office.

It is more surprising that Chamberlain should have confirmed in their offices those followers of Eden whom he referred to disparagingly as the 'Boys' Brigade': Oliver Stanley (Board of Trade), W. S. Morrison (Agriculture), Walter Elliot (Secretary for Scotland), W. Ormsby-Gore (Colonial Secretary) and Malcolm MacDonald (Dominions Secretary). Their opposition to his direction of foreign affairs did not develop until later in 1937, but he had no reason to welcome them as colleagues. The explanation lies partly in the lack of alternatives – even Duff Cooper, whom he disliked personally, and nearly dropped for his incompetence at the War Office, was given the Admiralty[18] – and partly in Chamberlain's confidence that the loyalty and cohesion of the senior group would be enough to carry the majority. The absence of a grand gesture such as the appointment of Churchill needs no explanation. Even if Chamberlain had foreseen the sort of role which Churchill might ultimately play, as Baldwin did in 1935,[19] it was not suited to the circumstances as he understood them.

Chamberlain's senior ministers had been in office almost continually for six years, and the majority for eleven out of the previous thirteen. He was sixty-eight and the average age of the Inner Cabinet was sixty-one. The most notable feature of the Cabinet is this difference of age: on one side of the decade 46–56 were Chamberlain, Halifax, Simon, Hoare, Inskip, Lord Hailsham, Lord Zetland, Lord Stanhope, Lord Maugham (who succeeded Hailsham), Sir Kingsley Wood and Ernest Brown; on the other, Eden, Malcolm MacDonald, Lord de la Warr, Hore-Belisha, Elliot, Stanley, Duff Cooper and Morrison; in between, only Ormsby-Gore and Lord Swinton. In no Cabinet of this century was age confronted so sharply with relative youth, and the line-up was remarkably similar to the individual distinctions of approach to foreign affairs. Without making too much of the generation gap alone, it can reasonably be said that the 'Conservative' half of the Cabinet had spent their formative years in the period before 1914, while for the rest the First World War and its aftermath had been the central experience. The consequence was, as an ardent follower of Eden thought – 'the Cabinet are in fact far to the right of the House of Commons and the country'.[20]

In terms of age and to a lesser extent of experience, the Inner Cabinet of 1938 confronted the Foreign Secretary of 1937 and the three Service ministers across a gulf of personality. Yet often it was the younger men who were conservative, holding to traditional policies where Chamberlain went boldly in new ways. In this arena of potential conflict, the structure of advice and the pressures exerted by officials, Foreign Office, Civil Service and Chiefs of Staff take on special significance. The influence of outside agencies, political pressure-groups, leader writers and columnists of the 'quality' Press and coteries associated with the Cliveden set or the *Round Table* is less certain.

The political élite in the 1930s was more concerned with policy-making and the exercise of power than with the possession of power in constitutional terms; and in order to understand the evolution of policy it is necessary to study the interaction of circumstances and personalities at certain critical moments. There is an obvious formal hierarchy in which each component has a statutory function: at the top, Prime Minister and Cabinet, and the junior ministers of the Government; then the diplomatic machine, the Foreign Office and all its membership overseas; the bureaucratic machine, or the other departments involved in policy-making, primarily the Cabinet Secretariat and the Treasury, but also frequently the Board of Trade, Colonial and Dominions Offices and the India Office; finally, the military apparatus, the Service ministries and their Chiefs of Staff, the Committee of Imperial Defence and its subcommittees, the military attachés in foreign capitals, overseas commanders; and the obscure network of MI5 and MI6. To set out their separate functions would be otiose because the inter-action of influence varies under different governments and with the personalities of different officials. Not all were subject equally to the general assumptions and value judgments about Britain's status and aims set out earlier, and no ideal relationship of all of them in policy-making existed, no yard-stick by which performance could be judged, except that of success. In the continual flux of government, success at any given moment is not easy to measure.

Inside and outside the Cabinet room ministers walked in the shadow of the ubiquitous Sir Maurice Hankey, Secretary of the Cabinet since 1916, Assistant Secretary of the Committee of Imperial Defence from 1908, Secretary since 1912 and Clerk of the Privy Council since 1922. The influence which he and Sir Warren Fisher, the other senior civil servant of equivalent status and experience, wielded over more than twenty years requires a separate study[21] and it is sufficient here to suggest their effect on foreign policy in 1937–8. The importance of Hankey's role in strategic planning has never been denied, even by Lord Chatfield, First Sea Lord after 1933, who said of him that, 'he did all a Secretary could do, but it must be remembered that he was only a Secretary'.[22] The close trust and reliance which Baldwin, both as Lord President and as Prime Minister in 1953–7, placed in him was shown when Hankey was made chairman of the vastly important Defence Requirements Sub-Committee of the CID, and he was primarily responsible for its 1934 Report. The attempt of Warren Fisher and Chamberlain to reach a détente with Japan and thus cut back on Far Eastern defences was anathema to him, and after its defeat it was he who visited Australia and New Zealand to reassure their governments about Britain's commitments to Imperial defence. He led the opposition to the proposed Ministries of Supply and Defence in 1935 and 1936, and only accepted reluctantly Inskip's appointment to the office of Co-ordinator.

Up to 1936 he was the prime defender of the Army in its continued European role and he showed little enthusiasm for the concept of a deterrent Air Force. After the occupation of the Rhineland, however, in proportion to France's military decay, he changed his attitude. Basing himself always on the principles of the Defence Requirements Committee Report that Britain should never be dragged into a war fought in Europe and the Pacific, he gave his powerful support to Chamberlain's overtures to Italy as a means of diminishing the number of her enemies. In March 1938 he castigated what he called Eden's folly in rejecting a *rapprochement* with Italy which he believed might have fulfilled Stresa, held Austria independent and freed British forces in the Mediterranean and Red Sea.[23] Well aware of France's situation, he advocated immediate recognition of Abyssinia (Mussolini's *quid pro quo* for an agreement) before Hitler came to terms with Italy instead. Hankey's revision of his earlier view contributed to the weakness of the War Office in the face of successive Treasury economies and perhaps also to the supine state of the Army Council who had looked to him before as their principal advocate among the politicians.

Chamberlain trusted Hankey and recalled him from retirement in September 1938 to advise on preparations for a possible war. A year later, when war came, he appointed him to the War Cabinet. Only Churchill disliked him, resented the scope of his influence, and dismissed him in March 1942. Although Hankey's last few months before his retirement in July 1938 were spent largely in inter-departmental disputes and although, as his staff noticed, he had so much business in his hands that he was rarely free to talk,[24] his residual power in terms of information retrieval, continuity, experience and plain wisdom was unrivalled. Only ministers who had sat for years on the CID could match him in argument. He had the immense advantage of having begun the 1919 'War Book', giving the procedure for the working of the Cabinet Secretariat and all Government departments on the outbreak of, and in time of, war. He had made successive British delegations at the various international gatherings after the Peace Conference into virtually a standing Secretariat and he had more knowledge than anyone alive of the Dominion and Colonial political networks. A decline of efficiency in the Cabinet Secretariat and the CID was noticeable as soon as he retired; but, of much greater importance, the tendency which grew during 1937 for the Cabinet to make decisions in advance of strategic advice, ran parallel to the rift signified by the separate appointments of Edward Bridges to the Cabinet Office and Major-General Ismay to the CID.

The distribution of influence among the policy-making élite of the Foreign Office* had changed since the days when Austen Chamberlain had exercised substantial freedom from the super-

* In a study as limited to Cabinet policy-making as this, only a tentative sketch of opinion in the Foreign Office, as it existed at certain moments, can be given. The history of its changing composition, in terms of effective advice and actual policy-making, can only be the result of many separate studies. Among the printed evidence on the attitudes of personalities as regards policy towards Europe in 1933–7, the Harvey diaries and Medlicott, *Britain and Germany, the Search for Agreement 1930–37* (London 1969), are of considerable help. See also Watt, *Personalities and Policies*; Gilbert and Gott, *The Appeasers*; Martin Gilbert, *The Roots of Appeasement* (London 1966); Colvin, *Vansittart in Office*, Valentine Lawford, *Bound for Diplomacy* (London 1963); and the various diplomatic memoirs: Sir Nevile Henderson, *Failure of a Mission* and *Water Under the Bridges* (London 1945); Sir Ivone Kirkpatrick, *The Inner Circle* (London 1959); Lord Strang (Head of the Central Department of the Foreign Office 1937–39), *The Foreign Office* (London 1955) and *Home and Abroad* (London 1956); Lord Vansittart, *The Mist Procession* (London 1958); and the obituaries written by Sir Orme Sargent for the *Dictionary of National Biography* on Henderson and Phipps.

vision of his Cabinet colleagues and even the Prime Minister. Under the permanent head of the Office, Sir Eyre Crowe, it would have been inconceivable for heads of departments or ambassadors in foreign capitals to by-pass the normal channels of advice or to correspond directly with members of the Cabinet other than the Foreign Secretary. But a series of short-lasting ministers followed after 1929; Arthur Henderson, much preoccupied with Geneva, Lord Reading whose tenure lasted only four months, and Hoare who was forced to resign after less than a year in 1935. Simon, it is true, lasted three and a half years, but he was disliked by his colleagues and mistrusted by many of his permanent officials. Moreover, the permanent head in the 1930s, Sir Robert Vansittart, proved to be a prima donna whose memoranda to the Cabinet not only overstated his case but frequently overreached the limits of officials' power which had been accepted in Crowe's time. His close acquaintance with Baldwin and his incursions into more direct policy-making, such as his negotiation with Laval in Paris immediately before the Hoare–Laval Pact was signed in 1935, helped to break down the traditional pattern. At the same time, heads of departments acquired greater power and freedom and although Vansittart's activities were curbed to some extent by the new Foreign Secretary, Eden, in 1936[25] the latter was young and neither powerful enough in Cabinet nor masterful enough in Whitehall to restore the former balance.

The problems posed by German expansion in the 1930s enhanced the divisive tendencies present in any Government department and alternative policies became associated with competing factions. There was no doubt in the Office of the danger from Germany after 1934, nor of Vansittart's endorsement of the Defence Requirements Committee's first report.[26] Equally there was general agreement that many of Germany's grievances in the early 1930s were genuine.[27] Differences centred on the question of whether war to preserve Britain's vital interests was inevitable, or whether it could best be avoided either by a deterrent policy to contain German ambitions, or by one designed to appease Germany's claims. Among the dozen most senior officials, opinion changed a good deal between 1934 and 1937, and Vansittart himself changed tactics in a way which later laid him open to discredit (see below, page 72n). By the latter date three distinct groupings can be identified, each faction bidding for political support as the threat of war grew more urgent, and not necessarily through the Foreign Secretary. By striving to convince Cabinet and Prime Minister that their divergent policies were correct, they undermined the monolithic authority which the Office had formerly possessed. Vansittart's language in particular made it hard for ministers to avoid the conclusion that the distinctions were as much the product of temperamental conflicts as of diplomatic analysis.

The group who believed in a policy of containment rather than appeasement of Germany – which did not exclude modifications of the 1919 peace settlement – included Vansittart, Sir Orme Sargent, the Assistant Under-secretary, R. A. Leeper and J. W. Baxter, both counsellors in the Office, Ralph Wigram, head of the Central Department 1933–6, Laurence Collier, head of the Northern Department, and Sir Eric Phipps, Ambassador in Berlin 1933–7 and in Paris afterwards. These believed in the rearmament programme as a deterrent, in strengthening the links with France, and in maintaining amicable relations with Russia. They feared that to meet German grievances wholesale would be to set up an Anglo-German understanding at the expense of France, who would then make her own settlement; and they did not accept that appeasement, even the surrender of Britain's interests in the independence of Austria, the revision of the Peace Treaty in regard to Germany's claims from Poland and the improvement of status of the Sudeten Germans in Czechoslovakia, would set a term to German expansion.

To some extent, the second group existed simply in opposition to the harshness of a view which seemed to postpone reconciliation with Germany indefinitely. Sir Alexander Cadogan, deputy under-secretary from 1936–7, cannot be classified simply as an 'appeaser' and he was Eden's choice to succeed Vansittart.[28] Nor can William Strang, though he drifted into appeasement in 1938. In the line-up of advisers on policy towards Italy in November 1937, for example, they were both ranged with Eden and Oliver Harvey, the Foreign Secretary's Private Secretary, *against* those who wanted a détente – Vansittart, Sargent and Leeper.[29] But the group included those who would later be the disciples of Chamberlain and Halifax – Sir Nevile Henderson, Ambassador in Berlin after 1937, Lord Perth, Ambassador in Rome since 1933, Basil Newton, Minister in Prague, and Lord Chilston, Ambassador in Moscow 1933–8. By 1938 these men held almost a monopoly of advice presented from the countries most closely concerned with the Czecho-slovak problem; and in 1938 they were joined by Phipps, whose estimates of French morale became gloomier at each stage of the crisis. As Sir Horace Wilson was quick to point out, they took the same stand as Vansittart himself in 1936.* The Francophiles,† on the other hand, were the survivors of the Baldwin regime and, as a policy of immediate détente with Germany and Italy was adopted to the detriment of Anglo-French relations, their influence declined.

There was a third group, much more closely associated with Eden, owing him personal loyalty and committed to the policy of keeping both Germany and Italy guessing. Oliver Harvey, Lord Cranborne, Eden's junior minister, and J. P. L. Thomas, his parliamentary private secretary, formed, on the evidence of Harvey's diary, a pressure group which saw Eden not only in terms of alternative policy but as a candidate to replace Chamberlain as Prime Minister. Their tactics can be compared with the Churchill group (see below, page 98) and they were sometimes equally over-sanguine of the relative importance of their man. 'Whenever he took a firm line, the Cabinet gave way because they couldn't face his resignation,'[30] Harvey wrote only a fortnight before Eden and Cranborne resigned, alone. Harvey in particular tried to bolster Eden into playing a part

---

* 'I am unable to understand in what way the Government, before Munich, differed materially from what Vansittart advocated when Permanent Head of the F.O. In the summer of 1936 he visited Berlin and wrote a report on his visit. His conclusion was that we had better try "an act of faith" in regard to Germany. Of course he advocated large-scale rearmament but that had by then become accepted policy. In December 1936, V. wrote a paper (C8998/8998/18 (FO371/19949) – of which Wilson's account is a reasonable summary) on the world situation and British rearmament. His first point was that we should try to keep Italy friendly. His second . . . the act of faith to which he had referred in his report of the Berlin visit. His third point was that we must press on with rearmament. Finally he said that we required time until 1939. He said it was the task of the F.O. to hold the situation till then. This is precisely the policy that Chamberlain put into practice and it is difficult to see why V. should, in 1937/8, play the obstructive critic.' (Wilson Memorandum) (The comparison was fair, but the circumstances had changed beyond recognition.)

† Vansittart was a close friend of Alexis Léger, Chef du Cabinet at the French Foreign Ministry, and close relation, as well as friend, of Phipps, the British Ambassador in Paris.

for which he was unfitted and probably unwilling:* Eden was not the man to present an alternative policy at public meetings up and down the country as Lloyd George had done in 1929, or Baldwin in 1924.

On policy-making, as Foreign Office advice emerged, this latter group had little effect after Eden went. They were persuasive advocates of the line which he defended through 1937 but they suffered as he did from the disadvantage that the policy of keeping Germany guessing was a long-term one, dependent on parity of armaments. Given all the delays of the rearmament programme and the rapid pace of German expansion in 1936–8, their advice seemed to both the other groups, and especially to the Cabinet, permanently and obstinately negative.† The quick answer, like 'hot' information about German motives, proved much more attractive.

The alternative aspects of British policy towards Germany can be seen in the preparation of a Foreign Office paper[31] for the Cabinet Foreign Policy Committee in July 1937. This document, which forecast the likely action Germany would take in central Europe in the next eighteen months, was not followed by debate, but it was an important source of information for the decisions taken during the rest of 1937, and was itself a subject of fierce inter-departmental argument. Nevile Henderson sent a memorandum to Sargent which he had composed in May, before his appointment to Berlin, advocating an understanding with Germany, bought at the price of 'peaceful expansion and evolution in the East'. Eastern Europe, he thought

emphatically is neither definitely settled for all time nor is it a vital British interest, and the German is certainly more civilised than the Slav, and in the end, if properly handled, also less potentially dangerous to British interests—one might even go so far as to assert that it is not even just to endeavour to prevent

---

* *Diaries of Oliver Harvey*, p. 129. 'It seemed clear to me that his role was to constitute himself the leader and spokesman of that floating vote which the Government had now lost, and thus became an alternative head of National Government for all those, and they were a majority, who did not want the P.M.'s present Conservative trend any more than a Labour Government.' Baldwin tried also to groom him as an opponent to Chamberlain (cf. Middlemas and Barnes, *Baldwin*, pp. 1042–4).
† Their argument has been taken further: since it was so unconstructive, it left no alternative but a stalemate, followed by war (cf. R. Skidelsky in his review of the Harvey diary, *Spectator*, 25 July 1970). The evidence that such realism existed is scanty.

Germany from completing her unity or from being prepared for
war against the Slav, provided her preparations are such as to
reassure the British Empire that they are not simultaneously
designed against it.[32]

Such views were at once attacked by the other side. Vansittart
wrote to Sargent: 'Sir N.H.'s contribution is much more than a
bit wide of the mark. . . . It must be thoroughly dissected and
shown [as] above all contrary to the policy of HMG.' It was.
The paper which followed carried a classic statement of the
Vansittart–Sargent case: Britain *was* interested in the fate of
central Europe and would not condone German expansion in
the east. 'Europe is in a tense and potentially unstable condition.
What keeps it from immediate collapse is the closeness of the
Anglo-French connexion.'[33]

Henderson was an extremist who had shown himself politically jejune even before he reached Berlin,* and his appointment was soon bitterly regretted not only by Vansittart, who
had advised on his new posting.† He had his own channel of
communication, however, with the Prime Minister which he
did not hesitate to use, and in that quarter his opinions proved
more and more acceptable.

The variations in Foreign Office thinking, as well as the
reactions to the intervention of outsiders in the 1930s, can be
gauged from similar comments made on the memorandum
written by Lord Lothian after his second interview with Hitler
and Goering, on 10 May 1937.[34] Whatever their own
differences, Baxter, Sargent, Cadogan and Vansittart all pointed
out Lothian's naïveté in assuming that concessions broadside
in Eastern Europe would check German ambitions *tout court*
or that they could be made without serious repercussions in
France and Russia. There is here and elsewhere evidence of
how the unofficial visitors to Germany were resented – reflection
both of the pride of the Office and its normally superior
expertise. Lothian's participation had been welcomed, because

* Harvey recorded Henderson's grandiose accounts of what he hoped to do by
private negotiation with Prince Paul of Yugoslavia: 'I hope we are not sending
another Ribbentrop to Berlin.' (*Diaries of Oliver Harvey*, p. 41).
† A decision which, according to the accounts given by Eden and Vansittart's
biographer, seems to have been made in an atmosphere of complete unreality.
'Sir Nevile has done his stint in South America – he shall have his reward' (Colvin,
Vansittart in Office, p. 146) – Berlin ranking higher in the pecking-order than
Buenos Aires.

of his American connections, during the discordant negotiations with the United States in 1934,[35] but the only reason for taking seriously his 1937 memorandum seems to have been that he had also circulated it to Dominion Prime Ministers during the Imperial Conference, to whom it was useful ammunition in their demand for disengagement from European commitments.

The policy-making activities of the Foreign Office involve the collection and analysis of information about all aspects of foreign affairs and the processing of this into a coherent body of advice to the Foreign Secretary, recommending certain courses of action. A great deal, of course, is decided and acted on at lower levels within the Office but the Minister himself has often to judge between conflicting courses recommended by separate departments. The advice tendered may be rejected by the Foreign Secretary or Cabinet, for other reasons, and the information supplied may be tested against other sources. The Office, in short, may be overridden but it and the Foreign Secretary are rarely dispensed with.

After Chamberlain became Prime Minister it suffered from four important disadvantages in relation to other sources of influence. Because of the divergent recommendations about policy towards Germany and the way in which all groups played politics at Cabinet level, its authority was divided. Ministers could and did set one rank of experts against another. Secondly, the existence of opposed forces acted like a brake on *any* course of action so that impatience with the Foreign Office became a common characteristic among the politicians. Thirdly, since the normal scope of communications with the Cabinet lay through the Foreign Secretary alone, the battle to convince him added an extra stage of argument, in contrast with the workings of the CID where the Prime Minister took the chair and whose reports were made direct to the Cabinet. The anomalous positions of 'Chief Adviser' to the Government emphasised the disadvantage. Sir Horace Wilson, Chief Industrial Adviser, maintained a direct relationship with Chamberlain, as did Sir Warren Fisher, Head of the Treasury and the Civil Service. Vansittart had exerted similar influence with Baldwin but not with Chamberlain, and it was not recovered even when he was made Chief Diplomatic Adviser. Finally, Dominion spokesmen, by right of membership of the

CID and through the High Commissioners in London, were able to communicate directly with the Cabinet in 1937–8, over and above the Dominions Office.

Multiplication of channels of advice was a characteristic of the 1930s: the Baldwin Cabinet also relied on unofficial sources for information about Nazi Germany. But the tendencies to side-track the experts, and more dangerously, to conflate into a mish-mash distinct recommendations were symptoms of a larger change of balance. Whether or not the Foreign Office failed, the Chamberlain Cabinet came to believe it had, and acted accordingly.

Vansittart's inability to convince either Eden or Chamberlain of the need to strengthen the German conservative opposition to Hitler, and his dismissal in December 1937, illustrate both the limitations under which officials worked and their insecurity in the face of Chamberlain's determination. One of Vansittart's unofficial contacts was Dr Carl Goerdeler, who had resigned from his post as Chief Burgomaster of Leipzig in April 1937 in protest partly against Nazi extremism and partly because of the economic dangers aroused by Hitler's four-year rearmament programme. Goerdeler made a world tour in the early summer of 1937, sponsored by a Stuttgart industrialist, and with the support of the Economics Minister, Dr Schacht, Admiral Canaris, head of German counter-intelligence, and to some extent of Goering.[36] In July 1937 he met Eden, Halifax and Vansittart separately in London. Eden, preoccupied with non-intervention in Spain, seems by his own account to have taken no interest. Halifax kept Chamberlain informed,* but he too was involved with the overture to Mussolini, and no discussion of the visit was held by the Foreign Policy Committee or the Cabinet. Vansittart saw Goerdeler three times.[37] Goerdeler insisted on the significance of the struggle in Germany between the Nazi Party and the moderates (who included part of the High Command, himself, Schacht, and most of the leaders of industry and finance) who were disturbed at the down-turn in the economy and wished to settle with the Western powers on the lines of a colonial and economic agreement. He gave a good deal of evidence from the industrial side in support of his contentions and, although there was little hard information

---

* Halifax took over the Foreign Office in the last week in August, while Eden was away.

about the political direction of Germany, Goerdeler provided a substantive warning against any easy détente with Germany. He advised the British to maintain the same firm policy which Vansittart himself had advocated since 1936.

Early in July, Vansittart began to work this information into his contribution to the memorandum on Germany but it does not appear in FP 36/36. According to his biographer, he marked the section on the German moderates 'suppressed by Eden'.[38] Of course Eden, Halifax and Chamberlain were all aware of Goerdeler's views; but for quite different reasons none of them wished to introduce this issue into political debate in the summer of 1937. The use of the word 'suppressed' may have been hyperbole, but the episode shows the real limits on the power of any member of the Foreign Office to bring advice or information to the political forum without the support of the Foreign Secretary.

Mistrustful of his permanent under-secretary's enthusiasms and punctilious for the proper channels of advice,* Eden had clipped Vansittart's wings after the Hoare–Laval affair and late in 1936 he urged him to take the Paris Embassy. Vansittart refused.† Six months later, Eden tried again and, lacking the determination to transfer his entrenched adviser, asked Chamberlain to replace him. His own choice was Cadogan, but Chamberlain, at the instigation of Warren Fisher, wanted to bring in Sir Findlater Stewart from the India Office.[39]

Vansittart could survive the disapproval of his Foreign Secretary although he was conscious of his own diminishing influence. He could also survive the efforts of his civil service colleagues, notably Sir Horace Wilson and Warren Fisher who in May 1937 tried to bring pressure to bear on Eden's parliamentary private secretary, J. P. L. Thomas, to undermine Vansittart's alleged influence[40] and also, apparently, to frighten him directly by reference to his future honours – or lack of them.[41] But when in December Chamberlain decided that he, too, had had enough of a permanent official whose advice continually crossed his own inclinations ('I never know how Van interprets my

---

* Witness his strong disapproval of the proposal that Baldwin should visit Hitler unofficially in June 1936. (Middlemas and Barnes, *Baldwin*, pp. 957–8.)

† Avon, *Facing the Dictators* p. 521. 'Vansittart would be welcome in Paris. It was also true that a new figure as Permanent Under-Secretary would now make more impact on Whitehall.' (Also, *Diaries of Oliver Harvey*, p. 22.)

messages or what comments he adds,'[42] he wrote during Eden's absence at the Nine-Power Treaty conference in Brussels), Vansittart was cut down without recourse.

After all the months that S.B. wasted in futile attempts to push Van out of the F.O., it is amusing to record that I have done it in three days. Of course, it is deadly secret at present.... Van has accepted my proposal. Indeed I did not give him any alternative! I think the change will make a great difference in the F.O. and when Anthony can work out his ideas with a sane, slow man, like Alick Cadogan, he will be much steadier. Van had the effect of multiplying the extent of Anthony's natural vibrations and I am afraid his instincts were all against my policy.... I suspect that in Rome and Berlin, the rejoicings will be loud and deep.[43]

Such was the incapacity of an official to stand up to ministerial power. The new appointment bore the title of Chief Diplomatic Adviser to the Government. Vansittart could, in theory, have acquired greater capacity, like Horace Wilson, but he had lost his executive functions and although he could sit on the CID and the Foreign Policy Committee he was no longer able to give direct instructions to British ambassadors abroad, nor was he in continued command of the inflow of information.[44] Later in 1938 he was able to work on Halifax, the Foreign Secretary, but not sufficiently to outweigh the power of the Prime Minister (see below, page 321).

Vansittart's freelance style was abruptly expunged from the Foreign Office after December 1937. The group linked with Eden also lost influence after his resignation. Cadogan, modest, self-effacing and industrious, tied himself to Halifax and only in the crisis of September 1938 forgot himself so far as to bring personal pressure to bear on his chief. Vansittart's exclusion made no practical difference, perhaps, but it was symbolic. Ernst Woermann, Counsellor of the German Embassy in London, took the point. Vansittart was regarded as 'an exponent of a one-sidedly French orientation of British foreign policy', he wrote, 'and this did not fit in with Chamberlain's attempts to promote better relations with other countries'.[45]

The new orientation confirmed the altered status of the Foreign Office in the intangible hierarchy of influence. A dozen quotations from Chamberlain's letters and diary could be given to show his disparagement of diplomatic personnel and the significant fact that he conflated – or was unaware of the existence of – the separate factions. Typically, he wrote after a speech by Eden:

It contained some unfortunate passages, from my point of view, and shows again a characteristic of the Foreign Office mind which I have frequently noticed before. They never can keep the major objects of foreign policy in mind, with the result that they make obstructions for themselves by endeavouring to give smart answers to some provocative foreign statement.[46]

Such prejudice alone did not determine the making of foreign policy, but Chamberlain and Halifax, the most powerful ministers in 1938, were peculiar in inter-war history in that they had gained their experience in fields quite remote from foreign affairs. The imposition of a 'higher criticism' – finance over strategy, political considerations over diplomatic advice – owed something to their relative freedom from the assumption that foreign affairs was a mystery to be guarded by devoted and exclusive high priests.

In this, Chamberlain's style was similar to Lloyd George's. The criticism of his relationship with Eden and the Foreign Office looked for precedent to the immediately preceding conditions of 1923–36. Although the experience of 1937–9 was to ensure that subordination of the Foreign Office was not repeated, that was at first by no means a foregone conclusion. Diplomacy like any other department of government must serve a common end, determined by the Cabinet. The Prime Minister must be ultimate judge of priorities if he is to be Prime Minister at all. As R. A. Butler, junior minister to Halifax after Eden's resignation, explained when he visited the German Embassy on 24 February 1938 to say that pro-French prejudice would now be annulled: 'It had been perfectly plain to all intelligent observers that there would have to be a showdown between these two groups after Baldwin left, and the first indication of this had been the side-tracking of Sir Robert Vansittart.'[47]

To explain adequately the effect on foreign policy of the network of the civil service, Treasury, Board of Trade, the Colonial, Dominions and India Offices, would require a description full of variables of great complexity. But these bodies were concerned less frequently than the Foreign Office and at this period their influence over foreign policy was exercised by a few individuals, whose views can briefly be described, although the role of the two principal civil servants has often been overlaid in the past with comments more impassioned than scholarly.

Sir Norman Warren Fisher, Permanent Secretary of the Treasury, became also Head of the Civil Service by a Treasury minute of 1919. Almost as long-lived in high office as Hankey, Fisher did not retire until 1939. As Head of the Civil Service he had technical power of approval over Foreign Office promotions, including the appointments of ambassadors, and his use of this has been called a subversive influence in foreign policy.

Fisher, however, was as staunch an advocate of rearmament as Hankey himself, though from a different strategic point of view, and he shared Vansittart's conviction of the threat of German militarism. P. J. Grigg, private secretary to Churchill when Chancellor of the Exchequer, saw him as 'a kind of unofficial Minister of Defence'.[48] Fisher took a major part in originating the 1935 Defence White Paper, seeing it as the means to set out publicly the implications of rearmament, and, firmly as he defended Treasury control of the programme in the period 1934-7, he set his face against any economies of the essential decisions. He was disappointed at the way Chamberlain 'toned down some of the asperities' of the 1935 White Paper and appealed to Baldwin over the Chancellor's head.[49]

Fisher saw clearly that the original DRC programme would be vastly easier to achieve if tension with Japan could be lessened. He fought a vigorous battle with Hankey, Chairman of the DRC, in February 1934 to get this recommendation written into the conclusions[50] and in the end he carried the argument into the Cabinet via the Chancellor. Perhaps Chamberlain's long struggle to recast the balance of the Services and the Far Eastern strategy of 1934 had other origins as well, but it is reasonable to suggest that the policy of 'making eyes at Japan' had its roots in the Treasury.

Fisher's policy ran almost parallel to Chamberlain's for at least three years before 1937, and they complemented each other when considering the balance between the roles of the Air Force and the Army. After Chamberlain became Prime

Minister, the rationing of the Services, which the unfortunate Inskip had to implement, the subordinating of the Co-ordinator's work, and the abandonment of the concept of a Continental army were all fruits of their alliance. The result was an emphasis on the defensive fighter screen, backed by arguments similar to those put forward in support of the pre-1914 Dreadnought, which Fisher repeated most strongly in October 1938 (below p. 424) and again in the Defence White Paper of 1939.

Because Fisher's strategic views were so closely tied to Chamberlain's, it is very difficult to assign him an individual role. The greater the Prime Minister's dominance appears in 1937–9, the less Fisher stands out. Like Hankey, Fisher was against the setting-up of a Ministry of Defence or Supply, but for different reasons. He believed, as Chamberlain did, that the Services alone had neither the ability nor the breadth of strategic vision to evolve a coherent defence programme; he wished to keep residual power in Treasury hands. But the conclusion that he and the other civilian officials were able to impose on the Chiefs of Staff 'a unity of strategy which they were unable or unwilling, or had not the capacity, to achieve'[51] seems too strong in the light of the part played by Chamberlain, set out in the next chapter. As with Vansittart (though not perhaps with Hankey, whose access to *all* ministers at any time gave him an enormous advantage), Fisher's influence was limited by his capacity to convince his political master; and where his master was as clear and resourceful as Chamberlain it was only to his subordinates in the civil service that he seemed an all-powerful manipulator.

The criticism which should be made of the Treasury is not, as Chamberlain sometimes feared, that the cheapest form of rearmament was preferred to the best. The Treasury, after all, was the only department concerned with over-all value for money and the relaxation of its control in the First World War had led to a great deal of waste which might have been avoided. But its influence over the rearmament programme after 1937, as transmitted by Chamberlain, became excessive, dominating the arguments of Chiefs of Staff and Foreign Office. The state of the economy and the claims of the social services were allowed to take priority in Cabinet discussions. The argument that the Army and, to a lesser extent, the Navy could be neglected in favour of the Air Force prevailed although there could be no assurance that Britain would never have to fight a Continental war against Germany. Chamberlain and Fisher believed in rearmament, certainly, but the conclusions of the Treasury strategy were essentially defensive and anti-European. Coming to terms with Japan meant alienating the United States. Priority for home defence meant withdrawing promised resources from France. Imposition of a fixed budget for the Services meant that each would compete for scarce resources at the eventual expense of the duty their armaments were supposed to perform. It was not failure of the Chiefs of Staff which caused the change but a shift of influence within the Cabinet; and strategic policy, in its widest sense, was subject to dictation from the Treasury boardroom in a way which had not occurred before 1937.[51a]

The role played by Sir Horace Wilson, Chief Industrial Adviser to the Government, is more difficult to assess. The evidence of official archives suggests that his activities were more subordinate than were alleged in the polemical wartime book, *Guilty Men*.[52] He had been brought into Downing Street in 1935 by Baldwin as a 'wise counsellor', somewhat against his own will. His experience was confined primarily to labour relations, and as Permanent Under-Secretary to the Ministry of Labour he had taken a heavy part in the General Strike and most attempts at Government conciliation since Lloyd George's abortive National Industrial Conference of 1919. His reputation as a skilled and subtle negotiator was unrivalled in Whitehall. From 1931 to 1939 the bulk of his work concerned domestic policy or his duties as unofficial counsellor to the Prime Minister.[53] Involvement in foreign policy developed only slowly, out of commitments like his membership (after March 1936) of the Principal Supply Officers Committee. There, though Treasury representative, he covered in practice the whole field of rearmament.

In Wilson, Chamberlain inherited a 'fluid person', as Thomas Jones had once described himself, of great seniority and experience, with an exceptionally lucid mind, who had no department to distract him and owed the Prime Minister primary loyalty. Wilson was the perfect man for unofficial duties which no member of the Cabinet Secretariat, not even Hankey – identified with existing Government policy – could fulfil. Chamberlain could use him as an emissary to the German Embassy, who would deliver an impressionistic view of British aims, informing the other side without the commitment inherent in diplomatic interchanges; at the same time he would sense the atmosphere of German thinking. Inevitably, the German documents record what seemed favourable to them: thus Theodore Kordt, counsellor to the Embassy – 'He is a man who compels respect from everyone who comes into contact with him. He is an embodiment of Moltke's ideal: "be more than you seem".'* Considering the way Chamberlain developed his policy, Wilson must have been eminently useful.

Naturally, his activities were resented in the Foreign Office. Eden noticed that 'contrary to custom' there were no members of the Foreign Service among Chamberlain's private secretaries. 'To have any specialised knowledge of foreign affairs was to be quite out of fashion; it was the day of the uninhibited amateur.'[54] The criticism is just; but Chamberlain could have answered that he needed a counter to the specialists of an Office he profoundly mistrusted, who seemed to him perpetually to cloud large issues with irrelevant information. This was how Wilson regarded his duty: 'H.W. frequently had to state the opposite point of view [from Vansittart], if only [because] "I knew that otherwise the P.M.'s policy would be negatived, though not by anything that Germany or Italy might do." '[55] He supplied a higher criticism, irritating to Eden but not apparently to Halifax, who wrote later:

So far from a feeling that Horace Wilson interfered and made things difficult between the Prime Minister and the Foreign Secretary, I always found him extremely helpful when the pressure of work was heavy, in ensuring that I was fully acquainted with the thoughts of the Prime Minister and *vice versa,* and that neither was unconsciously drifting into any misunderstanding of the other's mind.[56]

Wilson suffered from the fact that he made no defence against his accusers after the war. He had left several damaging hostages to fortune in the records of his visits to the German Embassy; and he took part in the manoeuvres which preceded Eden's resignation as well as Vansittart's 'elevation'. Yet until

* Dirksen papers (Moscow 1948) vol. 2, no. 5, 29 Aug 1938. The feelings were reciprocated; viz. Wilson's comment on Kordt: 'He had always worked for a peaceful solution. So had von Dirksen, the German Ambassador' (Wilson Memorandum).

the summer of 1938 and the Munich Conference he seems to have been no more than the efficient civil servant carrying out the Prime Minister's instructions to the limit and he would have attracted less odium if Chamberlain had not used him in a capacity more suited to the American political system than the British. Perhaps the fairest comment is Lord Woolton's:

He had more detailed knowledge of what was happening in Government circles than anyone else. He was deeply conscious of the strain under which Prime Ministers work, with the perpetual flow of papers, minutes and reports coming to them from every department. His insight and his high competence as a civil servant were invaluable, but I believe the greatest help he gave to the Prime Minister was that of his sympathy.... With his knowledge and his understanding, he enabled the Prime Ministers to have somebody to whom they could talk and upon whom they could rely.[57]

A few other officials were occasionally concerned in foreign policy making. In 1938, for example, the Department of Overseas Trade (part of the Board of Trade) became involved in a plan to increase British trade and political standing in southeast Europe. Sir Frederick Leith-Ross, Chief Economic Adviser and Government representative at most of the international conferences of the inter-war years, and R. H. Hudson, the junior minister, took part. Although the moving force came from Sir Maurice Ingram of the Foreign Office, Leith-Ross took the chair of the Committee set up to carry it out. Likewise there were the 'economic men' of the Treasury, such as Sir David Waley, Principal Assistant Secretary, who spent most of his career in financial negotiations with foreign governments, in his capacity as representative of the Overseas Department. But, apart from those of the Economic Relations section of the Foreign Office, their functions were normally advisory. When Leith-Ross began to take a large part in the negotiations with Schacht about the return of German colonies, in 1937, he became the object of fierce rivalry from the diplomats.

In assessing British policy before 1939 it is essential to understand the weight given by the Cabinet to the advice of the military staffs. Theoretically, the Cabinet was kept continuously aware of Service advice about the strategic implications of all their decisions. Contingency planning for any likely situation in foreign and imperial affairs, and the preparation of defence forces to meet the obligations laid down by the Cabinet, are the cardinal duties of the three departments and the Chiefs of Staff. At the request of the Cabinet they provide expert assessments of any particular problem or alter their dispositions to undertake new commitments or relinquish old. To enable this reciprocal relationship to work smoothly, the CID had developed a structure analogous to the Cabinet. Normally the Prime Minister took the chair with the other members of the Foreign Policy Committee, the First Lord of the Admiralty and the Secretaries for War and Air. The three Chiefs of Staff, Warren Fisher, Cadogan, and Lord Zetland, Secretary for India, usually attended, and any Dominion minister available in London. The CID had its own structure of sub-committees, notably the Chiefs of Staff (formed in 1924), the Overseas Defence and Coastal Defence Committees, and *ad hoc* bodies like the DRC or the Air Defence Research Committee of 1935. It possessed its own secretariat, headed by Hankey, and the presence of so many members of the Cabinet should have ensured a sensitive and speedy response to its strategic debates.

The organisation was believed to work satisfactorily and in 1929 Ramsay MacDonald took it as his model when setting up his 'economic general staff', the Economic Advisory Council. During the inter-war years, however, practice changed substantially and the structure failed in one major respect: it rarely engrossed the three Services sufficiently to produce a unified opinion. Inter-Service disputes, usually over the allocation of scarce resources but sometimes over questions of inter-departmental control, such as the perennial quarrel between Admiralty and Air Ministry over the Fleet Air Arm, continued in spite of the co-ordinating work of Inskip and the liaison activities of the civil servants on the Principal Supply Officers Committee. Political arguments about the balance between the roles of Air Force and Army were magnified within the Service hierarchy and each limited increase of Government money for rearmament produced unedifying squabbles and a great deal of factitious reasoning.

Politicians tended to play one Service against another, even as early as 1934 when, in spite of the care taken to maintain the balance of the recommendations of the Defence Require-

ments Committee, the Navy and Army were left to settle with
the Chancellor in turn for what they could get, after the Air
Force had had its due. The efforts of Navy and Air Force to
hold their places in the ratio of the rationed budget after the
defeat of the War Office claims during 1937 actually facilitated
the imposition of rationing (see Chapter 4). But to say this is
not to argue that it was the duty of the Services to speak as a
single body, offering a total defence policy.[58] This is the function
of the Cabinet, as Hankey argued when the creation of a
Ministry of Defence was proposed: 'No one can carry the guns
except the P.M. . . . only the P.M. could settle the great issues
and even his decisions might not hold.'[59] Baldwin had taken
the chair of the CID regularly after Curzon's death and
established the tradition that it was the Prime Minister's duty*
because, as he told the House of Commons in March 1934:
'When war comes, the Prime Minister must be familiar with
that work; therefore I hope very much that whatever work a
Prime Minister may let go, he will not let that go.'† Inskip
was appointed as a substitute in 1936 only because the work
had become too heavy to combine with the other duties
of Prime Minister. Even those, such as Churchill, who proposed
to set up a Ministry of Defence, never suggested that the over-all
planning of strategy should be relinquished to the Services,
only that the old system permitted and even encouraged an
inefficiency and sluggishness which Britain in the 1930s could
no longer afford.

Another weakness of the system was that the CID had ceased
to be the forum where the Dominions themselves discussed
Imperial Defence. While Dominion ministers could attend the
CID at will and did so regularly until the Dominion Prime
Ministers meeting of May 1935, Canada and South Africa
refused to do so at the Imperial Conference of 1937.‡ The
result was that the frequent interventions made by the
Dominions in 1937–9 were channelled through the High Com-

* During the governments of Lloyd George and Bonar Law, it had been taken by
Lord Balfour and then Lord Curzon.
† Hansard, 5th series, vol. 287, col. 1322, 21 Mar 1934. Also CAB 27/600 (Defence
Co-ordination Review, 1936): 'Even in peace, it was essential that [the PM]
should deal with the larger issues.'
‡ Although Pirow, the South African Defence Minister, spent some time in
London in July 1937, he was concerned solely with the arrangements of the
Simonstown naval base and the defence of east Africa.

missioners or by visiting statesmen direct to the Cabinet or Foreign Secretary. Dominion fears and prejudices made their impact without the softening process of bureaucratic screening or absorption into more general strategic appreciation.*

The potential influence of the CID as an institution was weakened even more by the relationship between the Service staffs and the politicians. The Service advisers were as much an élite as the diplomats but they were not men who had spent their lives advising and influencing ministers. Given the composition of the officer hierarchy and the fact that all three Chiefs of Staff in 1937, Admiral Sir R. Backhouse, Air Marshal Sir C. Newall, and General Lord Gort, had been of field rank before 1918, there was little chance of the sort of social mixture achieved even in Conservative Cabinets. The traditions of the Services, especially at the end of a decade which had seen the run-down of officers under the restricted establishment of the Ten Year Rule era, encouraged absurdly ostrich-like behaviour, notably the purblind reaction of the War Office to mechanisation. In any case, even when the staffs surmounted their esoteric rivalries, they spoke with certain shared assumptions in mind. A degree of respect, for example, was shown towards other disciplined élites: some of the naval commanders (Admiral Drayer, Commander in Chief Far-Eastern Fleet, and Lord Chatfield, Chief of Naval Staff) and the Chief of the Imperial General Staff, Field-Marshal Montgomery-Massingbird, sympathised with Japan's exasperation with the chaotic state of China in the period 1932–4† and believed, for different reasons from the Treasury, in Britain's urgent need to come to terms with the one impressive power of the Far East. A similar fellow-feeling is suggested by the contacts between General Milch, Goering's Chief of Staff, and the British Air Staff in 1936–7.[60]

The Chiefs of Staff may have been inclined to an exaggerated respect for the strength of countries dominated by an officer caste, which would help to explain their low estimate of the Soviet Red Army, shorn of 60 per cent of its officers in the Stalin purges, and the excessive trust they placed later in the

---

* See below, pp. 383 and 391, for particular examples.
† C. Thorne, 'The Shanghai crisis of 1932: the background to British policy', *American Historical Review*, Oct 1970. Similar tendencies can be observed in the United States services, particularly the views of the Commander-in-Chief, Asiatic Fleet, and also General Bilotte, the French Commander-in-Chief Indo-China.

D

gallant but outdated Polish forces. Consciousness of belonging to a separate profession showed most strongly in their relations with politicians. Trained in one world, they scorned the behaviour of another. They were not like Hankey, who had ceased his active service as Colonel in the Marines in 1908. Only Lord Chatfield took a strong political part and there was no Alanbrooke with status and capacity to stand up to the Prime Minister. In the 1930s the staffs never insisted on their views to the point of resignation, as the Board of Admiralty had done to coerce the Cabinet during the 'cruiser crisis' in 1925. In December 1937, in contrast, the Secretary of State for War, Hore-Belisha, with the Prime Minister's full support, sacked the entire Army Council for incompetence and obstruction and appointed his own afresh, promoting Lord Gort over the heads of Ironside and Dill, and bringing in a naval officer as Master General of the Ordnance.

Their restraint, even when ignored collectively, has been taken for excessive prudence or timeserving. It might better be called disdain. As Sir Cyril Deverell, CIGS in 1938, said, 'The Army must stand together and show a solid front to the politicians.'[61] Too many senior officers remembered the conflict between Lloyd George and the General Staff during the First World War and the long-lasting public obloquy which they believed had been foisted on the latter. Lord Beatty had once written: 'these politicians are all alike, a disgusting breed without real patriotism',[62] and the attitude of impotent fury shown by the War Office staff towards Hore-Belisha for his reliance on the advice of Captain Liddell Hart was equally instructive.[63]

The Chiefs of Staff were at a disadvantage also when confronted by the permanent civil service. On the Defence Requirements Committee the balance was held by Hankey, Fisher and Vansittart, and although the Chief of Air Staff, Sir Adrian Ellington, frequently disagreed with them, he and his colleagues lacked the power to outweigh the official triumvirate. Some of the resentment which was their response to the politicians can be seen in the diary of Major-General Pownall, Director of Military Intelligence in the CID Secretariat after 1936. His particular *bête-noir* was Chamberlain who, he wrote in July 1934, has shown himself strangely obtuse in strategical questions, even ignorant—quite apart from his own departmental difficulties (which are quite easy to understand) his attitude is not readily explicable. He hates battle-ships because they are expensive, as they are, but that is not a strategical argument for doing away with them. And others manage to find the money somehow. Indeed in America a naval construction programme is regarded as a means of relieving unemployment; surely the same condition applies to us?[64]

He was equally contemptuous of the Treasury arguments in favour of 'limited liability' in January 1936 –

They cannot or will not realise that if war with Germany comes again . . . we shall again be fighting for our lives. Our effort *must* be the maximum by land, sea and air. We cannot say our contribution is 'so and so' and no more, because we cannot lose the war without the extinction of the Empire. The idea of the half-hearted war is the most pernicious and dangerous in the world. It will be 100 per cent—and even then we may well lose it. . . . The Chancellor's cold, hard, calculating, semi-detached attitude was terrible to listen to.[65]

Subordination of the military advisers had been avoided in Baldwin's time because he was willing to listen to the full complexity of the cases put by individual Services.* But when Chamberlain took the chair at CID meetings Warren Fisher was, metaphorically, at his side. Since Hankey had come close to Chamberlain's way of thinking by 1937, a great deal of the Services' residual power to over-awe the Cabinet disappeared. The CID was not itself a decision-making body, but the opposition which Hankey and the Chiefs of Staff had mustered against the Air Pact in February 1935 had been substantial.† The weight given to them then by Cabinet and Foreign Office was more than would have been warranted in 1938.

A strong new institution had been set up which also detracted from the power of the Chiefs of Staff. The Defence Policy and Requirements Committee, composed originally of Baldwin, the

* Witness his formal and informal contacts with Hankey, Chatfield, Ellington and Weir (Middlemas and Barnes, *Baldwin, passim*). The last instance was his work in resolving the Fleet Air Arm dispute in 1937 (*Baldwin*, pp. 1020–2).
† Another case was the Chief of Naval Staff's opposition to the Cabinet decision to send the whole Home Fleet to Gibraltar in August 1935, during the Abyssinian crisis. Pownall called this 'a very interesting example of the military people holding back the statesmen' (Diary, 22 Aug. See also *Baldwin*, pp. 793–6).

Lord President, Chamberlain, the Chancellor, Simon, the Foreign
Secretary, as well as the three Service ministers, had been
created by Baldwin in 1935, on Hankey's advice, largely to
further the rearmament programme and sidetrack the political
opposition of Simon and MacDonald in the Cabinet. When
Baldwin became Prime Minister, the weight of Service advice
continued to impinge on the innermost reaches of the Cabinet.*
Chamberlain, however, had a more quizzical approach: at
heart he suspected the Services of empire-building. He wrote in
April 1937:

> The public, of course, has no idea of what is going on behind
> the scenes, nor of the constant, harassing rear-guard action that
> I am fighting against the services all the time. No one is more
> convinced than I am of the necessity for rearmament and for
> speed in making ourselves safe. But the services very naturally,
> seeing how good the going is now and reflecting that the reaction
> is sure to follow, want to be 100 per cent or 200 per cent safe
> on everything.[66]

Once again he was in accord with Warren Fisher.

A slow but radical change in the effective disposition of
power took place. The principle of rationing, which was adopted
in February 1938, was tantamount to a rejection of the earlier
convention that the military advisers should be given certain
defined terms of reference and that they should then inform the
Cabinet of what was necessary in terms of men and material to
fulfil these commitments. The Cabinet might, and frequently
did, subordinate this advice to the greater needs of the civilian
economy, the political situation or the contrary advice of the
Treasury, but they had not attempted, even during Chamberlain's campaign in June 1934, to lay down and divide up the
resources of the Services. After 1937, this was no longer the
case and it is significant that during the crisis summer of 1938
the CID met rarely. Grand strategy was made elsewhere. In
March 1938 the Foreign Policy Committee was in a position to
make vital decisions about Czechoslovakia before the military
advice had even been discussed.

---

* The 1936 Defence Co-ordination Review recommended the further development of the CID 'so as to improve the examination of the broadest aspects of
defence, to co-ordinate executive action, and to take the initiative for causing any
specific questions to be examined which appear necessary' (CAB 27/600).

The role of Government Intelligence services in the formation
of policy is rarely discussed, because of the almost total lack of
reliable documentation. The Secret Service is necessarily secret
and will remain so. Yet the quality of information about foreign
powers, their military and economic strength and their policy
intentions is a vital matter, of much greater concern than the
efficiency of the process by which decisions are made. The most
perfect machine ceases to function if fed with the wrong fuel.

The network of information services in the 1930s suffered
from the intertwined disadvantages of overlapping and lack
of professionalism. The latter was the more serious, because
conflicting reports tended to cancel each other out at higher
levels of government; and because after 1935 some provision
was made for co-ordination.* The main Government departments concerned with foreign affairs each had their own
service. In addition to the normal resources of diplomacy there
was the 'secret' side of the Foreign Office. Then, as now, there
were First Secretaries in Embassies who were not established
officials, whose task was to co-ordinate and evaluate the information coming in from a network of informants or spies, which
they had either set up or which they operated and paid. Sometimes the contacts built up by the Foreign Office were made at
a higher level than paid spies, or arose out of German initiatives.
The visits of Konrad Henlein, leader of the Sudeten Germans,
to London in December 1935, July 1936 and March and October
1937 were arranged through Group Captain Christie, director of
intelligence at the Air Ministry,[67] and like those of Goerdeler
and von Kleist later they helped to make up the over-all picture
of British interpretation.

Vansittart developed these contacts inside Germany to the
point where they were known in Whitehall as his 'private
detective agency'. Even in the minutes of the Inner Cabinet,
his sources were always referred to simply as 'secret'. They
included Admiral Canaris, Chief of the Abwehr (German
counter-intelligence), the brothers Kordt and General Milch,
although the latter's revelations about the strength of the
German air force in 1936, which so impressed the Cabinet that

* An Intelligence Co-ordinating Committee was proposed by the War Office in
Oct 1935. Creation of a formal body was postponed by the CID but awareness of
the problem of overlapping was at least the first step in unofficial coordination.
(Pownall diary, 28 Oct 1935.)

they were confined to a file more secret than the minutes, were suspect.* Many of Vansittart's inspired guesses were accurate, but he used the secret nature of his information to bolster up the exaggerated language of his memoranda and frequently it lost its effect on his Cabinet audience. Such interventions were not popular with the new Prime Minister, who once called them 'unchecked reports from non-official sources'.[68]

The Foreign Office did not possess an economic section until 1934 – another of the causes for disagreement with Warren Fisher – and this deficiency had to be made up by the apparatus of the Department of Overseas Trade or Industrial Intelligence, headed by Sir Desmond Morton, which was a useful and generally accurate source of German and Italian military and industrial production.† All the Service departments had their attachés in the principal foreign capitals, their duty being to report as fully and deeply as possible on the size and effectiveness of those countries' defence forces. They varied in success in their ability to absorb information and make contacts with their opposite Services. Britain was fortunate having in Berlin Colonel Mason MacFarlane, the high-spirited Military Attaché,‡ and his assistant, Major Strong,[69] who found freely-speaking contacts in the German High Command and became the recipients of a deal of information about the German preparations to implement the policy outlined by Hitler at the Hossbach Conference in November 1937. This information was generally accurate and certainly better, on most occasions, than that of the French who relied heavily on what was passed to them by British Intelligence (see below, page 274).

The activities of MI5, the intelligence branch of the Secret Service, and MI6, the counter-espionage department, can only be deduced from occasional references in Cabinet and private

---

* In the extraordinarily intertwined network of conspiracy in the Third Reich, figures of aircraft production were, as Austen Chamberlain once said about Lloyd George's statistics, used as adjectives. Vansittart had been warned, in even greater secrecy, to distrust Milch's 'official' confidential leaks and he cautioned Hankey to do the same.

† Morton, with the agreement of MacDonald and then Baldwin, was Churchill's main source of facts about the German air force. (Middlemas and Barnes *Baldwin*, pp. 787, 819; also Robert Rhodes James, *Churchill, A Study in Failure* (London 1970) p. 236.)

‡ According to a correspondence in *The Times*, in March 1970, MacFarlane once asked War Office permission to shoot Hitler with a sniper's rifle from the British Embassy during a military parade. Whether the action or the venue was more undesirable, is not recorded: permission was refused.

papers. At times in recent history the Secret Service has worked independently of the politicians, but in 1938 the relationship seems to have been satisfactory; there were no complaints, to judge from evidence such as the close contact between Colonel Campbell, Military Attaché in Paris, and Colonel Gauché, head of the French Secret Service. It is worth mentioning that in 1936 Group Captain F. W. Winterbottom, head of the Air Intelligence Section of MI5, was able to make an analysis of German psychological penetration of France in the light of a list of collaborators in German pay he had been shown.[70] On the evidence of the Cabinet papers, however, the most notable information provided by Intelligence in the period 1936–8 came after the Munich settlement and was almost wholly ignored (see below, page 434).

There is no means of knowing how much inaccurate information was sent into the processing operation up to 1937 by British agents, some of it, like Milch's earlier figures, deliberately planted at German or Italian instigation. British security procedures were lax; it was the era when Harold Philby and Burgess and Maclean were appointed, and when security checking had barely evolved from the assumption that patriotism and probity were automatically part of the make-up of all entrants. Lack of professionalism was a serious defect because the Intelligence services were popularly supposed to be the most efficient in the world – an attitude which encouraged over-confidence. Even more seriously, few embassies abroad made proper security provisions. In Rome, in the middle of the Abyssinian crisis in 1935, an Italian safe-breaker was infiltrated into the British Embassy. He removed copies of all diplomatic correspondence and passed them not only to the Italian Intelligence, but also to the Soviet Minister in Rome. British codes and cyphers were broken and the information passed by the Italians to Germany, so that Goering's Research Office, which was responsible for the interception of diplomatic communications, was able to read everything which passed between London and Berlin.*

---

* Watt, *Personalities and Policies*, p. 200. The Foreign Office index refers to a paper (Y775/775/650) concerning an inquiry into a leakage of information from the Rome Embassy in 1937 but the original has been destroyed. It may never be known whether the code books had been changed before the British overtures to Germany in 1937.

The factual information coming out of Germany on production of war supplies and productive capacity seems rarely to have been seriously at fault. The figures at the disposal of the Chiefs of Staff in writing their report on the military situation in Europe in March 1938 were sound.[71] But British governments worked in the dark when they considered the political motivation of the Nazi leadership. Not only was the Hitlerian circle difficult to penetrate, but Hitler himself gave few hints of what he really thought and his policy was almost impossible to deduce from the cloudy meanderings of second- and third-hand reports. Without an expert understanding of the Nazi hierarchy, which few even in Germany in the volatile society of 1937 could provide, there was nothing but rule of thumb and intuition by which to measure the standing, for example, of the German moderates and the opposition to Hitler, or the place of Goering and Ribbentrop in the ever-shifting balance of Hitler's confidence. The year 1937 proved to be critical for Hitler's policy towards Britain. The Foreign Office realised this but failed to penetrate the curtain.[72] As late as 15 February 1938, after Hitler's purge of the High Command which was the outward expression of his new policy in Europe, Harvey could write mistakenly, of Hitler's attitude towards Austria, that 'he felt he must bring off some coup to reassure himself after his recent and damaging internal crisis'.[73]

To circumvent this ignorance of Hitler's plans* ministers often grasped eagerly at opinions from those who had visited him, such as Lord Lothian and Lord Allen of Hurtwood, Lloyd George and Thomas Jones. Sometimes the visitors worked partly at the Prime Minister's request, like Ernest Tennant or Burgon Bickersteth,[74] and sometimes, like Philip Conwell Evans (see below, page 298), they were questioned afterwards by the Foreign Office, irrespective of the purpose of the visit. Lord Londonderry was too openly pro-German to offer much more than the Nazi propaganda already available and Lord Lothian was prone to statements of his deep impression by the sincerity of Herr Hitler, whom he regarded as a prophet.[75]

* There is no reason to think that the plans expressed in *Mein Kampf* were not available. The book was not published in English until 1939, and only a few ministers (Baldwin among them) read German, but at least one summary was made available to the Cabinet before 1934, with the key passages translated, by the Foreign Office.

The sum total of influence on the Cabinet of all Hitler's visitors was less than is sometimes suggested,[76] but the gap of understanding remained and was shown up particularly in 1938, at the time of the May crisis, and at the end of August when, because of the conflict of opinion between Nevile Henderson in Berlin and the rest of the Foreign Office, the Cabinet were presented with almost irreconcilable deductions from a sketchy, but broadly similar set of facts.

One last limitation of Intelligence existed. However strongly they argued, the defenders of the view that Hitler was far gone in his expansionist programme, and that appeasement could never succeed, were restricted by the incapacity of ministers to accept the starkness of what they were saying. Hard-pressed men, faced with an intractable problem and the unthinkable risk of war, preferred to accept what suited their hopes. As Air-Commodore Slessor, Deputy Director of Air Staff at this time, noticed, there was a strong tendency to prefer supposedly 'hot' information, especially when official sources failed to offer what was wanted.[77] It is, perhaps, a virtue not to accept failure merely on advice; but it took the *Anschluss,* Munich and the invasion of Czechoslovakia in March 1939 before the members of Chamberlain's Cabinet accepted the logic of arguments which Hitler had in fact outlined in his plan at the Hossbach Conference in November 1937.

More attention has been given in the past to the influence of advice coming from outside the Government than to the official machinery, a reflection partly on the greater availability of private papers and printed sources, partly because the German propaganda offensive drew into the sphere of foreign affairs individuals and groups who would not normally have been considered part of the policy-making group, and partly because of the climate of opinion which has favoured the growth of conspiracy theories about the evolution and practice of 'appeasement'.

The most that can be said of this is 'not proven'. The juxtaposition of comments by the 'appeasers', leading articles in certain newspapers, house-parties at Cliveden, dinners at All Souls, and actual political decisions is quite inadequate as a method of showing that influence existed. It requires to be

shown that agencies outside the Government machine exercised
a powerful or even exclusive influence at specific moments
before these decisions were taken – which the evidence of the
Cabinet archives simply does not substantiate. These sources give
very little credit at all to external pressures. To some extent
this may be an inevitable result of the process of minuting by
the Cabinet Secretariat, but the private papers of close participants, Chamberlain himself, Halifax, Inskip, Hoare, Vansittart
and the published works of Eden and Simon do not suggest a
Cabinet open to the variable winds of the Press, public or private
opinion. The dominant group of senior ministers were elderly
and encased in years of office. The Inner Cabinet did not take
sufficient account of expert advice from the Foreign Office and
the Service Departments, let alone from outsiders. Unconsciously
they may have been affected by the prevailing climate of public
opinion as regards their inherent attitude to Germany,[78] but
this is a less important factor than their plasticity in the hands
of Chamberlain. Whatever their feelings towards the Nazi
regime they had followed the Eden–Baldwin line up to the end
of 1936; within six months they accepted with equal ease the
policy Chamberlain pushed through until the Munich crisis.
Above all, there is no sign that Chamberlain was deflected by
outside opinions: his own private comments suggest a high
degree of resistance to any unofficial intervention.

The British Government in 1937–8 certainly appears less
sensitive to public opinion than were the governments of either
France or the United States. The withdrawn nature of the
Inner Cabinet was intensified by the élitism of the Foreign Office
and the Service Departments. Decision-making was impervious
to outsiders unless they had social or political links strong
enough to outweigh this disadvantage.* Thus pressure groups
within the Conservative Party were the only ones to have access
to the Prime Minister and his senior ministers.

They centred in this period on the ex-ministers, Churchill,
Amery, Austen Chamberlain and, after February 1938, Eden.
Until the end of 1936 Churchill had managed to lead a
charmed life in spite of his excessive and archaic opposition to
the Government of India Act. He had been made a member of

* The influence of the Crown at this time was negligible. Chamberlain and Simon
had been two of those most fervently against Edward VIII's attempts to influence
the Foreign Office but they had no cause to complain of George VI.

the Air Defence Research sub-committee of the CID by Baldwin, and despite his subsequent withdrawal continued to be supplied with secret information. By virtue of his former colleagues' consent, as well as his own stature, he occupied a privileged position, but almost destroyed it by his romantic espousal of the King's cause during the abdication crisis. Although Chamberlain showed him a certain respect in 1937, there was none of the affection and cross-fertilisation of ideas which existed when Churchill had headed a deputation of senior party leaders on the question of rearmament in July 1936.[79] His views in 1936–7 appeared even more eclectic than usual: in March 1936 he approached Lord Robert Cecil, President of the League of Nations Union, to offer his co-operation in the defence of parliamentary democracy,[80] but as he was still wedded to the principle of vigorous rearmament Cecil remained sceptical of his 'queer manoeuvres'. During the abdication crisis he wrote to Cecil again, proclaiming his faith in the Little Entente and an Eastern Locarno under the League – views which, eighteen months after the assassination of Barthou, must have seemed remarkably out of date.

Leopold Amery, on the other hand, who had resigned from the Shadow Cabinet in 1930 a year before Churchill, and who shared many of his assumptions, was arguing in the opposite direction, against any attempt to re-create the Anglo-Franco-Soviet encirclement of Germany which 'might well make war inevitable'.[81] Austen Chamberlain remained the elder statesman in the shadows, powerful but remote from active politics, writing grimly to Gilbert Murray of his fears about the German designs on Austria, French weakness and the frail existence of collective security.[82]

None of these men offered an alternative foreign policy which could be cast in a public campaign. The group of soldiers, businessmen and politicians who met under Amery's chairmanship confined themselves to setting up the Army League as a means of strengthening the War Office in the political spectrum.* Eden, though backed by the prestige of Baldwin and the Salisbury family, and his own able junior, J. P. L. Thomas, and

* Leopold Amery, *My Political Life*, vol. III (London 1955) pp. 199–200. The group included Field-Marshals Milne and Chetwode, Lieutenant-General Sir Ronald Charles, Edward Beddington-Behrens, Lord Lloyd, Victor Cazalet, Lord Illiffe and Sir Harry Hague.

encouraged especially by Oliver Harvey, carefully avoided outright opposition to Chamberlain's policy and after Munich even
considered rejoining the Government.[83] If anything, he linked
his position with Amery rather than Churchill.

Churchill appeared to be the only credible alternative Prime
Minister in 1937–8 but, after the failure of the Arms and the
Covenant campaign in 1936, his own group of followers,
Duncan Sandys, Robert Boothby and Oliver Locker-Lampson,
became an inward-looking clique, exploiting parliamentary
opportunities rather than challenging Chamberlain's foreign
policy. Churchill's own opinions, during the early stages of the
Czechoslovak crisis, were not distinct enough from Government
policy to be the substance of opposition (see below, page 291).

Nevertheless these were impressive names and it is significant
that the Focus campaign against pro-Nazi tendencies in Britain,
inspired by Eugene Spier, chose to approach them rather than
the opposition within the Cabinet. Their weakness was the party
position which was also the source of their strength. Chamberlain made loyalty the test of admission to the governing club
and his hold over the majority of the Conservative Party was so
great that his opponents might conceivably form an alternative
Government, only if Chamberlain fell by other hands.

The other groups (outside the Labour Party) who advocated
a positive theme in foreign policy straddled the political divisions.
The 'new imperialists', as they have been called,* included
Lord Lothian, Geoffrey Dawson, Amery, the Astor family,
Lionel Curtis and Field-Marshal Smuts. They had a common
experience, dating back in most cases to Lord Milner's 'kinder-
garten' in South Africa before 1905, which gave a wider setting
to their views on what Britain's foreign policy should achieve.
Ownership, or direction of *The Times, Observer* and the *Round
Table*, and friendship and intellectual comity with many
Dominion statesmen gave them power to advise and strong
reason to do so. They constituted a significant 'high level
bridge' between Dominion opinion and the Cabinet, and their
unofficial contacts with the latter ensured that even when the
High Commissioners and Prime Ministers were not in London

* The phrase originated with the anonymous author of the *History of the Times*
vol. 4 (London 1952) ch. 1.

the Dominions were not forgotten.* Not so much anti-European as isolationist, in the sense that Lord Salisbury had shunned Continental ties, they recognised few British interests in Europe and none in the centre or south-east. These attitudes and their association in particular with the 'Cliveden set' lined them with the 'appeasers'. Lord Halifax, though not in any other sense an associate, was as aware of Indian opinion as they were of the white Dominions; and Chamberlain's affinity with his father's tariff imperialism made him peculiarly sensitive to such advice – especially since it usually coincided with his own judgement.

Somewhat to the left of the Tory Party, the Next Five Years Group, founded in 1935 – including Harold Macmillan, Lord Allen, Sir Arthur Salter and Norman Angell among others – rejected the 'new imperialist' theme as 'morally insufferable, politically suicidal and technically impossible'.[84] They were far better versed in European affairs but they did not line up with Churchill or Amery, distrusting cries for an Anglo-French alliance or old-fashioned balance-of-power thinking. Their original manifesto declared its belief in collective security 'with Germany, if she is willing – but if not, without her – . . . strong and effective against any breach of the peace'. By 1937 some were still inclined towards a settlement with Germany, although Lord Allen was no longer typical when he spoke to Ribbentrop of his profound sympathy for Germany and his belief in 'a very genuine understanding'.[85]

Further left in the overlapping grades, the League of Nations Union, which had organised the Peace Ballot in 1934–5, spoke with a confused voice, symptom of the uncertainty implicit in the questionnaire and in the variety of meanings attributable by then to the concept of the League itself. Even in 1934, one of its founders, Gilbert Murray, was contending that revision of the Treaty of Versailles had gone far enough. 'No conceivable alteration of treaties now would satisfy or seriously appease the feelings of Germany. . . .'[86] Other members disagreed. As

* Lord Lothian's views on the aims of British policy in 1937 are worth quoting: 'Detachment is the only basis upon which we shall be able to find a common policy with the Dominions and move towards that informal naval cooperation with the United States – i.e. the United States in the Pacific and ourselves in the Atlantic – which is the best way of preventing the dictatorships establishing themselves on the oceanic highways and therefore the best security for free institutions over half the world.' (Butler, *Lord Lothian*, p. 214.)

late as the end of 1936 Cecil clung to his illusions: 'Time is on our side. Nazism and Fascism cannot last. Even in oriental Russia Stalin feels the necessity of making some concession to democracy. And there must remain considerable deposits of sanity in Germany and Italy, which have not been destroyed by these few years of tyranny.'[87] The extent to which the Cabinet took notice of either may be expressed rather roughly in the Prime Minister's own words:

> I can find no polite words to express my opinion of the League of Nations Union ... the kind of person who is really enthusiastic about the League is almost invariably a crank and a Liberal, and as such will always pursue the impracticable and obstruct all practical means of attaining the object in view. But fortunately the majority of the nation does not agree with them....[88]

It is unlikely that the efforts of pro-German sympathisers were more successful in cajoling Cabinet ministers except those who were already predisposed to accept their accounts. The apologistic activities of some members of the Anglo-German Group,* the straightforward pro-Nazi propaganda of The Link,† like the private war against them mounted by Spier and the Focus group, represented a battle for public, not Cabinet, opinion. That a sympathetic attitude towards Germany had been built up in articulate society, long before Hitler's rise to power, and largely through the agency of the *Wirtschafts-politische Gesellschaft*, headed by Dr Gärtner, is not in doubt.[89]

---

* Arthur Marwick, *Clifford Allen, the Open Conspirator* (Edinburgh 1964 pp. 159–60), and Watt, *Personalities and Policies*, pp. 124–7. Founded in 1929, the Anglo-German Association was dissolved six years later after the majority of its members had spoken out against the Nazi ascendency. The Anglo-German Group represented the efforts of a number of men, some of Quaker origins, some members of the Labour Party and some of the Royal Institute of International Affairs to educate British opinion to a better understanding of Nazi Germany. They included Lord Allen, Charles Roden Buxton, Lord Noel Buxton, W. Arnold Foster (also of the League of Nations Union), Sir Walter Layton, proprietor of the *News Chronicle* and the *Economist*, and the latter's foreign editor, Vernon Bartlett, and Philip Conwell-Evans.

† A basically anti-Semitic organisation founded in 1935 to promote Anglo-German friendship. Several of its members crop up in the lists of more overtly anti-Semitic bodies (cf. Hilary Blume, *Anti-Semitism in Britain in the 1930s*, shortly to be published.) Seven members signed a letter to *The Times* after Munich, commending the settlement, (below, p. 407n). Conservative MPs were prominent: Colonel Moore, Sir Arnold Wilson, Lord Londonderry, Colonel Victor Cazalet, Lord Rothermere and Lord Mount Temple, president of the late Anglo-German Fellowship.

Nor is the part played by pro-German sympathisers in organising the visits to Hitler during 1935–7; but all this work had been done by the time Chamberlain came to power. Cabinet policy after 1937 owed its dynamism to other influences.

The influence of the 'quality' press was both more pervasive and difficult to gauge than any political grouping, and its study has been exaggerated by the natural overestimate of their own power, propagated by press lords, editors and journalists alike.* The difficulties of making a satisfactory study are legion: beginning with the arbitrary assumption that only the 'quality' papers – *The Times, Daily Telegraph, Manchester Guardian, Observer, Sunday Times* and the provincial *Birmingham Post, Yorkshire Post, Glasgow Herald* and *Scotsman* – took part in the debate on foreign policy. It is not within the scope of this book to analyse the Press or public opinion in 1937–8; nor would it be possible to do so from official archives and private collections. Ministers did not quote the latest editorials at Cabinet meetings even if they had read them in preference to the Foreign Office brief for the agenda. Downing Street rarely acknowledges its debt to Fleet Street. There is, in fact, no evidence here on which to construct more than a few assumptions. What Cabinet ministers read is so far almost unknown. They may have relied on the heavily Tory section, *The Times* and *Telegraph*, which both came out strongly against Eden after his resignation, or they may have balanced them with the more isolationist *Daily Express* and *Daily Mail*, or the Liberal *News Chronicle*, or the left-wing papers, the *Daily Herald, New Statesman*, the *New Leader*, or even the Communist *Daily Worker*. But whatever their papers were, they represented only one part of the mass of documentation all Cabinet ministers have to read. One may assume, reasonably enough, that news reporting was as potent a factor in informing the political élite as the official summaries circulated to the Cabinet; also that leader-writing was – as it still is – an art-form intended to influence certain groups or to create a forum for deliberately

* An instance can be found in the influence which Geoffrey Dawson claimed to have had on Baldwin during the abdication crisis. (Sir Evelyn Wrench, *Geoffrey Dawson and Our Times* (London 1955) pp. 342–6.) As the crisis proceeded, however, Baldwin wished to see him less and less and offered only enough information to keep him quiet (see Middlemas and Barnes, *Baldwin*, pp. 989–90, 1004).

stimulated discussion. Dawson, for example, might use the centre page of *The Times* instead of directing a private letter to the Prime Minister. During the abdication and the Hoare–Laval crisis he had twice tried 'to show a way out' to Baldwin; the famous editorial of 7 September 1938 was clearly written on his own initiative and against the wishes of his senior editor.[90]

But the latter case suggests that there was a different relationship between the Press and the politicians than Dawson imagined. That leader, with its message of secession for the Sudeten Germans, which caused heart-burnings in Printing House Square and a diplomatic furore abroad, could have made no difference to any member of the Government, because the Inner Cabinet had envisaged the possibility nearly six months earlier. It is probably true that the long-term *suppressio veri* effected by Dawson and his deputy editor, Barrington Ward, in the interests of a better Anglo-German understanding was more important than the *suggestio falsi* which only occasionally broke through,* but the effect was on British public opinion rather than on the Cabinet.

The manner of slanting and cutting of news from Germany is well documented. Given that many foreign governments regarded *The Times* as an official source, the composite effect of taking its views as an indication of Government policy may have led the French in particular to misunderstanding. The Press certainly had power at home: the lack of news coverage given to the Focus campaign which, considering its distinguished membership, can only have been deliberate, was a major reason for its failure to move the general public.[91] On the other hand, if the proposition put forward by Hugh Cudlipp is correct,[92] newspapers can only succeed in their campaigns if

---

* The messages from Ebbutt, *The Times* correspondent in Berlin, were frequently omitted or selectively pruned. Yet Dawson was outraged when, in spite of this, Ebbutt was expelled from Germany in August 1937. He wrote to his correspondent in Geneva: 'It would really interest me to know precisely what it is in *The Times* that has produced this new antagonism in Germany. I do my utmost night after night to keep out of the papers anything that might hurt their susceptibilities ... I shall be more grateful than I can say for any explanation and guidance for I have always been convinced that the peace of the world depends more than anything else upon our getting into reasonable relations with Germany.' (Wrench, *Dawson*, p. 361.) *The Times* was not the only paper where foreign correspondents were at loggerheads with their editorial boards. The same was true of Ian Colvin and the *News Chronicle*, G. E. R. Gedye and M. W. Fodor of the *Manchester Guardian* and Victor Gordon-Lennox of the *Daily Telegraph*.

their readership is predisposed to accept them. This then becomes a tautology.

In any case, news coverage increased and decreased in proportion to events and crises of which ministers were already aware. In *Britain by Mass Observation,* the authors gave a table showing the amount of column inches in six national dailies devoted to foreign news in the period August/September 1938.[93] Admittedly it was the height of the holiday season, but increases to anything over the mean accompanied or followed crises where the Cabinet decisions had already been taken. The *continuity* of information on which the foreign policy of the Government was based remained the prerogative of the Foreign Office.*

Newspaper proprietors used their personal contacts with ministers. Dawson enjoyed with Chamberlain the same sort of privileged position which Lords Beaverbrook and Rothermere had had with Lloyd George. It is unlikely that he did more than reinforce Chamberlain's natural inclinations. Knowing enough of the Prime Minister's mind to predict the outcome with reasonable accuracy, he was the Government's unofficial harbinger rather than its oracle.

The Chamberlain Government itself exercised a more substantial influence over the Press than had existed earlier. In November 1937, for example, Eden had tried to curtail a correspondence in *The Times* about the return of German colonies which he thought was encouraging the dictators to press more extreme claims. 'I asked Dawson some time ago to stop this correspondence, but without success.'[94] In contrast, Halifax had no trouble in suppressing a projected correspondence unwelcome to the Government at the time of Munich (see below, page 289). The Government was able to impose restrictions on the BBC coverage of news, despite the protests of Sir John Reith, the Director-General: 'The BBC was told to say nothing that night [after Eden's resignation] about

---

* None of this is intended to deny influence to what may be called the academic school of protest. Books like *Britain and the Dictators* (1938) by R. W. Seton-Watson; *Czechs and Germans* (1938) by Elizabeth Wiskemann; *Vanity Fair* (1938) and *Disgrace Abounding* (1939) by Douglas Reed; *South of Hitler* (1938) by M. W. Fodor; *Fallen Bastions* (1939) by G. E. R. Gedye, and the publications of the Left Book Club sold their editions to an avid readership. Whether they made converts among the politicians is less certain.

Germany and Italy.'[95] In the final fortnight before Munich, Hoare's secret briefing-sessions with newspaper proprietors and editors by-passed the parliamentary lobby and virtually dictated the Government view.

The National Government had ceased to be national in any sense after the retirement of Ramsay MacDonald; and the Labour Party Opposition disagreed with it on almost every issue in foreign policy after 1931. With Chamberlain and Attlee as leaders, party differences were sharpened, leading to several undesirable effects. Although the Labour movement was by no means united in 1937 in its attitude towards foreign policy, there was no useful cross-fertilisation of opinion with the Government, such as had existed between Labour Governments and Conservative Opposition in 1923–4, over European policy, or in 1929–30 over American.

Through the 1930s, consensus within the Labour movement subsisted in a few propositions: that the Government's nationalistic policy ignored the League of Nations; that peace could only come through disarmament and collective security; and that total resistance should be offered to the war-like policy of an arms race. The 1933 Labour Party Conference unanimously passed a resolution:

> To pledge itself to take no part in war and to resist it with the whole force of the Labour movement, to seek consultation forthwith with the Trade Union and Co-operative Movements with a view to deciding and announcing to the country what steps, including a general strike, are to be taken to organise the opposition of the organised working class movement in the event of war, or threat of war.[96]

Although the trade unions began to turn against Hitler in 1934 because of his attacks on the labour movement in Germany, the Labour Party fought nearly every by-election from Arthur Henderson's victory at Clay Cross in August 1933, through East Fulham, to Lowestoft in February 1934, and again from October 1934 until March 1935, on pacifist lines, attacking the Government, in Stafford Cripps' words, for 'a new and desperately dangerous policy, abandoning the very hopes which the Government had told us time and time again are the only hopes that stand between us and the annihilation of civilisation ... and a new race in armaments'.[97] Although the Government did not lose all these by-elections, the swing against it averaged 19 per cent in the first series and 24.4 per cent in the second – disastrous figures by any standard. Meanwhile the Parliamentary Labour Party voted solidly against the Service Estimates each year between 1934 and 1937, and against the Defence White Paper up till 1938. A fair example of their position was Attlee's statement on the critical Air estimates of 1934: 'We deny the need for these armaments; we deny the proposition that an increased British air force will make for the peace of the world and we reject altogether the claim for parity.'[98]

The way in which all Labour Party thinking was linked to disarmament vitiated it in the eyes of the Baldwin Government. Attlee's reasoning – 'It is impossible for us to get any kind of security through rearmament'[99] – struck clean across the attempt to create a deterrent to back up British foreign policy. The only points of agreement between the parties were, curiously enough, the embargo on the supply of arms to China and Japan in 1933 (which was mainly Chamberlain's work) and the proposal (finally rejected by the Labour Party) for an all-party discussion on the defence situation in July 1936.[100]

The coherence of Labour policy disappeared after 1936, as wide differences began to appear over the sanctions policy against Italy. The chief advocate of unilateral disarmament, George Lansbury, leader of the parliamentary party, was destroyed politically by the savage tongue of Ernest Bevin at the Party Conference in 1935. Some members welcomed Hitler's introduction of conscription as evidence that Versailles was finally dead; and cheered the occupation of the Rhineland and Hitler's 'final' offers. Dalton's often-quoted comment on public opinion* was true of most sections of the Labour movement, but there was a vast difference between those who accepted the need for rearmament to back up collective security and the rest, notably Cripps, Lansbury and Harold Laski, who saw

---

* *Hansard*, 5th series, vol. 310, col. 1454. 'Public opinion in this country would not support, and certainly the Labour Party would not support, the taking of military sanctions, or even economic sanctions, against Germany, at this time. . . .'

contemporary events in terms of the struggle between Socialism and Capitalism. 'I do not think', Cripps said in November 1936, 'it would be a bad thing for the British working classes if Germany defeated us. It would be a disaster for profit makers and capitalists but not necessarily for the working classes.'[101]

The Government, less sensitive to fine shades of interpretation, tended to lump all together with Cripps' other well-known outburst to a trade-union gathering at Eastleigh in March 1937. 'Today you have the most glorious opportunity that the workers have ever had ... refuse to make munitions, refuse to make armaments.' After the Hoare–Laval fiasco the Labour Party had reacted violently against the Baldwin Government, and Chamberlain's 'mid-summer of madness' speech against sanctions in June 1936 broke any remaining understanding between him and what he called 'an ignorant, unprepared, and heavily committed Opposition'.[102] Although trade-union support produced a vote of 1,836,000 to 519,000 in favour of the Government's policy of non-intervention in Spain at the Labour Party Conference in October 1936, it was more clear to insiders* than to the Cabinet that this majority represented a victory for moderate common sense.

The Labour Party might have agreed to a rearmament policy, in the sense of the 1936 Conference resolution about 'defence forces ... consistent with our country's responsibility as a Member of the League of Nations, the preservation of the people's rights and liberties, the continuance of democratic institutions and the observance of International Law'[103] – but not one drawn up by a Tory-dominated National Government. Attlee summed up that debate: 'There is no suggestion here that we should support the Government's rearmament policy.'[104] The conflict lasted into 1937–8, scarcely modified by the decision no longer to vote against the Service Estimates but to abstain. The voting on that proposition, in July 1937, was 45 to 39: Attlee, Greenwood and Morrison voted with the

---

* According to Hugh Dalton, those who opposed the resolution were 'wallowing in sheer emotion, in vicarious valour. They had no clue in their minds to the risks and the realities, for Britain, of a general war. Nor did they, even dimly, comprehend how unrepresentative they were, on this issue, of the great mass of their fellow-countrymen.' (Hugh Dalton, *The Fateful Years* (London 1957), p. 102).

minority. Labour policy, as well as Liberal,* represented nothing constructive to Conservative ministers, even when some of them, like Halifax after Munich, spoke of reorganising the Government to bring in 'some of the better Labour men'.

Because of the gulf between the parties, it became difficult sensibly to discuss the rearmament programme in the House of Commons, even in 1933–5. Since there was no bridge of reasoned argument to cross the ideological gap, the successive announcements of the programme had to come either as sudden shocks – Baldwin's parity speech and 'the bomber will always get through' – or as carefully mounted campaigns, like the 1935 election. Later, the temptation to sidetrack public opinion became greater and the exaggerated violence of Opposition arguments led the Government simply to ignore both it and the House of Commons as a forum of debate. It is extremely unlikely that the Government would have worked like the proverbial mole in 1937 and 1938, if a dialogue on foreign policy had been possible before.

Nor were the proper functions of an Opposition exercised. Even in the absence of friendly contacts 'behind the Speaker's chair', the Opposition could have influenced Government policy cumulatively in the House of Commons and by appeals to the public beyond. For this to have had effect, the alternative had to be one which Government could conceivably accept. In the 1930s, whatever their electoral success or impassioned rhetoric, the Labour Party did not present a foreign policy acceptable to the National Government, which regarded their reason as illusion and their answers as surrender. This was a loss in real terms. Worse, it emphasised the exclusiveness of the inner group and it polarised debates which should have cut across party lines. Every time Labour Party spokesmen mentioned Russia, the understanding which they asked for appeared

---

* Liberal attitudes towards rearmament may be seen in a statement by Sir Herbert Samuel, the Liberal leader, on the Air Estimates, July 1934: 'What is the case in regard to Germany? Nothing that we have so far seen or heard would suggest that our present Air Force is not adequate to meet any peril at the present time from that quarter. I believe that the British nation views this step not merely with regret, but with resentment and anger. . . .' (*Hansard*, 5th series, vol. 292, cols 2360–3, July 1934). Much later, Chamberlain commented on a critical letter by Gilbert Murray in *The Times*: 'It is that sort of spirit that makes one hate and despise the Liberals in a way I don't feel about Labour.' (Chamberlain letters, 6 Feb 1938.)

even more of an entanglement to the Conservative Government and the task of those in the Foreign Office who did not want Russia cold-shouldered became more difficult. The League and the ideal of collective security grew dim in Tory eyes in direct proportion to the fervent support given them from the left.

It is hard to define public opinion, except in terms of the leaders of opinion mentioned above. In Cabinet debates, ministers frequently invoked it in their support, offering no substantive evidence of its existence and no analysis of what they meant. The Peace Ballot, organised by the League of Nations Union in 1934–5, had been answered by over eleven million people and appeared to be a significant test of public opinion, but its effect in Government circles was marred by the contradictions involved in the final question. On the other hand, the Government was very well aware of voting behaviour as expressed in by-elections. The reverses of 1933 and 1934 provided the material reason for not holding an election on the rearmament programme until November 1935, just as the marked swing to Labour in the autumn of 1938 became the Conservative Party's overt reason for not holding an election after Munich.

Electoral calculations were those which mattered to the Party managers and particularly to Chamberlain, who had largely built up the Research Department after 1930. He had appointed Joseph Ball as director in 1930, and he was using Sir Joseph, as he had become, still in 1937–9* to provide private forecasts of public opinion. Likewise, George Steward, the press officer at 10 Downing Street, reported regularly† on the state of 'public opinion' as conveyed through the collective medium of the Press. Yet there is no evidence, during Chamberlain's tenure of office as Prime Minister, of a concerted effort to educate the public to accept his policy, as Baldwin had done

---

* Ball had been Director of Publicity in Central Office from 1923–30 and he is believed to have had connections with MI5. He had acted as go-between for Major Guy Kindersley during the Zinoviev letter affair (see J. C. C. Davidson, *Memoirs of a Conservative* (London 1969) p. 204). In June and July 1939 he took part in the talks between Sir Horace Wilson and Staatsrat Wohlthat in London. (Gilbert and Gott, *The Appeasers*, p. 216–17.) He retired in 1939.

† At the time of greatest agitation against his National Defence Loan in April 1937 Chamberlain wrote: 'On the other hand, Steward reports that in the country there is increased support for the budget and the chief fear is lest I should give way too hastily to Stock Exchange clamours.' (Diary, 29 Apr 1937.)

several times in his own political life; and Chamberlain's
authoritarian attitude to protest, whether from the public or
from the Opposition, may be found in a letter of 5 June 1938,
in which he referred to Labour backbenchers as 'a pack of
wild beasts. . . . I think what enables me to come through such
an ordeal successfully is the fact that I am completely convinced that the course I am taking is right and therefore
cannot be influenced by the attacks of my critics.'

Brief, self-confident, intellectually arrogant, that comment
could serve as an epigraph to an analysis of outside influence.

4 Positive Thinking

In a long entry in his diary, written on 19 February 1938, the day before Eden's resignation, Chamberlain set down the principles which he had tried to follow in the year since he had begun to take over from Baldwin: 'From the first, I have been trying to improve relations with the two storm centres of Berlin and Rome. It seemed to me that we were drifting into worse and worse positions with both, with the prospect of having ultimately to face two enemies at once.'[1]

The desperate weakness of France, the isolationism of the United States, and the crippling cost of rearmament, he believed, dictated his first moves in 'making friendly representations to Germany' as soon as he became Prime Minister.

British policy towards Germany at the end of 1936 showed that the Foreign Office was well aware of the dangers represented by Nazi foreign policy since Hitler had come to power. Two separate attempts to create a détente had failed and diplomatic efforts had been replaced by a wary insistence on British rearmament as the prior condition to any concession. Yet, in the midst of the 'cunctation' policy, there was a reluctance to let opportunities slip by, expressed for example by Sargent and Wigram in a memorandum of November 1935 which advocated coming to terms with Germany in Western Europe as a means of moderating her ambitions in the East.[2] About the same time, Vansittart had replied to George V's expressed wish for a settlement with Germany, in a note to the King's private secretary:

Any arrangement with Germany would have to be paid for and handsomely paid for. Otherwise it will not even work temporarily, let alone hold permanently, and nothing that will not fulfil the latter requisite is really greatly worthwhile. Now I am convinced that modern Germany is highly expansive and will become highly explosive if it is sought to cramp her everywhere. But the inevitable expansion can only take place either in Europe or Africa. Therefore if we are to undertake eventually and seriously any negotiation, we must be prepared to pay in one of these two quarters.[3]

In 1936 he repeated the theme: 'If it can't be in Africa, it will be in Europe. And I would prefer it to be Africa, in regions with which we were always well able to dispense.'[4] The sacrifice would have to come out of British territory and in his memorandum of 1 December 1936, with its 'act of faith' in regard to Germany, he made it quite clear that he preferred a colonial settlement to economic or European concessions.[5]

This general Foreign Office view about colonies was corroborated from Germany in March 1935. At his meeting with Simon and Eden, Hitler had made colonial readjustment one of his main demands,[6] and 'colonial equality of rights' figured largely in the statement made at the time of the Rhineland occupation. Accordingly, a sub-committee of the CID was set up under Lord Plymouth in March 1936 to investigate what territory might be used to bargain with. In June, Plymouth reported that there was nothing which did not conflict with some British strategic interest, but that if something had to be given away it was best to join with France and cede Togoland and the Cameroons, in West Africa.

Eden wished simply to refuse, before German appetites grew larger. Nevertheless, when the matter was taken to the Foreign Policy Committee of the Cabinet in July, the Foreign Office advised that a total refusal would make 'a genuine settlement with Germany' impossible.[7] Tanganyika should not be given back under any circumstances, being strategically too important, and to transfer territories mandated to Britain by the League of Nations was morally and politically objectionable; but 'if wider considerations are held to outweigh these grave objections', and if France joined in the concessions, then the Government should consider the Plymouth recommendations. However, Eden warned:

Germany's desires cannot be satisfied in the colonial sphere, either politically or economically. Such contributions as are possible in the colonial sphere should be combined with an attack on the wider and more fundamental problems underlying the political and economic discontents of the world.

Lord Halifax duly made a routine announcement to quell speculation,[8] and gave a public assurance about the future of

Tanganyika. Then, in August, Dr Schacht, the Reich Economics Minister, had conversations with Blum in Paris in which he pressed hard for the restitution of colonies. Anxious not to let the moment pass, Blum turned to Eden, who refused. An invitation had been sent by the Locarno powers to Germany, at the end of July, to join a conference on the Western Pact, and Eden argued that colonies could be included in these discussions.[9]

Hitler accepted this invitation in September 1936, but made impossible conditions. Unease in the Foreign Office at the implications of abandoning the Western Pact, continued pressure by France, and an attempt to hold the status quo until British rearmament was complete* were responsible for bringing the question of colonies up again, early in 1937. On 13 January 1937 in his forecast for the year, Eden warned the Cabinet that economic circumstances in Germany might force Hitler into a foreign adventure. After Hitler's annual Reichstag speech, he concluded that the position of Czechoslovakia was uncertain and he offered to submit a paper on Germany's likely policy, which would include a reference to colonies.[10]

The Foreign Office was beginning to see negotiations over colonies less as the precursor of a 'general settlement' than as a means of buying off trouble in central Europe until 1939 – by which time rearmament was supposed to be complete. There was also a degree of inter-departmental rivalry: Sir Frederick Leith-Ross had been authorised to hold talks with Schacht in February,[11] and the Foreign Office were afraid of being committed by the Treasury to an understanding, when Schacht might at any moment be repudiated by his Government.†

The Foreign Policy Committee discussed Anglo-German relations at two important meetings on 18 March and 6 April. Eden reiterated his argument that discussions on colonies should cease unless Britain really meant to make a concession; otherwise, the Government should combine with France, not

---

* 'To the Foreign Office falls therefore the task of holding the situation until at least 1939,' Vansittart wrote on 31 Dec 1936. 'There is no certainty of our being able to do so, though we are doing our utmost by negotiating with Germany, and endeavouring to regain lost ground with Italy . . . .' (C 8998/8998/18 (FO 371/19949)).

† *Diaries of Oliver Harvey*, p. 20. Although favourable to negotiations over colonies, the Foreign Office was generally opposed to those with Schacht; Cadogan was undecided (C2124 (FO 371/20734)).

to make territorial surrender to match France's return of Togoland and Cameroons, but (on the advice of the economic
section of the Foreign Office) to give access to raw materials or
an 'open-door' policy in British possessions in tropical Africa.

The Committee was full of doubts: Japan would have to be
excluded from a trade agreement or she would swamp the
African market; France would complain, and the Dominions
might well object to Britain giving up a League of Nations
mandate, in case they were asked to do the same – Australia in
the Pacific, or South Africa in the former German South-West
Africa. At this stage, Ormsby-Gore, the Colonial Secretary,
Inskip and Duff Cooper were uncertain, and Halifax wanted
to know the extent of German claims and what guarantees
would be given in return. He did not want discussion to
take place 'until British public opinion was convinced that
this was the only outstanding question which prevented a full,
final and general settlement being reached'. Similarly, Chamberlain saw a transfer of territory as the culmination of the détente
with Germany, not the starting-point for prolonged bargaining.

Nevertheless, Chamberlain also saw the chance to secure a
settlement with Germany before more damaging crises arose in
Eastern Europe. As the Foreign Office had been aware for a
long time, Hitler was likely to champion the cause of the
Sudeten Germans in Czechoslovakia, and France might ask
Britain to accept a share in her guarantee to the Czechs under
the 1925 Treaty.* There was thus a good reason to take
seriously Halifax's rather naïve remarks:

he did not believe that it was possible indefinitely to keep
Germany out of Africa without a war, or perhaps even with a
war. If it could be done privately he would like to gather all
the powers interested in Africa together, and see whether it might
not be possible to have some repartition of Africa in which
Germany could find a place.[12]

---

* Eden had discussed this situation with Vansittart, Cadogan, Sargent and
Harvey on 22 Feb. Phipps, from Paris, was against making any démarche urging
President Beneš to come to terms with Germany: but Sir Charles Bentinck, Minister in Prague until 1937, favoured it. The new Minister, Basil Newton, was
finally instructed to say that Britain wished the two states to be good neighbours – no more, for fear of committing Britain to something which Beneš would
later misuse. (*Diaries of Oliver Harvey*, p. 18)

Chamberlain's views were nothing if not definite. He 'did not share the view that when Germany had possessed colonies, she had maltreated and exploited the native population. He thought that on this matter the German colonial administration had been unjustly maligned.' He shared with Halifax a somewhat apocalyptic approach: and he spoke of 'the gravity of the general situation and the necessity of seizing any opportunity of ameliorating it'.

No one questioned the willingness of Germany to take the bait, but Eden feared Chamberlain was moving too fast, asking for more than Schacht could give and relying too much on a man without connections in the German Foreign Office. It was the first of their many later clashes. Yet in spite of the fact that Chamberlain was still only Chancellor, he carried the meeting and Eden agreed to concoct a despatch to France based on his recommendations.

On 14 April Eden put forward a Foreign Office appraisal of the state of Germany[13] which substantiated the argument that concessions in Africa could divert Germany from creating trouble in central Europe. He emphasised the effects of German rearmament on the civilian economy and supply of raw materials, and gave evidence that the Army General Staff was opposed to intervention in Spain. On the other hand, the German Foreign Office was thought to be planning to involve Italy and France so much in the Spanish Civil War that they could not intervene in central Europe. 'The occasion would then be seized by Germany of inspiring a revolt of the German minority in Czechoslovakia and of using this pretext for an invasion of that country. . . .'

A month later, when France postponed a definite answer on the question of colonies until after Schacht's next visit, on 26 May, it was clear that Blum disliked the idea of ceding French territory. Eden was equally reluctant to talk alone with Schacht unless Britain intended something more positive, such as giving Gambia to France in compensation for her losses elsewhere. There were also strong moral objections.* On the other hand, the majority, led by Chamberlain, wished to keep the

---

* Ormsby-Gore said of Gambia: 'He saw the greatest possible difficulty in transferring the colony against the wishes of the natives. This would be quite inconsistent with modern views on the subject of our responsibility for backward peoples'. (10 May 1937, CAB 27/622.) Nevertheless, the Committee instructed Hankey to look up earlier proposals for transfer at the end of the First World War.

talks in being as a means of discovering Germany's full *desiderata* in Europe. Yvon Delbos, the French Foreign Minister, visited London on 16 May to ask for a British representative to attend the talks with Schacht, and the Foreign Policy Committee agreed to send an official as an observer. Phipps was instructed to show just sufficient approval to keep the discussions going.

The French Government appeared to be trying to cut the losses of the past three years *vis-à-vis* Germany, and was perhaps attempting to diminish German involvement in Spain; but their desire for British co-operation did not extend to making unilateral sacrifices of French territory. Britain had to do the same if Schacht's mission was to be used to come to terms over European security. Broadly speaking, this is what Chamberlain wanted: and it did not matter to him whether he dealt with Schacht or Neurath. To Eden it did: worried by the Prime Minister's haste and the prospect of a firm promise without any corresponding German guarantee of future good behaviour, he was isolated in the debate and he gave an impression of carping hesitation which was to recur significantly in the autumn.

When Chamberlain finally took over from Baldwin in May, he issued an invitation to Neurath, to visit London. Neurath accepted without enthusiasm, then cancelled it at short notice, ostensibly because of a torpedo attack by Spanish Republican forces on the German cruiser *Leipzig,* off Oran. Henderson believed that the real reasons lay in the jealousy of Neurath shown by Ribbentrop, the German Ambassador in London, and the fact that Hitler himself had never approved of the visit.[13a] The setback had serious repercussions. The semi-official negotiations on colonies which Leith-Ross was then conducting in Geneva ceased.[14] At the same time, Chamberlain went through the depressing experience of the Imperial Conference (which was explained only in very veiled terms to the Cabinet on 17 June). Within a fortnight of becoming Prime Minister his long-term policy of reconciliation seemed prematurely to have failed.

Early in July he wrote:

The Germans and Italians are as exasperating as they can be and it is rather difficult to reconcile their expressions of desire for one's friendship with the incredible insolence and licence of their press. But I still get the impression that neither of them wants to go to war and accordingly we have played for time and avoided a break [in Spain].

He no longer expected Neurath to come to Britain but hoped instead for a more amenable reply after the summer: 'If only we could get on terms with the Germans I would not care a rap for Mussolini.'[15] Perennially optimistic, he could see the long distance and plan the tactical moves for the immediate future. But he was less certain of the middle ground, into which his Government would move, hemmed in and shackled by all their cumulative short-term decisions. Already, in a series of important decisions about the defence programme, taken deliberately and carefully since February, the Government had committed itself to a direction which undermined Eden's policy and limited Chamberlain's own freedom to revise his, if he had to.

Defence policy was hammered out in full Cabinet, in contrast to the discussions about colonial appeasement, which had taken place in the smaller Foreign Policy Committee.* (Indeed, Chamberlain's extension of the latter in June suggests that he wished at first to involve more of his colleagues in the new positive policy.) Fully to understand the scope of what was done it is necessary to go back to January 1937. Throughout, the underlying argument concerned the role of the Army in Europe and harked back to the inter-Service rivalry of 1934.

Baldwin relinquished much of his authority over defence in January 1937,† and the debates which took place in February confirmed the position of the Air Force as the spear-head of rearmament. Chamberlain was, after all, in Vansittart's phrase, a 'thirty-niner'‡ though in a much more restricted sense than Eden. But Chamberlain began to alter the share of the Navy

---

* CAB 27/622. The membership of the committee under Baldwin comprised: Chamberlain, Simon, Halifax, Eden, Hailsham, Inskip and MacDonald. Under Chamberlain — the same plus Duff Cooper, Ormsby-Gore, Hoare, Stanley and Zetland.

† Formally, of course, he retained authority until he retired in June, but the operative decisions were taken by Chamberlain, whose statement that economic factors must determine the future course of rearmament was accepted on 20 Jan (CAB 23/87) (cf. also Middlemas and Barnes, *Baldwin*, pp. 1025–9.)

‡ That is, one who looked to the defence programme to provide complete protection against direct attack by 1939.

and the Army in the cake, as he had wanted to do in 1934.

The claims of the War Office had been building up steadily since at least 1936.[16] At that time the Regular Army had been accepted, on paper, as 'a properly equipped force of five divisions, one of them mobile, ready to proceed overseas wherever it may be wanted.'[17] If required on the continent, it would be available in $x + 15$ days. The role of the Territorial Army had not been satisfactorily defined, partly because War Office armaments productive capacity was already over-extended in providing for the Regular Army, thanks to earlier doubts about its role and several years of inefficient direction by a series of second-rate Secretaries for War, and partly because of the objections of the Treasury to any formal commitment to equip the TA on a war footing. The Army Council had, however, hoped eventually to equip and train the TA so that twelve divisions could be sent to Europe in successive groups in four, six and eight months after the outbreak of war.

At the end of 1936, Duff Cooper announced that the War Office was ready to embark on this programme and on 16 December he asked also for authority to broaden the base of supply, to prepare the ground for expansion of recruiting after mobilisation. Chamberlain at once pointed out that these claims amounted to full equipment for seventeen divisions and rejected them in favour of Air Force and naval priorities, arguing that even in a European war there would be no Continental role for the Army because of substitution by the other two Services.

The issue was referred to the Chiefs of Staff, who reported late in January 1937[18] that the Air Force alone could not stop a German attack, nor could Britain rely wholly on France – with or without the support of Belgium – to provide land forces to defend the Channel ports. Britain must send a Regular Army contingent supported by proper reserves within four months, which could only be supplied by the TA. The Chiefs of Staff expressed grave concern at the likely speed of modern mechanised war and about the inadequate preparations to cover the remainder of Imperial Defence. For once the three, Chatfield, Ellington and Deverell, were more or less united, and in view of later allegations about their incompetence it is worth stating that their case was a cogent one.

As usual, Inskip produced a compromise[19] to meet both the

strategic arguments and the financial limitations: twelve TA divisions should have a continental *standard* of equipment, but only in sufficient quantity for training. In the event of war this would be pooled, enabling two divisions to support the Field Force after four months. Although it was obvious that this would leave the remaining ten with nothing, the Cabinet approved his scheme on 3 February, after making heavy and largely unjustified criticisms of the Chiefs of Staff. No one, however, carped at confirming a five-division Field Force with a European role.

Further debate was postponed until the War Office had worked out the cost of the modified plan. They did not report until April, and by then two decisions had been made which largely destroyed their case. On 10 February, in a debate on the general implications of defence, Chamberlain made his announcement about the need for legal authority to borrow for the rearmament programme, and he went on to say that he intended, by specifying the sums involved, to tie the Government down to these limits. Secondly, in a major review of British defences, in relation to Germany and Italy,[19a] the Chiefs of Staff came to markedly more optimistic conclusions about home defence than they had expressed in the paper on the role of the Army. Without actually agreeing with Chamberlain that the Navy and Air Force would fill the Army's European role altogether, they played down their concern for a properly equipped Territorial Army.

The TA standard of equipment came before the Cabinet during April and May. Chamberlain was by then very much in command, and the dice were loaded against the War Office. Duff Cooper was asking for three categories of increased expenditure: £204 million for equipment and reserves for the Field Force and Regular Army requirements in Britain, such as Air Defence and coastal defence; £9 million for training equipment for the twelve TA divisions under Inskip's scheme; and £43 million for full war equipment for four TA divisions who were to be ready for active service on a four-months' basis. Duff Cooper had some support from Inskip but none from the Chancellor, who spoke suspiciously of 'hypotheses one day, practice the next', and cited past history as if the Army were the only Service to have expanded since 1933. The War Office, he said, had begun by asking for a small perfect army, then for perfect reserves; now they had doubled both. The £204 million alone contrasted with the £134 million provided by the DRC in 1934 and would push the total defence bill far beyond £1500 million. He would soon have to prepare 'a fixed limit to which the services would have to conform'.[20]

Later, Chamberlain agreed with Inskip to accept the first two demands but not the third. Inskip admitted, 'there was no alternative but to accept what the Chancellor would agree to'. Chamberlain defended his regulation of priorities.

He could not accept the question at issue as being a purely military matter ... he himself definitely did challenge the policy of their military advice ... he did not believe that we could, or ought, or in the event would be allowed by the country, to enter a continental war with the intention of fighting on the same lines as in the last war.[21]

Historic memory and the consensus of the vast mass of his countrymen perhaps supported him; but his case rested on assumptions about the strength of France and the ability of the Air Force and Navy to substitute for the Army which were not discussed at all.

The Army was thus left without the prospect of proper trained reserves in time of war, and its capacity to train new recruits had been undermined. No wonder that Duff Cooper asked, despairingly, what then was the role of the Army? Chamberlain snapped up the question and referred it, together with an Admiralty request for the New Standard (an increase from fifteen to twenty-two battleships) to the Defence Plans (Policy) Committee.*

Returning the long-accepted concept of the Field Force to the melting-pot was only the first stage of revising the strategy of the Baldwin Government. Within a month Chamberlain was Prime Minister, using Inskip and Simon, the new Chancellor, to remould the whole financial structure of rearmament. On 30 June, Simon proposed a radically new procedure involving a defence review almost as far-reaching as that of 1934. The Service Departments were to state the time required to complete their current programmes and to give their estimate of costs in each year, and for continuing expenditure on

---

* A ministerial body consisting of the same members as the Defence Policy and Requirements Committee (see above, p. 89) but including the Chiefs of Staff.

E

maintenance and renewal afterwards. These figures were then to go to the Treasury, who would pass them with comments and suggested totals to the Defence Policy and Requirements Committee, the purely ministerial body set up in 1935, who would decide priorities and set maximum totals for each Service in each year, which would not be exceeded without Cabinet authority. Finally, all other decisions (e.g. on the Navy's New Standard and the TA war equipment) would be postponed. 'Otherwise, we might find in time of crisis that we had incapacitated ourselves from the ability to make the necessary effort'.[22]

Whether the full rigours of the scheme were not clear or whether they were already resigned to the imposition of Treasury criteria, the Service ministers merely tried to shift the venue from the purely political DPRC to the DPPC instead. Chamberlain refused. Even when Chancellor, he said, he had meant to institute a global total for defence. Lord Swinton was the only one to fight strongly against this procedure; Inskip appeared to be worried more about the delays involved in the complicated process and Hore-Belisha, Duff Cooper's successor at the War Office,* showed himself content to hold the little that his predecessor had gained. Even that was put in jeopardy, because Simon made a distinction between schemes approved by Cabinet and Treasury and those by Cabinet alone. The latter, including the increases of the Regular Army, were to go through the mill as well as all the new demands.†

The system of rationing wrested from the Service advisers a large part of their traditional functions. Until then, whatever the financial exigencies, they had been able to argue that since the Cabinet laid down their obligations the Cabinet must provide the resources which they, as experts, declared to be necessary. If these could not be provided, then the Cabinet must modify the commitments. Now the resources were to be laid down from above by the politicians on the DPRC, without benefit of expert advice, and the Services were to be left to make what response they could.

---

* Chamberlain mentioned Hore-Belisha, who was 'doing what I put him there for and has already stirred the old dry bones up till they fairly rattle. Things are even worse at the War Office than I feared and I foresee that I am going to have a fierce struggle there before we can settle down to rebuild on sounder foundations.' (Letters, 1 Aug.)
† In late July, Hore-Belisha applied for authority to spend £43 million in order to proceed with long-term Regular Army contracts but he was turned down.

On 29 July, just before the summer recess, Inskip gave the Cabinet some idea of the totals the Treasury had in mind, to prepare them for the shock in the autumn. The calculations were shattering. The 1936 programme, without any extras at all, would cost £240 million a year in maintenance alone after completion in 1941, and this 'seemed likely to constitute a permanent financial burden which was altogether beyond what this country could find from revenue'.[23]

The wheels of the new procedure ground too slowly and in any case, as Simon told the Cabinet on 27 October, the Treasury had found itself unable to give 'a figure the nation could afford'.[24] He implied that the nation could afford very little: there had been no sinking fund to reduce the National Debt since 1931, and the Governor of the Bank of England was deeply worried about the inflationary effect even of a £60 million loan in compensation for the abolition of mining royalties. Simon feared that the DPRC might have wrangled well into the autumn and instead he referred the whole affair to Inskip.

With the aid of Hankey, Sir Arthur Robinson (chairman of the CID Supply Board), Sir Horace Wilson, two Treasury officials and the Chiefs of Staff, Inskip began the invidious task of bridging the impossible gap between the Service estimates and the Treasury totals. The predominance of Treasury officials and the lack of any higher court of appeal than the Co-ordinator's miniscule Department gave a fair indication of what was to come, yet the Cabinet offered very little criticism. Swinton actually welcomed the new procedure, thinking that it would make possible an over-all review, 'taking account of finance, international trade and real strategic considerations'.[25] He asked if Inskip would produce 'his conception of the real strategic necessities'. But this was not the intention of what already constituted the inner group.

Through October Inskip laboured on his report, neither alone nor unscathed, because the Chiefs of Staff, in a last attempt to make themselves heard, used a report on 'British relative strength in the world as of January 1938'[26] to convey their feelings:

Our Naval, Military and Air Forces in their present state of development are still far from sufficient to meet our defence commitments which now extend from Western Europe through the Mediterranean into the Far East.... Without overlooking the assistance which we shall hope to obtain from France and possibly other allies, we cannot foresee the time when our defence forces will be strong enough to safeguard our territory, trade and vital interests against Germany, Italy and Japan simultaneously. We cannot therefore exaggerate the importance from the point of view of Imperial Defence of any political or international action that can be taken to reduce the numbers of our potential enemies and to gain the support of great allies.[27]

This counsel of despair, far removed from the advice of the Defence Requirements Committee in 1934, put the onus on the Foreign Office and the diplomats.

The Chiefs of Staff report was in flat contradiction with Eden's aims. At this time, he was still urging on the completion of the rearmament programme as the essential buttress to his foreign policy.* He had, in fact, given the Chiefs of Staff a verbal account of his aims and he seems to have been curiously unaware of the implications of the Treasury defence review. Instead, he showed resentment at what he took to be military dictation of foreign policy.[28] He admitted the Chiefs of Staff contention that Britain could not face all three enemies at once, and that France with her strong army but weak air force was Britain's only substantial ally, but he denied that this should rule British policy. He mistook the Chiefs of Staff reaction for a plea for appeasement and he took pains to show that while to try and detach one of the three enemies was a reasonable objective, it could also lead to concession and humiliation and the destruction of confidence of friendly nations in Britain. His whole opposition to Chamberlain's policy rested on a defence force strong enough not only to repel a German attack but, in the sense the word had been accepted since 1934, to act as a deterrent to German aggression against any other British interest.

None of this was relevant to the Chiefs of Staff report. Eden's reassurances of what was being done with Germany and Italy gave them no relief. What they complained of was the imposi-

---

* The Foreign Office had been complaining for a long time about the slow pace of rearmament. Vansittart had written on 11 Feb 1937, apropos of the latest CID review: 'this is a dreadful record of all-round improvidence, despite all the warnings put out by the F.O. for years past'. He noted particularly the shortage of long-range bombers — the teeth of the deterrent — after all the Government's pledges of parity. (C1406/205/62 (FO 371/20701).)

tion of rationing and the total dominance of the politicians; and
their fears were increased when Chamberlain scaled down the
definition of air parity: 'he did not intend to repeat Lord
Baldwin's words . . . and he would make it clear that the Government did not consider it necessary to have precise equality
[with Germany] in every class of aircraft'.[29] The dismissal of
the entire Army Council and the CIGS, Sir Cyril Deverell, by
Hore-Belisha, on the advice of the civilian businessman, Lord
Weir, in December was the final outrage to Service morale.

On 22 December Inskip presented his report, 'Defence
Expenditure in Future Years'.[30] He set out two alternatives:
first, the continuation of existing programmes, costing £1,500
million over the period of 1937–41; which, he argued, was the
most the country could afford considering the cost of maintenance after 1941: second, the same, but including the Navy's
New Standard and the Air Force Scheme J (an increase over
F), costing £1,800 million; this was not acceptable. He was
prepared to add something for the Navy over and above the
£1,500 million, though nothing like the 'staggering cost' of the
New Standard, and he would concede a larger number of
fighters for the Air Force Home Defence.* Nothing was left
over for the Army, and Inskip recommended that its role be
changed – a bland statement which moved at least one member
of the CID Secretariat to fury.† The new list of priorities
read: 1. the defence of Britain; 2. her trade routes; 3. defence
of overseas territories and aid to Dominions; lastly: 'our fourth
objective, which can only be provided after the other objectives have been met, should be co-operation in the defence of
the territories of any allies we may have in war'.[31]

Hore-Belisha had attended the French army manoeuvres in
September and had told the Cabinet then that the already
'virtually impregnable' Maginot Line was to be extended to
Dunkirk and that a 'renaissance of French morale' had taken
place. France, he had said, no longer expected a large Field
Force and really only needed two mechanised divisions.[32]
Inskip now used this over-optimistic report to deny the British

* The Chief of Air Staff claimed that unless Britain built more bombers air policy
would seem 'defeatist' (CP 316/37). Inskip recommended only fighter increases,
but offered the Cabinet a slight modification towards bombers if they so desired.
They did not. The deterrent policy was finally abandoned (22 Dec, CAB 23/90A).
† Pownall diary, 18 Feb 1938: 'See how the role has altered to fit the purse. The
tail wagging the dog.'

Army a Continental role; and, whatever sympathy he may have shown to the other Services in his judgements, he elevated the Chiefs of Staff forebodings into a principle of government. 'Adequate provision', he wrote, 'will only be achieved when our long-term foreign policy has succeeded in changing the present assumptions as to our potential enemies.'[33] This was said in spite of his own warning:

> if France were again to be in danger of being over-run by land armies, the situation might arise when, as in the last war, we had to improvise an army to assist her. Should this happen, the Government of the day would certainly be criticised for having neglected to provide against so obvious a contingency.*

Curiously enough, it was Duff Cooper, the First Lord, and Swinton, Secretary for Air, rather than Hore-Belisha, who challenged the report. Duff Cooper asked for more destroyers and submarines to make up for the rejected New Standard, and Swinton rehearsed the difficulties inherent in the supply of aircraft on a purely short-term basis. He demanded numerical parity, at least in front-line aircraft, and sufficient long-range bombers to match those which could reach Britain direct from Germany.† Eden, Halifax and Hoare supported him, and Chamberlain was constrained to agree to some departure from the report, if such necessity could be proved. The door was open for the Air Force, but only just.

Hore-Belisha, on the other hand, welcomed the new role of the Army and congratulated Inskip. The influence of Liddell Hart,‡ his unofficial adviser from August 1937 to May 1938, was responsible for many of the best things Hore-Belisha did,

---

* CP 313/37, para. 75. In this connection, Inskip told the Cabinet that he had had a letter from Vansittart, giving a similar warning 'before he went on leave'. The Cassandra of the Foreign Office understood the implications of the report for France as well as the Service Chiefs did.

† Air Staff strategy comprised both defence and a counter-strike: if the latter were abandoned, then an 'ideal defence' – i.e. forty-five or more fighter squadrons – would be required.

‡ Captain (Sir) Basil Liddell Hart, military correspondent of the *Daily Telegraph* for many years, the brilliant strategist whose book *The Strategy of Indirect Approach* made perhaps the most original contribution to military science since Clausewitz, took up his unofficial post at Hore-Belisha's request. Among other recommendations, Hore-Belisha accepted Hart's memorandum on Army reorganisation in preference to that of his own staff, and sought his advice on subjects ranging from anti-aircraft defence to the promotion and retirement of senior officers. Even after the dismissal of Deverell and the Army Council in Dec 1937, Liddell Hart's influence was strongly resented. (See Liddell Hart, *Memoirs*.)

but it was cast against any thought of repeating the style of warfare of 1914–18. To abandon what appeared to be a carbon copy of the old British Expeditionary Force as a preliminary to creating a new, mechanised, highly mobile strike-force may, in isolation, have seemed an admirable exercise; but it ignored the Locarno powers' declaration of March 1936; and the negation of the five-division Field Force was immediately to give rise to French suspicions of British motives. Admittedly the Army in 1938 lacked tanks, and the War Office showed little understanding of what mechanised warfare could mean, but neither Liddell Hart nor Hore-Belisha, in their iconoclastic fervour against the old structure, realised how little Chamberlain and the Treasury would be prepared to give in order to create the new model Army they desired.*

So no one defended the Field Force, and Hoare, the Home Secretary, actually tried to snatch the TA – now everybody's dogsbody – for civil-defence duties. Eden alone confessed to 'some apprehension' about the inability to despatch troops to France, but he admitted that the report was 'irresistible'. He consoled himself with the thought that the situation was very different from 1914, and with the advice that France must be warned of the decision so that the two allies could plan together on the basis of the two mechanised divisions, which the Blum Government apparently did need.

It is worth asking whether Chamberlain was right in giving priority to finance – the fourth, often forgotten, arm of defence. The contrast was never so black and white as he and Simon painted it. Defence costs had only cut very slightly into the 'civilian' budget in 1937, and Britain was in no sense on a war economy, as Germany was supposed to be. For all the alarmist fears of interested ministers and the Governor of the

---

* An indication of how faithfully Hore-Belisha accepted Chamberlain's arguments may be found in a letter he wrote to Chamberlain in Jan 1938 setting out the new schedule of orders for tanks: 846 light reconnaissance were then on order, but only 50 heavy cruiser tanks, with a further 65 of more modern design scheduled for Jan 1939. In addition there were 60 infantry tanks (slow-moving tanks to support infantry) for Oct 1938 and another 65 in 1939. All these were allocated for Imperial Defence. Hore-Belisha accepted that no medium tanks were required, and added: 'the real saving of course is in the consequence of a continental policy. These were bound to be progressive and inestimable in their full extent.' (PREM 1/241, 31 Jan 1938). There was no provision even to *design* a heavy tank for use in a European war.

Bank of England, the rearmament programme had a beneficial effect on the level of economic activity up to 1939 and neither the social services nor the export trade suffered until March 1939.* The Government had scarcely more grounds for baulking at the likely cost of maintenance after 1941, because the assumption that rearmament would be 'finished', ill-judged as it was, should never have been allowed to exclude considerations of a rolling defence budget.

It is not by any means clear what Chamberlain meant when referring to 'economic strength'. The First World War had been paid for out of loans, internal and foreign, in preference to taxation, and he may have feared both a shortage of rentier capital and an unstable tax-base on which to finance the next. Yet in other terms, notably in the reduction of unemployment, rearmament could be seen as a positive economic gain. Chamberlain's attitude becomes more comprehensible, however, if related to the policy of balanced budgets from 1932–7, of which he was inordinately proud. They expressed his arguments about the maintenance of foreign and domestic confidence and about strength – or the ability to control inflation – and they related directly to the experience of 1931. As Chamberlain had said in his Budget speech in 1933:

Look round the world today and you see that badly unbalanced Budgets are the rule rather than the exception. Everywhere there appear Budget deficits piling up, yet they do not produce those favourable results which it is claimed would happen to us. On the contrary, I find that Budget deficits repeated year after year may be accompanied by deepening depression and by a constantly falling price level.... Of all countries passing through these difficult times the one that has stood the test with the greatest measure of success is the United Kingdom.... We owe our freedom from the fear [that things are going to get worse] to the fact that we have balanced our Budget.[34]

* From 1932–5, defence spending remained roughly stable (9.7 per cent to 11.2 per cent of total Government expenditure). From 1935–6 it rose steadily, reaching 30 per cent by 1938–9. The £1,500 million programme of Feb 1937 helped to intensify the boom during the period of recovery and to insulate the economy in the short recession of 1937–8. Chamberlain's borrowing of a substantial proportion of the total after 1937, rather than raising the money by taxation, had only a short-lived inflationary tendency before 1939. Shortages of skilled labour appeared early in 1937 and of raw materials soon after, affecting, for example, steel supplies to the motor industry, but these subsided during the recession and only became serious again early in 1939. (H. W. Richardson, *Economic Recovery in Britain 1932–9* (London 1967) pp. 231–5.)

Although the argument about confidence lost much of its relevance after the crisis of 1931, the Treasury case was still a formidable one. As Simon said in October 1937, it was their duty 'to consider the comparative claims upon the resources of the country in the widest terms, including the necessities of overseas trade, manpower etc. . . .', to achieve, in fact, 'the best use of our national resources'.[35] At its simplest this meant saving money: as Sir Richard Hopkins had noted in 1932, 'If we really get rid of the bomber as a threat to the civil population, we might save a considerable sum on the home defence air force.'[35a] But, in the widest sense, the Treasury had to ensure the economic base for a long war. In preparing the Defence Loans Bill of 1937, for example, Hopkins drafted a statement for Chamberlain to make, in which he pointed regretfully to the need for further borrowing; 'nevertheless we have the satisfaction of knowing that for the past six years we have been building up our credit to a degree of stability which would have withstood, had it been necessary, far greater demands than those that are now contemplated.'[35b]

This argument, of course, was unanswerable, as the Government found after 1939. Yet it was not the only argument, and one criticism to be made of policy-making in 1937–9 is that, because Chamberlain was Prime Minister, the Treasury view was heard to the exclusion of Service opinion. The imbalance became worse because of a circular process: the more the Treasury emphasised the need to fortify the economy for a long war, the more the Chiefs of Staff themselves tended to think in terms of a war of attrition waged primarily by blockade and air defence (p. 293 below); and the more hostile the Cabinet became to a policy of military cooperation with France.

The second justification for the fears of Chamberlain and Simon can be found in a comparison with the economies of France and the United States. The remarkable recovery and success of the New Deal in the United States ran out in the summer of 1937, when signs of a turn-down appeared. In the next nine months occurred one of the most rapid recessions in American history, when production fell by a third, national income by thirteen per cent, and unemployment rose from six to ten millions. To observers in Britain this was not only a terrible blow to the theory of the New Deal, but proof that the Treasury aims of deflation, though harsh, had been correct.

France provided other examples of dangers which British

devotion to orthodoxy seemed to have avoided. Although little affected by the 1929–32 depression, the French economy remained grievously unstable in the mid-1930s. Her share of world trade declined and this was not checked either by the deflationary policy of the Laval Government in 1935 or the 'Blum experiment' of 1936–7. France abandoned the gold standard in September 1936 and devalued by twenty-five per cent. The revival which followed petered out early in 1937. Inelasticity, shortages of skilled labour, rising prices and an unstable currency offered evidence of a major recession to come in 1938.

If these were the economic reasons behind rationing, they were never spelt out to the Cabinet. None of the service ministers questioned the assumptions of the Treasury case, nor the right of the Chancellor to dictate priorities. Halifax's sombre conclusion that the financial limits on the Service Budget 'threw the burden on diplomacy'[36] was not challenged.

The details of the revised estimates were not prescribed until 16 February 1938, but the principles of rationing and the transfer of the burden to diplomatic action were accepted after Christmas 1937. They governed and limited British policy in the crises of March and September 1938, just as they dictated the isolationist strategy which was to meet the only type of war that the Cabinet envisaged. They were imposed largely by Chamberlain's direction and they owed surprisingly little to consideration of existing commitments. Seldom have the defences of a nation been rearranged with such concentration on economic grounds.

Eden scarcely took part in the long defence debate and appears to have been remarkably unaware of its implications. The story of foreign policy-making in the second half of 1937 can, however, be written in terms of the clash between him and Chamberlain, to which the strategic changes formed only the back-cloth. While Eden held to the policy of keeping Germany guessing long enough to give Britain time to rearm, so that he could negotiate from a position of strength, Chamberlain, conscious of time running out, preferred to settle the outstanding accounts at once, with Germany if possible but, if not, with Italy as a lever to open doors in Berlin. Different assumptions lay behind the personal antagonisms of the two men. At the same time a struggle for control of the Foreign Office came to a head, and, in the end, the future both of appeasement and Chamberlain's style of government was hammered out.

In spite of the failure of Chamberlain's first plan in June 1937, the Cabinet continued to expect progress with Germany rather than Italy. A secret letter from Lord Perth, Ambassador in Rome, indicating the extent of Italian hostility, was circulated to the Cabinet on 7 July, and Chamberlain's response was that 'the real counter to attack Italy's disquieting attitude is to get on better terms with Germany'.[37] A week later the Cabinet was instructing the CID to consider the military implications of Italy being unreliable or actually hostile – a contingency which was also considered in the composite Foreign Office report on the possibility of German action in central Europe.[38]

It was all the more surprising that an overture came from Mussolini. On 21 July Count Dino Grandi, the Italian Ambassador in London, told Eden that Mussolini had no aggressive designs in the Mediterranean, nor in Spain.* This seems to have affected Chamberlain's thinking more than the evidence warranted, although any sign of sunshine after the depressing experience of June was likely to be welcomed. Chamberlain agreed to see Grandi on 27 July, when he received a good impression of Italian intentions.† Afterwards he wrote directly to Mussolini, phrasing his letter in vague but friendly terms. 'I did not show my letter to the Foreign Secretary for I had the feeling that he would object to it.'[39] Mussolini sent a 'very cordial reply'.

Eden made no complaint at the time when he heard about the letter, and he was away on holiday when the second conversation with Grandi took place, in the first week of August. In an outburst of enthusiasm, Chamberlain foresaw a sudden thaw in the frigid pattern of Europe. The Foreign Office

was coming along nicely, though I can see that if left to

---

* Avon, *Facing the Dictators*, p. 450. The message, Grandi said, had been given him earlier by Mussolini, to deliver at his discretion, and he had chosen to do so following a speech of Eden's on British aims in the Mediterranean. The reason was dubious: in spite of the failure of non-intervention, the war in Spain was going badly for Italy and in mid-August the Italian Government had to decide on sending 5000 more troops to maintain its existing formations. (*Ciano's Diary 1937–38*, ed. M. Muggeridge (London, 1952) p. 6.)

† Grandi made only one positive demand—for *de jure* recognition of the Italian conquest of Abyssinia. (Avon, *Facing the Dictators*, p. 452.)

themselves there would be a danger of their letting pass the critical moment. As it is I can look back with great satisfaction at the extraordinary relaxation of tension in Europe since I first saw Grandi. Grandi himself says it is 90 per cent due to me and it gives one a sense of wonderful power that the Premiership gives you. As Chancellor of the Exchequer I could hardly have moved a pebble: now I have only to raise a finger and the whole face of Europe is changed![40]

On his return, Eden looked on these proceedings with misgiving. He told Vansittart that he must see all future correspondence between 10 Downing Street and Rome, and he insisted that Britain's *desiderata* in the Mediterranean – Italian withdrawal from Majorca and removal of the mechanised divisions from Libya – took place before any talk of recognising Abyssinia. Chamberlain may have fed on reports from Lord Perth that his letter had

> produced an enormous impression in Italy and he at any rate believes that if we can follow it up, we can to a great extent, if not entirely, restore Anglo-Italian relations to what they were before the Abyssinian adventure. If so, we shall have made a very important step towards European appeasement.[41]

But his Foreign Secretary refused to accept that the involvement of the dictators in Spain was a minor question, and struggled to hold back what he regarded as intemperate optimism in Downing Street.*

The events of August justified the Foreign Secretary's caution. Tension rose in the Mediterranean as Italian submarines, disguised as Spanish vessels, attacked British and French merchantmen running supplies to Barcelona and Valencia for the Republicans. On 28 August the French Foreign Minister, Delbos, asked for a general meeting of the Mediterranean powers, and the preparations began for what became the Nyon Conference. Eden wished Italy to take part and France wanted Russia: in the end Italy refused to attend and the agreement to patrol the Mediterranean against submarine attacks was worked out at Nyon on 10/11 September, between France and Britain

---

* For a very full account of their growing estrangement on the Italian question, see Avon, *Facing the Dictators*, pp. 454–76. Vansittart was the only Foreign Office official to query Perth's over-optimistic account, given in person at a conference in London on 10 Aug (R 5532/1/22).

alone, with limited support from Russia and the smaller east
Mediterranean states. Italy was offered a large but unimportant
area in the patrol – to hunt her own submarines – and, after
intense recrimination, accepted it in October.

The Nyon Conference greatly increased Franco-British
co-operation and ended in something approaching full-scale
staff talks. Italy was shown to be isolated and vulnerable.
Mussolini began to move closer into the German orbit although
it was not until later in September that the German press rallied
to his aid. But what mattered to Chamberlain was precisely this
danger: 'we have had a great success at Nyon but at the
expense of Anglo-Italian relations....'[42] He congratulated
Eden but he would not endorse the policy whole-heartedly. At
the last Cabinet before Nyon, on 8 September, the rift between
them showed quite plainly.

Chamberlain's argument was that Italy was afraid of Britain
and that to reach a speedy Anglo-Italian agreement would
make it possible to weaken the Rome–Berlin Axis, thus turning
the German flank. He proposed to bring up recognition of
Abyssinia at Geneva where, because Abyssinia was no longer a
sovereign state, individual nations could act on their own initiative in order to outweigh the scruples of what he called 'extreme
supporters of the League'[43] (such as New Zealand, a member
of the League Council). Given the support of France, recognition could then be seen as part of 'general appeasement', and
the Spanish question could still be linked to it: if Britain got
what she wanted, then she would do what she could for Italy.

Eden remained suspicious: 'Italy was unstable and untrustworthy.' He repeated that he would only link Nyon with
Abyssinia if the Cabinet insisted. This the others did –
MacDonald, Stanley, Duff Cooper, Halifax, each one keen to
take the chance.

Afterwards, Eden seemed unsure of his ground. He knew
that the Prime Minister was sympathetic to an Italian proposal
to refer the submarine affair to the virtually redundant Non-
Intervention Committee, and he pushed ahead to Nyon to
forestall him.[44] It was as well he did not know what Chamberlain wrote, on 12 September:

I am not too happy about the Foreign Office who seem to me
to have no imagination and no courage. I must say A.E.'s awfully

good in accepting my suggestions without grumbling but it is wearing to have always to begin at the beginning again and sometimes even to re-write their despatches for them. I am terribly afraid lest we should let the Italian situation slip back to where it was before I intervened. The F.O. persist in seeing Mussolini only as a sort of Machiavelli putting on a false mask of friendship in order to further nefarious ambition. If we treat him like that we shall get nowhere with him and we shall have to pay for our mistrust by appallingly costly defences in the Mediterranean.[45]

Involvement in the Spanish question widened the divisions between Foreign Secretary and Prime Minister, between Eden's realistic mistrust of Italian offers and Chamberlain's overriding awareness that time with Germany was short. It was ironic that at that moment both men's assumptions were probably correct. Mussolini had no intention of cutting down his army in Spain, and recognition of Italy's African conquest, though flattering, had no strategic significance. On the other hand, in September 1937, there might have been an outside chance for British negotiations with Germany to succeed. The compromise decision of the Cabinet to link Spain and Abyssinia* condemned them to an artificial co-operation which only delayed a definite decision and intensified their personal disagreements.† As autumn turned into winter, the 'dual policy' polarised every issue, and the questions of whether the Italian change of heart was genuine and, if so, whether it should override involvement in Spain – Eden's test case for facing the dictators – became inextricably confused with the original plan for a settlement with Germany until both solutions were decisively too late.

During September and October Anglo-Italian relations warmed slowly, while Cabinet debates revealed that only a minority sided with Eden. Chamberlain always showed himself conscious of time lost and great chances slipping away, and Halifax began to take on the appearance of the Prime

* In his 'Notes' for 1937–9 (Templewood Papers X5) Hoare wrote: 'Eden introduced the Spanish settlement policy without the Cabinet's approval.' In fact, it was Chamberlain who linked the withdrawal of Italian troops with British recognition of Abyssinia, on 8 Sept (CAB 23/89).
† Chamberlain fully understood the political implications of a quarrel with his Foreign Secretary. Eden was due to address a large meeting at Llandudno on 15 Oct. Chamberlain asked him to cancel his speech, giving the reason that he didn't want Eden to become a 'party hack'. He went so far as to bring Hacking, the Conservative Party chairman, into the argument but eventually gave way.

Minister's front man in the running argument with Eden.*
The Foreign Office itself was split. Meeting on 7 November to
discuss a conversation between Leeper and Grandi, in which
the latter had made a powerful appeal for an immediate
approach 'as this is the eleventh hour', the senior officials
divided: Leeper, Vansittart and Sargent in favour, Cadogan,
Harvey, Eden and Cranborne against.[46]

Meanwhile, as a result of a conversation between Henderson
and Goering at the Nuremberg Nazi Party Rally in September,
where Goering had complained about the danger of the German
people always thinking of Britain as an enemy,[47] an invitation
came in October to Halifax, in his capacity as Master of the
Middleton hounds, to attend the International Sporting and
Hunting Exhibition in Berlin in November. There was no doubt
of the political intention of this curious stratagem. All the
emotional capital locked up in June by the cancellation of
Neurath's visit was released.

A serious dispute broke out between the Foreign Office and
the Prime Minister. Halifax, quite correctly, said he would go
only if Eden consented.[48] Eden did so reluctantly, under the
impression that Halifax would meet Hitler in Berlin; later,
when he realised that Halifax was to be lured to Berchtesgaden, Eden suspected a move to put Britain in the position of
humble suitor for German favours. He was then in Brussels at
the Nine-Power Conference on the Far Eastern crisis and,
worried at the public reception of the visit after the announcement of the Anti-Comintern Pact on 6 November, he returned
to protest to Chamberlain – an uneasy interview which ended
in a quarrel about the slowness of rearmament and an almost
contemptuous dismissal by the Prime Minister. Eden began to
suspect that Chamberlain's prejudice against the Foreign Office
lay behind the build-up of Halifax and that the announcement
of the visit had been leaked deliberately before he came back
from Brussels to prevent cancellation. The effect on France of
the exaggerated hopes vented in the British press† worried him
even more.

* 'With all his virtues, Anthony does want support and guidance and they are
not forthcoming from the F.O.' (Chamberlain letters, 16 Oct 1937).
† The *Evening Standard* diplomatic correspondent suggested on 13 Nov that in
return for a ten-year truce on the colonial issue 'Hitler would expect the British
Government to deal him a free hand in Central Europe'. This was immediately
denied by the Foreign Office. (Gilbert and Gott, *The Appeasers*, p. 72.)

Meanwhile, Delbos was warning the Foreign Office against any encouragement of Nazi ambitions towards Czechoslovakia. Fully alive to this danger, Eden primed Halifax with a memorandum by William Strang, of the Central Department, which analysed and corrected Henderson's 'too loose and yielding' exposition of what British policy should be.* He had already sent Cranborne, his Under-Secretary, to argue against the visit with the Prime Minister and he now sent his Parliamentary Secretary, J. P. L. Thomas, to confront Horace Wilson, who replied blandly that the Prime Minister 'was saving Eden from himself'.[49]

Chamberlain was determined that the visit should take place, and Eden gave way. Chamberlain was horrified that the opportunity might be thrown away. 'I won't allow that. And I appointed a meeting with Edward and Anthony and it is now fixed that Edward will go. . . . But really, that F.O.! I am only waiting for my opportunity to stir it up with a long pole.'[50] He was relying on Nevile Henderson to check what he called 'Hitler's impatience' and he was particularly irritated by Eden's speech in the House of Commons debate on the Address: 'Anthony should never have been provoked into a retort which throws Germans and Italians together in self-defence, when our policy is so obviously to try and divide them.'[51]

At that time he still hoped Hitler would come to Berlin. 'I can hardly believe that the Führer would miss such an opportunity. At any rate this will be the acid test of his good faith.'[52] Yet when Hitler refused, Chamberlain did not waver. After another battle with the Foreign Office over Halifax's instructions, he wrote: 'I am satisfied that he won't spoil the effect of his visit by any tactlessness when he comes to talk with Hitler. I am quite sure the country approves what I am doing.'[53]

In the light of this scarcely disguised antagonism for Eden, it is hardly surprising that the Cabinet meeting on 5 November

---

* Avon, *Facing the Dictators*, p. 513. In the memorandum (C 7027 (FO 371/20736)) Strang wrote, 'Even if it were in our interest to strike a bargain with Germany, it would in present circumstances be impossible to do so. Public sentiment here and our existing international obligations are all against it.' He envisaged a settlement with at least one of the three potential enemies, Italy, Germany or Japan, and wished to obtain an assurance from Germany not to intervene if Britain became involved in war with Italy, but an alliance with Germany 'was out of the question'. Sargent, Cadogan and Vansittart concurred; all noted that Henderson had exceeded his instructions when speaking with the Nazi leaders at the Party Rally.

was not consulted about the forthcoming visit. But the struggle to imprint divergent policies on Halifax continued. From Berlin, Henderson pleaded directly with him to do something positive to meet German demands in Austria and Czechoslovakia.

> Morally even we cannot deny the right of Germans living in large blocks on the German frontier to decide their own fate. If they were Hungarians or Croats everyone in England would be clamouring for it. We should, even if we don't like it, sympathise with German aspirations for unity, provided all change be based on the clearly established principle of self-determination.[54]

Eden and the Foreign Office, on the other hand, were at pains to discourage any mention of Austria or Czechoslovakia.

Whose advice would predominate was not seen until Halifax returned. Eden saw him first* and thought that nothing had changed on either side as a result of the vague, valueless discussion,† but he accepted that Hitler was more interested than he had imagined in the return of the colonies, either by force or legal restitution. Otherwise the visit seemed to Eden to have confirmed the prejudices of both sides and done more harm than good, because Halifax had failed to deliver any warning against aggression in central or south-eastern Europe. Instead, he had talked dangerously of

> possible alterations in the European order which might be destined to come about with the passage of time. Amongst these questions were Danzig, Austria, Czechoslovakia. England was interested to see that any alterations should come through the course of peaceful evolution and that methods should be avoided which might cause far reaching disturbances, which neither the Chancellor nor other countries desired.[55]

Hitler had given a vaguely benevolent but non-committal reply, and the Foreign Office at once became uneasy, taking the reaction as evidence that he was no longer interested in a general settlement or immediate negotiation. A colonial settle-

---

* Chamberlain regarded that as a formality: 'I shall see him tomorrow, after honour has been satisfied by a visit to the F.O.'. (Chamberlain letters, 21 Nov.)
† Eden found Halifax's account less complete than the notes taken by the interpreter, Paul Schmidt, which were forwarded to Henderson by Neurath. (*DGFP*, series *D*, vol. 1, no. 31, pp. 54–67.) Lord Birkenhead's biography, pp. 369–72, reveals Halifax's limitations when faced with Hitler, and his constant use of the metaphor of 'speaking different languages' to disguise his lack of comprehension. It is clear also from this account that Halifax's full conclusions (Hickleton papers, 21 Nov) were intended for Chamberlain, not Eden.

ment might still be acceptable, but they feared it would no longer be seen as worth a bargain in Eastern Europe.[56]

Halifax had also seen Neurath, Goering, Goebbels, Schacht and Blomberg – a fair cross-section of German opinion which should have enabled him to detect at least any differences between Hitler and the rest. In the composite account which he gave the Cabinet on 24 November, however, he showed no signs of such awareness. Goering had told him that there was no reason for Germany to fight to gain colonies; Hitler appeared satisfied with the Austro-German agreement made in July and had said that Czechoslovakia 'only needed to treat the Germans living within her borders well and they would be entirely happy'.[57] Halifax also quoted General Blomberg's opinion that Anglo-German relations were more important than the colonial question – but he saw no contradiction between this and what Goering had said. He concluded that Germany did not plan an immediate adventure but would increase her strength and then move covertly in central Europe; and he deduced that an Anglo-German understanding was still possible.

> The whole thing comes back to this [he wrote to Chamberlain]. However much we may dislike the idea of Nazi beaver-like propaganda etc., in Central Europe, neither we nor the French are going to be able to stop it and it would therefore seem short-sighted to forgo the chance of a German settlement by holding out for something we are almost certainly going to find ourselves powerless to secure.[58]

Colonies were thus linked to the context of a general settlement, which would include assurances about the League, central Europe and progress with disarmament or the abolition of bombers, on the lines of the Anglo-German Naval Treaty. Germany, too, would gain. Chamberlain told his colleagues: 'There would be nothing to prevent the Germans from continuing what Lord Halifax had called "their beaver-like activities" but he would regard that as less harmful than, say, a military invasion of Austria.'[59]

It would be wrong to pinpoint this as the first clear statement of 'appeasement' or to contrast it too sharply with Eden's alternative policy. The Foreign Secretary had scarcely shown himself a buttress of Czechoslovakian or Austrian independence

in the past.[60] Late in 1936 he had foreseen that a German–
Czechoslovak conflict would draw in France and most likely
Britain, but had not proposed a specific answer. 'The Sudeten
problem was not one in which we could properly arbitrate
or give more than general advice to Czechs and Germans.'[61]
His instructions to Newton, on taking up his post as Minister in
Prague in March 1937, had been to refrain from putting
pressure on Czechoslovakia, and only indirectly to suggest that
Britain would welcome action to meet the grievances of the
Sudeten Germans. Eden's 'prudent but not disinterested' attitude
towards Austria during 1937 had a good deal less than the force
of the Stresa front.[61a] Chamberlain's advocacy of an Anglo-
Italian agreement seemed to the Cabinet a better defence of
Austrian independence. Eden may not have been willing to
concede the reality of German eastwards expansion so long as it
had the appearance of peaceful penetration, even in return for
a general settlement; but neither did he suggest a credible
alternative. By November 1937 it was late in the day for
'keeping Germany guessing'.

In any case, Chamberlain did not expose his whole policy to
Cabinet discussion. Halifax had invited Neurath again to London.
This was the 'second step, if the first came off'.[62] On 26
November, Chamberlain gave his estimate of what should be
done, and showed how significantly he had misunderstood
the nature of Hitler's ambitions for the future of Germans beyond
the frontiers of the Reich:

> It was not part of my plan that we should make, or receive, any
> offers. What I wanted to do was to convince Hitler of our
> sincerity and to ascertain what objectives he had in mind. . . . Both
> Hitler and Goering said separately and emphatically that they
> had no desire or intention of making war and I think we may take
> this as correct, at any rate for the present. Of course they want to
> dominate Eastern Europe; they want as close a union with Austria
> as they can get, without incorporating her in the Reich, and they
> want much the same thing for the Sudeten Deutsch as we did for
> the Uitlanders in the Transvaal.

Germany would have to be satisfied with territory 'carved
out of Belgian Congo and Angola'. The core of the letter was in
the sentence

> But I don't see why we shouldn't say to Germany 'Give us

satisfactory assurances that you won't use force to deal with the Austrians and Czechoslovakians and we will give you similar assurances that we won't use force to prevent the changes you want, if you can get them by peaceful means. . . .' In short I see clearly enough the lines on which we should aim at progress but the time required to arrive at satisfactory conclusions will be long and we must expect setbacks.[63]

In the rather leisurely schedule of conversations with France which followed this important letter, Eden and Chamberlain seemed like two horses harnessed to a cart, both pulling in different directions. Eden had already arranged a meeting with Delbos, at which Czechoslovakia was to be on the agenda. Both of them had sent messages to Beneš, the Czech President, designed to strengthen him in his negotiations with Germany.[64] But the solidarity of Foreign Ministers could not withstand the urgent requirements of their leaders. Chautemps wished to speak to Chamberlain first: Delbos's views on Czechoslovakia were no more welcome to him than Eden's were to Chamberlain.[65]

The talks took place on 29/30 November.* The French seemed to be impressed with Halifax's account of his visit and his advice that they should jointly encourage the Czechs to meet the legitimate grievances of the Sudeten Germans, while still holding the return of colonies as a bait for a more general settlement. Chautemps was prepared to be much more conciliatory than Delbos towards Germany, and it was agreed that when Delbos visited Prague he should find out what concessions Beneš was prepared to make to the Sudeten Germans. This report would then form the basis for a Franco-British approach to Germany. But no one was sure whether Germany would actually reply to these 'friendly and persistent efforts', and they feared that Hitler might reject the overture and claim that the Sudeten question was a matter entirely for the two countries concerned.

The French were helpful about Austrian independence, and recalled the spirit of Stresa; but on its corollary, the détente with Italy, they were less accommodating. They asked for the cessation of anti-French propaganda in the Italian press and the withdrawal of troops from Libya which menaced

---

* The account given here is taken from Chamberlain's report to the Cabinet, 1 Dec (CAB 23/90A), and the Foreign Policy Committee on 24 Jan (FP 36/40) since these indicate what British ministers thought were the important points.

Tunisia. Chautemps was careful to emphasise that he was far ahead of French public opinion, even in discussing the subject of colonies* and he welcomed Chamberlain's private assurance that France would not be called on for greater sacrifices than Britain.† In principle, the two sides agreed to find out what Germany really wanted and tactfully to sound out the willingness of Portugal and Belgium (who had received no territory from the Peace Settlement) to participate in the sacrifice.

Conflicting accounts were prepared for public opinion in London and Paris, but French and British ministers parted without any serious misconceptions, and Eden and Chamberlain were probably right to think that the first major conference since March 1936 had strengthened the entente. The French had even confessed to the weakness of their air force, perhaps out of surprise at the rate of British production; they testified to the strength of their army but admitted that 'the air force had fallen a little behind hand in consequence, but they were going to spend a great deal of money'[66] – in purchases from the United States.

So long as relations with Germany were the chief preoccupation, Eden was able to keep pace with the Prime Minister. The Foreign Office, indeed, now believed that another Nazi coup in Austria was imminent. In a memorandum of 4 December, Vansittart argued that

the Nazi party radicals in the Reich believed that after the Austrian *anschluss* has been effected, favourable conditions would exist for starting a kind of second Spain in Czechoslovakia, i.e. a rebellion by German and Hungarian minorities and perhaps other sections of the people, fanned and secretly helped by German equipment and volunteers against the allegedly 'Communist' Czech Government. That situation, it is argued, should soon prove whether any military action would be forthcoming by Czechoslovakia's allies before Germany need declare any war. The party is strongly inclined to bank on Great Britain's abhorrence of war

* In public, and to the American Ambassador, William C. Bullitt, he claimed to have stopped any barter of colonies, which he called 'throwing the hungry tiger a huge tenderloin in order to improve the condition of his stomach'. (*FRUS 1937*, vol. 2, pp. 186–8.)

† There is some conflict of evidence over what Chamberlain actually promised. In a letter to Hilda of 5 Dec he said that the French had been relieved by the assurance that they would not have to give back colonies; later (diary, 18 Feb 1938) he envisaged a joint settlement. The reason may be that the plan to carve up the empires of Belgium and Portugal was not yet complete.

proving effectual in holding France back. . . . The policy of Beneš is, of course, contributing to these calculations. . . .[67]

Vansittart recommended therefore 'some sort of step towards conciliation in Czechoslovakia, if a complete upheaval is to be avoided'.

Eden told Chamberlain that he did not care to press France too hard to make colonial concessions, nor Czechoslovakia to give away too much. If territory had to be returned, 'he would prefer to give back all the ex-German colonies including Tanganyika'.[68] On Chamberlain's deduction that the détente with Italy must be pursued in order to safeguard Austrian independence, he did not comment. European foreign policy was not discussed again in Cabinet or Foreign Policy Committee until nearly the end of January, and as a result the heads of their disagreement over Italian policy were not made obvious to the rest of the Cabinet, who would have been astounded to know that Eden's closest friends were urging him to resign rather than let the Cabinet 'use A.E.'s popularity and sabotage his foreign policy'.[69]

Instead, the dual policy of alternate approaches to Germany and Italy was adopted almost without opposition on 1 December,* after the French ministers' visit. Whether Chautemps and Delbos had assented wholeheartedly or not, they had given it sufficient weight for Britain to go ahead. With his clear vision of the future, Chamberlain began detailed preparations for an all-round settlement in which Britain was to be both initiator and dominant partner. While the final act of rationing was imposed on the Services, and while diplomacy was being given its role of diminishing the number of Britain's enemies, he cleared the ground.

I am having a series of quiet talks with colleagues individually in which I just put before them certain considerations. At the end of the talk I see that they can't find any answer and that they are ready to agree with me. Presently I shall have them all together in Cabinet Committee and by that time most of them will already have been concerted.[70]

---

* Only Eden, Duff Cooper and Stanley showed uneasiness. (Stanley suggested that rearmament should be made a priority to tide over the approaching recession.) The Foreign Office supported this dual policy, though without much enthusiasm. The danger of facing three enemies at once, so Cadogan wrote in January, was sufficient stimulus to try. (R329/23/22 (FO 371/22402).)

Each time he turned towards Italy, however, he clashed with Eden.* Before Christmas, they had a long talk about the prospects of a détente:

I told A. that I feared we were getting ourselves into a deadlock and, if we stuck to it, that we could not open conversations till the League had given us permission, since the League and Italy were again at daggers drawn. I therefore asked him to study the question and make some suggestion for a way out.[71]

Eden did not immediately object, and before he went on holiday he discussed with Cadogan and Sargent two possible ways of approaching the problem. The first was to trade *de jure* recognition of Abyssinia for some withdrawal of Italian troops from Spain. Alternatively, Eden should go to Geneva, win Delbos's support for recognition and then start on the *de jure* talks with a clear conscience. All three preferred the second since it did not involve trading a moral principle for material advantage. Chamberlain thought both ideas were bad, but the second worst: 'We should be signing away the best card for nothing and moreover we should call down on ourselves a condemnation more scathing than that aroused by the Hoare–Laval proposals.'[72] So he summoned Cadogan, after Eden had left, 'and turned them down in favour of a method of my own, which I hope A. will agree'.[73] Recuperating in the south of France, staying with the Churchills, Eden knew nothing of this.

Meanwhile, after a discussion with Avenol, Secretary of the League of Nations, on 8 January,[74] Chamberlain evolved a scheme for the readjustment of the whole of tropical Africa, which he produced to the Foreign Affairs Committee, a fortnight later. By then Eden was back, and had quarrelled violently with him over the Roosevelt telegram (below, page 144). Eden had produced a paper discussing the most urgent points on the European scene, but Chamberlain pre-empted the debate by claiming

The desirability of showing the Germans at the earliest possible moment that we were giving serious consideration to the position arising out of Lord Halifax's visit. Some time had elapsed since that visit and as time went on the Germans might well become

---

* 'It makes me almost despair to see how the Italians see only one side of things and that entirely distorted ... when I get back to London I must see if I can do anything more' (Chamberlain letters, 1 Jan 1938).

suspicious that we had abandoned our original intention of follow-ing up Lord Halifax's conversations. This suspicion might be confirmed and intensified if we entered into conversations with Italy—and also that if talks did begin with Italy, it would be better if it were known that negotiations were under way with Germany. . . .

'The Colonial question was, in German eyes, the only out-standing problem remaining between the two countries,' so he launched what he called:

the opening of an entirely new chapter in the history of African colonial development, to be introduced and accepted by the general agreement of the powers interested in Africa. The new conception would be based on complete equality of the powers concerned and of their all being subjected to certain limitations in regard to the African territory to be administered by them under the scheme. Germany would be brought into the arrangement by becoming one of the African colonial powers in question and by being given certain territories to administer. His idea was that two lines should be drawn across Africa, the northern line roughly to the South of the Sahara, the Anglo-Egyptian Sudan, Abyssinia and Italian Somaliland, and the southern line running roughly to the South of Portuguese West Africa, the Belgian Congo, Tan-ganyika and Portuguese East Africa. There should be general agreement among the powers concerned that all the territories between the two lines should be submitted to the proposed new rules and regulations covering the administration of the territories. . . .[75]

This startling innovation, at the expense largely of Portugal and Belgium,* but also of Britain's professed strategic interest in Tanganyika, was the first of Chamberlain's many inventive schemes to circumvent German intransigence. His colleagues, unprepared for so grandiose a scheme, debated details, making a mental tour of the African colonies in search of an alterna-tive to the loss of Tanganyika. Eden made two substantial criticisms: the plan might be taken out of context as if it were a unilateral settlement – as Nevile Henderson was strongly advising should be done; secondly, he feared the effect on Portugal, Belgium and France – 'it was most unwise of us to think that we could get away with this question on the backs of other powers'.

* Belgium was prepared to make some concessions in west Africa, so Ormsby-Gore assured the Committee after a consultation with the King of the Belgians.

Hoare was also worried but the remainder were content to accept the plan as a bargaining gambit to widen the scope of negotiation. The differences narrowed down to the style of approach and all were able to agree to Chamberlain's suggestion that Germany should be given the British requirements for a general settlement to examine while Germany's own colonial demands were under consideration in London. Yet it is hard to believe that Eden was content with the Prime Minister's proposal that a draft telegram, embodying the British scheme, should be put to Henderson, and that he should be summoned to the next Cabinet meeting to give his advice in person. The implication that a single ambassador was being set up as a counter to the Foreign Secretary was unmistakable.

Eden's position was intensely difficult, as his prickly behaviour showed. There was as yet no obvious ground of disagreement with the Prime Minister other than the Roosevelt telegram about which he could not speak in the full Cabinet. He was by now very sceptical of the chance of any general settlement with Germany,[76] yet he was understandably unwilling to draw out argument into a head-on clash on that issue when he was already in conflict over Britain's Italian and American policy. In spite of the efforts of Harvey to get him to resign, there was no fundamental difference of aim in regard to Germany – Eden's memoranda led to the same general conclusions as Chamberlain's scheme, even if the two men disagreed about priorities. It was hard to argue with such a dominant leader in public, especially when Chamberlain could normally sway the rest of his colleagues, who did not seem to realise what was involved in bringing Henderson home and who still knew very little about the Roosevelt telegram.

Because Eden had no recognisably alternative policy on Germany and no cause to rally his friends except what the majority of the Cabinet regarded as peripheral, he appeared to be continually trying to undermine the Prime Minister's best efforts, without much justification. This, at least, was what Chamberlain thought, and as the inner group took their lead from him Eden's political position weakened steadily. It did not help him that on his holiday in France he had been stiffened against the talks with Italy by Churchill and Lloyd George,[77] who were still very much bogeymen to senior members of the Cabinet.

The affair of the Roosevelt telegram had no long-term effect on future British policy, but it focused the dispute into the first major power struggle in Chamberlain's Cabinet. Roosevelt's very tentative invitation to Chamberlain to visit the United States had been rejected, with Eden's agreement, in September 1937.* Eden continued to work towards an Anglo-American intervention in the Far East, however, and he welcomed Roosevelt's 'quarantine speech' on 5 October, with its famous phrase: 'when an epidemic of physical disease starts to spread, the community approves and joins in the quarantine of the patient in order to protect the health of the community against the spread'.[78] Anathema to the mass of isolationist opinion in the United States, who took it for a call to sanctions against Japan, the speech was well received abroad, particularly in France. Chamberlain acknowledged it politely in public, but wrote privately:

> In the present state of European affairs with two dictators in a thoroughly nasty temper, we simply cannot afford to quarrel with Japan, and I very much fear, therefore, that after a lot of ballyhoo the Americans will somehow fade out and leave us to carry all the blame and the odium.[79]

His estimate of Roosevelt's intentions, or lack of them, was shrewd, but he was prepared to use any American aid so long as no sanctions were intended. In this sense he was a supporter of the Nine-Power Conference; and he urged on the Anglo-American trade agreement in November: 'because I reckoned it would help to educate US opinion to act more and more with us and because I felt it would frighten the totalitarians'.[80]

Eden was more sanguine; he found no sign of firm American resolve in Brussels, despite his long talks with Roosevelt's European envoy, Norman Davis, but he believed that a valuable opportunity had been lost when the conference broke up,† and he went on working for Anglo-American co-operation in the Far East. Considering how little the United States had responded

---

* *FRUS*, 1937, vol. 1, p. 113. The invitation was despatched on 28 July and it reached Chamberlain in Scotland in August. By then full-scale war had broken out between Japan and China, and American help in stopping the growth of tension had become irrelevant. Chamberlain waited until 28 Sept and sent a non-committal reply.

† 'The last good chance to work out a stable settlement between China and Japan.' (H. Feis, *The Road to Pearl Harbour* (Princeton 1950) p. 16.)

before, the result was surprising. Following a series of Japanese attacks on British and American shipping, Sir Ronald Lindsay, British Ambassador in Washington, was summoned to see Roosevelt on 16 December. The President spoke of naval staff talks, a blockade of Japan and sending a special emissary to London. Admittedly Cordell Hull refused to embark on joint action,[81] but Eden's livelier hopes seemed confirmed when Roosevelt's messenger, Captain Ingersoll, came to London on 1 January, offering an exchange of naval information so that plans in the Pacific could be co-ordinated. The hesitation of the United States Navy Department appeared to be outweighed by the President's personal involvement. But whereas Eden was prepared to see in the telegram the long-delayed opening of the democratic front against the dictators, Chamberlain used Hull's gloomy prognostications to prove the opposite.*

In his telegram, Roosevelt proposed to make a major speech to the international Diplomatic Corps at the White House about the dangers to world peace, followed by a request for a conference to cover international relations, arms limitation, access to raw materials, the rules of war and the inequalities of the 1919 Peace Settlement. The proposal (substantially watered down by Hull[82]) was made solely to Britain and a reply, conveying HMG's 'cordial approval and whole-hearted support', was required before 17 January; otherwise the President would not proceed. Chamberlain dealt with the message himself on 13 January, and made no attempt to consult Eden who was still in France. Bearing in mind the opinion he had formed long before about American isolationism, reinforced by the reference to American 'freedom from political involvement' mentioned in Roosevelt's own text, and well aware that British involvement in the proposal might anger Hitler and Mussolini and nullify his own plans, Chamberlain ignored strong recommendations from Lindsay and Cadogan and sent a chilly reply, which the American Under-Secretary, Sumner Welles, called 'a douche of cold water'. Cadogan at once called Eden home.

Furious at the set-back to what he called 'two years of Anglo-

---

* Eden gave a rosy account of the Lindsay-Roosevelt interview to the Cabinet on 22 Dec. Chamberlain, in contrast, dwelt on the impracticable nature of sanctions as proposed by Roosevelt and Morgenthau who, he thought, were under the impression that they involved no risk of war. Britain must 'bring home to President Roosevelt the realities of the situation' — the weakness of both democracies, if involved in war with Japan. (CAB 23/90A.)

American co-operation' Eden had a stiff, angry interview with Chamberlain at Chequers on 16 January. He complained especially because Chamberlain had mentioned *de jure* recognition of Abyssinia in his reply, and he sent his own telegrams to Lindsay to undo some of the damage. Assailed by Horace Wilson, and well aware that Chamberlain had deliberately not invited his opinion, Eden persuaded the Prime Minister to summon the Foreign Policy Committee. On 18 January came the formal American answer, conveying Roosevelt's obvious disappointment and a stern warning against *de jure* recognition. Lindsay commented: 'It would rouse a feeling of disgust ... it would be represented as a corrupt bargain, completed in Europe at the expense of interests in the Far East in which the United States was intimately concerned.'[83] This confirmed Eden in his resistance. At a second confrontation, Chamberlain produced a letter from his sister-in-law, Lady Chamberlain, who conveyed an unofficial message from Ciano that the 'psychological' moment for a settlement with Mussolini had come,* and he used the letter to emphasise the extreme urgency of the Italian negotiations.

Eden and Cranborne were ready to resign, even before the Foreign Policy Committee began its series of meetings on 19, 20 and 21 January,[83a] but, as both Cadogan and Chamberlain pointed out, they could not go out on something which, of its nature, could not be explained in public. Even with the possible support of Stanley, Ormsby-Gore, MacDonald and Elliot in the Cabinet, Eden's dilemma was acute, for he could hardly encourage Delbos to recognise Abyssinia, when he knew privately the extent of American disapproval, nor could he let MacDonald propose it to the Dominions. He argued vigorously against Chamberlain, Halifax, Simon and Inskip, warning them of the risk of losing American co-operation, but he failed to move them. Eventually, out of exhaustion and the impossibility of continuing government with the Prime Minister and Foreign

---

* In spite of the heat aroused by this incident, Chamberlain need not be blamed for using his sister-in-law's letter improperly at first. He was used to writing long letters to his family, usually conveying something of his policy; in this case he had told Ivy more than Eden knew. She showed it, injudiciously, to Ciano who may, as Eden suggested, have already known its contents through Italian Intelligence. Ciano used his opportunity. Willingness to believe Ciano is much more to be criticised, as is the Prime Minister's use of the letters later to overrule Eden in the Foreign Policy Committee.

Secretary so opposed, the Committee sent four telegrams; two to the President, giving British consent to his proposal and explaining that *de jure* recognition was only intended as part of a general settlement; and two to Lindsay, indicating something of their disagreements and the urgency of coming to terms with Italy.

It was not surprising, in view of this delay, that Roosevelt also postponed his plans. Chamberlain pressed him, on 28 January, for a firm indication of whether he would go ahead or whether British overtures to Italy and Germany could proceed. Roosevelt indicated vague approval so long as recognition was not given for nothing. His great scheme was never put into effect.

A substantial breach had occurred in the machinery of British policy-making, however much the inner group might try to disguise it. In so far as he reckoned the dictators' unwillingness to come to terms, Eden was probably right about Mussolini and certainly about Hitler (see below, page 173). Yet, paradoxically, Chamberlain assessed American intentions more accurately. There were many reasons, quite apart from British dilatoriness, for Roosevelt to postpone his *beau geste*. The American historians, Langer and Gleason, conclude that:

> Mr Roosevelt and his advisers sympathised with the British and wished them well in whatever efforts they felt constrained to make in the direction of peaceful adjustment, but there was never any question of approving or supporting their specific policy and certainly no thought of assuming any political or military commitment in connection with it.[84]

Welles was over-optimistic after the quarantine speech, and Eden underrated the extent of Hull's restrictive influence.[85] Even if Britain had accepted the Roosevelt offer, it would hardly have made much difference to Hitler who had accepted as early as October 1937 the implications of ultimate hostilities with the United States (see below, page 170). The most that could have happened was yet another conference – interminable talk and powerless resolutions.

Eden and Chamberlain made *post facto* justifications to the Cabinet on 24 January, like opposing advocates in court.[86] Eden's account was fair and loyal, while that of the Prime Minister, who spoke of 'those rather preposterous proposals', was polemic – a symptom of the ruthless attitude which he took up until Eden's resignation removed the cause of what he regarded as desperate delay. The final disagreement about the talks with Italy concerned less important divisions of opinion but, unlike the American issue, it was one on which resignation was possible.

No new issues came up before the feverish Cabinets of 19–20 February. Eden tried hard to further the colonial offer to Germany while at the same time scotching the private negotiations between Chamberlain and Grandi, which occupied more and more of the Prime Minister's enthusiasm. Very little response, however, came from Berlin. The Foreign Policy Committee, meeting on 3 February, listened to Henderson's outline of what he had already done to recommend the Prime Minister's 'magnanimous plan' to Neurath and Ribbentrop, and how he would commend it directly to Hitler.[87] Neurath had made no demur to discussing air disarmament and a twenty-year agreement with Czechoslovakia but he had dismissed the question of Germany's return to the League and was distinctly unco-operative about Austrian independence. Nevertheless Henderson returned to Berlin with a clear and straightforward brief: to offer 'collaboration in appeasement' and to 'mention Czechoslovakia and Austria', but to couple both with agreements on colonies and disarmament of bombers. France (whose security arrangements would be severely upset by German encroachment in central Europe) was yet to be told of Henderson's instructions. 'Equality of sacrifice' remained the theme.

There was very little here that would not have been acceptable to Vansittart or Sargent in 1936. But as Vansittart said on another occasion, 'the Germans will never accept this now'. Henderson's instructions had been drafted by the Foreign Policy Committee, not the Foreign Office, although, so long as a settlement was negotiated as a package deal, the Office did not actually object to the attempt.[88] But before Henderson had even reached Berlin, Ribbentrop had replaced Neurath as Foreign Minister, and Hitler, having rid the high command of Blomberg and Fritsch, became his own War Minister. Faced with this the Cabinet met on 9 February to decide whether or not to go ahead. Eden pointed out that the moderate General Beck was still Chief of Staff and that the others were not wholly eclipsed.* He preferred to push on, aware already of the smell of trouble from Austria. Halifax, more timorous, wished instead to ask Ribbentrop's advice. The overture was put off until the next Cabinet, by which time they knew of Schuschnigg's visit to Hitler on the twelfth and his capitulation to the demands made at Berchtesgaden. Although Italy was well aware of what was happening, Mussolini had made no move, and Eden drew the conclusion that it was too late to do anything – the first round had gone to Germany.†

While forebodings grew about Germany's obscure actions, the Italian talks caused acute dissension. Chamberlain had moved much further in private than Eden or his colleagues realised. He wrote on 30 January: 'It will be as well, for the Japanese are getting more and more insolent and brutal.'[89] That day Eden saw him and urged the importance of including Spain in the discussions. 'He appeared to agree.'[90] But the safeguards Eden clung to seemed irrelevant to Chamberlain, especially when set beside the news straight from Rome conveyed by Lady Chamberlain. Roosevelt's 'bombshell' was safely out of the way by early February‡ and, though Chamberlain admitted that he had been caught out by the fall of Neurath, he was ready when Grandi returned from holiday in the first week of February and asked to see him. From this moment he began to use Joseph Ball, Horace Wilson's private source of information, as an intermediary with the Italian Embassy§ – a fact of which Eden was not aware until much later.

Meanwhile Eden had found support for his safeguards from the like-minded Delbos, and some encouragement from Grandi

---

* Hore-Belisha made a curious analogy with Stalin's purge of the Red Army and suggested that the German Army would lick its wounds for several months. The significance of the purge (see Chapter 5) was not noticed at once. Harvey regarded it as 'an uneasy compromise between the Party leaders and the Army' (*Diaries of Oliver Harvey*, p. 84), and thought that Hitler had had to give way to the latter in refusing a demand from Mussolini for a guarantee of further help in Spain.

† 16 Feb, CAB 23/92. Eden was determined not to get involved at this late stage, by recommending anything to Austria which could be held against Britain afterwards. According to Harvey the Foreign Office rather shortsightedly regarded the situation as 'more Musso's funeral than ours'. (*Diaries of Oliver Harvey*, p. 90).

‡ Chamberlain letters, 6 Feb: 'The bomb is still unexploded and there seems little doubt that my prompt action averted what might have been an awkward moment.'

§ Chamberlain acknowledged the fact in his diary on 18 Feb: 'I did not ask H.W. who the intermediary was and he did not actually tell me, but I assumed it was Joseph Ball who has once or twice before given me information of what Grandi, whom he knows well, is doing or thinking.'

whom he saw on 5 February. He was angry about Lady
Chamberlain's gossip to Ciano which, justly, he took to be an
incitement to Mussolini to make fresh demands and he complained to Chamberlain about the press campaign in favour
of immediate talks, which he believed was inspired by Ball.[91]
He insisted that withdrawal of volunteers from Spain must
proceed, *pari passu,* with recognition of Abyssinia.

These differences appeared quite openly in the Cabinet on
9 February. The Italians were using Grandi's perceptive information skilfully; soon Lord Perth reported a message from
Ciano urging haste in view of 'possible future happenings'. The
same suggestion reached Chamberlain via Lady Chamberlain;
what was easy now would be harder later. 'Things are happening in Europe which will make it impossible tomorrow.'[92]
Perth could not or would not elucidate the meaning of Ciano's
statement. Perhaps Germany's designs on Austria did not occur
to him – more likely he indulged in wishful thinking about
the chances of appeasement. Chamberlain thought it clear that
'Mussolini was furious' at Hitler's success with Schuschnigg[93]
and wished to know whether Britain was a friend or not: if
the latter, he must make terms with Hitler. Chamberlain
rejected a Foreign Office assessment based on secret information[94] which suggested that this had already happened, and
he refused to accept that the *Anschluss* was imminent.*

In that frame of mind he took up the request which Ball
brought from Grandi and decided to see the Italian Ambassador
himself. Whether he realised at that moment how far apart
he stood from his Foreign Secretary is doubtful. He was very
angry with accounts of a split in the Cabinet given in the *Daily
Express* and *Daily Mirror*[95] and denied them, apparently with
a straight face; he seems genuinely to have been surprised by
Eden's shocked reaction to his request. When they met at lunch
on 17 February, Eden resisted the Prime Minister's wish to
attend the meeting and called on Cadogan for support.
Chamberlain brought in the advice of Margesson, Conservative
Chief Whip, and Hankey, and insisted. Later in the day,
Eden sent a note, firmly requiring him not to commit the
Government to the talks.

---

* Once again both protagonists were right and also wrong. Hitler did not give the
order for *Anschluss* until forty-eight hours before it took place. Yet Eden and the
Foreign Office had foreseen it as early as Sept 1937 (R2320/989/3 (FO 371/21119)).

This note [Chamberlain wrote] convinced me that the issue between us must be faced, and faced at once. In my view, to intimate now to Grandi that this was not the moment for conversations would be to convince Mussolini that he must consider talks with us 'off' and act accordingly. I had no doubt at all that in his disappointment and exasperation at having been fooled with, as he would think, so long, Italian public opinion would be raised to a white heat against us. There might indeed be some overt act of hostility and in any case the dictatorships would be driven closer together, the last threads of Austrian independence would be lost, the Balkan countries would feel compelled to turn towards their powerful neighbours, Czechoslovakia would be swallowed, France would either have to submit to German domination or fight, in which case we should almost certainly be drawn in. I could not face the responsibility of allowing such a series of catastrophes to happen and I told Horace Wilson on Friday morning that I was determined to stand firm, even though it meant losing my Foreign Secretary.[96]

Thereafter there was no way out. In spite of support for Eden's anti-Italian line from the Conservative Party Foreign Affairs Committee, composed of backbench MPs, including Churchill, the interview took place. Grandi played up to his appointed role, denied collusion with Germany over Austria and provided Chamberlain with all the arguments necessary to overbear Eden's objections.* Mussolini, Grandi said, could not move troops to the Austrian frontier as he had done in 1934, unless certain of Britain's attitude; and he swore that the opening of talks would safeguard Austria's future.

The two British ministers were then left alone to ransack their previous arguments. Eden reaffirmed his mistrust of Mussolini, his fear that a secret agreement had been made to dismember Austria, and the patent imperviousness of Italy to requests for withdrawal from Spain. Chamberlain, bent on starting the talks at once, began angrily to reproach him with losing yet another chance. Finally Grandi was put off and the Cabinet called for the nineteenth.

At the first session, each put his case. Chamberlain's account of recent history was coloured by his hopes, but his statement that Italy had signed allegiance to the Anti-Comintern Pact

---

* 'Germany was now at the Brenner,' Chamberlain reported Grandi to the Cabinet. 'It was impossible for Italy to be left alone in the world with two great potential enemies, Germany and Britain' (19 Feb, CAB 23/92).

F

only because of British hesitation, and his use of Lady Chamberlain's letters, were undeniably effective. There was other evidence
besides his trust in Grandi. Perth had said, on the authority of
the Russian and Czechoslovak ministers in Rome, that no
peace was possible in central Europe until Italy and Britain
could agree.[97]

Eden's case was less persuasive because the principle behind
their differences was still not clear to the Cabinet as a whole,
and his argument consisted, inevitably, in a denial of what
the Prime Minister said, rather than an alternative. He was
handicapped by lack of hard information on collusion between
the dictators, and by the fact that Grandi's overture did not
look like 'political blackmail' to the others. Most members of
the Cabinet indulged in wishful thinking and few of them
understood all the implications of the earlier quarrel over the
Roosevelt telegram. After he had heard the views of all twenty,
Chamberlain thought that fourteen supported him unequivocally, and four – MacDonald, Morrison, Zetland and Elliot –
with some reserve. The minutes of the debate read less categorically, but it was dominated by the former Foreign Secretaries and the emphasis on the need to restore British influence.
Simon said: 'Everywhere in Europe people were realising that we
were impotent. There would be great advantages at the present
time in any positive step.' Hoare swore that for twelve years
Britain had always been too late. The alternative to talks now
was no talks at all, an arms race and a divided Europe. 'We
should have to prepare now for a war emergency.' Elliot and
Zetland gave some support to Eden, but he was clearly vastly
outnumbered. At the end he said he would resign. Probably
the majority had no idea of how far things had gone, for
Morrison and Stanley wavered, thinking they might also resign.
Chamberlain announced that 'he himself held the opposite view
so strongly that he could not accept any other decision' and
adjourned till the next day.

During the evening Halifax tried to make a peaceful compromise, but Eden and Chamberlain met privately and agreed
that the gulf was unbridgeable. At all costs the Prime Minister
had to avoid more than a single resignation, and he must have
been relieved that Eden assured him he would go, whatever
attempts were made to hold him by his friends. Quite apart
from private interventions, a formal Committee of mediators,

Halifax, MacDonald, Morrison, Inskip and Stanley, wrought on him the next day, without effect. The Cabinet was deeply divided and, if Eden had not been firm*, Chamberlain might have lost a substantial part of his authority. Right to the end there was some doubt as to whether Stanley and MacDonald† might not join Eden; but only Eden, Cranborne and J. P. L. Thomas actually resigned.

I am in no doubt [Chamberlain wrote the next day in his diary] Anthony was right. Some members of the Cabinet were very much alarmed at the disastrous effect... to me it was really a relief that the peace-makers were unsuccessful. A. would never have been able to carry through the negotiations with any conviction and in his hands they might well have failed. Now, at least, they have a fair prospect of success.

The feelings of Hankey, expressed in a letter to his son on 1 March,‡ show how his own originally distinct attitude to foreign policy had coalesced with that of Chamberlain. The trouble, he felt, had begun in Baldwin's day and in the Foreign Office itself. Everyone in the Cabinet, except Eden and 'his little clique at the Foreign Office', saw that the reduction of Britain's enemies might best be achieved by detaching Italy, whose interests in a free and open Mediterranean, Red Sea, and an independent Austria, were so similar to our own. What Hankey called Eden's bluff, as well as his faith in the League, had both been destroyed by Mussolini; and Eden's hatred for him was, Hankey believed, the only factor in delaying talks. Chamberlain had been too patient, too long – Hitler was to visit Rome in May and, with each day, recognition of Abyssinia,

* Ormsby-Gore, while admitting 'the Prime Minister's undoubted right to take a more initiating part in foreign affairs' (CAB 23/90A) offered his own post as Secretary of State for the Colonies to Eden because he felt so strongly that he should be retained in the Cabinet. 'I could see', Eden wrote, 'that the P.M. did not much like the idea.' (Avon, *Facing the Dictators*, p. 593).
† Stanley urged the rest to change the policy and keep the Foreign Secretary. Halifax replied that that would be tantamount to asking the Prime Minister to resign. Stanley 'was very stiff and said that he did not think that he himself would go on in the new situation created by the acceptance of Eden's resignation'. His opposition to Chamberlain may be detected from this point. (Templewood Papers X3.)
‡ Hankey ended the letter, finding 'something fine' in the manner of Eden's resignation. But like Ormsby-Gore and most of the Cabinet, he took it for granted that in such a disagreement the Prime Minister must prevail. (I am grateful to Captain Stephen Roskill for showing me this letter.)

the only card that Britain held, fell in value. Now that he had gone, Hankey felt 'we might escape this horrible war'.

Eden's resignation was not, except in the most superficial sense, what Ciano called a victory for fascism. There had been several different levels of conflict as well as the main point of principle; between the old guard of the Baldwin era, whose deterrent-backed foreign policy was cut down by the introduction of rationing for the Services, and those who 'put the burden on diplomacy'; between the traditional style of the Foreign Office and the hasty private diplomacy of the Prime Minister; between Eden's wishful firmness and Chamberlain's wishful realism. It could be seen in terms of incompatible personalities (though Eden rejected Chamberlain's parallel with Lloyd George and Curzon), whose headstrong conflicts polarised foreign policy. But the distinction was also one of profoundly different interpretations: between Eden's well-documented and fully justified caution in dealing with the dictators and the Prime Minister's awareness – of greater, but not sufficient realism – that time was running out for *any* policy to avert war. In brief, the whole policy of appeasement was at stake.

Whether these conflicts did fatal damage to the British initiative is considered in the next chapter. Here it may be said that although Chamberlain's credulity may seem remarkable, and his back-stage methods undesirable, neither was wrong in the *immediate* context. If Mussolini had moved his troops at the time of the *Anschluss,* Chamberlain's way would have been acclaimed by historians. The failure to evaluate the situation in March was much more serious than what occurred in February.

Freed of the incubus of a Foreign Secretary they could not control Chamberlain and Halifax moved on a broad front in the first week of March. Instructions were sent to Lord Perth about preliminaries for the talks. Chamberlain thought it 'desirable that agreement with Italy should be reached as rapidly as possible and that it would be most unfortunate if the conversations were unduly prolonged with the discussion of details'.[98] Halifax weakened Eden's safeguards at once by making it clear that Spain was to be put on the agenda only formally. It would be discussed by the Non-Intervention Committee, and Perth was to bring it up only as a threat if the talks went badly, or if there was any need to publish documents. By early March, Halifax was prepared to say frankly to the House of Commons that the Government was not going to insist on the pledge to link the Italian agreement with Spain.[99]

The existence of an opposition within the Cabinet was confirmed. MacDonald, Ormsby-Gore and even Simon found the new policy hard to swallow. They were only a little mollified by Chamberlain's further assurances from Grandi, and Halifax's ambivalent definition of withdrawal from Spain: 'The scheme should be working and withdrawal under it should be taking place, and generally speaking all the arrangements were being observed loyally and in good faith.'[100]

The veil over German intentions grew thicker. As he ran through his colonial policy for the benefit of the Cabinet on 2 March*, Chamberlain was not inclined to expatiate widely on the prospects. On 9 March, when Halifax reported Henderson's disastrous interview with Hitler, the scheme seemed almost dead. Hitler and Ribbentrop had been at their worst, virulently anti-British, bent on getting their own way in central Europe, and interested neither in colonies nor in a joint approach from France and Britain about Austria. Halifax had sent a mildly reproachful message back to Ribbentrop: 'We had taken a reasonable line about Central Europe and had done our best to steady opinion as to Austria and to use our influence in Czechoslovakia in favour of a settlement of the German differences.'[101] The faintest hint of a threat was allowed to show through: 'If once war should start in Central Europe, it was impossible to say where it might not end, or who might not be involved.'

Firmness, even at this hour, would be vitiated by Henderson's behaviour in Berlin, according to the dissenters, Stanley, Ormsby-Gore and Hailsham; but the opposition had no inkling of the *Anschluss*. Chamberlain had quoted a most 'reliable source' that no requests relating to Austria had been made to Mussolini by Germany.[102] Henderson was no better informed of the date.[103] Ten days later came the invasion and the incorporation of Austria into the Reich.

Until that moment there had been no substantive reason for

---

* It is significant that this was the first Cabinet discussion of the scheme to divide up tropical Africa which Chamberlain had put to the Foreign Policy Committee on 24 Jan.

a reappraisal of the policy which the Cabinet had adopted during 1937. Two choices opened up in March 1938: either to abandon the whole project for appeasement – drawing on the evidence of German unwillingness to negotiate and the confirmation of malevolence implied in the *Anschluss*; or to pursue it wholeheartedly to its conclusion. The evidence for the latter was held to be overwhelming. Mussolini had failed to prop up the Schuschnigg Goverment, as he was believed to have done in 1934. On Grandi's evidence it was argued that if an Anglo-Italian agreement had been concluded in January Mussolini would have acted differently. Czechoslovakia was now at risk and, since the French Government swore that they would stand by their ally, German aggression might precipitate European war. At the same time, the Cabinet was faced with another problem: if Germany had rejected the bait of African colonies before, would she now accept a pragmatic solution of the Sudeten question? Or would the situation, as Harvey suspected, tempt Hitler 'to make a fresh coup because he believes the P.M. and Halifax would stand aside, and France would not dare to move without us'?[104]

5 The German Negative

In the aftermath of the *Anschluss,* the British Government was offered a rare moment of introspection and choice. Their decision to work for the continued appeasement of Germany and for the Anglo-Italian agreement, excluding consideration of the Grand Alliance or the mistrustful firmness of the Eden–Baldwin line was based as much on their view of Hitler's motives as on their analysis of the British predicament. Was their estimate of what British policy could achieve accurate? Was it true, as Henderson and Perth suggested, and as Grandi only too eagerly insinuated, that the *Anschluss* had occurred because of their failure to conclude an agreement with Italy? Was Hitler ever likely to listen to the scheme for carving up colonial Africa and lumping it in the balance with the problems of central and south-eastern Europe? Was the Government right to conclude that once Austria 'was out of the way' only the racialist pattern of German expansion would continue, so that the Sudeten problem could in some way be separated from German ambitions to seize the whole of Czechoslovakia?

To attempt more than a sketch of the evolution of Nazi foreign policy in the 1930s is beyond the scope of this study,[1] but in order to gauge whether British policy had any chance of success and to illuminate the reasons behind Chamberlain's policy, something must be said about the process of policy-formation under the Nazi regime, and about Hitler's attitude towards Britain and to the Czechoslovakia question in 1936–8. By the beginning of 1938 German policy had reached a stage where the impact of Britain's efforts was much slighter than in 1936, and it is an irony that this change should have occurred simultaneously with the final British conversion to appeasement.

The events of 1936–8 are important not only because of this transformation, but because of the emergence of Hitler as the supreme arbiter of foreign policy in the Third Reich. How far his intentions were clear-cut and ordered in priorities, even then, is a matter of intense argument[2] but it is not necessary to establish here, from the undoubtedly sketchy documents of these two years, questions so large as whether or not he planned explicitly for war against the Western powers in 1939.

According to the orthodox school of British historians, Hitler came to power with the long-term aim of achieving *Weltmacht* for Germany on lines similar to those set out in *Mein Kampf*. Premeditation lay behind all his striking successes up to 1937, and after the *Anschluss* the sequence then led on to the dismemberment of Czechoslovakia in two stages and to the war of 1939. If this view is accepted, then the whole of Chamberlain's policy, from 1937 onwards, was futile. Britain should have learned the truth at each successive crisis, and the inaction over the Rhineland, the failure to abandon appeasement in March 1938 and the signing of the Munich settlement constitute the most damning indictment of modern history. If, on the other hand, the thesis put forward by the opposition – notably A. J. P. Taylor – is accepted, British policy becomes much more a matter of debate. If Hitler was basically a traditionalist, following the style of policy of Bismarck and Stresemann, and the professional diplomats of the German Foreign Office in order to free his country from the burden of the Treaty of Versailles, restore the army, and 'make Germany the greatest power in Europe from her natural weight';[3] if he exploited the follies of Western statesmen, and gambled and stumbled by mistake into war, then there is no need to condemn Chamberlain's Government root and branch, but to search for the moments when alternative policies might have checked Hitler's progress, or where lack of information or plain ineptitude led to wrong decisions.

These two viewpoints, though widely opposed, are not mutually exclusive. Contemporary German historians tend to take a middle course, emphasising the dogmatic nature of Hitler's long-term plans, but also the absence of a definite order of priorities or of a time schedule in the period before the middle of 1936. His priorities could, and did, change: war with the United States, for example, though a recognised end, was reserved for the indefinite future until it was first admitted, late in 1937, as a likely consequence of anti-British activity (see below, page 170). In the sense that the list was tailored to circumstances and the time schedule fixed as much by accretion of decisions as deliberate forethought, Germany's foreign policy was shaped by its leader's opportunism. In the early days at least he was 'never so sure of himself and his position as both his enemies and his friends thought. He was a man playing in a game of chance, a German roulette, that most men would not join if they could, and in which the stakes shook even Hitler.'[4] But it is also true that Hitler believed superstitiously that he would not live to be an old man* and that his political work must be finished, like his architectural monstrosities, before the late 1940s. He was forty-eight in 1937, the year of his 'political testament' at the Hossbach Conference – and in May 1938 he made his will. Doctor Morell's hormone-injection treatment, on which Hitler set great store, was less and less effective. Moreover, certain test cases – the success of the Roehm purge, the occupation of the Rhineland and German participation in the Spanish Civil War – gave him confidence for the next steps, while some of the original principles themselves, like the future relationship with Britain, changed; and others, such as war with France, altered in immediate importance as internal and external events suggested.

Hitler's apparent indecisiveness, taken with his sudden urgent incursions into policy, can be seen either as signs of vacillation or a brooding authoritarianism. Speer, offended by his lack of discipline, called it a sign of the artistic temperament.[5] In domestic policy he rarely gave a clear lead; and the bureaucrats, in particular Dr Hans Lammers, who saw him nearly every day, tended to build up his vague pronouncements into coherent decisions. Within this style of government, a determined subordinate such as Himmler was able to build up the police state almost without direction or restraint. In foreign affairs Hitler relied heavily on Otto Dietrich, the Reich Press chief, with whom he discussed international affairs.[6] Like his adjutant, Captain Wiedemann, Dietrich was intellectually superior to most of the Nazi leaders, and the success of Hitler's inspired guesswork owed much more to these paladins of the inner court than to the Foreign Office or Ribbentrop's private bureau, the Dienstelle. The fact that Hitler ignored many of the patterns of *Mein Kampf* suggests that he had a pragmatic surface even if the guiding themes of his political life were

---

* Speer, *Inside the Third Reich*, pp. 103–4. 'It seems to me that Hitler's plans and aims never changed. Sickness and the fear of death merely made him advance his deadlines' (Speer, p. 107).

dogmatically followed.* Nevertheless, all the important initiatives in foreign policy in the period 1936–8 appeared to come from Hitler himself.

Indecisiveness was a weapon in itself. Behind the mask, Hitler could divide and rule his subordinates. In a confused period when substantial power still rested with the High Command, the Foreign Ministry and big business, as well as the Nazi Party and the SS, he retained the final capacity of decision. His spectacular interventions indicated not only growing confidence in his own ability, but his freedom from one centre of power as against another, and the means by which he isolated and destroyed, successively, the alternatives in foreign policy associated with each.

Towards Britain, before 1936, Hitler showed a curious respect, based on his conception of racial affinity and the deduction from past history that she was a natural ally like Italy, just as France was a natural enemy. In the autumn of 1935, during the Abyssinian crisis, Speer heard him say: 'it is a terribly difficult decision. I would prefer to join the English. But how often in history the English have proved perfidious. If I go with them, then everything is over for good between Italy and us. Afterwards the English will drop us and we will fall between two stools.'[7] The experiences of the First World War had convinced him that Germany had lost because she had been betrayed and because she had made the initial mistake of fighting the British Empire. This would not be repeated. In his *Second Book* he spoke of the significant value of Anglo-Saxon blood and traditions, and the sagacity of the British nation in its acquisition of an empire for the provision of raw materials and the colonisation of surplus population.[8] There was no essential conflict, he believed, between Germany and Britain, whose stable empire had now ceased to expand.† Instead, Germany's animus lay against her inveterate encircling enemies, France and Russia. His policy was to remould Europe, and since in his scheme Europe was no concern of Britain

---

* cf. A. Hillgruber, *Hitlers Strategie*. According to Speer, Hitler refused to publish his *Second Book* – 'What political complications it would make for me' – and also refused to be pinned down to the detailed programme of *Mein Kampf* (*Inside the Third Reich*, pp. 86 and 122).

† In a conversation with Sir Eric Phipps, the British Ambassador in Jan 1935, Hitler showed himself most solicitous for the welfare of the Empire, especially for the future of India within the scope of British rule (C600/55/18 (FO 371/18823)).

the two should recognise their common links. As he told Sefton Delmer at the Brown House in Munich in 1931, 'You take the sea, and we the land, or the Red Flag will fly from London to Vladivostok.'

Britain's designated role remained that of Nordic blood-ally until at least 1935. She was not involved in the fight for *lebensraum* nor the extension of the racial principle to all Germans living beyond the frontiers of the Empire of 1914. Britain was not even part of the ultimate aim of changing both the geographical distribution of the world and the biological nature of mankind. German rearmament was not initially directed against her. The army was to be restored to face the great Continental powers on the frontiers east and west; the air force was to give it support and create opportunities by long-range bombing of Paris, Moscow and Warsaw, not London. The Anglo-German Naval Treaty of 1935 was seen in German eyes as a defensive as well as a conciliatory measure. Whereas Hitler's plans always provided for war against France, there is no indication of his willingness even to contemplate war with Britain before 1937.

But British Governments of the 1930s failed to fulfil Hitler's requirements. However deviously, they held to the entente with France and built up an air deterrent to rival Germany's own striking-force. All the preparations for rearmament which flowed from the decisions of 1934 confirmed the recommendations of the Defence Requirements Committee report that Germany was to be regarded as the ultimate enemy. Worst of all, to Hitler, was the continuing British involvement in Europe. The creation of the Stresa Front, short-lived though its strength was, was a most serious blow to his confidence in the ability of Germany to break loose from the shackles of Versailles. In spite of the overtures to Germany concerning colonies (see above, page 110) the part played by Britain in imposing sanctions on Italy, in the questionnaire addressed to Hitler after the Rhineland, and in Baldwin's refusal to visit Germany in July 1936, confirmed the apparent rejection of the separate but equal status which Hitler had offered to the British Empire.

Since Britain was neither a suitor nor a partner, she was increasingly ignored. There had been nothing to attract Germany in the British proposals of March 1936, and there were no more overtures from Hitler after the brilliant promises which accompanied the reoccupation of the Rhineland. That event, as Eden complained, destroyed the best British bargaining-counter.[9] There is no specific documentary evidence that Germany would have retreated in March 1936 if France and Britain had resisted, but Hitler did say, according to Schmidt, 'the 48 hours after the march ... were the most nerve-racking in my life. If the French had then marched ... we would have had to withdraw,' and Speer verifies it.[10] Britain did nothing, and without her support France dared not move troops. This was the first test case of British strength. Afterwards, if Britain wanted peace, then she would have to come to terms with German desires.

In the period of 'secret preparations for aggression'[11] the change was veiled, but in 1936 Hitler began to take greater risks which, in their military and economic consequences, could not easily be concealed. By then his own position as leader had been vastly strengthened inside and outside Germany. His diplomatic successes, won in the main against the advice of the centres of political power like the High Command and heavy industry, were outstanding. Germany had achieved large-scale rearmament of the army and air force and had consolidated the navy within the favourable scale laid down by the Anglo-German Treaty. She had withdrawn from the League of Nations, leaving behind sufficient burden of guilt for her return to become another bargaining-counter in the armoury. A wide rent had been torn in the system of French security in Eastern Europe by the German–Polish Agreement of 1934, which had also safeguarded Germany's own weak eastern frontier. Meanwhile Mussolini, who had previously avoided too close a relationship with Germany, had been driven to it by the exigencies of sanctions and the steady drain of the Abyssinian campaign. The German–Italian agreement was signed in October 1936 after the Rhineland had been occupied; and militarisation of the zone was to enable the building in 1937–8 of a Western wall against the threat of French invasion by which Germany had been humbled in 1920 and 1923. Finally, the anti-Comintern pact had been signed with Japan, and although largely an exercise in propaganda, an attempt to draw the sting of the Franco-Soviet Pact, it would provide another source of trouble in a new quarter of the world for Britain and the United States. 'In less than four years Hitler had achieved full freedom of movement for Germany and had practically invalidated the Treaty of Versailles . . . he might have been taken for a politician of genius.'[12]

The next stage, the 'transition to expansion', did not immediately reveal a new attitude towards Britain. Ciano, the Italian foreign minister, had from Hitler a copy of the British plan of January 1936 for the overture to Germany but his reaction to the anti-German tone of much of the evidence in it is not known.[13] So long as Edward VIII was King, Hitler placed an absurdly over-optimistic reliance on what he could do to maintain friendly relations.[14] Besides, Hitler was by no means so certain of total power in his own house as external achievements suggested.* The year 1936 was one of conflict between the claims of the civilian side of the economy and the rearmament programme, which centred on the personalities of Hjalmar Schacht, the Finance Minister, and Hermann Goering, who was promoted in April to be final authority on questions of raw materials and currency. Schacht opposed the rearmament programme as fatal to future progress on the lines of his own 'economic miracle' of 1934–5, but Goering eventually overrode him. Hitler's personal intervention was necessary on two occasions and the debate in which both sides sought foreign influence to outweigh their opponents within Germany (page 76 above) did not end with the introduction of the Four Year Plan in August, but only with the enforced resignation of Schacht in November 1937.

The Four Year Plan, however, began to undermine Schacht's position. Goering was put in charge of it in October 1936, and when Hitler delegated this authority he spoke of 'the lack of understanding on the part of the Reich Ministry of Economics and the opposition of the German business world', as he handed the document to Albert Speer, the last of only four Nazi leaders to have a copy.[15] Here, the future economic

---

* An indication of the position can be found in the 'provisional war directive' issued by the Commander-in-Chief of the Wehrmacht, Werner von Blomberg, shortly after the ratification of the Franco-Soviet Pact in May 1936. The directive envisaged war on two fronts against France, Russia and Czechoslovakia. Although this represented a significant advance on the previous plan (code name Schulung) of Mar 1935, there was still no intention to provoke war deliberately. Hitler's influence is to be found rather in the extension of conscription from one to two years, and the deliberate press and propaganda campaign against Russia which the plan also included.

objectives were laid down: increases in the self-sufficiency of German agriculture, the creation of an autarky in raw materials, the building-up of new industry, especially synthetics, and the subordination of civil life to military development. These were preparations for a prolonged war, and the political preface and the devastating conclusion of the document left no doubt either of its authorship or its intention: 'I thus set the planning task: 1. The German army must be operational within four years. 2. The German economy must be fit for war within four years.'[16]

These plans were directed against Soviet Russia and the threat of an all-encroaching communism. The date of war was not set, nor was it to be of Germany's choosing. When he announced the plan at the Nuremberg Party Rally on 9 September, Hitler still confined himself to speaking of the fear of 'Bolshevik invasions'. But the effect of the plan, at the end of four years, would be the same whether Germany fought East or West and whether Hitler waited or chose the date for war. Autarky meant that Germany ceased to be interested in Britain's colonial offers. Britain herself was now lumped with other European powers 'disintegrated through that democratic form of life, infected by Marxism and thus likely to collapse in the foreseeable future'.[17]

At the end of 1936 the British Government still assumed that a permanent détente with Germany was ultimately possible and that it would be based on parity of military strength and the settlement of outstanding differences. To a large extent their estimate was founded on the belief that Hitler was not always the prime mover, nor the final arbiter in German external policy; they were wrong in the second premise, and shortly to be proved wrong in the first.

Four centres of power in the Reich can be discerned in the three years after the Roehm purge in 1934 eliminated the SA, the revolutionary wing of the Nazi movement. First, was the officer class, including the majority of the High Command, led by the Commander in Chief, Blomberg. These were associated with the second group consisting of Schacht, the bankers and the heads of big business, particularly of the heavy industries in the Rhineland and the Ruhr. Opposition by both groups to the total concentration on rearmament continued after the announcement of the Four Year Plan and remained formidable despite the centralised growth of the third, the Nazi Party and the fourth, the SS, led by Himmler. Roehm and the SA had, after all, been sacrificed largely to retain the formerly enthusiastic support of the officer class for the new regime. But the conflict which lay between the advocates of an economy based on international trade and those favouring autarky was resolved by the personal intervention of Hitler in launching the Four Year Plan. The big business group split, as I. G. Farben, the giant chemical firm, and others saw what profits could be made out of the new emphasis on synthetics. The High Command also divided, since many of the generals objected to Schacht's restrictive control of the military budget, conscious that raw materials mattered more for equipment of the Wehrmacht than 'normal' foreign trade.[18] The power struggle continued for more than a year but was resolved to Hitler's satisfaction at the end of 1937.

There were, however, other agencies in the making of foreign policy. The Foreign Office had remained, ever since the time of the Weimar Republic, an aristocratic province, led by von Neurath, Foreign Minister from 1932–8. Hitler had once condemned it as 'an intellectual garbage dump' and he by-passed it when he could by employing men like Ribbentrop. But the calibre of junior Nazi party leaders was low and the choices for embassies abroad, when they excluded Foreign Office officials, were unimpressive and frequently unwise. Much of the resistance to Hitler was to be found among individuals in the diplomatic élite. Neurath himself was a revisionist, by negotiation rather than by force. He lacked the stamina to stand up to Hitler and suffered a heart attack after the Hossbach Conference, but greater resolution came from men such as Ulrich von Hassell, the brothers Kordt and von Weizsäcker, State Secretary from 1938, a Nationalist and a Catholic, who attempted to influence the regime from within. The force of their opposition, however, and of links like that between Weizsäcker and General Ludwig Beck, dates from 1938 rather than the critically important period when Hitler's policy towards Britain was still fluid. At the same time, outside the Foreign Office altogether, Ribbentrop created his own apparatus, the Dienstelle Ribbentrop, initially only an information office editing foreign news, but a potentially powerful body because of Hitler's reliance on it and its director, and his contempt for the official channels.

Goering, organiser of the secret police before Himmler, director of the Four Year Plan and Commander-in-Chief of the air force, spanned all the centres of power, yet his role in foreign policy making was indeterminate. He grew more conservative during the 1930s and, like most of the members of his staff, particularly Staatsrat Wohlthat, his commissioner for the Four Year Plan, he preferred that Germany should have indirect hegemony over Eastern Europe and an economic empire rather than the physical acquisition of *lebensraum*. The invitation to Halifax in November 1937 had been made on his initiative and he welcomed the idea of a colonial empire offered by Chamberlain in 1938. At the time of Munich, Goering opposed Ribbentrop's violent demands for war.

On the other hand, he was lazy, afraid of Hitler, cowardly and submissive in the Führer's presence. He was useful, as Hitler said, as a respectable bully, 'brutal and ice-cold' in the Roehm purge[19] or in the flaying of Austria after the *Anschluss*; his influence in foreign affairs was slight. He used the information provided by his own Research Department to maintain his position and weaken by blackmail that of others,* and he preferred to curb the activities of Ribbentrop rather than to advance his own. His own part, his qualified support for Goerdeler's first visit to London and the mistimed invitation to Halifax may only have been the result of misinterpretation of Hitler's opaque strategy.

There were thus no alternative policies which Hitler could not circumvent or countermand. Even against the opponents of the Four Year Plan he had vast advantages. Objection to the exercise of his powers was more widespread than to him as leader. Few, before 1938, wished Hitler overthrown or dead — he had given almost all levels of German society too much success in his first five years. The opposition was scattered and varied: ranging from the inertia or institutional drag of the bureaucracy, reinforced by the hostility of individuals like Admiral Canaris, head of counter-intelligence, as far as the independent behaviour of individual Gauleiters who ran their districts in frequent disagreement with the Party chiefs in

* The information that Blomberg's wife had been a prostitute, which led to the Commander-in-Chief's downfall, was provided by Goering's department.

Berlin. But the ability of the professional civil service or Foreign Office to bemuse and divert the Party machine represented a brake on what was done rather than an alternative. After 1936, none of Hitler's major initiatives in foreign policy was blocked or altered by the centres of power beyond the Nazi circle.

The capacity of resistance might have been of the greatest interest to the British Government. A direct onslaught on Hitler's leadership or a weakening of his support among the German people might have provided the occasion for a British démarche, impossible in other circumstances. In the period 1936–7 however, there was no discernible movement of popular opinion. Resistance grew in plenty to the activities of the secret police, the persecution of the Jews and the suppression of the Confessing Church, but valiant though the churchmen were, whether Roman Catholic or Protestant, they made no appreciable impact on Hitler's aggressive pre-war *foreign* policy. The conditions did not exist. There was no popular sympathy to rouse against achievements which had been acclaimed as matters of national honour since Stresemann's day. Hitler held a monopoly of patriotism and of the weapons of the State – the police, press and terror. Rearmament at this time meant full employment, rather than privation; only when war seemed a reality in September 1938 did the Nazi leaders – or the British Government – detect a sullen unwillingness in the German people for the ultimate struggle.[20]

The secret nature of Hitler's directives and the manipulation of propaganda ensured that foreign policy would not become a matter of public debate. Resistance could only come from individuals within the hierarchy, like Admiral Canaris, Weizsäcker or General Beck, or within the old governing élite, members of the same ruling class whom President Hindenberg had recalled to form von Papen's Cabinet of Barons in 1932, after the fall of the Weimar Republic. Authoritarian, intensely nationalist in temperament, sympathetic to the idea of the corporate state, the conservatives remained uneasy at the pretensions of the upstart Hitler, while compelled to admire his achievements. They were of use to Hitler, at least until 1937; and, although they opposed him, by doing so through the existing system they probably helped to prolong its life. Goerdeler, Popitz, von Hassell, von Moltke, later the associates of von Stauffenberg in the conspiracy against Hitler's life, did not turn to the idea of a coup against him until later in 1938, by which time the military and economic direction of foreign policy had been largely determined.

The British found it hard to judge the quality or reliability of this resistance. When Goerdeler and von Kleist visited London the Foreign Office and the Cabinet saw the same traditional Prussians whom Britain had fought in 1914 (see below, page 306). Early in March 1938 Goerdeler met Vansittart, to warn him of the rumours of the Hossbach Conference, which he had heard from Generals Beck and Fritsch. They discussed the Sudeten German problem and, instead of sympathising with the British argument that a degree of autonomy could be given within the Czech state, Goerdeler showed himself indistinguishable from the Nazis: 'the area was German, it had a common frontier with Germany and must be incorporated in the Reich'.[21] The Foreign Office might well ask: did they want to see Hitler – a man who might yet be reasonable – replaced with old-style Prussian nationalists?*

This conflict of opinion highlighted the British confusion between opposition to Germany's expansion in Europe and to Hitler's regime as such. That they would risk losing all the credit that had been built up by two years of concession remained the overriding argument against siding with the resistance; but there is no doubt also that the Chamberlain Government took it for granted that Hitler's power was so surely based by 1938 that it would be worse to attempt to dislodge him than to come to terms.

Unfortunately for the British, as Hitler's confidence in his political power and his ability in foreign affairs increased, anti-British sentiment flared in Germany. Hitler was secure at home, backed by the weapons of tyranny, terror and concentration camps. The Nazi Party centralised and co-ordinated the national life, even the arts under Goebbels' Chamber of Culture. After Hitler's decree of 17 June 1936, Himmler and Heydrich built the SS into a unified state police, with a military wing on the lines of Hitler's bodyguard, the Liebstandarte Adolf Hitler. Such discontent as existed was largely displaced by the waves of

---

* cf. C8520/1941/18 (FO 371/21732), comments by I. Mallett on Kleist and Goerdeler. Also, typically, apropos of rumours of a conspiracy in Feb 1938, 'we have heard a great deal about their proposed coup d'état, but there have been few signs of it yet' (C6578/62/18 (FO 371/21663)).

anti-Semitism and the vivid successes of foreign policy. In this mood of success, Hitler treated the British lack of response with petulance, like a rejected suitor. He had hoped that Ribbentrop, Ambassador in London since October 1936, would bring about a political understanding on the lines of the Anglo-German Naval Treaty, with separate spheres of influence delimited by agreement and historical necessity. Ribbentrop signally failed.

The precise moment of Hitler's change in outlook towards Britain cannot be pin-pointed but it was already present when the 'period of expansion' began.[22] The long political exposition of the military directive of June 1937 showed the new style at work.[23] Preoccupation with war on two fronts against the Franco-Soviet-Czechoslovak combination remained, but the document also provided for punitive action in Spain and a fresh initiative in Austria to forestall any chance of a Hapsburg restoration. Moreover, preparations were ordered 'to enable the military exploitation of politically favourable opportunities should they occur'. During the summer of 1937 the anti-Soviet campaign slackened, while Neurath's visit to Britain in June was cancelled.* Hitler's speeches grew noticeably more anti-British, to the disquiet of the High Command, particularly the navy staff, who were totally unprepared to face war with Britain.

The British reaction to the Spanish Civil War provided the next test case for Hitler, after the Rhineland, which determined his final opinion. Non-intervention amounted in his eyes to non-commitment. Had the British Government undertaken even the limited scheme to impose their policy suggested by Eden in January 1937, Hitler might have been influenced.† Instead his private intentions developed continuously through 1937 always one step faster than the Chamberlain Government could run. The colonial question was no more than a stalking-horse; Schacht's overtures, and Neurath's responses were both used to deceive and humiliate the British Government. The actual acquisition of African territory meant little. As early as July

---

* According to Wiedemann, Hitler's policy towards Britain had changed before the cancellation of the visit. The *Leipzig* incident merely provided a suitable excuse. (*Der Mann, der Feldherr werden wollte* (Berlin 1964) p. 102.)
† Eden proposed that the British Navy should patrol the approaches to every port in Spain to enforce non-intervention. (Middlemas and Barnes, *Baldwin*, p. 1023.)

1935 Hitler had told General Beck that the colonies would have to wait 'until England one day wants something from us'[24] while during the Hossbach Conference he said: 'Serious discussion of the question of the return of colonies to us could only be considered at a moment when Britain was in difficulties and the German Reich armed and strong.'[25]

Hitler kept the colonial question alive sufficiently to confuse Halifax, to whom he said that it was the only direct issue left.[26] Halifax accepted what he said and convinced the British Cabinet, so that Chamberlain evolved his scheme for partition of central Africa, unaware that it would automatically be rejected.* So long as it remained on the agenda, however, changes in the status of Austria by negotiation were acceptable in London, and the use of moral blackmail was available for Hitler to win his essential demands. As Jacobsen says: 'he could obtain the greatest gains at the least price in Central Europe, since the area of raw materials would be contiguous to the Reich'.[27] Hence the equivocal reply to Henderson in March 1938; until the order for invasion of Austria was given, there was still some profit in the offer of British mediation.

Another indication of how rapidly Hitler abandoned his willingness to negotiate a settlement with Britain can be found in his response to Roosevelt's 'quarantine speech' in October 1937 (above, page 144). Dieckhoff, the German Ambassador in Washington, warned that, though the United States would remain aloof, a conflict which menaced the existence of Britain would lead to intervention.† The threat does not seem to have disturbed Hitler who, according to Erich Kordt, had already shrugged off any concern about the effects of German policy in Asia, with the observation that the United States was incapable of military leadership or positive action.[28] He had a low opinion of the fighting qualities of what he called 'a mass of immigrants from many nations and races'.[29] By the

---

* The Government's ignorance was partially excusable. Weizsäcker was then urging the setting up of an Anglo-German Commission to study the German claims (*DGFP*, series D, vol. 1, no. 21, p. 40) while Schacht had argued for the transfer of Cameroons and Togoland, part of the Belgian Congo and Angola, during Halifax's visit. The Foreign Secretary's failure to distinguish between the competing sectors of German opinion, and his uncritical acceptance of Hitler's statements, had long and serious consequences.

† *DGFP*, series D, vol. 1, pp. 639–41: 'The weight of the United States will be thrown into the scales on the side of Britain, at the very beginning of the conflict, or shortly thereafter' (p. 641).

end of 1937 he had accepted the United States as an ultimate enemy.[30]

The conference of German leaders held in Berlin on 5 November 1937 holds a key place in any description of Hitler's pre-war strategy. The minute taken by his adjutant Colonel Hossbach, and approved by Field Marshal von Blomberg afterwards, became a crucial document in the legal arguments of the Nuremberg trial because it offered evidence that a war of aggression had been deliberately planned. Taken in its context, however, it represents a further stage in the evolution of a continuous and coherent policy.

Apart from Hitler and Hossbach, Neurath and the High Command were present – Blomberg, General Fritsch, Commander-in-Chief of the army, Admiral Raeder, Commander-in-Chief of the navy, Goering, Commander-in-Chief of the Luftwaffe. Hitler excluded the experts from what was intended initially to be a discussion of the rearmament programme[31] and gave what he called, in the event of his death, 'his last will and testament' – 'the fruit of thorough deliberation and the experiences of his four and a half years of power'.[32]

The theme is well known. Because of the expansion of population and the narrow limits of their territory, the German people must, as a matter of great urgency, be given *lebensraum*. This was the ultimate political aim; the creation of an autarkic economy would not suffice. In contradiction to what he had said in July 1936, Hitler now declared 'participation in world trade was inevitable . . . autarky was untenable in regard both to food and to the economy as a whole'. Nor could rearmament provide a satisfactory long-term basis for a sound economy. 'The only remedy, and one which might appear to us as visionary, lay in the acquisition of a greater living space – a quest which has at all times been the origin of the formation of states and of the migration of peoples.'

Space had to be found in Europe, not in a colonial empire of subject races; and force was necessary, despite its attendant risks. The obvious candidates for takeover were Austria and Czechoslovakia; their acquisition and the consequent expulsion of part of their population would give the Reich a source of food for five to six million people, and a far more defensible frontier. If nothing favourable occurred in the political situation earlier, then the conquest must be completed by 1943–5; but Hitler looked either to the demoralisation of France or a possible conflict between Italy, France and Britain to provide the opportunity he required.

He 'believed that almost certainly Britain, and probably France as well, had already tacitly written off the Czechs and were reconciled to the fact that this question would be cleared up in due course by Germany'. If Britain did not act to prevent it, nor would France. Once the attack had been launched, the conquest must be made quickly, before Russia could move to the defence of Czechoslovakia.

Blomberg and Fritsch criticised the plan, on military and political grounds, because it would make enemies of France and Britain. Their opposition placed them on the wrong side at the decisive moment. Whether the conference was called in order to achieve this result, to test out opinion and mark down the dissenters, or simply to isolate Schacht and prod the High Command into more intensive rearmament, is still argued;[33] but Hitler's polemic warned them all of what to expect, without setting any specific date. What followed not only fitted in with the programme, but expressed the changes which had occurred since 1936.

Already, on 3 November, Goebbels had issued a new directive instructing the German press to prepare the public for a new role in foreign policy.[34] The Hossbach Conference went on to settle the disputed question of allocation of steel for rearmament in favour of the navy,[35] a clear sign of new emphasis, and, during 1938, Raeder was instructed to build up the number of battleships (see below, page 302). Until then the German Admiralty had accepted the logic of the Anglo-German Naval Treaty and planned a navy to fight Russia and France, but early in 1938 Plan Z was adopted, providing *inter alia* for six new battleships each of 50,000 tons.

Such planning was clearly directed against the Western powers. No significant changes occurred in the army before the construction of the Western Wall defences of 1938. But by late 1937 'the military plans of the Third Reich had been revised and were now based on a definite offensive pattern'.[36] The directive issued to all three Services on 21 December, which set out the case of Deployment Green – 'an offensive war against Czechoslovakia so that the solution of the German problem of living space can be carried to a victorious end, even if one or other of the great powers intervenes against us'[37] – reflected exactly the theme of the Hossbach Conference and showed that the High Command had swallowed their objections to the military risks, provided that the political circumstances did not force them into a war on two fronts.

The details of the Hossbach Conference were not known in Britain until Goerdeler's visit in March 1938[38] and its significance was not widely understood in Britain or France even then, although the news of the reallocation of steel had reached the French Embassy at once.[39] But the winter of 1937–8 offered definite signs of a change in the structure of Nazi leadership. Schacht was forced to resign and the news was published in the *Berliner Tageblatt* on 21 November. In January 1938 the High Command was purged. Hitler's personal involvement in the charges of scandal against Blomberg's wife and homosexuality against Fritsch is clear. Blomberg resigned and Hitler relieved Fritsch of his command without even waiting for a court of inquiry. In itself, the episode could be seen as part of an obscure power-game, with Goering and Himmler asserting their claims or those of the SS. But Goering was not promoted and Fritsch's place was taken by Brauschitsch, a weak man, whose wife was an ardent Nazi. General Halder became Chief of the General Staff, and the Wehrmacht structure was remoulded. Hitler himself became Supreme Commander, and he created a new institution, the OKW (Ober Kommando der Wehrmacht), with the subservient General Keitel in command, to form his personal staff.

The tall trees had been cut down. Of the opposition, only Generals Beck and Adam remained. On 4 February, Neurath was moved to the otiose post of President of a non-effective Council and replaced by Ribbentrop. The Wilhelmstrasse, like the Wehrmacht, capitulated at once; and Hitler was left in a position to codify his political direction of foreign and strategic policy. The Hossbach programme was translated into the institutional structure of the Reich. As Alfred Jodl, Keitel's Chief of Staff and Hitler's new strategic adviser, wrote on 31 January: 'Führer wants to divert the searchlights from the Wehrmacht, keep Europe on tenterhooks and, by recasting various roles, give the impression of a concentration of strength, not of a moment of weakness. Schuschnigg must not take courage, but fright.'[40]

After November 1937, the conquests of Austria and Czecho-

slovakia were dogmatic aims of Hitler's policy, but the dates
were left vague. What limited capacity Britain had to affect
German policy was diminished further by the elimination of
the opposition to Hitler. Britain had been defined as an enemy
at the Hossbach Conference: 'German policy had to reckon
with two hate-inspired antagonists, Britain and France, to
whom a German colossus in the centre of Europe was a thorn in
the flesh, and both countries were opposed to any further
strengthening of Germany's position either in Europe or overseas.'[41] Britain was weak. She could only protect her Empire
by alliances with others and her prestige had been greatly
undermined by events in Ireland, India, and in the Far East,
vis-à-vis Japan, and in the Mediterranean vis-à-vis Italy. 'With
[only] forty-five million Britons, in spite of its theoretical sound-
ness, the position of the Empire could not in the long run be
maintained by power politics.'[42]

This was far from the 'natural ally' of 1935. On the other
hand, Hitler was 'convinced of Britain's non-participation' in
Central European affairs, and he was not yet prepared to
envisage war. Indeed, 'regret at not having made an ally of
England ran like a red thread through all the years of his rule'.[43]
If Germany had to fight France, he stated in November 1937,
the army must not march through Belgium 'because it would
certainly entail the hostility of Britain'.[44]

By the time that the British Cabinet had formulated their
colonial offer in central Africa, no long-term influence over
German foreign policy was possible, and the elevation of
Ribbentrop as Foreign Minister spelt the message out. Rich,
socially ambitious, prejudiced, potentially violent, Ribbentrop
had a certain social flair which distinguished him in the Nazi
Party, and Hitler believed that he understood and was respected
by the British.* To a limited extent, as Ambassador in
1936–8, Ribbentrop lived up to expectations and was lionised
by some sections of London society, but his dream of an Anglo-
German understanding came to nothing and was replaced by
an equally irrational Anglophobia.[45] Because Hitler believed
him to be an expert, Ribbentrop's misconceptions of British

---

* Hitler seems to have combined contempt for Ribbentrop as a man with acknowledgement of his supposed expertise about England (Speer, *Inside the Third Reich*,
pp. 97 and 109). Of course, as Speer points out, very few of Hitler's entourage had
ever been abroad, and such a reputation was easy to acquire.

opinion were significant. From 1937 onwards, he confirmed his master's prejudices, especially that Britain would probably not intervene in central Europe. As a trusted source of information, he provided the third test which Hitler needed before making his decisions about Britain in 1938. On 2 January 1938, he sent a most important *Memorandum for the Führer:* 'Conclusions concerning the future development of German–British relations',[46] summing up the results of two years' intermittent observation.

Briefly, Ribbentrop concluded that since Germany wished to expand in central Europe hope of an understanding with Britain was at an end. The future, and the likelihood of war between them, depended on whether Britain would follow France in defence of her Eastern allies. Britain, he thought, would not consent to be dragged in if conditions were unfavourable for the Empire, and if Italy and Japan declared themselves hostile. 'Over a local problem in central Europe, even if it were to add considerably to Germany's strength, England would, in my opinion, not risk a struggle for the survival of her Empire.' What Ribbentrop most feared was an Anglo-Italian *rapprochement* or a successful outcome to Sir Robert Craigie's mission in Tokyo. Germany must cement the Anti-Comintern Pact and:

continue to foster England's belief that a settlement and an understanding between Germany and England are still possible eventually. Such a prospect might, for example, have a restraining effect on any possible intention to intervene on the part of the British Government, should Germany become involved in a local conflict with central Europe, which does not vitally concern England.

So long as the dividing-line between the German alliances and the Western alliance did not become rigid, war might be avoided; but it depended on the political leadership in Britain:

It is conceivable that a British Prime Minister—if he is not afflicted with the psychosis regarding German strength and lust for power, but in principle believes in the possibility of German and British friendship—would still prefer to seek a generous, sober settlement which would satisfy German aspirations without endangering vital and purely British interests. [The test case would be] an unequivocal British concession regarding the Austro-Czechoslovak question....

Ribbentrop's pessimism led him to conclude that 'every day that our political calculations are not actuated by the fundamental idea that England is our most dangerous enemy, *would be a gain for our enemies'*. As Foreign Minister, he was able to confirm this impression on Hitler by personal contact and through the operations of the Dienstelle Ribbentrop. Thus by January 1938, when Henderson presented the British plan, the direction of German policy had passed the stage at which such an offer would be treated seriously. Only compliance with German ambitions sufficed, in Hitler's eyes, to justify the continued existence of the British Empire. Germany would demonstrate her strength and Britain would come to heel. But war was not yet premeditated.

The *Anschluss* came earlier than had been planned because of Italy's shifting allegiance. The protracted Abyssinian crisis had begun to close the gap which Mussolini had been careful to maintain between Rome and Berlin during the 1930s. The Stresa Front had been the last moment at which an Anglo-Italian understanding was possible. As Mussolini told von Bülow-Schwante, Head of the Protocol Department at the Foreign Ministry, in October 1937, 'He had doubted any intervention by England in the Abyssinian war . . . On the basis of these considerations [Britain's pacifism and Britain's economic prosperity] he had, as he said, literally become impudent and had ventured the blow against Abyssinia.'[47] He announced the Rome–Berlin Axis in November 1936, by which time involvement in the Spanish Civil War had created another ground for discord with the Western powers. Germany's one-time 'natural allies' had been driven apart in precisely the areas – Red Sea, Mediterranean and North Africa – where members of Chamberlain's school of thought such as Hankey imagined their interests were similar, and it is reasonable to conclude that Mussolini's 'very strong aversion to England'[48] was genuine. There was no intention of heeding British efforts in Spain: the Gentlemen's Agreement of January 1937 and the Nyon Agreement both failed to diminish the supply of Italian 'volunteers'.

Late in 1937 Mussolini moved steadily towards closer association with Hitler – a move which Hitler desired, failing the alliance with England. In September Mussolini visited Berlin, reaffirmed the principles of solidarity and the Anti-Comintern Pact and resistance against 'any attempt at disturbance by third powers', and came to a general agreement on relative spheres of influence. 'Italy will not be impeded by Germany in the Mediterranean whereas, on the other hand, the special German interests in Austria will not be impaired by Italy.'[49] Hitler carefully avoided direct discussion of the future of Austria, but by 11 February 1938 Ciano could record in his diary: 'Mussolini . . . has become more radical. He told me this morning [the day of Schuschnigg's visit to Berchtesgaden] that he is in favour of the nazification of Austria. Anything that is not thorough-going is not safe.'[50]

Nazification of Austria had been on the cards when the High Command was purged, but it is doubtful if Hitler had really been determined, as he said later, to win for the six and a half million Austrian-Germans the right of self-determination, as early as January 1938.[51] Since the failure of the *putsch* in 1934, von Papen, the Ambassador in Vienna, had been instructed to work quietly towards a Nazi takeover. The military decision to invade was made at short notice, only after Schuschnigg's attempt to reverse his surrender at Berchtesgaden by calling a plebiscite. Firm assurances from Mussolini were not received until the evening of 11 March. Hitler's almost hysterical relief and the sudden decision to incorporate Austria in the Reich were signs that the timing of the *Anschluss* was another piece of inspired opportunism.

Yet in spite of the gamble and the assimilation of Austria, the preparations for a takeover in Czechoslovakia went ahead at once. France and Britain had not intervened to save Austria – indeed, Nevile Henderson had indicated only too clearly that Britain would welcome alteration in Austria's status, if it were done peaceably. But Czechoslovakia, with its network of defensive alliances with France and Russia, was less tractable – and, unlike Austria, not a willing bride for the Reich.

Direct German support for irredentist movements in Czechoslovakia had varied during the first five years of Nazi rule. Konrad Henlein, a gymnastics instructor, had been leader of the Sudeten German Home Front since its formation in 1933 after the banning of the Nazi Party. The Front, which became the Sudeten German Party (SDP), included opinions ranging from those who merely wished to rescue the German minority from the existing disabilities, to others who insisted on complete incorporation in Germany. The style of Henlein's SDP was not wholly welcome in Berlin:[52] the Party and SS leaders, Himmler, Bormann and Goebbels would have preferred a full-blooded Nazi leader, like K. H. Frank, rather than the apparently moderate Henlein, but Hess, who was in charge of relations with external German groups, subsidised the SDP in the elections of 1935, which gave it over sixty per cent of the German vote and made it the largest party in Czechoslovakia.

A quality which made Henlein attractive to Hitler was his ability to convince the British that he was a moderate. He had visited London twice, in December 1935 and July 1936, and on the latter occasion won the support of Vansittart for his current programme of reforms. Events in 1936–7, however, seemed to place a moderate solution out of reach of Henlein or the Czech Government. Negotiations between Albrecht Haushofer, a member of the Dienstelle, and President Beneš came to nothing, and a Czechoslovak attempt to conciliate the German minority in 1937 did not prevent a marked shift towards Berlin in the SDP. This had its reaction: when Henlein paid his third visit to London in October 1937, Vansittart told him that Britain would seek far-reaching autonomy for the Sudeten Germans but would stand by France if Germany sought to incorporate them in the Reich. Henlein, however, was finding it hard to hold the middle ground between mere reformism and *Anschluss* and he came to rely more and more on Nazi support at the end of 1937, not entirely to the delight of Hitler, who feared precipitate action like the 1934 *putsch* in Austria. Henlein was not necessarily a Nazi agent, even though he wrote to Hitler, on 19 November 1937, that the SDP had to plead in public for the preservation of the Czechoslovak state, but that at heart it believed in National Socialism and incorporation of all Bohemia and Silesia in the Reich.[53] Such views only became politically welcome in 1938 as Hitler's strategy unrolled; and in February 1938 Eisenlohr, German Minister in Prague, was still advising Henlein to join the Czech Government and work for a compromise.[54]

Shortly after the *Anschluss*, on 28 March, Henlein visited Hitler and received more definite, but still undated, instructions.[55] Hitler now stated his intention to settle the Sudeten question 'in the not too distant future' and gave Henlein the vague title of Statthalter or Viceroy. The method was indirect:

'demands should be made by the SDP which are unacceptable to the Czechoslovak Government . . . we must always demand so much that we can never be satisfied'. Führer and Viceroy were agreed: but this was still some way from a plan for military takeover. On 21 April Hitler discussed Case Green with Keitel[56] and concluded that because of opposition from the Western powers the attack could not come out of a clear sky. As in November, and despite the success of the *Anschluss,* the pretext must be found through diplomacy. Even then, lightning military action would be needed to force submission in a matter of days, before a European war could break out.

This last point was vital to the British if their policy was to have any effect at all. If the manner of the attack was not certain, then the method might be diverted into peaceable channels. If Hitler still feared war on two fronts, arising out of the treaties of mutual security, then an Anglo-French démarche might carry weight.[57] Russia had not yet been finally excluded; the Western Wall defences had scarcely been started; failing the correct political circumstances, the German final date remained that of 1943.

But in assessing German motives, the British suffered from several major disadvantages. Although the diversity of German power-centres was understood in the Foreign Office, Halifax's visit in November 1937 led to a serious confusion of thinking at Cabinet level which persisted into 1938, and masked the growing dominance of Hitler by conflating his public statements with those of his subordinates. Secondly, past policies, such as Eden's obsession with non-intervention in the Spanish Civil War, left the Cabinet with a legacy of commitments difficult to meet or to evade when Chamberlain sought to canalise his own greater obsession into the Italian Agreement. Neither aim really related to the question of Anglo-German relations in 1938 nor to Germany's long-term drive for *lebensraum* but they served to delay British decisions until the time of the *Anschluss.* Worse, the British solutions had been reached through sufficient conflict and heart-searching for them to acquire a form of internal self-justification just at the moment when they became thoroughly out of date. The illusion of a permanent settlement, on terms favourable to Britain, persisted long after its continued rejection warranted. Finally, the Cabinet were unable to see any alternatives. Given their style of thinking, Eden's policy had been discredited by its failure to produce results, and Churchill's was ruled out as tantamount to preventive war. Assassination was not seriously canvassed, and support of the German resistance was held to involve too dangerous a risk.

The *Anschluss* might have provided the occasion for the British to reappraise Chamberlain's strategy. Instead of reflecting on the changed face of Nazi leadership, on the exclusion of men with whom compromise had seemed possible, the British Government chose carefully and deliberately to continue. Of the six months which followed, two questions need to be asked: was there any chance of their plans for Czechoslovakia giving what Britain most required – the permanent avoidance of European war? And, if not, when and how would they accept that war as inevitable?

6 March 1938

While the German mechanised units invaded Austria on 11 March 1938, Chamberlain and Halifax were giving a farewell lunch at 10 Downing Street to Ribbentrop who was returning to Berlin to take up his full-time duties as Foreign Minister. Chamberlain hoped to impress on him that Germany had only to co-operate with Britain to get most of what Hitler wanted in Austria: 'If she did so, she would find us not unreasonable.'[1]

When they heard the news, Ribbentrop was summoned back. He was, apparently, ignorant of the invasion. Later, Schuschnigg, the Austrian Prime Minister, telephoned for help. What would Britain do if he were asked to resign? Halifax replied sombrely, as if Austria's fate had never been a British interest, that he could advise no action which might expose his country to dangers 'against which the British Government could not guarantee protection'.[2]

When the Cabinet met in emergency session on 12 March, Chamberlain concluded gloomily that the *Anschluss* had been inevitable, 'unless the Powers had been able to say – "If you make war on Austria, you will have to deal with us" '. However much Austrian independence had mattered to the framework of European and British security, that had never been a possibility. Chamberlain ended his summing-up with a curiously matter-of-fact conclusion: 'At any rate, that question was now out of the way.'

Indications that he gave more weight to the manner of the German takeover than to its effect, and that he made light of past British attempts to preserve Austria as a bulwark between the two dictators, are pointers to the style of policy perpetuated by his Government in 1938. Conviction that an agreement *could* and must be reached with Germany was not in any way discouraged by the *Anschluss*. The probable direction of German ambitions had been forecast by the Foreign Office nearly a month before, when Schuschnigg had been summoned to meet Hitler and brow-beaten into submitting to demands for the inclusion of leading Nazis in his Government. Chamberlain had said then:

> Once more an urgent decision had been achieved by force. Europe had received another lesson as to the methods by which Germany would pursue her aims. It was difficult to believe that this was the last, or that the eventual result would not be the absorption of Austria and probably some action in Czechoslovakia. That produced a dangerous situation. It might lead [the Little Entente] to give up all hope of resistance to the hegemony of Germany. It would seem that this must be unpalatable to Signor Mussolini and that an opportunity offered to encourage him to make a more determined stand.[3]

But Mussolini had declined to stand firm. Next time the Cabinet were determined that if concessions were to be made to Nazi Germany they should be made by agreement, not by force. Spurred on by the prospect of another European war in defence of Czechoslovakia, following the shock of the incorporation of Austria into the Reich, the British Government took a definite and, by contrast with her policy in the twenty years since 1918, remarkably swift and emphatic initiative, whose planning was completed within ten days.

In public and in the House of Commons, the Government deplored the methods used by Germany to take over Austria, and the shock to world opinion, rather than the thing itself. In the Cabinet, the debate proceeded on three connected lines – reviews of defence policy, of the attitude towards Italy, and plans for defusing the Czechoslovak time-bomb. The minutes of these discussions illustrate not only how the *Anschluss* had brought to a head general issues of British foreign policy, but also the impetus given to the formation of an inner group within the Cabinet. Policy decisions of great importance were taken more and more in the Foreign Policy Committee, which acquired increased significance as Chamberlain began to use it to the exclusion of the rest of the Cabinet.

The defence debate was not allowed to develop into a criticism of past policy decisions. The Chiefs of Staff Committee was instructed to examine what would happen if Germany attacked Czechoslovakia, in the light of the *Anschluss* and of the treaty network with France.[4] But the decisions of the Foreign Policy Committee* were reached at successive meetings on 15, 18 and 21 March without benefit of the military advice.

Nor did the full Cabinet redress the balance. Lord Swinton asked immediately for a substantial increase in the air defence establishment, only to be faced by Inskip and Simon's insistence on the fixed total of the rationed budget. This moment, apparently of extreme danger in Europe, was the occasion for Simon's morbid preoccupation with the poor state of the Government's relations with the trade unions. Too sensitive to the fear of industrial discontent to envisage anything more than consultation with the unions about a voluntary scheme for dilution of skilled labour, Chamberlain was keen to play down the suggestion that the *Anschluss* had radically altered the European scene. Both he and Halifax refused to accept the pleas of Hore-Belisha for an increase in the manpower and equipment of the Regular Army on the ground that there might not be five years to complete the current programme and that the danger of war over Austria was immediate. All that senior ministers would concede was the necessity of a fresh review.

The second stage of debate concerned the opening of conversations with Italy. However desirable a breach in the Rome–Berlin axis seemed, in the aftermath of the *Anschluss*, it was not a simple matter of accepting the offers made by the Italian Ambassador, Count Dino Grandi. The Government were still tied to Eden's pledge that the talks should be linked to a definite withdrawal of Italian 'volunteers' from the Spanish Civil War. In private, Chamberlain regretted the pledge,† believing that Mussolini's inaction over Austria had been the result of British delay; but attempts to water it down roused the disapproval of the younger members of the Cabinet who had

* The Foreign Policy Committee was composed of Chamberlain, Halifax, Sir John Simon (Chancellor of the Exchequer), Sir Samuel Hoare (Home Secretary), Malcolm MacDonald (Dominions Secretary), Sir Thomas Inskip (Minister for Co-ordination of Defence), Lord Hailsham (Lord Chancellor), W. Ormsby-Gore (Colonial Secretary), Oliver Stanley (President of Board of Trade).

† At the meeting of the Foreign Policy Committee on 15 Mar, he said: 'H.M.G. have never defined the precise meaning which they placed upon this expression — "settlement of the Spanish question" ... he did not think that ... the Government were necessarily pledged to the view that the Spanish question must be settled *before* the Anglo-Italian agreement could be executed.' (CAB 27/623 (Foreign Policy Committee) 15 Mar.) But Chamberlain had confirmed the pledge himself in the House of Commons on 21 Feb.

stood by Eden and who pointed to the widespread suspicion that Hitler had made a bargain with Mussolini not to interfere in Austria. They coupled Spain with France and Czechoslovakia: 'If we could give France assurances that, in the event of an attack by Germany on Czechoslovakia, we should stand by the side of France in resisting that aggression, this would be a valuable *quid pro quo* for any concession which we might require from France in regard to the Spanish difficulty.'[5]

Here was one answer to the problem of French security against Germany. After the *Anschluss,* a firm request had been received from France for a joint declaration to Germany that the two Governments 'could not remain indifferent to any German action on Czechoslovakia'.[6]

Senior British ministers, however, regarded their French counterparts with a mixture of contempt, hostility and ignorance. The political situation in France was unstable: the Chautemps Government was likely to collapse at any moment* and talk of resisting aggression on Czechoslovakia, in the total absence of joint planning, or even mutual confidence, was mere whistling down the wind. Hoare assumed blandly that the French Government would concede to any British pressure and Halifax asserted casually that French ministers could be 'summoned to London' as soon as they had a stable government.

The policy towards Czechoslovakia, which determined the course of British foreign policy until September, was decided during the four days 18–22 March. On 18 March, Halifax submitted a lengthy Foreign Office paper† to the Foreign

---

* Chautemps resigned on 13 March and was replaced by Léon Blum's radical government, with Paul Boncour as Foreign Minister.

† 18 Mar, CAB 27/623. Several distinct points of view had been compressed into the paper (FP 36/56). Sargent's view was that Germany was trying to create a number of vassal states: 'in any future war, not only will these not be [our] allies, they won't even be neutrals'. He recommended staff talks with France, and strengthening the links with Russia, Poland, Greece and Turkey, and, if possible, with the United States — 'to try and save the British Empire'. Strang, in contrast, believed in a plebiscite to satisfy the Sudeten Germans, followed by an Anglo-French guarantee of Czech security. Gladwyn Jebb stressed French weakness: 'the suggestion that we and the French alone should fly to the rescue of the Czechs boils down to something . . . resembling suicide'. He suggested that Britain should give France a tacit understanding not to support the Czechs, and he even spoke of 'the incorporation of Czechoslovakia in the Reich'.

Summing up, Cadogan said that the Sudeten question 'would not be an issue on which we should be on very strong ground for plunging Europe into war'. He

Policy Committee, which laid out the issues with great clarity.

The Memorandum assumed that Germany would 'by fair means or foul continue to work for the eventual incorporation within the Reich of the German minority in Czechoslovakia. . . . They would also aim at breaking the Czech connection with France and the Soviet Union'; also that although the Sudeten Germans were not wholly united, the pull from across the frontier would be expected to increase. Already their leader, Konrad Henlein, was suspected by the Foreign Office of being in the pay of the Nazis.

The Memorandum also pointed out that Czechoslovak security had been gravely weakened by the *Anschluss* and that the country was now open to attack along the unfortified Austrian border. Germany 'now controls Czechoslovakia's only effective communications with the sea and can easily establish an economic stranglehold'.

Anything Britain could do to avoid a repetition of the *Anschluss* must include measures 'to establish Czechoslovakia's moral position *vis-à-vis* public opinion in this country and in the world generally'. This meant that 'The Czech Government must satisfy His Majesty's Government and British public opinion, not only that the Sudeten Germans enjoy the treatment to which they are entitled, but also such treatment as will leave the German Government with no reasonable cause for complaint.'

As Halifax pointed out, however, to give the Czechs help would be to increase British commitments, which were still only those of one League member to another. If given, it must be clear and unequivocal. 'Mere statements that we are interested in peace in Central Europe, or not indifferent to German action in Central Europe, have no longer any deterrent effect.'

Distrust of France prompted the next argument. A new commitment might decrease the chances of war; but it might also bring war earlier if it encouraged France to take action in defence of Czechoslovakia which otherwise her Government would not have risked. The guarantee might also provoke

came down against both the extremes – Sargent and Jebb – and recommended: no fresh commitment to Czechoslovakia, more rearmament, fulfilment of the Anglo-Italian agreement, and a renewed pledge to France, to help her 'pull herself together' (C 1865 and 1866/132/18 (FO 371/21674)).

Hitler – and Britain dare not bluff. She could undertake nothing which she could not fulfil.

Bearing all this in mind, Halifax set three possible courses before the Foreign Policy Committee. The first, which had also been advocated by Churchill in the House of Commons during the debate on the *Anschluss* on 14 March, was to form a Grand Alliance against Germany. The Foreign Office thought it an attractive proposal, subject to the decisive objection that it would require multi-lateral negotiation and a formal treaty for which there was insufficient time. The second consisted of a new commitment, either directly to Czechoslovakia or as reinforcement of the treaty network between her two partners France and Russia. The disadvantage was that this would involve Britain in accelerated rearmament and perhaps turning over the economy to a war basis. The third choice was to do nothing publicly but with France's aid to persuade Czechoslovakia 'to make the best terms she can with Germany, while she can perhaps still do so in more favourable conditions than would obtain later'.

Halifax had given some thought to an undertaking to assist France against Germany if her territory were attacked by Germany, but he advised the Committee not to give it unless Czechoslovakia first solved the Sudeten problem and unless France also undertook to ask British approval before going to war in fulfilment of the 1925 Treaty. Such conditions bordered on the impossible, and, since the Government was unlikely to be able to avoid all the risks so neatly, Halifax chose the third case, in spite of the danger to the entente and the fear that France might come to terms with Germany at Britain's expense. He set out his argument in a way which merits quotation because it is as clear a statement of what was at stake as anything written in the next six months.

In a Minute written in 1908 Sir Eyre Crowe said 'Political and strategical preparedness must go hand in hand. Failure of such harmony must lead either to military disaster or political retreat.' The question may well be asked whether we should embark upon a course, one of the risks of which is, in attempting to circumscribe German territorial expansion in Central Europe, we should plunge into a war in which we might be defeated and lose all. It may well be true that Germany's superiority in arms may be greater a year or two hence than it is now, but this is not a good argument for risking disaster now. The ground upon which it is sought to justify the undoubted risk which we would be assuming, is that unless we make a stand now Germany will march uninterruptedly to hegemony in Europe, which will be but a first step towards a deliberate challenge to the British Empire. There is much force in this argument and yet it may well be based upon a more confident prediction of future events than the experience of history will support. Who is to say what the future holds? Would the annexation of non-German territory or the establishment of political influence over it necessarily be a source of over-powering strength to Germany, even though organised with new techniques and a new spirit to which national socialism has given birth? It cannot be contended that the future is not black, but there is at least an element of uncertainty in the diagnosis, and on the strength of that uncertainty we might at least refrain from embarking on the more hazardous courses.[7]

To the credit of the Foreign Secretary – or rather of his officials – the opposing case was also set out:

If Germany dominated Central Europe . . . it may be foreseen that this in its turn will lead to the isolation of Great Britain with France and Western Europe, with all the consequent loss of its prestige and even security. It will also represent an extension of the application of the Nazi theory of government over a large area of Europe and the further discrediting of free institutions. It may be argued that in order to prevent such developments, the two great democracies must rally their forces and make a stand at an early date before the position deteriorates still further; and the obvious point on which to make such a stand is over the continued independence of Czechoslovakia.

The arguments at the time of Munich in September 1938 were almost precisely the same. Halifax left no doubt on which side he stood. If some Commission of Enquiry into the Sudeten German question were to recommend a drastic solution such as a plebiscite – that is, voluntary transfer of the German-speaking provinces to the Reich – there would be less objection to giving a guarantee to France. Basil Newton, the British Minister in Prague, had recently suggested that 'having regard to her geographical situation, her history and the racial divisions of her population, Czechoslovakia's present political situation is not fundamentally tenable'.[8] Halifax was convinced that Britain could not fight for something so unstable; but if the

British 'went to great lengths in bringing the Czech government to agree to measures which will settle the Sudeten question in conformity with the realities of the situation, unpleasant as those realities may be,' that was different.

There was no reason to doubt that this document was in close accord with Chamberlain's own policy, as he set it out in a letter to his sister on 20 March, pointing out the utterly impracticable nature of the Grand Alliance:

> You have only to look at the map to see that nothing that France or we could do, could possibly save Czechoslovakia from being over-run by the Germans if they wanted to do it. The Austrian frontier is practically open; the great Skoda munition works are within easy bombing distance of the German aerodromes, the railways all pass through German territory, Russia is a hundred miles away. Therefore, we could not help Czechoslovakia—she would simply be a pretext for going to war with Germany. That we could not think of, unless we had a reasonable prospect of being able to beat her to her knees in reasonable time and of that I see no sign. I have therefore abandoned any idea of giving guarantees to Czechoslovakia or the French in connection with her obligations to that country.[9]

Chamberlain's views had developed to a more definite point than those of his Foreign Secretary. He was prepared to approach Hitler:

> and say something like this. 'We gave you fair warning that if you used violence to Austria, you would shock public opinion to such an extent as to give rise to the most disagreeable repercussions, but you obstinately went your own way and now you can see for yourselves how right we were. We can't go on talking about colonies... everyone is thinking that you are going to repeat the Austrian coup in Czechoslovakia. I know you say you aren't, but nobody believes you. The best thing you can do is tell us exactly what you want for your Sudeten Germans. If it is reasonable we will urge the Czechs to accept and if they do, you must give assurances that you will let them alone in the future.' I am not sure that in such circumstances I might not be willing to join in some joint guarantee with Germany of Czech independence.*

* Chamberlain letters, 20 Mar 1938. Chamberlain's notion of a guarantee seems to have been peculiarly fluid. A joint guarantee with Germany was almost exactly the reverse of the original proposal for a guarantee with France.

Halifax had spoken already of a plebiscite for the Sudeten Germans. Given Chamberlain's willingness to approach Hitler, the plan for the solution of the Czech question was now nearly complete. But the Prime Minister opened his mind only cautiously to his colleagues in the Foreign Policy Committee on 20 March. It was by no means certain that they would be receptive to a scheme for solving the Czech question in so arbitrary and high-handed a fashion, even if this was likely to remove the danger of France and Britain being drawn into a European war.

He wondered [Chamberlain told the Committee] whether it would not be possible to make some arrangement which would prove more acceptable to Germany. Apart from other considerations, this would have the advantage that it would be more likely to secure permanency.... Herr Hitler had said that all he wished for was some measure of local autonomy for the Sudeten territory, something in fact similar to the arrangements which had been made between the United Kingdom and Eire, and he had said that if this could be done Germany would be prepared to guarantee the independence of Czechoslovakia. It was, of course, possible that in the interval Herr Hitler might have changed his mind, but at all events the possibility of some arrangement of this kind might be worth exploring.*

During the discussion, ministers showed a strong disinclination to offer a guarantee to France, unless she first not merely asked, but obtained, British approval before going to the help of Czechoslovakia. Halifax suggested that Germany might simply reject the guarantee on the ground that the Sudeten question was a domestic matter between Czechs and Germans. Basing himself on Newton's reports, Chamberlain said that 'the seizure of the whole of Czechoslovakia would not be in accordance with Herr Hitler's policy, which was to include all Germans in the Reich but not to include other nationalities'. Only Sir Maurice Hankey, Secretary of the Cabinet and of the Committee of Imperial Defence, protested at an interpretation which destroyed the geographical and economic coherence of the Czechoslovak state.†

* 20 Mar, CAB 27/623. The parallel with Eire was misconceived. Eire was already a Free State and on the point of declaring independence of Britain.
† 'Her manufacturing districts and the agricultural districts were naturally dependant.' The Foreign Office took the same point (C1932/132/18 (FO 371/21674)).

Each member of the Committee stated his point of view. No one spoke for the Grand Alliance; only Stanley and Hoare wished to give some support to France. Malcolm MacDonald took his cue from the reluctance of the Dominions to become involved. 'If we found ourselves engaged in a European war to prevent Germans living in the Sudeten districts of Czechoslovakia from being reunited with Germany, on this issue the British Commonwealth might well break in pieces.' While Australia and New Zealand would almost certainly follow the British lead, South Africa and Canada would not.

Lord Hailsham preferred to trust in the Locarno Pact. He conceded 'the plain fact that we could not in our own interest afford to see France over-run', but argued that if Britain did not commit herself she 'could keep both France and Germany guessing as to what our attitude in any particular circumstances would be and no doubt this in itself [would have] a restraining effect both upon France and Germany'. This plausible argument was wearing thin since its first use at the time of the German withdrawal from the League of Nations four years before.

The Chiefs of Staff report was not yet available but Inskip was not deterred from concluding that Germany could over-run Czechoslovakia in a week. In his opinion Britain's only effective sanction against Germany was a naval blockade which would take two to three years to be effective. Nothing could protect, or preserve, Czechoslovakia.

Halifax doubted if France would do more than hold the Maginot line: her air force was hopeless. Contemptuously, he added:

No doubt the French authorities would face up to the fact, but when he had put the difficulties to M. Corbin [the French Ambassador], the latter had replied to the effect that these were matters which could profitably be discussed with us. Mr Winston Churchill had a plan under which the French army was to act on the defensive behind the Maginot Line and there detain large German forces, while Czechoslovakia engaged Germany's remaining forces. This seemed to have no relation to the realities of the situation.

The line taken by the majority allowed for, and even encouraged German expansion in Eastern Europe. Halifax said: 'much of the argument for the need of a deterrent rested on the assumption that when Germany secured the hegemony over Central Europe, she would then pick a quarrel with France and ourselves. He did not agree.' Indeed, the more Britain linked herself to France and Russia, the more Germany would feel encircled and reject what he called 'a real settlement'. He distinguished between 'Germany's racial efforts, which no one could question, and a lust for conflict on a Napoleonic scale which he himself did not credit'.

The opposition, Stanley and Hoare, conceded that 'not a soul in this country could give any direct guarantee to Czechoslovakia herself', and Ormsby-Gore added that 'Any specific commitment to Czechoslovakia would split public opinion in this country from top to bottom.'

For the others, Halifax's contention that a new commitment might mean war 'in the very near future', sufficed. The nation, he said, could, of course, mobilise all her friends and resources and embark on a full-scale campaign against Germany; but it would be much wiser and in tune with British public opinion if the Government announced that they were already overcommitted; and then persuaded France that the best thing was for Czechoslovakia to make what terms she could. Britain then 'would use any influence we might have with Germany, to induce her to take up a reasonable attitude'.

Chamberlain closed the discussion and dismissed the idea of any help from the United States. The pious aspirations of Secretary of State, Cordell Hull, meant nothing; nor did the entente with France whose army, he thought, might be in good condition, but whose air force and economic and political situation were all hopeless. There was no other resort except Anglo-German understanding: 'If Germany could obtain her desiderata by peaceable methods, there was no reason to suppose that she would reject such a procedure in favour of one based on violence. It should be noted that throughout the Austrian adventure Herr Hitler had studiously refrained from saying, or doing, anything to provoke us. It indicated a desire to keep on good terms with us.'

Simon suggested shrewdly that if the Sudeten Germans knew the Prime Minister's mind, they would demand a complete transfer of their areas; and Chamberlain replied prophetically: 'Ultimately this would no doubt be so, but he thought that in the first place our objectives should be the retention by

Czechoslovakia of the Sudeten areas with some measure of local autonomy.'

Under French and British pressure, Czechoslovakia was to come to terms, cut off the rejected tissue and cauterise the wound. No one questioned the assumptions, least of all about the nature of the Czech state. They took it for granted that, even by victory over Germany, it would be impossible to re-create. 'It was not a case of re-establishing an ancient political entity. Czechoslovakia was a modern and very artificial creation, with no real roots in the past.' Not even Hoare, friend of Jan Masaryk, protested at such ignorance of European history.

A day before they were given the military advice of the Chiefs of Staff, in opposition to the advice of the Foreign Office, without knowledge of the attitude of France, and wholly ignorant of that of Russia – third party to the Czechoslovak treaty arrangements – the Foreign Policy Committee had taken the road to Munich, openly, deliberately, and by general agreement. There was a discussion about the questions of how to ensure that solution of the Sudeten question was orderly and not reached by force of arms; how to explain to France that Britain offered nothing, but asked a great deal; how to find out what were Germany's desiderata in Czechoslovakia. Halifax, who wished to send instructions at once to Sir Nevile Henderson, was persuaded to wait three days, at least until the full Cabinet had approved the new policy; but there was no move to delay the decision itself until the military advice was ready.

The Chiefs of Staff report, 'The Military Implications of German Aggression against Czechoslovakia',[10] was handed round to the Committee on 21 March, but its conclusions closely substantiated what Inskip and Chamberlain had said about the impossibility of preventing a German attack, and it made little difference to what had already been decided. The document was reserved for presentation to the Cabinet. The meeting then concentrated on giving a less gloomy cast to Halifax's revised memorandum[11] and the draft communication which was to be made to France. The length of time spent on the presentation of these documents shows how carefully the impact on public opinion and the House of Commons was considered. Sir William Malkin, the Foreign Office Legal Adviser, had carefully rehearsed the obligations of Britain under

Locarno, but Simon advised him to check again : 'the critics of the Government would be only too eager to make party capital out of any slip.'[12]

The impact of the plan on France was likely to be, in Vansittart's words, 'catastrophic'. Halifax saw no way round: 'because France would be shocked, was no reason why we should refrain from pursuing a policy on the correctness of which we were fully satisfied'.[13] As he said bluntly later: 'The French were never ready to face up to realities, they delighted in vain words and protestations.'[13a] Reaffirmation of the British commitment to the Locarno Pact salved one or two consciences. Stanley alone fought for some more substantial offer. He argued for nearly half the meeting until out-weighed by the rest and by the sheer negative weight of the Chiefs of Staff report.

At the end, Chamberlain revised the order of the draft so that it should take on a more optimistic note, and it was despatched to Phipps, to be delivered to the French Government on the twenty-third – too late for a protest before the Prime Minister made his announcement in the House of Commons, on the twenty-fourth. Likewise, at twenty-four hours' notice, the Dominions were to be told. The statement prepared for the House itself was, as Halifax said, to be 'dressed up rather better' because his junior minister, R. A. Butler, had warned that members might find it thin and disappointing.

These messages depended on the authority of the Cabinet, which was to meet on Tuesday the twenty-second, but the main body was not given much chance to disagree with the Committee. The Chiefs of Staff report, 'an extremely melancholy document but [one which] no Government could afford to overlook', took pride of place in Halifax's introductory speech,* and the Cabinet were given merely the gist of the messages to France and the House of Commons statement. Military considerations thus became supreme *after* the vital decisions had been taken, in order to justify them to the wider circle of government. Halifax read out in full the unequivocal warning:

---

* 22 Mar 1938, CAB 23/93. According to the minutes of the Foreign Policy Committee, the Cabinet was not to be asked for a formal decision, but only to be told 'with a view to the general feeling being ascertained on the policy proposed' (21 Mar, CAB 27/623).

We conclude that no pressure that we and our allies can bring
to bear, either by sea or land or in the air, could prevent Germany
from invading and over-running Bohemia, and from inflicting
decisive defeat on the Czech armies. We should then be faced with
the necessity of undertaking a war against Germany for the purpose of restoring Czechoslovakia's lost integrity and this object
would only be achieved by the defeat of Germany and as the outcome of a prolonged struggle. In the world situation today, it
seems to us if such a struggle were to take place, it is more than
probable that both Italy and Japan will seize the opportunity to
further their own ends and that in consequence the problem we
have to envisage is not that of a limited European war only,
but of a world war.[14]

Chamberlain and Halifax judged the temper of their colleagues correctly. Although there was considerable opposition
to the new policy, the Chiefs of Staff report was not queried,
nor were there complaints that the advice of the Dominions
and the Ambassadors in Berlin, Paris and Prague had not been
laid in front of them. No one inquired why Italy, apparently so
close to agreement at the time of Eden's resignation, should
now be presumed hostile rather than friendly by the Chiefs of
Staff. No one questioned the military assumptions as a whole,
nor the extremely poor assessment of the military strength of
France and Czechoslovakia in relation to Germany. The pre-
disposition of the majority towards inaction can be seen when
their response is compared to the many occasions where they
had attacked the military advice when the Chiefs of Staff had
advised rearmament or other positive forms of action in the
past. Only one (unnamed) voice was raised to ask why they
had been deliberately told to leave Russia out of their calculations – and he was given no answer.

Yet it was a contested debate. Duff Cooper, the First Lord
of the Admiralty, reading the documents the night before,
had thought the message to France 'a cold refusal of support'.
'The Parliamentary statement read like a declaration of isolation.'[15] With Stanley, he fought for a more friendly gesture to
France, and an admission that, whatever the policy, 'when
France fought Germany, we should have to fight too, whether
we liked it or not, so that we might as well say so'. But
Chamberlain, without disclosing that the Foreign Policy Committee had already decided to move towards a direct solution

of the Sudeten question, insisted that the Cabinet must approve the general policy, and at once. He rehearsed the argument that Germany could eliminate seventy-five per cent of Czech trade by economic pressure. A belligerent attitude by Britain would then appear ridiculous. The Chiefs of Staff report showed that the threat of blockade by British sea-power was irrelevant. Britain could do nothing for Czechoslovakia. As for France, 'it was difficult to believe that, if the subject were discussed seriously between the two nations, the French would not be glad to find some method to relieve them of their engagement'.[16]

Powerful though his case was, it did not entirely blanket the opposition in the Cabinet, grounded in doubts which had not, apparently, troubled the Foreign Policy Committee. The House of Commons might think the statement to be an open invitation to Hitler's aggression; Britain might lose the friendship of France, and later have to fight Germany alone. Was Germany so powerful? Hitler might have his own troubles, and the other likely enemy, Japan, was preoccupied with war against China. Did not Russia propose to carry out her part of the 1935 Treaty? As for British military weakness – would the position relative to Germany be any better in 1939, especially if, during that time, all the small states of Eastern Europe collapsed? The Balkan countries, Yugoslavia, Rumania, Hungary, Turkey and Greece, might, as Halifax and the Chiefs of Staff alleged, be of little use as allies, but under German rule they would give her great strength in oil and other raw materials. If Germany was not ready for war now, as the report suggested, would she not be more ready in 1940?

Those who put such questions* advocated a number of possible lines of action. The Government could tell the House of Commons that the democratic powers must stand together: and that staff talks would be held with France. Alternatively, Czechoslovakia could be told that if she was prepared to make reasonable proposals for the Sudeten Germans, Britain should support them and insist on Germany taking part in the negotiations. In that case, the Government could ask Germany for a twelve months' guarantee for Czechoslovakia. Or, if it was not possible to help Czechoslovakia directly, at least Britain should keep Germany guessing as to future actions, especially in sup-

* This part of the discussion was minuted only in a general way, with no attribution to specific ministers.

port of France. Finally, if nothing else could be done, the memorandum to France and the statement to the House of Commons should both show the utmost cordiality and goodwill towards France and sympathy for Czechoslovakia.

Taken one after another, the proposals diminished in strength, and the minutes drily record: 'the view that was accepted more generally and increasingly as the discussion continued, was that the policy proposed by the Foreign Secretary and supported by the Prime Minister was the best available in the circumstances'. Chamberlain and Halifax said, rather portentously, that they had actually wanted to give a guarantee to France but had been deterred by what they called 'the investigations of the Foreign Policy Committee'. They added, the last resort of argument, that public opinion in Britain was not ready for such firm action – and cited the views of 'an important figure in the City of London' as evidence. As for other factors, 'while there was no suggestion that the foreign policy of this country should be subordinated to the views of the Dominions, the Cabinet were impressed that the policy of further commitments would be very unpopular in all the Dominions, except possibly New Zealand, and might lead to a crisis in our relations with some of them'. Moreover, if war did break out, and Britain came to the help of France, not only would Czechoslovakia fall but the French would merely sit and defend the Maginot Line. German bombers would devastate London and the undefended south coast – 'a responsibility that no Government ought to take' – two months before the British Army could appear, effectively, on the Continent.

These arguments will be evaluated later. At the time, they prevailed. The opposition made no impact except that, at the end, following a satisfactory account of the projected programme of the Air Force for 1939, the rule that the normal course of trade should not be impeded by rearmament was cancelled.

When the French were told, and the policy made public in the House of Commons, in the 'declaration' of 24 March, the overriding impression was of British caution, even indecisiveness. Behind the public appearance, however, the Government set in motion a foreign policy more positive than anything which had been tried out since the conclusion of the Anglo-German Naval Treaty in 1935. Many complicated questions had been

evaded in the ten days since the *Anschluss,* but at least it seemed
to the inner group of ministers that Britain had a policy that
was commensurate with her real standing and power in the
world. It remained to be seen if France would take part, if
Germany would listen and if Czechoslovakia would give
way quickly and quietly. But there was no undue haste: other
crises in the 1930s had burst on unprepared governments who
had been forced to react to them. On this occasion, the Government had taken the initiative.

The plan to solve the Sudeten German question was the last
of Chamberlain's diplomatic initiatives and the most effective.
It merits a detailed study, even though the ground is well
trodden, because the history of the next six months confirms
much of what has been said above about the making of British
foreign policy, and the predominance of the Prime Minister,
and because its ultimate 'success' can be judged by the events
and the aftermath of the Munich Conference as the abortive
overtures to Germany in 1937 cannot.

7 The Public Face

The *Anschluss* and the prospect of a German attack on Czecho-slovakia brought the British Cabinet hideously close to the first open power-struggle with Germany since the rise of Hitler; and it raised the spectre of the war on two fronts against which the Defence Requirements Committee had warned in 1934. The enthusiasm which had backed up successive attempts to reach a détente with Germany was now transferred to the achievement of the Anglo-Italian agreement in order to wean Mussolini away from the Rome–Berlin Axis, while the Government set out to solve the Sudeten German question and thereby defuse the immediate threat to European security.

It is not surprising that British policy-making, vigorous and far-ranging as it had been since the middle of 1937, became charged with a sense of impending doom, so that Czecho-slovakia's problems became, in the narrowing circumstances of the next six months, the focal point of British politics. Politicians frequently speak of 'last chances' and 'final solutions', and their terminology is rarely justified. In this case it is significant that although the Government was apparently running its Italian and Czech policies in tandem, and trying to pacify Germany and detach Italy from her at the same time, the manoeuvres were in fact transparent to both sides and mutually contra-dictory. In the last resort, the British believed that if Italy was to have an alternative to the Axis, it would have to lie in a security arrangement which included not only Britain but the Balkans, Czechoslovakia and a benign France. None of these results could follow from the British Government's admission of future German penetration of Czechoslovakia and the Balkans, which could lead only to the destruction of the Little Entente and the alienation of Italy.

At the same time, the implications of what the Government already intended to extract from France were not likely to encourage reciprocal gratitude towards Britain. They intended to freeze France's hopes of British military help, not merely in the case of a war fought on behalf of Czechoslovakia but in the case of any German aggression on the Western frontier; and secondly they wished to induce her to betray the alliances freely made in 1925 and 1935. Finally, without any formal consultation, Russia was to be doubly spurned, by rejecting out of hand Litvinov's proposal for a Four-Power Conference and by sapping the will to fight of France, her only Western partner. It may be that, in the interests of Britain alone, the policy was viable and it is true that it is the only one which was likely to attract Dominion support, but it was a weighty thing to undertake without retrospective analysis of the failures of 1934 and 1937. All this, urgent though it was, was still only the prelude to the Anglo-German understanding which had eluded British policy since 1933. Without that receding goal, it was appeasement indeed. The question of whether Germany was interested, at any price, was not asked in the hectic third week of March. Instead, the Government devoted a large amount of time to making its public policy apparently less frigid towards France and more palatable to the House of Commons.

Russia was spared this courtesy. On 17 March Litvinov, the Russian envoy at Geneva, had proposed a conference of the major powers concerned with the Czechoslovak minority dispute. Litvinov had also given a press conference to say that 'means would be found' to fulfil the Russo-Czechoslovak agreement, but his remark that Russia would look to the machinery of the League in the first instance did not arouse much confidence in London.[1] The Soviet Union appears to have thought of the League as a mechanism for coercing difficult minor powers and for resolving the sort of conflicts which in the last twenty years have been handled by the United Nations. Serious consideration of the suggestion depended on the credibility of Russia's readiness to carry out her 1935 agreement, after the purges of the high command in 1936 and 1937 which, according to British information, had rendered the Red Army virtually incapable of anything but a defensive campaign.* The Soviet air force was believed to be of unknown quality,

* The British Ambassador, Lord Chilston, reported on 19 Apr that the purges and shootings had affected 65 per cent of senior Red Army officers. The Military Attaché, Colonel Firebrace, did not believe that at that stage the Russian regime was capable of waging war beyond the Soviet frontiers (*DBFP*, series 3, vol. 1, no. 148, pp. 161–2).

and the permission of both Rumania and Poland would have to be obtained before Russia could launch an offensive against Germany by land or even by air.

The British considered the Russian suggestion in these military terms in the Chiefs of Staff report of 21 March[2] but the Cabinet did not debate their assessment at all. The idea that the League might prove effective found little support from Sir William Malkin, the Foreign Office Legal Adviser, but the Vansittart–Sargent faction firmly recommended cultivating friendship with Poland and Russia, and Sargent himself envisaged something like benevolent neutrality on Russia's part.[3] Ivan Maisky, Russian Ambassador in London, promised a large contingent of aircraft and Vansittart pointed out how effective the Soviet air force had shown itself in the Spanish Civil War.[4] On the other hand, Cadogan forecast trouble with the Labour Party opposition and minuted: 'The Russian object is to precipitate confusion and war in Europe: they will not participate usefully themselves; they will hope for the world revolution as a result (and a very likely one too).'[5] This is perhaps the clearest statement of the ideological barrier on the British side. Russia was to be useful only 'behind us', if Britain were to call the German bluff – a solution which had already been ruled out. Cadogan's final draft for the Foreign Policy Committee was a cool brush-off. Litvinov's offer, according to the Cabinet minutes, was never discussed. Chamberlain's well-known letter with its picture of 'the Russians stealthily and cunningly pulling the strings behind the scenes to get us involved in war with Germany (our Secret Service doesn't spend all of its time looking out of the window)'[6] offers an explanation; but the files of the Secret Service which might substantiate this charge are still closed against research.

In contrast, the text of the message to France was given the benefit of a major drafting exercise in diplomatic tact. After all, the Foreign Office had been in favour of renewing the pledges to France.[7] To send something akin to a démarche might have undermined the entente so much that Britain could no longer look for French support against German attack. Yet to be too encouraging was thought unwise: France might take a bold stance in her interpretation of the 1925 or 1935 treaties, thus arousing all Germany's fears of encirclement and leading directly to a war which could, in British terms, have been avoided and in which Britain might not merely be involved for the sake of Czechoslovakia – with all that that implied for the Empire – but find herself fighting on the same side as Soviet Russia.

The Cabinet meeting of 22 March let the Foreign Policy Committee draft pass unscathed. The Francophiles, Stanley, Duff Cooper and Ormsby-Gore disliked it, but no one attempted to redraft it as Stanley had done earlier. France was not expected to like the terms, only to accept that, however disagreeable, there was no alternative. To prepare the way, Halifax had already given a very guarded answer to Corbin's formal request for an answer whether Britain would, in fact, stand by France if she became engaged in war with Germany. Corbin had said:

There was the greatest danger of the process that we had witnessed in Austria being continued by one means or other on the part of Germany with one country after another in Central and Eastern Europe and resulting in a growing disinclination of these countries to make any stand against this sequence of events.[8]

But a firm warning was precisely what the British, fearful of a commitment which would be held against them by France and Czechoslovakia, would not give.

The message which was finally transmitted to Paris pointed out that as recently as November 1937, Delbos (then Foreign Minister) had confirmed France's willingness to accept her treaty obligations – words which had been repeated to Halifax by Corbin after the *Anschluss*. Having put the onus squarely on France, the limits of British commitment were then rehearsed. Britain would 'come to the assistance of France in the event of an unprovoked act of aggression on her by Germany', and an offer of air staff talks was made. But this was all, because the Government regarded its present commitments as

no mean contribution to the maintenance of peace in Europe and, though they had no intention of withdrawing from them, they cannot see their way to add to them.... H.M.G. could certainly not go so far as to state what their action might be in the event of an attack upon Czechoslovakia by Germany. They are accordingly not in a position to undertake an obligation in advance to render military assistance to France in cases and circumstances not covered by the Treaty of Locarno.[9]

Some salve might be found in the declaration, which Chamberlain was to repeat to the House of Commons:

His Majesty's Government would not however pretend that, where peace and war are concerned, legal obligations are alone involved and that if war broke out it would be likely to be confined to those who have assumed such obligations. It would be quite impossible to say where it might end and what Governments might become involved. The inexorable pressure of facts, revealing threats to vital interests, might well prove more powerful than formal pronouncements and in that event it would be well within the bounds of probability that other countries, besides those which were parties to the original disputes, would almost immediately be involved. This is especially true in the case of two countries with long associations of friendship like Great Britain and France, which are devoted to the same ideals of democratic liberty and determined to uphold them.

But that was modified by the last part of the message which emphasised both the military weakness of Czechoslovakia now that the Austrian frontier lay open, and the fact that the status of the country could not be restored, even after a victorious war against Germany. British involvement would, accordingly, be more strictly limited than France might have imagined.

Their main contribution, in the early stages of the war, would be exercise of economic pressure by means of sea power, and this, as experience has shown, is slow in operation and tardy in its effects.... His Majesty's Government feel, therefore, that every possible step should be taken both by the French Government and by His Majesty's Government to help remove the causes of friction or even of conflict by using their good offices with the Government of Czechoslovakia to bring about a settlement of questions affecting the position of the German minority.

How that was to be done was not stated, but Halifax's covering note to Phipps advised him:

If a settlement is to be reached of the problem of the German minority in Czechoslovakia, it will be necessary at some stage to bring the German Government into the negotiation.... The establishment of good relations between Czechoslovakia and Germany depends on the latter being satisfied as to the regime provided by the Czech Government for that minority, or at any rate being deprived of legitimate grievances in relation thereto.... No mention is made in the aide-memoire [to France] of any approach to Germany, as that can only come at a later stage. But if we ever reach that stage, I should hope that the

French Government would not be able to say that we had given them no warning that we contemplated bringing Germany into discussion. . . .[10]

Similar instructions went to Newton in Prague, recalling to the Czech Government the minimal extent of British obligations and urging them 'to remove the causes of friction or even of conflict arising out of the present minority problem in Czechoslovakia'.[11]

Warming up the new policy for the House of Commons and the British public was equally difficult. Too strong a line on Czechoslovakia might at the same moment offend Germany, encourage France and inspire Czech resistance to German claims. Too weak an announcement would be taken, as the Foreign Policy Committee feared and as some members of the Cabinet complained, for an invitation to German aggression.

Halifax helped Chamberlain to draft his speech and they showed it to the Cabinet, first on the twenty-second and then, in its final version, on the twenty-third, the day before the debate. Those who had expressed fears about 'losing the friendship of France' made unfavourable comparisons between the timidity of the statement and the much tougher reaction of the Baldwin Government to the reoccupation of the Rhineland in 1936.[12] However, Halifax suggested that the Labour Opposition and trade unions were more worried about events in Spain than Czechoslovakia. Chamberlain had already reassured Walter Citrine, General Secretary of the TUC; and he intended to offset any public outcry by giving Parliament the impression that the Italians 'were playing the game'.

For those who were still upset that the Government's public response was timid, and who feared a diehard reaction from the Tory backbenchers, there was consolation in the fact that the implications of cancelling the rule that rearmament should not interfere with normal trade were already being worked out in Whitehall, where civilian departments were discussing joint preparations for defence.

Even so, it was thought wise to prepare the ground. Negotiations had gone on for several days between Chamberlain, Attlee and Archibald Sinclair, the Liberal leader, for 'a formula of policy that will command the assent of the whole House'.[12a] It seemed clear that whatever attitude was taken up in relation to Spain, most shades of opinion in the House of Commons would at least not condemn outright what the Government regarded as the far more important statement on central Europe. To do so would prejudice the talks with Italy. Nothing of the actual plan for solving the Sudeten problem was to be mentioned. Quite apart from the obvious impossibility of revealing what had been said to France, any mention of an overture to Germany or putting pressure on the Czechs would have ensured a hostile reception. Nor, in fact, did anyone other than Chamberlain and Halifax yet imagine that Britain would take more than an oblique, advisory part where discretion, influence and secrecy were essential to success.

Chamberlain's speech on 24 March was moderate. He emphasised that he was expressing the Government's 'attitude' towards events in central Europe, rather than its 'policy'. British policy in general he defined as 'the maintenance and preservation of peace and the establishment of a sense of confidence that peace will, in fact, be maintained'.[13] He repeated his view of the fallible nature of the League, the reasons why no greater guarantee could be given to France. On the subject of Czechoslovakia he made a declaration identical with that in the memorandum to France.

Almost in the same breath, Chamberlain dismissed the Russian offer of a Four-Power Conference; and whatever hopes some members of the Labour Party still placed in Russian foreign policy, probably the least contentious part of his speech was that in which he said

their proposal would appear to involve less a consultation with a view to settlement than a concerting of action against an eventuality that has not yet arisen. Its object would appear to be to negotiate such mutual undertakings in advance to resist aggression as I have referred to, which for reasons I have already given, H.M.G. for their part are unwilling to accept.[14]

After hinting that the Government would 'at all times be able to render any help in their power' to the Czechs 'to meet the reasonable wishes of the German minority', Chamberlain moved on to Spanish affairs and a proud, but selective, account of the acceleration of the rearmament programme. Afterwards the brunt of the Opposition attack was directed, as he had forecast, against the overtures to Italy, but the tone was much less bitter than that of the debate on Austria ten days before. It was by no means clear what the Labour Party wanted for Czechoslovakia: Chamberlain's previous speech on 14 March had been apparently enough to satisfy Henderson, son of the former Foreign Secretary;[15] and on 24 March Major Milner, a prominent Labour backbencher, could still declare that 'we all hope for appeasement'.[16]

Among the Conservative critics, Churchill thundered, in one of his finest speeches: 'I have watched this famous island descending incontinently, fruitlessly, the stairway which leads to a dark gulf. It is a fine broad stairway at the beginning, but after a bit the carpet ends. A little further on, there are only flagstones, and a little further on still these break beneath your feet.'[17] But his complaint was not made on a vital distinction of policy; rather the Government's failure to make the full deterrent use of a declaration of support for France. About Czechoslovakia, he was ambiguous: Britain was not obliged to go to war for her sake under the Covenant; 'but we are obliged not to be neutral in the sense of being indifferent if Czechoslovakia is the victim of unprovoked aggression'. The impression he made on the House of Commons was uncertain and evanescent: 'When Mr Churchill sat down there was deep silence for a moment: then the show was over. The House broke into a hubbub of noise; Members rattled their papers and shuffled their way into the lobby.'[18] Other Conservative critics were satisfied with Chamberlain's declaration. Leopold Amery wrote at the time: 'I was still very uncertain how we could do anything with Czechoslovakia and whether we might not have to resign ourselves to falling back, with Italian support, on holding Yugoslavia and the Balkans, and letting Germany find her elbow room in the rest of the Danubian area and in Eastern Europe.'[19]

Duff Cooper thought: 'The P.M.'s speech ... was a great success. It was very different in tone and emphasis from the draft the Cabinet were asked to consider last Tuesday. Without saying so definitely, he quite clearly implied that if France went to war, we should go too. This was all that I wanted.'[20] From the left wing of the Conservative Party, Harold Macmillan commented: 'this new assertion of Britain's interest in Central Europe seemed to show a more robust attitude'.[21]

Given the fact that the declaration was not intended to

be more than the first stage of a complicated diplomatic manoeuvre, the Cabinet could congratulate themselves on its reception. The reaction of the Press was very heartening: thus *The Times*: 'public opinion will be overwhelmingly with the Government. . . . It will receive with deep approval the final passages of Mr Chamberlain's speech. . . . There is good reason to believe that, as Mr Chamberlain has presented it, it answers the ideals, the hopes and the resolution that prevail here and throughout the Empire.'[22] The parliamentary correspondent added: 'All suggestions of a revolt in the Conservative Party . . . were entirely dispatched by the P.M.'s speech.' The *Manchester Guardian* noted: 'Mr Chamberlain has overcome the enemies in his own camp . . . those who wanted him to show some resolution . . . accept this statement as a valid new commitment and the sign of the resolution they were looking for.'* They could scarcely have been more wrong.

Surprisingly, the *Daily Herald* attacked the League which, it declared, 'has for the moment ceased to be an instrument of collective security. . . . As a method of enforcing peace and restraining aggression, the League in practice no longer exists.'[23] The Beaverbrook newspapers remained as isolationist as ever, as if they had indeed been spokesmen for the Empire they so ardently defended. Powerful support for the Government came from J. M. Keynes. In the *New Statesman* he urged that Czechoslovakia should 'at least attempt to negotiate with Germany a reasonable solution to the problem of the Sudeten Germans, even if this means a rectification of the Bohemian frontier. Racial frontiers are safer and better today than geophysical ones. . . .'[24]

Chamberlain had every right to be satisfied with the reception at home. However, the elimination of Eden had not entirely purged the opposition within the Government. Chamberlain wrote on 20 March 'what a comfort [Halifax] is to me and how thankful I am that I have not to deal with Anthony in these troubled times',[25] but he recounted intrigues and dark conspiracies centred on Churchill, Beaverbrook, Hore-Belisha and Boothby, and his suspicions of sections of the French Government, 'I suspect in closish touch with our Opposition'. His prickly awareness suggests an unhealthy degree of

---

* *Manchester Guardian*, 25 Mar. The editorial, on the other hand, was more critical: 'at best Mr. Chamberlain has only half a policy'.

preoccupation with his popular standing. Personalities and political loyalty had always meant much to him, ever since his unhappy experience of the wartime coalition. Now loyalty was being confused with approval and policy identified with his own political strength.

The same hypersensitive consciousness can be seen in the way he appeared to rely excessively on the support of friends. He delighted in a round-robin from a number of Conservative MPs expressing their personal loyalty. Hore-Belisha, perhaps to offset suspicion, had given him a bust of Pitt, 'to show that he considers me as *l'héritier de Pitt'*.[26] Chamberlain sent an effusive note of thanks – 'I was never troubled by the foolish stories of divisions in the Cabinet. I should trust my colleagues to tell me first if they disagreed with me and your loyalty has always been beyond suspicion.'[27] The Prime Minister was even glad of a reassuring word from the tiny group of Clydeside MPs.

These weaknesses would not be very significant if Chamberlain's personality had been a less powerful ingredient in the making of foreign policy in 1938. During the previous winter, he had frequently set out what he thought to be the effect of his actions on Europe in a way which, even in private letters, was exaggerated to the point of vanity. In domestic politics this judgement might have been valid, but this transposition of the British for the European scene indicates a major failure of political insight. Thus he could write, after his House of Commons speech on 24 March, that it had been not only a 'remarkable success' but that it had made 'a vast impact on Europe'.[28] Congratulations indeed flowed in – from the Pope and Nevile Henderson, from Lord Tweedsmuir, Governor-General of Canada, and from Hacking, the Conservative Party chairman, who thought that Chamberlain had soundly frightened 'the weak-kneed Liberals who felt safe with Baldwin'.[29] These were not sources to be accepted uncritically, yet they were.

Foreign opinion was by no means as favourable as Chamberlain supposed. True, Blum wrote from Paris to thank him, perhaps ironically, for his declaration on 'the bonds which unite us'.[30] But his Government was about to fall and he would be replaced by the supposedly less pliant Daladier. Phipps meanwhile reported that the official French line was unchanged :

Paul Boncour (the Foreign Minister) 'maintains his belief that a definite warning to Germany by the two countries regarding consequence of aggression on Czechoslovakia, would be the best means of avoiding war'.[31] Boncour swore that if Germany attacked the Czechs, France would summon the League Council and occupy the Rhineland. He denied that the German minorities in Czechoslovakia were ill-treated and he objected strongly to any Franco-British approach to Germany. This would be 'a terribly dangerous precedent for all countries with any German minorities and would moreover be resented by the Czechoslovak Government itself'.[32]

In Prague the reaction, according to British sources, was equivocal. Newton reported the assurances of the Foreign Minister 'that the Czech Government asked nothing of H.M.G. They realised how difficult it was for Britain to extend its commitments and were quite satisfied with British sympathy and understanding.' But, he continued: 'One or two subsequent remarks . . . show that the Czech Government rely on their French alliance and eventual British support for France.' Later he talked to President Beneš who told him 'that he looked forward to a growing recognition of identity of interest of Britain and Czechoslovakia in resisting German aggression'.[33]

There was no mistaking the German reception. The Chargé d'Affaires in London, Woermann, reported Chamberlain's speech to Berlin:

these last statements continue to indicate as highly probable that Britain would in any event take part in a war arising over Czechoslovakia, if France were to intervene in fulfilment of her Treaty obligations . . . there is thus implied a kind of warning to Germany and an emphatic proffer of help to France. However, and with particular regard to the fact that British policy is conducted in the closest agreement with the Dominions, the possibility still remains now, as before, that according to the circumstances of the moment it might not in such a case come to a British intervention or not to an immediate one.[34]

Hitler's speech on 28 March reflected this shrewd appreciation.

The situation [cannot] be tolerated indefinitely. Germany is on the rise and is becoming continually greater, and prouder and more self-respecting. Is it to be wondered at that these people look more and more with burning eyes to Germany and throng more and more round the loudspeakers to hear what is happening in Germany? They have only one hope—Germany must save us.... I have given warning and declared publicly that Germany *cannot* be and *will not* be indefinitely a spectator of the oppression of her fellow countrymen....[35]

Considering how far Hitler's plans had matured, Britain now would have to work hard to bring Germany to negotiate with the Czechs, even if a direct approach were made to Berlin.

The British saw no need to worry about the United States. The Chiefs of Staff report on German action had not even mentioned the attitude of the United States to Europe, although it discussed the implications of the Sino-Japanese war. Eden's enthusiasm for Roosevelt's offer in January was buried and forgotten. In a letter written after the *Anschluss*, Chamberlain noted 'what a fool Roosevelt would have looked if he had launched his precious proposal. What would he have thought of us if we had encouraged him to publish it, as Anthony [Eden] was so eager to do? And how we too would have made ourselves the laughing stock of the world.'[36] Indeed, American attitudes remained ambiguous where Europe was concerned. W. Thomas Bullitt, United States Ambassador in Paris, believed in Franco-German reconciliation, and Kennedy in London seemed ready to pay any price to avoid European war. The United States Minister in Prague, Wilbur J. Carr, appointed at the age of sixty-seven by Roosevelt in what seems to have been a fit of absence of mind, asked a visiting State Department official at the end of March what American policy towards Czechoslovakia was. 'He learned only that opinion was divided at home: some State Department people were hostile to German ambitions, others were convinced that Chamberlain was on the right path and that the United States should follow his lead.'[37]

After the declaration of 24 March, the British Government had three consecutive aims: to complete the Anglo-Italian agreement; to accelerate the rearmament programme towards its primarily defensive role; and, by solving the Sudeten German problem, to create the necessary conditions for an Anglo-German settlement. To its own satisfaction the Government had time and strength to pursue these policies together. Any

contradictions between them were less evident than the logic of
past policy and present circumstances. To begin with, though,
the first two were paramount. The Government's approach to
the third was oblique, even devious and always secret. When
the Cabinet discussed what Halifax called his 'secret memorandum' in the first week of April, the Foreign Secretary was still
taking the line that Britain did not know enough about the
Czech problem to be able to suggest a solution both equitable
and of value to Germany. It was France who was to take the
main part in the joint approach to Prague, to induce President
Beneš to come to terms with Germany while it was still possible.

The gap between the public debate on foreign policy, conducted in the House of Commons and the Press, and the Government's private plans began to widen significantly after the last
week of March 1938. In answer to a question at the Cabinet
meeting on 6 April about the future of Czechoslovakia, Halifax
admitted that Hitler might want more: 'the Sudeten Germans
were so mixed up with the Czech population, that a strictly fair
and equitable solution was very difficult'.[38] The last two
words in the Cabinet minutes are written in on top of the typed
report, which reads: 'a strictly fair and equitable solution was
not a possibility'. The palimpsest represents the public face,
the original the reality of British policy over the next five
months.

8 The Conversion of France

Unchecked by a House of Commons ignorant of how far they were prepared to go in coercing Czechoslovakia, the Cabinet were able to follow their aims without serious internal discord and virtually without complaint from Press or public until the end of May 1938. During this time, however, British intentions were misunderstood, mistrusted or simply ignored by Germany, whose leaders were preoccupied not only with plans for the invasion of Czechoslovakia, but with the problem of assimilating Austria while at the same time maintaining the Rome–Berlin Axis. The British Government's plans were, in fact, as much at variance with German thinking as they had been when the colonial offer was made in January, but, since the preliminary stages most concerned France and Italy, this was neither understood nor allowed for in London.

Three distinct issues were dealt with in London during April: the Anglo-Italian agreement was concluded; the relationship with France was forcibly redefined to an extent which allowed the British to take charge of the joint approach to Czechoslovakia; and the pattern of defence was argued out in a way which limited almost to nothing British participation in any Continental struggle. The result of a month's intense effort was to eliminate all other choices of approach towards Germany and to concentrate British policy-making on the Czech problem alone.

How much the agreement with Italy meant to Chamberlain is clear from his belief that Mussolini might have acted differently if it had been in force at the time of the *Anschluss*, and from the haste in which the Foreign Policy Committee attempted to finalise it before Hitler could repair what they imagined to be the damage done to Germany's relationship with Italy. Under the impression that Hitler intended to patch up the Axis by a visit to Rome on 15 April, the Government overrode the objections put forward by New Zealand, the only Dominion actually to protest at giving *de jure* recognition of Abyssinia before a full withdrawal of Italian forces from Spain had taken place. In the end, New Zealand announced that, although a member of the League Council, she would abstain at Geneva rather than vote against the resolution on Abyssinia. The difficulties created by the personal appearance at Geneva of the Emperor, Haile Selassie, seem to have been discounted after the British had made arrangements with Avenol, Secetary-General of the League, about procedure to be adopted during the debate.[1] In case the Government could not carry the main resolution, even after these preparations, the Foreign Policy Committee decided to subscribe to a policy of declaratory statements by individual nations, to get the same result.

Their reward came promptly: on 13 April the completed Anglo-Italian Agreement was read to the Cabinet. The British had gained security of the status quo in the Mediterranean, an exchange of military information about the Middle East and a guarantee of non-interference in the Near East (that is, in Palestine); but all this still depended, so Halifax said, on British satisfaction about the Spanish question; and, on the Italian side, on the actual recognition of Abyssinia. The Agreement was published on 27 April and Chamberlain assured his colleagues that it had made 'a deep impression'.[2]

Chamberlain's part may be gauged from a letter written just after the completed British document had been returned to Rome.

You should have seen the draft put up to me by the F.O.! It would have frozen a polar bear! And when I had warmed it up to what I thought was nearer the appropriate temperature, they wrote a note saying that it was 'only too likely that Mussolini would want to publish it'. Of course, that was what I intended. . . .[3]

In the ephemeral circumstances of the time, the Cabinet could congratulate themselves that this estimate was not inaccurate. Hitler's state visit to Rome took place on 3 May, and in spite of elaborate ritual it failed to recapture the mood of 1936. Hitler and Ribbentrop pressed on a reluctant Mussolini the advantages of a formal treaty, but with suave words Ciano rendered the German document meaningless. Mussolini appeared anxious to keep open his relationship with at least one of the Stresa powers. Moreover the *Anschluss* had awakened the separatist ambitions of the German minority in the south Tyrol who, in Ciano's words, were getting 'too uppish'. It was only a month since Italy had been prepared to threaten war, if Germany moved the frontier post south one single yard.[4] Ribbentrop persisted, tactlessly and inelegantly, only to be relegated by Mussolini to 'that category of Germans who are a disaster to their country'.[5] Hitler, indeed, had to spend much of his time melting the ice. But Mussolini regarded British friendship only as a useful standby. Doubts and difficulties arose between Britain and Italy during the summer as soon as Italian concession in Spain could no longer be avoided.[6] Yet it is curious that, after the violent haste of February and March, the British Government should have been content to think they had neutralised anti-British feeling in Italy without exerting themselves until July actually to bring the Agreement into effect. Such was the degree of concentration on the Czech problem, and the strategic significance attributed to the *Anschluss* which, by revealing the long, only partly defended, frontier between Austria and Czechoslovakia, had freed Hitler from dependence on Italian acquiescence in a military coup.

Chamberlain's letter of 16 April ended with the words: 'We can't do anything with Hitler just yet but we are trying to get the Czechs to face up to realities and settle their minority problem and if we should be successful it might presently be possible to start again in Berlin.'[7]

The Cabinet had already considered Halifax's 'secret memorandum',* and discussion continued for a week there and in the Foreign Policy Committee. The plan extended far beyond giving advice to President Beneš. Apart from the joint Anglo-French approach to Prague, Halifax foreshadowed direct dealings with Germany:

He did not contemplate any immediate approach to Berlin but ... the time would come when it might be of some advantage to impress upon the German Government the fact that the Czechoslovak Government was giving their careful consideration to the problem and expressing our hope that Germany would exercise patience in the matter. Great care would, however, have to be

---

* CP 76/38, 13 Mar. Foreign Office opinion was now substantially in favour of the first stage of Government policy on Czechoslovakia. Even the Eden group agreed that Czech independence could only be preserved if Hitler feared a European war, 'and that we could not threaten in our present state of armament.' (*Diaries of Oliver Harvey*, p. 133.)

taken to avoid giving Germany the impression that we were actively supporting any particular proposals made by the Czecho-slovak Government.[8]

He asked for this authority, promising his colleagues that he would be careful not to let Beneš draw Britain into a public expression of opinion on the details of any proposals for the future of the Sudeten areas, in case these should be given the colour of British approval. So long as there was hope of the Czech Government doing its own work by negotiation with Henlein and the SDP, there might be no need for Britain to intervene directly in Berlin.* But the Foreign Policy Committee also worked urgently in the first week of April to bring France into line – to forestall the danger of the Czech Government delay-ing, under the impression that Germany was occupied consol-idating her conquest of Austria, thus ignoring the fact that frontier incidents might create the conditions for a German invasion.

Britain could bring no effective pressure on the Czechs by her-self: she had nothing to offer that was not politically inexpedient, and nothing to withdraw. All the urgency was channelled into the effort to make France fit the plan. Evaluation of the internal struggle between the Czech Government and Henlein's Sudeten party waited on the double task of forcing France to abandon her belligerent defence of the treaty with Czechoslovakia and persuading the new Daladier Government of the attractive nature of the British plan.

What seemed simple in the Euclidian geometry of British policy-making, however, looked vastly different in the three-dimensional pattern of Europe. Even if France agreed, success depended entirely on reasonable progress in the talks between Henlein and the Czech Government. But what if the Germans refused to accept a settlement? There were some ministers, such as Hoare, who still believed it useful for Britain to keep

---

* Unofficial pressure had already been exerted. An (unidentified) member of the Cabinet had seen Jan Masaryk, the Czech Minister in London, and told him that it would be necessary for Czechoslovakia to put her house in order. Halifax thought that Masaryk's reply indicated some concession on the part of Beneš. (*DBFP*, series 3, vol. 1, pp. 113–14.) Masaryk also wrote to Hoare for 'direct blunt concrete advice' on whether or not to make concessions; and Hoare replied on 25 Mar, 'speaking as an old friend', that the Czech Government should ask Britain and France to use their good offices. (Templewood, *Nine Troubled Years*, pp. 292–5.)

Germany guessing. But the Cabinet had already suggested (on 2 April) that the Czech Government should declare the utmost extent to which it could go in concession and ask France and Britain to act as mediators in Berlin on their behalf. There was a danger here: to be linked to specific details and to have to defend them, as Stanley pointed out, would put Britain in a delicate position. Could the Cabinet avoid having influence without responsibility?

None of this made the approach to France any easier. Halifax had already sent a rejoinder to 'correct any misinterpretations' of French hopes arising out of the original shattering message of 23 March.* Now he delayed, uncertain of the strength of Daladier's Government and content to hedge on the subject of Britain's attitude to the Henlein talks. The fact that Chamberlain consented to this delay suggests that he hoped progress in the Prague talks might itself ease the unenviable task of making the French face what the British considered to be reality.

In their general attitude to Germany, the Foreign Policy Committee was timid. They approved when Halifax advised them to emphasize in Berlin the chances of Britain being drawn in if war broke out, but to discourage this interpretation elsewhere – that is, in Prague and Paris.[9] No doubt they preferred to ignore the fact that the German Ministers in both capitals were unlikely not to sense the contradiction and draw their own conclusions, even if Nevile Henderson did not do the job for them. No formal attempt was made to enlighten Germany about British plans until on 22 April R. A. Butler, Halifax's Under-Secretary, held a conversation with the Chargé d'Affaires, Woermann, and Theodore Kordt, the Military Attaché in London. The British desire for good relations with Germany was stressed in the most general terms, according to Kordt – Butler, 'as it were, the spokesman of the younger generation in England', hoped to inspire confidence which his seniors could not provide. But he was elliptical when being most explicit: 'We probably could not yet speak frankly about certain subjects. ... Immediately thereafter he said that England was aware that Germany would attain "her next goal". The manner in which

---

* A visit from Churchill seems to have raised French hopes of a full-blooded entente. On 20 Mar, Halifax told the Cabinet that he was asking Phipps to dispel such dangerous rumours (CAB 23/93).

this was done was, however, decisive for the reaction in England.'[10]

Meanwhile, as a preliminary to the talks with France, the Cabinet completed the year-long strategic debate. The result was a good forecast of the style of foreign policy to come; and the discussions showed that neither Britain nor France was going to be able to avoid joint military discussions.

In the immediate shock wave after the *Anschluss*, pressure built up from the Service advisers and inside the Cabinet for a revision of the rationed budget. The direction – towards greater provision for the Air Force and anti-aircraft defence – indicates that the predominant fear was of German bomber-attack on the defenceless south-east of England. First reactions were soon followed by more general claims. Sensing perhaps that, in such a mood, the Cabinet might revoke the rationing system, Chamberlain opened the door in principle for increases in fighter strength and for anti-aircraft defence, so long as no impression was given in public that war was likely in a few weeks. Another detailed review of the Service proposals began, this time taking into account the views of the trade unions.

At once the Service ministers raised their opening bids. On 14 March, Swinton asked for the Air Force Scheme K* to be put into effect, at an increased cost of £567 million; also for sufficient labour to work all aircraft factories on double shifts (thereby raising output by thirty-three per cent in three months). The War Office asked for extensions for the Territorial Army as well as increases for anti-aircraft defence; the Navy claimed that the money was better spent on warship construction. Chamberlain played one against the other and disposed of the Admiralty request for a third battleship in 1938 at once. The argument narrowed to a fight between Scheme K and the TA – much as it had done in January. The warnings of Ernest Brown, Minister of Labour, about the likely state of the labour market if the Government resorted to compulsion added weight to Treasury criticisms. Evidently, the abandonment of the rule against interference with normal trade had not yet been accepted

---

* 14 Mar, CAB 23/92. Scheme K provided for a total front line strength of 2182 aircraft – 1320 bombers, 544 fighters of modern design – which was to be achieved by May 1940, a full year earlier than the completion date of Scheme F, which had been adopted in 1936.

in practice. Simon said bluntly that Scheme K would mean the end of rationing because the February limit (now of £1570 million) could not be held. Extreme methods must be permissible in war but, used in peace, they would destroy financial stability before war even began.

It was not enough for Swinton to state that, according to the Air Staff, Scheme K was insufficient to meet a full German attack, and should not be regarded as more than basic insurance cover. Inskip threw his weight behind Simon. Like Ernest Brown, he was afraid of trades union reaction to requests for dilution of skilled labour. When Chamberlain, in a sensible and moderate speech, suggested that the Cabinet should not at this stage accept Scheme K, but begin talks with the unions and employers about increase of labour for the aircraft factories on voluntary lines, only Lord Winterton, Chancellor of the Duchy of Lancaster and spokesman for the Air Ministry in the Commons, complained of the inability to fulfil the pledge of parity given by Baldwin in 1934.* Swinton's prestige in the Cabinet had declined sharply in the early part of 1938, mainly because of publication of the Cadman Report on civil aviation which made severe criticisms of the Air Ministry. Winterton was very junior, impulsive and generally considered a lightweight. The rest were satisfied with a bromide statement from Halifax that no new situation existed, and a CID proposal to buy war material, including Douglas aircraft, from the United States and Canada.†

The real issues were not so easily settled. The question of whether the Air Force should retain its bombing offensive component or confine itself to the defensive fighter-strength, which was the logical outcome of the Cabinet's earlier decisions, did not have to be decided immediately, but the role of the Army could not be postponed. The claims of the War Office for an effective field force gained strength from the need to give France something more tangible than vague assurances of support if she was to join in coercing the Czechs. The French were bound to

---

* 'That in air strength and air power this country shall no longer be in a position inferior to any country within striking distance of our shores' (*Hansard*, 5th series, vol. 286, col. 2078. 8 Mar 1934).
† Something which Hankey and Baldwin had been striving for as early as the summer of 1936, and which the British representatives at the 1937 Imperial Conference had been denied.

ask what help would be forthcoming and were expected to require staff talks covering all three services. Here the Chiefs of Staff got cold feet. Having been overridden so often by the politicians, they passed responsibility and indicated only that they thought staff talks unnecessary except for the Air Force – a two-division field-force was too small to need them, and naval strategy could be co-ordinated nearer the outbreak of war.[11] In the end, the question was left open for the Cabinet to decide.

Chamberlain made the most of this hesitation by contrasting the pusillanimous military advice with the Government's plan. He told the Cabinet, on 6 April, that as Chairman of the CID he had had to push the Chiefs of Staff:

it had been with a good deal of hesitation that they had been induced to agree to conversations more or less *sub rosa* between Air Attachés. To him it seemed to be an anomalous position that the Government should have accepted obligations but taken no steps to make them good. He could not have reconciled the acceptance of such obligations with the frequent rejection of French approaches which only meant that our action would not be decided until the emergency arose. His opinion in this matter had been reinforced by what had happened in Austria. In modern warfare the aggressor was able to move with such rapidity that there was no time for making plans. Wider consultation should take place, to know what part the other could play.[12]

He hoped, also, that the fact that Britain was instigating staff talks would soften the shock when France realised just how little actual support would be given. The talks should begin 'as soon as there was a stable Government in France', and the military must find out what the French intended to do if Germany attacked Czechoslovakia. Chamberlain added sardonically that 'he understood from Mr Churchill that the French plans contemplated holding to the Maginot Line but at the same time to undertake offensive operations in another area'. The Cabinet, who had had a fortnight to study the relative assessment of European armed forces in the Chiefs of Staff paper of 21 March, cannot have placed much faith in Churchill's judgement. Earlier in March, the French Military Attaché, General Lelong, had been asked what France proposed to do. Lelong replied that the French did not intend to cross the Upper Rhine nor to campaign in the Black Forest. He evaded a further question as to whether they would attack the Palatinate.[13] The War Office staff drew the conclusion that they would be content to hold the Maginot Line and that the air force might possibly bomb the Ruhr.

Further evidence that France intended to play a purely defensive part was given in the military report of 21 March. Against the French figure of an army of a hundred divisions, the Chiefs of Staff reckoned that only fifty-three actually existed; French tanks were spread widely among infantry formations rather than concentrated on armoured divisions; and the air force, the most powerful in the world in 1935, now amounted to a front-line strength of only 297 fighters and 456 bombers, the majority obsolescent. The implication was that, unless Germany chose to split her forces, attacking France at the same time as Czechoslovakia, France's ability to defend her ally in any way was minimal.*

Given such a disparity between French strength and declared strategy, the need for staff talks was obvious. The lack of past co-operation and present information in itself became an admirable bargaining-counter during the political talks about Czechoslovakia. The hesitation which Halifax had shown earlier diminished as the attractions of a fuller 'reconciliation' with France grew. If the Daladier Government could be made to realise that it was better to clear away the muddle of the previous two years, and to accept that British aid, though confined to a naval blockade of Germany, a purely token field force, and some air cover, would at least be guaranteed on a basis of joint planning, then, Chamberlain and Halifax assumed, the French, conscious of their own military inadequacy, would gratefully join in solving the Czech question.

This thinking lay behind the Cabinet's acceptance of staff talks in principle, and the rest was exceedingly simple. Hore-Belisha had already been told by Simon to cut his War Office estimates by £82 million and he had duly produced a new Army scheme which was attacked on all sides, at the Cabinet meeting on 27 April, for its excessive cuts in the Field Force and the Territorial Army. Mildly enough, Hore-Belisha replied that the Cabinet had ordered him to make his cuts somewhere, and

---

* COS 698. These conclusions were substantially correct—see Royal Institute of International Affairs Survey for 1937, vol. 3, p. 576; Georges Bonnet, *Quai d'Orsay* (London 1965) pp. 164–5 (covering the minutes of the Permanent Committee for National Defence meeting on 15 Mar), and 179–80; and the evidence given at the Riom trials in 1942.

on the basis that the scheme would occupy the full manufacturing capacity of the War Office for two years (in itself a major condemnation of the previous five years' policy) the cuts went through. The Army at last had a role – determined for it by the superior bargaining power of everyone else.

The question of the Air Force was decided differently. The protagonists put forward their revised schemes: Swinton, a new scheme L* giving all the advantages of K plus full reserves; Simon and Inskip, lenient on the expansion of the existing scheme F, but utterly opposed to L or K. Whatever else Inskip was prepared to allow, he was adamant that the total of the defence budget should not pass beyond the February ration. If the Air Force got their increase, then the other Services must contract. Simon claimed that Scheme L would require an extra hundred thousand men, skilled and unskilled; even if the Treasury raised the £1570 million limit, this scale of industrial transference was impossible unless the economy were put on a war footing.

Chamberlain asked Swinton whether in practice parity could not be gained under a modified scheme F by 1939 or 1940. 'Could we produce a formidable force while carrying out a programme designed to strengthen our *defensive* strength so that we should not be at the mercy of a foreign power?'[14]

The drift was clear: minimum standards would replace parity and full reserves. Under scheme L Britain would have had fewer machines than Germany by 1939, but better fighters and bombers than in 1938, and must therefore have been relatively stronger. Scheme F was at this time a short-term affair, and to accelerate the existing programme the Air Ministry needed a long and accurately programmed timetable. At that moment Germany had between 1080 and 1350 bombers compared to Britain's 800, many of which could only reach Germany from French soil. Germany enforced conscription in industry. According to Swinton, Scheme L, though the minimum insurance

* Scheme	Bombers	Fighters	Recon.	Army Co-op.	Total
F	990	420	194	132	1736
K	1320	544	194	132	2190
L	1352	608	281	132	2373 (excluding Fleet Air Arm)

advised by the Air Staff, was barely enough to achieve parity even on known German numbers. But the alternative was to 'confess to permanent and total weakness'.

The crux of the argument lay in two quite separate concepts of air power. Swinton still believed in the deterrent effect of a bomber counter-strike. Scheme L perpetuated roughly the existing balance between bombers and fighters. Chamberlain had never been convinced of the value of the deterrent; and the discrepancy was resolved by economic rather than strategic arguments. Simon advanced a statement to which the Prime Minister was peculiarly sympathetic. 'These figures could not be reached unless we turned ourselves into a different kind of nation.' Germany had got rid of her war debt and her internal debts through inflation, had cut her social services, controlled wages and lowered the standard of living. Britain could not do these things and must be content with 'the sound business method of not expanding the business till we were in a position to do so'.

When the debate was finally resolved, on 27 April, in comparison with the economies made at the War Office, the Air Ministry did well. Swinton told the Cabinet that he planned to finish scheme L by 31 March 1940. After a special review of industrial capacity made by Sir Charles Bruce-Gardner, Chairman of the Society of British Aircraft Constructors, he could assure the Cabinet that there would be no difficulty regarding plant or premises, and manpower would be alright, given political goodwill. So far, the Treasury-dominated sub-committee had conceded Swinton's case. But the actual excess over the rationed total was limited to two years; the five-year total defence programme was pegged at £1650 million and the Cabinet was not permitted to consider itself bound beyond 1940. The whole 'acceleration of rearmament' after the *Anschluss* was something of an illusion because the increases were won largely at the expense of the War Office and the principle of rationing was enforced as firmly as before.

These strategic dispositions confirmed the isolationist nature of British foreign policy. They meant that nothing but a token force which would have a wholly inadequate supply of undergunned, lightly armoured tanks would be sent to Europe. Fully trained reserves would be limited to fifty per cent of battle strength, and provision for training greater numbers did not exist. British participation in a general war against Germany –

as distinct from a German attack on Britain – would amount to a naval blockade and an unspecified quantity of supporting aircraft. The whole burden of actually beating Germany on land devolved on France. This strategy was the creation of the Cabinet, not the Chiefs of Staff. After presenting their major analysis on 21 March, the latter were not asked to report again until September,* and the CID occupied its meetings during the summer with matters of secondary importance.

Already, on 13 April, the CID had delivered the portentous judgement (defended to the Cabinet by a united front of Chamberlain, Halifax and Inskip) that it was not certain Britain could send a field force to France at all.[15] The inner group of ministers had balanced the modest increase for the RAF against further cuts in the Army. They were also well aware that by threatening to deprive France of any physical support at all they might compel her to fall into line over Czechoslovakia. As Chamberlain said, in a burst of candour, France should know about the Army at once lest she should be under any illusions – it might even encourage her to complete the Maginot Line.[16]

The staff talks were to be severely restricted to the basis of the Locarno declaration of 19 March 1936. The choices posed in the Chiefs of Staff report of 21 March – the grand alliance or the guarantee to France – were to be excluded. So also should discussion of the Mediterranean situation, because of the Italian agreement, and the Far East, because of the Sino-Japanese war. No naval talks were provided for because they might give a handle to Germany to denounce the Anglo-German Naval Treaty, still highly valued by the Admiralty.† Yet, having also told France that there would be virtually no army in the event of war, the Cabinet decided that somehow 'they should avoid the idea that Britain was not contributing anything'.

Discussion of procedure was concerned largely with the threat of a German attack on Britain and showed such national selfishness that the future of Anglo-French co-operation must have seemed, to an impartial observer, short and hopeless. An explana-

---

* The reports on anti-aircraft and anti-submarine defence, after the May crisis (COS 733–5) represented an emergency review, not a full strategic appreciation.
† 'This Agreement has been of incalculable value to us,' wrote the Deputy Chief of Naval Staff; 'and I think that when summing up what we stand to lose if we antagonise Germany . . . the loss of this should occupy a foremost place.' (COS 701 (CAB 53/37).)

tion may lie in the type of war which they envisaged: 'not...
the repetition of 1914, but...most likely an attempted knock-
out blow. In view of the strength of the Maginot Line, this is
less likely to be directed against France than against the
industrial and other resources of this country, which are especially vulnerable to air attack.'[17] But, they might have asked,
why not then approve scheme L? One answer was that the air
talks with France were to be 'fairly full'. The Government was to
tell France frankly that the 'primary object of our air striking
force is the defence of this country' but that, of course, a contribution would be made to the defence of France. As if this were
not enough, the Cabinet was to ask for French help if the main
attack *did* turn against Britain. Rarely, if ever, can there have
been a less enthusiastic or more blinkered approach to an ally.
It needed a Balfour to do justice to the mission – 'for a task so
complex as this I feel a trained diplomatist is required. But I
will do my best.'[18]

Balfour, at least, might have added levity to the gloomy and
self-righteous message which Halifax transmitted to Phipps on
11 April, as soon as he judged the new French Cabinet – then
only two days old – could stand a renewal of the memorandum
of 23 March. The narrowly defensive nature of the British
strategic outlook permeated his request that

> every step that is possible should be taken to avoid an outbreak
> [of war] which in present circumstances might carry with it a
> very considerable risk for both France and Great Britain....
> Unless the French and Czech Governments can be brought to
> face the realities of the present position, it is to be feared that
> the Czech Government will not realise the necessity of making
> drastic concessions to the German minority, but will content
> themselves with superficial measures...while the French Govern-
> ment, for their part, will fail to appreciate the necessity of using
> their undoubted influence in Prague to promote a supreme effort
> on the part of the Czech Government to find a solution to the
> problem on the settlement of which the continued existence of
> Czechoslovakia as an independent state, within her present
> frontiers, may well depend.[19]

The British may have imagined that they could impose their
version of the situation on France and Czechoslovakia by sheer
force of argument. But as Chamberlain had written, six years
before, at Lausanne, 'the foreigner simply can't contemplate get-

224 The Conversion of France

ting down to business without using preliminary sparring and skirmishing'.[20] In this case, France returned a non-committal answer; and the immediate hope of a favourable response in Prague was destroyed when Newton forwarded the Czech Government's proposals for concessions to the SDP on 19 April. The difference between their conception of minority reform and the demands of the Sudeten Germans was far greater than the British Government had suspected. The proposed Statute of Minorities, which offered new language regulations and a small degree of fiscal manipulation in favour of minorities was quite insufficient. Five days later Henlein responded with his famous programme, delivered in a speech at Carlsbad at the annual general meeting of the SDP.* Short of a demand for a plebis-cite or direct secession no more complete severance from the Czech state could have been imagined.

The Carlsbad programme seriously worried the Cabinet, who at this stage, in spite of the regular supply of information by the Foreign Office,† understood very little of the complexities of the situation inside Czechoslovakia. They had accepted that the Sudeten German problem was, in Chamberlain's words, like that of the Uitlanders in the Transvaal – a gross oversimplification – and they regarded Henlein as a Jameson without inquiring into his relations with the more extreme Nazis like Karl Frank. Enlightenment came later, and only partially erased the picture of the honest, moderate reformist which Henlein had given on his visits to London.

In their estimate of the reaction in France, the Cabinet were more perceptive. They were not convinced by bold statements that France would spring to Czechoslovakia's defence. Indeed, spurred by Halifax's brusque disparagement of the French,[21] the majority showed themselves much more contemptuous of Daladier's assurances than the evidence warranted. Later in the

---

* It comprised: full equality of status between Czechs and Germans, guaranteed by recognising the Sudeten Germans as constituting a 'legal personality'; definition and legal recognition of the German regions within Czechoslovakia; full self-government in German areas; legal protection for all Germans living outside the Sudeten area; removal of injustices inflicted on the Sudeten Germans in 1918 and reparations for damages; German officials for German regions; liberty to profess German nationality and German political philosophy.

† Files C4851–9818/1941/18 *passim*. These cover the whole period down to Sept 1938, but the complexity of the situation in Czechoslovakia does not seem to have filtered through the Foreign Secretary's papers to the Cabinet as a whole.

summer they had to revise this opinion; but at the time it seemed clear enough. Daladier had appointed Georges Bonnet, whom Phipps's reports revealed to be an advocate of appeasing Germany, as Foreign Minister in preference to Paul Boncour. Although the British did not know it, Boncour had stood by his earlier assurances to Czechoslovakia.[22] He wrote himself out of the job; Daladier, convinced that Hitler was planning the destruction of Czechoslovakia at the risk of a futile war,* turned to Bonnet. The British were certainly not wrong to conclude that he was setting the stage for a defeat with honour in which the blame would fall on them – a repetition, in fact, of the Rhineland situation. Bonnet later told Bullitt that 'it was his conviction that the British Government would not go to war on behalf of Czechoslovakia', and Bullitt got the impression that Bonnet 'fiercely desires to avoid war at all costs'.[23]

On 27 April, soon after the Anglo-French talks had been arranged, Phipps reported that Bonnet was deeply worried that Germany intended to settle with Czechoslovakia 'this summer at the latest'. Bonnet feared that the deadline might be May and told Phipps that it was 'essential that Czechoslovakia should be discussed tomorrow, in London, fundamentally',[24] thereby justifying the British view that the French, at heart, wished to be freed of the incumbrance of their treaty obligations.

Before the French and British ministers met, for the first time in two years, the final disposition of the combined diplomatic and strategic policy was made at the long Cabinet meeting on 27 April. First, Halifax warned that the most dangerous element in the talks was that France would ask again for a precise statement about British reaction to German aggression in Czechoslovakia. It was essential that the vagueness of the declaration of 24 March should not be put to this test. Halifax intended to tell the French that there was no such thing as a limited war. War with Germany meant total war, for which neither Britain nor France was ready, which might last years and after which it would be impossible to re-establish Czechoslovakia. They must persuade Germany that she could not get away with aggression, but equally they must not sponsor Czech proposals for fear of humiliation if Hitler rejected them. 'That need not prevent us

---

* Daladier told William Bullitt that 'he considered the position of Czechoslovakia entirely hopeless since the annexation of Austria.' (9 May. *FRUS* (1938), vol. 1, p. 493.)

from saying to Germany that she could apparently get 60 per cent of what she required by negotiation and asking why she chose the risk of a European war in order to get 100 per cent.'[25]

However he might lay down the basis for the talks, Halifax could not cover every contingency and he did not deny that if the French asked them for army staff talks, it would be difficult to forbid it. Giving a promise that they would not overstep the two-division maximum for the field force, he and Chamberlain got Cabinet agreement to concede the point if necessary.* They were to make good capital out of this later.

The French came to London without demur. (Not until after Munich did British ministers go to Paris.) Chamberlain and Halifax held nearly all the cards at the joint meetings on 28 and 29 April. The French were desperate for staff talks in all three Services and the British knew it. For the British to concede was to give away the shadow only, because they knew how few armaments they had to offer. In return, they could demand not merely French consent to a joint démarche in Prague, but British leadership of the manoeuvre. The alternative for France was isolation, faced with a renascent Germany – the reality of the security nightmare which had haunted her since 1918.

When the discussions began at Downing Street on 28 April,[26] the British ministers played their cards carefully and won. Their opinion of the French ministers was low. Chamberlain thought Daladier 'simple and straightforward, though not perhaps so strong as his reputation', and he distrusted Bonnet, whom he had known since 1932. 'He is clever, dull, ambitious and an intriguer. The French are not very fortunate in their Foreign Secretaries.'[27] To begin with, Chamberlain, master of committee procedure, was able to manage the agenda so that the military aspect of joint co-operation was taken first – ensuring that the political debate was grounded on the British interpretation of military realities, and not, as Daladier wanted, on the premiss that the Sudeten claims were only one element in Hitler's march to *Weltmacht*. It was possible thus to deal with Czechoslovakia in isolation rather than embarking on a

---

* Simon and Winterton were much worried in case two divisions might be taken as a firm promise. Lord Maugham went further: he was anxious not to upset Germany by the despatch of the air mission to the United States or by any staff talks at all, in case Hitler was driven, as he said, 'too fast'.

debate about the merits of the grand alliance against Germany.

Chamberlain was able to make substantial political capital out of concessions. He began by outlining what the Cabinet had agreed to offer in the event of war – a naval blockade and air support, possibly two divisions not necessarily equipped for modern warfare, and air staff talks. Daladier angrily demanded staff talks for all the services and two mechanised divisions. Primed already, Chamberlain gave way with apparent ill-grace, as if it had been wrung from him: the military attachés might discuss the employment of the two divisions and, in principle, 'as opportunity offered', naval talks might also take place. At the same time, however, Halifax emphasised the military position: 'If the German Government determined to take hostile steps against the Czechoslovak state, it would be impossible . . . to prevent these steps from achieving immediate success.'

Daladier refused to accept this: Czechoslovakia possessed a reputable army which could be doubled by mobilisation; Russia might be able to overcome Polish and Hungarian objections to the passage of aircraft and bomb Germany direct. 'War could only be avoided', he went on, 'if the British and French made their determination quite clear to maintain the peace of Europe by respecting the rights and liberties of independent people'[28] – the firm stand which both countries had failed to make in March 1936 over the Rhineland. What, he asked, would Britain do if France joined her, forced Czechoslovakia to comply with Henlein's demands, and if, despite the surrender, Hitler still attacked? It was a shrewd, almost unavoidable thrust, and Chamberlain chose to ignore it, saying simply that he could not go beyond his statement of 24 March. Faced with this impenetrable oracle, the French had either to accept, or go home. Whatever they did would reveal their real interest in these talks as clearly as if they had laid their cards on the table. By staying, they gave way, and admitted tacitly that they could not face the isolation which the other alternative implied. Instead they asked how Britain proposed to coerce Czechoslovakia.

Halifax wanted to see Hitler and ask him to influence Henlein. Of those present only he seems to have felt confident in direct dealings with the Nazis. Neither Chamberlain nor the French liked the idea, and Daladier refused to take negotiations out of Czech hands. Chamberlain produced a compromise : Britain would explain that she was trying to find an answer through an Anglo-French approach, and would ask outright for Hitler's own proposals. At the same time, or as a second stage, a warning would be delivered: stating that if the negotiations failed, and if Germany then attacked, and France became involved, Britain could not guarantee to remain neutral.

The wording of this warning appeared to be sharper than the declaration of 24 March, but French acceptance left the control and timing of the approach to Germany and even the delivery of the warning entirely in British hands. Reporting the talks to the Cabinet on 4 May, Halifax made no secret of the fact that the French had given way on the points that mattered. Rather coyly, he disguised the extent of the disagreement during the negotiations. Chamberlain was much more explicit in private: 'Fortunately,' he told his sister, 'the papers have no hint of how near we came to a break over Czechoslovakia.'[29]

The Foreign Office transmitted instructions almost before the French had left London.[30] Nevile Henderson was told to see Ribbentrop, on his return with Hitler from Italy, to inform him that France and Britain were using their influence in Prague; that they hoped Germany would moderate the demands of the Sudeten Germans and work with the British who, without wishing to interfere, were doing their best in the service of peace in Europe. At the same time, he was to find what Germany really wanted, so that the Czechs might be pushed in the right direction.

Later the tempo quickened. A second message instructed Henderson to ask for an immediate interview with Goering, in case what Halifax called his 'notorious antipathy towards Britain' tempted him to reject the overture out of hand. But there was no mention at all of the warning which had been promised in the talks with the French and, to meet suspicions in Paris, Phipps was told to make it clear to Bonnet 'that the second stage has not, of course, been overlooked'.[31] Yet a month was to pass before it was given, and Halifax's hesitation was a conclusive moment of weakness in the British plan.

An excess of optimism may have been responsible. Halifax had been given an unduly rosy picture of what would be acceptable in Berlin by von Dirksen, the German Ambassador in London.[32] He had also discussed Czech concessions to the SDP with Jan Masaryk, the Czech Minister, who made the curious remark that his father Thomas, virtual founder of the Czech state, 'had never wished to have the Sudeten Germans in the Czechoslovak state, but they had been "forced on him by Mr Lloyd George" '.* This was treated with caution but it seemed to show that Beneš was ready to go a long way to meet Sudeten demands. Halifax outlined his policy to the Cabinet on 4 May:

His general line was to say to the Czechoslovak Government that they had got to go as long a way as they could to meet the Sudeten Deutsch and to remind the Germans that they too were required to make a settlement and that they must help. It would be very useful if the Germans would tell us at some time what would satisfy them. But we would have to be very careful to assume no responsibilities. At the end of the negotiations the position might be reached where they could say to the Germans that they could get say 75 per cent of what they wanted by peaceful means and urge on them the folly of risking war in order to get 100 per cent.[33]

Chamberlain added: 'much depended on our being able to establish good relations in this matter with Germany on a proper footing, so that we could use our good offices with them'. But this was an illusion; for the good relations which were to give Britain influence were in fact the aim, not the premise, of the whole plan to solve the Czech problem. The means were beginning to assume a greater significance than the end.

The response from Germany was sour and ill-omened. Goering was upset that staff talks had been arranged with France and he told Henderson roughly that he wished the Anglo-German naval agreement had never been signed. Henderson did not say that staff talks had been bargained in return for French acquiescence in the British plan, and for a while it seemed that the overture would simply be rejected. On 7 May (in Ribbentrop's absence) the Political Director of the Foreign Ministry replied tartly that the Sudeten German question was one of purely internal significance.

Worse news came from Prague, where Krofta, the Foreign Minister, rebutted Newton's bleak description of Western military inadequacy and Czech helplessness. Krofta believed that the SDP would never be content until they regained their position as 'masters in this country'.[34] He gave the impression that

* *DBFP*, series 3, vol. 1, pp. 235–8. At the Cabinet meeting on 4 May, Halifax said that he had consulted Lord Lothian, Lloyd George's Private Secretary in 1918, who denied what Masaryk said. Hankey also refuted it. (CAB 23/93.)

his Government would resist, relying on France and on their own innate strength, and that he did not care greatly whether Britain offered help or not. Nor could Newton find much support for the view that Henlein's Carlsbad programme represented the full SDP case: he had an interview with Eisenlohr, the German Minister in Prague, on 9 May:

> my intuitive impression from his general attitude was that the Sudeten German party might continue indefinitely to extract from the Czech Government the maximum concessions obtainable under whatever pressure could be applied and that then, however favourable the position achieved might be, they would feel perfectly free to secede and break up the Czechoslovak state, if it suited their purpose or that of the German Reich to do so.[35]

The Cabinet had to balance the fear that Henlein was only the front man for Nazi extremists against the very different reports from Henderson in Berlin. Henlein and Hitler, Henderson thought, were 'both moderate compared to many of their followers and Beneš' sole hope, in my opinion and in the interests of his country, is to make such a maximum offer that these two cannot well decline it'.[36] It was a judgement the Cabinet were singularly unfitted to make.

To judge by his letters early in May, Chamberlain was pleased enough with the progress of the British plan. He was not disturbed by Hitler's visit to Italy because he had expected him to dislike and try to undo the Anglo-Italian Agreement; as late as 15 May he expected no immediate trouble over Czechoslovakia and had heard nothing to upset his conclusions about Hitler and Mussolini.[37] Nevertheless, he realised that the favourable omens were unlikely to last; and he repeated his calculated indiscretion of 1936 at a meeting with a number of foreign journalists at Lady Astor's London house. Boldly he told a mainly American audience that Czechoslovakia could not continue in her existing form. 'Within adjusted boundaries', however, her integrity should be guaranteed by a Four Power Pact.* It is inconceivable, on any estimate of Chamberlain's character, that this action was not carefully calculated. By indirect publicity, he intended to undercut Czechoslovak pretensions, warning them of the ultimate fate if they delayed; and

---

* *New York Times*, 15 May. Chamberlain had not told Eden, the Foreign Secretary in 1936. He did not consult Halifax in 1938.

he indicated to Germany, in a way impossible through normal channels, that Britain was prepared to go the whole way in coercion. His words were the logical consequence of the policy adopted in March.

In his eagerness to cut down the time spent in bargaining, Chamberlain laid himself open to the charge of precipitately abandoning the Czechs. But, since Britain had no substantive hold over them, his speed can at least be understood. To the Germans, however, British actions were transparently contradictory. Newton was vigorously screwing on the pressure, while Henderson equivocated with the Nazi leaders in Berlin, in response to Halifax's instructions of 11 May – 'While we are emphasising in Prague the weakness of the military situation, we hope to make the German Government think long before doing anything likely to break the peace.'[38] As F. S. Northedge points out, this 'rested on the curious assumption that they could be kept separate'.[39] Ribbentrop was well aware of what Newton had said in Prague, because on his return from Italy he told Henderson that Hitler would be compelled very shortly to take action if the Czechs allowed things to drift.

Yet this did not really matter to Chamberlain. Henderson's report of his interview, with its advice to the Czechs to make 'a serious effort to compound with Germany while there is yet time', was not unwelcome in London. The inner group of British ministers agreed with Ribbentrop that the Carlsbad programme was fair. They had talked, even in March, of the Czechs' 'unforgivable treatment' of their minorities. They were content with Ribbentrop's statement that responsibility for the settlement should be left to Henlein, with the German Government standing guard for the Sudeten Germans. The right of self-determination, by plebiscite if necessary, had been discussed. Henderson's recommendation that the Sudeten provinces should be ceded to Germany,* though obviously unwelcome, did not go beyond the worst which Chamberlain had already envisaged. When Henderson said that 'far from resenting our interference, Herr von Ribbentrop not only welcomed it, but regards it as the

---

* 'The existence of a dissatisfied bloc of foreigners in a modern state is a liability rather than an asset ... in the case of Czechoslovakia, a small and defenceless country, the arguments for a composition are immeasurably stronger, even though her very weakness and our own responsibility for her creation make them the more distasteful.' (*DBFP*, series 3, vol. 1, pp. 296–7.)

only hope of [a] peaceful solution',[40] he was not so wilfully blind
as has frequently been made out.

Whether Ribbentrop really understood the underlying aims
of British policy is less certain. When Halifax tried to explain it
to Dirksen, who was much more favourable to Britain than the
Foreign Minister, Dirksen replied that Germany could not take
part in any negotiations in Prague, nor guarantee the outcome.[41] Still, British ministers had reason to hope that the
direct approach to Germany had been useful. They did not
demand more than that the German reply would be – 'Go ahead
if you wish: if you can bring Czechoslovakia to terms acceptable to us, well and good: if not, we will act ourselves.' But
Ribbentrop had not chosen to define what was acceptable; nor
would he put pressure on Henlein to moderate his demands.

The negotiations in Czechoslovakia had their own momentum,
markedly different from that of Anglo-German or Anglo-Czech
relations. In the six weeks since the meeting at which Henlein
had been appointed 'viceroy', Hitler had not precisely determined his plans and timetable for 'settling' the Czechoslovak
problem.[42] Henlein kept the level of SDP demands steady
through March and early April and even asked the German
Foreign Office to help lower the political temperature among
his over-eager supporters. The Carlsbad programme was an
advance on previous demands, but it did not ask for secession
nor any form of control by Germany itself. It was not regarded
as excessive by the British Foreign Office,[43] and Henlein's third
visit to London, on 12–13 May, was arranged by Vansittart and
Colonel Christie with Halifax's agreement.[44] Henlein met
Churchill and Sinclair and also Professor Lindemann and
impressed them all with his desire for compromise, preferably
in some form of provincial autonomy but, if not, through a
plebiscite for secession, conducted under British auspices.[45] After
a private dinner with him, Vansittart called Henlein 'a wise
and reasonable man', and minuted: 'we shall be helping both
Herr Henlein and ourselves by putting really strong pressure on
Berlin not to interfere with any acceptable solution.'[46] Not
even Christie, of the Secret Service, seems to have suspected how
close were Henlein's relations with the German leaders.

Masaryk 'professed himself content with a settlement on these
lines'.[47] Henlein had visited Hitler on his way but only if it is
assumed that he was simply Hitler's mouthpiece can the visit be

seen as a brilliant confidence trick. If he was free to play his hand largely as he chose, under Hitler's general authority, then he may have been speaking the truth.[48] His own position was insecure, and to keep the field clear of great powers on either side was the only way for him to bring off the coup in the negotiations with the Czech Government which would let him become Führer of an autonomous Sudetenland.

Unfortunately for the British, what was said in London bore no relation to the progress of the SDP – Czech Government talks in Prague. The Czech Government let it be known that the Carlsbad programme went well beyond what they were prepared, at that time, to concede. Newton reported that Krofta was obstinate and narrow-minded – 'the possibility of any reconstruction of the Constitution went beyond his range of vision'.[49] British influence was not yet so strong that Newton could freely obtain access to Hodza, the Slovak Prime Minister, who was the most sympathetic of Czechoslovak leaders to the German claims, nor to Beneš himself.

Even after the talks with France and the British démarche of 4 May, Newton made little impression in Prague. The Czech Government appeared to be pliant when talking to him, but firm elsewhere; and, in so far as he could judge, public opinion was stiffening against any further discussion with the SDP. On 13 May the Czech Government announced that it would negotiate with the SDP on the proposed Nationalities Statute, but this was followed by the formation of a Sudeten Defence Force, which at once began to take control in the German areas. In a series of gloomy reports in the third week of May, Newton pointed out that if the Czech police and troops imposed order too harshly after the anti-German incidents which were occurring frequently during the preparation for the local elections on 22 May, they might bring about intervention from Germany itself.[50] On 17 May a large number of leading Czech intellectuals had signed a manifesto calling on the people to maintain their unity and the tradition of democratic liberty.[51] Not for the first time there were rumours that if the politicians made concessions the Czech army might take over.

In these circumstances, Ribbentrop's warning that Hitler would shortly move against Czechoslovakia assumed quite a different aspect. Moreover, the British Government were becoming aware of a cold draught at their backs. General Hertzog,

Prime Minister of South Africa, had complained strongly that the Anglo-French talks and their results were 'most disappointing and disturbing and if persisted in, must spell disaster to Europe'.[52] At the time, Halifax tried to make light of this letter, but ministers were not to be allowed to forget that action with, or in support of, France was more likely to produce disunity than a coherent Imperial response.

Up to then, the Government had been optimistic. Foreign Office correspondence during the week after the eleventh indicated nothing unusual. Lord Perth and Henderson both indicated that Germany was not planning a surprise move. On 17 May Newton, after a three-hour talk with Beneš, professed himself reasonably confident of the Czech Government's readiness for concession in the next round of negotiations with the SDP. On the same day Chamberlain also wrote to his sister to say that the situation looked better, and Halifax told the Cabinet that at a meeting with the League Council a week earlier in Geneva Bonnet had told him, quite explicitly, that he wished Britain to put greater pressure on Czechoslovakia 'in order to save France from the cruel dilemma between dishonouring her agreement or becoming involved in war'.[53]

There was an illusion in London that a détente with Germany was about to begin. Yet, on 19 May, Henderson sent the first of several highly alarming reports of German troop-movements near the Bohemian border and in southern Austria, with a commentary predicting that immediate invasion would follow any incidents or bloodshed in the Sudeten areas.[54] The May crisis had begun.

What had caused it is still a matter for dispute among historians[55] and, in the absence of clear evidence of Hitler's plans in the vital days of 15–22 May, likely to remain so. The two most plausible versions are, first, that Henlein visited Hitler on 15 May and gave him a report of his London visit which emphasised the extent and value of British co-operation, the sympathetic attitude of the Government and political circles, and the willingness of France to apply pressure to the Czechs. Hitler was thus inspired to plan a lightning coup and order troop movements for the next weekend. This version derives substance from some German records,[56] but it has been suggested that Henlein did not actually visit Hitler until 22 May, after the crisis was over. If this is true, he may have been trying to retain his freedom of action. The creation of an autonomous German province within Czechoslovakia was obviously acceptable in London and Henlein believed (according to Masaryk) that an attempted coup by Germany would mean war with Britain and France whose outcome, either way, would exclude his own ambitions. If, on the one hand, he did not see Hitler until after the crisis, this could mean that he had deliberately avoided the meeting; or, if before, he may have tried to warn him and failed. Events in the Sudeten area were moving too fast for Henlein to control, with or without German assistance. The manifesto of the intellectuals had been timed carefully before the local elections due on 22 May, and had been followed by a crop of incidents and an increase in press attacks against Germany. Eisenlohr, whose judgement was shrewd, sent a warning on 13 May[57], shortly before Henlein's return, about the hysterical situation in which most Sudeten Germans hoped for, and expected, union with Germany. 'Hardly anyone thinks any longer of autonomy . . . almost the whole population hopes for the *Anschluss* with the German Reich and expects it in the immediate future . . . the mass are intoxicated by the overwhelming success in Austria; they will neither await nor accept any other form of political solution.' Although he guessed that the Anglo-French démarche had forced the Czech Government to accept the need for some compromise and given Hodza strength against 'his recalcitrant colleagues', Eisenlohr feared that the Sudeten Party could not guarantee discipline among its followers. 'It is no longer possible to calculate the full effects of the passions that have been let loose.'[58]

Eisenlohr was a conservative, like Weizsäcker and von Hassell, opposed to Hitler's wider ambitions. But in any case the May crisis was not the invasion as it had been tentatively sketched out by Hitler in March. Troop movements may have been ordered in response to Eisenlohr's warning, to keep the peace and prevent a premature outbreak like the abortive 1934 *putsch* in Austria. Hitler himself may possibly have been under pressure to satisfy the psychological needs both of the Sudeten Germans and his own army – as Nevile Henderson imagined: 'Extremists are pressing for an immediate show-down in the confident hope that Western powers will once more accept a *fait accompli*'[59] – a view with which, for once, Vansittart concurred.

The origin of the crisis is less relevant to this study than the British reaction. Knowing and suspecting nothing beforehand, the Government was sharply jolted and faced, unequivocally, with the reality of war. At once, they had to respond with the precise judgement appropriate to a situation where seconds mattered and the vague hopes and understandings of the previous six weeks were completely out of place. Henderson's report of the troop movements was confirmed by the consuls in Munich and Dresden,[60] though it was denied on 20 May by the German Foreign Ministry, and Keitel, Chief of Staff. On 21 May, Newton reported that the Czech Government believed the reports and had begun to mobilise.*

Seen from London, the crisis followed a pattern that was eventually flattering to British judgement. In his original alarmed warning of 19 May, Henderson had stated: 'in the event of a serious incident Sudeten appeal for intervention would be irresistible. There is, I beg you to believe, no bluff in announced intention of Germany to intervene in case of serious blood-shed.'[61] He saw Ribbentrop the next day, and a torrent of anti-Czech fury flowed over him. 'The Czechs', Ribbentrop swore, 'were mad and if they persisted in their present attitude they would be destroyed . . . Germany would not wait much longer and if provocation continued, her 75 millions would act as one man.' Henderson thought this 'extremely critical'. But in the middle of the tirade Ribbentrop included the phrase that 'the German Government appreciated the intentions of H.M.G.' – even though these efforts 'had led to no result whatever . . .'.[62]

The Foreign Policy Committee did not meet. The Foreign Office asked Henderson to check his facts, and Colonel MacFarlane and Major Strong went on a long motor-tour of Saxony and Silesia to inspect. They found no evidence of troop concentration. Vansittart advised firmness,[63] and Chamberlain and Halifax took the decision to send the warning promised as the second stage of the agreement with Daladier. They in-

* They actually decided to put into force the first stage permitted by the Czech Defence Act, the calling-up of one class of certain army specialists. In the prevailing atmosphere this amounted to mobilisation. Until the twentieth, the Czech Government had been waiting to start further negotiations with the SDP, but Henlein had already gone to Austria, for reasons which are still obscure. When he returned on the twenty-third, he refused to hold a meeting with the Government so long as the Sudeten German areas remained 'unprotected'.

structed Henderson to see Ribbentrop once more, on the afternoon of 21 May. At this meeting, Henderson formally regretted that the Sudeten Party was not willing to negotiate with the Czech Government and delivered the threat that if war broke out, and if France fulfilled her obligations, as expected, 'HMG could not guarantee that they would not be forced to become involved also'.[64] The Ambassador proved less impressive than his message; at first, Ribbentrop blustered about Czech provocation. Later, conscious of the unanimity of Henderson and François-Poncet, the French Ambassador, he changed his tone. Though he still refused to use his influence with Henlein, he went so far as to suggest that the British should use theirs with Beneš. Meanwhile Bonnet was telling a press conference in Paris that France would undoubtedly stand by her treaty obligations to Czechoslovakia if Germany attacked,[65] and in Moscow Litvinov reiterated Russia's full acceptance of her duty.

Belated though they were, these warnings and Halifax's chilly conversation with von Dirksen seemed to the British to have astounded Hitler and his colleagues.* But, once the bargain with France had been kept, and following hot on Henderson's previous instructions, came other messages from London virtually nullifying the effect. Henderson's own rather lurid report of what Ribbentrop had said was partly to blame.[66] On 22 May, Halifax told Newton to ask the Czech Government to minimise trouble. A similar order went to Henderson, with an admonition to utter no more than vague threats in the future. The French had already warned the Czech Minister in Paris of the serious way in which his country's mobilisation was regarded, *especially* because of the Czech failure to consult France first. Despite Bonnet's press statement, Halifax sent a prim note to Paris repeating most of the caveats of late March.

It is of utmost importance that the French Government should not be under any illusion as to the attitude of His Majesty's Government so far as it can be forecast at the moment, in the event of failure to bring about a peaceful settlement of the Czecho-slovak question. His Majesty's Government have given the most serious warnings to Berlin and these should have prospects of success in deterring German Government from any extreme courses.

---

* According to Henderson, Ribbentrop 'was clearly perturbed by the reference to the Prime Minister's speech on 24 Mar.' (*DBFP*, series 3, vol. 1, p. 335.)

But it might be highly dangerous if the French Government were to read more into those warnings than is justified by their terms.[67]

He asked particularly that the British Government should be consulted on any action France might take in the future. Halifax need not have worried: the French were just as keen to take what evasive action they could. The next day Daladier was to tell Welczeck, the German Ambassador in Paris, that 'speaking frankly as a French ex-service man' he feared a likely European war and 'the utter destruction of European civilization. Into the battle zones, devastated and denuded of men, Cossack and Mongol hordes would then pour, bringing to Europe a new "culture". This must be prevented, even if it entailed great sacrifices.'[68] Only three years after the Treaty of 1935, these were strange words to describe the Russian ally. French anxiety, however, was assuaged by information from Poland and Rumania that neither Russian troops nor air force would be allowed to pass over their territory.

There is no evidence to bear out a theory of tough collective action successfully wielded at the critical moment – save possibly on the part of Russia. As far as Britain went, what had occurred was that the warning, the almost automatic second stage of the plan agreed with France at the end of April, already delayed a month, had been put into effect, to stave off the immediate danger of war. The warning could hardly have been avoided any longer, but it was modified and disowned in practice by both parties as soon as possible, before its long-term effect could properly be judged. The intention had never been to bolster up what both Britain and France regarded as Czechoslovakia's temerity in mobilising – and very soon steps were taken to see that the action which had almost precipitated war should not occur again.

At first the Cabinet were inclined to hush up the whole affair. Halifax evolved an anodyne statement for the House of Commons and decided not to see the Czech Minister in case Germany might think that Prague was being given preferential treatment. He would not even intervene directly in Prague: 'to do so when we were under no obligations to come to Czechoslovakia's aid in the event of German aggression, might well put us in a false position'.[69] Czechoslovakia was not to have any moral satisfaction for her egregious folly.

However, over the next days, as the reaction to the May crisis within Germany became clear,* British ministers proved not unwilling to claim credit for the stand which they had not actually made. Two letters of Chamberlain show the change brought about after a single week of world-wide British popularity. On 22 May, he was utterly low. Opposition attacks in the House of Commons had rattled him and his first thought, he told his sister, was to hand over power – but there was no one to take over without 'undermining confidence'.[70] The German press, he complained, made no mention of 'our efforts' to induce the Czechs to meet the Sudeten Germans half-way.

The fact is that the Germans, who are bullies by nature, are too conscious of their strength and our weakness, and until we are as strong as they are, we shall always be kept in a state of chronic anxiety. What with the opposition... and the League of Nations Union, and other war-like pacifists, our task of keeping the peace isn't an easy, or an enviable one.

A week later, he viewed the crisis differently.

The more I hear about last weekend, the more I feel what a damned close run thing it was. It is all very well for the German press to make light of it in order to establish that British firmness had nothing to do with the crisis... but if that be so, why did Ribbentrop abuse Henderson for spreading reports? I cannot doubt in my own mind, 1. That the German Government made all preparations for a coup. 2. That in the end they decided, after getting our warning, that the risks were too great. 3. That the general view that this was just what had happened made them conscious that they had lost prestige, and 4. That they are ventilating their spite on us because they feel that we have got the credit for giving them a check... but the incident shows how utterly untrustworthy and dishonest the German Government is, and it illuminates the difficulties in the way of the peace-maker... one thing is very clear to us, though we can say nothing about it. The Anschluss and the Anglo-Italian Agreement together, have

* British Intelligence reported that troop movements in Germany were stopped on 22 May. MI5 attributed this climb-down at least partly to the Anglo-French warning. So did the War Office and the Foreign Office. (Pownall diary, 23 May; *The Ironside Diaries 1937–40*, ed. R. Macleod and Denis Kelly (London 1962) p. 57; *Diaries of Oliver Harvey*, p. 144.)

given the Rome–Berlin Axis a nasty jar and in our future continental and European policy we may hope for a good deal of
quiet help from Italy.[71]

This was the version impressed on the Cabinet, on 25 May,
when Halifax told them that the German Government was
resentful of comments in their own and the French press that the
crisis had been avoided by British diplomatic firmness. Ministers,
already conditioned to the convention that major decisions on
foreign affairs were taken by the inner group, were delighted.

The fact that this assumption was widely accepted is significant in the history of the formation of policy after the May
crisis. It helped to build up the belief that Britain had greater
strength and bargaining power than her actual military capacity
warranted. It boosted the illusion that diplomatic efforts alone
could be effective, without military backing, and it also added
to the political stature of Chamberlain and Halifax. When the
Prime Minister told the Cabinet, late in September, that it
was his earnest belief that he had personal influence with Hitler
and that Hitler trusted him, the Cabinet were ready to accept
his word, having seen it accredited in May.

What they did not, and could not then realise, was that
Hitler had abandoned any vestigial belief in British acquiescence
in his solution of the Czech question. His reaction is discussed
in Chapter 10; there is room for doubt just how firm was the
deadline for invasion of Czechoslovakia on 1 October, which
was set out in his directive of 30 May,[72] but it is certain that
British help in doing the job for him was no longer desirable.
Moreover, the British Government was only just beginning to
realise that the Czech problem had two aspects – not merely
the demands of the Sudeten minority, but the very existence
of the treaties with France and Russia. Was Hitler aiming
at a racial solution – inclusion of all Germans in the frontiers of
the Reich – or was he concerned with the strategic dangers of
'encirclement' and the territorial prize of the whole of Czechoslovakia?

After the May crisis, the British were placed in a wholly
false position, with far greater leeway to make up than before,
if the Government still intended to solve the Czech problem
without war. The old policy might have been reviewed once the
warning had been given; instead, the way in which the leader-

ship reacted served only to reinforce the illusory hopes current at the time of Henlein's visit. For two months thereafter, the British Cabinet, with no dissentient voices* and with France at their heels, was to march woodenly like a company of grenadiers further and further from a genuine appreciation of German strategy, into a position of its own creation, from which it seemed it could only withdraw at the price either of the war which it had declared intolerable from the beginning, or by complete subservience to German demands.

The balance sheet, two months after the *Anschluss,* was not encouraging. Admittedly, there was the constructive gain of the entente with Italy, although the agreement had not yet been put into effect. On the other side, lay the demoralisation of France – the real tragedy of the first stage of the British plan. French subservience was necessary for the plan to work, and by military and political pressure worthy of a better aim it was achieved. By the end of the May crisis, in spite of Russia's reaffirmation of the 1935 Treaty, France had, to all intents and purposes, reneged on both her Eastern European treaties. In the process, she had lost some of her influence in Czechoslovakia, revealed her mistrust of Russia and, in Bonnet's statement, with its evident fear of war, given a great hostage to the British. The British Government was not entirely to blame; Daladier and Bonnet had shown a defeatist side† and the majority of the French Cabinet followed their lead. Well before the crisis the right-wing French press were attacking the treaties and *Gringoire* printed the emotive headline, 'Veux-tu mourir pour la Tchécoslovaquie?' on 10 April.[73] France had devalued her European prestige. Yet these sacrifices had no value: she would have to face a continental war whether Britain sent military aid or not. In the cause of avoiding war, Britain had helped to weaken French morale so greatly that the risks of war were multiplied.

---

* In *Old Men Forget* (pp. 221–2) Duff Cooper claimed not to have believed in the Government's interpretation of the May crisis. The Cabinet minutes do not indicate any complaint at the time.

† Halifax met Bonnet and the French delegation at Geneva during the League debate on Ethiopia, in the third week of May. He derived the 'very definite impression . . . that they would welcome *any* pressure we put on Beneš to reach agreement and so avoid a head-on collision which would place France in the dilemma of fighting or dishonouring her signature'. (*Diaries of Oliver Harvey,* p. 142.)

9 The Hunting of the Snark

If the Czech Government had hoped, by their partial mobilisation, to create a favourable front among the signatories of the treaties, they were soon disillusioned. Believing that French and British tenacity had forced the Germans to climb down, the Czechs resisted pressure to come to terms with the Sudeten Party and refused to rescind the summons to the reservists. In contrast, the SDP appeared willing to resume the interrupted negotiations. Sympathy in the British Cabinet swung even further away from the Czech point of view. Aiming to reduce Czech obstinacy, and persuade a Germany now, as they hoped, more pliant, British ministers were predisposed to cast Beneš as the villain obstructing the peaceable, rational settlement which the rest of Europe desired.

This opinion was reinforced by Halifax's presentation of the situation and of his future plans to the Cabinet on 25 May. No radical rethinking was to take place.

If we had turned the first corner successfully we ought to be getting ready for the second.... The French Government were constantly talking of the dilemma in which they were placed between the risk of war and dishonour. The British view was that a war would be an unprofitable one, and that was the French view also.... The French engagement had been entered into many years ago in totally different circumstances, when Germany was still disarmed and they had, so to speak, a backdoor approach to Germany through the Rhineland. It was desirable, therefore, if possible, to obtain a release for the French from their obligations and its contingent consequences. If the present negotiations went well and a permanent settlement was reached, *cadit quaestio*. We could hardly dare hope, however, for that, and it was quite possible that things might become ugly again. It was true that a firm attitude on our part might conceivably be successful again, but if a really bad incident occurred and a number of lives were lost, there was the possibility of our finding ourselves in trouble.

He [Halifax] had been considering how the whole question could be liquidated. He did not think it was possible for His Majesty's Government to pledge themselves to support any particular solution of the Sudeten question in Czechoslovakia, ... They were not equipped with the necessary knowledge; and, in addition, such a pledge would bring us very near to a military commitment. Consequently, if at some point in the negotiations a strong demand should be made for a plebiscite, he doubted if it could well be resisted with sufficient support from public opinion here.[1]

Halifax realised that it would be damaging to Beneš if a plebiscite were granted as the result of German intimidation, and he suggested that Beneš should make the offer 'of his own free will', realising presumably, that no other offer was any use 'if large blocks of the citizens of the country were to remain discontented'.

Halifax's scheme was no more than the extension of what had been regarded in March as the worst of the available choices for Czechoslovakia. He had already discussed a plebiscite with Cadogan, Vansittart and Hoare and none of them had dissented.* Both Halifax and Chamberlain doubted whether any solution short of self-determination could provide a lasting answer. Nevertheless, the transition from an agreed policy of oblique interference to one of direct dictation was so swift and uncontested that it can only be explained by the fact that during the May crisis the Cabinet had looked into the pit. The danger of European war could not be allowed to recur, not from personal fear or dislike of what a later generation would call brinkmanship, and which they regarded as bluff, but because if Britain's bluff *was* called there was a real danger of losing the war which would inevitably follow. The effect of the May crisis, in spite of the initially favourable cast put upon it by British politicians, was to inspire them with even more urgent determination to come to terms with Germany and thus to sweep away the earlier stages of bargaining, so that they were reduced to final bids almost before the real game of bluff had begun.

The Sudeten problem was deliberately lumped together with the underlying strategic question. Without resolving whether the racial demands of the Sudeten Germans for inclusion in the Reich or the fear of encirclement as a strategic danger counted most with Germany, and without thinking of playing concessions

* *Diaries of Oliver Harvey*, p. 144. Foreign Office objections to a plebiscite were not formalised until the memorandum of 4 July (p. 245, below).

in one sphere against advantage in another, Britain proposed to throw her weight behind the self-determination of the Sudeten areas *and* the neutralisation of the Czechoslovak state. Halifax said that

> he did not feel that we could ask the French, Czechoslovak or Russian Governments to renounce their alliances; he would, however, like to see the Czechoslovak state move into a position of neutrality which, like the neutrality of Switzerland, would be witnessed by the big nations concerned. Under such a system the Alliances would automatically disappear.[2]

In practice, of course, independence for the Sudeten areas or their inclusion in Germany amounted to strategic neutralisation, in terms of Czechoslovakia's ability to resist aggression. An *equitable* settlement of a problem which had been critical for ninety years was impossible. (After Munich, there was still a German minority in Czechoslovakia, 377,830 strong, while 1,661,616 Czechs and Slovaks had been transferred to the Reich.[3]) Much more serious would be the economic result of transfer, however the Sudeten areas were determined.* The economic stranglehold which Germany would obtain would make Czechoslovakia politically dependent, whatever safeguards the Western powers obtained.

In itself, however, partition would not unravel the danger of a general war. The British Cabinet realised that, with possession of the Austrian frontier, and the proximity of Poland and Hungary, both looking for the 'return' of minority territory, Germany's means to reduce Czechoslovakia by economic pressure already existed.[4] They had no objection to peaceful penetration, only to an Austrian-style *Anschluss*, which would be resisted by force, leading to war. Unless the security treaties were nullified, this danger would remain. Even after Munich, Czechoslovakia retained the great Skoda armaments complex and a secondary ring of fortifications. Germany still feared Czech military capacity in October 1938: the German army was ordered to increase its hold over predominantly Czech areas where the main railway lines of Bohemia and Moravia ran, up until the signature of the border settlement on 20 November,[5] because the German High Command believed that in the event of war

---

* Luza, *Transfer of the Sudeten Germans*, pp. 163–4.

the Czechs could still raise an army of 750,000 men and an air force of 1,360 planes – enough to pin down twenty-five German divisions.* If the security treaties had survived after 1938, Russia would still legitimately have been able to bomb Berlin from Czech airfields, or France to invade the Rhineland. Adequately to appease German demands, the British had to do more than reduce Czechoslovakia to the status of Belgium (whose safety was still guaranteed by the Locarno powers although she could not come to the aid of the others); Luxemburg, a state with no foreign policy of its own at all, was the better example.[6]

The antipathy towards Beneš and the Czech Government which the British Cabinet showed more and more openly during the summer of 1938 had two causes. The British Cabinet simply did not know very much about Czechoslovakia – a fact which lends a certain poignancy to Chamberlain's famous utterance about 'a far-away country' and 'people of whom we know nothing'.† Successive British Ministers in Prague, especially Newton, had been hostile to what they thought were Czech pretensions to international status. Newton's reports in the previous year had sharpened British uneasiness about the stability of the Czech state. Within the Foreign Office itself, Vansittart was not so preoccupied with Germany that he excluded fair treatment of Czechoslovakia; but in his negotiations with Henlein (through the Secret Service) he seems to have been concerned primarily with reaching a quick solution. Hence his invitation, via Colonel Christie, to Henlein to visit Britain in May.‡ The Foreign Office objections to a plebiscite were not set out formally, for example, until early July, and this able document was

* *DGFP*, series D, vol. 4, p. 58 and n. No. 88 (pp. 109–10) indicates Hitler's continuing concern with the needs of the General Staff and desire to keep military communications open.

† As late as Apr 1938, Halifax relied on a Foreign Office memorandum of 8 Apr 1936, when giving the Cabinet information about the German minority problem – a document heavily slanted against the Czechoslovak Government on the grounds of oppression in land tenure, language, education, and internal politics. He blamed Czech policy for the fact that Henlein had turned to Hitler and took for granted that Henlein must be met half-way. 'Even the adoption of a liberal policy cannot guarantee the eventual survival of the Czech state, but it might, if effected soon, greatly improve its chances.' (R971/971/72, embodied in FP 36/62 CAB 27/623.)

‡ Christie was the principal Foreign Office contact with Henlein; but in June Ward Price, editor of the *Sunday Dispatch*, reported an interview with him to Vansittart.

never put to the Cabinet.[7] Among Cabinet ministers only Hoare, who was a friend of Masaryk, showed any real understanding of the difficulties facing the Czech Government. There is no question that the minorities in Czechoslovakia were well treated by middle European standards,[8] yet Hoare alone recognised the fact in the Cabinet debates – 'before the war no nation had treated their minorities worse than the Poles and since the war none worse than the Magyars'.[9] The almost complete absence of concern that the transfer of the Sudeten areas would jeopardise the economy of Czechoslovakia was partly caused by Cabinet ignorance about the distribution of industry and population.*

The second reason for British callousness was much more simple. Time, which had seemed sufficient in March, was short in June – and the Czechs were blamed for it. Henlein's claims had been seen as moderate and reasonable, when he visited London in May. Even before the May crisis, the British had been irritated by the Czech Government's delay in bringing forward legislation for minorities; afterwards, their refusal to reopen negotiations was taken for obstinacy or worse on the part of Beneš. The British had no real doubt, then or later, that, given the immovable attitude of Germany, the Czechs would concede in the end. The more that Beneš conceded grudgingly, the more the British assumed that he was hedging. By the late summer of 1938 they were no longer prepared to tolerate what they believed was his dangerous game of bluff.

Ignorance and arrogance on the part of the British Government combined to make the part odious to contemporary commentators. But they were genuinely uncertain about the very important estimate of how long the Czechs could withstand a German attack. The optimistic accounts from Brigadier Stronge, Military Attaché in Prague, of the high state of morale and the efficiency of Czechoslovak mobilisation during the May crisis were countered by MacFarlane from Berlin.[10] In March the Chiefs of Staff had hazarded a guess that the Czechs could resist for only two or three weeks.[11] Daladier suggested two to three months, confirming what Stronge believed; but then General Gamelin, French Chief of Staff, told Bullitt that the *Anschluss* had made any effective defence of Czechoslovakia

---

* An ignorance not shared, for example, by Churchill, who made the point very effectively in the debate on the Munich agreement (*Hansard*, 5th series, vol. 339, col. 365. 5 Oct).

impossible.[12] The margin of error was vast, yet it was a vital judgement to make because if the Germans could overrun the country in a matter of days France might have her excuse for not intervening, which would not suffice if the war dragged on. Not unnaturally the British were disposed to accept the shorter answer.

A plebiscite of the Sudeten areas offered them the easy way out. If Halifax's advice were taken, Beneš could make a grand gesture and free himself from the charge of surrender to German demands. The result would be clear-cut – the May elections had shown a ninety-per-cent vote for the SDP in the likely plebiscite areas. A plebiscite would give the colour of a democratic decision: the Saar, after all, had chosen to become German in 1935 under the auspices of the League and in pursuance of the Peace Treaty. It would achieve the compromise which the British believed possible: satisfaction of Germany, the SDP, and, provided some form of guarantee for the remainder of Czechoslovakia, involving modification of the treaties, could be evolved, the Czechs themselves. At this stage the details of how the voting would be held, and in which areas, worried them no more than the economic and strategic objections. The objections to a guarantee, to be expected from the Dominions and British public opinion, would be small in comparison. France would be freed from her distasteful obligations,* and the smashing of the Little Entente would leave her more dependent on Britain. Russia would be divorced from her only remaining link in Europe.

To prepare the ground, Halifax proposed to send William Strang, of the Central Department of the Foreign Office, to Prague at once to report directly on 'the atmosphere in that city'. He would return by way of Berlin. Strang's visit was a confession of ignorance but at least it was preferable to reliance on private sources such as Lord Lothian. 'In the meantime the Foreign Office would be examining the ideas of a plebiscite and of a system of neutrality.'[13]

There was only a short discussion in the Cabinet on 25 May, the gist of which was that Czech neutrality was desirable, but

---

* 'In reply to a question as to whether the French themselves had any idea as to how to escape from their dilemma, the Foreign Secretary said that they had communicated nothing to him. He thought that M. Bonnet would be glad of any suggestions,' (25 May, CAB 23/93.)

I

that a plebiscite would be difficult for the British public to swallow. Chamberlain was not ready to put his full weight behind a plebiscite – 'what he had been thinking of was, that the Sudeten Germans should remain in Czechoslovakia, but a contented people. If the Germans could be satisfied with the Czechoslovak state from the point of view of their foreign policy, it might be possible to get a settlement in Europe.'[14] How, he did not say.

Later on the twenty-fifth, Halifax saw Masaryk again and pressed him very hard, saying that the least price Czechoslovakia must pay was regional autonomy on the Swiss model; but although he advised the Czechs to consider taking up a position of neutrality he made no mention of a plebiscite. He had already seen Dirksen on the twenty-third in order to assure him that the Government was not being unduly partial towards Czecho-slovakia, and had asked him to help in restraining the German press from misinterpretations of British actions in the May crisis.[15] Fresh instructions were sent to Newton and Phipps and on 31 May something nearer to an ultimatum. Newton was to tell Beneš that the British Government considered he should accept the proposals put forward by the SDP on 30 May. This was tantamount to insisting on acceptance of the Carlsbad programme. Halifax thought that they 'commended themselves as reasonable here to persons of widely differing political thought and I think it of the highest importance that the Czech Govern-ment should accept them as a basis of discussion . . . [if not] there will be increasing danger of a serious and perhaps disastrous deterioration in the situation'.[16]

Concerned as they were with action arising from earlier plans, intensified by the May crisis, the Cabinet assumed that no radical change had taken place in other elements of the Czech situation. Lulled, perhaps, by the apparent willingness of the SDP to negotiate, and impressed by the forward thinking of the Foreign Secretary, they continued to imagine that, after a scare on a large but limited scale, and thanks largely to British firmness, Anglo-German relations had returned to the hopeful state of early May. Consequently, no real rethinking seemed necessary and none was asked for. They were not disturbed by the differ-ing advice from within the Foreign Office because Halifax sum-marised it in his own way; and there was nothing in the attitude of France, the United States or the Dominions to contradict

them (see Chapter 10). They were certainly not suspicious that
the terms of reference of their original decision in March had
altered, so that they now resembled explorers following a path
by means of a map which no longer covered the territory
which they had reached.

Thus self-satisfied, the Cabinet formalised the balance between
the armed services, and by perpetuating the defensive aspect
made any renewal of the spurious valour of the May crisis
almost inconceivable. In the process, occurred a resounding
political storm which, as in Eden's case, emphasised and defined
more clearly the lines of power in the Cabinet.

No open discord had shown between Chamberlain and Lord
Swinton up to May 1938, but the arguments over Schemes K
and L had been vigorous and the Prime Minister had not forgotten that the decision to go ahead with Scheme L represented
a substantial short-term victory for the Air Force over the
Treasury; nor that the Cadman Report had been damaging to
the Government as well as the Air Ministry. In the debate
announcing Scheme L in the Commons, Lord Winterton, the
junior Minister, made a lamentable showing and Chamberlain
decided that both he and Swinton should resign, on the ground
that not to have a Service minister in the House of Commons
was too great a liability. Swinton was bitterly hurt about his
enforced resignation, believing that he had been dismissed to
give Chamberlain unchallenged supremacy in the Cabinet.
Chamberlain saw it differently: he wrote that 'The whole affair
confirmed the view I had already come to, that when a Department is under such continuous bombardment as the Air Ministry
has been, it is impossible to maintain its position with the Head
in another place.'[17] He did not doubt that he had been right,
but there were other things at stake. Ormsby-Gore went also:
on his father's death, he had become Lord Harlech, but he
could easily have been retained in the House of Lords. There
were rumours that the promotion of Kingsley Wood to the Air
Ministry was only a preliminary to wider reconstruction and
The Times, apparently inspired, called for a broader base to
the Government.[18] True or not, the effect within the Cabinet
was as Swinton thought. Opposition was reduced by the loss of
two of its best spokesmen to Duff Cooper, Elliot, MacDonald
and Stanley. Kingsley Wood at no point in the next six months

raised his voice against the general tenor of Chamberlain's policy, and the air programme went quietly ahead. On 18 May the new Secretary of State was able to report to the Cabinet that the mission to the United States had ordered 200 reconnaissance and 200 Lockheed training aircraft. On 25 May, in a debate on the Air Force, Chamberlain categorically refused to set up a Ministry of Supply, with all that that implied in terms of good industrial relations, and no further disagreement over the air programme occurred until the end of January 1939.

The Admiralty and the War Office, however, did not accept the defence settlement of 6 April which had traded Scheme L for the field force. The extent of the Army's reduction may be seen in General Ironside's comments on 29 May on the decision to form six anti-aircraft divisions which, he said

> seals the fate of the Territorial Army, as an army able to go into the field...all our guns, money and energy will be expended in making these divisions.... We now have no army fit to send abroad to our foreign stations; we have swallowed up our reserve...never again shall we even contemplate a force for a foreign country. Our contribution is to be the navy and the RAF.[19]

The anger of the War Office Staff was impotent; they were compelled, on this basis, to carry through the staff talks with France, which dragged unsatisfactorily through May and June. Meanwhile, stubbornly reluctant to upset the tidy balance of the defence budget, ministers continually harped on the fact that no *actual* promise of a two-division field force existed. The analogy of the secret undertakings before 1914, and distrust about naval talks 'in preparation for war', were used as arguments against the field force, as the appalling difficulties of Anglo-French co-operation after so many years' neglect and mutual mistrust were revealed.

Yet gradually a certain entente emerged from the talks themselves. On 6 July Inskip asked diffidently that they should be extended to cover food supplies, oil, coal, non-ferrous metals and minerals, textiles, raw materials and shipping tonnage; provided of course that they were on the basis of a 'fairly hypothetical contingency that no commitments or agreements be entered into, and that no question arises of taking a final decision now on actions to be taken if the contingency materialises, which remains a matter solely for the Government of the day'.[20] Likewise, with infinite caution he wanted to inform the French that in a *given* situation they would be informed of British distribution of ships and that they would do likewise. But this was the limit: Duff Cooper, much more warily, thought that since it was much more likely that France would fight without us 'it would be desirable for them to make their normal arrangements on that basis'.

The Admiralty still regarded contingency planning with France as a danger to the Anglo-German Naval Treaty and to the future of Anglo-Italian co-operation in the Mediterranean (see above, page 222n). They did not, however, intend to let the growth of the Air Force pass without bidding for their own increases in capital ships. Unfortunately, as so often in the past, they had been relegated to the end of the line, and it was perhaps only the exhausted state of the War Office that gave some success to Duff Cooper's campaign. Stirred by the debate on financial assistance to China, with its corollary of trouble with Japan (page 257, below), in which Halifax quoted the American Ambassador's words – 'the British Empire has enough trouble on its hands without gratuitously taking on more'[21] – Cooper pressed for the New Standard. During the subsequent arguments with Simon, Inskip and Chamberlain, he became highly unpopular, but he did raise the basic question of the right balance between the military advisers and the Treasury. 'I suggest', he wrote in his diary, 'that the sensible plan must be to ascertain your needs for defence first, and then enquire as to your means of meeting them. If it is really the case that they cannot be met, then there must be some fundamental change of policy. . . .'[22] Although Simon persuaded him not to circulate a memorandum on the general subject to the Cabinet, he raised, in its most acute form, a debate on the principle of rationing the Services out of the agreed total, as against the prior determination of strategic need. Inskip sought to exclude the New Standard on a financial basis;[23] but Duff Cooper was able to reply that there was a £20 million budget surplus. To the discomfort of his audience, he also warned that, for the first time in history, Britain was numerically inferior in capital ships to Japan, and only just ahead of Germany. In their global strategy, the Admiralty were already depending on hypothetical French assistance, yet the Dominions had been promised, as recently as the Imperial

Conference of 1937, that Britain could send a fleet to the Far East. There had been no mention then of shortages or of rationing.

Despite some help from Hoare, a former First Lord, and Stanley, Duff Cooper made no ground against the Prime Minister on the principle of rationing. However, when that had been firmly restated, Duff Cooper was allowed, as a sop, to discuss with Inskip and Simon the total for the next five years. In the event, Duff Cooper and Inskip split the difference and settled on a basis of £410 million for the period up to 1942, which the Admiralty could divide as it chose. In accordance with Chamberlain's advice, no specific pledge of the New Standard was given. Afterwards, Duff Cooper recorded his satisfaction: 'my people thought they could just do with £405 million, but I succeeded in getting £410. The Controller and the others were very pleased.'[24]

The long-term result was to confirm for the Navy as well a purely defensive strategy against aggression by Germany and Japan – the British equivalent of the 'Maginot Line mentality' of France. Each Service had won something, for even the Army hoped to emerge at the end of its long tunnel remodelled, re-staffed and re-equipped. But none of these revisions were aimed at parity or deterrence, the goals of the mid-thirties. The principle of rationing took precedence over the claims of any single Service so that each gained only at another's expense. Chamberlain and the Treasury were prepared to make concessions, even if they involved slightly increasing the total figure, but they would in no way alter the over-all system, nor the style of foreign policy built upon it.

Like the dove sent out from the ark, William Strang returned bringing the hoped-for news from his breakneck visit to Prague and Berlin. On 1 June, Halifax relayed his report to the Cabinet. Strang thought that Germany did not want 'a surgical operation' if a decent settlement with Czechoslovakia could be obtained without one; but he confirmed Halifax's earlier deduction that Germany was now as keen to dissolve the treaties as to win autonomy for the Sudeten population; and Henderson, too, confirmed the strategic danger of Czechoslovakia 'thrust into the heart of Germany'.[25]

According to Foreign Office information the German army

was not ready for a European war and had advised the political leaders to be prudent. Germany was more aware of her own weakness than of Britain's. Vansittart had secret information that Henlein would stick to the Carlsbad proposals if he could get a quick settlement,[26] and Henderson and Newton had advised turning the screw on Hodza as well as Beneš. Drawing on the now canonised version of the May crisis, Halifax concluded: 'for the moment we have stopped the German aggression, but all depended on a Czech settlement'.[27]

The Cabinet was satisfied; the subject of Czechoslovakia did not come up again for a fortnight. During that time the Foreign Office carried on with activities designed at once to mollify the Germans and to force the Czechs to settle quickly. Following Halifax's somewhat desperate message on 31 May,* though not necessarily as the result of British pressure, the situation in Prague improved. The Sudeten leaders had already resumed negotiations and, during June and July, Sudeten claims increased and the Czechs, little by little, gave way.† The only worry in the Cabinet was that the French were not fulfilling their side of the bargain. Halifax was only barely satisfied with a report that Bonnet had warned the Czech Government that if they continued to be unreasonable France's interpretation of her Treaty obligations might change.[27a] Halifax kept watch and asked Phipps for precise information on what Bonnet was actually saying – a fair indication of the estimate in which the British Government held their potential 'ally'.

When the Cabinet next discussed Czechoslovakia, on 15 June, they were told that the Czech Government had accepted the Carlsbad programme as the basis for negotiation – Hodza had told Newton that he was making good progress among his colleagues and Masaryk had returned to London in an optimistic mood. Things were moving so well, it seemed, that Halifax did not see the need to try to prevent the Czech Government raising the requirement of military service from two to three years, despite the angry clamour of the German press.

* *DBFP*, series 3, vol. 1, p. 418. Newton was to warn the Czechs that if they did not accept the Carlsbad programme, their obstinacy would 'exercise an immediate and adverse effect upon the interest taken in the problem . . . and upon the sympathy felt for the Czechoslovak Government'.
† On 24 May Hodza met Henlein. Meanwhile, more extreme claims were being put forward by Dr E. Kundt, the chairman of the SDP parliamentary club in succession to K. H. Frank, one of the main negotiators on behalf of the SDP.

The negotiations were completely unreal. The British had no inkling that Kundt and Henlein were raising their demands always beyond the reach of the Czech Government; and in their ignorance, they transmitted the plan for neutralising Czechoslovakia to the French on 17 June.

By reducing what Germany professes to regard as provocative elements in the Czech system of treaties, [the plan would] tend to promote stability in Central Europe and lessen the chances of France being called upon to fulfil her obligations to Czechoslovakia in possibly unfavourable circumstances... The easiest and least disturbing course would be to invite Czechoslovakia to remodel her treaty relations—

so that Czechoslovakia would not be bound to assist Russia and France in the event of a German attack. Germany would undertake not to infringe Czech integrity but to assist Czechoslovakia if attacked, and Czechoslovakia would pledge herself not to use her territory for aggression against other states, as a passage or base of operations.[28] Bonnet was asked to suggest an alternative. His reply was most cautious: France promised nothing but to 'consider' the scheme – secrecy was essential; 'it would be disastrous if Germany were to hear of this plan'.[29]

Both the timing and the tone of the British note were dictated by the discussion in the Foreign Policy Committee on 16 June, where Halifax made it very clear that 'drastic modification' of the treaties 'was probably Germany's real objective'.* The Foreign Office had already prepared a draft scheme which had been sent for comment to Newton and Henderson the week before.[30] Once more, French activity was needed in Prague, and since the talks between France and Italy were on the point of breaking down, France was presumed to be in a psychological state suitable for treaty revision on a substantial scale. Halifax's memorandum[31] took it for granted that France would not be sorry to be relieved of her fears of carrying out an obligation assumed in the very different circumstances of 1925.

The analogy with the plans made for a colonial settlement in 1937 is obvious; constructive appeasement could go no further than for both Western powers to resolve all the possible

---

* 16 June, CAB 27/624; FP 36/63. Halifax's authority was derived from Newton, via Strang – another indication of how far the British minister in Prague influenced the Cabinet.

German demands in advance. There were two ways of proceeding: by 'guaranteed neutralisation' on the Swiss model (thus automatically debarring Czechoslovakia from treaty relationships with France and Russia) or, less drastic, by modification of the treaties, as had been done when Belgium withdrew from the Locarno Pact in 1936. Halifax evidently preferred the first, and thought it doubtful if Germany would be satisfied with less than the complete dissolution of any agreement which permitted the use of Czechoslovak territory for military purposes. Yet he had to admit that this would break up the remains of the Little Entente and would be difficult for France to accept. Vansittart, while accepting the second proposition, strongly objected to the first[32] and the Foreign Policy Committee took his advice, keeping the more radical scheme in reserve.

No one opposed Halifax's tactics, but the question of a guarantee to the future demilitarised Czech state was highly contentious. The Committee accepted that some form of security would have to replace what they had destroyed; but they were not keen to be saddled with an obligation carrying even the remote risk of action. Halifax stated that Britain could only take part in a joint guarantee: that is, one where each partner would act only if all the others did, and not in a several guarantee where each would be pledged to fulfil the obligations, regardless of the rest. With an eye to the House of Commons, Simon complained that Britain could have complete freedom of action to back out. Halifax's answer to the charge of 'window-dressing' – it would show that Britain 'was interested in Czechoslovakia' – was less than convincing.

During the drafting of the neutralisation plan, prepared with the legal expertise of the Foreign Office adviser, Sir William Malkin, it was by no means clear exactly what ministers wished for. They argued about the precise nature of the Belgian example and how the new scheme would operate if Germany attacked Russia, and Russia asked for a base on Czech territory.* Hoare spoke of 'neutrality within the League of Nations'

---

* Chamberlain wished Czechoslovakia's rights under the Covenant to be preserved. Halifax indicated that Czechoslovakia would not be able to offer bases to Russia under the new scheme, but would still be able to do so under the Covenant. What they wanted to avoid was an attack on Germany by Russia, where Russia could use Czech territory: the Committee believed that their scheme prevented this.

and, while accepting that Beneš should make 'the maximum concessions in such matters as local autonomy', he stuck at a plan which might so alienate France that she would simply stop trying to coerce the Czechs. Stanley also fought a rearguard action, pending unofficial soundings of French opinion. He was overborne by the flat assertion that Bonnet wished to be free of the encumbering treaty. Halifax, fearing the breakdown of negotiations in Czechoslovakia, wished to have the next stage of the plan ready for use at once. Later in the meeting, Halifax suggested that if the talks in Czechoslovakia did fail Britain should offer a mediator and he suggested two possible choices (neither of whose names are given in the minutes). This first mention of the mission, later to be led by Lord Runciman, was received without enthusiasm.

Until 10 August, when the French negative was received,* the Government remained in a state of serene anticipation. Although they were almost entirely dependent on French support for the neutralisation plan, no one was prepared to admit that if France actually abandoned her efforts in Prague the British could do nothing but sit idly by. Their optimism relied on the apparent submission of Daladier in April and on Halifax's well-justified faith in Bonnet's aversion to strong tactics. During June and July at least, neither assumption was seriously tested. On 18 June Chamberlain told his sister that the talks in Prague were going well. His mind had already jumped ahead to Spain: 'the mess we have got to clear up next...what I am after is to persuade the Italians to join with me in bringing about a truce'.[33] In spite of the fact that Ciano had flatly refused to resume talks with France or to consider an armistice in Spain, the Prime Minister believed that 'if only we could get an armistice, all this bombing of civilians and ships would cease, and what suffering and misery would be saved'.[34] It fitted the guiding assumption of his political philosophy that men would rather be unfree and alive than free but tormented or dead.

June was a more constructive month for new ideas in British foreign policy than any since the end of 1937. Chamberlain could write – foreshadowing his remark before the German invasion of Norway in 1940 – 'They [the Germans] have missed

* *DBFP*, series 3, vol. 2, pp. 71–4. Bonnet replied that such a plan was inopportune. Until then, French acquiescence had been assumed.

the bus and may never again have such a favourable chance of asserting their domination over Central and Eastern Europe.'[35] Faith in the accepted version of the May crisis was undiminished, and the initiatives that flourished for a while point to how far senior British ministers believed they still held freedom of action and influence, just as the period of gloom which followed exposed their real limitations.

The attractive illusions grew out of belated attempts to replace military power by economic penetration. In May, the Government made an £18 million loan to Turkey for the purchase of warships, as Chamberlain said, to bind Turkey morally to Britain: 'the first time we have ever used our financial resources for political purposes' – Germany 'would be frantic if they knew what we were thinking about next!'[36] Later he quoted the judgement of the British Ambassador in Istanbul, Sir Percy Lorraine, that Turkey 'was in our pocket'.[37] Since Halifax was encouraging the Foreign Policy Committee to do the same for Greece, for a moment any member with a knowledge of the 1920s must have reflected that the British Government was aspiring to assume the role played by Sir Basil Zaharoff, who sold arms indiscriminately to both inveterate enemies of the Near East.

At the same time the British watched the Far East. But an attempt to prop up the failing regime of Chiang Kai-shek against the Japanese advance and at the same time safeguard the wide British trading empire based on the foreign concessions in China, was open to enormous objection. The Admiralty feared, as they had done during the Shanghai crisis of 1932, a war against Japan in which Britain might lose both Hong Kong and Singapore. A scheme for a loan of £20 million to the Kuomintang Government was finally put forward early in July by Halifax.[38] Opinion divided evenly. Some of the Cabinet were well aware of the value of British trade and the appeal of economic rather than military aid to China. Others, including Simon, pointed to the dangerous situation in Europe, the Chiefs of Staff warning against war on two fronts, and the likelihood that the loan was only the first of many, in an open-ended commitment. Chamberlain finally decided that the loan would be construed as intervention, and might encourage Germany to take Czechoslovakia while Britain was occupied elsewhere. Halifax dutifully withdrew the plan. It was unfortunate for the British that once more Russia, who was supplying China with munitions, appeared as champion of the free world against aggression.

The third of these plans was the most interesting. Early in May, under the auspices of Sir Maurice Ingram, counsellor in the Foreign Office, and R. H. Hudson, junior minister at the Board of Trade, in charge of the Department of Overseas Trade, a scheme was worked out for British economic penetration in south-eastern Europe as a counter to German political and economic aggression. Halifax presented a paper to the Foreign Policy Committee on 2 June and left no doubt that he supported enthusiastically a plan which in principle represented a substantial divergence from earlier British policy in the Balkans.[39]

Halifax wanted a political not an economic evaluation:

> we were now confronted with a probability that German influence had penetrated throughout the whole of Central and South-Eastern Europe in the economic sphere, leading to the likelihood of Germany dominating this great area in the political sphere. It seemed most desirable in the interests of the preservation of European peace that an attempt should be made to check this process before it was too late, and that if this could be done our own position would itself be greatly strengthened.[40]

This would also depress those 'extremist elements' in Germany and lessen the dangers of a general war.

The problem might be stated as a political tug-of-war between Germany and the smaller countries on her Eastern and South-Eastern frontiers, and the object of his Memorandum was to show that we might add an extra man to the small countries' team by throwing into the scale the great political and economic strength and resources of Britain.

Halifax contended that German domination went beyond economic and political factors, into the sphere of culture and language. The defunct Danubian Federation of the early 1930s might serve as a model for a Zollverein or customs union. He was, perhaps, not entirely wrong to see it as a question of morale: 'unless we could in some way provide these small countries with an alternative *point d'appui* for them to look up to, they would undoubtedly drift into Germany's orbit'. After all, Chamberlain had made the same point about Turkey. According to MacDonald: 'As a result of political and diplomatic activity, we had succeeded in convincing Turkey that we were a great and powerful nation, able and willing to throw our weight and resources into the balance against Germany. In his opinion the more that we could do in directions such as this, the better.' Yet all of them had agreed, only two months earlier, that Germany could have a puppet Nazi government in Rumania whenever she wished.

The debate is of interest because it shows how the Inner Cabinet envisaged British influence at work, and the freedom of action which they thought they still had. Their grasp of the economic and political realities of the Balkans contrasts oddly with the *simpliste* view of Czechoslovakia. In a less urgent case, the expertise of the departments was allowed full scope. But the scheme opened up old political divisions in the Cabinet, going back to the 1920s, as the principle of Government intervention in the free market came under fire, and as the strange alliance of Foreign Office and Board of Trade faced the Treasury. Simon, the Chancellor, thought that the Balkan states feared German supremacy, but doubted whether economic assistance alone could do much to prevent political change. Stanley, President of the Board of Trade, admitted that if Germany were already in the field she would be hard to outbid, but argued that even a small number of reciprocal trade agreements would encourage a spirit of independence. Chamberlain was in a dilemma. Accepting East European imports at favourable rates ran counter to his financial principles, to say nothing of the hostility the Dominions were bound to show; he was sceptical of Britain's capacity, yet the political implications, where they could be separated from mere fantasy, obviously appealed to him.

The details proved to be the sticking-point. Imports of meat from Hungary, for example, would be opposed by the Ministry of Agriculture because of the political and economic effect on Britain. Chamberlain mentioned Balkan tobacco: to accept imports up to two per cent of the British total would be a useful gambit; but would 'the man in the street' ever smoke it?* Only a rich and powerful country could accept such losses without a balancing margin elsewhere. The nub of the argument was

---

* Halifax cited the case of Rhodesian tobacco, which the public had duly accepted. But then, Chamberlain replied, the manufacturers had realised that it was in their commercial interest to advertise it. Balkan tobacco would reduce the supply from Rhodesia.

the price the Government was prepared to pay for buying not in the cheapest but politically the most advantageous market, and whether, as Stanley claimed, the psychological value was sufficient. R. H. Hudson explained that all the schemes were impracticable on a purely budgetary basis; the Cabinet would have to override the financial, political or public objections. He read out the notes of a talk with Giannini, Head of the Economic Department of the Italian Foreign Office,* which indicated that Italy also wanted to counter the influence of Germany in Yugoslavia and Hungary; and he suggested the use of such agencies as the Government Supply Organisation, or the Export Credits Guarantee Department.†

Chamberlain was cool but not hostile to the idea of playing Germany's own game. In spite of Simon's unwillingness to undermine the basis of ECGD, Stanley's request for a permanent department on the lines of the 1918 Economic Offensive Committee had its effect and, although Chamberlain imposed a series of safeguards restricting the freedom of the original scheme, he allowed the setting-up of an interdepartmental group under the ubiquitous Sir Frederick Leith-Ross, which was later given the title of Economic Pressure on Germany Committee.[41]

With time, it was to do effective work. Even in 1938 it had sufficient power, after its first meeting, to ask for and win increased power to initiate schemes where export credits were involved. But it came far too late in the day to help the Czechoslovak policy of a Government which had shown in all the defence debates that it would not consider dramatic but expensive essays in unorthodox external policy. The scheme would have represented a substantial break with earlier British commercial and foreign policy. Ten years before, perhaps even in 1934, economic penetration might have been a substantial help in building up the Little Entente; but British policy then

* Ingram had recently returned from seven years' service as commercial attaché in Rome.

† The ECGD had arranged to give credits to Poland to the limit thought safe and justified, within their terms of reference, by the Treasury. Poland wanted more, for the renewal of the braking system of the state railways, the establishment of an electricity grid and the withdrawal of munitions factories from near the German border. If the Supply Organisation could place armaments orders in Poland, Hudson suggested, the ECGD might be able to extend the credits. Similar work could be done in Yugoslavia and Bulgaria.

had had no use for any commitment east of the Rhineland. In 1938, Britain started with too many handicaps.

During the discussion, Chamberlain allowed himself to speculate on whether, as Germany grew stronger and more stable, she might not become more peaceable. 'Might not a great improvement in Germany's economic situation, result in her becoming quieter and less interested in political adventures?' Why then oppose her drive towards south-east Europe? The logical progression of such a view was to permit or ignore the claim for *lebensraum*, or to argue that if Britain did intervene the result would be a struggle for mastery between the great powers of the West, followed by the eruption of Bolshevism in a defeated Germany. Just as Daladier feared 'the Cossack and Mongol hordes', so Chamberlain remembered the Communist disturbances in Germany in 1918.

These activities were stimulating, yet none of the plans had had the required effect. In June, therefore, the Government attempted to consummate the Anglo-Italian Agreement. Italy showed not the slightest sign of compliance with the conditions laid down publicly; so on 16 June Chamberlain put forward a new formula, weakening Eden's line on the withdrawal of troops from Spain:

If an armistice could be arranged with the reasonable prospect of its leading to the establishment of peace, and with appropriate guarantees against the entry of supplies and men and material to either side during its continuance, and if therefore the Italian Government were to withdraw a substantial part of their troops and material from Spain, then H.M.G. would be prepared to regard that as a settlement of the Spanish question.

Reliance on words such as 'reasonable', 'appropriate' and 'substantial', could mean that in a different, more urgent situation, reinterpretation might rob the definition of its meaning. Time was short. On 22 June Halifax warned that completion could not wait on resumption of talks between France and Italy. Yet Britain had no means to coerce Italy: only two days later, as Chamberlain faced an angry House of Commons, he had to admit that there was no way to prevent the bombing and sinking of ships by Franco's Nationalist forces – aided by Italian aircraft – except by war. Privately, he wrote that that would mean war with both Germany and Italy, and the throwing-away, merely for the sake of Spain, of what he called his 'great influence' on the Continent.[42]

This frustrating position was sharply emphasised on 6 July by an exceedingly rude letter from Mussolini himself, complaining that Italy had carried out her part of the bargain but that Britain had not. The Foreign Office put the blame on Italian irritation at their slow military progress in Spain, and saw the letter as an attempt to split Britain from France. Explaining the reversal did not help, and Chamberlain wrote gloomily on 9 July: 'Mussolini is behaving just like a spoilt child, and it is difficult to know how to deal with him.'[43] There were graver signs for the Government's Italian policy. Mussolini had sent 2,000 volunteers to Spain in June, twice the usual monthly supply, and the same number followed in July. Whatever the feelings of that imponderable mass, the Italian people, whom Chamberlain imagined to be delighted with the Anglo-Italian Agreement,[44] Mussolini showed no signs of grace and neither he nor Ciano had any intention of surrendering what they had gained in Spain.* The British made no further overtures to Italy until the last stages of the September crisis.

Meanwhile, so Newton reported, Beneš had promised to bring in a new programme of reform in mid-July. Yet Halifax told the Cabinet on 22 June that he had secret information that the Czech Government was holding back and that the Slovak Prime Minister, Hodza, who was keener than Beneš to settle quickly at the expense of Bohemia, was disappointed. Halifax offered to see Masaryk once more and tighten the screw again. He already had 'a wise British subject available to slip off to continental Europe to try and get the parties together again'.[45] See-sawing between partly good and faintly ominous, the news for the next four weeks was never distinct enough either way for the senior ministers to think it necessary to recapitulate and reassess their strategy. Pressure on Prague, fair words in Berlin, blunt talk in Paris; the pattern did not alter, although in the Foreign Office a debate took place on the preconditions and

---

* *Ciano's Diary 1937–38*, p. 130, 22 June 1938 – '[Mussolini] absolutely refuses to compromise [on Spain] – we shall not modify our policy towards Franco in the slightest degree and the agreement with London will come into force when God pleases. If indeed it ever will.'

timing of the mediating mission which was regarded as a most likely development.

No Government can react to all shifts of opinion as they appear through the opaque medium of diplomatic prose. No one had yet suggested that the whole plan, as conceived in March, had gone wrong. Yet, secure in their illusions, the Government abandoned self-analysis. The Foreign Policy Committee met for the last time on 16 June,* before being replaced, in practice, by the inner group of four – Chamberlain, Halifax, Simon and Hoare. For the rest of the Cabinet, the complicated, partial and contradictory nature of the information was simplified and reduced to a pattern. It is not, of course, the business of other ministers to run the Foreign Office, and the Foreign Secretary must process the diplomatic advice and information for their benefit. Nevertheless, in the early summer the majority of the Government was given an unduly coherent and optimistic view of the European situation. If the conflicting nature of the reports which Halifax received had been appreciated, some demand for a general debate might have been heard before the end of August.

During the diplomatic manoeuvres of June and July, the grievances of the Sudeten Germans took priority. Newton's despatches confirmed the impression that both sides in Czechoslovakia, though 'fundamentally opposed',[46] were taking seriously the points at issue in the Carlsbad programme rather than making new extreme demands.

On 30 June, Halifax explained to the Cabinet that, as Hitler was not likely to insist on a plebiscite, and would accept a settlement if Henlein could reach one, Britain would probably have to take a hand by 'congratulating both sides on the concessions they had made and then leading them on to a final settlement'. A week later, more convinced that a mediator would be needed, he suggested that, in case the Czechs rejected the mission, it would be necessary to present it in some form of disguise. At that time the Foreign Office did not believe that the comprehensive statute projected by the Czechs would satisfy Henlein, let alone the German Government; but the thinking behind the Runciman mission was, nevertheless, based on the assump-

* It did not reconvene until after Munich.

tion that negotiation was acceptable and a compromise possible. There was no suspicion in London that Hitler would run the risk of war.

Disillusion struck deeply in mid-July. On top of the trouble with Italy, came the rejection of Hodza's proposed reforms by his own Cabinet on 14 July. After the prolonged game of blind-man's buff, the weeks of waiting and patient pressure on the Czechs seemed to have been wholly wasted and to have revealed nakedly the limits of British and French power in central Europe. The setback seemed to justify the forward planning of the Cabinet for neutralising Czechoslovakia, and their preparation of the way for a mediator. All the information in the week after-wards suggested that only in these ways could the Czech problem be settled, before the Nazi Party Rally at Nuremberg on 12 September, when Hitler's oratory, combined with the end of the harvest, might set the stage for a violent solution instead.

Otherwise, the Czechs themselves might precipitate the crisis. After a long conversation with Beneš on 16 July, Newton reported that the Government was so deeply divided that it was unlikely to be able to come to terms with the Sudeten leaders in the future; instead, united only on the points agreed with the SDP in June, it might decide to introduce the original Minorities Statute without further consultation – a course of action which Halifax had already condemned in outspoken terms.[47]

Even worse, the news from Germany in mid-July suggested that steady mobilisation was going on. Strang believed Hitler intended military action in the autumn, and Vansittart agreed.[48] They feared Germany was about to drive a wedge between Britain and France. 'Germany . . . does not think it should wait any longer. . . . It may find itself unable to counter the increased economic influence [sic] of Britain and France in Hungary and the Balkans.' Other information, from German sources, showed that all road-building had stopped, except on the French and Bohemian frontiers. The West Wall was to be completed by 1 November and Hitler had given orders to prevent repetition of the breakdown of army mobility at the time of the Anschluss.[49]

Yet at this point, too close for coincidence, the German Government suddenly took advantage of the offer held out by the British since the May crisis. The overture came a roundabout way, through Hoare's brother, Oliver, and Lady Snowden: 'neither exactly the go-betweens one would choose,' Harvey commented.[50] Neurath was believed to be in the secret, but not Ribbentrop. The affair therefore appeared to be 'safe'. On 16 July Chamberlain wrote to his sister: 'Word came to us through unofficial channels that Hitler wanted to know what we should say if he were to send over one of his "top men" for unofficial conversations. We made an equally cautious, but friendly, reply and an emissary is coming over tomorrow.'[51]

The emissary was Captain Wiedemann, Hitler's ADC. Through Princess Hohenlohe, a known sympathiser, it was arranged that he should meet Halifax and Cadogan on 18 July. 'What this means', Chamberlain wrote, 'I don't know but this is the most encouraging news from Berlin that I have heard of yet and I hope signifies that at any rate they mean to behave respectably for the present.' Optimistically, he speculated on whether Hitler meant to steal a march on 'his dear ally' Italy.[52]

The Wiedemann visit was a probe, designed to test the strength of the entente with France, but the British understood it differently. Chamberlain imagined Hitler had realised at last (as he had so signally failed to do before the *Anschluss*) that he had everything to gain by peaceful means. Obsessed by the importance which they themselves put on their plan, British ministers supposed that Germany now realised the great advantages offered if their chestnuts were taken for them from the fire.

The ostensible reason for the visit, Chamberlain told the Cabinet on 20 July, was that Hitler wished to send Goering to London for talks on the whole range of Anglo-German relations. Wiedemann was merely to prepare the way. It seems likely that the visit would have taken place in total secrecy, but Wiedemann was seen at the airport and the *Daily Herald* gave an account which Chamberlain called 'misleading'* – the Cabinet was therefore given the information which otherwise they might not have had.

Wiedemann saw Halifax at his house on 18 July and assured him that the German Government was not going to attack Czechoslovakia 'in present circumstances' but that such a pledge could not be binding 'for all time'.[53] It was not so much the

---

* Chamberlain letters, 24 July. Chamberlain was furious that the visit had been discovered by the Press.

assurances – which he judged might be valid for at most a year – as the motive behind the visit which interested Chamberlain, who concluded: 'probably H.M.G. would have to intervene in some way; if Germany was in the mood depicted, it was possible that their Government might accept'.[54]

Under this impression of Germany rather than the belligerent one depicted by the Foreign Office, Chamberlain and Halifax put the next stage of their plan into operation. They had been waiting for something like Wiedemann's visit to send their mediator on the road to Prague.* Halifax accompanied the King and Queen on 19 July on a state visit to Paris, which was intended publicly to demonstrate, and privately to re-create Anglo-French solidarity. He met Bonnet and Daladier and explained the theme of the mission, which Lord Runciman had rather unenthusiastically agreed to lead. Less hopes were put on the scheme in Paris than the two ministers professed at home. Halifax suggested merely that the British Government's responsibility 'would begin and end with finding [Runciman] and turning him loose in Prague to make the best he could of the business'.[55] What precisely the French imagined could come of so vague a mission, they did not reveal. Halifax reminded them, yet again, of Dominion reluctance to co-operate with Britain in any guarantee to France. Presumably the French were glad of anything which gave substance to the shadow of the entente. They welcomed the British initiative and promised to support it in Prague.

At first the Czech Government rebelled. Beneš had not been warned of what was coming and was shocked by what, with justification, he called a direct infringement of Czech sovereignty.[56] Hodza complained that the dispatch of the mission reduced the legitimate Government to the level of the Sudeten Party; yet, under continuous pressure, he agreed to lay the matter before the Czech Cabinet. There, after two days, and with a reluctance overborne by pressure amounting to threats, the mission was conceded, with sufficient ambiguity to allow the British Government to claim that the Czechs had actually requested it. Chamberlain was able to make an announcement in the House of Commons on 26 July, stating

* Sir Horace Wilson prepared a short list of possible names on 22 June: Runciman, H. A. L. Fisher, Lord Macmillan, Lord Riverdale and Sir Norman Raeburn (PREM 1/265).

that Runciman would impress the world with the true facts of the minority claims and produce a climate of opinion ready for a solution: 'issues which have hitherto appeared intractable may prove under the influence of such a mediator to be less obstinate than we have thought'.[57]

The underlying purpose was set out in Halifax's instructions to Henderson. 'You will see ... that the Czech Government accept the idea ... [of Runciman] acting independently of H.M.G. to elaborate proposals that might harmonise the views of the Czech Government and the Sudeten Party. ... It will be less difficult for the Czech Government to collaborate on these lines, if it can be represented that initiative in proposal had been theirs – and that H.M.G. had acceded to it.'[58] Henderson was to urge the German Government to bless the scheme and induce the Sudeten Party to accept it.

The mission had a second, less clearly stated purpose. If the situation required, at some future date, Runciman's report could serve as the next line of defence against total breakdown. He could produce a scheme which the British Government might sponsor, and then, with German acquiescence, impose directly on the Czech Government as a reasonable and rational solution.* Otherwise, something so naïve, even absurd, as sending Runciman with his diminutive delegation – four officials including Ashton-Gwatkin, of the Foreign Office Central Department – could hardly be taken seriously. Henderson's reply gives colour to this interpretation. He had no faith in the mission as a mediating factor, because he did not believe that Henlein would accept any report recommending only reform within the Czech state; but he saw it as a means of bringing yet more pressure to bear on what he called the 'pig-headed race' and on Beneš, 'not the least pigheaded among them'.[59]

Significantly, in his next speech in the House of Lords, Halifax did not repeat the warnings of 24 March or 21 May, but instead appealed to Germany: 'since we are pressing the Czech Government to be generous and conciliatory, we confidently count on Germany to give similar advice where she may, with a view to avoiding a deadlock, the consequences of which might be in-

---

* See, for example, L. Creswell's minute, with the phrase 'we would leave them to their fate if they do not accept the Runciman proposals' (C8520/1941/18 (FO 371/21732)).

calculable'.[60] Even if the assumptions about Wiedemann's visit had been correct, this was much weaker stuff than before.

The last Cabinet meeting for five weeks took place on 27 July. Chamberlain was perceptibly overtired after a hard parliamentary session and the abrupt way in which he and Halifax presented the Runciman mission to the Cabinet as a *fait accompli* indicates a lapse in his normally confident touch. This was surely the time to bring his colleagues up to date with the doubts and complexities behind the decision to send the mission; but it was allowed to pass. Halifax told them simply but inaccurately that, on his return from France, he had sent a telegram to Prague, suggesting a British mediator, and that this had been accepted. He denied that the mission had an official brief and he quoted Runciman's own phrase: 'the Government were pushing me out in a dinghy in mid-Atlantic'.[61] None of these statements was entirely true and they encouraged a quite unjustified sense of euphoria about the reaction of the Czech Government. No doubt the two leaders wanted to keep their freedom of action, even if necessary to disavow Runciman altogether, but they were responsible for leaving their colleagues largely ignorant and out of touch until the serious shocks of late August began to undermine the consensus of opinion which had, until then, given strength to the plans of the inner group.

It is more surprising that no one at that meeting questioned the terms of reference of the Runciman mission. What could they expect to achieve? Perhaps the Cabinet believed that Czechoslovakia *had* actually requested the mission, and that both sides would listen to the force of reason, as in the nineteenth century Queen Victoria was sometimes asked to arbitrate frontier disputes. Perhaps they trusted in residual prestige to ensure that, Britain having once taken the matter in hand, all the conflicting forces would stand still while the rule of reason produced a solution acceptable to all sides. Did Halifax consider whether his appeals to Ciano and Ribbentrop for a sympathetic response were likely to draw more than their contempt? It seems unlikely.*

Runciman left for Prague on 2 August, but the German

---

* He assured the Cabinet that Kundt was in favour of the mission and he added that some of his Foreign Office advisers [i.e. Vansittart and Sargent] had revised their gloomy forecasts and now believed that the 'war party' in Germany had been checked again, as in the May crisis.

Government showed no sign of interest in his mission. Weizsäcker had already complained that the news had been leaked to the press before Henderson had told the German Foreign Office – and was not in the least mollified by the apology sent by Halifax on 28 July.[62] British policy was forced to proceed in the dark and throughout early August there was no certainty of either the German or Czech reaction. Hitler's actions were more than usually obscure. One face seemed responsive to the British efforts; the other menaced Czechoslovakia sufficiently to convince the Western peace-makers that each chance was the last chance, each concession the only means to avoid war. His real preoccupations were quite unrelated to the efforts of the Runciman mission (see below, page 301).

Runciman set to work as if the Sudeten problem was an intractable dispute between employers and trade unions. At first, days went by simply in acquiring information and meeting the leaders of both sides. Then as each proposal was marketed around, its attractions melted away. The golden mean, like the pursuit of the rainbow's end, was always just out of his reach. If there had been no limit to the debate, he might have found an answer, but not in August 1938, when Henlein's power to restrain his impatient party was gradually slipping away. Henlein and Frank were received together by Hitler on 31 July. Already Henlein was spouting the crudest Pan-Germanism and when Hitler ordered Frank to 'hold out and wait' on 1 August Henlein's individual supremacy was at an end.[63]

Runciman's main difficulty was that the Czechs, having reluctantly accepted his mission, proceeded to instruct him and argue the merits of their case as if the clock had been put back to March. Part of the urgency built up by British demands was actually dissipated, and Czech resistance to Sudeten claims increased in direct proportion to Runciman's inability to coerce either side. The Sudeten Party played the same game, and Runciman was not even able to see Henlein until 18 August.*

By the middle of August the mission, white hope of July,

---

* The Foreign Office did its best, through Colonel Christie, to bring Henlein to terms. It was even suggested that he should act as mediator with Hitler on Runciman's behalf (*DBFP*, series 3, vol. 2, pp. 199–200). But the British were out of their depth – their efforts were countered from Berlin. Henlein was now virtually under German control. A final meeting was arranged between him and Christie by Vansittart, but when it took place in Zurich on 17 Aug., Henlein proved to be arrogant and unsympathetic. (C8118/1941/18 (FO 371/21731).)

had ceased to have immediate relevance. British policy was influenced by Runciman's own pessimism* and was dictated, to a great extent, by their estimate of German motives. After the diplomatic débâcle of 11 August (below, page 273) Halifax actually had to restrain Runciman from submitting an independent report, on the grounds that to do so would lay the blame specifically on the two parties and would, by implication, pledge British support for the side which accepted the report first.[64] What the Foreign Secretary really wanted was a private report to the British Cabinet which could be kept in reserve, as a weapon for publication, to coerce either side.

There was a moment late in August when Runciman reported that there was some hope of bringing the two sides together. The Czechs had drawn up a list of substantial concessions, and if Beneš would only 'do the large thing' and present them to the Sudeten leaders Runciman thought he might get their agreement.[65] Beneš did see the Sudeten leaders, on 24 August, and proposed his 'Third Plan'.† In the last week of August this improvement became a reason for the British to contain themselves and to wait a little longer for Runciman to fulfil his instructions than they might otherwise have done.[66]

In London, however, the inner group were suddenly initiated into the reality of the German drive towards war. More definite warnings of Germany's military preparations, accompanied by the rumour of a date for the invasion of Czechoslovakia, were given in a telegram from Henderson on 28 July.[67] The Ambassador indicated that manoeuvres on a large scale had been scheduled for 15 August; and his report was confirmed by the fact that the German news agency, DNB, published a Government communiqué forbidding the access of foreign military attachés to eastern Germany.

A much fuller account came on 3 August with a detailed report from the British Military Attaché in Berlin, Colonel Mason MacFarlane, who had excellent sources of information in the German General Staff among men who disliked Hitler's

---

* Newton reported on 17 Aug that, despite Runciman's hard work, he was only partially able to hold a situation in which the Czech attitude was hardening and Sudeten complaints growing. (*DBFP*, series 3, vol. 2, p. 100.)

† The Third Plan comprised the division of Czechoslovakia into twenty areas of which three would have some measure of German autonomy; a loan for depressed German areas; and some constitutional reform.

plans and hoped that Britain could still prevent war by diplomatic means. MacFarlane gave news of a partial test mobilisation scheduled for a date after 8 September, which would affect seven or eight divisions in Germany and all troops in Austria. This, he said, was on a scale unknown even before 1914. Added to the widespread retention of second-year men with the colours until the autumn, it was 'desperately provocative . . . it is hard to see how Czechoslovakia can fail to mobilise in reply'. The General Staff, he thought, opposed the extremist policy, and von Brauschitsch was only carrying out the orders of the politicians. MacFarlane's informant, Hauptmann E. von Albedyl, Chief of the Attache Gruppe was 'absolutely convinced that the German public as a whole, were violently opposed to war'.[68]

This memorandum was incorporated by Henderson in a note of 3 August, but the Ambassador drew somewhat different conclusions. He agreed that the military timetable indicated a date between the Nuremberg Rally and the end of October, but he judged that the frankness of the German War Office was a bluff – the threat was real, but it was not necessarily tied to war with Czechoslovakia on a given date. For the moment Hitler was happy for Britain to go ahead and try to solve the Czech question for him first.[69]

Two entirely different courses of action opened out from these reports. Britain could either be firm and repeat the warning of 21 May, hoping that internal disagreements in Germany would produce the same result as before; or she could hasten at all costs the Runciman report and keep Germany as sweet as possible in the meantime. MacFarlane preferred the former; Henderson, so long convinced that Hitler was a moderate, holding the 'War Party' in check, the latter. On 3 August Henderson wrote that 'the extremists have now overcome Hitler's hesitations'; and he added later: the 'possibility that he may [use force] has now become more real'.[70] He was fitting the military information into his own understanding of the political balance between Hitler and the rest of the Nazi leaders and the generals. If he were right, Hitler could still be weaned away from war.

On 6 August Henderson delivered a long note, setting out his considered judgement. Since it represents one side of the debate on which the Cabinet had to adjudicate at the end of August it is worth quoting. He did not believe that Hitler wanted a general war, although that was a possibility if the Czech problem was not solved. He accepted that if Britain 'showed [her] teeth' Hitler would not dare to attack. But

> that would be the greatest tragedy of all...though it might be acclaimed as final, in fact it would merely mean postponing the evil day. *We do not want another May 21st.* A second such rebuff to Hitler would never be forgotten or forgiven and *Der Tag* would become as inevitable as in the years preceding 1914. [Britain had undertaken in March] a *major* operation calculated to prove that even the most vital problems were capable of settlement without recourse to force. We cannot hope to prove this thesis if we allow the Czechs to fob us off.... I just sit and pray that Lord Runciman will live up to the role of an impartial British Liberal statesman. I cannot believe that he would allow himself to be influenced by ancient history or even arguments about strategic frontiers and economics, in preference to high moral principles. The great and courageous game which you [the Government] and the Prime Minister are playing, will be lost.... Just as I was convinced years ago, that Austria must inevitably come into Germany sooner or later, so I am convinced that the Sudetens must do so in the end.... One may hate to see Germany encouraged; yet the moral principle is in the end of far far greater importance.[71]

It is doubtful from this masterpiece of appeasement literature whether Henderson understood fully the springs of the Prime Minister's policy, but the conclusion was clear. The Cabinet must 'get the pronouncement out of Lord Runciman before the Nuremberg Party Congress...Germany does not want war this year; that is my definite opinion...and we should treat with them on that basis'.[72]

MacFarlane visited London in the first week of August, and spent some time trying to correct Henderson's presentation of the military information. The War Office staff, having known him as a consistent optimist, were impressed with his sombre account of the military preparations in eastern Germany. He repeated, however, that the German public did not want war and that he had evidence of increasing discontent with the regime.[73] British Intelligence confirmed the reluctance of the General Staff and that Keitel had said, *à propos* the May crisis and the British warning, 'thank God, the English have certainly helped us this time'.[74] The picture was still confused, but gradually a counter to Henderson was building up – which was to be effective early in September.

It was unfortunate that Chamberlain was ill during the middle of August. On holiday at Scourie in Sutherland, fishing with the Duke of Westminster, he had felt extremely ill and seen a local doctor. He came back to London on the tenth, when he saw the physicians Lord Horder and Bedford Russell. His trouble was mainly due to sinus, but it was painful and depressing, and it left him in no fit condition for the important decisions of that week, although being in London he could decide on his European policy by conversation – a fact which, he suggested, was 'a great relief' to Halifax.[75] He remained there another week, in a state of considerable depression, before returning to continue his holiday. The débâcle which took place suggests that his influence on the Foreign Secretary was not so valuable as he imagined.

Halifax, who stayed in London most of the time, apart from short visits to Garrowby, his estate in Yorkshire, had already replied to Henderson's first urgent warnings on 5 August; 'like you, I have no intention of [going to war] over Czecho-slovakia if I can avoid it'.[76] At that time he had been content to repeat the arguments accepted long before by the Cabinet, such as the impossibility of re-creating the Czech state after a major war. However, on 11 August, with Chamberlain's concur-rence, he sent a direct appeal to Hitler, asking him to desist from military preparations in the interests of the peace of Europe.

To appeal to a Head of State, over and above his Foreign Minister, to alter the internal security arrangements of his coun-try, is not a diplomatic manoeuvre to be undertaken lightly. Yet, in spite of Henderson's advice to the contrary, Halifax sent this request to Berlin and asked the British Ambassador not to take it personally to Berchtesgaden where Hitler was, in case of publicity, but send it through his Chancellery, with a cover-ing letter and a German translation. Only a copy was to go to Ribbentrop and the Foreign Office.[77] Ribbentrop was out-raged; his vanity was hurt at the slur, and at the clumsy attempt to exploit the differences between Hitler and his Foreign Ministry, and he did his best to turn the occasion into a major diplomatic incident. The appeal was rejected at once by his Under-Secretary Woermann, on the grounds that it had been broadcast by Radio Luxemburg before Hitler had received it. Hitler himself took no action, except to say that he would consult with Ribbentrop, but the latter's reply, dated 21 August, was a model of freezing discourtesy. It was not even directed to Halifax's appeal, but to the announcement of Runciman's mission on 28 July, at which he still took grave offence, refusing to co-operate in any way or take any responsibility for it because it 'came about without [German] participation'.[78]

The evaluation made of German feeling at the time of Wiedemann's visit was nullified. Ribbentrop stressed the fact that British policy had so far totally failed in Prague and had actually encouraged the Czechs to greater resistance. As for Halifax's appeal, it 'had given rise to the greatest astonishment here ... it goes without saying that we cannot allow ourselves to enter upon any discussion about internal military measures'. Ribbentrop ended with a peculiarly offensive reference to the anti-German comment in the English press – 'I should like ... to direct your personal attention to this particular question.'[79]

While Halifax was digesting this rebuke, two more telegrams heightened the British predicament. MacFarlane reported that he had heard of a council held at Doberitz, where Hitler had announced his intention to attack Czechoslovakia at the end of September. 'The General Staff are staggered by the fact that it has been taken so quietly abroad.' MacFarlane's informant begged for firm deterrent action from Britain, but Henderson minuted that this man's views were 'clearly biased and largely propaganda'.[80]

The French, who were normally given MacFarlane's information via their Military Attaché in London, General Lelong, became seriously alarmed. Cambon, the Chargé d'Affaires, came to see Halifax on 25 August to ask whether Britain would consider it desirable to repeat the warnings of 24 March and 21 May. He did not ask for an answer immediately, but Halifax gave him one which Henderson would have approved wholeheartedly. Britain had appointed Runciman, and sent the appeal of 11 August; 'I have no doubt therefore that the French Government would feel that we had done everything that was possible, in the sense of a discreet repetition of warning, and I was myself sensible, as no doubt they would be, of the dangers of diluting the effect of warnings by excessive repetition.'[81]

The equivocal answer was reinforced, as usual, by vague

warnings of the attitude of the Dominions. The correct policy was: 'to keep Germany guessing and prevent them from thinking that the danger of any extension of hostilities [after Czechoslovakia had been attacked] was in any way negligible'.[82] Even then, Halifax reminded Cambon of the assurances given by Bonnet on 23 May[83] (confirmed to Phipps on 16 July) that France would take no action that might inspire a German attack without consultation with Britain.[84] So far as France was concerned, all the concessions of April and their trust in being relieved thereafter from their obligation had been wasted : the position remained as it had been at the end of March.

The French might be kept guessing, but to allow the deadline of the Nuremberg Rally – which Henderson now accepted as important – to run out without further British action would be to undo all the Government's attempts to come to terms with Germany since 1937. Yet action depended entirely on the assessment of German motives, and opinions conflicted on interpretation and answers. Between a policy of deterrence on one side and pacification on the other, there was no clear way to judge. The situation was complicated by the visit to London of von Kleist, a Prussian land-owner, on 17 August.

Von Kleist represented the same conservative faction in Germany as the opposition of Schacht and Goerdeler. Like them, Kleist disliked the ideological content of foreign policy inherent in the Nazi ethic, without deploring Hitler's specific policy for the future of the Sudeten areas. But, like all Hitler's opponents, he was against any policy which involved the risk of war against France and Britain. Kleist met Vansittart on 18 August. Whether he had come of his own accord, or, as Vansittart's minutes of the conversation suggest, at the Chief Diplomatic Adviser's personal suggestion, is not certain. Vansittart called him 'a well-informed German acquaintance of mine, who is in close touch with influential sources'.[85]

The burden of Kleist's remarks was that war was now certain – an opinion which Vansittart took pains to establish in detail – and that Hitler was 'the only real extremist'. Encouragement was constantly given him by Ribbentrop 'who keeps telling him that when it comes to the showdown, neither France nor England will do anything'; but Ribbentrop was only 'an evil yes-man ... Hitler has made up his mind for himself'. After 27 September, despite the opposition of the generals, it would be too late to alter the military plans already made. Determined British influence could only divert Hitler's war machine before the middle of September, or, more safely, before the Party Rally. Kleist offered two ways out: either to convince Hitler, beyond any warning so far issued, that France and Britain were not bluffing over Czechoslovakia; or a dramatic appeal to the public in Germany itself. The country was 'sick of the present regime' and afraid of the prospect of war; 'I wish that one of your leading statesmen ... would appeal to this element in Germany, emphasising the horrors of war, and the inevitable general catastrophe to which it would lead.'

Vansittart could not test how accurate von Kleist's predictions were.* He queried the second remedy, as being likely to reunite Germany rather than inspire revolt, and though von Kleist stuck to his proposal, what Vansittart carried away was the first – the warning – 'which', he reminded Halifax, 'is the same as that which I have reported to you as being the desire and the almost open request of a number of other German moderates who have been in communication with me during these past weeks'.[86]

Considerable discussion has taken place over the significance of Kleist's second suggestion and the reaction of British politicians to so unusual a demand. Chamberlain's response is well known: 'I take it that von Kleist is violently anti-Hitler and is extremely anxious to stir up his friends in Germany to make an attempt at his overthrow. He reminds me of the Jacobites of the Court of France in King William's time, and I think we must discount a good deal of what he says.'[87]

It has been suggested that he had a deep-seated respect for the legitimate authority of Hitler, and therefore shunned the plotters; but it is more likely that Chamberlain intended the simile to highlight the fact that German Conservatives were a right-wing aristocratic group, without much popular support. Although he may not have understood fully the power of ideology in Nazi thinking, he did understand a great deal about

---

* There had been talk of plots against Hitler since the beginning of 1938, when Neurath and the generals had been dismissed. Goerdeler's correspondent in the United States told Ashton-Gwatkin that 'the army officers had been too honest and sincere'. This was mid-June. A typical Foreign Office reaction was: 'we have heard a great deal about their proposed army coup d'état, but there have been few signs of it yet'. (C6578/62/18 (FO 371/21663).)

political power. It is often said that in such a dictatorship outside help was needed before the plotters could overthrow the
Government. This may be true of an attempt at assassination,
but so far as the British then knew assassination was not the
issue. Chamberlain knew the power he himself possessed, even
within a democratic state. To back an unknown group against
the power of a total despot, might be to invite precisely the
direct war with Germany which Ribbentrop had already threatened and which the whole British plan was designed to prevent.
Moreover, if Hitler did fall, there was no obvious successor.
Goerdeler, Kleist and the generals might come to power or
Germany might revert to the chaos of 1918. Compared with a
military clique of Prussian officers or the threat of Bolshevik
revolution, the relative stability of Hitler's regime may have
seemed preferable.*

There is no evidence that Kleist's second plan was discussed
in detail, but his request for a firm warning added (as Vansittart
intended it should) to the weight of opinion piling up on one
side of the controversy which had begun a fortnight before.
Most of the evidence presented by the Foreign Office was in
favour of a warning[88] – indeed, only Henderson argued strongly
against any form of diplomatic démarche. The inner group may
have been predisposed to be firm : they met on 24 August and
agreed to repeat the substance of the earlier warning, and
Simon did so, at a speech at Lanark, three days later. But
this was for public consumption, as much in Britain as abroad.
All the senior ministers would have agreed with Kleist that
something much more stringent than this was required if a
deterrent was to be provided at this stage.

Rather more about Chamberlain's views on whether to warn
Germany or appease her can be gauged from a talk between
Horace Wilson and Theodore Kordt, the German Chargé
d'Affaires in London, on 22 August. If Wilson was reported
correctly – and there is no reason to suppose otherwise – he said:

Britain and Germany were in fact the two countries in which
the greatest order reigned and which were the best governed.
Both were built up on the national principle . . . the only working
principle of human relationship. The reverse of this, Bolshevism,

* See Sir I. Mallet's comment on Vansittart's note of this interview: 'The events
of June 1934 [the Röhm purge] and February 1938 do not lead one to attach
much hope to energetic action by the army.' (C8520/1941/18 (FO 371/21732).)

meant anarchy and barbarism. It would be the height of folly, if these two leading white races were to exterminate each other in war. Bolshevism would be the only gainer thereby.... A constructive solution of the Czech question by peaceful means would pave the way for Germany to exercise large-scale policy in the South-East... neither had Britain any intention of opposing a development of Germany's economy in a south-easterly direction. Her only wish was that she should not be debarred from trade there.[89]

This may have been 'a highly coloured version of the official British attitude'.[90] Yet, considering what has already been said of Wilson's relationship with the Prime Minister, it is unlikely that he exceeded his instructions. During August and September, Wilson was in constant touch with the Prime Minister by letter and telephone, and acted fully on his behalf – to the extent of rewriting a major speech which Halifax was to give on 1 September.[91]

But the statement to Kordt was not a proposal nor a programme of action. When that came it would have to be precise and crystal clear. All Chamberlain's instincts were to postpone decisions until the picture built up by information left no doubt what Britain should do. The reports from Germany had still to be resolved; Runciman might yet pull a settlement out of failure. Only at the very end of the month did the reports take on an aspect so menacing that further delay became impossible.

On 30 August Newton reported that, despite Beneš' willingness to hand over the details of his Third Plan, Runciman (who had seen them) regarded them as inadequate. Runciman feared that publication might actually do harm and he suggested that Henlein be told he was ready to produce his own report by 15 September.[92] The inference was that Runciman could outbid Beneš and, with Henlein's support, present a scheme for Britain to impose when the deadline was close enough to unnerve the Czech Government.

Meanwhile, MacFarlane reported, most pessimistically, that Hitler was certain to attack if nothing had been done by 12 September, the day of the Party Rally. He confirmed a number of Kleist's points, mainly that the German moderates regarded the British attitude as all-important, and he made a forlorn plea for a final warning, which must take place before Nuremburg. 'Whether or not we decide to say so, must be settled at once.'[93]

Finally, on 30 August, Lieutenant-Colonel Campbell, Military Attaché in Paris, had an interview with the head of the Deuxième Bureau, Colonel Gauché. The French Secret Service was convinced that Germany was mobilising and ready for an immediate attack. 'It rests entirely with the political side, if it is to be averted,' Gauché said, adding that Italy would join up with Germany in the event of war. This was the frank view of the whole French General Staff.[94]

Now presumably the Prime Minister would take counsel with his Cabinet, rethink his plans and decide what they should do. For the first time in five weeks, on 30 August, the full Cabinet met.

K

10 Revaluations

Cabinet Ministers were recalled to London from their summer holidays to decide on subtle issues whose complexity they only partly understood. They had ended the session in July, reasonably confident of the success of the Government's plans for Czechoslovakia, trusting in a favourable response from Germany, the persuasive power of Runciman and the concessions of Beneš. They had not been kept in touch with the alarming reports of early August nor told of Halifax's abortive appeal to Hitler* and the majority were not aware that the Prime Minister and Foreign Secretary had already come to the conclusion that Hitler now intended war within a certain time-limit, unless the extremer Sudeten demands were met. They certainly had no idea that Chamberlain had already decided to make a personal visit to Hitler (see below, page 300). In this state of ignorance, they were likely to prejudge the debate on whether or not to issue a more categoric warning to Hitler, partly because Simon had made his Lanark speech only three days before, and partly because nothing in the external factors affecting foreign policy appeared to have changed sufficiently for them to abandon their extreme caution of early July. The essential question of what to do about the alarming reports from Germany, which was the subject of the meeting, was not fully debated in its context. But it would be too harsh to accuse the inner group of deliberate deception: most of the factors which were taken into account really had not altered significantly during the summer, or had developed aspects which were so obscure as to preclude informed argument.

The Dominions, certainly, were no less isolationist than they had been in the immediate aftermath of the *Anschluss* in

---

* Halifax's account of the previous month's diplomatic activity, at the meeting on 30 Aug, brought his colleagues up to date in a highly selective fashion (CAB 23/94).

March. In contrast to the colonial administrations* they were kept in constant touch with what the Government was doing by Malcolm MacDonald – but he was not a member of the inner group. The information he passed on was what had been approved by the whole Cabinet: to some extent, therefore, the British indirectly evoked the response which the Dominions gave. Of course the British Cabinet was sensitive to what Dominion Prime Ministers and the High Commissioners in London said, but the use that Halifax or Chamberlain made of it before the September crisis indicates that they were content with the views as they were.† There is no trace of an attempt to convert the Dominions nor to work up opinion on any specific issue.‡ All the same, there was no reason to suppose that Halifax exaggerated the isolationism of the Empire: a variety of statements during the summer confirmed the fact that the attitudes of Canada, South Africa and Australia remained wholly unsympathetic to any further British commitment, especially in Eastern Europe.

On 11 March, Hertzog, Prime Minister of South Africa, had set the tone by threatening that if Britain became involved in a European war, after a course of diplomacy 'of which South Africa could not wholly approve', then South Africa would not consider herself bound to come in.[1] His protest, on 11 May, against the Anglo-French staff talks was a stronger indication of his Government's views than the broadly satisfactory talks about South African coastal defence which took place during the summer, between Pirow, the South African Defence Minister,

---

* To have kept all the colonies informed would have been an immense and wasteful labour. But their opinions were ignored and the debates of their legislative councils were quite unreal. Consultation took place only in relation to the individual circumstances of their defence; such as in the case of east Africa, where, during 1938, the Government tried to involve South Africa to spread the burden. Even the Government of India was not fully informed: it did not hear, for example, of the system of rationing which had been imposed on the British defence ministries in Feb, until at least the end of Apr (Pownall diary, 25 Apr).

† It is worth noting the contrast between the way the British Government listened to Dominion opinion in 1938 and earlier, say at the time of the Abyssinian crisis of 1935. In that case, it made virtually no difference to British attitudes towards the imposition of an oil sanction on Italy. In 1938, the contrast was pointed by what was at stake. Whereas in 1935 the worst outcome would have been war with Italy, in 1938 it was likely to be European or world war – in which case, Britain would need Dominion help.

‡ Communications between the Cabinet and the Dominions appear to have come under the direct aegis of the Prime Minister only in Sept 1938 (PREM 1/242).

and the CID Secretariat. It was reinforced on 1 September, when the South African Government became alarmed at British information about German military preparations, by a statement tantamount to a declaration of neutrality, supported by Pirow and even Field-Marshal Smuts.[2]

Canada was thought to be equally recalcitrant. On 30 June the Cabinet had discussed whether or not to attempt to create a reserve potential for aircraft construction there. Not least of the reasons given was that 'if Canada could become interested in the provision of aircraft to this country, the aloofness of that Dominion from Imperial Defence and its dissociation from the problems of the United Kingdom, might be reduced'.[3]

Even New Zealand who had opposed Britain's actions over recognition of Abyssinia, offered little support for a firm stand against Germany. Robert Menzies, then the Australian Attorney-General, came back from a visit to Germany in July convinced that 'it would be wrong had Europe drifted into a war in which the merits were distributed' and he was to be much more outspoken in September. The Australian Government instructed Stanley Bruce, their High Commissioner, to pass on the view that the Czech Government should be urged to make a public statement at once of 'the most liberal concessions it could offer'.[4]

Voices from India also penetrated to the heart of British foreign policy making. On 13 July, when the loan to China was being discussed, Lord Zetland, Secretary for India, quoted a warning from Pandit Nehru 'who had told him that he had found people on the continent of Europe expressing doubt as to whether we were in a position to take a strong line'.[5] Nehru was prepared to concede that the Nyon Agreement of 1937 and the Government's conduct during the May crisis showed evidence of British power, but he remained sceptical of the future. The Aga Khan, leader of the Ismaili Mohammedans and representative of Muslim opinion in the Near East, was known to be in favour of a negotiated settlement in central and eastern Europe and his proposals had already been pressed into use by Chamberlain and Halifax in their conversations with Germany.[6]

France, Britain's only material ally, presented the same uncertain picture as before. After four months of alternate wheedling, cajoling, exhortation and blackmail, the Daladier Government seemed to have acquiesced in British policy, yet the vital question of the obligation to Czechoslovakia was still obscure, hidden by the curtain of Bonnet's diplomatic defences. The French had promised that they would not do anything irrevocable without informing Britain first. The British were also confident that the French wanted to be rid of their entanglement in Czechoslovakia. But, though Daladier had blessed the Runciman mission, he had given no answer to the question of what would happen if the Sudeten problem and the existence of the treaties had not been resolved by negotiation before Germany attacked. By the end of August, this was critical. As Sir Cyril Newall, Chief of Air Staff, wrote to Ismay on 9 September, if France declared war, 'it is quite obvious that we shall not be able to stand out'.[7] The other two Chiefs of Staff, Backhouse and Gort, concurred. Yet they were by no means confident that France could stand up to Germany: in reply to his questions, Phipps was told on 13 August that France possessed 340 fighters, 570 bombers and 210 other aircraft in the first line.[8] General Gamelin was to claim 100 divisions for the army when he came to London on 26 September. The Chiefs of Staff, on the other hand, in their report of 21 March,[9] had allowed only 53 divisions after mobilisation and a front-line strength of 297 fighters, 456 bombers and 248 others. The British had reason to be suspicious,* even without the obvious prevarication of Bonnet who had told Bullitt, the American Ambassador, that 'France could not preserve her honour if she ran away from war' in June,[10] and Halifax precisely the opposite at Geneva in May (see above, page 241).

Russia, whose offer of a four-power conference had been rejected brusquely in March, was not seen as a potential source of strength. The inner group relied entirely on information from Lord Chilston and Colonel Firebrace which through the summer of 1938 confirmed the low opinion of Soviet military power accepted in March.[10a] The Chiefs of Staff, in their revisions of the likely line-up in a European war, did not alter their evaluation : Russia, they said, was 'in no condition to wage offensive war effectively, and will go to almost any lengths ...

* According to the evidence given by La Chambre, the Air Minister, at the Riom trial, France possessed a total of only 700 aircraft of all classes in Sept 1938, most of which were obsolete, and no reserves (Cot, *Le Procès de la République*). French production was seriously retarded by a strike in the aircraft industry which lasted for most of Aug 1938.

[short of German invasion of Russian territory] to avoid hostilities'.[11] On this basis, Chamberlain and Halifax convinced
themselves that Litvinov's original offer had been intended as
mischief-making bluff. Vansittart made many efforts to prevent the
exclusion of Russia (see below, pages 297 and 354) and Churchill
appealed to Chamberlain on 31 August for a joint note of warning from Britain, France and Russia,[12] but these interventions
were received as coldly as Maisky's assurance (1 September)
to Vansittart that Soviet isolationism 'would not go too far',
and his promise that Russia would help the Czechs 'if Czechoslovakia was not abandoned by the Western powers'.[13] The
Cabinet were not surprised that Litvinov should state in July
that Russia would take no action, even when France was
engaged in war, except to lay the matter before the League
of Nations.[14] The apparent dedication of Russia to collective
security was, rightly or wrongly, ignored by the inner group; and
it was not even debated formally in the Cabinet.

In July, Chamberlain had noticed a change in American
attitudes. He wrote on the ninth: 'Kennedy has come back
with the most roseate accounts of the change in American
opinion in our favour and of the President's desire to do something to help.'[15] On 20 July he told the Cabinet of talks with
Myron Taylor, United States representative at the Evian
Conference, 'almost of an historic character'.[16] But this help,
as Kennedy's own naïve attempts to visit Germany and achieve
a personal diplomatic triumph[17] indicate, would have been in
support of a negotiated settlement on the British lines, not of
any repetition of the warning to Germany. In any case Kennedy
was not always representative of the thinking of Roosevelt or the
State Department. Most other American diplomats in Europe
spent the weeks after the May crisis dissociating the United
States from the least suspicion of interest in European affairs.
Kennedy's offers were at first rebuffed by the German Foreign
Office.[18] It is doubtful whether any of this encouraged
Chamberlain to modify his long-term distrust of American policy,
and his statement to the Cabinet on 20 July suggests that he was
pleased to see signs of Roosevelt's growing awareness of reality
rather than that he put any faith in the outcome.

His deductions were confirmed by the incident of Roosevelt's
speech at Queen's University, Ontario, on 18 August. Roosevelt
declared that the United States would not sit idly by if another

empire attempted to dominate Canada, and that the day had passed when 'controversies beyond the seas' did not interest or harm the peoples of the Americas.[19] His words were hailed by the French press as a guarantee for the whole British Empire and, by implication, for themselves. German newspapers raised a storm of ridicule, and the statement was soon set in perspective by Roosevelt in a letter to Lord Tweedsmuir, Governor-General of Canada, insisting that the guarantee applied only to Canada and that any United States President could have said the same at any time during the last fifty years. Roosevelt had not intended to do more than make 'some small effect in Berlin'.[20]

Chamberlain and Halifax understood quite well that the State Department aimed, during the summer, at creating a state of doubt about American policy, sufficient only to deter Germany from extreme provocation in Czechoslovakia. On 24 August Halifax said as much to the United States Chargé d'Affaires, Herschel Johnson.[21] Kennedy's enthusiasm was nothing on which to base a policy of bluff. In reply to a hint from Chamberlain on 30 August that an American guarantee would strengthen a British warning to Hitler, he at first said that German invasion would be 'hell' but, if France and Britain were involved, so probably would be the United States. Roosevelt had 'decided to go in with Chamberlain; whatever course Chamberlain decided to adopt, he would think right'. But this firm statement had to be modified substantially the next day, when Kennedy told Halifax that though 'shocked' the United States would not think it necessary to plunge Europe into war, because of German aggression.[22] Chamberlain was right to tell the Cabinet that the foreign policy of the United States was that of the mugwump; at the same moment, Kennedy was writing to his own Secretary of State, Cordell Hull, that Chamberlain would try to keep France out and was, himself, the 'best bet' against war.[23] Unwitting and unwilling allies, Britain and the United States reinforced each other: American isolationism encouraged the drive towards appeasement of Germany, without giving it any of the substance needed for success, and the existence of the British plans encouraged the United States' belief that it was unnecessary to take a more positive part.

There remained the enemies, as defined by the Defence Requirements Committee report of 1934. Japan's involvement in the war with China was, if anything, greater at the end of

August than it had been in mid-July, when the loan to China had been rejected. Not until October, in the wake of Munich, did the Japanese launch an all-out offensive to cut off the Kuomintang Government from the outside world. British policy towards Japan was therefore confined to claims for compensation and appeals by Sir Robert Craigie, the Ambassador in Tokyo, for an agreement respecting British rights and investments in China. Craigie ran a difficult course between the still-powerful trading lobby in the House of Commons and the self-evident lack of British military strength in the Far East; he wrote on 22 August: 'Violent criticism of Japan and hints of economic pressure do infinite harm because they undermine the position of our friends and are dismissed by our enemies, as either bluff or derogatory to Japan's dignity.'[24] British policy in Europe, however, was unaffected by the argument.

Mussolini's stance was equivocal. On the one hand he had complained about British backsliding, while intensifying Italian efforts to win the war in Spain. On the other, there was evidence in June of Italian anxiety about German domination of the Balkans (see above, page 260). Believing that the Italian promises, made in 1937, still had some meaning, and unwilling either to press too hard for fulfilment of the Anglo-Italian agreement or to abandon it, the inner group of the British Cabinet put consideration of policy towards Italy on one side, pending the solution of the Czech question. They were aware that Hitler persisted in his overtures to Mussolini yet they still considered themselves bound by limits of House of Commons and public tolerance on the subject of Spain – a subject which, as Chamberlain was to emphasise in September, troubled the trade unions and the Labour Party far more than Czechoslovakia. Until the most urgent point in the September crisis, the Cabinet were content to hope that the timorous side of Mussolini's nature would prevent him from complete commitment to Hitler; and, with considerable foresight, the Foreign Office made sure that Italy was kept informed of what went on in Prague.[25]

Nothing in the international situation, except the questions of Germany and Czechoslovakia which they had been summoned to discuss, was likely to force the Cabinet to change their plans. But after a month of vacation, ministers could be expected to be sensitive to the pressures of what they defined as public opinion.

If a strong current was running, either in favour of, or against, the Government's policy, they who had shown themselves well aware of public reaction in March could be counted on to bring it up as evidence during the meeting on 30 August.

The fact that no one did so is evidence both of the stability – or perhaps, uninformed nature – of public opinion in July and August and of the way in which ministers tended to react to it, using it in their defence but ignoring or making light of it when the evidence contradicted their own estimates. An accurate study of public opinion in 1938 was not easy to arrive at. A Mass Observation poll taken at the end of March 1938 had suggested that only 28 per cent were satisfied with the Government's foreign policy, 32 per cent were dissatisfied, and the very high proportion of 42 per cent uncertain.[26] A more extensive series of questions, put by Gallup at the same time, showed heavy opposition to the Government, but a great deal of doubt on the crucial point of Britain's attitude towards Czechoslovakia.* On the other hand, Mass Observation's poll in August indicated that 40 per cent of those questioned (admittedly during the holiday period) were taking less interest in foreign affairs than in March, an estimate confirmed by the amount of space devoted to foreign affairs in six of the main national daily newspapers.†

---

* The questions posed in Feb 1938 were:

	Yes	No	Don't know
		Percentages	
Do you favour Mr Chamberlain's foreign policy?	26	58	16
Do you think Mr Eden was right to resign?	71	19	10
Do you agree with Mr Eden's reasons?	69	19	12

But in March—

	Yes	No	Don't know
Should Britain provide assistance to Czechoslovakia if Germany acts as in the case of Austria?	33	43	24

(*Public Opinion Quarterly*, Mar 1940 (School of Public Affairs, Princeton))

† Amount of news-space given to foreign affairs in six national dailies; expressed in column inches.

25 Aug	400		12 Sept	2800 \ (Nuremburg Party
27 ,,	400		13 ,,	3700 / Rally)
29 ,,	1300 (Lanark speech)		15 ,,	4000 (Berchtesgaden visit)
31 ,,	1600 (Henlein-Ashton-Gwatkin meeting)		17 ,,	3200
			19 ,,	3500 (Anglo-French talks)
1 Sept	600		21 ,,	2800
2 ,,	500		23 ,,	4900 (Godesberg meeting)
7 ,,	400		26 ,,	4800 (Czech refusal of Godesberg terms)
8 ,,	1200 (SDP break off negotiations)		27 ,,	6000 (Hitler's speech)
10 ,,	900		29 ,,	8000 (Munich)

(Figures from Madge and Harrisson, *Britain by Mass Observation*, p. 23.)

The individual expressions of ministers suggest that the atmosphere of crisis would need to be far more grave before they reacted to public demand.

The lack of urgency in the Press at the end of August was caused at least partly by the manner in which many of their foreign correspondents' warnings had been ignored. The Beaverbrook papers were instructed to play down the crisis in Europe while the crusade for the Empire lingered on; isolation was the theme, and Beaverbrook himself felt no regret at the dismemberment of Czechoslovakia after Munich. 'Well, isn't Czechoslovakia a far-away country?' he said when Arthur Christiansen, editor of the *Daily Express* complained.[27] Lord Rothermere, likewise, influenced the editorial policy of the *Daily Mail* and conducted a correspondence with Ribbentrop whose views he passed on to Chamberlain as if they were revelations from the holy of holies.[28] Against their autocratic control, individual journalists were helpless. Ian Colvin, Berlin correspondent of the *News Chronicle,* sent back a series of warnings similar to those of Colonel MacFarlane in August, but his anxieties were not reflected in the paper and he made his impact instead on the Conservative Opposition, particularly Lord Lloyd.[29] The Berry family kept the *Daily Telegraph* faithful to the Government into the centre of the crisis in spite of Victor Gordon-Lennox, the foreign editor. The practice of Dawson and Barrington Ward of *The Times* of suppressing part of the most urgent messages from their European correspondents continued (see above, page 102), in the interests of providing what they regarded as a balanced view which should not unduly alarm or distress the German leaders. The *Manchester Guardian* reflected the ambiguous position of Liberals in Parliament, and the tenor of foreign news-reporting frequently clashed with editorial policy. More surprising, a section of the intellectual left wing joined the appeasement chorus. Lord Allen and Lord Noel Buxton had always favoured a settlement with Germany, but on 27 August Kingsley Martin, editor of the *New Statesman,* published an alarmist piece about the forthcoming Nuremberg Rally which recommended, in forthright terms, that if Runciman could not solve the Sudeten question in time, then 'the question of frontier revision, difficult though it is, should at once be tackled. The strategical value of the Bohemian frontier should not be made the occasion of a world war. We should not guarantee the status quo.'[30]

Some of the Government's advisers relied on press comments to back up their conclusions. Nevile Henderson wrote to Cadogan on 6 September: 'I do wish it might be possible to get at any rate *The Times,* Camrose, Beaverbrook Press etc., to write up Hitler as the apostle of peace. It will be terribly short sighted if this is not done.'[31] Yet the famous, or infamous *Times* leader of 7 September, proposing openly 'the secession of that fringe of alien populations who are contiguous to the nation with which they are united by race',[32] even if based on what Chamberlain had told the gathering of American journalists at Cliveden in July, represented less than the Prime Minister himself was already willing to concede. Later in the crisis, the Government not only led the way, but through Hoare's press conferences briefed the editors and proprietors of newspapers rather than the parliamentary lobby and set out for them the issues and the confines of the debate. The extreme limit of Government direction was probably reached – if Duff Cooper's story is accurate – when Halifax persuaded Dawson to 'bottle up' a correspondence on the secession of the Sudeten areas which *The Times* intended to start after 12 September.[33]

In any case, given Chamberlain's character, it is most unlikely, at this late date in the execution of the Government's plans, when he was recovering from his illness and confined by the extreme urgency of the situation, that he would allow himself to be influenced by the Press or public. The only shift of opinion which mattered in terms of the balance in the Cabinet was that of Halifax, which can be quite clearly attributed to the influence brought to bear on him successively by Vansittart, Cadogan, Horace Wilson and Chamberlain himself.

In the House of Commons nothing had changed. The debate on 26 July, about the sending of the Runciman mission, does not reveal the sort of major shift of alignment which ministers, wary of the autumn session, might have taken to heart. The Liberal view, expressed by Sinclair, was that while the Czechs should go as far as possible in concessions 'consistent with the safety of their state', British policy should be to resist 'unjust and aggressive demands'.[34] This was not likely to cause the Government to lose their sleep. Of the Labour Party, only the maverick Josiah Wedgwood came out with a fighting speech: 'Every time you sacrifice one of your potential allies to this pathetic desire to appease the tyrants, you merely bring nearer and make more inevitable that war which you pretend you are trying to avoid. ...'[35] The official line of the Labour Party was less decisive. Geoffrey Mander, summing up the debate, paid an unusual tribute to Chamberlain's love of peace. Collective security and the League still bulked largely in Opposition thinking: Mander suspected that Runciman had been foisted on the Czechs and feared that concessions to the SDP would undermine internal security, but his only recommendation was that Czechs and Germans should be left to sort out their differences, free of outside interference – an impossible ideal.[36]

Even in private, the Labour Party diminished its own influence by excessive caution. As near to the end as 29 September, Philip Noel-Baker begged Attlee to sign a telegram jointly with Churchill, Lord Robert Cecil, Sinclair, Eden and Lord Lloyd, warning Chamberlain to make no more concessions at Munich and threatening a parliamentary revolt. 'Attlee refused to sign without the approval of his party.'[37] In July the Labour Party had presented a memorandum on defence, complaining that the RAF lagged behind Germany in aircraft design and technology.[38] What might have been the start of a fruitful political co-operation (like that between the Government and the combined Opposition in July 1936)* was vitiated by accumulated mistrust on both sides and the Labour Party's exclusive insistence on principles of collective security under the League.

Even if there had been an all-party backbench revolt, Chamberlain was not a Prime Mininster to blench; on 25 June he had written to his sister, describing the Labour Opposition, in their fury over bombing in Spain, as 'a pack of wild beasts ...I think what enables me to come through such an ordeal successfully, is the fact that I am completely convinced that the course I am taking is right, and therefore cannot be influenced by the attacks of my critics'.[39]

The impact of more congenial 'informed opinion' on foreign policy-making cannot easily be traced in the Cabinet archives. From the evidence of the minutes of the full Cabinet and its committees, the 1937 balance had not changed: if policy owed anything to influence outside the Cabinet, it was to advice from

* Above, p. 97.

within the Government machine, Treasury, Foreign Office, or Chiefs of Staff. The correspondence in the files of the Private Office, however, shows that outside suggestions, at least from the Conservative opposition, *were* taken seriously, in proportion to the increasing gravity of the Czechoslovak crisis.

Those who were listened to did not include the Eden group. Oliver Harvey had been right in thinking that Eden could have built up an unrivalled position in public esteem during the first half of 1938. If he had done so, his right to assail the Government in September would have been unquestioned, and his power might have been decisive in changing Chamberlain's strategy. Only Eden could have undermined public enthusiasm for the visits to Hitler or the Munich settlement itself. He chose not to do so. He continually disappointed Harvey; his caution, even after Munich, sometimes irritated his audiences and his own loyal supporters.[40] The Group, which at this time included J. P. L. Thomas, Lord Cranborne, Harold Macmillan, Harold Nicolson, Lord Wolmer, Sir Edward Spears, Ronald Cartland, Anthony Crossley and Richard Law, preferred to work for gradual amendment of Government policy and sedulously avoided association with Churchill.[41] Eden himself appears to have been ready to rejoin the Government, on suitable terms, at any moment after February 1939.[42]

In contrast, Churchill retained his curiously privileged position, even when most outspoken in attack and in spite of the fact that his public reputation took two serious knocks in the summer of 1938. His stand against abandonment of the rights to use the Irish ports, which had been retained by the 1921 Treaty, was widely criticised and often misunderstood; and the 'Sandys affair' brought to the surface old suspicions about his lack of balanced judgement. (Duncan Sandys, one of his closest followers, became involved in June and July in a breach-of-privilege case concerning his use of confidential military information, in the House of Commons. Churchill, who was nominally a signatory of the Committee of Privileges report, proceeded to attack it in the House.) As Churchill's most recent biographer remarks, 'parliamentary reputations are as susceptible to minor incidents as to great ones, and their significance should not be ignored'.[43]

Churchill's published statements on Czechoslovakia were a good deal more ambiguous than is suggested by his own account in *The Gathering Storm*. On 23 June he published an article[44] suggesting that the negotiations in Czechoslovakia were likely to end on a basis of home rule for the Sudetens within the Czech state, provided that Britain and France combined their good offices. 'The Czech Government owe it to France and Britain that nothing which reason and justice can claim should be withheld.' He deprecated the suggestion that Henlein and his party sought an *Anschluss* with the Nazi state. Then, in another article, coinciding with the debate of 26 July, he wrote,

> All the essential elements of a good and lasting settlement are present unless it is wrecked by obstinacy on the one hand, or mischievous fomentations upon the other. . . . The assurances lately received from Herr Hitler must be welcomed in a sincere spirit and must be matched by renewed efforts on the part of the British and French Governments to secure a just and fair solution.*

In private Churchill remained on terms of respect with Chamberlain, who could write, in spite of the Sandys affair, 'Sandys was only a dummy. Winston was the real mover and he saw, or thought he saw, an opportunity of giving the Government a good shake. . . . [But] it is just his restless ambition that keeps him incessantly criticising any administration of which he is not a member.'[45] The constructive side may be found in the memoranda Churchill sent to Downing Street during 1938[46] and in particular in the correspondence of late August when Churchill seems almost to have converted Halifax to a plan for a joint warning to Germany, to be signed by Britain, France and Russia, accompanied by movements of the Fleet and the raising of certain destroyer flotillas to war strength.[47] Later in the crisis, he was never far from Downing Street, and the Inner Cabinet actually found him waiting outside the door of the Prime Minister's room in the House of Commons after the critical meeting of 10 September.[48]

No one else in the Conservative Party could make his presence felt, physically. Amery wrote to Chamberlain on occasion; there is no evidence that he made any impression. Robert Boothby had more success, because he furnished useful information about

---

* *Step by Step*, p. 266. At the time of Kleist's visit in August, Churchill showed himself so sympathetic to the idea of a plot to put in a right-wing regime in place of Hitler that he wrote to Kleist, suggesting that the British Government could offer such a regime a colonial settlement, trade facilities and even the possibility of negotiations about the Polish Corridor. (*DBFP*, series 3, col. 2, pp. 687–9.)

the state of Czechoslovakia and about German opinion.[49] Two of his letters were even mentioned to the Cabinet. But although the information was useful, his analysis was no more acceptable than the resolutions of the League of Nations Union which appear in the same files, or letters from Lord Robert Cecil and Gilbert Murray lamenting that the League was not handling the crisis.[50] Among dozens of letters from sources as widely different as Lord Tyrrell, former Ambassador in Paris, Lord Kemsley, the newspaper proprietor, the Comtesse de Baillet-Latour, and Captain Victor Cazalet, the only ones which appear to have received Chamberlain's close attention were from his friend Sir Patrick Hannon, and from Lord Brocket who, by chance, had sat next to Ribbentrop at a tea-party during the Nuremberg Party Rally.[51] The views of the 'new imperialists', Lord Lothian, Lionel Curtis, the Astors, were of course, still acceptable and unchanged. But one outside intervention was interesting and effective. On 1 September Horace Wilson reported an interview with Lord Weir, who advised that Chamberlain should make a 'personal approach' to Hitler.[52]

Since March 1938, the Chiefs of Staff had maintained a regular review of the situation in the event of war with Germany. On 26 April, they analysed the general political assumptions behind their report of 21 March.[53] It appeared that war was most likely to arise 'from the present practice of conducting foreign policy by bluff and counter-bluff'. The United States was unlikely to support Britain except in the case of a war against Japan as well as Germany; Russia was 'in no condition to wage offensive war effectively'; Italy could be discounted in the first stage, until the reactions of Germany and Japan were certain; Japan was more likely to attack Russia than British possessions in the Far East. As for a German attack on Czechoslovakia – France must join or be relegated to the status of a second-class power; and Britain would have to follow, whatever the legal obligation.

The Chiefs of Staff were not asked to submit a full review of the situation again until 12 September, but they continued to make plans for a war emergency, and for civil defence in the event of a German attack.[54] On 5 August, they made the gloomy forecast: 'To sum up, we shall be faced by an enemy who has fully prepared for war on a national scale, possesses the initiative, has superiority in air and land forces, but is inferior at sea and in general economic strength.'[55] They recommended concentration on defensive measures, the weakening of Germany by blockade and economic pressure, reliance on Empire resources while British industrial and military power was built up, and finally, and only then, a counter-offensive. Reliance on the long war of attrition owed much to the uncertain state of mind which eighteen months' political dictation had created. There was nothing here to cause the Cabinet to change their minds nor to question their prior strategic assumptions.*

If Hankey had still been in the Cabinet Office, he might have safeguarded the interests of the War Office and the existence of the field force. He had retired in July, after some months in which his influence was diminished by an unsuccessful battle with the Treasury over the question of whether his successor should be a civil servant or a staff appointment. Hankey lost to Warren Fisher: Major-General Ismay was promoted secretary of the CID and Edward Bridges, a Treasury official, to the Cabinet post.

The new arrangement took several months before it became as effective as the old. Between May and September there was no pressure of the kind which Hankey, with his twenty years' experience, had always been able to bring to bear, even on the Prime Minister, in the interests of the Services. But it is doubtful whether Hankey would have offered alternative advice. He had concurred in Chamberlain's foreign policy during 1937 and supported him during the crisis of Eden's resignation. The views which he expressed in September 1938 show quite clearly that, even if he had not actually been in touch with the Prime

---

* Fear of a 'knock-out blow' by Germany was also a powerful deterrent to a policy of continental warfare during 1938 and was accepted uncritically by military advisers and politicians. It provides another explanation of British reluctance to commit either troops or aircraft to the support of France, and British insistence on reciprocal arrangements for French air cover in the event of German attack across the Channel. But the fears were greatly exaggerated. Germany did not plan a knock-out blow (see below, p. 302; and Sir Charles Webster and Noble Frankland, *History of the Second World War* (*U.K. Military Series*), *The Strategic Air Offensive against Germany*, vol. 1 (London 1961) p. 78–80). The figures of German bombers, which were accurate as well as frightening, did not necessarily signify that all could bomb London with impunity. Case Blue (war against Britain), which was considered in the summer of 1938, envisaged clear limits on range and bomb loads, even for south-east England. Both sides grossly overestimated the effects of bombing, in casualties and on civilian morale.

Minister in his retirement, he still followed the line he took.*

The only flicker of revolt against the subservient role assigned to the military advisers by the system of rationing came from the War Office staff. Using the argument that the rationed limit had already been broken by the Air Force, Lord Gort, the CIGS, and his staff argued that, whatever the commitment made in peacetime, when war broke out it would be necessary to build up a force strong enough to defend the north-west sector of Belgium and France, covering the Channel ports. Though their view was the logical corollary of the long-term understanding that Britain could not afford to see France beaten, it was severely repressed.

In this case, pressure was siphoned off at ministerial level, in what General Pownall called 'the oriental intrigues in the War Office'.[56] Hore-Belisha the Secretary for War relied heavily on the advice of Liddell Hart, his private adviser from August 1937 to May 1938. Liddell Hart was deeply worried that too much had already been promised to France – worried 'whether we can regain any control over the policy – which has in a practical sense committed us – by an undertaking that will modify the risks which [France's] present undertaking entails for us as well as for them'.[57] Defensive theory held the day.† Had Hore-Belisha struggled in the Cabinet as Duff Cooper and Swinton had done, the problem of support for France would at least have been discussed. But he accepted Treasury cuts in estimates without question and the tanks which were being built throughout 1938 were those he had allocated 'for imperial defence purposes' in January – light reconnaissance, light cruiser and armoured personnel-carriers.[58] Only later in the year did Hore-Belisha begin to swing towards acceptance of a Continental commitment, and this change of opinion was not reflected in

* Hankey believed that the Czech question should not involve Britain. At Locarno, Britain had refused to take part in the treaty between France and Czechoslovakia, fearing just such a situation as that of 1938. Britain had remained uncommitted and had been proved right. There was no reason to alter the policy except, as the Government had done, to underwrite France, in Britain's own interests. Even that much, he thought, exceeded the strict interpretation of Britain's obligations, and should be honoured only when France was attacked. (I am indebted to Captain Roskill for this account of Hankey's opinion in September 1938.)

† After lunching with Liddell Hart on 31 May, Oliver Harvey recorded: 'His theory is that the defence is stronger than the attack, and that even a relatively modest defence may be adequate . . .' (*Diaries of Oliver Harvey*, p. 146).

the advice tendered to the Cabinet until the reality of the Munich crisis accelerated the trend and opened the way for the War Office staff to bring greater influence to bear on their reluctant minister. Until at least the middle of September the official War Office line was to welcome the 'freedom' which the strict limits on the role of the Army allowed them.

By the end of August 1938, the disposition of the conflicting groups in the Foreign Office had been modified. The resignation of Eden's followers, Cranborne and Thomas, had largely nullified the influence of those who owed him personal allegiance. The remainder of the officials, who had been divided roughly into two camps, for and against a tough line with Germany in 1937, were still separated on the same issue of principle, but the placing of individuals had altered. In September Cadogan joined Vansittart and Sargent in advocating a renewed warning to Germany, while Nevile Henderson, Harvey,* Strang and the 'new diplomat', Horace Wilson, confirmed the importance of appeasement.

This distinction explains the undercurrents of the crisis of the inner group early in September. Vansittart and Cadogan, with Churchill's help, were able to bring great influence to bear on Halifax, which Wilson and Henderson combatted directly by reference to the Prime Minister. The growth of the power of the two Chief Advisers – Vansittart and Wilson – is an interesting feature of the Whitehall scene during July and August, while the Cabinet and Foreign Policy Committee did not meet.

Eden's resignation freed Vansittart from the crippling restraint of a Foreign Secretary who mistrusted him. Halifax was amenable to any advice put forthrightly enough. Aloof but tolerant, he could always be jolted by reference to his duty or to the moral implications of diplomatic decisions. Cadogan avoided such methods until later on in the September crisis, but Vansittart never scrupled to use what ammunition he had to destroy the opposition. His attack on Henderson's 'defeatist attitude' is a fair sample of his invective: 'I have never once in any despatch of his, seen the faintest indication that he had any idea of ever

---

* 'The important thing is to convince Hitler that *actual progress* is being made so that he shall not commit himself to some irrevocable action when he speaks at the Nuremberg *Parteitag*.' Strang took the same view. (*Diaries of Oliver Harvey* (6 Sept) pp. 169–70.)

putting any curb or bound to Germany's march to Weltmacht. There is here and everywhere a tendency observable towards a mere impotent putting-off of inevitable evil days.'[59] Gradually, he recovered some of the power he had lost when kicked upstairs in December 1937; and since he remained on friendly personal terms with Cadogan the conflict between them was less than their overlapping roles might have implied. Vansittart had two extra-mural sources of power: his contacts in Germany, which became essential information to the inner group of the Cabinet in making their analysis of Hitler's policy, and his friendship with French officials, especially Alexis Léger, Secretary General of the Foreign Ministry. Léger and the members of the French Government who opposed Bonnet's defeatist policy formed a powerful group, with influence in Prague: Churchill's visits to Paris in August and September materially stiffened Beneš' resistance to the Anglo-French demands (see below, page 359). As the British became aware of Daladier's dependence on a narrow majority of his ministers, they listened all the more to those known to have friends in Paris, however little their views were to the Prime Minister's taste. Britain's dependence on French attitudes restored the eminence of the Francophiles just as the submission of France in April had depressed them.

The central European policy of the Vansittart-Sargent group was now substantially firmer than it had been during the overtures to Germany in December 1936. Vansittart had written of 'putting really strong pressure on Berlin not to interfere with any acceptable solution'[60] even before the May crisis. During July, he warned Halifax that Italian military aid to Franco was undiminished and he opposed the idea that Italy should be asked to assist France and Britain in the Czech negotiations.

She has really nothing to do with it and her presence would only tend to stiffen the German attitude, for Signor Mussolini is still, so far as we can judge, entirely on the Rome–Berlin Axis. Moreover such an idea would be the thin edge of the German wedge for excluding Russia from Europe. This is one of the main planks in Germany's long range policy and we ought on no account to play the German game, which would be fatal for us and Europe in general, for the reasons which I have enlarged upon in previous minutes.[61]

But in spite of his request for a renewal of the warnings to

Germany in mid-August – 'Safety would be better served, if we
spoke earlier. Otherwise the military programme will have gone
too far. Personally I feel most strongly that we should act *now*'*
– nothing happened. The advice he gave after von Kleist's visit
seems to have made no impact. Only at the very end of August
did Halifax waver, perhaps as a result of Vansittart's memorandum giving the views of Professor Conwell-Evans, an ardent
member of the Anglo-German Fellowship, who was teaching in
Germany at this time. Conwell-Evans had just seen Ribbentrop
and was convinced that Hitler was going to war between the end
of September and mid-October, not to remedy Sudeten grievances, but (as Vansittart had always claimed in the past) 'to
incorporate Bohemia and part of Moravia', that is, to break
up the Czech state. According to Conwell-Evans,

> Hitler dismisses all the objections of his generals and of the
> moderates with the statement that France and Great Britain will
> remain neutral... [but] if Hitler knows beforehand that France
> and Great Britain will fight, and if we mobilise the fleet in the
> North Sea, he will even now hesitate. If a firm declaration on
> our part is now accompanied by a very good offer of home rule,
> there is good hope that Hitler cannot fight, for the German people
> is opposed to war and German opposition will then become too
> strong for Hitler to disregard.... This plan will at least save
> the independence of the Czechs as a separate people, while it
> will also bring the necessary pressure on Mr Beneš. In this
> manner we shall not lose prestige. Hitler's own plan for war will
> fail but at the same time he also will not lose prestige to any
> undue or intolerable extent; and that is a point of vital
> importance.[62]

The only point where Conwell-Evans' advice differed from
Vansittart's was on the timing: whereas Evans recommended
a warning between 10 and 18 September, Vansittart put it
earlier than the Nuremberg Rally.

These views were substantiated by most of the principal
officials of the Foreign Office, but their effect was countered
at a higher level by the Prime Minister and Sir Horace Wilson.
There was a heavy legacy of suspicion in Chamberlain's mind
about Vansittart's unofficial activities. Hankey had thought him

* Vansittart papers. Almost exactly a year later, on 30 June 1939, he wrote:
'I have always been convinced that if we had mobilised the fleet early in August
1938, instead of late in September, history would have been very different.'

a malign influence and had never forgiven him for his part in the Hoare–Laval affair; he believed that Vansittart was working against Chamberlain in 1937, and suspected, almost certainly correctly, that he was leaking Foreign Office information to Léger and the French ministers in opposition to Bonnet – Reynaud and Mandel.

Wilson's position was much stronger than it had been in 1937. As he wrote himself, 'H.J. [Wilson] frequently had to state the opposite point of view. I knew that otherwise the P.M.'s policy would be negatived, though not by anything that Germany or Italy might do.'[63] He recorded a meeting in Halifax's room at the Foreign Office

> while Runciman was still struggling in Prague. V. arguing in favour of what would have been tantamount to a declaration then and there, that we would go to war with Germany if she attacked Czechoslovakia. H. J. [Wilson] wanted first to know views of Chiefs of Staff. 'I thought it would be hard not to place upon him a good deal of the responsibility for it. I am unable to understand in what way the Government before, and at Munich, differed materially from what V. advocated, while permanent head of the F.O.'[64]

Throughout August, Wilson was in constant touch with Chamberlain by letter and telephone, and on two occasions at least he exercised the Prime Minister's mandate in a way which gave great and lasting offence. First, he curbed Halifax's inclination to take up Churchill's suggestion of a four-power joint note to Germany, because he was worried that the inclusion of Russia would make Hitler angry, and because he thought it a bluff which might be called;[65] then, after the Cabinet meeting on 30 August, he took the leading part in preventing Halifax from changing his mind and sending a warning regardless of the Cabinet decision (see below, page 321). Halifax seemed unable to stand up to the combination of Wilson and Chamberlain, and he gave way.

The Prime Minister held the substance of power. It was Henderson who was summoned to London to advise the Cabinet in person on 30 August; Henderson, of whom Vansittart had written a fortnight before: 'Sir Nevile Henderson is not well-informed ... while wishing to avoid standing up, and anxious to run away, he makes no attempt to say how far he would run, where he would stop – if anywhere – and how, and when, and why.'[66] Vansittart himself had been excluded from sessions of the Foreign Policy Committee in favour of Cadogan, although he later attended the formal sessions of the Committee on the Czechoslovak Question (as the inner group was called, after 12 September). No clearer indication could have been given of the type of advice which Chamberlain wanted aired in public; and in private, it should be noted, it was in a conversation with Wilson, late at night at 10 Downing Street on 28 August that Chamberlain decided to make his personal visit to Hitler[67] – a decision mentioned only to Henderson before the Cabinet met.

In this way, the unwelcome commentaries provided by the Foreign Office were reduced almost to insignificance. For those in favour of a tough line, the only way to restore the balance after the Cabinet meeting of 30 August was to work on Halifax and to hope that the return of the Cabinet later in September would reinforce his latent opposition to the Prime Minister. The subsequent struggle reflected these factors, for it lay, not between the inner group and the dissident juniors, but between Halifax and Chamberlain.

The issue of whether or not to give the categoric warning to Hitler was of fundamental importance. Although in theory, whatever was decided, the Government's long-term policy towards Germany remained the same – that is, solution of the Sudeten question, and modification of the security treaties as the preliminaries to an Anglo-German understanding – the whole policy of appeasement was in question. Rearmament could not now be speeded up sufficiently to affect the strength of British diplomacy. Those who wanted to make the threat had to face the contingency of war with forces that the Chiefs of Staff declared to be adequate only for a defensive campaign. Those who played for time had the trump card that theirs was the only certain way to avoid war.

If Henderson's opinion was correct then there was time to play with; in contrast, 'keeping Germany guessing' was a card of steadily diminishing value. When time ran out a month later it was worth nothing. In any case, the debate as framed by the two sides in London was itself something of an illusion. The situation in Germany after the May crisis had developed in a way which largely excluded British influence.

Hitler's exact intentions in August 1938 are not easy to discover. During the May crisis, Keitel had revised the plans for Case Green, taking into account the rumours of Czech mobilisation. He emphasised that the requirement of four clear days was vital, so that the Wehrmacht could concentrate on the invasion without having to worry about an attack on the Rhine or the eastern frontier.[68] After the crisis, Hitler retired to Berchtesgaden, in fury, for five days, and then issued the famous directive 'It is my unalterable decision to smash Czechoslovakia by military action in the near future. It is the business of the political leadership to await or bring about the suitable moment from a political and military point of view.'[69]

There is room for doubt about whether the date of 1 October was set irrevocably. In the past, Hitler had frequently couched his general dogmas in circumstantial political plans which bore no relation to what later happened. In this case, as A. J. P. Taylor has pointed out, the outline of the political developments was inaccurate.[70] On the other hand, military preparations *were* set in motion; and the whole argument between Hitler and the generals which occupied the summer was based on the assumption that the armed services were to be ready on that date to face the Czechs and, if necessary, France and Britain.

Hitler was a pragmatist, even a pupil of Machiavelli, yet the dogmatic character of his programme should also be emphasised.[71] It is perfectly possible to envisage him in the three months after the May crisis, obsessed with military preparations for the West Wall and the invasion of Czechoslovakia, fighting the resistance of the High Command, and ignoring quite deliberately the mediating processes of bureaucracy and diplomacy. It is also possible to see his awareness, on certain occasions, that military planning had to be set in a political context. In his instruction to Keitel on 21 April[72] he had insisted on the need for a pretext for invasion. The directive after the May crisis argued the same case, dealing with the possibility of an attack after a period of prolonged tension, or after a diplomatic incident, either of which could justify German action and cause confusion among the allies while the Wehrmacht won its lightning campaign.[73] The fact that this did not happen does not vitiate the importance of Hitler's preparations. His occasional awareness of the diplomatic context of the Czech question is also one explanation for his acceptance of the invitation to the Munich Conference, at a time when all the military plans were complete.

Some of the generals, Beck and Adam in particular, stood up to Hitler, on the grounds that the war with Czechoslovakia could not be won quickly, that France would stand by her treaty, and that Britain would fight as well. Beck produced a series of memoranda during the summer, and Brauschitsch, Halder and Goering appeared to be convinced that Germany was not ready for such a war. A meeting of the high command, held on 10 August, showed a majority in favour of Beck. Brauschitsch informed Hitler, who at once summoned a conference of younger commanders. In an impassioned three-hour speech, he won their support, in spite of the objections of some of General Adam's staff that the West Wall could not be held against France for more than three weeks.[74] Brauschitsch gave in and Beck resigned, though the news was kept secret until after Munich. General Halder replaced him – a secret conspirator, later joined by Beck; and opposition to Hitler was directed into obscure paths which British Intelligence could not easily penetrate, and whose importance the British Cabinet could not properly assess.

Although the argument between Hitler and the generals was conducted in terms of military strategy, it involved a political 'calculation of risk'[75] as to whether France, Russia and Britain, or any of them, would go to war. Wiedemann's remark to Beck, on 29 July, that Hitler was determined on war even if France and Britain intervened, may be discounted as propaganda; but Ribbentrop certainly believed that this was Hitler's position.[76]

Hitler was enraged that England had betrayed him during the May crisis.[77] Since his suit had been rejected, he was ready, with vindictive logic, to destroy the nation whose favours he had sought. There were no more overtures, until August 1939; and on 24 May 1938, even before the directive for Case Green, he ordered Admiral Raeder, Commander-in-Chief of the navy, to prepare a new plan (later Plan Z) and to speed up existing warship construction, since Britain was now to be considered one of Germany's deadliest enemies.[78]

Hitler had excellent reasons for assuming that France and Britain would shirk the fight. Willingly or not, the democratic powers had provided almost an embarrassment of evidence –

Henderson's marginal comments, watering down the significance of the messages he transmitted; Daladier's conversation with Welczeck about the Russian alliance; and Bonnet's repeated duplicity and ambiguity, to say nothing of the estimates provided by the German secret service, from decoded British and French telegrams.* Then there was the patent deficiency of French morale and the obsolete character of the French air force, evident enough to the German attachés in Paris. On the clear evidence of the published estimates, British forces were not to be feared during the early stages of war.

This is not to say that Hitler welcomed the prospect – only that he was not afraid of accepting a challenge which he had come to believe was inevitable, sooner or later. So the building of the West Wall, later called the Siegfried Line, went ahead. Jodl said at the Nuremberg trial after the war that the Wall was like an unfinished building-site at the time of Munich, but this may be taken as exculpation from the charge of premeditated war. In late August, the Limes plan for extension of the Wall to fight a defensive action against France was prolonged into the autumn. At a military conference on 27–8 August,[79] Hitler discounted the strength of the French and British armies, greatly over-estimated the effect of possible Italian intervention and overrode the objections of Brauschitsch and Adam who feared that Holland and Belgium would also become enemies.

It has been suggested that the timetable involved in the Limes plan, which was extended after Hitler had made a tour of the West Wall in the last week of August, restricted his freedom of action to launch an attack on Czechoslovakia to a short period at the very end of September,† and therefore indicates a cautionary, pragmatic approach. It can also mean, as we have seen, that military planning for Case Green was meant to be much more thorough than in the case of the *Anschluss*. The plans for Case Green were not altered despite all the generals'

---

* It has been assumed (cf. Watt, *Personalities and Policies*, p. 200) that the breaking of the British cipher code in the Rome Embassy in 1936 allowed Germany full insight into British Foreign Office communications. There are no German or British records available to test whether this was still true in 1938 (see p. 93n).

† The supply trains for the Limes Plan were to run until 20 September. Railway timetables for German mobilisation were only to be in full operation after 21 September, allowing for an attack on Czechoslovakia on 1 October. This is held by Robertson, *Hitler's Pre-War Policy*, p. 136, to have eliminated the possibility of a surprise attack at the time of the Party Rally at Nuremberg.

opposition, until, at the conference held on 3 September, between Hitler, Brauschitsch and Keitel,[80] the final details of troop movements after the critical date of 28 September were discussed. Here, despite Brauschitsch's objections, Hitler took the major part in actual military planning, ordered increases in the fortifications of the West Wall, and stated flatly that the OKW must have finalised its plans by noon on 27 September.

The debatable question of whether Hitler intended to use force if the Czechoslovak question was not solved by 1 October has been wrongly posed. He had decided to use force in any case. During the summer, he laid the military foundations for the operation in his capacity as Minister of War. In this situation, it did not matter greatly whether Ribbentrop wanted a European war or whether the generals opposed it; so long as Hitler retained power, he went his own way. This interpretation would explain why he told Dirksen that he did not wish to speak to British diplomats at the time of the Party Rally[81] – at that stage, he was not interested in a negotiated settlement, whatever solution the British brought.

On the other hand, Hitler was careful to seek support from Mussolini; and on 7 September he sent a personal message, warning the Duce that Britain was 'determined to get rid of one or other of the two totalitarian nations as soon as she has completed her rearmament'.* For the present, she was 'trying to prevent or postpone at all costs any European conflict which might lead to a weakening of the whole position of the democratic powers'. Mussolini was presumably meant to deduce that it was better to cripple the entente powers in 1938 before they in turn took on the dictators. The message continued:

The Führer looks upon the current negotiations sceptically. The danger lies in the fact that the intentions of the Czech Government and the British to attempt to gain time can no longer be concealed, either from the Germans or from the remaining nationalities in Czechoslovakia. For, while the time is frittered away in discussion, the exact opposite to the declared aims is taking place.

* *DGFP*, series D, vol. 2, pp. 671–3. This note was handed to Mussolini by Prince Philip of Hesse, son-in-law of the King of Italy and special envoy between the dictators. As the editors of the German documents write, 'this presumably represents a statement of the Führer's policy intended for Mussolini personally' (p. 671n).

He asked for Mussolini's co-operation and promised that 'in spite of all threats from Britain and France, even at the risk of war with both these powers' he would intervene at once in any case of 'fresh intolerable provocation'. He did not wish, he said, to take the initiative, nor to state a definite time 'because he does not know this himself'. That must wait for his speech at the Party Rally.

The evidence of Hitler's relations with Henlein and the SDP, though far from clear, also suggests that he was set on engineering the sort of political crisis in Czechoslovakia which would make Case Green possible at the given date. The instructions had not changed. Indeed, in response to the SDP's repeated requests for guidance, Ribbentrop replied, testily, on 18 August that 'Henlein had already received clear instructions . . . the answer [to Beneš' proposal] was contained in the general instructions . . . namely, always to negotiate and not to let the link be broken, on the other hand always to demand more than could be granted by the other side.'[82] This doctrine was reiterated at the interview between Hitler and Henlein on 2 September.[83] Similar directions went to K. H. Frank. When the appointed hour came, Germany would solve the problem herself.

Taking all this into account, a British warning, even if it had been more stringent than that of 21 May, could have had little direct effect on Hitler's policy. Henderson may well have been right to think that it would have provoked rather than restrained him. But Henderson was quite wrong to imagine that Hitler was still a moderate, prisoner of the extremists, open to British reason and negotiation. This leaves the question of the opposition: would an appeal to the German people have toppled the regime, as Kleist suggested? An answer must be hypothetical, since no one in London seriously suggested a public démarche, and the conspirators themselves were so devious in their approaches that the second and third-hand reports of their activities were bound to make them seem half-hearted.

The balance of power was not wholly in Hitler's favour even after Beck's resignation. Goering had now taken the position formerly occupied by Schacht, and during 1938 he and his staff on the Four-Year Plan, led by Wohlthat, took the revisionist line. This implied hegemony in Europe, domination of the south-east, but no war against the West. Some of the generals, like Milch, Goering's Chief of Staff, sympathised, even if they did not move into more open opposition and conspiracy. Goering would have been the most likely successor to Hitler if the September plot had succeeded, because he was the only leader acceptable both to the Nazi Party and the old élite. He had inspired Halifax's visit in the previous November and it could still be said that this group favoured a negotiated settlement with Britain. As late as 29 September, on the morning of Chamberlain's invitation to Munich, Goering was the principal counter to Ribbentrop's passionate desire for war.[84]

The conspirators took the deadline of 1 October entirely seriously. Opposition to Hitler within the framework of government in the Third Reich had patently failed by the time Beck resigned. In the fortnight afterwards, therefore, plans were made swiftly for Hitler's arrest. The leaders were Halder, the Commander-in-Chief, Beck, General von Witzleben (commander of the Berlin district), Hans Gisevius (in charge of Berlin police), Brauschitch, von Runstedt and, of course, the political opposition, Schacht, the Kordt brothers, Weizsäcker, von Hassell and Goerdeler.[85]

As is now known, the plot was cancelled shortly before the appointed hour, because of Chamberlain's announcement of his first flight to meet Hitler. The British had been told of the plot, in very general terms, by Kordt on 5 September, at the instigation of Weizsäcker,[86] but no details of dates or methods were given. Chamberlain treated the news with the same scepticism as he had shown towards Kleist's pleas in August. Whether he was justified, is almost impossible to assess: the generals and Neurath had failed to stand up to Hitler in the winter of 1937–8 when they were still in power and they failed again in 1944. Patriotism in the face of the enemy evidently ranked higher in 1938 than disapproval of the regime. They could not make a revolution at a time when the international situation was critical for Germany – especially since Chamberlain's visit was taken as a German diplomatic triumph. Halder may have been tougher than Beck and Brauschitsch, but Gerhard Ritter concludes that, even so, 'it was a gamble with little chance of success'.[87] Jodl was eager to emphasise the significance of the plot in his evidence at the Nuremberg trial, but, again, he had the motive of denying that the whole high command was involved in the drive towards world war.

Hitler was also well aware that plotting was taking place.

More than once he declared that he would smash 'the spirit of Zossen' – where the headquarters of the General Staff was.[88] He had his own secret service and the information provided by Otto Dietrich. Simply because we do not know the measures that had been prepared to safeguard the Führer's position it should not be presumed that he was merely the passive object of the conspiracy.

Given these circumstances, the British were fighting a war of illusion in August 1938. They knew that the German leadership suspected Britain would not fight,[89] but the questions which the Cabinet debated – whether Hitler was an extremist or a moderate, and whether he wished to free the Sudeten Germans or destroy the Czech state – though relevant, were also unreal outside the British context. The debate between the two sides in the Government was restricted to the question of whether to warn Hitler off or to go to the extreme length of concession, rather than the consequential question of whether, at that stage, Britain was ready to fight. This is not to say that the result of their deliberations was unimportant. Whether the warning of 21 May had diverted Hitler or not during the May crisis, the fact of British involvement had certainly jolted his preconceived ideas. It might have done so again, as Halifax was inclined to argue in the first week of September.* That Hitler did ultimately accept the invitation to Munich, and a negotiated settlement, is proof he could be diverted from a purely military solution. The British illusion lay in the failure honestly to face the stark question of the inevitability of war, and in their persistent belief that co-existence with Germany, on British terms, was still within the limit of practical politics.

* As Speer also argues, in retrospect: 'his aims could only have been thwarted by superior counterforces ... and in 1938 no such forces were visible' (*Inside the Third Reich*, p. 109).

11 Narrow Choices

Sudden recall of the Cabinet only a month after the long summer recess had begun would have been sufficiently alarming to disturb the Press and arouse the public. The Cabinet Secretariat therefore took considerable pains, then and later, to avoid the appearance of anything unusual and the meeting on 30 August was designated as a Conference of Ministers. With the exception of Hailsham who was on a cruise to South Africa, Edward Stanley who was in Canada, and Leslie Burgin in Switzerland, however, all the Cabinet were present, having been summoned with the utmost discretion. The atmosphere among his colleagues, Inskip thought, was one of mild surprise.

The meeting was summoned ostensibly to bring ministers fully up to date with the latest information provided by the Foreign Office, and to decide on the next step in the plan to solve the Czech question. Whether the Prime Minister would have allowed a radical examination of the whole purpose of the plan is an open question: no such demand was made. Chamberlain did not dictate the next step to his unwilling colleagues – they deliberately chose it for him. But it is clear from the fact that he had already evolved the idea of his visit to Hitler, and spoken about it to Nevile Henderson, and from the type of information given and the manner of decision asked for, that the meeting was carefully weighted to produce what the Prime Minister had intended to do.

The Cabinet was asked to choose between the rival interpretations of the German military build-up, between Henderson and MacFarlane, between Vansittart's interpretation that only a stern warning could deter Hitler from war and the contrasting opinion that war would be more likely as a result of firmness. Facts were not much in doubt; the military preparations were now too well documented. But was the time limited to three weeks or three months?

The firm line was undermined from the beginning. To a great extent, the authority of the Foreign Office had been devalued in the collective consciousness of the Cabinet by Chamberlain's persistently hostile attitude. Halifax now admitted to Chamberlain that 'some of his F.O. advisers who had formerly thought the Czechoslovak situation very bad, now believed that the "war party" in Germany had been checked'.[1] The complete lack of comment on Henderson's attendance at the meeting on 30 August can only be explained by a general feeling that the advice of the man on the spot was necessary to clear up the obscurities in the views presented to them.* They did not know – even Halifax did not yet know – of the planned visit to Hitler. But Henderson was told before the meeting; and Henderson not only impressed ministers with an immediate sense of authenticity in interpreting Hitler's policy but helped to phrase the questions on which the discussions took place.

It was taken for granted that Britain had now outrun the time in which the Government could expect to induce the Czechs to settle with Germany. Because of Germany's unreasonable attitude and the tactics of Beneš there appeared to be no alternative except a direct approach to Berlin, involving Britain much more deeply than the original scheme. The way this evidence was presented was sufficiently ambiguous to permit the hypothesis that, if the Czech Government moved far and fast enough under British pressure, the attack would not take place. The concept of a warning became confused. It could be taken either as a straightforward threat that if Germany attacked Czechoslovakia Britain would stand by France and fight; or it could be seen as a tactical move, in support of a new approach to Berlin and renewed pressure on the Czechs. Those in favour of the warning did not make the distinction, hoping perhaps to have the best of both interpretations.

No one yet expressed the ultimate fear that Hitler would invade *whatever* the terms offered by Czechoslovakia. The fear of war shadowed the Conference of Ministers, as it had every meeting since the *Anschluss*, but it was still held in check by the presumption of Hitler's rational behaviour. They believed that he would prefer his gains, whether racial, territorial or strategic, peacefully rather than risk a situation in which he would have to

* The only other precedent for summoning an Ambassador to address the Cabinet, in Chamberlain's time, was after the *Anschluss*, when Palairet gave his description of the scene in Vienna. But he was not asked to help the Cabinet make up its mind on a major issue of policy.

face the Western powers. That being so, ministers imagined that they had only to find the perfect balance, within the time allowed.

So, no one suggested a preventive war. It would have been remarkable if it had been discussed, considering the attitude of the Dominions and the United States, and the defence dispositions made during the previous year. But *any* course of action, other than a direct approach to Germany, now seemed likely to involve Britain in war. Even to reverse the decisions of March, to withdraw into isolation, leaving the field to France, might mean war. Whatever had been said by France, the Cabinet still could not be certain that she would not fulfil the obligations of the treaty with Czechoslovakia; and no minister (with the possible exception of Lord Maugham) denied that if France were attacked Britain would have to assist under the terms of Locarno, in a war for which Britain was militarily and psychologically unprepared.

Chamberlain's opening remarks came as a serious shock, after a month spent by the Cabinet in the illusory optimism of late July. This may explain why Halifax gave a very selective account of the diplomatic activity of August, rehearsing the reports of German military preparations, but skating briefly over the dismal story of the rejection of his own appeal to Hitler, and Ribbentrop's 'unhelpful attitude'. However, he made it clear that Germany was now poised to invade Czechoslovakia and he quoted the authority of the German Ministers in Rumania, Yugoslavia and Russia. Hitler would attempt to put responsibility for a general war on France.[2]

Halifax claimed, with excessive optimism, that Runciman was personally responsible for the restoration of talks between the Sudeten leaders and the Czech Government. Ashton-Gwatkin had returned on 25 August full of the news that Beneš was prepared to go to the extent of setting up three autonomous German regions within the Czech borders. But Halifax did not quote Runciman's last gloomy message, that this would not be sufficient. Instead he pointed out that Kundt, who was in charge of the negotiations with Beneš, was apparently pleased with the stage which they had reached.

In his summing-up,* Halifax shared Henderson's view that

---

* Halifax also said he had considered sending 'an eminent person' to meet Hitler face to face; he had asked Runciman, who had refused. This information can

Hitler was not adamant on settling the Czech question in 1938, but was prepared to do so and would use every resort of bluff, backed ultimately by force. He rejected the idea of a deterrent warning, because a mere repetition of the 24 March and Lanark speeches would not be strong enough. Nothing would serve but the clear statement that if Hitler invaded Czechoslovakia Britain would go to war. But something so categoric might incite the Czechs to break off negotiations with the SDP, leaving Britain to fight on the worst possible ground. Intervention could not save Czechoslovakia. Even if the Western powers won, and forced Germany to restore the conquered territory, 'it was unlikely that any peace reached at the end of such a war, would recreate Czechoslovakia as it exists today'.[3]

Halifax found the French argument, that 'we were in effect concerned with the attempt of the dictator countries to attain their ends by force', unjustifiable. By giving it the character of a preventive-war plan, he went far to discredit it. Moreover he scaled down the likelihood of France fighting at all. He did not anticipate the French doing more than mobilising and holding the Maginot Line. Cambon, the French Chargé d'Affaires, had told him that 'French opinion would come round to the view that some action might be taken'.[4] The inference was obvious: Britain should not get involved unless Germany invaded France – a most unlikely development. The rapid construction of the West Wall, Halifax believed, was proof 'that Hitler's intentions are primarily defensive'.

In the light of Halifax's private doubts about British appeasement, which induced him to speak out against Chamberlain during the next week, his attitude on 30 August is hard to understand. A week later, he was first in line of those who wanted to issue a warning: yet at this meeting, while admitting that the Foreign Office had received messages from moderate Germans, he dismissed this whole question almost casually: 'he received these messages with some reserve' – regimes did not fall in this way. He had also considered asking the Admiralty to make a dramatic manoeuvre with the Fleet but had rejected the idea, partly because Duff Cooper had been away, and partly

hardly have been intended to prepare the Cabinet for the idea of Chamberlain's visit to Hitler, since Halifax had not yet been told, but Halifax may have wanted to go himself, as he had done in November 1937, and had wished to do again in April 1938.

L

because it was 'so out of line with the rest of our actions'. Britain should carry on, firm to the declarations already made. Beneš must make his offer public before the Party Rally. What then was to be done towards Germany? 'In effect we should keep Hitler guessing.'

Halifax was in no doubt of the significance of the position he had taken up. At the end, in a sombre paragraph, he said : 'he wished it to be clearly understood that if this policy failed, the Government would be told that if only they had the courage of their convictions, they would have stopped the trouble. They would also be accused of deserting the principle of collective security and so forth. But those criticisms left him unmoved.'

Chamberlain followed, rounding off and filling in the argument. He had been impressed, he admitted frankly, by the arguments for a severe démarche. He even quoted the letter from Boothby, full of information from German industrialists, all leading up to the conclusion that, unless warned off, Hitler would move straightforwardly towards invasion.[5] But then came Chamberlain's conclusive argument – 'no state, certainly no democratic state, ought to make a threat of war unless it was both ready to carry it out and prepared to do so'. Baldwin had used the same argument to Flandin after Germany's reoccupation of the Rhineland in March 1936. Two and half years later it was less self-evidently true, but no one challenged it, nor Chamberlain's amazing analogy with the Schleswig-Holstein question of 1863 when Palmerston's so-called 'neglect of sound principles' had led to evil results and war.

All Chamberlain's thinking lay against a warning on the lines of 21 May. Hitler, he explained patiently, was a man of withdrawn, 'exalted' character, who could not be expected to keep to normal diplomatic rules. He might call the bluff and Britain would have to fight, or be humiliated. War would be a worse test even than in May, because of the deterioration of France, and the growing hostility of Italy. Public opinion might support the Government now, but faced with war it could change. As for the Dominions – 'the policy of an immediate declaration or threat might well result in disunity in the country and in the Empire'. Finally, more profoundly, even if the threat worked, as he believed it had on 21 May, that would not be the end: Hitler would return to the attack, frustrated, and bluff would eventually give way to humiliation.

Chamberlain followed his precept and put his colleagues through his own process of reasoning. He was, perhaps, the only one there who had thought the question through and come up with the answer that all other courses of action meant war. Nevertheless, it is surprising that the subsequent debate failed to penetrate such assumptions as 'the deterioration of France' and 'the growing hostility of Italy'. Issues have to be simplified for ministers not attuned to the daily routine of foreign affairs; inevitably, certain aspects are pointed up and emphasised to the exclusion of others. But the absence of the critical faculty was remarkable. Halifax and Chamberlain occupied quite different positions from the last Cabinet meeting in July, yet their senior colleagues accepted the change without demur. Simon, Inskip and Hoare, all agreed. Lord Maugham went further, echoing one of Henderson's more damaging interpretations – 'if Czechoslovakia had not done her best', then Britain should think twice about helping France. MacDonald, speaking for the Dominions, thought it politically impossible to make a threat without their approval. 'He had little doubt that the Dominions would be in favour of holding this country back.' Since the United States and British Empire were the only forces in the world which at some future date might have to hold back the dictators, the Government 'should not break up the Commonwealth now'.

Henderson substantiated what Halifax had said. He had received, he admitted, evidence that Hitler had decided to use force, but this came from enemies of the regime. 'In Germany important secrets were well-kept.' The opposition to Hitler would be unlikely to know the facts. Without explaining how Hitler could keep secret from the High Command his military preparations for an invasion only four weeks ahead, Henderson offered his own judgement that Hitler had decided to deal with the Czechs before the winter, but had not fixed on the means or the date. What Henderson feared was not Hitler's lack of regard for Russia and his willingness to fight the Western powers, but the thought that, if he were allowed to get away with an invasion of Czechoslovakia, he would blackmail Britain forever, tear up the Anglo-German Naval Treaty, and challenge British supremacy of the seas. To prevent this, a negotiated settlement had to be made at once. If Beneš did not publish his concessions before the Nuremberg Rally, Hitler would either demand a plebiscite or threaten force. It followed that the

Government must compel Beneš. A warning to Germany would infallibly confuse the issue and diminish the chances of success.

Like the reflection in a distorting mirror, Henderson's account of the British predicament was recognisable but unpalatable to the opposition group in the Cabinet. However, he succeeded in eliminating entirely the arguments in favour of an out-and-out threat to Germany and the opposition looked to other tactics.

Duff Cooper, who had sailed back from the Baltic in the Admiralty yacht *Enchantress* to be in time for this meeting, put the alternative case. Conquest of Czechoslovakia would not weaken, but strengthen Germany, just as the conquest of Germany had for Napoleon. The United States would be discouraged and lapse into total isolation. If war did break out, the Czechs would fight well; in any case, it was not a question of helping Czechoslovakia because 'if there was a European war, we should inevitably be involved in it'. He wanted to make a gesture: to bring back the battle cruiser *Repulse* from the Mediterranean, and advance the fleet manoeuvres, due in a fortnight, by six days.

Faint support came from De La Warr, who wanted that elusive phantom 'a policy of moderate action, combined with a show of resolute strength'; and from Walter Elliot and Winterton, who wanted just *something* done. In a different vein, Oliver Stanley conceded the strength of Chamberlain's argument but declined to bring pressure on France to keep her from fulfilling her treaty. Stanley was the only member to think of France. Of the rest, Kingsley Wood followed the Prime Minister's line. He appealed to the obscure authority of public opinion and declared that a threat to Germany would 'divide' it with the 'majority' against. Hore-Belisha accepted that 'public opinion would not support strong action' and saw 'no way of preventing the Sudeten Germans from joining their compatriots'. Morrison, Stanhope, Brown and Colville simply agreed with the Foreign Secretary.

Halifax let it be seen that he was 'surprised' at the stand made by Stanley and Cooper. He was not contradicted. Perhaps the opposition did not realise that this was their last opportunity to influence policy as a whole. Despite the speeding-up of events during the next few days, the Cabinet did not meet again until 12 September, and then in circumstances in which rational debate about the basic principles of their plan was difficult, if not impossible.

After this meeting, authority over foreign affairs was vested, in very vague terms, in the inner group, of whose existence the Cabinet was now officially informed. During the next twelve days, all decisions were taken by Halifax and Chamberlain, Simon and Hoare; and Duff Cooper was not the only minister to complain of exclusion. The minority may be blamed for not attempting to exercise more control, but the inner group certainly exceeded their stated mandate. Chamberlain had declared that policy would be to keep Germany guessing; he said nothing of a direct personal approach. At this time, according to his letters, he intended to keep 'Plan Z' in reserve.

I keep racking my brains to try and devise some means of averting the catastrophe, if it should seem to be upon us. I thought of one so unconventional and daring that it rather took Halifax's breath away. But since Henderson thought it might save the situation at the eleventh hour, I haven't abandoned it, but I hope all the time that it won't be necessary to try it.[6]

The Cabinet did not realise that delegation of authority would soon be taken to cover a deal with Germany, including a plebiscite. All Inskip carried away from the meeting was the belief that 'we were to keep Hitler guessing while we pressed Beneš to get on with the negotiations'.[7]

The care taken by Chamberlain in managing this meeting of the Cabinet indicates the importance he placed on having a unanimous base for his policy. But already the inner group's plans were far in advance of the Government's public statements, and at some point Chamberlain was likely to find he had left even his closest colleagues behind. Halifax was not told of the plan to visit Hitler until 1 September, two days after the Cabinet meeting. Hoare and Simon were told during the following week.[8] Halifax disliked the idea but was overborne. Chamberlain and Wilson argued with him patiently for four days, but the support of the other two, and of the Cabinet as a whole, was taken for granted.

The meaning of Chamberlain's 'autocracy' lies not in the lack of consultation, which took place openly enough, but in his assumption that, having gone through the process of reasoning, all his ministers must inevitably come to the same answer. If they did not, then they were taken for 'weak-kneed liberals' or members of 'the boys' brigade'. Halifax's doubts were of a different order, and Chamberlain put himself out, to a very rare degree, to cajole and appeal for his Foreign Secretary's goodwill.

It is also true that the opposition, having made a token protest, offered themselves up like sacrificial lambs. After Eden and Swinton had gone, the others, Stanley, Cooper, De La Warr, Ormsby-Gore, Winterton and occasionally Malcolm MacDonald and Hore-Belisha, spoke their minds; but all, with the possible exception of Stanley, acquiesced in the policy chosen. They were not excluded and ignored: they chose to be so. They did not once vote, nor carry their dissent to the point of asking the Secretary to minute it.*

The response of the younger men and their failure to press their opposition was becoming a familiar phenomenon, almost a customary reaction. Inskip summed up the discussion on 30 August, not unfairly: 'There was no real difference of opinion, although Duff Cooper and Oliver Stanley both professed to want to force the issue with Hitler. While professing this view, they each had a "but" at the end of their observations.'[9]

Certainly, after the May crisis, the full Cabinet was not kept closely informed of the plans for Czechoslovakia, but in the ordinary course of events, with the rest of foreign and all domestic policy to consider, ministers had plenty to confuse them. Czechoslovakia was rarely off the agenda, and yet the dissenters did not call for more information, nor make their protests heard. Only in their memoirs they gave currency to the idea of a frustrated opposition, rigidly excluded by a domineering Prime Minister – who was, by then, dead. They had had the worst of all worlds, having been inadequate to affect the decisions yet close enough to the centre to be damned with the same public obloquy as the inner group.

They complained, then and later, that Chamberlain had relied on his friends. It was natural, given his style of leadership, that Chamberlain should work best with those who shared his assumptions and aims rather than the group with whom he was

---

* Stanley, for example, could have reopened the terms of the Note to France of 23 March, in full Cabinet, after his protest had been overridden in the Foreign Policy Committee, but he failed to do so.

temperamentally as well as politically at odds. Simon and Hoare were not only sycophants. Both had been Foreign Secretaries; both were of high intellectual calibre; both were senior men whose ministerial experience dated back to the early 1920s. Halifax he trusted above all: 'what a comfort he is to me, and how thankful I am that I have not to deal with A [Eden] in these troubled times,' he had written on 21 March; on 22 May – 'I thank God for Halifax.'[10] To these, Horace Wilson should be added. Minister, friend, confidant, ADC and political weathercock for the Prime Minister, Wilson played a part at least as important as if he had been a member of the inner group during September.

Whatever the complaints, there was in practice no danger to Chamberlain's policy so long as it was, or could be represented as, successful. The inner group was a committee of all the talents. Outsiders might presume that it was a mere cabal, but they did not know. Those not inside the 'narrow circle'* could not easily judge: as Lord Dunglass, the Prime Minister's PPS, wrote: 'he *never* talked about this kind of matter to anybody outside the Cabinet and very few in'.[11]

Within three days of defining British policy as 'keeping Hitler guessing', Chamberlain wrote from Scotland:

While our Foreign Office keep repeating that we must 'keep Hitler guessing' that is exactly what he does to us and we have no definite knowledge of his intentions. Nevertheless, I have a feeling that things have gone in such a way as to make it more difficult for them to use force, and I hope it may yet be possible to avoid even the unprecedented step to which I alluded in my last [letter].[12]

Events in Prague at that moment seemed to justify Chamberlain's optimism. After the Cabinet meeting on 30 August, Halifax had sent a telegram, stating that German war preparations made it essential for the Czech Government to agree with the Sudeten Germans without further delay.[13] Beneš must be warned 'with all the earnestness at [Newton's] command' to clear himself and his Government 'of the suspicions ... that, counting on foreign support, they are merely

* Pownall diary, 25 September: 'The work has chiefly been done by the "narrow circle" – Prime Minister, Halifax, Inskip, Hoare, Simon. Some at least are jealous of this and our Secretary of State [Hore-Belisha] is among them.'

manoeuvring for position and spinning out the negotiations without any sincere intention of facing the immediate and vital issues'. The seven points* would no longer suffice. The full Carlsbad programme must be endorsed – a view in which Runciman concurred.

Newton had a long interview with the President on 3 September. 'I wished', he said, 'to emphasise that it was vital for Czechoslovakia to accept great sacrifices and even if necessary, considerable risks now, in order to avoid much greater risks leading to disaster. Dr Beneš seemed painfully impressed. . . .'[14]

Beneš had already received demands from the SDP much more radical and destructive than the suggestions of his Third Plan. After the British démarche he gave way and evolved a new scheme which amounted to autonomous self-administration for all the nationalities in the Czech state. The cantonal system, which the British had discussed in June, had at last been reached. The Fourth Plan, as it became known, was presented by Hodza to Kundt on 7 September.

In the first week of September, however, three quite separate dangers threatened the policy agreed by the Cabinet. The assumption which had been made about Czech and French attitudes was rendered suspect. Meanwhile, an internal political crisis developed in Whitehall; and in Britain public opinion which, for all ministers' *dicta* had remained obscure, began to make itself felt.

Czechoslovak opinion was by no means entirely represented by her President and Prime Minister. Resistance to concession was only to be expected and it took two forms, internal military opposition and a reliance on the support of the allies. The British Military Attaché in Prague, Colonel Stronge, reported on 3 September that it would be 'quite unprecedented in modern times' if Hitler were to override Czechoslovakia in as little as three weeks. The Czech army might be in a numerical inferiority of $1:4\frac{1}{2}$ but 'there is no material reason why they should not put up a really protracted resistance single-handed'. Morale was the vital factor: 'if it holds [the war] may drag on for months'.[15]

A war of several months would make irrelevant any conclu-

* The 'Third Plan' put by Beneš to Ashton-Gwatkin, and repeated to Halifax on 25 August.

sions based on the fact that France and Russia could not intervene in time. Moreover the military might well replace the civilian government and revive Czech morale. So far as the British knew, the Czech Government could not rely on support from Russia. According to Bonnet's version of an interview with Litvinov on 6 September, Russia would bring the matter to Geneva but only when France was already involved. Russia, in Bonnet's words, was 'showing much more caution in this matter than she wishes either of us to show';[16] Rumania and Poland would not permit Soviet aircraft to fly over their territory to help Czechoslovakia.*

But could the Czechs rely on France? The British Cabinet had taken at their face value Halifax's assurances and Bonnet's statements that France wished to be free of her treaty obligations. But no way had been found to dissolve them in time. Could France now stand out and actually say 'no'? On 31 August Corbin asked for an interview with Halifax. The French Government, he said, supported the Lanark statement and realised that Britain could go no further. Runciman should finish his mission and Beneš should accept the findings, if necessary under French pressure. The key to the whole situation was elsewhere: if Germany intervened or provoked incidents in Czechoslovakia, it would be 'an illusion to believe that conflict could be limited'. Corbin went on to reveal France's fear of an Italian attack on Algeria and Tunisia, if France were occupied in confronting Germany. Consequently, in addition to certain military preparations designed to counter the effect of German mobilisation, France hoped to make use in Berlin and the Little Entente capitals of the promised action Britain might take.[17]

These hints of a stronger line and the first of many demands for a British declaration took substance from the statements of Daladier† – in spite of a message from Bonnet that 'if M. Beneš will not accept Lord Runciman's verdict, then France will consider herself released from her engagement to Czechoslovakia'.[18] They were echoed by what Phipps called the 'alarm-

---

* This interpretation was substantially confirmed by Potemkin, the Deputy Foreign Minister in Moscow, to Lord Chilston on 8 September (*DBFP*, series 3, vol. 2, p. 266). Nevertheless, the Poles and Rumanians had no means of stopping the Soviet air force, if a decision to cross their territory had been made.

† On 8 September Daladier told Phipps that if Hitler 'could only be made to realise that German aggression means a general war, he would abstain and perhaps seek to gain his ends by means of economic pressure'. (*DBFP*, series 3, vol. 2, p. 269.)

ist rumours' of the opposition within the French Cabinet – Blum, Flandin, Herriot, Mandel and Reynaud. In a talk with Phipps on 4 September, Léger said that no French politician would dare to leave on record that he had agreed to discussing revision of the Czech treaty. Later, when Beneš appealed to the French Minister in Prague, Bonnet refused to instruct him in the same inflexible terms that Halifax had used to Newton.[19] The French Government, having been kept in the dark as to Runciman's fears, were taken aback by the sudden British démarche in Prague, of which they had had no warning; Corbin took a distinctly stiff tone when he pressed Halifax twice, on 7 and 9 September, for a clear indication in Berlin to dispel what he called the 'dangerous misunderstanding' about Britain's attitude.[20] Despite the vacillations Bonnet emphasised the firm side of the French attitude to the German Ambassador[21] and by 8 September, after another conversation with Daladier, Phipps was convinced 'that French action would follow pretty soon on any German attack on Czechoslovakia'.[22]

In itself this was not sufficient to induce the British to give Germany a firm warning, but it gave extra significance to the growing dispute between Halifax and Chamberlain. Uneasy about the proposed visit to Hitler and sympathetic already to Churchill's plan for a joint Allied note to Germany, Halifax swung into the orbit of the hard-liners in the Foreign Office,* although not necessarily into support of the attitude of France.

After drafting the memorandum based on Conwell-Evans' report, Vansittart continued to bombard Halifax with advice. On 7 September, after *The Times* leading article advocating partition, he condemned both that and the Government's policy:

The policy of keeping Germany guessing is the policy that obtained in 1914. We did keep the Germans guessing and they ended by guessing wrong and war followed. We have now got into a position where tremendous pressure has been put upon Beneš and nothing equivalent on the Germans. A good many people feel, and more are likely to feel, that we have already gone a

* A report was received in the Foreign Office from Christie (Secret Service) on 5 September, giving information from 'important members of German heavy industry' that Hitler had scheduled the invasion for the end of September, but that opposition in Germany to the idea of war was very strong. The industrialists feared the effect of an Anglo-French blockade; the Secret Service recommended the British Government to take a strong line. (C9876/1941/18 (FO 371/21737).)

long way in putting pressure on Beneš, and that the resulting offer ... goes almost too far. ... *The Times* leading article definitely encourages them to turn it down and leads to a most dangerous misconception of the British attitude.[23]

During the absence of the Prime Minister in Scotland, Vansittart persuaded Halifax to come south from Garrowby on Saturday, 3 September and, according to Inskip :

persuaded Halifax that a note ought to be sent to the effect that we would come in if France honoured her obligations in Czechoslovakia. ... R.V. whose position at the Foreign Office is quite anomalous (a legacy from Anthony Eden) had become thoroughly worked up ... by Sunday 4 September I understood from the P.M. that Halifax had become unsettled — no doubt under R.V.'s influence, and had drafted a note.[24]

The vehicle for this note had already been provided by the German opposition to Hitler. On 31 August the State Secretary, Weizsäcker, had tried to persuade Henderson on his return from London, to see and warn Hitler at the Nuremberg Rally. Henderson was more impressed by a threat from Ribbentrop that any repetition of 21 May would only infuriate Hitler and he refused to take the risky initiative of requesting an audience unless he had a change of British policy to announce. On 2 September he asked Halifax for authority to make his plans for Nuremberg as seemed best at the time.[25]

On Sunday, 4 September, Halifax met Wilson, Vansittart, Sargent and Cadogan at the Foreign Office. Cadogan was in favour of a private warning to be delivered by Henderson during the Rally.[26] Vansittart pressed for an official démarche; but the time was not yet ready for the Foreign Office to circumvent the Cabinet decision; Wilson invoked the Prime Minister's authority against the scheme. The only action taken was to give Henderson permission to act as he chose. However, Halifax's dissatisfaction was increased on 5 September when, at Weizsäcker's instigation, Theodore Kordt, Counsellor at the German Embassy, called on Horace Wilson to give much firmer details of the right-wing conspiracy than had yet been available. This was the first indication that a tough attitude by Britain and France would give the conspirators their chance on the day of German mobilisation.

With Halifax's agreement, Vansittart and Cadogan decided

to summon the Prime Minister back from Scotland. Kordt was introduced to Halifax on the seventh. His information confirmed what Kleist had said; the date for the invasion of Czechoslovakia was 1 October.[27] But when Kordt advised them to broadcast to the German nation, he met precisely the same objections as Vansittart had given Kleist (see above, page 276).

On the eighth, Chamberlain came to London and called Simon, Halifax, Wilson and Cadogan together at 11 am in the Cabinet Room. At that moment, according to Inskip, Halifax was ready to enforce a warning despite Henderson's reluctance to deliver it. The meeting dragged on all day. Runciman was against it;[28] and Cadogan wrote: 'The Prime Minister thought a warning not a bad idea; and mentioned that he wanted to visit Hitler.'[29] After a second meeting on the ninth Inskip heard that 'ultimately though it [the warning] was sent to Nevile Henderson, instructions were given not to deliver it until further orders'.[30] Henderson was told to ask for an interview, not with Hitler but with Ribbentrop. Halifax had been overruled.

The Foreign Office front began to disintegrate. Vansittart continued to attack the proposal to visit Hitler* but Cadogan acquiesced. Inskip wrote: 'R.V. had fought the idea tooth and nail. "It was Henry IV going to Canossa over again". I was a little tepid about the proposal and merely said it could do no harm. I was pledged to secrecy, as surprise and timing were vital to its success.'[31]

Once Chamberlain was acquainted with the atmosphere in London, he outbid all opposition by emphasising to his colleagues the plan to visit Hitler. He told Kingsley Wood and MacDonald and, having gathered control quickly, summoned a Cabinet meeting for Monday, 12 September, in case he needed authority for the visit earlier than he thought.

Halifax carried out his new instructions rigidly, as if he had never wavered in the path of loyalty. Anglo-French relations were deliberately turned back to the cold definitions of April. When Corbin visited him again on 9 September, the French request for a warning was buried with the arguments deployed earlier in Cabinet. When Corbin protested that if German

* Vansittart even asked Eden to return from holiday in Ireland to speak to Halifax. The interview took place on 9 September. Eden apparently asked for nothing with which Halifax, in his aggressive mood, could not agree, except to take the Labour opposition into the Cabinet's confidence (Avon, *The Reckoning*, pp. 21–2.)

aggression were not resisted it would be their turn next, he received from Halifax a broadside of freezing contempt: 'with that argument I had never been able to feel any sympathy; nor did I think that the conclusions of it could be justified'.[32]

British hostility to France's point of view was shown even more clearly when Bonnet made his well-known request to Phipps on 10 September, 'as a friend' : 'supposing the Germans attack Czechoslovakia and France mobilised, as she at once would. Supposing France then turned to Great Britain and said "We are going to march; will you march with us?" What would our answer be? Bonnet said it was tremendously important to know and, if the question were put, it would be tremendously important that the answer should be immediate and quite plain one way or the other'.[33] Phipps replied equivocally. When Bonnet pressed him to write a private, unrecorded letter to Halifax, Phipps commented: 'Bonnet, perhaps more than Daladier, and certainly more than Mandel, Reynaud and Co. is desperately anxious for a possible way out of this impasse without being *obliged* to fight.'[34]

Meanwhile, in Britain, opinion began to stir, as if the public had at last understood that a crisis had begun. The news from Europe was not especially alarming, and from Czechoslovakia, in the brief aftermath of the Fourth Plan, actually good, but the Press was acutely sensitive to the approach of the Nuremberg Rally. On 7 September *The Times* exploded the holiday atmosphere with its leader recommending partition of Czechoslovakia, preferably by plebiscite. Dawson believed firmly in neutralising Czechoslovakia,[35] and his close link with Chamberlain may well have shown him what was in the wind. Halifax, after all, was to commend a plebiscite to Corbin only two days later. Although the Foreign Office repudiated the *Times* article, at Masaryk's request, Halifax lunched with Dawson afterwards and indicated his sympathy with the theme.[36]

The Times provoked a reaction in other newspapers much less agreeable to the Cabinet. The *Daily Telegraph* of 10 September declared roundly that 'peace is not to be preserved by indifference to the coercion of a small nation by a powerful neighbour'. At the other end of the political spectrum the *Daily Herald* warned of a 'united British people' ready to take up Hitler's challenge, and at the weekend the *Observer*

(11 September) proclaimed that German invasion 'would be without exception and by far the greatest crime that ever was committed in the world's history'. Suddenly the conflict was thrown open to the public and, fresh from their summer holidays, readers became aware of a real danger that they might be involved in war.

Mass Observation noted the sudden increase in column space devoted to foreign affairs in the six main national daily papers (see above, page 287); the change was not lost on German observers. Selzam, Counsellor at the Embassy in London, reported on 10 September –

Whole London and provincial press represents political situation today—clearly from official information—as extremely grave. It gives expression throughout to supposition that Führer incorrectly informed about attitude of British Government and public opinion...even *Daily Mail* and *Daily Express* have abandoned hitherto dissenting attitude.[37]

Two days later, with probably much greater satisfaction, Kordt confirmed the warning –

The complete change which British public opinion has undergone during the last fortnight places British Government in a position to implement tomorrow the policy announced today.... It has become known that Attlee, leader of Opposition, as well as Churchill and Eden...have given full support to the Government's policy. In consequence there is at present no opposition to Chamberlain.*

Still, as Harvey noted, *The Times*'s opinion 'was broadcast in Germany and it has been represented everywhere as a *ballon d'essai* and as foreshadowing a fresh surrender by HMG'.[38]

The administration showed itself remarkably inert. Halifax appears to have been the only member of the inner group seriously affected by the change.[39] At the Cabinet meeting on 12 September, Chamberlain asked Ministers merely to try 'to keep public opinion steady'. The TUC, at its annual conference in Blackpool, had adopted a resolution calling for collective defence against aggression, urging the Government to leave no doubt that they would support France and Russia. The Labour Party were pressing for an unequivocal declaration of British policy on Czechoslovakia: consequently some public statement

* *DGFP*, series D, vol. 2, pp. 742–3. 'Chamberlain', in this context, refers to the public statement made at Lanark.

had to be made. With the support of both Eden and Churchill, Chamberlain had made a statement to the House of Commons lobby correspondents, on the eleventh; 'Germany cannot with impunity carry out a rapid and successful military campaign against Czechoslovakia, without fear of interference by France and by Great Britain.'[40] But the significance of that was not to be read in the context of British policy. The thinking of the inner group was now so far in advance of the public, and the choices were constrained within such narrow limits, that outside opinion was ignored.

Meanwhile Henderson had been sent the revised message to give to Ribbentrop on 10 September. The Nuremberg Rally was under way and Henderson was living in the sleeping-compartment of his railway carriage; the message reached him by train from Ivone Kirkpatrick, First Secretary in Berlin. It was carefully phrased and, in the circumstances of Henderson's request for the interview, could be interpreted as marginally firmer than the Lanark speech. Admittedly, the Government only asked for German co-operation in avoiding trouble, but they allowed themselves to appear 'greatly disturbed'. Much stress was put on British achievements so far in Prague; and a new and slightly more precise definition of likely British involvement was given: if France went to war under the 1925 Treaty, 'it seems to H.M.G. inevitable that the sequence of events must result in a general conflict, from which Great Britain could not stand aside'.[41]

However mild the rebuke seems now, Henderson was appalled. He telephoned from Nuremberg at 8.30 am and 'urged with all the force at his command that he should not be instructed to make the official *démarche* proposed in telegram no. 354'.[42] Twice during the day he reinforced his refusal and asked to be allowed to transmit the sense of the message verbally only. 'The most fatal thing would be any repetition, or appearance of repetition, of 21 May threat . . . I have made the British position clear as daylight to people who count. I cannot do more here.'[43]

The Inner Cabinet met that morning,* and discussed whether or not to let Henderson do as he wished. 'We came to

* This was the last meeting not to be formally minuted. The best account is that of Templewood, *Nine Troubled Years*.

the conclusion that another warning after the many that [Hitler] had received, was more likely than not to excite him and push him into war.'[44] Cadogan commented briefly – 'The Ministers decided to hold their hand. I think it right. Van furious.'[45] All agreed that Chamberlain should put his plan for a visit to Hitler to the full Cabinet for approval; and later in the day Chamberlain wrote to Runciman, telling him of what was to come.[46]

The Vansittart–Halifax counter-attack finally ceased. Halifax had fought for some form of warning[47] but he initialled the countermand: 'On understanding that you have in fact already conveyed to Herr von Ribbentrop and others the substance of what you were instructed to say . . . and that you are clear they can be under no misapprehension I agree you need make no further communication.'*

Perhaps only Chamberlain saw his way clearly now. On the eleventh he wrote to his sister:

I fully realise that if eventually things go wrong, and the aggression takes place, there will be many, including Winston, who will say that the British Government must bear the responsibility and that if only they had had the courage to tell Hitler now that if he used force we should at once declare war, that would have stopped him. By that time it would be impossible to prove the contrary, but I am satisfied that we should be wrong to allow the most vital decision that any country could take, the decision as to peace or war, to pass out of our own hands into those of the ruler of another country and a lunatic at that.[48]

* *DBFP*, series 3, vol. 2, p. 285. There appear to be no German documents recording what Henderson actually did say to Ribbentrop, which justified the Ambassador in accepting this condition. Henderson had already twice – and probably more often – deliberately undermined the force of his instructions. In June, in a conversation with Weizsäcker (*DGFP*, series D, vol. 2, p. 377) he had said that Britain had already told the Czechs that they would be abandoned if they did not give way before the war broke out; and at a party on 6 August, according to the German report, 'Henderson repeatedly emphasised . . . that Great Britain would not think of risking even one sailor or airman for Czechoslovakia, and that any reasonable solution would be agreed to, so long as it was not attempted by force.' (*DGFP*, series D, vol. 2, p. 536). During the Nuremberg Rally, he told a Nazi official that 'he personally had no sympathy at all with the Czechs' (*DGFP*, series D, vol. 2, p. 758). Probably the best indication of what happened at the Rally is given in Colvin, *Vansittart in Office*, p. 239 – where he records Henderson as saying 'I can't warn the Führer and talk policy to him at a Party occasion. If I did he wouldn't listen, wouldn't understand it. It would have the wrong effect and send him off the deep end. They must start with the Czechs.'

Churchill was waiting outside when the inner group finished their meeting on the tenth. He demanded an ultimatum to Hitler 'in advance upon anything proposed hitherto, based on the theory that France would fight'.[49] His information about French determination, however, was soon suspect: the next day, Bonnet asked the British delegation in Geneva for a definite expression of British intentions and indicated that his Government had no more intention of fighting Germany and Italy together than of jumping off the Eiffel Tower.[50]

While the inner group waited for the speech Hitler was due to make to the Rally on the evening of the twelfth, they concentrated on preparing for Chamberlain's visit. On the evening of the tenth, Wilson had discussed Plan Z, as the scheme was now called, with Halifax and Cadogan, and they began to draft an announcement for the inner group to consider. Nothing was yet to be said to the full Cabinet; Chamberlain himself had not finally made up his mind. In the meantime, he wrote, 'I do not want to do anything which would destroy its chance of success, because if it came off, it would go far beyond the present crisis and might prove the opportunity for bringing about a complete change in the international situation.'[51]

In the plain needs of the State, preparations for a defensive war had begun.* Inskip attended a conference of senior ministers on 8 September 'to consider steps for readiness for war without giving publicity' and another meeting of the Chiefs of Staff with Chamberlain and Halifax, 'called to discuss further measures short of mobilisation'.[52] Preparations extended overseas. The Dominions had been kept in touch, and even so unlikely a source as de Valera offered help.†

Chamberlain thought that this hectic week had been

enough to send most people off their heads, if their heads were not as firmly secured on as mine. You have no conception what the atmosphere is—every 10 minutes someone comes in with a box bringing some new and disturbing communication, while busy-

* Even at the end of August the War Office were taking as many preparatory measures as possible without publicity—such as the organisation of air defence and the preparations for the despatch of the two divisions to Europe (Pownall Diary, 30 August).
† Inskip breakfasted with him on his way to Geneva at de Valera's request: 'He was obviously worried about the idea of war and wanted help as to the best use to be made of their resources. "A few airplanes" was his idea. I discouraged this and suggested defences of the ports.' (Inskip diary, 8 September.)

bodies of all kinds intrude their advice and the papers do their best to ruin all one's efforts.[53]

He singled out a *Daily Mail* leader, urging the Government to send an ultimatum to Hitler, and ordered telegrams to be sent to Paris, Prague and Berlin to deny the report. Hoare confirmed the Prime Minister's suspicions. 'The trouble,' he wrote,

> was the anti-Chamberlain clique. They dine together at Admiralty House [i.e. Duff Cooper's headquarters] and Winston was usually there. Everything said in the Cabinet repeated. They all regard war as inevitable. Intrigue with dissident French Ministers in Paris ... difficulty in speaking freely to the Cabinet in these conditions....[54]

Yet the opposition had lost momentum. At the Cabinet meeting on 12 September, Halifax reported that Churchill was isolated; Eden 'expressed complete agreement with the line taken'.* Apparently even Lord Lloyd had told him that 'we could not go against Henderson's strongly expressed advice'. In the Cabinet itself no one took exception when Chamberlain explained that the absence of any meeting for a fortnight had been the result of the decision of 30 August, that 'the Cabinet should meet from time to time in order to hear from those directly concerned how matters were proceeding and to assure themselves of their unanimity'.[55]

When he had brought his colleagues up to date, Halifax rejected the case he had advanced only a few days before. Though he deplored the *Times* article, he quoted Henderson's own defence of the failure to deliver the warning. He mentioned that the Admiralty's action in bringing up the mine-sweeper flotilla to full strength had severely shaken the German Naval Attaché – but he endorsed the decision to refuse Duff Cooper's request to bring the seventh destroyer fleet up to strength.†

* This may not have been true – see Avon, *The Reckoning*, pp. 22–3. Halifax may have been under a misapprehension from his earlier meeting with Eden, on 9 September. The views of other individuals, including Vincent Massey, Ambassador Kennedy, Cambon and Attlee, were included in the Foreign Office brief for Halifax (C9818/1941/18 (FO 371/21737)). Attlee appeared satisfied with what he had been told privately, 'and had said that he would avoid giving any impression that this country was disunited'. So much for the future of collective security.
† Ambassador Kennedy had also asked Halifax whether he wished the United States to move two cruisers to Portland. Halifax replied coolly that this was 'a matter for the U.S. Government' (CAB 23/95, 12 Sept). (Kennedy was again out of

Halifax quoted a report (via the German Ambassador in Paris) that Hitler had contemptuously tossed aside a memorandum suggesting that the Western powers would fight. He was, Halifax thought, quite probably mad. 'Any serious prospect of getting Hitler back to a sane outlook, would probably be immediately destroyed by any action on our part which would involve him in what he would regard as a public humiliation'. If he had decided to invade Czechoslovakia, a warning might drive him over the edge. The speaker might have been Nevile Henderson.

Only Duff Cooper complained, calling the undelivered telegram No. 354 'a fair statement of the case'. He did not press the matter against Chamberlain's ruling. If he had, the Dominion replies would doubtless have overwhelmed him. Australia, according to MacDonald, 'had suggested we should advise the Czech Government to do something generous and that, unless they did so, we should wash our hands of them'. Halifax quoted Vincent Massey as saying that although 'a minority in Canada might be in favour of our taking some forward action, the majority would be against ... in the hope that we should not become involved in a war'.[56]

The only question discussed before they listened to the broadcast of Hitler's speech from Germany was the shape of the reply to France's repeated requests for a British declaration of intent. Halifax's verdict followed the same line as his earlier reply to Corbin: Britain could not automatically fight in defence of French obligations, 'which Britain did not share and which a large section of British public opinion had always disliked'.[57] Chamberlain added that the declarations of 24 March and 28 August 'represented the *probable* sequence of events rather than a definite commitment'.[58]

Again, no one dissented. Léger had sent a proposal for a four-power conference* which was assumed by the Cabinet to be another convincing sign of French weakness. Corbin had been told the day before that no warning was to be sent to Germany. Now MacDonald said: 'Difficulties would arise if we reached a decision [in the event of war] without allowing time

step: on 9 September, Roosevelt deliberately dismissed talk of an American line-up with Britain and France against Germany as '100 per cent wrong'. *New York Times*, 10 September).
* A proposal (to include Germany, Britain, France and Italy) which was vigorously opposed by his friend Vansittart because it would 'drive Russia out of Europe' and glorify Italy at her expense (Vansittart papers, 13 Sept).

for what the Dominions would regard as reasonable consultation.'[59] The ineffable Lord Maugham suggested that the Cabinet should tell France that Britain was weak and would intervene only if France was 'in danger of losing a war'.

The formal reply was that Bonnet's question 'cannot be dissociated from the circumstances in which it might be posed which are necessarily at this stage quite hypothetical'; and the inner group, who finished drafting the note shortly before Hitler's speech began, defined Anglo-French relations in terms worthy of Curzon at the height of his powers: 'While H.M.G. would never allow the security of France to be threatened, they are unable to make precise statements on the character of their future action, or the time at which it would be taken, in circumstances that they at present cannot foresee.'[60]

At the very end of this exhibition of xenophobia, Kingsley Wood asked, rather hesitantly, for a military appreciation of the situation – from the British point of view – in the event of an attack by Hitler against Czechoslovakia. Oliver Stanley also asked the Chiefs of Staff to define what would be the relative position in 1939 if Germany won and then prepared to expand in other directions. It was an extremely important point, as Inskip realised: 'O.S.'s idea was that preventive war now is better than a war in twelve months. He wanted a report from the C.O.S. to support this view, from which apparently he has never receded, though he has never insisted on it.'[61] But Stanley was not to be satisfied at all.*

'So', Inskip wrote, 'we separated to wait and see. Nothing was said about the P.M.'s dramatic plan – Plan Z as it was called – and K. W[ood] and I were told before the meeting, by Sir Horace Wilson, to be careful not to mention it either in, or out, of the Cabinet.'[62]

Full of violent imprecations against the Czechs, Hitler's speech proved to be less of a disaster for British policy than the Cabinet feared. 'Sound and fury,' wrote Hoare, 'but no bridges broken.'[63] In the district of Eger and at Carlsbad, however, the

---

* Inskip asked the Chiefs of Staff to prepare the paper at once. The first draft, made by the Joint Planning Committee (CAB 53/41, COS 766), was ready on 13 September, but it was not finally approved until the twenty-fourth. Even then, Inskip did not mention it in the Cabinet on the twenty-fifth, and its conclusions failed to penetrate in the crisis atmosphere of the last few days before Munich.

Czech police fired on crowds listening to the broadcast in the open air. Six were killed and twenty seriously wounded. Martial law was imposed at once by the Czech Government.

Before the news reached London, the Cabinet Committee on the Czechoslovak Crisis – to give the inner group its new formal title – had met, but only to defer action until they had studied the broadcast. Routine preparations for defence were speeded up by asking the Defence Departments what instructions they required, short of orders for full mobilisation.

While the senior ministers followed the advice to 'wait and see', the imposing façade of French solidarity began to crumble. Martial law in Czechoslovakia, an evasive reply from Russia to Bonnet's latest series of questions about the Soviet commitment, and finally the complete refusal of Britain to be drawn into a sympathetic declaration brought Bonnet to the point of capitulation. The Runciman mission offered him the only way out. If Runciman could issue a report which Britain and France might then sponsor, Czechoslovakia would *have* to accept. Bonnet begged for haste – 'the whole question of peace and war may only be a matter of minutes'.[64] He even told Phipps that he was grateful for the British note, cold though it was, since it would help to restrain 'certain bellicose French Ministers'.[65] Commenting on this undignified *volte-face*, Phipps added that 'His Excellency seems completely to have lost his nerve and to be ready for any solution to avoid war.'[66] By 13 September, after he had heard terrifying reports from the American pioneer aviator, Colonel Lindbergh, about German air superiority and a series of prophecies of disaster from General Gamelin, Bonnet showed such signs of collapse that Phipps asked for an interview with Daladier; and found him also so weak that he wrote to Halifax: 'I fear the French have been bluffing, although I have continually pointed out to them that one cannot bluff Hitler.'[67]

At the end, French resolve almost vanished. Bonnet cried in despair, 'We cannot sacrifice ten million men, in order to prevent three and a half million Sudetens joining the Reich.'[68] After a Cabinet meeting on the thirteenth, in which the opposition, Mandel, Reynaud, Blum and Campichi were overridden by the fears of the majority, Daladier submitted a formal proposal to the British Cabinet. In order to prevent an invasion by German troops and the war which would ensue, Runciman should publish his plan and bring the two sides together. Failing that, a three-power conference composed of 'Germany for the Sudetens, France for the Czechs, Britain for Lord Runciman', should be summoned at once, 'with a view to obtaining that pacific settlement advocated by Hitler'.[69] For the second time in 1938 the French Government delivered itself unconditionally to the British.

There was a distinct fear in London that they were already too late. Henderson had reported Hitler's speech with the rider: 'If the Czech Government cannot, or will not, give satisfaction, war will ensue whatever the consequences.'[70] That Henderson should now admit Hitler's readiness to fight both France and Britain was decisive:

> about 3 o'clock things began rattling round to war. German troop movements, fighting in Czechoslovakia, fierce German and Sudeten propaganda.... Daladier tried to telephone to P.M. who would not speak to him.[71] Phipps saw Daladier and reported he had undergone a remarkable change since the middle of the previous week. He declared that at all costs Germany must be stopped from moving. Some way out must be found. If Czechoslovakia was invaded, France would be 'faced with her obligations'. This seemed to appal Daladier. Similar reports had come from other sources to me. Everything showed that the French didn't want to fight, were not fit to fight and wouldn't fight.[72]

In London the Czech Committee was meeting to discuss and dismiss the earlier French proposal for a four-power conference. 'It was felt that the proposal would not be in any way attractive to Germany except in so far as it involved the exclusion of Russia.'[73] Equally, they feared publication of Runciman's report, in case it was taken to be an official British plan. Instead of being used to coerce the Czechs, as originally intended, the Report had become a hostage in the hands of France.

Before Daladier's despairing message arrived, the idea of a plebiscite was taken much further than France's initial acquiescence warranted.* 'It was clear that the proposal would be intensely disliked by the Czechs who would regard it as disintegration of their state and as leaving them exposed to Germany without any natural defensive frontier.'[74] Great though the objections were, and even though no decision was taken that

---

* By the fourteenth, however, Harvey could write: 'Outstanding factor is now this peace at any price French attitude which of course lets H.M.G. out ... ' (*Diaries of Oliver Harvey*, p. 179).

the British should initiate the scheme, the Committee's minutes record that 'the general feeling among Ministers was that they would have great reluctance in involving this country in war, if the alternative was a plebiscite, provided that a plebiscite on fair and reasonable terms could be obtained.'[75]

The devil was out. The plebiscite was a living thing which the British might not formally propose, but which, as a last resort, they would accept; and which they would propagate indirectly through the Press. In that meeting the inner group finally set their seal of approval on the strategy in which they would safeguard for Czechoslovakia only the means of transfer of the Sudeten areas to Germany and not the principle of transfer itself. This decision was taken, it should be emphasised, without reference to France or to the United States.*

The Cabinet Committee gave Chamberlain authority to make his approach to Hitler at once.[76] In the evening, at 10 pm, Chamberlain, Halifax, Cadogan and Horace Wilson met to discuss the detailed arrangements for Plan Z. Daladier's message had arrived. Wilson had spoken to Henderson by telephone, and learned that Ribbentrop would be returning that night to Berlin. The proposal for the Prime Minister's visit was sent for Henderson to deliver early the next morning.

The full Cabinet met on the fourteenth, for the second time since the crisis had begun, twelve hours after Chamberlain's dramatic scheme had been launched. According to Inskip, 'there was a feeling of rather sharp anxiety, as to whether Hitler would send a refusal'.[77] But Chamberlain still dominated his colleagues, swallowing up their anxieties by his enthusiasm and the imaginative scope which he gave to his plan. 'The vital element was surprise and as it was imperative that no hint of what was in contemplation should leak out, he had thought it better to postpone mentioning it until the last moment.'[78] He explained that he had originally intended to leave for Germany before telling Hitler that he was coming. Dramatic effect had given way to cooler calculations.

The success of the plan depended upon its being accurately

---

* Lindsay had reported from Washington that American opinion was in favour of making a firm stand against German aggression, and that 'any compromise may bring about a let-down of American friendliness' (DBFP, series 3, vol. 2, p. 301). In the absence of positive proposals, his message made no impression (Inskip diary, 14 September).

timed. If adopted too soon, it would be asked why this action had been taken before Lord Runciman had finished his task. On the other hand, if we waited too long, Herr Hitler might have taken some irrevocable action. Up to yesterday afternoon [13 September] ... he had had it in mind that the plan ... should be put into effect probably towards the end of the present week. On the preceding afternoon, however, events had started to move rapidly. ... He hoped that the Cabinet would feel that he had not gone beyond his proper duty in taking this action on the advice of those of his colleagues whom he had mentioned, but without consulting the full Cabinet.

Chamberlain's preparations for the interview are of sufficient importance to be quoted.*

He hoped that the idea would appeal to the Hitlerian mentality. Herr Hitler liked to see Heads of State, and it might be agreeable to his vanity that the British Prime Minister should take so unprecedented a step. But he also had in mind that you could say more to a man face to face than you could put in a letter, and he thought that doubts as to the British attitude would be better removed by discussion than by any other means ... it was essential that the present dispute should not be settled by force. We were neither pro-Czech nor pro-Sudeten German. Our business was to keep the peace and find a just and equitable settlement.

Chamberlain intended to point out how much Britain and France had done to put pressure on the Czechs and how much further Beneš had gone than they expected. He anticipated a tirade from Hitler about Beneš' faithlessness but he meant to continue with a proposal for an international Commission to supervise the fulfilment of the agreement, if it were reached; or, alternatively, that both sides should lay their cases before Runciman and accept him as arbitrator. Unfortunately,

he now felt that Herr Hitler might say that, while this might have been acceptable a week ago, nothing could now settle the matter except a Plebiscite. The Prime Minister thought that the Cabinet would have to consider very carefully what should be said to any such demand.

Some people might take the view that the demand for a Plebiscite should be rejected out of hand. That was not his view, nor the

* The main source of the brief which Chamberlain took to Berchtesgaden and Godesberg was Horace Wilson (PREM 1/266A), but Cadogan, Sargent and the Chiefs of Staff also took part. It is not clear whether Hankey gave advice.

view of the Foreign Secretary. He thought it was impossible for a democracy like ourselves to say that we would go to war to prevent the holding of a Plebiscite. Further, the presence within their boundaries of a homogeneous, disciplined and easily-moved people such as the Sudeten Germans, was not a source of strength to Czechslovakia. The Prime Minister added that he was aware of the enormous difficulties attending a Plebiscite. There was the initial difficulty of delimiting the areas to which the plebiscite should relate; there were mixed populations to be dealt with; there were also strategic and economic considerations; but he doubted whether Czechoslovakia would ever have peace so long as the Sudeten Germans were part of the country. He did not think it right that we should say that we would have nothing to do with the idea of a Plebiscite. . . .

But supposing that part of Czechoslovakia were given to Germany, what would happen to the rest of the country? It might be said that there would be a helpless little strip of territory liable at any moment to be gobbled up by Germany. The Czechs might take that view and might prefer to die fighting rather than accept a solution which would rob them of their natural frontiers.

The only answer which he could find was one which he was most unwilling to contemplate, namely, that this country should join in guaranteeing the integrity of the rest of Czechoslovakia. This would be a new liability, and he realised that we could not save Czechoslovakia if Germany decided to over-run it. The value of the guarantee would lie in its deterrent effect. The sort of arrangement contemplated was that Czechoslovakia should be guaranteed by France, Russia, Germany and ourselves, and should be relieved from liability to go to the assistance of the guarantor countries, and would thus become a neutral State. This would help to clear up the situation in Central Europe. . . .

The inducement to be held out to Herr Hitler in the proposed negotiations was the chance of securing better relations between Germany and England. This chance would be lost if Herr Hitler had recourse to force now.[79]

On past experience, a plebiscite was most unlikely to be acceptable to the Czechs and the proposed guarantee was self-evidently weak to the point of futility. The Czechs would have to be coerced with threats beyond anything so far imagined; yet France and Czechoslovakia were not to be informed until after the proposal had been accepted by Germany. Nevertheless, 'almost everyone spoke in favour of the P.M.'s bold stroke. Walter Elliot was inclined to complain that he had not been consulted. He . . . was rather obscure. No one else took this line. Nobody takes Winterton seriously. . . . J. Simon finished by his usual shower of compliments to the P.M.'[80] The last phrase is an understatement. Simon eulogised what he called 'this brilliant proposal' and added that 'if the Prime Minister came back with the seeds of peace with honour, he would be universally acclaimed as having carried out the greatest achievement of the last twenty years'.[81] The phrase stuck. At 3.30 pm the message from Hitler came. 'He was at the P.M.'s disposal and suggested Mrs C. should accompany him.'[82]

Chamberlain's plan was a logical extension of what had been envisaged in March. Since the Czech Government could not do the job itself, Britain and France would intervene to restrain Germany while at the same time imposing a settlement on them. Chamberlain could think that he had played his game like an angler, inching in a powerful fish with a thin, delicate line. All the adverse factors, the attitude of France, the United States and Russia, had been channelled or excluded in preparation for a situation where the Czech question could be solved conclusively, as a prelude to an Anglo-German détente.

Chamberlain had indeed won such freedom of action as the British predicament allowed. His Cabinet surrounded him and held up his hands; public and Parliament were soon to applaud his tenacity and courage. He had successfully taken for granted the compliance of the Cabinet.* He had a mandate from the Dominions: the Australian High Commissioner 'had telegraphed that morning, saying that opinion in that country would prefer almost any course to war'.[83] Among his opponents, even Duff Cooper acknowledged that war later on was preferable to war then.

On the other hand, Britain was now totally committed. Chamberlain's keen sense of the value of drama in political life made him well aware of the impact of the visit on international opinion, but his misunderstanding of the Nazi temperament prevented him from realising that his master stroke of diplomacy placed him in a most unflattering light in Berlin. If the French had always come to London, it was the British who always

---

* 'So I sent the fatal telegram and told the Cabinet the next morning what I had done. Of course they did not, for the most part, realise how it would strike the world but they approved.' (Chamberlain letters, 19 Sept.)

flew to Germany. The umbrella was a fatal symbol of bourgeois respectability. In the midst of German military preparations, it did not occur to the British to send at least the CIGS in full dress uniform; Chamberlain arrived surrounded by civilians in suits.

Moreover, by the token of the visit, Britain became identified with the necessity of a solution, as clearly as if the Government had endorsed Runciman's report. In the absence of co-ordinated action with France and Russia – the signatories of the treaties – British action amounted to direct intervention from which there could be no withdrawal. The myth of arbitration, preserved so long as Runciman worked, was destroyed. British policy was now to be controlled by factors beyond the power of the Cabinet to affect.

Chamberlain did not, of course, go unarmoured. He could point to the enforced acquiescence of France as well as to the concessions already made by Beneš. He could offer, if necessary, a plebiscite and British mediation. So long as Hitler was interested in negotiations, British goodwill might appear attractive. But even if that were possible Chamberlain had not foreseen the complexities which his apparently simple action involved. In the Cabinet meeting on 14 September, hesitant voices were raised to inquire about the future claims of the Polish and Hungarian minorities. The Prime Minister and Foreign Secretary skated over them with an assurance amounting either to wilful ignorance or deliberate deceit. They 'did not contemplate that any such demand would be made. ... Other minorities ... were content at the moment.'[84] There were also immensely complicated questions of means and principles: the Cabinet might cheerfully accept the idea of a plebiscite at some future date; but several ministers jibbed at calling one immediately. Stanley declared: 'No Government which proposed such a suggestion would stand for long, nor would it deserve to.'[85]

No one asked what would happen if Chamberlain failed or was humiliated. Kingsley Wood offered the suggestion that 'if it met with a rebuff, it would be recognised that we had done everything to avoid a catastrophe'. But that rebuff would mean war or total surrender. In either case, it might create a worse catastrophe if British intervention had lost her the support of France. After expatiating for months about the danger of placing Britain's freedom to declare war in the hands of an ally, the

Cabinet had allowed Chamberlain to risk it on the goodwill of an enemy. The answer, and some explanation of the catharsis which Hitler's acceptance of the visit caused among ministers, is to be found elsewhere. The 'rattling down to war' had stopped, like a film projector put into reverse. The Chiefs of Staff Report showed what they had been spared:

> no pressure we and France could bring to bear by sea, land or air could stop Germany over-running Bohemia and inflicting a decisive defeat on Czechoslovakia. The war would be an unlimited war in which, while we should initiate no air bombardment, sooner or later we must experience it to the tune of possibly 500–600 tons of bombs a day for two months, against our 200 tons, and France's 200 tons. Economic pressure by the navy would be our real hope. The Chiefs of Staff have no doubt that *after a long war,* this would prevail.[86]

12 The Lobster and the Pot

At the time, much was made of the venture of an elderly man flying for the first time to such an appointment. Thirty years after Blériot crossed the Channel there was neither danger nor much discomfort in the short flight from Heston to Munich. Yet the excitement was not misplaced: it was literally an unprecedented thing for a British Prime Minister to do. Chamberlain had always been sparing in political gestures. He had despised Lloyd George and MacDonald for their 'showmanship', but when he needed, he showed himself no less a master of the stage-management of occasion. The Press received the news with acclamation and relief, and the City smiled: share values rose again on the Stock Exchange.[1] Few in Whitehall were so churlish as to recall Vansittart's comparison with the Emperor Henry IV and Canossa – and none so pessimistic as to say so in public.

It would be wrong to depict Chamberlain as a helpless innocent, shuffling sheeplike among the crooked leaders of the Third Reich. He was used to rough bargaining and in the past, in British domestic politics, he had shown himself as tough and ruthless as any leader of the twentieth-century Conservative Party. It was unfortunate that his only previous experience of foreign negotiation should have been in the relatively mild climate of Lausanne in 1932, where concession appeared to be wisdom. On the other hand, he held powerful cards, and during the lull after Hitler's acceptance of the visit, a considerable share of initiative. As he flew over London – and confessed to 'some slight sinkings'[2] – he could be certain that, so long as the talks and any subsequent negotiations lasted, the invasion of Czechoslovakia would not take place.

But Chamberlain was in the position of a man playing poker for stakes which he could not afford. In such a situation, whatever the lie of the cards, bluff becomes difficult. With the self-evident and fully admitted spectre of war sitting behind him at the table, Chamberlain was naturally inclined to shorten the process of bidding and bargaining. As a result he was forced back almost at once to his ultimate proposal of a plebiscite. This was the British predicament – they had to play, but on the terms accepted by the Government they could not afford to lose.

The meetings at Berchtesgaden* and Godesberg are so well known that there is no need to do more than recapitulate briefly the main events. To answer the questions whether government policy changed as a result of the visit, whether Chamberlain's primacy in the Cabinet was weakened by opposition while in Germany and after his return, and what effect the British imagined they had had on Germany's demands, the story must be told from the point of view of the inner group and the Cabinet, and their advisers.

At first, the Cabinet was treated to second-hand consultation. 'It was', Inskip recorded, 'a complete surprise to read in the morning papers of the 16 September that he was on his way back. Mrs C. was not told by the F.O. and read of it in the papers. Strang, who had gone with him, telephoned to say it wasn't too bad, but otherwise nothing came through, throwing any light on the talks.'[3] The inner circle were better informed, from what Hoare called 'cryptic conversations with Horace Wilson on the telephone.'[4]

Chamberlain's account of the mission, which he gave to the inner group at 6.30 pm on 16 September, shortly after his return, set out the basis for future policy-formation, and was not challenged – nor, in the nature of the evidence, could it be.† He began by confirming the Cabinet's assumption about Hitler's timetable for the invasion.

Very soon after his arrival at Berchtesgaden he had appreciated that the position was well-nigh desperate. Everything was ready for an immediate blow. He did not mean that Herr Hitler had

* This name for Hitler's mountain resort has been chosen in preference to Obersalzberg, as being more commonly accepted in English.
† Chamberlain and Hitler talked together with only the interpreter, Paul Schmidt, present. The British delegation had no idea what had transpired until Chamberlain dictated his record after dinner (*Diaries of Oliver Harvey*, p. 183). The Germans were supposed to send a copy of Schmidt's record, as they had done after the Halifax visit in November 1937, but they refused to do so, alleging misuse of the transcript of the Ribbentrop-Henderson conversation in March 1938 (*Diaries of Oliver Harvey*, p. 185). Schmidt's record (*DGFP*, series D, vol. 2, pp. 786–98) shows that Chamberlain's own account was substantially accurate; indeed suggests that he was firmer than might be guessed from his own version.

definitely made up his mind that he would strike, but he thought that Herr Hitler definitely contemplated that he might strike at any moment. There were plenty of incidents to stoke up the fires, and the air was full of fantastic stories. In a word, the whole position was ripe for some irrevocable step.

Herr Hitler had said that the Sudeten Germans must come into the Reich. They wanted to come in, and he was determined that they should. If the Czechs said that they would not allow it, he would have to see that they did. 'As to the possible consequences, I would chance a world war', he had said. Herr Hitler had talked of this so much as an affair of a few hours that he [Chamberlain] began to speak a trifle sharply. He asked Herr Hitler whether he had wasted his time in coming and said that perhaps he had better go home.

On this, Herr Hitler, who had previously been rather inclined to rant, had quietened down, and his manner changed. Everything, he said, depended on the attitude of His Majesty's Government. Were they prepared to accept the principle of self-determination? This was a crucial question. The procedure could be settled afterwards.[5]

In one step, Hitler had effectively disposed of the alternative schemes of provincial autonomy, or Beneš' Fourth Plan. He could not have known whether Chamberlain was prepared to keep pace with him, but Chamberlain had at once played his best card. 'He was not authorised to give any such assurance without talking the matter over with his colleagues; it would also be necessary for him to consult with the French Government and Lord Runciman.'

So far, cautious; but with a frankness indicating either amazing lack of foresight or deliberate intention well beyond his assurances to the Cabinet, Chamberlain had gone on: 'speaking personally, the Prime Minister said that he did not object to the principle of self-determination, or, indeed, attach very much importance to it. What he wanted was a fair and peaceful settlement. It was the practical and not the theoretical difficulties of the situation which concerned him.'

So they had agreed that Chamberlain should return to London, consult his colleagues, and meet Hitler again. After a great deal of persuasion, 'Hitler had given a half-hearted assurance that he would not set the military machine in motion until this second discussion took place', but he had made it plain 'that incidents might make it impossible for him to restrain from strengthening the machine and his assurance was qualified to that extent.' Chamberlain's own impression, however, was that 'Herr Hitler would be careful not to start the machine pending the second conversation'.

At the same time, Chamberlain had tacitly acceded to Hitler's demand that the areas for transfer to Germany should be delimited on the principle of a bare German majority of inhabitants, 51 per cent as opposed to the 80 per cent majority which the Cabinet had previously discussed. The distinction was of great importance: transfer on an 80 per cent basis would involve removing 2,030,000 Germans from Czechoslovakia and roughly 15,000 square kilometres of land;[6] on a 51 per cent basis the figures would rise to 2,822,899 Germans, but to the much larger figure of 28,996 square kilometres;[*] the extra territory would include the towns of Olmütz and Gablonz and the Neumarkt which separated the central and southern Sudeten areas, as well as sections of the frontier fortifications. These were not 'theoretical difficulties' even if Chamberlain chose to ignore them. The British attempt to insist on an 80 per cent majority later (below, page 355) was futile because any chance of success had been undermined by the Berchtesgaden 'understanding'.[†]

In his report to the Cabinet on the seventeenth, and in notes circulated to ministers, Wilson put an advantageous gloss on the visit. Von Dirksen had told him

> that the visit had been most valuable ... it could not have been timed, or done in a better way. They all seemed to be impressed by the 'statesmanship' of what they evidently regard as a bold masterstroke of diplomacy. It clearly appealed to Hitler as something after his own heart and [Hitler's] subsequent long conversation with the Prime Minister had done nothing to lessen its effect.[‡]

Wilson was also at pains to emphasise how far Germany had

---

[*] Luza, *Transfer of the Sudeten Germans*, p. 158. CAB 27(646) (20 Sept) gives the figure for 51 per cent transfer as 2,600,000, the figure given in Henlein's demand of 15 September; the areas were to be occupied by German forces within twenty-four hours. (*DGFP*, series D, vol. 2, p. 801.)

[†] Schmidt's report makes it clear that Chamberlain tried to insist on the 80 per cent principle, but that his personal admission to the demand for succession in general could be taken as agreement to the 51 per cent basis.

[‡] Wilson: notes in the Thomas Jones collection (foreign affairs 1938) entitled 'Notes written somewhere over Germany, 16 September'. Hewel, Ribbentrop's personal secretary, also told Wilson that 'Hitler told me he felt he was speaking to a *man*.' This may be set beside Weizsäcker's comment that Hitler 'felt that he had manoeuvred the dry civilian into a corner'.

prepared for invasion. He emphasised that the German Foreign Office had already considered all the questions of local government and voting in the new areas of the Reich and that Gaus, Legal Adviser to the Nazi Government, had been included in the German delegation. 'When I suggested that we might have a little trouble with the French who would in any case take care to blame us, [Dirksen] said it could not be helped and that "anyhow the decision rested in that car," pointing to the Prime Minister's car just in front of us.'[7]

The Berchtesgaden visit cleared the air by reducing the British immediately, and without protest, to their final position of accepting secession of the Sudeten areas. Chamberlain may have hoped for more but the haste in offering his 'personal statement' suggests that he had expected to have to go this far, whatever he had agreed with the Cabinet beforehand. Whether he believed Hitler's attitude had been, as he said, not unreasonable, or whether he genuinely thought that there was no other choice but war, can only be guessed at.

Chamberlain had preserved the vestiges of long-term British policy by looking beyond the Czechoslovak question to future Anglo-German relations; but it was clear to Hitler as it was to him that the British now had to force the issue with France and Czechoslovakia. Thus Hitler was given a double advantage: if he chose to carry on by negotiation, he could get his desiderata bloodlessly if Chamberlain succeeded; or, if Chamberlain failed with the Czechs, he would have not only an excellent *casus belli* to invade but quite enough evidence of Czech intranssigence to keep France from fulfilling her treaty obligations by war.

Chamberlain gave no sign of suspecting what a hostage he had given, unless his insistent demand that Hitler should maintain the status quo revealed a basic mistrust. He took on voluntarily the job of trying to extract at any price – and within a week – the agreements he required. It is perhaps too much to say that he was caught in the situation he had created, or that he had completely surrendered freedom of choice; but, even taking into account the fact that partition was part of the British plan, and that the degree of disruption of Czechoslovakia did not unduly worry him, two questions which he should have asked and required an answer for were not put, or were pushed aside.

First and most important : would self-determination for the

M

Sudeten Germans form the basis of a sound Anglo-German settlement? This was the keystone of the whole scheme, reaching back into 1937. Chamberlain made no more than a gesture, and allowed himself to be rushed by Hitler's answer, that he would not take Anglo-German relations first because '300 Sudeten-Germans had been killed' in the Sudeten areas and a solution could no longer be delayed. No doubt Chamberlain received these figures with scepticism* but he accepted Hitler's contention that there was greater urgency than he had previously allowed. Anglo-German relations were not to be discussed again until after the Munich settlement had actually been signed.

The second question, although not of such long standing, was equally significant. If Germany took over the Sudeten areas, would Hitler then be satisfied with what was left of Czechoslovakia? Would he be content with the solution of the racial problem and the additional German security provided by the partial destruction of the Czech frontier defences? Or did he want the whole country, like Austria, as part of his drive towards *Weltmacht*? The British were not certain. Hitler had laid down fierce conditions, including the abrogation of the treaty with Russia. On the other hand, he had not shown any interest in non-German minorities. Pressed by Simon, who asked both these pertinent questions,† Chamberlain gave Hitler's statement that he would be satisfied; 'but he had not undertaken to make a specific declaration to that effect. . . . Herr Hitler might be prepared to repeat what he had already said.'[8]

In the Prime Minister's absence, some routine and rather desultory war preparations had been conducted. The CID had met to discuss the scheme of Sir John Anderson's committee for evacuating London, at ten to fourteen days' notice. Some acceleration of Service programmes was allowed and a new laxity prevailed – 'Sir Warren Fisher allowed plans for millions of pounds to be approved without more than a nod from him. It is easy to hark back and reflect on the objection to expenditure

---

* Wilson tried all day to obtain official confirmation of these figures but the German officials stalled. Later, Runciman denied that more than 75 deaths had occurred on both sides (Wilson Memorandum).

† Answering the first criticism, Chamberlain said only that 'He hoped that when this had been cleared up it would be possible to go back to the question of an Anglo-German understanding. This was very much in their minds.' (16 September, CAB 27/646.)

when war seemed far off. Now it is near, the Treasury control disappears.'[9] The CID also approved the sending of a mission to France to plan for the use of the advanced air striking-force. Later Inskip postponed it – 'The avoidance of publicity for our preparation was very much in all our minds . . . it was doubtful whether we were wise, but no one took a different line at our many discussions of preparations for war.'[10]

Uncertainty and lack of urgency clouded the pronouncements of the Chiefs of Staff. In the last fortnight before Munich, there was no concerted effort to make a military view heard. The memorandum of 24 September made the interesting suggestion that Germany was not likely to attempt a knock-out blow, but it was not pressed on the Cabinet;[11] instead the Chiefs of Staff took refuge in a form of fatalism, a reliance on eventual victory, by indirect means, 'after a long war'. No offensive plans were to be prepared until defences were complete and all Services brought up to war priority. 'Otherwise we would place ourselves in the position of a man who attacks a tiger before he has loaded his gun.'[12] Quick results were not to be expected: 'nevertheless the latent resources of the Empire and the doubtful morale of our opponents under the stress of war give us confidence as to the ultimate outcome'.[13]

Nothing had occurred of which Chamberlain could have disapproved. The Czech Committee met on the fifteenth to discuss the recall of Parliament and also the many questions which would arise if a plebiscite were held. Halifax, bold indeed, suggested 'that it might be desirable to make a very guarded approach to France saying that we appreciated her anxieties that a peaceful solution should be found, and leading them to express their point of view about a plebiscite without expressing any opinion on behalf of this country'.[14] Even this silken trap had to wait for the return of the Prime Minister. The Committee did, however, ask the War Office for a military assessment of whether a plebiscite could be held under fair conditions 'within a few weeks or months' if such a thing were demanded.[15] The sending of an international force, as well as British troops, was discussed. A plan put forward by *The Times* for transfer on the basis of existing ethnographical information, or the pattern of recent voting, found a good deal of support. In the Foreign Office, Harvey believed that 'a plebiscite is the utmost that we can possibly hope for', and

Strang thought that Czechoslovakia would be better without the Sudeten Germans, who could never be expected to settle down again as loyal citizens.[16] But the practical difficulties of a plebiscite were soon seen to be overwhelming and the suggestion of direct transfer offered an easier way out.

At the meeting of the inner group on the sixteenth,[17] Chamberlain began bluntly,

he was convinced that there was no longer any solution except by self-determination.... He was satisfied that it was impossible to go to war, in order to prevent self-determination, more especially now that Henlein said the Sudeten Germans wanted to go back to the Reich. The real question was should that return be carried out in an orderly or disorderly manner?[18]

The greatest difficulty, he thought, would be to obtain Czech agreement. As for France – he read out a letter from Flandin, the former Foreign Minister, to the effect that 'if the issue was one of a plebiscite France would not oppose it and would not go to war to prevent it'.[19] The best thing would be if Runciman were to say that 'it was impossible that the Sudetens and the Czechs would settle down together and that a plebiscite was the only way ... this might make matters easier for the Czech Government'. Runciman was to be useful at last.*

The inner group agreed with him on the general principle. But there was a great deal to be settled in detail: questions of the approach to the Czech Government and to France, and the method of transfer. Runciman had seen Beneš that morning and in answer to the President's pleas about the 'sacrifice of Czechoslovakia', had given him a very rough ride. 'He had told Dr Beneš that he thought the latter had done more than anyone else to sacrifice his country. Further, if he had not been a party to the "spoils" system [in the treatment of minorities] in its worst form, he would have avoided many of his worst difficulties.'[20]

Chamberlain and Runciman heightened the atmosphere as if they were working in concert to discredit the Czech Government. Chamberlain said 'that he felt sure that if he had not

* Runciman was in a poor state on his return from Prague. Harvey found him ashen-faced, worn out, and anxious to avoid argument. He was keen only 'to make the Prime Minister's position easier', and he had become strongly anti-Czech (*Diaries of Oliver Harvey*, p. 187).

gone to Berchtesgaden some violent action would have taken place'. Runciman added, 'Czechoslovakia provided horrid stories of irregularity, graft and corruption. The behaviour of the Government towards minorities had been outrageous. This was the case not merely with the Germans but also with the Hungarians. Altogether it was an ugly story.'

Poor, mild, democratic country – what would the upright Liberal have found in Rumania or Bulgaria? As for the Polish claims to Teschen, and Hungary's demands for all the southern border-lands, Runciman admitted that these areas would demand plebiscites themselves. Would Czechoslovakia then cease to exist? Halifax asked. Runciman replied, 'Once you started to examine the make-up of particular provinces, you found that they were all terribly mixed. If all the minorities got self-determination, the country would be reduced to a very small area.' Yet Chamberlain still repeated Hitler's promise 'that if a plebiscite was granted, he would not worry his head on what was left of Czechoslovakia. . . . This really represented Herr Hitler's view'.

However unfairly they slanted the argument against the Czechs, the British still relied on French help because, so long as the Czech Government had any lingering hope that France would fulfil the treaty, Beneš was unlikely to give way. The group decided not to send France any news of what had transpired at Berchtesgaden, 'as the only result would be that the gist . . . would immediately become known all over the world'. The British press was likewise kept in the dark. Dawson of *The Times* and Lord Beaverbrook had both seen Halifax and 'claimed that they were short of guidance'. Hoare was briefed to meet the proprietors and editors of newspapers when the Committee thought fit. No decision was made on whether to proceed by way of a plebiscite or a transfer of territory on some principle such as that suggested in *The Times*. The information which the Committee had, suggested that the latter was open to less objection from the Czechs themselves.*

When the full Cabinet met on 17 September, Chamberlain appeared 'astonishingly fresh and alert', and he gave a lively account of his visit, calling Hitler 'the commonest little dog he

---

* Beneš had taken pains to remind Runciman that Czechoslovakia could mobilise 400,000 men. He warned that a military government might take over to prevent a plebiscite being held (CAB 27/646, 16 September).

had ever seen'.[21] During the description of the interview with Hitler, however,

> his common appearance was somehow rather forgotten and the P.M. was impressed with his power.... The impression made by the P.M.'s story was a little painful. H. had made him listen to a boast that the German military machine was a terrible instrument, ready to move now, and that, once put in motion, could not be stopped. The P.M. said more than once to us he was just in time. It was plain that H. made all the running: he had, in fact, blackmailed the P.M.[22]

Chamberlain did not attempt to dispel this impression, but asked bluntly for agreement on the principle of self-determination at once. Opposition, which had died down in the relaxed atmosphere before the visit, flared again. The most far-sighted of the dissidents was De La Warr, who did not object to the principle of self-determination, but condemned the concessions involved in a plebiscite held immediately and under German control, not merely as 'unfair to the Czechs and dishonourable to ourselves after all that we have done in the last six months', but because unless an honourable peace was achieved war would follow in any case. If Britain did not stand firm, 'whenever Hitler threatened the world, we should have to concede what he asked for'. De La Warr was 'prepared to face war now, in order to free the world from the emotional threat of ultimata'.[23]

He was alone, and the Prime Minister disapproved strongly of what he had said. Duff Cooper began by talking belligerently of history and the balance of power, but ended lamely with the conclusion that putting off the evil day might gain time 'until the Nazis fell'. Stanley said he would fight, rather than surrender, but he did not regard the plebiscite as a surrender unless it was unfair – and that begged the question.

The rest agreed, whether enthusiastically or not. As so often, the ultramontane position was held by Lord Maugham, who quoted Canning on British interests and betrayed great hostility to France. Inskip feared that a war would bring 'changes in the state of Europe which might be satisfactory to no one, except Moscow and the Bolsheviks'. MacDonald appeared to agree with Runciman that Czechoslovakia had maltreated her minorities. Lord Zetland, Secretary for India, was terrified of war and Russia. The rest, Hailsham, Simon, Colville, Brown, Stanhope,

Morrison, Hore-Belisha, Kingsley Wood, agreed with the principle of partition, either by transfer or plebiscite. Halifax delivered one of his more abstruse pronouncements – 'He would fight for the great moralities which knew no geographical boundaries. But there was no greater urge to fight for Czechoslovakia than to fight Japan because of the bombing of civilians in Canton.' The Cabinet must have found it hard even to guess where the Foreign Secretary actually would stand and fight.

A majority in favour of partition was not enough to satisfy Chamberlain's feeling of urgency. The difficulties attendant on a plebiscite were too great to dispose of in one week of negotiation. Mere acceptance of principle was not something he could offer to Hitler. Also the minority, who had never entirely accepted his authority, now had a principle to fight for. For the first time he seems to have wished actually to exclude the critics: who were associated not only with Churchill and his group,* who regarded Berchtesgaden as 'the stupidest thing that has ever been done',[24] but with plans to work up opposition in France. Churchill was speaking in terms of the Grand Alliance, a ring of force against German aggression. A few junior members of the Government, notably Captain Crookshank, Secretary for Mines, were voicing their doubts about the Prime Minister's conduct of affairs. Churchill himself crossed to France on 19 September, and met Blum, Herriot, Reynaud (Minister of Finance) and Mandel (Minister of Colonies). Vansittart was intriguing busily and corresponding with Léger at the Quai d'Orsay.†

Chamberlain imposed his authority by explaining that in the next set of talks with Hitler he must retain freedom of action. He would not agree to a plebiscite without safeguards. The plebiscite might not be necessary at all and the Cabinet should not tie his hands too tightly in case he had to exceed his mandate, in order to stop a precipitate invasion. Bonnet and Daladier

---

* 'On Saturday', he wrote to his sister, 'we had two Cabinets lasting five hours and finally overcame all critics, some of whom had been concerting opposition beforehand' (Chamberlain letters, 19 September).

† According to Harvey, Vansittart attempted to exclude Bonnet from the French delegation of 19 September, fearing that his influence on Daladier would be fatal to the line he wished to take against Germany (*Diaries of Oliver Harvey*, p. 182). Phipps, in contrast, faithfully interpreted the policy of the inner group, by working on Bonnet's weakness and by alienating the opposition. To some extent, he helped by his reports to condition the British response.

were invited to London that night, and the meeting adjourned, the only sign of firmness being that the majority – Halifax very reluctantly – agreed to give an unspecified guarantee for the rump of Czechoslovakia after partition had occurred.

While Ministers waited for the French to arrive, Chamberlain saw the Labour leaders, Dalton, Morrison and Citrine. They were taken aback by his pessimistic account of the views of France and the lack of positive support from Russia. Litvinov had replied: 'that under the Treaty the Soviet Government were only bound to come to the aid of France after Czechoslovakia had become involved in the war on her behalf. The Russian Government therefore proposed to take no action until France had become involved in war, and then to take the matter up at Geneva.'* Chamberlain gave a fair account, but he did not try either to persuade the deputation or to educate them in the real meaning of what the Government was trying to do.

Not the least significant factor in the final weeks of the Czech affair is that whenever Anglo-French talks took place it was always the French who were summoned to London. Such was the British attitude to their ally, but the circumstances also gave the French the excuse – for domestic consumption – that they were being brow-beaten. They took full advantage: French capacity to say one thing in London and another in Paris seems continually to have amazed the inner group.

On the other hand, the insularity of British ministers was their most striking characteristic. They had taken the accuracy of Phipp's reports for granted – he had been a hard-liner when Ambassador in Berlin. The British either missed the point about France's need for a strong lead before showing a robust attitude herself,[25] or they ignored it deliberately. The Chiefs of Staff, after all, were convinced of France's capacity to fight[26] if the will was there. As Colonel Campbell wrote, 'Germany would by no means be able to hold the French, if they mean business'.[27]

Daladier and Bonnet arrived early on Sunday, 18 September, and met Chamberlain, Halifax, Simon and Hoare in talks which lasted until after midnight, interspersed with two meetings of the Inner Cabinet. Daladier was far from pleased about Chamberlain's plan to visit Hitler, 'and said he had been pressed to go

* 19 Sept, CAB 23/95. 'Russia unlikely to do anything effective. Deputation astonished at this' (Wilson Memorandum).

to Germany himself but had always replied that a British representative should go too'.[28]

Chamberlain opened the meeting with a full account of the proceedings at Berchtesgaden and of Runciman's mission. A curious ball-game followed, in which Chamberlain and the French bandied questions to and fro. To Chamberlain's probing, Daladier replied

> that they were anxious to hear the views of the British Government, who had by now had some days to deliberate over the position. To this the Prime Minister had replied that since the French were bound by treaty obligations and we were not, he thought it was for the French to express their views first. The French representatives in turn had found some means of passing the ball back into our court, and so matters had continued during the whole morning.[29]

At last, however, Daladier admitted that the real question 'was what we could do, in order to ensure peace, while saving as much as possible of the Czech state'.

Lunch followed. Chamberlain told the Inner Cabinet that 'the darkest hour was always before lunch' and during the meal the closed mistrust began to ease. Daladier said privately that though he objected strongly to the principle of self-determination by plebiscite, because it would raise the question of the other minorities, 'he thought that he could get M. Beneš to agree to a cession of territory in the particular case of the Sudeten Germans'.* Meanwhile, Bonnet was telling Halifax that the difficulties 'turned on whether Britain was prepared to join us in some form of international guarantee in Czechoslovakia'.

The British were, of course, ready with answers to both the guarantee and the question of direct transfer in preference to a plebiscite. Chamberlain summoned the inner group, who met at 2.45 pm for about three-quarters of an hour and agreed formally to a guarantee, not necessarily of the status quo after the transfer, but against aggression in general – revealing an attitude towards the claims of other minorities which would have angered the French – which, they decided, should be conditional on future Czechoslovak neutrality and on the Czech Government

* CAB 23/95. There is some conflict of evidence between the official printed version of this discussion (*DBFP*, series 3, vol. 2, pp. 373–400) and that given here, from the Cabinet report. The official version does not give what was said in private, which was the report on which the Cabinet made up their minds.

'agreeing to act on our advice on issues of peace or war'. They were uncertain as to who should give this guarantee. Germany might refuse, especially if Russia was already on the list. The minutes of the meeting show that there was no support for a plebiscite, although it was recognised that 'the transfer would be more difficult to justify to public opinion and it would be necessary to take steps to find out what people wished to be transferred'. Various suggestions were canvassed, of which an International Commission was the most popular. Halifax talked vaguely of 'some wise person to determine the proper frontier' without elucidating the meaning of 'wise' or 'proper'. No one defended the principle of the 80 per cent German majority, and Hitler's own formula of a 51 per cent majority – 'I do not deal in percentages,' he had said at Berchtesgaden – was taken for granted.

A sense of unreality* clouded all the discussions about majorities, rights of individuals and the transfer of property. It is hard to see anything more than a perfunctory regard for the interests of Czechoslovakia.† The danger of war was held to be so great and time so short that British ministers were not prepared to insist on any guarantees, any more than Chamberlain had struggled to retain the 80 per cent limit against Hitler in the relatively mild circumstances of Berchtesgaden. Haste and imprecision were major weaknesses, and were to become a desperate liability when Chamberlain was faced at Godesberg with a detailed map and Hitler's remarkable mastery of the details of Sudeten population and geography. Chamberlain had demanded nothing in return at Berchtesgaden. His initial failure to bargain was what Hoare was to single out, when it was all over, as the greatest mistake of all.

Before meeting the French again, the inner group decided to send a telegram to Beneš, as a token to show that the Sudeten

---

* Halifax, for example, suggested 'that a Jewish shop-keeper who wanted to remove from the Sudeten areas should be able to get something reasonable for the value of his shop', but he failed to explain what safeguards would ensure this under occupation by the German army.

† 'The possibility of holding a plebiscite is now being feverishly examined in the Foreign Office under instructions from No. 10 in order to bamboozle the British public,' Harvey wrote on 18 September. 'The least study shows however that it is impossible to hold a plebiscite in existing conditions without a vast army to control the whole area' (*Diaries of Oliver Harvey*, p. 185). The Army, so the Chiefs of Staff declared, could not be provided (CAB 53/41, COS 766). The date of Harvey's note indicates that this activity was no more than an exercise in public relations.

areas were being treated as a special case and that after the transfer Britain would give a guarantee. The Czechs had already declared that they were considering general mobilisation,[30] and Halifax 'thought that it should be stated pretty bluntly that if Dr Beneš did not leave himself in our hands, we should wash our hands of him'.[31] The lunchtime talk with the French was propitious: the afternoon discussion soon reached agreement that a formula for transfer must be adopted and put into effect by an International Commission. Both sides spoke happily of the Commission 'taking into account geographical, economic and strategic considerations' and they hoped, equally unfoundedly, that the other minorities' disputes, 'which did not present difficulties of the same order, might be settled by friendly negotiation'. Only the question of a guarantee remained, to meet, as Daladier freely admitted, France's fear of total German domination of central and south-east Europe.

Chamberlain made the most of his cards, speaking of a guarantee as a 'very serious additional liability for this country'. Daladier threatened not to urge the transfer scheme on Beneš, and the British representatives withdrew for another discussion. The gesture was purely formal – so much so that they occupied the time drafting the joint telegrams which France and Britain were to send to Beneš.* On their return, Chamberlain said with great solemnity that the inner group felt bound to take part in the guarantee. France would be presumed to be grateful for so great a concession. The French were then shown the draft telegram and the delegates adjourned for dinner. Afterwards, between 10.15 and midnight, the draft was accepted; Daladier and Bonnet left London early the next morning and the French Cabinet gave its approval before lunchtime on the nineteenth.

In Hoare's words 'the French made a very bad impression – Bonnet determined not to fight'.[32] Later historians have not been so harsh. Chamberlain, as F. S. Northedge points out,[33] had not told the French that at Berchtesgaden he had given his own personal blessing to the principle of cession. He had also stage-managed the discussions so as to give the illusion that the French had won by argument something the British were unwilling to concede. Chamberlain had thus extracted the maximum political capital so that he should have no hindrance when

---

* Halifax's first draft was amended during this discussion. Hoare called the draft 'much too defensive' (Templewood papers, X5).

he next met Hitler. France could no longer offer even moral
support to Czechoslovakia. But both sides skated over the logical
consequence that the Poles and Hungarians would press at once
for their share. Poland and Hungary may have been only jackals,
but the entente powers can hardly have forgotten the voracity
of the demands in all previous partitions of eastern Europe.
Nor can they have been wholly convinced that treating the
Sudeten lands as a special case would forestall German irredentist
claims in Poland and East Prussia.

Perhaps the most significant fact to emerge was the exclusion
of Russia. In spite of the warnings of Vansittart that to do so
would be

> playing the German game to the full and would moreover be
> grossly unfair to the Czechs, who would then only be getting a
> British guarantee in place of a Russian one; whereas the whole
> compensation to them (if indeed they see any anywhere) is that
> they will be getting a British guarantee in addition to those of
> both countries on whom they have hitherto considered themselves
> entitled to rely, if their existence were menaced.[34]

both France and Britain acted as if the 1935 Soviet–Czech and
Franco–Soviet treaties were irrelevant. Russia was not consulted,
and Bonnet's version of Litvinov's statement was taken as
authoritative. Yet on 23 September Russia was to threaten
Poland that if she attacked Czechoslovakia the non-aggression
pact between them would be regarded as null and void.[35]

The telegrams were delivered by Newton to Beneš on the
morning of the nineteenth. Harshly and unsympathetically the
two governments recommended a transfer of the Sudeten area
where more than 50 per cent of the inhabitants were German,
to be arranged under the auspices of an international body,
which would include a Czech representative. This body might
also deal with exchange of population and individual preferences, within a given time-limit. In return, the British and French
would join in an international guarantee of the new boundaries
against unprovoked aggression, which would be a general substitute for the existing military treaties.[36] The reply was required
as soon as possible, for Chamberlain had arranged a meeting
with Hitler for Wednesday the twenty-first.

Meanwhile, the Cabinet was summoned for the nineteenth,
less to advise than to consent. Ministers who came back from

the country noted that the Press, even the *Daily Herald,* was favourable to the Franco-British terms.[37] Nothing had been done in excess of what the majority of the Cabinet had agreed to two days before, but a slightly different temper showed itself. Inskip noticed that

> Hore-Belisha took a good deal of exception to the guarantee of the new C.Z. He got into a rather acrimonious discussion with the P.M. who was inclined to let the guarantee be given as a deterrent, however difficult it might be to give effect to it. I thought the P.M. seemed tired and dispirited at this Cabinet: especially when he found discussion continuing over the whole field, both of the Hitler talk and the Anglo-French proposals.[38]

Hore-Belisha contended that Czechoslovakia would be economically and strategically unsound and therefore unstable. If Poland and Hungary attacked, would Britain fight them as well? The guarantee was a 'postponement of the evil day and there was a risk that we were putting our signature to something which might involve us in dishonour'.[39] Against him, Lord Maugham tried to pare down the implications of the guarantee, while Hailsham declared it impossible to effect and likely to be rejected by the Dominions. At the end, Hore-Belisha was isolated; Duff Cooper supported the Anglo-French proposals and, although Oliver Stanley offered a number of useful safeguards, none of them were likely to be of much value without Hitler's co-operation.

The undercurrent was too slight to be called an incipient revolt and in any case it was suppressed with masterful sophistry by the Prime Minister himself. The guarantee, he said, was only against unprovoked aggression and who would define that? 'He appreciated the difficulties of seeing how we should implement the guarantee. Its main value would lie in its deterrent effect.'[40]

If the Cabinet could draw its own conclusions, so would Germany in due course. On the vital question of the size of area to be transferred, Chamberlain said that the 51 per cent proportion

> was in effect what Hitler had told him, and he felt that unless he was in a position to make a settlement on this basis, he might be in an awkward position when he met Herr Hitler.... [Moreover] it was of the utmost importance not to give M. Beneš any

ground for saying later that he would never have accepted this joint proposal, if he had known how much he might have to concede.[41]

To ensure that, the telegram had already been delivered to Beneš.

The failure of the opposition in the Cabinet to seize on the distinction between the 51 per cent and 80 per cent principles, or on the arbitrary time-limit for transfer, cannot entirely be excused by the way Chamberlain presented the case. Duff Cooper's statement that the scheme, if it was guaranteed, was preferable because it postponed the 'appalling prospect of war'[42] was typical. They accepted, without demur, Chamberlain's statement that 'he might even be able to get Herr Hitler to repeat his declaration that if he attained incorporation of the Sudeten Germans in the Reich, he would be satisfied'. Winterton could conclude 'that it was very satisfactory to find the Cabinet entirely united. . . .' Duff Cooper added the comment that 'any differences had only been as to emphasis and not to substance'.[43]

According to Halifax, everything now depended on the acquiescence of the Czechs. To a question about the possibility of resistance he answered blandly: 'M. Daladier had said that he regarded such a reply as impossible.'[44] Yet there was more doubt about the Czech reaction than at any other time during the whole five months since the *Anschluss*. Earlier British and French diplomatic activity had not been up against such a tight deadline. Although both countries had evidence of Beneš' weakness, there was no assurance that he would represent much longer the coalition of conflicting interests in the Czech Government. Masaryk had sworn that the Czechs would fight.[45] Newton had information that 'there is considerable agitation amongst army officers in favour of overthrowing the Government and setting up a military one'.[46]

The British Cabinet had realised, after Colonel Christie's last meeting with Henlein at the end of August (page 269, above), that there was little of value to be extracted from Runciman's access to the Sudeten Party, as distinct from direct dealings with Germany. Vansittart had learned from German sources that Henlein had 'lost faith' in Britain because of her 'ineffectual intervention'[47] and the Foreign Office had refused his curious offer to act as mediator between Runciman and Hitler because they suspected that he was merely attempting to bolster up his own declining political power.[48] They did not know that Hitler met Henlein and Frank on 12 September but the events of the next three days in the Sudeten areas confirmed their belief that the SDP had ceased to matter as a force distinct from German policy.

On the night of 12 September, after Hitler's speech at the Nuremberg Rally, Germans all over Czechoslovakia began to riot, attack the Czech police and loot Czech and Jewish shops. The 'rising' appeared to be carefully co-ordinated, although the evidence that it was inspired from Germany is dubious.[49] The trouble was crushed swiftly by the Czech government, using troops and the state police. Thrown back on to the defensive, the SDP issued an ultimatum with a six-hour time-limit, demanding withdrawal of the Czech armed forces and the repeal of martial law. Runciman's delegation made a futile attempt to prevent the breach, but although Henlein was confronted by Ashton-Gwatkin he refused to withdraw the ultimatum and subsequently crossed into Germany where, on 15 September, he announced that the Sudeten people, through him, implored the Reich to save them in their hour of misery.[50]

The rising may have had some effect on Chamberlain's choice of a date for his visit to Hitler. More important, it polarised the issue in Czechoslovakia, as far as the British understood it. Runciman's mission now had no *raison d'être*. The SDP itself fell into the background. With Hitler's qualified approval, Henlein had dissolved the SDP negotiating committee before he fled. Deserted by its leaders, the SDP split: Kundt reported 'a state of complete panic and uncertainty in the Sudeten German area'.[51] In this crisis, many Germans transferred their allegiance to more traditional parties and the German Social Democratic and the former Agrarian and Catholic parties came together on the basis of acceptance of Beneš' Fourth Plan. While Henlein was raising the Freikorps, the Sudeten 'liberation army in exile', to attack from within Germany, the remnants of his party seemed to be endorsing the perpetuation of the existing frontier.

With order firmly restored and a virtual military occupation of Sudeten areas, Beneš could tell Newton on 14 September that civil war would follow the imposition of a plebiscite.[52] Vice-President Bechyne declared: 'we shall have no plebiscite and no international police in this State. We have ourselves restored order and we can ourselves maintain it.'[53] For the first time since the May crisis, the Czechs seemed in command.

On 16 September, however, Hodza, the Slovak Prime Minister, told Newton that if it would satisfy Germany's territorial claims he would be prepared to cede the Egerland, the most German of the Sudeten provinces.[54] Such evidence of potential rifts in the Government was welcome in London where the subtleties of events were hard to comprehend. In spite of the long series of Foreign Office reports since July,[55] opinion within the Cabinet had not been weaned away from the stereotypes of 1937 – a fact for which Runciman's increasing anti-Czech prejudice must be held principally to blame. In any case, the overriding urgency of the negotiations with Germany reduced events in Czechoslovakia to subsidiary importance. The British did not care whether they were to coerce Beneš or Hodza into accepting the Anglo-French démarche. But a military coup, and government by a junta of generals, was to be feared because it might stiffen national morale so greatly that it would make probable the long diehard war of resistance predicted by Brigadier Stronge. Fighting behind their frontier fortifications, on internal lines of communication, the Czech army could perhaps hold up Germany long enough to shame France into coming to her aid.

Awareness of the temporary nature of Beneš' hold on public opinion may explain the feverish urgency of the Anglo–French diplomatic onslaught. Beneš attempted to play one against the other by invoking the Czech-German arbitration treaty of 1926.[56] The Treaty was of no value whatever but, as a delaying tactic, the appeal was clearly intended to bring the entente powers up against the German deadline, on Czechoslovakia's side.

Anger at being treated as they wished to treat Beneš produced a vehement reaction. Newton solemnly warned him of the danger of total destruction of Czechoslovakia and asked Halifax for authority to 'deliver a kind of ultimatum to President Beneš... [so that] he and his Government will feel able to bow to *force majeure*'.[57]

The patent irritation of the British allowed no sympathy whatever for Beneš, torn as he was between the hostility of his ally, France, and the patriotic impulses of the Czech army. He understood better than his generals that Poland and Hungary might join the war and that the Czech people as well as the state might be destroyed; but he feared to ask for Russian help. Trusting in the West, he could not take the great leap of despair which was to occur in the years after the Western betrayal and the German occupation. All he did was to ask if Russia would act if France fulfilled her treaty; and he received the same wary answer which Litvinov had given the French. He refused to appeal direct to Moscow, not least because, so long as France held to the agreement with Britain, Russian aid could only be unilateral, outside the Treaty and in the end potentially more dangerous for the future than a partial surrender to Germany.

This dilemma the British and French exploited. When Hodza tried to summon up the support of the opposition within the French Cabinet, on 20 September, he met the same unyielding hostility that Halifax showed in his reply to Newton. Lacroix, the French Minister in Prague, referred at once to Paris. There Churchill and General Spears, a Conservative MP and former Military Attaché in Paris, had been working on Osusky, the Czech Minister, as well as their friends Reynaud and Mandel. Undoubtedly Osusky's report had buoyed up optimism in Prague,* but the official French reply killed at once whatever manoeuvre was in progress.

Bonnet in fact asked the British for more than they dared to give. He suggested to Phipps that Halifax should sign a joint telegram declaring formally that if Beneš did not accept the Anglo-French terms, both nations would withdraw all support. The Foreign Office was wary of giving France such evidence of British coercion, and instead the shattering message went directly to Newton at 1.20 am on 21 September.

The Czech response, Halifax wrote, 'in no way meets the critical situation which the Anglo-French proposals were designed to avert and if adhered to would, when made public, in our opinion, lead to an immediate German invasion. You should urge the Czech Government to withdraw this reply and urgently consider an alternative that takes account of realities.'[58] If they did not, Chamberlain could not go to his appointment with Hitler and Britain 'could take no responsibility' for the situation which would follow. The Czech Govern-

---

* Halifax told the Cabinet on 21 September, 'Messages received from Paris . . . indicated that considerable pressure was being brought to bear on the French Government, whose position had appeared somewhat insecure' (CAB 23/95).

ment would then be 'free to take any action that they think appropriate to meet the situation that may thereafter develop'. The euphemism barely veiled the threat that Czechoslovakia would have to fight alone.

Armed with almost identical replies, Newton and Lacroix converged on Beneš at 2 am and wrestled with him again. To the last, Beneš attempted to extract by delay what advantage he could, by consulting his colleagues and then asking for a written Anglo-French declaration that the Western powers would stand by Czechoslovakia should Germany attack in spite of her surrender. He had to be content with a verbal promise that such a guarantee would be given in due course. At 6.30 am Hodza's private secretary telephoned Newton to say that the proposals had been accepted unofficially, and the wheels in London began to turn towards the meeting at Godesberg.*

Meanwhile, the encircling nations lost no time, like vultures drawn together in the sky by the sight of prey. Beck, the Polish Foreign Minister, had already made a demand for the 'return' of Teschen. The Hungarian claims for plebiscites all along the southern border were ready, only waiting for encouragement from Hitler. The Hungarian Minister in London pressed his country's claims on Halifax on the evening of 20 September;† the Poles followed suit on the twenty-first.

In London the Government prepared for the Godesberg meeting. Almost continuous conversations had been carried on between Malcolm MacDonald and the Dominion High Commissioners‡ since 12 September, and their views coincided at all points with the Government's plans.[59] MacDonald's reports were sent direct to the Prime Minister's private office, and these consultations were deemed to be of great importance. They helped to mould the attitude of mind in which the Godesberg diktat was received although it is also true to say that, since the

* The official reply was not approved by the Czech Cabinet as easily as Hodza had thought and it was 5 pm before Krofta finally handed over the note of acceptance.

† 'Hungary's claims were overwhelming and they had behaved with great moderation for which they should not be penalised.' Halifax was not discouraging: HMG were busy, but 'that did not mean that any claims which Hungarians might make would not be given due consideration, if it were raised at the appropriate time.' He gave the same answer to the Poles. (21 Sept, CAB 23/95.)

‡ Dulanty (Eire), Bruce (Australia), Sandford (New Zealand), te Water (South Africa), Massey (Canada).

High Commissioners relied heavily on MacDonald for their
information about the central European situation, the process
of 'consultation' was circular.

At three o'clock on the twentieth, the inner group met to
discuss the brief for Godesberg prepared by Sir Horace
Wilson.[59a] Chamberlain was to open by saying that Beneš had
now agreed to the transfer and that various steps required to
be taken; he would then ask what Hitler's views were. He had
no intention of making a final settlement without consulting
Beneš but he did not want Beneš to be brought in and would
therefore suggest leaving all the details to be discussed through
normal diplomatic channels. 'From the point of view of
public opinion in this country', it was very desirable to obtain
some concessions and he would try for a more favourable principle of transfer than the 51 per cent majority already accepted,
and for some withdrawal of German troops from the frontier.
The Sudeten German Freikorps should be disbanded at once.
Chamberlain did not show himself sanguine of success, and his
statement is difficult to reconcile with Wilson's views that they
should 'get the soldiers on each side in immediate charge of all
the details of the occupation'.[60] The Chiefs of Staff had said
that three divisions of British troops would be needed to police
the area sufficiently to hold a plebiscite[61] – self-evidently an
impossible force to produce in the time available. The real
objection to introducing German troops was that it would seem
'that Germany was being allowed to enter into possession at
once before she had made any concessions herself'.[62] The brief
discounted the idea of the SDP doing the work. A report that
Prince Max Hohenlohe would prefer German regular troops met
with a general feeling of agreement, and the group decided to
'persuade' Beneš to ask for German regulars to control the
predominantly German areas and leave the local police and
Czech troops in the mixed areas.

This arrangement was the only remaining decision Chamberlain needed before his flight. There followed a good deal of
rather academic discussion about the possible scope of the
Boundary Commission and principles of transfer, payments,
compensation and exchanges of population. They decided that
Germany should be asked to conclude a separate pact of non-
aggression and not to be a guarantor herself. Finally they argued
about the guarantee and whether Russia should be asked to be a

party to it. 'If Russia dropped out, it would be argued that we had merely substituted ourselves for Russia and that Czechoslovakia had received no advantage to counterbalance the loss of her strategic frontiers. A considerable body of opinion in this country would also favour the inclusion of Russia.'[63]

Chamberlain did not necessarily expect to get these concessions but that he could imagine asking for them is some indication of what he expected from the Godesberg meeting. His attitude was similar to his hope before the *Anschluss,* that if only Hitler would listen he could have the substance of what he wanted without trouble. But such bargaining should have been done at Berchtesgaden. Instead he had conceded too much, too quickly. Hitler's impatience for confirmation of the date of the next meeting (which Nevile Henderson reported on 20 September) could be taken to mean that Hitler was eager to resume negotiations; or that his demands were rising fast.

Chamberlain chose the first interpretation when he met the inner group again on the morning of the twenty-first,* but he showed himself worried for the first time about Hitler's demands for 'immediate steps', not in the predominantly German districts but in the 'mixed areas' where Hitler had spoken of a future plebiscite. The inner group were even more wary; and decided that if Hitler broached the question of combining the Polish and Hungarian minority claims with those of the Sudetens, or if he attempted to exclude Russia as a guarantor, Chamberlain should not give his assent but return to consult the full Cabinet. It was an important step and may be seen as the first intimation that the senior ministers realised how exposed the British position was.

At the next Cabinet meeting, Chamberlain emphasised the commitment he had made. The Polish and Hungarian representatives in Germany had already visited Hitler at Berchtesgaden. If Hitler tried to press for an all-round settlement of claims or if he objected to Russia as a guarantor, Chamberlain

---

* One last loose end remained to be tied up. Runciman's report was now ready for publication. He intended to recommend transfer according to the Anglo-French plan, since the time was long past when the Carlsbad proposals could have formed the basis of a settlement. Instead, the group decided to postpone it and to publish it later as a White Paper. Having lost all chance of glory as an arbitrator, Runciman was not even allowed the satisfaction of justifying his mission's secondary purpose.

promised he would refuse, and if necessary fly home 'to consult'.[64]

In spite of this safeguard, Duff Cooper and Stanley objected to Chamberlain's action in accepting in advance that German troops should move into the areas scheduled for immediate transfer. They were overborne by the conclusive advice of Inskip, Hore-Belisha and Lord Gort that to provide an acceptable British alternative would require more than half the Field Force and would take at least three weeks to assemble. The most they could extract was an undertaking that Chamberlain would not actually *suggest* that Germans should police the areas but begin by offering an international force.

Nevertheless, several members of the Government, both in the inner group and the Cabinet, were now seriously worried by the consequences of the way Chamberlain had handled the Berchtesgaden meeting. Their forebodings about Godesberg can be seen in these attempts to impose restrictions on the Prime Minister before he left. Stanley and Duff Cooper had sent letters to Halifax, protesting at the tone of the communications to Prague; Elliot was also restive.[65] But although Chamberlain might accept conditions about other minorities and the inclusion of Russia, he could scarcely be bound hand and foot. His colleagues did not have to carry the responsibility for the next encounter, nor for summing up any change in Hitler's demcanour on the spot – a factor recognised fairly enough by Simon, who said: 'The Prime Minister was the only person who was in a position to compare what Herr Hitler said on the first occasion, with what he might say in the resumed conversations. It was therefore essential, at the outset, at any rate, that [the negotiations] should be carried on by the P.M.'[66] In the meantime, contingency planning went ahead. Italy had been kept informed of the negotiations in Prague since July;[67] and Chamberlain could imagine that her inclusion as a guarantor might weaken the Rome–Berlin axis.[68] But no one asked – what if the talks went wrong? As Wilson wrote later, 'I doubt whether he thought much about the political implications of failure, until the morning after the first meeting at Godesberg, which had not gone at all well.'[69]

Until 22 September 1938 the six-months plan had been kept clearly in sight; it had been amended to suit circumstances where circumstances could not be forced to suit it. The overriding aim had not been lost, although Chamberlain's failure at Berchtesgaden to insist on the basic question of Anglo-German relations had seriously weakened it. The possibility of breakdown had been avoided with the same expert casuistry as the subject of war and it was still assumed, on 22 September, that Chamberlain should withdraw and consult his colleagues – the classic formula for breaking off a diplomatic initiative.

But could Britain withdraw? Could Chamberlain, having conceded the principle of self-determination at Berchtesgaden, simply leave Hitler to invade Czechoslovakia and start the very war that had been avoided at such cost? If Beneš surrendered, and war still broke out, then France could not avoid conflict and Britain would be doubly bound to come to her help. What would happen to British prestige if she tried to withdraw? Would the Dominions follow, if she did assume the responsibility? Like the father of an illegitimate child, the Cabinet were bound by the unscheduled growth of their conception. Short of the violent answers he had eschewed since 1937, Chamberlain had to persuade Hitler or give way to fresh demands.

On the afternoon of 22 September the British party, Chamberlain, Wilson, Strang and Sir William Malkin, the Foreign Office Legal Adviser, reached the Petersberg Hotel in Godesberg. At 4 pm they crossed the Rhine to meet Hitler at the Hotel Dreesen.* Chamberlain began as he had planned, by giving the terms he had won from the Czechs, broadly the same as Hitler had outlined at Berchtesgaden; he proposed the international commission; he mentioned the guarantee and carefully pointed out that Czechoslovakia would now be neutralised. Afterwards 'he leaned back ... with an expression of satisfaction, as much as to say "haven't I worked splendidly during these five days?" '[70]

The shock was all the greater because Hitler had listened without interruption. Flatly he replied that this was not enough. The Czech question consisted not only of Sudeten grievances but those of other minorities. Their demands needed sympathy and no peace could be established without their settlement. 'Neither the Sudetens, nor the Poles, nor the Hungarians wanted

* Chamberlain took Kirkpatrick with him, because the Germans had refused to send Schmidt's transcript of the first meeting.

to remain in Czechoslovakia and the Czechs were attempting by force to thwart them.'[71]

Chamberlain's agreement with his Cabinet was quite clear. This was the moment to break off and return home. Instead he told Hitler that he had 'hoped to show the world that the orderly operation of treaty revision could be achieved by peaceful means', and with fatal lack of foresight asked – did Hitler have any proposal? Hitler at once produced a map.* A frontier based on language distinctions should be drawn up at once behind which the Czechs should immediately withdraw. The German army would occupy these areas and a plebiscite would follow later in the mixed areas. All the Sudetens who had moved out since 1918 would be able to vote and no Czech who had moved in since could. No compensation would, or should, be paid.

Chamberlain hedged. How could this work fairly, he asked, and why the plebiscite? Hitler replied that it would prove to the world the just grievances of the Germans in Czechoslovakia – otherwise the solution could only be based on a military victory. Chamberlain repeated the plea he had made at the time of the *Anschluss*; why lose British friendship as well as German lives? But speed was essential, Hitler replied, and he began to expound the German proposals – giving an exhibition of technical mastery of every intricate detail of the Sudeten question, which took Chamberlain off balance and showed up the inadequacies of the British party's brief. At one point Wilson tried to rebut him: 'It was my first experience of his irritability. Hitler shouted for what seemed ten minutes and blazed and hissed "Czechen!" which meant, when Schmidt translated it – "if you had lived under the Czechs as I have, you would hate them too".'[72] Chamberlain's question met with scarcely better results. Then, timed as accurately as at Berchtesgaden, came the news of twelve German hostages shot at Eger. It did not matter whether it was true or false; Hitler used it to ram home the lesson that the Czechs must be taught to behave.

Drearily, Chamberlain's party returned to their hotel, having arranged to meet again the next day. Had the Prime Minister made a fatal mistake? Should he have broken off, as agreed, and returned home? Considering all the circumstances, to have

* The German plans at Godesberg were based closely on those of Henlein, dated 15 September (*DGFP*, series D, vol. 2, p. 801).

done so would have been taken as final, tantamount to a declaration that war was inevitable. If the assumptions behind his entire understanding of foreign policy are accepted, he was not wrong. But as with so many of his decisions in the past the cumulative effect of the way he had dealt with Hitler weakened his whole bargaining position. Back in the Petersberg, as Wilson saw, he was moved for the first time by doubt, even despair;[73] but he did not seek advice from his colleagues in London.

During the night Wilson thought of sending a formal note 'designed to force opposite side to define what they had in mind. At breakfast agreed to draft letter for P.M. to send to Hitler. H.J.W., Henderson and Strang delivered draft which P.M. improved to send.'[74] The message was substituted for the morning meeting and did something to repair the damage. In due course Hitler answered, taking the same position, insisting that the Czechs must begin to evacuate the Sudeten areas early on 26 September and complete it by 29 September. No International Commission was acceptable and no compensation was to be paid. His only concession was that German troops might not be sent in to the mixed areas until the plebiscite was held.

After asking for a copy of the map, Chamberlain announced that he would inform the Czech Government and return to London for consultation. This was the answer he could have given the night before. Giving it now added weight to Hitler's accusation that the Allies were going back on their admission of the principle of self-determination. Just as he had laid down the 51 per cent basis at Berchtesgaden, so Hitler had succeeded in defining the lines within which the argument was to be conducted. Chamberlain had a hard uphill fight even to get him to discuss a memorandum outlining the German proposals.

The tone of this memorandum was explicit and final. The new frontier would be established by 1 October. The Czech Government would release all political prisoners and discharge all Sudeten Germans in the armed forces. The German Government would arrange for a plebiscite by 25 September at the latest, on the 1918 voting-roll. Any problems could be settled by discussions between Germany and the Czech Government, or an International Commission. Since no time was provided these were no safeguards at all.

No directive exists to show Hitler's state of mind in the week between the two meetings with Chamberlain. Projecting the view taken here of his policy since 1936, three reasons may be offered for his acceptance of Chamberlain's first offer to come to Germany. It did not necessarily override his military preparations for invasion since nothing might come of it and the war machine was not set to move until 1 October, over a fortnight later. Secondly, it might herald the long-awaited British alliance on his terms, which he had hoped for in the past. It was also intensely flattering that the British, whose bourgeois decadence he had scorned at the Hossbach Conference in November 1937 should now come to Berlin bringing with them a certificate of respectibility for his regime. There is no reason to assume Hitler so hell-bent on war that he would ignore the chance of having Czechoslovakia delivered on his terms. But there was to be no bargaining. 'There are only two possibilities' was a phrase he used so often that it became a joke in the inner circle at Berchtesgaden.[75] Only he could raise the bids and at Godesberg, seizing the advantage he could gain by supporting the claims of Poland and Hungary, he did.

There were two imponderables: the attitude of Mussolini and the volatile nature of the Sudeten Germans. The SDP 'revolt' of 12–15 September had failed, but Henlein was now in Germany surrounded by a flood of refugees. To keep them busy, as much as to harass the Czechs, Henlein had formed the Sudeten Freikorps, under Hitler's personal direction, and launched them across the border. These guerilla raids conflicted with the plans of the German High Command, because Czech troops moved up to forward positions on the frontier. Freikorps activities were soon curtailed. Their only major success was to occupy the area around Asch on 20–21 September, but they were later supplanted by the German army.[76] If civil war were to break out inside Czechoslovakia, the Sudeten population might still have to be rescued in an operation distinct from the planned offensive. The fall of the Hodza Cabinet on 21 September and its replacement by another, more subservient to the military, under the premiership of General Jan Syrovy was a bad omen, even though the new Cabinet endorsed the surrender made by Hodza and Beneš. These factors were all arguments in favour of accepting a negotiated solution.

Mussolini's reaction to a German invasion mattered greatly to Hitler, who still admired the Italian dictator. On 19 September, Mussolini came out strongly in favour of secession of the Sudeten areas,[77] but it was a gesture not so clearly in Hitler's favour as it seemed. Oliver Harvey wrote, 'this is believed to be intended to show Hitler that he [Mussolini] will not stand for absorption of Czechoslovakia as a whole'.[78]

Against this background, the meeting between Hitler and Chamberlain on the twenty-third had certain unexpected overtones. The Czechs had asked the British and French for permission to order full mobilisation to defend the frontier. Halifax was inclined to give it but Chamberlain refused (below, page 372). Secure in the belief that the Czechs would wait, Chamberlain began by taking a much tougher line than he had done the day before. He had just called the German plan 'dictation, not negotiation', when Czechoslovak mobilisation was announced. According to the German record, the British 'were extremely taken aback and Chamberlain said that a development he had long feared had occurred'.[79] It can hardly have escaped Hitler's notice that Prague would be very unlikely to take the drastic step without consultation and he may at this point have thought Chamberlain a much more subtle man than he had imagined. If so, it would explain both his anger and the unease which he and Ribbentrop betrayed later in the meeting.

At the time he declared: 'In that event, things are settled'. Chamberlain protested vigorously that the mobilisation was a defensive, not offensive measure, and an angry argument developed. Finally Chamberlain said that he would go home 'with a heavy heart' at the wreck of his hopes for peace. Then Ribbentrop called attention to the memorandum, which had almost been forgotten. Chamberlain said he would transmit it to the Czech Government. Hitler, rather weakly, promised not to use force for the present, other than to deter Czech mobilisation. Chamberlain argued on, and produced the famous phrase that the time schedule made the document an ultimatum. Hitler replied that the word 'memorandum' was at the top of the page. He made a number of trivial concessions, and at 1.45 am they broke up. Hard though the passage had been, there was some slight sign of concession in Hitler's attitude. His blandishments at the end, when he spoke of Czechoslovakia as the last barrier to Anglo-German understanding, and described Chamberlain as the only man who had ever won concessions from him, may not have been the otiose flattery they seem. As Chamberlain left, however, he was 'satisfied Hitler was ready (and almost eager) to march'.[80] He was still like a lobster caught in a pot, for whom the way out was much smaller than the way in, while the sides of the cage turned in against him.

Kirkpatrick thought, that night, that Hitler saw Chamberlain as an 'impotent busybody who spoke the ridiculous jargon of an outmoded democracy'.[81] But Kirkpatrick strongly disapproved of Chamberlain's style of foreign policy. Hitler's cruel contempt for the 'man of peace' was not necessarily the result of anger at being deprived of military success.

Given Hitler's consummate technique as an actor, it is possible to see the whole Godesberg performance as an exercise in bluff. Chamberlain had thought him 'struck all of a heap' by the Berchtesgaden initiative.[82] Perhaps Hitler did admire the bold gesture, but he also learnt from it just how much the settlement of the Czech question meant to Britain. Until then he had thought of British intervention as a bargaining-counter, a temptation of the same unreal value to Germany as the concessions in central Africa. The British had overestimated his perception – and perhaps his interest in their motives as opposed to their friendship – all through, from March 1937 to September 1938. The imagined détente of May 1938 had been an illusion like that of May 1937. Not until Berchtesgaden did Hitler fully appreciate the British horror of war as an instrument of policy – a horror which had made his quarrel with Czechoslovakia a British interest though Czechoslovakia *in itself* could never become one. When he saw how far Chamberlain was prepared to go, when presented with the fatal personal agreement to partition, he did the obvious thing and raised the demand. At the last meeting at Godesberg he may have sensed that he had gone far enough; but he still wanted it done his way. The British and French had brought the Czechs this far; would they force on Beneš even the Godesberg *diktat*?

13 The Price of Peace

In London, the opposition in the Cabinet began to stir. In the time between Chamberlain's first visit to Hitler and Godesberg, public opinion seemed to have stiffened against the policy of concession at the expense of the Czechs. A poll conducted by Mass Observation on 22 September showed that 40 per cent of the sample regarded Chamberlain's policy as wrong; only 22 per cent were in favour, of whom a mere 10 per cent were for peace at any price; and the high figure of 28 per cent remained undecided.[1] Of the national newspapers, only *The Times* continued to give unqualified support to the Government. The high Tory *Daily Telegraph* spoke of 'Danegeld that Europe is to go on paying for ever afterwards in ever larger sums',[2] and the *Manchester Guardian* of a moral defeat.[3] Chamberlain himself had been booed on his departure from Heston airport. Churchill, Eden and Sinclair had all made public speeches attacking the Government, and in the House of Commons a curious coalition seemed to be developing between the Conservative opposition and the Labour Party. Theodore Kordt reported a significant swing in public opinion against Germany.[4]

There is no conclusive evidence to link this with a change of awareness in the Cabinet, but it coincided with the atmosphere of mistrust and caution in which its members had sought to limit the Prime Minister's freedom of action before he went to Godesberg. That temper developed into something which, although not exactly a Cabinet revolt, was tantamount to a rejection of the exclusive domination held by the Prime Minister since March. The vigour came, not from the junior ministers, but from Halifax, who resumed the independent line he had taken in early September. He did not choose the role voluntarily, but the fact that Chamberlain allowed the Cabinet to remain virtually cut off with only the vaguest news for two days, helped others to force him into a position of responsibility. Beyond Chamberlain's direct control, he fell once more under the influence of his civil servants.

The Czech Committee met during the afternoon of 22 September and Halifax, who was in the chair, defined the point at which they should break with Germany, in a manner perceptibly tougher than before: 'There was all the difference in the world between an immediate and orderly settlement of the Sudeten question ... and forcible annexation, to be followed by the activities of the Gestapo.'[5] He asked the others to consider two grave questions. Two days earlier, Britain had agreed with France to advise the Czechoslovak Government not to mobilise. Since then, the Sudeten German Freikorps had occupied the district of Asch. If this movement turned into a German attack, Britain would have to give the Czechs positive advice to mobilise. Cautiously enough not to prejudice the talks at Godesberg, the inner group prepared to consult France and to change their minds.[6]

Secondly, Halifax asked: what if the talks failed? Much depended on whether Germany crushed Czechoslovakia, while standing on the defensive on the French frontier. They discussed the Chiefs of Staff reports[7] on what France would do. Reactions were still defensive* but unmentionable questions were being opened up. An earlier Foreign Office plan involving almost total withdrawal was condemned out of hand as 'half hearted and ineffective'.[8] Already, as Inskip told them, the Chiefs of Staff had done everything short of mobilisation. They telephoned to Godesberg and told the delegation of the seizure of Asch, and waited for Chamberlain to authorise the next step.

At 9.30 they met again.† The French had replied, agreeing to the despatch of joint advice to Prague to mobilise; and this message waited on one hour's notice only. The only news from Godesberg had been a telephone conversation with Wilson who had said merely that the talks had been 'pretty difficult and they were all rather exhausted'.[9] He had given the text of the Prime Minister's statement to Hitler, and added much interpretative gloom. He telephoned again later to say that Chamberlain had been in direct touch with Newton and asked him to hold the Czech Government back from mobilisation. Apart

* 'Our most effective weapon was believed to be an economic blockade. It was not in the interests of this country to embark on unrestricted air warfare, unless Germany herself first embarked on this course.' (CAB 27/646.)
† General Ismay, Secretary of the CID, was now in attendance. An indication of their awareness that war was near may be seen in the fact that a military adviser was present at nearly all the meetings after 22 September.

from this, the Cabinet 'would have to go on for the time being with the information which [Wilson] had already given us'. Chamberlain was playing his cards very close to his chest.

The Committee hesitated about giving a free hand to the Czechs in case it damaged Chamberlain's position, but they asked for more information on what had happened during the day. At 10.30 Chamberlain talked direct to Halifax and at last the unpleasant truth was known. According to Halifax's account to the Committee, Chamberlain appeared to be thinking in terms of an ultimatum.[10] The Committee still wavered, but they asked Inskip what action would be taken by the Services if Britain were to break off the talks, and they agreed to advise ship-owners, privately, to delay the sailings of British merchantmen into the Baltic. The Standing Committee on Co-ordination of Departmental Action on the Outbreak of War was summoned to meet the next morning. Once more, and in earnest, Britain was 'rattling down to war'.

The inner group returned to the Foreign Office at 3 pm the next day, 23 September. In the morning, Halifax had asked Chamberlain to reverse his decision on Czechoslovak mobilisation. The reply, by letter, requesting further delay, did not arrive until 4 pm.[11] The rest of the Cabinet were now pressing for more information and the chance at least to consult their senior colleagues, and the seniors themselves were becoming intensely irritated at the way they were still being kept in the dark.* Only two messages came in during the morning and Wilson, promising more information, actually left things vague, not to say offensive – 'A short telegram will, we hope, be enough to go on in the light of previous messages – to enable the boys to go on playing marbles.'[12] The French wanted urgently to withdraw their advice to the Czechs not to mobilise[13] and the inner group waited only long enough to hear Chamberlain's 4 pm letter read before authorising Newton to go ahead, at 9 pm that night.[14] In addition, presumably in case the delegation at Godesberg tried to overrule them, 'Sir Robert Vansittart was authorised to tell Mr Masaryk that Mr Newton had been instructed to withdraw the advice to Czechoslovakia not to mobilise

---

* The most immediate complaint was that certain preparatory measures, leading up to full mobilisation, could not be taken without the authority of the whole Cabinet. The Chiefs of Staff demanded at least forty-eight hours' notice before a declaration of war (CAB 27/646).

and to urge upon him the importance of avoiding needless publicity in Czechoslovakia's own interest.'[15]

After another casual message from Wilson – 'We shall not speak again tonight: we have got a lot to do'[16] – Halifax's patience gave way. He believed that the talks 'should end on some simpler and stronger statement than on the available information the P.M. seemed to contemplate'.[17] He produced a draft, to be sent *en clair* by telephone 'in view of the urgency of getting a message to the P.M. before the latter left in the course of the next half hour for his final talk with Hitler'.

The message, which would have been inconceivable in terms of the situation before Chamberlain left, read:

It may help you if we give you some indication of what seems predominant public opinion as expressed in press and elsewhere. While mistrustful of our plan but prepared perhaps to accept it with reluctance as alternative to war, the great mass of public opinion seems to be hardening in sense of feeling that we have gone to the limit of concession and that it is up to the Chancellor to make some contribution. We of course can imagine immense difficulties with which you are confronted, but from point of view of your own position, that of Government and of the country, it seems to your colleagues of vital importance that you should not leave without making it plain to Chancellor if possible by special interview that, after great concessions made by Czechoslovak Government, for him to reject opportunity of peaceful solution in favour of one that must involve war would be an unpardonable crime against humanity.[18]

The message was agreed unanimously and Chamberlain received it before he left. His response was to make a last-minute attempt, via Wilson, to forestall the message to Prague. The inner group conceded the point,[19] but they were too late. Masaryk had already been sent the news, and mobilisation began at 10 pm. There is every likelihood that the inner group had foreseen what would happen, and chosen their own way to evade the Prime Minister's veto. Their independent attitude was the first real opposition to Chamberlain since Eden's resignation eight months before.

But when Chamberlain came back and gave his shattering description of the first meeting with Hitler, much of their spirit vanished. For the first time they were made fully aware of the narrow confines of the trap they had walked into and from

which they could not withdraw. Chamberlain's private consciousness of defeat extended to them all.

There were only two choices left, since rupture of negotiations had been avoided when Chamberlain began to discuss
Hitler's plan. One was to submit absolutely and to force the
Czechoslovaks to do the same. The second was to sit it out and
try to modify the Godesberg *diktat*. Chamberlain believed that
was hopeless because he himself had failed. He offered only
the first choice – to submit, and hope to escape without the
appearance of complete capitulation. His colleagues, however,
after the initial shock, refused to accept his definition of the
situation and preferred, with less experience of Hitler but greater
faith, to struggle for better terms. The drama of the next few
days lies in the conflict between Chamberlain and Wilson, who
had looked into the nether pit and thought that nothing but
capitulation could save Europe, and the rest, who refused to be
convinced.

Chamberlain had not expected revolt, but nor had he expected
Hitler's new terms. He set to work to persuade his colleagues
that Halifax had been wrong to define the situation as a contrast
between annexation plus the Gestapo, and peaceful and orderly
transfer. The underlying reality, in his opinion, was that Britain
wanted the Czechoslovak question resolved, and wanted Czechoslovakia neutral; eventual partition for the Sudetens had been
agreed by them all and they should accommodate their consciences to immediate partition, whilst playing for such safeguards as they could.

The problem was partly one of attitudes to public opinion and
propaganda. Chamberlain believed that he would be able to
mask the appearance of surrender sufficiently in national relief
that war had been avoided. The others were too aware of the
dangers. Even if they endorsed the Godesberg terms, would the
House of Commons, the Press and the people? As if Hoare–
Laval were come again, would 'public opinion' accept, as the
sensible solution, the appearance of servile surrender?

On 24 September, Saturday, immediately after his return,
Chamberlain met the inner group. What he told them is of
interest because he was able, for the last time, to express his
feelings without significant opposition. 'The most difficult part
was the immediate occupation by German troops, which was very

difficult to deal with politically; [but] having once agreed to cession, the sooner the transfer took place the better.'[20] German troops could keep better order than the Sudetens. He seemed satisfied that Hitler did not want more than racial self-determination, and that these were his last demands. Otherwise it would be war and the dismemberment of Czechoslovakia by Germany, Hungary and Poland. Above all, Chamberlain claimed, he had established some degree of personal influence over Hitler. 'He was satisfied that Herr Hitler would not go back on his word, once he had given it to him.'[21] That would make it the turning-point in Anglo-German relations.

The inner group reverted to their former loyalty. In a limited sense, of course, it was true that Hitler's proposed new frontier was better than a line drawn by force 'at the shortest point between Silesia and Austria'.[22] But the issue was not limited, unless they chose to do so. They were aware of the political disadvantages, in a rather paradoxical way: Hoare, for example, warned that the Government might have 'difficulties with the public' unless Germany made some concessions,[23] but no one seemed to believe that the Godesberg terms were bad enough to be a *casus belli*. Privately, Hoare wrote: 'He made them [the Germans] make some alterations; why did he not make them make more?'[24] But the inner group could not diminish responsibility by making Chamberlain a scapegoat.

Halifax's collapse was surprising, considering how far he had gone the day before. Cadogan, who thought Godesberg 'awful ... throwing away every last safeguard that we had', wrote,

I was completely horrified—he [Chamberlain] was quite calmly for total surrender. More horrified still to find that Hitler has evidently hypnotised him to a point. Still more horrified to find that P.M. has hypnotised Halifax, who capitulates totally. P.M. took nearly an hour to make his report and there was practically no discussion. John Simon—seeing which way the cat was jumping—said that after all it was a question of 'modalities' whether the Germans went in now or later! Ye Gods! ... I gave Halifax a note of what I thought, but it had no effect.[25]

To the full Cabinet, Chamberlain made the best case he could.[26] He emphasised factors of dubious optimism – that Hitler had not *insisted* on linking the Hungarian and Polish settlements with the Sudeten one; and, on the tone of the Godesberg meet-

N

ings, 'It was worth remembering the Germans were apt to express themselves curtly.' He declared that he had not approved the plans on behalf of Czechoslovakia; and that the final interview had been 'far more cordial'.

Chamberlain's gloss on the concessions he had been able to extract was much fuller and more subtle than at the earlier meeting.

In order to understand people's actions it was necessary to appreciate their motives and see how their minds worked. In his view, Herr Hitler had certain standards ... he had a narrow mind and was violently prejudiced on certain subjects; but he would not deliberately deceive a man whom he respected and with whom he had been in negotiation, and he was sure that Herr Hitler now felt some respect for him. When Herr Hitler announced that he meant to do something, it was certain that he would do it ... [Hitler had said that] once the present situation had been settled he had no more territorial ambitions in Europe. He had also said that if the present question could be settled peaceably, it might be a turning point in Anglo-German relations.[27]

To miss all this 'would be a great tragedy. ... A peaceful settlement of Europe depended upon an Anglo-German understanding. He thought that he had now established an influence over Herr Hitler and that the latter trusted him and was willing to work with him.'

Otherwise, only war remained.

That morning he had flown up the river over London. He had imagined a German bomber flying the same course. He had asked himself what degree of protection they could afford for the thousands of homes which he had seen stretched out below him, and he had felt that we were in no position to justify waging a war today, in order to prevent a war hereafter.

The man they had all followed for eighteen months was telling them to capitulate as the only alternative to war. It was Hailsham who asked whether, if Czechoslovakia refused the terms, Britain should hold out the hand of friendship to Germany. (Was he being ironic?) The meeting was characterised by a strong disinclination on the part of anyone to take any decision at all, except to follow the Prime Minister's suggestion and summon the French representatives to London. Yet all this did not signify agreement with what had been done. Duff

Cooper insisted on a 'precautionary measure', making the Navy ready for a blockade, and he asked why Chamberlain had failed to propose Russia as a guarantor of Czechoslovakia after the transfer. Hoare proposed that the British guarantee should come into force as soon as Hitler's proposals were accepted, and he noted, a little optimistically, 'the Cabinet stronger'.[28]

Chamberlain's authority over the meeting was still enough to postpone action. 'He did not think that we should find ourselves at war unless we first declared war.' But outside the Cabinet room, other forces brought themselves to bear. Hailsham and Duff Cooper began to work together;[29] and Winterton told Amery that four or five of his friends, including Duff Cooper, were thinking of resigning if Chamberlain recommended the proposals to the Czechs.[30] Eden begged the Cabinet to reject the Godesberg terms,* and Attlee wrote a cautious letter of disapproval, though he refused to join Churchill in a public protest.[31] Churchill saw Chamberlain and Halifax on the twenty-sixth but by then the meeting with Daladier had taken place and the tenor of policy had changed sufficiently for him to tell Lady Asquith that he was happier than he had been. During these days, he was at one remove from up-to-date information, as his reaction to the Munich visit suggests.[32] Perhaps the most far-sighted of the opponents was Cadogan who drove Halifax home and made the same personal and moral appeal that Vansittart had found useful earlier. He thought he had failed, but he had greater success than he knew. The next day Halifax said – 'I am very angry with you. You gave me a sleepless night . . . but I came to the conclusion you were right. In the Cabinet, when the P.M. asked me to lead off, I plumped for refusal of Hitler's terms.'[33]

Halifax's crisis of conscience was decisive. Daladier and Bonnet had not yet arrived, and there was no fresh news yet from Prague. But a shift in power in the Cabinet took place, putting in jeopardy the whole policy of appeasement. On 25 September at 10.30 am Halifax began by explaining that the day before, he 'had seen, or thought he had seen, certain things fairly clearly'.[34] He had not then thought the difference between Berchtesgaden and Godesberg justified war. But now

---

* Avon, *Reckoning*, p. 27. But see also Nicolson, *Diaries and Letters, 1930–1939*, vol. 1, p. 361: 'He doesn't wish to lead a revolt or to secure any resignations from the Cabinet.'

the old question of orderly, as opposed to violent, transfer was complicated by the claims of other minorities. He no longer trusted Hitler's promises nor the illusion of the Anglo-German *rapprochement*. 'He could not rid his mind of the fact that Herr Hitler had given us nothing, and that he was dictating terms just as though he had won a war but without having had to fight.'

Halifax was not aware of Hitler's long-term aims – he did not agree with Duff Cooper about the German drive towards *Weltmacht*, but he could see that

so long as Nazism lasted, peace would be uncertain. For this reason he did not feel that it would be right to put pressure on Czechoslovakia to accept. We could lay the case before them. If they rejected it he imagined that France would join in, and if France went in we should join with them. . . . He also remembered that Herr Hitler had said that he had gained his power by words and not by bayonets. He asked whether we were quite sure that he had not gained power by words in the present instance and that if he was driven to war, the result might be to help bring down the Nazi regime.

Where Halifax led, others grew bold. Hailsham ran through a long list of broken promises and 'last claims' starting in 1935 and finishing with the *Anschluss*. Like Winterton, he refused to put pressure on the Czechs. Duff Cooper forecast a violent reaction from the public, leading to the fall of the Government, if the Godesberg terms were published. Chamberlain should say that the terms were intolerable and that Britain would stand by the Czechs and with France. 'The future of Europe, of this country and of democracy was at stake.' This time he did not qualify his words.

Oliver Stanley took the same line: 'If these terms were accepted, Herr Hitler's price would only rise again and we should then find that we had bartered away many of the strong points in our position. No doubt war was horrible but it would be equally horrible in six months' time' – and worse if Germany had strengthened her position in Eastern Europe in the meantime. MacDonald was in favour of accepting the terms, shocking though they were, because the principle of transfer had been accepted at Berchtesgaden, but he would not recommend them to Prague. These six members of the Cabinet were joined by Elliot, De La Warr, Colville and Hore-Belisha.

Against them lay the passive majority, ready to recommend the Czechs to surrender: Lord Stanhope, Lord Maugham, Inskip, who sat on the fence as far as he could and tried to hide behind the hypothetical decisions of France, Lord Zetland, who evinced shock at the surrender but acceptance of anything in preference to world war, and Kingsley Wood who spoke of 'humiliation for which we must all take the responsibility – a responsibility extending back over many years' – a use of history which can hardly have appealed to his seniors who had been in office for most of that time.

Hoare wished neither to recommend nor to advise against, and was worried about the Dominion reaction, especially in Canada. He wanted to throw the responsibility back on the Chiefs of Staff before any commitment to stand with France. Simon preferred to wait for the French to jump first. Burgin and Brown were straightforwardly for telling the Czechs to accept; Morrison was cloudy and equivocal, but in practice with the Prime Minister.

Numerically, the opposition was in a minority of one, but the important point was that the inner group was split two and two. Chamberlain had to exercise the Prime Minister's prerogative of directing the debate, by emphasising that Britain was not accepting or rejecting the terms, but only acting as an intermediary. He played down the importance of Britain's role, as if the last six months' work had been purely altruistic. Britain, he said, could not deliver an ultimatum. On the other hand, 'no one was going to suggest we were debarred from putting before Czechoslovakia all the considerations which should properly be borne in mind in reaching a decision'.

After this disingenuous appraisal, he declared that there existed 'little difference of opinion among his colleagues. He did not think that it was necessary to take any immediate decision which went beyond the policy which had already been accepted by the Government.' He stressed the importance of minimising divisions in the Cabinet, in order to present a united front during the crisis. 'We might before long be involved in war. If that happened it was essential that we should enter war united, both as a country and as an Empire. It was of the utmost importance, therefore, that whatever steps we took, we should try to bring the whole country and Empire along with us and should allow public opinion to realise that all possible steps had been taken to avoid a conflict.'

It would be idle to deny the value of what he was saying, but the divisions patently existed and could not be papered over much longer, even by throwing all the onus on France, as he proposed to do in the forthcoming talks.* To hold the Government together, to keep it from odium at home and all commitments abroad, while coercing the Czechs by putting 'all the considerations' to them, and the French by refusing any guarantee, was an exercise in political sleight of hand reminiscent of Lloyd George's behaviour during the Chanak crisis in 1922. The stakes in 1938 were infinitely higher, and Chamberlain's courage in defence of his policy could not be denied.

Since he refused to recognise divisions or to count heads, and chose instead the lowest common denominator for action, there was nothing his colleagues could do but to accept or resign collectively. Chamberlain did not leave divisions to fester. He pursued Halifax importunately,[85] but failed to move him now that his mind had been made up. More than the doubts of the other nine, Halifax's refusal to follow Chamberlain made it impossible to *recommend* the Godesberg proposals to Prague. Nevertheless, if the Czechs were given advice which emphasised that Britain and France accepted them, the result would be the same. If, after that, Czechoslovakia went to war, then both Western powers would be freed from their obligations, contractual or moral.

In the three days after this Cabinet meeting, Chamberlain played his hand with remarkable stamina and persistence. The arrival of Daladier and Bonnet offered him the first of several ways out, and shortly before they arrived, on 25 September, he received confirmation that they were likely to be pliant in their demands. Phipps gave his 'purely personal impression'† that

---

* CAB 23/93. Chamberlain proposed that 'We should not say that if the proposals were rejected, we undertook to declare war on Germany. Equally we should not say that if the proposals were rejected, we should in no circumstances declare war on Germany. We should put before the representatives of the French and Czechoslovak Governments the full facts of the situation as we saw them in their true light.'
† He had already sent a message in which he doubted whether the French Government would get a sufficient majority in the Chamber and Senate to declare war. (*DBFP*, series 3, vol. 2, pp. 509–10.)

unless German aggression was so brutal, bloody and prolonged
... as to infuriate French public opinion to the extent of making
it lose its reason, war would be now most unpopular in France.
I think therefore that H.M.G. should realize the extreme danger of
even appearing to encourage small, but noisy and corrupt war
group here. All that is best in France is against war *almost* at any
price (hence the really deep, pathetic gratitude shown to our
Prime Minister). Unless we are sure of considerable initial successes,
we shall find all that is best in France, as well as all that is worst,
turn against us and accuse us of egging the French on to fight what
must have seemed from the outset a losing battle.[36]

These views from a trusted source were more acceptable than
the public declaration in the French press by Pierre Cot, the
Air Minister, that France would fulfil her commitments.

In these last few days three factors could have influenced
the British Cabinet – the attitude of Russia, the United States
and the Dominions; but in the narrow circle of the Cabinet
nothing in any of these was believed to have changed sufficiently.
Russia remained an enigma. Duff Cooper's attempt to query
the omission of Russia from the guarantors of the new, reduced
Czechoslovakia was the last mention minuted before Munich.
On 24 September, after meeting Litvinov at Geneva, R. A.
Butler reported the Russian state of mind, in terms slightly
stronger than what Bonnet had said earlier;[37] Russia would
come to the help of Czechoslovakia, if France honoured her
obligations. It was a statement which might have been probed,
but no one asked for greater definition, although a letter from
Robert Boothby, also from Geneva, offering a much tougher
interpretation, had been summarised and given to the inner
group.* Litvinov's proposal for a three-power meeting, preferably in Paris,[38] was discounted as likely to precipitate war before
the participants had made their preparations.[39] Litvinov may
have expected this response, since a similar proposal had been
rejected in March and he may have been content for Russia to
be relieved of responsibility.[40] The inference, though, is by no
means certain. Russia had already warned Poland not to move

* Boothby had also seen Litvinov at Geneva and reported him as saying that he
had seen the Czechs on two or three occasions in the previous week, and had
affirmed each time that if they were attacked by Germany, Russia 'would give
them effective aid. Help in the air would certainly be given, but it was more
doubtful whether it could be given on land. Mr Litvinov contemplated an appeal
to the League of Nations, partly in order to assist securing a passage for troops
through Rumania.' (23 Sept, CAB 27/646.)

against Czechoslovakia (page 354, above). On 20 September, Alexandrovsky, Soviet Minister in Prague, had assured Beneš that Russia would help, even if France did not, so long as the Czechs themselves resisted the German attack and asked for assistance.[41] This was confirmed by Klement Gottwald, the Czech Communist leader. But the promises were only verbal, and Newton did not know of them. As far as the British were concerned, they had no fresh reason to reconsider their view of Russia until General Gamelin gave them Marshal Voroshilov's assurances when he came to London on 26 September. After Godesberg, it does not seem that the British regarded Russian involvement as more than a bargaining-counter with France. Moreover, it was clear that the Czechs themselves were not interested in making a unilateral demand for help, fearing that the outcome would result in their becoming a Russian client state. They had signed the 1935 treaty before the full flowering of Stalinism, Russian intervention in the Spanish Civil War, or the purges of 1936–7. Czechoslovakia remained Western in the political assumptions of her leaders, to the end.[42]

Lindsay, the British Ambassador in Washington, had been optimistic about American attitudes earlier in September when Bullitt, American Ambassador in Paris, was taking a strong attitude towards German aggression[43] but these hopes, in which Chamberlain had shown no great interest, died. During the Berchtesgaden visit, Bullitt's reports were not calculated to arouse White House confidence in the stamina of the European powers.[44] Roosevelt himself lamented that Chamberlain wanted peace at any price. His attitude harshened perceptibly as it began to appear that Britain and France were dealing together to sell the Czechs down the river.[45] But his opposition to what he called 'the most terrible sacrifices' by the Czechs did not extend to encouraging 'vain resistance'.[46] The most that Roosevelt would do, was to suggest to Lindsay either a world conference, in which he would represent the United States, or a western blockade of Germany, with what negligible support the Neutrality Acts would allow the United States to give.[47] Roosevelt did consider proposing arbitration* but nothing came of this activ-

---

* J. P. Moffatt, of the State Department Western European section, drafted a scheme in which Roosevelt was to offer his services as mediator. There was a hint of treaty revision which was meant as a bait to Hitler. Cordell Hull agreed but Norman Davis took such exception to it, that it was allowed to die. (Offner, *American Appeasement*, pp. 262–3.)

ity except that, on 26 September, when it was too late to affect the Godesberg meeting, Roosevelt made a general appeal for peace and urged the four main parties to ensure a 'peaceful, fair and constructive settlement'. He robbed even this modest effort of effect by announcing at the same time that the United States 'had no political commitments'.[48] Chamberlain was so little impressed that Phipps had to remind him to send a reply. There is no evidence that the British expected anything or asked for anything from the United States until after the failure of the Wilson mission on 27 September.*

The attitudes of the Dominions were far more influential. On 16 September, after Berchtesgaden, Chamberlain had received letters from de Valera and Bruce, High Commissioner of Australia, expressing satisfaction, admiration and support for what had happened.[49] The High Commissioners met every day after 15 September to discuss events and receive information from MacDonald. Several of them wrote direct to Chamberlain[50] and their general reactions were given to the Czechoslovak Committee on 23 September, and to the Cabinet on the twenty-fifth and twenty-sixth. There was little variation from what had become an almost constant factor in the situation. On the twenty-third, according to MacDonald, Bruce of Australia was the only one who thought that if Germany annexed the Sudeten areas forcibly Britain should fight.[51] The rest, te Water (South Africa), Massey (Canada), Dulanty (Eire), disagreed. 'It would be very difficult to go to war on an issue concerned with method and not one with principle.' On the twenty-fifth MacDonald told the Cabinet that these three High Commissioners 'had all definitely taken the view that we had accepted the principle of transfer a week ago and that we ought now to accept proposals which merely concerned the method of giving effect to that principle. Mr Bruce [it appeared now] was inclined to take the same view....'[52]

A day later, he reported the same view more positively: 'in their view, acceptance of Herr Hitler's proposals was better than war'.[53]

* Roosevelt was pleased with the tone of Chamberlain's reply, but refused to accede to Chamberlain's suggestion that the broadcast he was due to make in London on the twenty-seventh should be relayed to various American cities—'lest it be misconstrued'. American radio networks were left free to transmit it if they chose (Offner, *American Appeasement*, p. 263).

The only variable was the attitude of France. Daladier and Bonnet had been delayed by a long Cabinet meeting in Paris at which, despite the efforts of the majority, the 'war group' had succeeded in foreclosing an agreement that if Hitler attacked Czechoslovakia, France would stand by her Treaty.[54] The men on both sides of the discussion which began in London at 9.25 pm on the twenty-fifth were thus tired before they began, eager to recriminate and impose blame on each other. Both had also heard from Masaryk that Czechoslovakia had rejected the Godesberg terms. 'The nation of St Wenceslas, John Hus, and Thomas Masaryk will not be a nation of slaves.'*

The conduct of the meeting by the British representatives† resembled the story in Aesop's fable of the rivalry of sun and wind, each trying to make a traveller take off his cloak. The British played both roles: first as the wind, which having raged and tormented the man only made him draw his cloak tighter about him; then as the sun, whose benign warmth persuaded him to disrobe.

The meeting began badly; Daladier complained that his Government had not had a copy of the Godesberg terms until 10.30 am that morning. His Cabinet intended to stand by the International Commission and the plebiscite in areas of Czech majority; 'In the view of the French Government, it was no longer a question of reaching a fair arrangement. Herr Hitler's object was to destroy Czechoslovakia and to dominate Europe.'

Chamberlain disparaged his fears, and then questioned him in minute detail on precisely how France proposed to take military action if the Godesberg Memorandum were rejected and if Hitler invaded. Would she defend the Maginot Line only, or attack Germany by land? Daladier proved evasive but quoted impressive figures of Russian strength and suggested that

---

* *DBFP*, series 3, vol. 2, p. 519. The report was unconfirmed when the Anglo-French talks began. Halifax attempted to prevent Masaryk from publishing this reply, because it would end all hope of negotiation. The next day it became clear that Masaryk had exceeded his instructions, in order to influence the Anglo-French meeting. (*DBFP*, series 3, vol. 2, p. 536. *DGFP*, series D, vol. 2, p. 933.)

† The account given here is taken from the Prime Minister's report to the Cabinet, at 11.30 pm, just after the talks were adjourned and (for the meeting on the twenty-sixth) from the report to the Cabinet of that day. The vital private conversation between Chamberlain and Daladier is not given in the published documents, which refer only to 'a short verbal report to the Cabinet', referring to the Wilson visit (*DBFP*, series 3, vol. 2, p. 537n).

France would attempt a land offensive and perhaps bomb military and industrial centres in the Rhineland. Angrily, he put direct questions to Chamberlain. Did Britain accept Hitler's plan? Would they press it on the Czech Government? Did they think France would take no action?

Turn and turn about, they wrangled, like men fighting in a dark alley, searching for each other's weakness. As Chamberlain admitted: 'it was not for us to say what decision France should take, but it was important to know what France intended to do'. Finally he asked for General Gamelin, French Chief of Staff, to come over on Monday the twenty-sixth 'as it was imperative to ascertain whether the French really intended to carry out any serious offensive hostilities against Germany. General Gamelin was in a position to speak on behalf of all France's three fighting services.'

However arrogant and unsympathetic the British attitude, it was understandable, given the long fear of war which had dogged their plans for the previous six months, that they should search for security. Although the French Ministers' words appear resolute in the print of the official record, they made a poor showing to those who were actually present. Hoare thought them 'weak and secretive' yet 'resentful' of the cross-examination;[55] Horace Wilson called the meeting 'painful. Daladier in a panic.'[56] Chamberlain 'thought it significant that never once had the French put the question – if we go to war with Germany, will you come in too?'[57] Daladier may have evaded the answer; equally, there is no sign of a British attempt to make the imaginative effort of understanding subconscious fears which they clearly expected the French to make for them.

Daladier's insistence on the International Commission was swept away by the flat assertion that Hitler simply would not accept it. He tried to awaken a response in British self-interest, by suggesting that Hitler would move on to take Rumania, and Turkey, before attacking France but no point of agreement was reached before they adjourned for the night.

The Cabinet met straight afterwards: Duff Cooper, who was contemplating resignation, complained that the British had simply contested the French point of view and put nothing in its place. For an hour the others speculated on what Daladier's words really meant and their doubts grew steadily. Inskip queried whether Gamelin could answer 'what was strictly a political question, namely what decision such a Government would take if and when hostilities broke out'.[58] Years of mistrust of weak and variable French Cabinets, dating back to Laval and beyond, lay behind such remarks.

Chamberlain had a scheme which might avoid war even though, as he suspected, Czechoslovakia had already decided to reject the Godesberg memorandum. 'He suggested that, basing himself on the personal conversations he had had with Herr Hitler, he should write a personal letter to the Führer, saying that he had received intimation that the Prague Government were likely to reject Hitler's proposals and making one last appeal to him.'[59] A joint Commission consisting of Germany, Czechoslovakia and Britain should be set up to see how to put into most orderly and speedy effect the proposals already accepted by Czechoslovakia, 'without shocking public opinion'. Thus the world would see how hard Britain had worked for peace; and the Dominions might rally round. Horace Wilson would take the letter. If it failed, then, as his confidential adviser, Wilson 'should be authorised to give a personal message from the P.M. to the effect that, if this appeal was refused, France would go to war and that if that happened it seemed certain that we should be drawn in'. If Hitler was bluffing, this would offer him a way out. If not, it was war. Without disagreement, the Cabinet gave him his mandate.

The style of this scheme was peculiarly Chamberlain's. It drew on his accumulated balance of prestige in Germany in order to satisfy all the competing claims. With luck, the formal Czechoslovak rejection had been held up by the Foreign Office; France, he assured the Cabinet, could be persuaded to agree. Germany had already been forewarned.* Wilson's mission can thus be seen not just as a last desperate throw, but also as a coolly calculated exercise in personal diplomacy on the very edge of chaos.

Gamelin arrived on the morning of 26 September, and turned out to be much more forthcoming and belligerent than the British had expected. He met Chamberlain and Halifax first and later talked with the Service Ministers and the Chiefs of Staff.

---

* An unnamed source, almost certainly Wilson, had told the German embassy, after Masaryk's announcement: 'The PM has sent me to transmit the following strictly confidential message—"the news . . . does not amount to the last word" '. (*DGFP*, series D, vol. 2, p. 933).

If Germany attacked Czechoslovakia, he said, France would declare war and attack Germany in about three days. He rated highly Czechoslovakia's capacity to resist and he assured the British that the French air force would bomb industrial targets in the Ruhr and Saar.* The inner group showed no sign of being shaken by what he said. They had already found a way to discover the answer to Simon's 'political question'. Chamberlain had decided to meet Daladier alone, away from the constraints of the French Foreign Ministry officials,[59a] and after seeing Gamelin Chamberlain asked Daladier to 10 Downing Street with only Corbin to interpret.

Daladier seemed pleased with the idea of the Wilson mission. Then Chamberlain showed him how the warning to Hitler would be phrased: 'The French Government have informed us that, if the Czechs reject the memorandum and Germany attacks Czechoslovakia, they will fulfil their obligations to Czechoslovakia. Should the forces of France in consequence become engaged in active hostilities against Germany, *we shall feel obliged to support them.*'[60]

At last, after so many months, the British had given their word – the guarantee that France had striven for ever since 1919. It was no wonder Daladier replied that 'he was absolutely in accord with the proposed statement' and, when Chamberlain asked if he had more to say, went on: 'Speaking frankly, he did not feel that he had expressed himself well the previous evening. He now stated that if Germany attacked Czechoslovakia and hostilities ensued, the French *intended to go to war*. . . . There was still one last opportunity for negotiation, but if that failed, France and this country stood together.'

Chamberlain, too, might justly be pleased. From the chaos of Godesberg, he had re-created the entente on a firm understanding with France and a new plan to deal with Germany. Once more he appeared to hold the initiative. The Cabinet approved unanimously. But no one had minuted the private discussion.

* 26 September, CAB 23/95. The British estimate, made by the CID, on 25 September (CAB 53/41, COS 770) broadly confirmed Gamelin's information about French and German dispositions on the Western and Czechoslovak fronts, but the most important factors, according to the CID, were that Germany had run down her strength on the Italian frontier, implying that she felt secure of Italian complicity; and secondly the emphasis to be put on the fact that the Western front was held 'comparatively lightly . . . implying that they do *not* believe the French will march'. This interpretation added to the British doubts of French intentions.

The guarantee did not appear in the official records of the Anglo-French meeting; and although Daladier had agreed on the wording of the warning the two Prime Ministers had not put it in a formal document. After Munich, and to the end of his life, Daladier denied that the pledge had ever been given.* Subsequent British actions may have caused him to doubt whether anything of significance had been said.

A state of euphoria transmitted itself to the Foreign Office, where Leeper drafted and Halifax authorised a communiqué† stating that if 'in spite of all efforts made by the British Prime Minister, a German attack is made upon Czechoslovakia, the immediate result must be that France will be bound to come to her assistance and Great Britain and Russia will certainly stand by France'.[61] So vehement a declaration was remarkable, even if it gave a vehicle for Halifax's long-suppressed opposition. Russia had not been consulted; nor had Bonnet, who tried to discredit it.[62] *Le Matin* in Paris called it a 'clever lie'.

Meanwhile, as Wilson left for Berlin, preparations for war were stepped up. Parliament was to be recalled for the twenty-eighth. Chamberlain arranged to make a broadcast in the evening of the twenty-seventh.‡ Hoare's meetings with Press proprietors and editors became more frequent. A mood of unity and purpose seemed to be growing in the Cabinet: Duff Cooper, reassured by a word from Daladier, apologised for his criticism of the Prime Minister's policy and indicated that he wished to withdraw his threat of resignation.[63] At Chamberlain's request, Hankey returned to the scene of his former glory. 'I am to parade for duty tomorrow at the Cabinet Office, apparently as a temporary personal adviser to him and the P.M.,'[63a] he wrote. (Chamberlain intended to put him in the War Cabinet if war broke out; but, although Inskip and Bridges, the Cabinet Secretary, approved, Ismay, Hankey's successor at the CID, did not. The plan was dropped when the Munich Conference made it redundant.) Chamberlain also met the Chiefs of Staff and the

---

* L. Thompson, *Munich*, p. 205. Yet Hoare described it as 'a specific pledge of a British expeditionary force to France, if France went to war with Germany' (*Nine Troubled Years*, p. 315).
† According to Robbins, *Munich, 1938*, p. 297, this was another example of officials making policy. Considering the guarantee offered by Chamberlain, this conclusion seems unwarranted.
‡ In Wilson's absence, Vansittart was to help draft this, with Sir Stephen Tallents BBC Public Relations Controller and Steward, Press Officer at 10 Downing Street.

Service ministers on the afternoon of the twenty-sixth, and as Hore-Belisha said 'more decisions were taken in an hour, than in weeks'.[64] Permission to call up anti-aircraft defence personnel was given and trench-digging and the issue of gas-masks was begun by the Home Office. Mobilisation of the fleet was postponed but then accepted at a meeting of the Inner Cabinet the next day, on the advice of Admiral Backhouse, Chief of Naval Staff. The Executive Committee of the League of Nations Union, meeting on the evening of the twenty-sixth, declared itself in favour of resistance to the latest German demands and the same evening saw a huge Labour Party Rally, at the Albert Hall, adopt a similar resolution.

Wilson's mission started badly: he was unable to meet Hitler until shortly before the major speech he was to make in the Berlin Sportpalast on the evening of 26 September. Hitler was excited and emotional and barely listened to Chamberlain's letter: when he heard that the Czechs were going to reject his terms, he began to walk out, and although his staff persuaded him to stay he refused to depart in any way from the Godesberg Memorandum. He would talk with the Czechs but Beneš must hand over the designated areas by 1 October. Wilson thought it useless to continue and dangerous to deliver 'the special oral message which he had been authorised to give and which Herr Hitler might have regarded as an ultimatum – and this might have made the character of his speech more inflammatory'.[64a] Instead he asked for another audience the next day.

The massed crowds in the monumental Sportpalast listened eagerly to Hitler's violent words: 'The Czechoslovak state began with a single lie, and the father of this lie was named Beneš... there is no such thing as a Czechoslovak nation but only Czechs and Slovaks, and the Slovaks do not wish to have anything to do with the Czechs. . . .' If freedom were not at once given to the Sudeten Germans, 'we will go and fetch this freedom for ourselves'.[65] Through the cloud of demonic possession, however, a thread of reason could be detected: Hitler thanked Chamberlain for his intervention and gave an assurance 'that the moment when Czechoslovakia solves her problems . . . I have no further interest in the Czech state. And that is guaranteed to him – we want no Czechs!'

The British believed, from what Wilson had told them and

from Hitler's reply to Roosevelt's peace appeal, that, unless a definite reply were received from Prague by 2 pm on the twenty-eighth, Hitler would declare war. It was extraordinary, therefore, that when the inner group met at 10 pm on the twenty-sixth Simon should say that it was a 'mark time' speech and Vansittart should agree that it did not justify immediate mobilisation. It was the measure of how much the Cabinet had staked on Wilson – and, by derivation, on their faith in Chamberlain's influence with Hitler.

Wilson met Hitler again at 11 pm on the twenty-seventh. He spoke no German and can scarcely have been sanguine of success, yet he did his best as an emissary who bore Chamberlain's authority: 'Sir Horace Wilson has my full confidence and you can take anything he says as coming from me.'[66] But Hitler was totally impervious to Wilson's tactful approach. He replied simply that he had no message 'except to thank Chamberlain for what he had tried to do'.[67] There were two courses left: 'either the Czechs accepted the terms or he would totally destroy them'. So Wilson delivered the warning which Chamberlain had shown to Daladier.

> Hitler replied, 'That means England will attack Germany.' I interrupted and said he had misunderstood the message. I then repeated it slowly. Hitler had by now worked himself up into (for him) a mild passion and once more said, that if Czechoslovakia rejected the terms—and he supposed they would now that they were assured of the support of England and France—he would smash them.[68]

Yet Hitler also pursued Wilson with careful questions, and emphasised that he was not going to attack France first.* If France and England attacked Germany, that would be their responsibility and the responsibility of the Czechs. Finally Hitler said, 'he could not believe that Germany and England could find themselves at war, and he urged the Prime Minister to do all he could to induce Czechoslovakia to accept his memorandum'.[69]

The omens were uncertain. Hitler might be offering Britain another chance to avoid war or he might be trying to suborn the Western powers into a position of total humiliation.

---

* This was confirmed by Ribbentrop, who took no other part in the discussion. (27 Sept, CAB 23/95.)

Wilson flew home at once, having accepted the first inter-pretation, and interrupted a meeting which had started between Chamberlain and Halifax after lunch and then broadened out into a conference with Inskip, and other advisers. They had heard exceptionally gloomy reports from Colonel MacFarlane on the state of Czech morale,* and from Lord Gort, the CIGS, who said that the Chiefs of Staff were worried, after their meet-ing with Gamelin, that the French might not be able to take effective action in a war. Mobilisation of the Navy was therefore agreed on.

The debate had become more and more depressing during the afternoon, with only eighteen hours to go to the German deadline. Chamberlain and Halifax finally agreed to send a telegram to the French inviting consultation before launching any military operation.[70] Suspicion that the French would be dilatory was not the only weakness in the new-found entente. Phipps had already reported that Bonnet was asking pertinent and detailed questions about the situation under the Chamberlain guarantee – if France went to war, would Britain mobilise immediately? would she introduce conscription? and would she agree to pool her economic and financial resources with those of France?[71] They were reasonable questions which ought to have been answered at once; but they also suggested uneasy feelings about the practical value of what Daladier had said.

The next visitor was equally sombre. The High Commissioners had been asking all day for an appointment to put their views. MacDonald told them to do so in writing, but Stanley Bruce, of Australia, was reluctant to do so because 'any view now committed to writing would be likely to take the line that the terms of the German memorandum were not a sufficient cause for a world war'.[72] Instead, he tried to persuade Chamberlain

---

* After a short motor-tour of Czechoslovakia, MacFarlane had returned to London, convinced 'that morale appeared to him poor and much of the material preparations were not completed. The Customs frontier guards were definitely scared stiff. On the Southern frontier . . . the Czechs appeared to him to be very ill prepared. . . . The French Military Attaché in Berlin was doubtful of the value of the resistance which the Czech army would put up. He [MacFarlane] thought that it would be very rash to base any policy on the assumption that the Czechs would fight like tigers.' From an erstwhile optimist, his conclusion was extremely unsettling. He gave no support to the hope that Hitler might stop at the 'language line' if he invaded and 'thought that there would be more enthusiasm [in Germany] for war, than seemed possible a month ago'. (CAB 27/646.)

to take a stronger line. It was, he said, 'really a challenge between the idea of force and peaceful negotiation, and the challenge must be taken up'.[73] But his assurance that, if the British chose the challenge, 'it was likely that the Dominions would come to share it', was less than convincing. Chamberlain might well have asked: how long before that happened, and in what strength?

Finally came Wilson. Hitler, it appeared, 'had been very quiet and almost cordial... he felt that we were being made dupes by the Czech Government. He regretted that, after accepting the need for a cession of the Sudeten territory, we appeared to be heading for a world war, simply because the Czech Government was so dilatory.'* Wilson clearly thought it wrong to hold out, and he suggested 'that a telegram should be despatched to Prague, suggesting to the Czech Government that they should tacitly accept occupation by the German troops of the areas up to the red line. This, he felt, was very likely the last opportunity of avoiding war.'

The inner group had come a long way since the day before. Even before hearing the advice of MacFarlane and Bruce, Halifax and Chamberlain had drafted telegrams to be sent to Berlin, Prague and Paris, 'urging upon the Czech Government acceptance, as far as possible, of Herr Hitler's terms (and to notify Berlin of such acceptance) before 2.0 pm on Wednesday'.[74] Now the trusted envoy, fresh with the latest experience of Hitler, advised the same† and explained sadly that Hitler had torn to pieces the 'special oral message' on which Daladier had set store. Chamberlain decided to send the telegrams at 6.45 pm and to hold a Cabinet meeting at 9.45 pm to hear Wilson's account and endorse what he had done.

He and Halifax were persuaded of the necessity of forcing the Godesberg terms on the Czechs. But could the rest of the Cabinet reverse a decision taken only two days earlier, with such heart-searching? How many resignations would follow? What of the House of Commons, and the public speech which

* CAB 27/646. In his own memorandum, Wilson described his first interview as a 'very violent hour'.
† Even before leaving Berlin, Wilson had asked the United States Ambassador to urge Roosevelt to persuade Chamberlain to keep Britain out of the war. (*FRUS* (1938) vol. 1, pp. 638–84.)

the Prime Minister could not now avoid? Chamberlain no longer seemed the dominant leader.* In the Cabinet Room that afternoon and evening, the sands began to run out.

Vansittart and Cadogan were still fighting a rearguard action to prevent Halifax agreeing to total surrender, but their views were subordinated to the advice of the Chiefs of Staff, which backed up the Chamberlain–Wilson thesis that war should be avoided at any cost. The military appreciation of the situation, if Britain went to war with Germany over Czechoslovakia, confirmed that the country could only fight a defensive war.[75] It is true that the Air Staff had realised by this time that the danger of Germany employing the 'knock-out blow' was slight,[76] but Inskip failed to put this point to the Cabinet with the significance it warranted, and the advice of the War Office, submitted on 27 September, was much more in line.

The War Office predicted early German success in the offensive against Czechoslovakia and heavy air-raids on France and Britain.[77] Nothing could be expected from Russia; Italy was more likely to come in on the German side than in a war fought in six to eighteen months' time. More important, they made a series of political judgements about the unhelpful attitude of the Dominions and the domestic situation. The House of Commons was 'likely to be bellicose. Their attitude may well drive the Government into war, a fact that is more unfortunate in that members have no knowledge of the military situation. . . .' While it was true that the Government had offered a guarantee to France, which could not be dishonoured without endangering their political future, and also that gallant defence by the Czechs would arouse great sympathy, the 'obvious advantages if we are to go to war at once, whilst the German defence is thin on the West . . . are evanescent.' Six months' preparation would be needed to face what the War Office called 'a war of the first magnitude'; and even then Britain would only be secure against defeat. She would not be strong enough,

even combined with France, to gain a positive victory unless strong additional aid were forthcoming from elsewhere. . . . From the military point of view the balance of advantage is definitely in

* Wilson thought him tired and uncertain what he would say to the House of Commons the next day — Ambassador Hugh Wilson (Berlin) to Hull. (*FRUS* (1938) vol. 1, p. 650.)

favour of postponement. . . . Our real object is not to save Czechoslovakia—that is impossible in any event—but to end the days of
the Nazi regime. This is not our selected moment, it is theirs; we
are in bad condition to wage even a defensive war at the present
time; the grouping of the powers at the moment makes well
nigh hopeless the waging of a successful offensive war.

It is not certain that Chamberlain studied this paper but in
all essentials it conformed to his thinking. Merely to state that
war should be avoided, however, solved nothing. The British
were still searching for the magic key to open their prison door.

At 6.45 pm Chamberlain sent Henderson a plan offering a
new timetable for occupation, which he hoped would be acceptable to both sides.[78] Although it provided for the occupation
of most of Asch and Eger on 1 October, partition would not
be completed before 31 October, and to the Germans it was
mere whistling down the wind. At no point in the time after
Godesberg did the inner group consider an appeal to the
German opposition, even though Henderson reported that
German public opinion was not ready for war.[79]

At 8 pm Chamberlain had to make his broadcast. In a tired,
flat voice which has reverberated on records down the years,
he gave vent to his sense of hopelessness.

How horrible, fantastic, incredible it is that we should be digging
trenches and trying on gas masks here, because of a quarrel in a
far away country between people of whom we know nothing. It
seems still more impossible that a quarrel which has already been
settled in principle, should be the subject of war.

Perhaps many in Britain, on reflection, would have agreed
with him, and with the reminder that 'however much we may
sympathise with the smaller nation confronted by a big and
powerful neighbour, we cannot in all circumstances undertake
to involve the whole British Empire in war, simply on her
account'. Yet Chamberlain had a unique occasion to educate
the British people – and he let it pass. It was entirely in character
with his policy and philosophy that he should have sought to
project his own disillusion, instead of uttering a rallying-cry.
It may have been honesty not to try to sell the dismemberment
of Czechoslovakia as a British master-stroke, but it was the sign
of a man who understood little of public moods, not to create a

counter to the German boast of fifty millions united behind Hitler, when war was less than a day's notice away.

It is true of any prolonged crisis that the skies never wholly darken until after the final minute of the eleventh hour, and men making decisions must be as careful of deceitful hopes as of ultimate threats. There was evidence, still, that Hitler was uneasy and unsure. After his first interview with Wilson, Hitler had sent Chamberlain a letter, laying stress on the importance of the plebiscite and offering to give a firm and formal guarantee for the remainder of Czechoslovakia.[80] At this stage Chamberlain could hardly do anything but take this at its face value, less for its promises than for what it revealed of Hitler's intentions. On that note, the last Cabinet at which any decision could be made began at 9.30 pm.

Chamberlain justified the fact that he had already advised Prague to capitulate by explaining the salient facts and quoting Henderson's most recent advice; 'unless at the eleventh hour we advise Czechoslovakia to make the best terms she could with Berlin, we should be exposing her to the fate of Abyssinia'.[81] He emphasised what MacFarlane and the High Commissioners had said, and he read out similar telegrams from Lyons, the Australian Prime Minister, and Hertzog.

Wilson was asked to give his account of his visit. Calmly and precisely he repeated the story. Hitler believed Beneš was lying and that he would continue to prevaricate, under the impression that Britain and France would ultimately support him. This delusion amazed Hitler, who was well aware from tapped telephone-messages* that Masaryk was the chief source of Beneš' information. '[Hitler] asked why we allowed our policy to be settled as the result of the influence of Russia, exerted at Paris and Prague. He had repeated that at this hour there were only two alternatives, and he had asked us to do all we could to find a settlement and avoid war.'[82]

The only alternative to acceptance of the Godesberg terms, Wilson suggested, was that the Czechs should withdraw their army and allow Germany to occupy the transfer areas, leaving

---

* By now it was obvious that the Czechs' first refusal of the Godesberg terms (which Masaryk had announced before the Anglo-French talks on the twenty-fifth) had originated in London; Masaryk had attempted to force his view on his Government by telephone, thereby giving a hostage to the German interceptors. There is some doubt as to whether the Syrovy Cabinet considered the Godesberg Memorandum at all before the evening of 26 September.

the International Commission to determine the mixed areas by plebiscite; thus taking up the advantages of the British guarantee and of Hitler's declaration that he had no more territorial claims in Europe. If Beneš could agree to this by 2 pm the next day, he believed that the Germans would co-operate.

Wilson's case was subtle and persuasive but the opposition could not stomach the implications. 'There were however other facts...,' Duff Cooper contended: a firmer spirit in France, and the appeal from Roosevelt. If they waited for the Dominions to be unanimous, Britain would never go to war. Wilson's proposal was a betrayal of the agreement made with Daladier and could only be carried out by telling Czechoslovakia 'that unless she adopted it, we should refuse to come to her help. This course was quite unjustified and he could not be associated with it.'

Alive to the great danger that others would resign with Duff Cooper, Chamberlain began to explain that this plan had been agreed by the inner group as the last chance to avoid war. 'He did not propose that we should advise Czechoslovakia... but merely that we should put this suggestion before them.'

On that tentative point Halifax stepped in. He refused to endorse the plan, or the telegram which had already been drafted asking for the withdrawal of Czech troops.[83] He would not back down on the promise to France, nor capitulate to Germany. 'We could not force the Czech Government to do what we believe to be wrong.' At last Halifax had grounded his policy in the 'great moral issues'. Wearily, Chamberlain answered: 'If that was the general view of his colleagues, he was prepared to leave it at that.'

It was no wonder that when Ambassador Kennedy, who had been seeking an interview with Chamberlain all day, caught up with him at 10.30 pm, he found him utterly depressed. Kennedy asked what he thought about another appeal to Roosevelt. Chamberlain barely reacted; there was nothing to lose.[84]

At this moment there were fourteen hours to go before the German time-limit elapsed. If Hitler were to stand by his own date of 1 October, he had three days in hand, but the British had learned nothing to cause them to doubt that what he had said at Godesberg – 2 pm on the twenty-eighth – was the literal truth. There was dogged courage in Chamberlain's determination still to find a way out, even though his Cabinet, led by

Halifax, had resigned themselves to a war based on an Anglo-French alliance.

Late in the evening, Newton reported the formal rejection of the Godesberg terms by Czechoslovakia, and the Syrovy Government's request to Britain and France to hold to what they had agreed after Berchtesgaden.[85] At the same time, the news from Paris opened up a most dangerous avenue. The French Cabinet had met that morning (27 September). Divided and uncertain, torn between mobilisation and surrender, they were wide open to suspicions that Britain would not fulfil Chamberlain's promise. Bonnet made the most of the fact that he had had no answer to his three requests for specific British pledges (above, p. 391). After a day of tormented and factious argument, it seemed as though the Government would fall. As Daladier's position weakened, Bonnet's advice predominated. Bullitt thought the situation so bad that he asked Washington for a firm message.[86] About midnight, Phipps reported that the French had not found the latest message from Prague conciliatory enough towards Germany, and that the French Ambassador in Berlin, François-Poncet, would be instructed to put forward another plan, offering larger areas for German occupation.[87] Before Chamberlain went to bed he had reason to believe that the military assurances of France were no longer reliable and that the morning might reveal Britain facing Germany alone without an ally in the world.*

As options were closed, however, others offered themselves. By 27 September, Roosevelt had realised, from the messages the State Department received from Europe, that war was imminent and he called a special meeting of his advisers – Hull, Welles, and Assistant Secretary A. A. Berle. Out of their conference emerged an appeal to Hitler, which, according to Bullitt, delighted Daladier, in the midst of his divided Cabinet. It was probably true that 'Roosevelt's chief concern was to encourage

* By now, according to Harvey, the Foreign Office no longer trusted Phipps's 'defeatist' reports. He was therefore instructed to ask all Consuls in France to report direct to London, to by-pass the Embassy. 'Almost all these reports are unanimous in saying the French are resolute and resigned to the necessity of making a stand now' (*Diaries of Oliver Harvey*, p. 200). But it was Phipps on whom Chamberlain and Halifax relied. Phipps confirmed his previous reports on 28 September: 'the only party that favours war are the Communists. . . . France is prepared to march to the last man to defend herself if attacked, but will not fight with any heart in a hopeless offensive war against Germany, for which she is not prepared' (FO 408/68, pp. 211–12).

further negotiation without committing the United States (and thereby arousing Congressional and public wrath) to European political settlements',[88] but the President also appealed to Mussolini* – a factor of considerable importance, because the British had also taken care to keep this line of communication open. Dieckhoff, German Ambassador in Washington, was aware of something significant in Roosevelt's actions, for he cabled on 27 September that Hitler could get 'practically all he is demanding' if he negotiated, but that in a war the United States would side with Britain.[89]

The British Foreign Office had received an encouraging message from Mussolini on 16 September and had carefully fanned the flame.† The Cabinet were, of course, aware that Italy might join Germany immediately war broke out, and when Italian troops were moved into Libya the Mediterranean fleet was directed to Egyptian waters.[90] But they were also sensitive to the fact that the Anglo-Italian agreement was still in being.[91] On the twenty-sixth, after Hitler's Sportpalast speech, Lord Perth, Ambassador in Rome, had asked if he should see Ciano, so that Mussolini might use his mediating influence with Hitler.[92] At that time, no action was taken, but late on the twenty-seventh Chamberlain sent instructions to arrange an interview with Ciano the next morning.‡

During the night, diplomatic activity continued incessantly, and with singularly little effect. Bonnet instructed François-Poncet to offer yet more Czech territory, as Phipps had forecast. Unable to obtain an audience with Hitler, the French Ambassador was reduced to waiting disconsolately with Henderson for a summons which did not come until 11.15 am.

* This message was sent by Hull to Ambassador Phillips in Rome (*FRUS* (1938), vol. 1, p. 677) and although it did not reach Mussolini till 4 pm on the twenty-eighth, its details were known to both him and Ciano before 10 am on that decisive morning. According to Phillips, the State Department had deliberately used a simple code, so that the Italians should break it. The United States Embassy confirmed at 9.30 am, that the contents were known to the Italian Foreign Office (Phillips to Hull, *FRUS* (1938), vol. 1, pp. 703–4).

† *Diaries of Oliver Harvey*, p. 181. The message came via Grandi. Afterwards Halifax told Perth to keep Mussolini informed of what went on at Berchtesgaden. He also passed on the suggestion that Poland and Hungary would receive their due 'at the appropriate time' (FO 408/68, pp. 176–7).

‡ Curiously enough, the same step was suggested by Lyons, the Australian Prime Minister, very early on the 28th; Lyons offered to send Bruce to Rome if it would help (PREM 1/242).

Chamberlain got up at 7 am to draft the telephone messages to Rome and Berlin which embodied his final initiative. He did not even consult Halifax, whose opposition at the evening meeting had shaken him severely, but he did show the drafts to Wilson – 'one more try'.[93] Lord Perth saw Ciano at 10.20 am and managed to alarm him sufficiently with prophecies of disaster. Mussolini, Perth said, was 'the only man who could now induce Hitler to accept a pacific solution'.[94] When he realised that this was an official démarche, Ciano replied, 'It is a question of hours, not days', and went to see Mussolini at once. Ciano was told to ring Attolico, the Italian Ambassador in Berlin, and instruct him to ask Hitler at once for twenty-four hours' delay.

Ambassador followed ambassador in the rooms of the Berlin Chancellery, in grave disarray, out of breath and constantly obstructing each other, to get to Hitler's notice. 'That day', Schmidt wrote, 'the Chancellery was more like the camp of an army in the field, than the centre of an organised Government'.[95] The important messages got through; Attolico broke in on François-Poncet, who was retailing the new French proposals, and Hitler gave Mussolini his twenty-four hours. Meanwhile, at 11.30, Chamberlain's formal notes were telephoned to Rome and Berlin.* Hitler's letter, the Prime Minister said, convinced him that Germany could get 'all essentials without war and without delay'. He offered to go at once to Berlin to discuss the transfer arrangements with Hitler and the Czechoslovak representatives and, if Hitler desired, those of France and Italy. Agreement could be reached within a week. 'However much you still distrust the Prague Government's intentions, you cannot doubt the power of the British and French Governments to see that the promises are carried out fairly and fully and forthwith.'[96]

This message has always been regarded as the highest pitch of appeasement. Afterwards the British could only trust in the rational chord in Hitler's mentality and in their slender credit-balance with Italy, or perhaps in Mussolini's reluctance to

---

* At the same time, Wilson was telling the London representative of the Dienststelle Ribbentrop that everything depended on the manner in which Hitler's demands were met. 'If we were to give way on the former', the representative wrote, 'Britain would be prepared to push through all our demands' (*DGFP*, series D, vol. 2, p. 989).

commit Italy to war. The offer was accepted: the telegram to
Rome stimulated Mussolini, either by appealing to his vanity in
offering him a place at the high table in Europe, or by playing
on his fears sufficiently for him to press Hitler to agree to the
proposed conference. Hitler's answer was finally given, not to
Henderson but to the Italians, at 2.40 pm, on the condition that
Mussolini came to the meeting as well. Invitations went to
Daladier, who accepted at once, and Chamberlain, who was
in the middle of his speech, opening the House of Commons
debate on foreign affairs. Cadogan ran with it from the Foreign
Office and there followed the famous 'chain of appeasement'
as the message was handed down from the gallery to the Prime
Minister, to make his climactic announcement.

Why did Hitler concede at that moment? He was under constant
pressure from the High Command, from Goering, Raeder,
Brauschitsch and Halder not to invade Czechoslovakia because
the army was not ready for a European war.[97] Operation
Green was likely now to be the opening campaign, not the
climax. Probably only Ribbentrop among Hitler's immediate
entourage really desired war. The conservative opposition in the
Foreign Ministry was in touch with Mussolini, and Goering and
Ribbentrop came near to quarrelling in the Chancellery on the
morning of the twenty-eighth. Probably the most important
reason, though, was that Hitler was by no means certain of
Mussolini's attitude and may well have judged that a mortgage
on the Italian dictator's political future was more important for
his own long-term ambitions than a military victory in central
Europe. His profound admiration for Mussolini has been noted
earlier* and Hitler may have needed only the right stimulus
from the right man. Perhaps, also, bearing in mind Dieckhoff's
report about the United States and world war, the dictator who
had raised the bids at Godesberg now called his opponent's
hand, because he thought the game had gone on long enough.
After all, he had written to Chamberlain on the twenty-sixth,
in rational terms, asking him to 'bring the Government in
Prague to reason at this very last hour'.[97a]
Acceptance of the conference gave Germany most of what
Hitler had demanded at Godesberg, but for the British what

* It survived until 1944, when he propped up Mussolini's pathetic republic in
northern Italy.

signified was that they were not at war. Diverted from total surrender by his Cabinet, Chamberlain had nevertheless brought out of the week after Godesberg something better than the disaster that his colleagues had come to accept as inevitable. The sequel was typical of Chamberlain's political style: neither they nor the inner group were consulted again before Munich; nor, once Daladier had accepted, was France. Nothing was done to jeopardise the illusion that Britain was once more the impartial arbiter of the European scene. While the Germans concerted policy with Mussolini, Britain made no arrangements to secure a common front with France.* At the Munich Conference, Chamberlain and Daladier arrived, behaved, and left as if they had no more in common than total strangers.

There were still dangers: a military coup might occur in Czechoslovakia, and the government might resist German troops, whatever France and Britain did. The British were aware that feverish negotiation was taking place, in an attempt to appease the Polish claim to Teschen, in order to safeguard the Czech rear. But the Syrovy Government soon proved to be only a front for Beneš and gave way steadily as he had done, always conceding too little and too late to affect the issue. In any case, the British gave the Czechs very little chance. At 6.45 on the evening of the twenty-eighth, Newton told Beneš merely that Chamberlain would go to Munich 'with the interests of Czechoslovakia fully in mind'.[98] Later, Halifax insisted that the Czechoslovak Government must accept the British plan in principle at once.[99] Surrounded by a disintegrating Government, Beneš appealed weakly to Chamberlain to permit nothing which would harm Czechoslovakia more than the original Anglo-French proposals, and at 10.40 pm acceded to the demand.

The other potential danger was a revolt of British public opinion, which might force the House of Commons to take a belligerent attitude. But the reaction to the news of Hitler's acceptance was quite different from what the War Office had forecast. Like an animal whose nervous preparation for battle dissolves in displacement symptoms when the danger is removed,

---

* Phipps did finally answer Bonnet's requests for information, made three days before. Britain would not introduce conscription except in defence against a German attack; the fleet had been mobilised; but pooling of resources, such as Bonnet suggested, would require Parliamentary approval (*DBFP*, series 3, vol. 2, p. 602). This was hardly calculated to inspire the entente.

the House of Commons and the public manifested a variety of responses ranging from the hysteria of relief to the busy digging of trenches in London's parks.

The Conference took place at Munich in an atmosphere of pervasive confusion. Chamberlain blamed the Germans 'for the length of the proceedings and the inefficiency of the arrangements,'[100] but the British had done little to ensure their smooth working. He and Wilson represented Britain; Daladier and Léger, France; Mussolini, and Ciano, Italy; Hitler, Ribbentrop and Weizsäcker, Germany. The Germans had, in fact, taken some care with the arrangements. Wilson noticed that the delegates were 'seated not at a conference table, but in chairs in a rough circle, too widely distributed to have informal contact with our French friends – about whom we were anxious'.[101] Schmidt acted as interpreter, master of ceremonies and referee, all in one. Mussolini spoke other languages than his own, so Italian was excluded from the repertoire. Czech was not needed – the two Czechoslovak representatives stayed in their hotel all day. When Chamberlain asked for their attendance, he was brusquely denied it, and neither he nor Daladier protested. The Conference in being was worth more to both of them than the appearance of consultation.

What the British did not appreciate was the way the policy divisions in the German leadership had been resolved before the Conference. Kordt, Weizsäcker and Neurath, aided by Goering himself, had drafted a memorandum (subsequently approved by Hitler) setting out the procedure to be adopted, and they had presented this to Mussolini, via Attolico, the Italian Ambassador in Berlin.[102] Mussolini took charge of the conference, to Chamberlain's delight, and by using the memorandum ensured that the Goering faction would predominate over Ribbentrop. At the same time, however, Mussolini provided Hitler with a grievance which he could exploit later when dissatisfied with the reception of the Munich agreement.

All that Chamberlain noticed was that 'Mussolini's attitude all through was extremely quiet and reserved. He seemed to be cowed by Hitler, but undoubtedly he was most anxious for a peaceful settlement and he played an indispensable part in attaining it ... his manner to me was more than friendly....'[103]

Britain and France agreed to accept his document as a basis for discussion. The French only saw fit to attend the morning session, perhaps with *post facto* justification in mind. Their absence, as that of the Czechs, made little difference. The only issue on which Chamberlain stood firm was when Mussolini called for Poland and Hungary to be given the same terms as the Sudeten areas. This was beyond even the Godesberg *diktat*, and he refused, successfully. The three heads of state reached agreement by midnight, but copies of the papers were not ready for signature until 2 am. The ceremony for the signature turned to farce, as the top of the grand inkwell fell off and no ink was found inside.

That is one short version of what happened, as if the principals were merely actors in a play written days before, fulfilling with one or two slight exceptions their appointed roles. The Czechs were soon disposed of : but Daladier refused to go to Prague taking the Munich agreement. He and Chamberlain arranged to see the Czech representatives instead, and Mastny, who was waiting in his hotel, was called in, given the terms and an explanatory map, and advised to accept. Ashton-Gwatkin was sent to Prague the next day 'to help tell the Czechoslovak Government'.

Meanwhile Chamberlain put forward the last stage of his plan as if he at least had never lost sight of his ultimate aim of an Anglo-German détente. He asked Hitler for a final private meeting on the thirtieth and told Strang to prepare a document on Anglo-German relations, drawing an analogy with the Anglo-German Naval Treaty. Strang, who thought this precedent was undesirable, objected and asked Chamberlain to consult Daladier. 'He saw no reason whatever for saying anything to the French.'[104]

Chamberlain and Hitler met for the last time, alone in the dictator's room, where they wrapped each other in mutual felicitations on the outcome of the Conference. Chamberlain hoped Czechoslovakia would not 'be mad enough to refuse the terms or attempt resistance' but, if they did, he begged Hitler not to bomb the Czech cities. Hitler made a polite lack of response. Then they talked of Spain, air disarmament, trade; particularly, Chamberlain asked for the chance of greater British participation in trade in south-eastern Europe. Russia was not

mentioned,* and the subject of colonies was not brought up at
all. At the end Chamberlain seemed delighted with the way
the talks had gone and produced the celebrated document of
agreement which Hitler readily agreed to sign.†

Afterwards the delegation flew home. Unlike Godesberg, it
was roses all the way. Chamberlain told the crowds that when
he left he had hoped to be able to return and say 'out of this
nettle, danger, we pluck this flower, safety'. Later, he wrote to
his sister:

> Even the descriptions of the papers give no idea of the scenes
> in the streets as I drove from Heston to the Palace. They were
> lined from one end to the other, with people of every class
> shouting themselves hoarse, leaping on the running-board, banging
> on the windows and thrusting their hands into the car to be
> shaken. The scenes culminated in Downing Street, where I spoke
> to the multitudes below, from the same window I believe as that
> from which Dizzy announced peace with honour sixty years
> ago.

Simon's unlucky phrase had stuck and he unwisely gave way
to emotion in his choice of words.‡ Then to Buckingham Palace,
summoned especially by the King, and finally to Chequers for
the weekend, 'nearer to a nervous breakdown than I have ever
been in my life'.[105]

Far more significant than his chance phrase about peace with
honour was Chamberlain's remark to Swinton: 'Can't you see?
I have made peace.'[106] For Chamberlain, even if not for Halifax

---

* Soviet participation in the guarantee was not mentioned during the Conference
either (2 October, CAB 27/646).

† 'We, the German Fuehrer and Chancellor, and the British Prime Minister,
have had a further meeting today, and are agreed in recognising that the question
of Anglo-German relations is of the first importance for the two countries and for
Europe.

'We regard the Agreement signed last night and the Anglo-German Naval
Agreement as symbolic of the desire of our two peoples never to go to war with one
another again.

'We are resolved that the method of consultation shall be the method adopted
to deal with any other questions that may concern our two countries, and we are
determined to continue our efforts to remove possible sources of difference, and
thus to contribute to assure the peace of Europe.'

‡ Wilson wrote: 'In the stress of the emotion caused later the same day by ecstatic
welcome, visit to Buckingham Palace, reception by colleagues at Downing Street,
he seemed for once to allow his feelings to outrun his usual caution in speaking
and he used words which reflected his feelings, rather than his judgment ...'
(Wilson Memorandum).

and the rest of the Cabinet, this was fundamental. At the worst point of 1940, shortly before he died, he still justified his action: 'never for one single instant have I doubted the rightness of what I did at Munich....'[107]

On a lower plane, it was possible to argue that the terms agreed at Munich were materially better than those offered at Godesberg. In the formal sense, this is accurate. Chamberlain set out the difference at great length to his Cabinet colleagues on 30 September. Most of the Anglo-French plan, agreed on after Berchtesgaden, had been accepted by Germany and Italy. The International Commission* would be set up to represent Czechoslovakia and the four great powers, fix the line of German occupation and, in the mixed zones, to define the areas where a plebiscite was to be held. Moreover, it would ensure that 'international bodies' rather than German troops occupied these areas until the plebiscite was complete, by 30 November. It was to determine the conditions of evacuation and it was to ensure the right of individuals, valid for six months, to opt for transfer either into or out of the Reich. Then there was the new guarantee: in addition to the Franco-British pledge, Germany and Italy undertook to make their own, when the Polish and Hungarian minority questions had been settled by agreement. In appearance, these were substantial gains for the Western powers. Something much less would probably have been acceptable to Chamberlain and Daladier, but with such concessions from the stern line of Godesberg, they could face the world, and their respective parliaments and public.

However it was publicised, though, the differences were only in the letter of the agreement. The Cabinet did not query the unseemly speed of the Conference itself, nor the wording of the agreement which was so loosely drafted as to defy sound interpretation. While the vital plebiscite areas were defined differently from the Godesberg Memorandum, they were not yet de-limited. That depended on the International Commission, whose own efficacy was in no way guaranteed. The Commission was given no provision for voting, let alone for safe-guarding the interests of Czechoslovakia in a situation where Mussolini was now working wholly with Germany, and France manifestly not with Britain. The Czechoslovak representatives could hardly recover power

* Consisting of Nevile Henderson, Weizsäcker, François-Poncet, Attolico and a Czech representative.

and prestige after the treatment of their colleagues during the Munich Conference. Germany was bound to dominate. What security was there that Germany would seek fair play and not press her great advantage?

Only Duff Cooper expressed uneasiness. He admitted that Munich represented a great gain but 'he was afraid that we might get into the position in which we were drawn into making further concessions'.[108] He had already offered and withdrawn his resignation. He waited until he had studied the terms; then did resign, not the only jarring note in the paean of praise which surrounded Chamberlain* but the most outspoken. Most others within the political élite accepted the Munich agreement with reservations but sufficient faith, until the conduct of Germany, Italy, and the Poles and Hungarians dispelled the illusion. It was not until 11 October that Vansittart wrote:

> In my opinion the proceedings of the International Commission have been scandalous. It never even made an attempt to get a compromise between population figures of 1910 and 1918, *as instructed*. It has simply reproduced Godesberg, after we had flattered ourselves publicly on having got away from it. Over three-quarters of a million Czechs are now apparently to be under German rule. It is a shame.[109]

At first, however, while Daladier, to his great surprise, was fêted in Paris, Chamberlain could savour his rest at Chequers and the congratulations of his political colleagues, the Press and Britain's friends abroad. He had defined the duty of the conference at Munich in terms worthy of the great post-1918 international meetings. 'The Czechoslovak question was a European question and the great powers had not only the right to settle it but the duty also. It was his wish to apply the authority of the great powers in the correct manner.'†

Simon saw it in the same way when Chamberlain came home: 'Before the Prime Minister spoke, he should express on behalf of the whole Cabinet their profound admiration for the un-

---

* Stanley also complained, but not to the extent of resignation (PREM 1/266A).
† 30 Sept, CAB 23/95. It is worth comparing this with his statement in 1939: 'The great triumph is that it [Munich] has shown that representatives of four great powers can find it possible to agree on a way of carrying out a difficult and delicate operation by discussion instead of by force of arms, and thereby they have averted a catastrophe which could have ended civilization as we have known it.' (N. Chamberlain, *The Struggle for Peace* (London 1939) pp. 309–11.)

paralleled efforts that the Prime Minister had made and for the success that he had achieved. He would also like to say how proud they were to be associated with the Prime Minister as his colleagues at this time.'[110]

The personal reception Chamberlain received probably surpassed that of any other peace-time British Prime Minister in the present century. The greater part of it, for all the heart-felt gratitude of simple men and women, which his first biographer set out, was evanescent. Some was almost seditious.* It is worth noting that Hankey and Lord Weir, neither of them noted for easy sentiment, commended his success. The Press, likewise, lauded him, even the Sunday papers, three days after the event. *The Times, Express* and *Mail* were predictably fulsome, but the *Daily Herald, News Chronicle* and *Manchester Guardian* also laid aside criticisms of the Munich agreement and their laments for the Czechs, in favour of the greater relief that Hitler's will had been thwarted; as the *Guardian* put it – 'Great as are the injustices that Czecho-Slovakia suffers under the Munich Agreement . . . they cannot be measured against the horrors that might have extinguished not only Czecho-Slovakia, but the whole of Western civilisation.'[111]

Similar, but more personal messages came from the Dominions: tributes and thanks from Hertzog, te Water and Lyons. MacKenzie King would have Chamberlain believe that 'the heart of Canada is rejoicing tonight'; he and his colleagues showed 'unbounded admiration of the service you have rendered mankind'.[112]

Phipps wrote privately to Chamberlain that Daladier's reception in Paris had surpassed even his own. Nothing like it had been seen since the Armistice.

This morning [30 September] at Munich Daladier felt grave misgivings as to the reception that awaited him there. This shows how surrounded he has been of late by the War Party—the mad and criminal War Party who, having missed every preventive train

---

* The Link, the group dedicated to better Anglo-German understanding, many of whose members figured also in the lists of anti-semitic organisations in the 1930s, published a letter in *The Times* on 12 October, which included the phrase that Munich was 'nothing more than the rectification of one of the most flagrant injustices of the Peace Treaties.' It was signed *inter alia*, by Captain Ramsey, Nesta Webster, Admiral Sir Barry Domville, Lord Londonderry, Lord Redesdale, and Lord Mount Temple.

o

since Hitler's succession to power, that might have led to a not too expensive terminus of victory, wished to embark on a train at this late hour that could have led to utter destruction and chaos. The evil forces working for war combined with foolish and misguided though patriotic forces; and I have the distinct impression lately that those forces both here and in England were working their hardest to undermine your efforts. The true France knows what you have done and will give you the greatest welcome ever accorded to a foreign statesman, if and when you come to Paris....[113]

Nor was the attitude of the United States, the great imponderable, any different. On 11 October Roosevelt wrote to Mac-Kenzie King to say that he was delighted war had been averted; and more outspokenly to Ambassador Phillips – 'I want you to know that I am not a bit upset over the final result.'[114] The rest of his staff followed suit. Secretary Hull spoke of 'a universal sense of relief' and Sumner Welles of the chance to establish 'a new world order based upon justice and upon law'. This was, after all, why Roosevelt had cabled Chamberlain the enigmatic phrase, 'good man', when he heard Hitler had accepted the invitation to Munich.[115] As Arnold Offner writes, 'mistakenly or not, diplomats in Washington sought, if not peace at any price, peace with honour; but above all peace'.[116]

One of the most valuable attributes in politics is the ability never to relax one's guard. Chamberlain would have to face the House of Commons, after his weekend at Chequers, whether he broke down or not. Baldwin's advice, which reached Chamberlain at Chequers, was shrewd: 'You have everything in your hands now, for a time, and you can do anything you like. Use that time well, for it won't last.'[117] The sequel, not the justification, would be the test of what had been done.

If there were fruits to be picked or lessons to be learned from Munich, it would have to be soon. All the public rejoicing and private eulogy was illusory if the wrong deductions were made. What, after all, were these sources of praise worth? The Foreign Office had ceased to trust Phipps' view of France; the Dominions had their own obvious interests to think of, and had been fed so long and so assiduously with the British version of international events that their judgements were hardly definitive.

Chamberlain had never trusted the United States before: should he now, when Roosevelt's conclusions seemed to match his own? The debate which began in London in October 1938 and continued until the German invasion of Prague in March 1939 provides a better test of British policy of the previous eighteen months.

14 Reckoning

The events leading up to the Munich Agreement have been told here in considerable detail because they provide a test case of what was suggested earlier in this book. The foreign and strategic policy of the Chamberlain Government was demonstrably different from that of its predecessor. The structure of decision-making resembled a pyramid, with the Prime Minister at the top, rather than the broader, less angular mouldings of the Baldwin Cabinet. Thus, as the stages of the Czechoslovak crisis developed, power was restricted to a steadily narrowing group until, at the end, after Halifax's revolt, the initiative rested solely with Chamberlain. Equally, after March 1937, the tenor of foreign policy was remarkably consistent with Chamberlain's earlier views, although by the time that the Pyrrhic victory had been won at Munich there were strong signs that the means had become the end.

Close study of policy making after the *Anschluss* suggests other general propositions. Only in the narrowest sense did the Chamberlain Cabinet hold to the principle enunciated thirty years earlier by Sir Eyre Crowe: 'Politicial and strategic preparations must go hand in hand. Failure of such harmony must lead either to military disaster or political retreat.' The plans for settlement with Germany, and to resolve the threat to European peace latent in the Sudeten German problem, were married to a strategy of defence which emphasised the extra-European aspects of British policy and interests. Much more closely than in 1934–6, the British seemed to accept the role of separate spheres of influence projected for them by Hitler. British policy during the Czechoslovak crisis can be depicted as an attempt to shuffle off residual responsibilities to France and diplomatic commitments in Europe. But this combination of policy and strategy allowed no contingency for failure. The historic British interest in the security of north-west Europe was not denied but only obscured after 1936. Incapacity to engage in continental war became an overriding reason for avoiding one at any cost; but the existence of an umbilical cord across the Channel worked to the ultimate detriment of plans for an Anglo-German détente. The charge of complacency must be a major criticism of British policy before Munich – for the inability to remedy the weakness through which, for reasons beyond the control of the Cabinet, the nakedness of the position might be exposed.

The Munich Agreement gave relief from many awkward questions. During the post mortem no one was rash enough to ask whether, if Hitler *had* invaded Czechoslovakia, Britain and France would have stood back and let him take his prize unscathed. Yet the relief was only temporary. Munich was a stage in the continuing interaction of forces governing British foreign policy. To take it as a climax is to forestall the questions. Did the British try to draw the supposed benefits from what they had done? Did Munich, as F. S. Northedge says, complete the education of the British in the ways of depraved men,[1] or did it confirm them in their view that rational appeasement was still worth pursuing? The Government's actions in the six months after Munich need to be analysed in terms of the justification they offered, as well as in the light of the detailed history leading up to it.

Many of the more polemical criticisms of Munich need not be repeated here. Given the British predicament in 1937 and the assumptions of Chamberlain, Halifax and the majority of their advisers, the policy of an Anglo-German détente was self-evidently desirable. Few of them – certainly not Chamberlain – can be depicted *before* 1938 as gullible men, motivated by 'a false reptile prudence, the result not of caution, but of fear'. Aware of Britain's multiple weaknesses and the risks of war, they sought a foreign policy in harmony with her resources and interests. The product was a tactical rather than a fundamental debate, in which, as D. C. Watt says, Munich became 'a shameful but inevitable consequence of the attempt to have isolationism but call it collective security'.[2] On this view, appeasement is to be condemned more because it was evolved too late to take advantage of Hitler's initial friendliness to Britain than for its inherent immorality.

The policy can be attacked, however, on more tangible grounds, of lack of coherence in planning and policy-formation. Taken *seriatim,* the successive stages of British foreign policy in 1937–8 lowered the country's bargaining power without gaining any consequent advantage from Germany. At some point, therefore, a moment should have been reached where the Government reviewed their policy in its entirety, weighing its lack of success against their original aims and the changing balance of power in Europe. The first chance of major stock-taking came after the *Anschluss,* and was ignored. By any standard, Munich was another.

A second equally serious charge is that, in their quest for the elusive balance between aims and scarce resources, Chamberlain's Government deliberately reordered the priorities of defence and imposed on the unwilling Chiefs of Staff a set of Treasury criteria based on a conception of what the nation could afford with a future long war in mind. But defence decisions cannot be ruled exclusively by economic standards; and it is noticeable that, after Munich, Warren Fisher at least argued for building up the air force as a deterrent against future German aggression (page 424 below). Before laying down either what the country can afford, or what type of defence preparations to make, the national interest itself must be defined. This is the only standard which can rule questions of priority between military and civilian claims, or the efficiency of one defence system against another.

Thirdly, the policy of appeasement was secretive and rash. To override the Foreign Office and the advice of civil servants and military experts is not necessarily wrong, if the end is successful; but to fail to educate public opinion was not merely arrogant but short-sighted, in a democratic country. The failure of Chamberlain's Government to enlist public support or to prepare for the possibility of failure laid it open to the accusation that its members saw opinion in terms of their own attitudes and assumptions; and that they ignored the weight that a united national consciousness might have added to the bald calculations of British and German military strengths. Moreover, as they practised it, appeasement was frequently unguarded. The British indicated quite clearly to Hitler not only their weakness but their intention to develop a foreign policy commensurate with that weakness. No attempt was made to rearrange the annual Service estimates nor to infiltrate rumours of the capacity of the eight-gun fighter into Germany – that would have been bluff. In their patent haste to come to terms – especially at Berchtesgaden in September 1938 – they betrayed naïveté yet thought their approach attractively honest. Even to get to Munich they had to fight a hard way back from Godesberg, harder than might have been necessary if only a shadow of the policy of 'keeping Germany guessing' had survived. At a more general level, also, the policy gives the impression of improvisation and shortsightedness. Could the optimistic view of the rewards of appeasement really have survived a debate, after May 1938, if Chamberlain had not defended it? Could Germany have been appeased except at the expense of France and Russia? – a question which was not asked, in principle, at all. And could Britain in the long run have avoided alienating the United States to whom some of Chamberlain's followers looked to provide a form of Atlanticism as Britain's alternative role?

Finally, in their estimate of German aims, Chamberlain's Cabinet made a profound error in 1938: they assumed that Hitler would act on the same rational assumptions which they held. They continued to imagine that Germany still had the same interests in peace and the furtherance of international trade, when the plain evidence of the *Anschluss* and the Four-Year Plan should have suggested otherwise. They accepted Chamberlain's belief that Hitler would keep his word, even though he himself had seen Germany as the 'bully of Europe' in 1937. They failed to see the contradictions in the policy of appeasement and they failed to see in Nazism a greater threat to British and European interests than they feared from Soviet Russia.

Chamberlain's Government made its own defence of its foreign policy, after Munich. War had been averted and, given our assessment of Hitler's military plans, that remains an acceptable proposition. In succeeding weeks, however, and until 1940, the Government developed four substantive themes: that Munich had made it possible to create a mood of national unity on foreign policy for the first time since the breakdown of the Disarmament Conference in 1934; that it had given time to prepare Britain's strength against future threats; that it cleared away the principal central European *casus belli* and prepared the ground for a firm Anglo-German understanding; and that the settlement imposed on Czechoslovakia would also act as a restraint on Hitler – proof to the world of his moderation if he held to it, proof equally of his malevolence if he did not.* As George VI wrote to Chamberlain in October 1940: 'Your efforts to preserve peace were not in vain for they established, in the eyes of the civilised world, our entire innocence of the crime which Hitler was determined to commit.'³

These justifications have frequently been repeated. Yet none of them was well founded and they became true only after the German invasion of Czechoslovakia in March 1939, after the guarantee to France and Poland and the attempt to create a grand alliance, which had first been canvassed after the *Anschluss* two years before. The critical test of Chamberlain's policy must be that it was not modified freely and deliberately in October 1938, after a comprehensive review of policy in the light of Munich, but was changed by force, against Chamberlain's will, as a result of sinister events in Europe six months later.

However temporarily, a genuine mood of national unity seems to have been created in the last week of September 1938. Although not so pervasive and determined as the atmosphere a year later – if the comments of observers and the Press are taken at their face value – it represented a substantial advance in the entente between Government and public which is an essential preliminary to a state of war. Yet the Government made no perceptible effort to sustain the mood, either by education in the need for rearmament and alliances abroad, or by actions designed to inject a sense of urgency such as the establishment of a Ministry of Supply. Chamberlain himself should have been aware of the need to convince the people that a war was their war: as Director General of National Service during the First World War, in 1916–17, he had seen the widespread feelings of apathy and hostility and had read the reports of the Industrial Unrest Commissions which gave colour to working-class grievances of blatant war-profiteering and inequality of sacrifice. Even if, as he said, Munich had brought peace, it was surely wise to prepare for possible failure.

Instead, as Chamberlain wrote in October: 'A lot of people seem to me to be losing their heads and talking and thinking

* The Anglo-German Naval Treaty of 1935 was intended to do precisely this, and it is interesting that Chamberlain used the parallel in the document which he and Hitler signed after the Munich Conference was over.

as though Munich had made war more instead of less imminent.'[4] Cabinet debates in the autumn scarcely touched on public reaction to their policies. Proposals for conscription and a Ministry of Supply were rejected, in spite of the protests of many backbench Conservatives and the Churchill and Amery groups, for reasons which had little to do with the outward image of what the Government were trying to do. The National Voluntary scheme, approved in November, offered only a register of service on a voluntary basis which scarcely met the need to give an outlet for the feelings aroused by the dangers of the September crisis.

The Press generally supported the official line through the autumn and, in most cases, until March 1939 – thus providing a partial explanation for the fact that the Government ignored its own public relations. The BBC proved to be more independent and the Government reacted as it had done before Munich by attempting to dictate. In November, the BBC was asked to tone down the anti-Nazi content of its programmes, and the same message was sent to the Australian Broadcasting Service.[5] The failure to make a constructive use of the BBC is more surprising; yet misunderstanding of the power of broadcasting recurred at the beginning of the war, when F. W. Ogilvie, director general after Reith, had to fight against the requisitioning of part of Broadcasting House for Government departments, and against a 1941 recommendation of the National Expenditure Committee that the morning home programmes should be cut as part of the fuel economy campaign.

The Government may well have been right to assume that the public relied largely on the news service of the Press and BBC for views on foreign policy and that they would react independently only on domestic issues. If it is true that the Press reflects the preoccupations of its readers, then the opinion columns and correspondence in the six months after Munich suggest that there was no need of an education programme in support of Government policy – unless appeasement were likely to fail. It may have been an illusion, held only by members of the political élite, that Czechoslovakia was also a moral issue; it was not self-evident at the time that, as Sir John Wheeler-Bennett wrote later, 'because we were too weak to protect ourselves, we were forced to sacrifice a small power to slavery'.[6] In the absence of a comprehensive study of public opinion in

1938, it is hard to say. The Cabinet did not show itself aware of any such public storm as the Baldwin Government had faced over the Hoare–Laval pact on Abyssinia – when the majority of ministers, in response to the public outcry, had demanded and got the Foreign Secretary's resignation. If there had been feelings of shame and guilt, surely in the circumstances of the thirties they would have flamed more fiercely for a white European nation with a long history and a democratic tradition going back to the Middle Ages? When protest occurred, it was isolated: Duff Cooper's resignation raised far less outcry than Eden's (see above, page 287n) – though Eden's reasons had been obscure even to the House of Commons.

It seems fair to say that a section of public opinion was vastly relieved by the outcome of Munich and that many people lapsed into the sort of contented ignorance which Mass Observation had noted before the crisis began. The Government's line was easy to adopt since it required the least effort. Czechoslovakia *was* far away in these terms and it required no great effort of memory to see that, whatever the rights and wrongs of the case, experience since the turn of the century indicated that when the interests of great powers conflicted smaller powers went to the wall.

Majority opinion among the electorate may have written off the League of Nations far more extensively than the Labour Party imagined. Government and public may have been in alliance in 1938–9 against those schooled by two decades of agreement about collective security and the power then imagined to be inherent in the League. Realists who recognised strategic landmarks, economic barriers and racial divisions may have sided unconsciously with traditionalists in opposition to those who saw in democratic movements the principle of frontier demarcation. Conflict between these categories lay at the heart of the Czechoslovak problem, and in Britain after Munich the moral attitude of individuals may have been predetermined by their political affiliation.

In any case, the abstract question of morality diminished, in Cabinet debates, in direct proportion to actual involvement in the plan to solve the Sudeten question. To find a parallel to September 1938, it is necessary to go back to the very different circumstances of the pact between Charles II and Louis XIV in 1670 to carve up Holland by the Treaty of Dover – perhaps the second most 'shameful' act of British foreign policy. Morality has no meaning when it is not acknowledged by participants to exist.

Yet Government showed itself much more sensitive to movements of public opinion reflected in electoral terms. Immediately after Munich the cry for a general election was raised. As Hoare put it to Chamberlain: 'With the present House of Commons, and with Parliament nearing its end, you will not get a fair run for a policy of peace. Every set-back, and there may be many, will be exploited against you, and with the House of Commons already breaking into cliques, the situation may soon become intolerable.'[7] Rather more high-mindedly, Halifax wrote on 11 October: 'My instinct therefore does on the whole lead me to feel that this is the psychological moment for endeavouring to get national unity and that, if for any reason it is not taken, it may be a long time before another occurs.'[8]

The arguments against an election were, nevertheless, too strong. Mass Observation surveys and the Gallup Poll showed a steady and serious weakness in the Government's position.* More important to the Conservative Party managers, the by-elections during the autumn of 1938 provided a significant index of the disunity of public opinion over foreign policy. Thirteen by-elections were held between 1 October and 28 February 1939. Ten showed a movement against the Government which was at its heaviest during October and November, the months of greatest recrimination about the Munich settlement. The six by-elections† held then show an average swing of 5.7 per cent against the National Government and two of the seats, Bridgewater and Dartford, were actually lost by the Conservatives: the former to an Independent, Vernon Bartlett, who turned a Conservative majority of 10,569 over Labour into an Independ-

---

* On 22 September 1938, a Mass Observation sample showed that 40 per cent thought Chamberlain's policy was wrong and that Czechoslovakia was being treated badly. At the time of Munich the figures were 54 per cent in favour, 10 per cent against, 36 per cent mixed or didn't know; however, in early October they were again 50 per cent for, 42 per cent against. The sample was very small and the results should be taken with caution. The Gallup Poll of February 1939, on the question of whether the sample would vote for or against the Government, was 50 per cent for, 44 per cent against, 6 per cent don't know.

† Oxford, 27 October, 6.4 per cent away from National Government; Bridgewater, 18 November, 10.1 per cent; Dartford, 8 November, 4.2 per cent; Doncaster, 17 November, 3.7 per cent in favour of Labour; Walsall, 16 November, 0.2 per cent away from Government; West Lewisham, 25 November, 7.6 per cent.

ent majority of 2332, and claimed it as a victory for the Eden policy against that of Chamberlain. Given the remarkably high poll of 84 per cent (the highest since 1935, according to *The Times*) he was probably correct. At Dartford the swing was only 4.2 per cent but the Labour candidate obtained a majority of 4238 on a higher poll than at the previous general election.

The most notable contest of the autumn, because of the publicity it acquired, then and later, was fought at Oxford, where on 27 October Quintin Hogg, son of the Lord Chancellor, defended the seat on the specific issue of foreign policy and the Munich Agreement. He won with a majority reduced from 6645 to 3434. What is significant is that an Independent Progressive, A. D. Lindsay, the Master of Balliol, an inexperienced candidate replaced the Labour one, Patrick Gordon-Walker, and raised the Opposition's sector of the vote from the 9661 of 1935 to 12,363. Hogg, in his speech after the poll, claimed: 'It is not my victory. It is Mr Chamberlain's victory. It is a victory for democracy, for peace by negotiation, and it is victory for a united Britain,'[9] and this was the gloss the Government chose to accept; but it is not surprising that Hoare's election cry was wasted. Opposition of this proportion on the single issue of foreign policy would hardly, if translated to the whole electorate, have returned a Labour majority, but it would profoundly have weakened the National Government.*

In his first plea for an election, which he made, to Chamberlain's surprise, during the journey back from Heston airport after Munich, Halifax wanted to bring in some Labour members 'if they would join'.[10] This represented his first move to detach himself from the Munich policy.[11] But Chamberlain rebutted all suggestions of bridging the gap between Government and the Labour Party and also denied the need to bring back Eden or include the Tory opposition. On 16 October he wrote:

What makes him [Eden] think it possible to get unity is my insistence on the necessity for rearmament and the news that I

* The results early in 1939 were, with one exception, better for the Government, though still a poor prognosis for an election. At West Perth, the Countess of Atholl resigned the Conservative seat and stood as an independent. She lost (22 December) but the Conservative share of the poll fell sharply by 7.7 per cent. Later swings were: Fylde, 1 December 2.4 per cent, East Norfolk, 27 January 5.9 per cent, and Holderness, 17 February 21.6 per cent, Ripon, 25 February 7.9 per cent, and Batley, 25 February 1.8 per cent, all swings against the Conservative candidates.

didn't like Hitler personally. He leaves out, or chooses not to see for the moment, that the conciliatory part of the policy is just as important as the rearming. [If Eden was in] he would do what he did before, always agree in theory, but always disagree in practice. ...I have had trouble enough in my present Cabinet.[12]

Instead of making a public gesture, Chamberlain contented himself with trivial reshuffles in October and January 1939: Lord Stanhope replaced Duff Cooper, Runciman took Hailsham's place; and Sir John Anderson became Lord Privy Seal with responsibility for civil defence. Discontent among the junior ministers grew loud enough for Chamberlain almost to regret his decision about the election. Yet in what he called 'an uneasy and disgruntled House', he looked round in December in vain for able alternatives. Inskip was replaced in the second reshuffle, in January 1939, by Lord Chatfield and W. S. Morrison together. There was nothing here to excite public support nor reconcile the factious state of parliamentary politics.

In March 1939, Gilbert Murray put his finger on the weak point in Chamberlain's public appearance. 'Whether Neville's actual policy was right or wrong, he has somehow failed to explain himself and that is a very dangerous position, when national unity is so important.'[13] Some indication of what the Government lost by not conducting a campaign of national unity on a clear, firm policy may be found in the Gallup Polls of 1939. Asked, on 4 August, whether they would fulfil the pledge to Poland, 76 per cent of the sample agreed, and only 13 per cent opposed it, with 11 per cent unsure. Such a decisive answer was denied to the Government's own popularity, which scarcely rose between February and December 1939 and dropped again in February 1940* when the figure of 22 per cent 'don't know' was a shattering comment on public uncertainty during the first six months of war.

To evaluate the Government's second claim, that Munich provided a breathing-space to repair Britain's military weakness, it is not enough to compare the situation in September 1939

---

* On the question of would the person vote for the Government or not, the replies were

	For	Against	Don't Know
February 1939	50%	44%	6%
December 1939	54	30	16
February 1940	51	27	22

with that of a hypothetical war in 1938. It is of course true that
Russia might have fought beside France in September 1938; on
the evidence of her military performance later, however, the
low assumption of her capacity may have been justified. But
the thirty Czechoslovak divisions would almost certainly have
resisted longer and done more damage to Germany than the
Polish forces in 1939.* Even after a German victory, Czechoslovakia would have been hard to occupy and hold down, and
Rumanian oil might not have become available to Germany. The
multiple gains coming from the seizure of Czechoslovakia in
March 1939, especially in munitions and the capacity of the
Skoda works, would have had to be won in 1938 at substantial
cost. Victory in the East would have taken longer, and Germany's
strength in 1938 was relatively less: thus she would not necessarily have been poised to attack the West a year later. In any
case, France, whose morale was demonstrably higher in 1938,
might already have assaulted the unfinished West Wall, and
taken the Ruhr. An Anglo-French blockade of the North
Sea and Mediterranean would have denied Germany external
sources of raw materials. Belgium might have been held, the
Battle of Britain might never have taken place (since few German
aircraft could have bombed London from *German* bases in
1938). Italy, seeing which way the conflict was going, might
not have intervened on Germany's side; depending on other
factors as well, Japan might well have steered clear. As they had
in 1914, the majority of the Dominions would have given aid
to Britain. Help from America would have been unnecessary.

All this is hypothetical, however, and based on the assumption
that war was inevitable in 1939. The question here is whether the
Government took steps to repair the deficiencies revealed by the
Munich crisis or not. Later, General Ismay was to say that
Britain could have fought and beaten Germany in 1938.[14] At
the time, the Chiefs of Staff expressed very grave doubts about
the Forces' capacity to fulfil their role, and about the ability
of the French to hold up against the combined strength of
Germany and Italy.[15] No further explanation of that imbalance

* Hitler ordered a test bombardment of the Czechoslovak frontier defences
shortly after Munich and, according to Speer, was impressed with their strength.
But there is also evidence to support the view that these defences would not have
lasted long (*DGFP*, series D, vol. 4, p. 531, November 1938).

is needed; did the Government listen to the warning and try to remedy it?

On the evidence of official statements and the political decisions taken, the impetus given to the rearmament programme after Munich was slight and confined chiefly to increases in air-raid precautions, anti-aircraft defence and radar – all made under the assumption that Germany would try to deliver the famous 'knock-out blow'. The Defence Preparations and Acceleration Committee was set up, under Inskip, to review the structure of defence,[16] but financial stringency was scarcely eased at all.

As Chamberlain told the Cabinet on 3 October:

Ever since he had been Chancellor of the Exchequer he had been oppressed with the sense that the burden of armaments might break our backs. This had been one of the factors which had led him to the view that it was necessary to try and resolve the causes which were responsible for the armament race. He thought that we were now in a more hopeful position and that the contacts which had been established with the dictator powers opened up the possibility that we might be able to reach some agreement which would stop the armament race.[17]

On the same assumption, the question of a Ministry of Supply was postponed indefinitely by the Cabinet on 26 October, and Chamberlain laid down the principle that, whereas acceleration of existing programmes was permissible, new expenditure was not – 'as though one result of the Munich Agreement had been that it would be necessary for us to *add* to our rearmament programme'.[18] These decisions had nothing to do with the difficulty of explaining to the House of Commons and the public why increases should be necessary after 'peace with honour' had been won; although, in fact, during the debate on defence on 1 November, Chamberlain refused to admit urgency:

I want Hon Members to remember that our programme of rearmament is a five-year programme and we are now only in the third year of that programme. To argue that because anything has not been completed in the third year the programme has broken down, is to lose sight altogether of the fact that it was never intended to be completed in three years. I doubt whether it would have been possible if we had endeavoured to do so at the beginning of the programme, to squeeze a five year programme into three years.[19]

Even as late as 21 February 1939 he was saying: 'Our armaments, vast as they are, are armaments for defence and defence alone, and if it be true that others have no more intention of aggression than we have, well then the conclusion that we must come to is that we are all piling up these ruinous armaments under a misunderstanding....'[20]

This could be explained as only the public face, statements tailored to a parliamentary situation where the Labour Party still vehemently opposed rearmament.* Chamberlain told the King in mid-October that 'future policy must be the cultivation of friendly relations combined with intensified rearmament. One must be strong in order to negotiate.'[21]

But, in real terms, the defensive balance of the Services did not change. The old priorities were confirmed by the Defence Preparations Committee which reported on 7 November.† Priority was given once more to the Air Force, in its defensive aspect. The concentration was on fighters (to prevent the 'knock-out blow'). As few bombers as possible were to be built, so long as the factories and plant were not actually idle, and Chamberlain and Simon allied themselves against the development of new heavy bombers, making a disparaging analogy with the development of the Dreadnought before 1914. Chamberlain allowed himself a highly questionable shooting metaphor: 'he could not help feeling that it would be more difficult to grass the whole covey of small birds than to bring down one large bird'.[22]

On the credit side, Kingsley Wood gave the Air Force what he called 'the highest priority [in] the strengthening of our fighter force, that force which is designed to meet the invading bomber in the air'.[23] The actual operational total of fighters did not increase beyond 1500, but by September 1939 it included at least twenty-six squadrons of eight-gun fighters.‡ These, of course, served to win the Battle of Britain. In addition, partly

---

* Arthur Greenwood attacked the modest defence increases on 6 December 1938: 'There is the experience of the great war to guide us and we are not in a mood to tolerate any Derby scheme or any attempt to establish conscription by back-stairs methods' (*Hansard*, 5th series, vol. 342, col. 1047). Attlee spoke of the goal of 'total disarmament' on 14 March, 1939 and the whole weight of the Labour Party was thrown against the introduction of conscription, as late as the end of April 1939.

† CP 247/38. (The members of the Committee were Inskip, Simon, Brown (Labour Minister) and the three Service ministers.)

‡ In September 1938 the aim under Scheme L was 1750 first-line aircraft with full reserves by 31 March 1939, and 2373 by 31 March 1940—a final total of 12,000 planes. (Royal Institute of International Affairs, *Survey 1939, The Eve of War*, Pt 9.)

due to the pressure of the Tory opposition in Parliament and partly to the work of the Air Staff, the bomber counter-strike was not wholly neglected. The monthly rate of production, which had been 30 fighters and 120 bombers in 1938, rose to 130 and 320 at the outbreak of war. The radar screen was also extended to cover the whole coast between the Humber and the Isle of Wight. None of this, however, was sufficient in 1939 to catch up with, let alone overhaul, the German rate or the German total.* The margin of defensive strength was exceedingly fine and Britain remained substantially less protected than the Government's public statements suggested. As in earlier years, the rate of production depended largely on industrial labour factors and the Government showed no desire for compulsion or total financial commitment before May 1939.

Britain was relatively well off in naval strength in relation to Germany and Italy, except in submarines. In December, however, Germany announced her intention of building up to parity in submarines, under the option given in the Anglo-German Naval Agreement; and evidence of the existence of Plan Z became incontrovertible.† At the time, the warnings of the Chief of Naval Staff were ignored,[24] but the review undertaken between November 1938 and February 1939 did produce CID approval for a new scale; which in August 1939 became the full Two-Power Standard that the Admiralty had asked for as far back as 1936. With the exception of submarines, the naval balance at the outbreak of war was satisfactory – in European terms. But again it must be concluded that Munich made little difference: the increases in capital ships were made with the vast Japanese fleet, British commitments to the Dominions and the defence of Singapore in mind.

The most notable British effort in the six months after Munich went into ARP and anti-aircraft defence. Even so, it was the end of March 1939 before a Civil Defence Bill made adequate finance available, and before practical schemes of evacuation of

* German total front-line strength rose from 2928 to 3750 in this year and the total monthly rate from 450 to 700. But reserves were much less than those of the British, in some squadrons as little as 10 per cent. 1938/9 proved to be the peak year of German growth of aircraft production.
† German production speeded up in 1938/9, with the completion of 2 battle cruisers and 2 pocket battle-ships. Raeder's long term plan Z, designed to be completed by 1941, consisted of 13 battle ships, 33 cruisers, 4 aircraft carriers and 250 U-boats; but it had not actually progressed far by September 1939.

major cities were evolved. Anti-aircraft defence had been by far the worst-equipped Service in September 1938. Only 100 guns, nearly all of obsolete three-inch pattern, guarded London, and perhaps 150 the rest of England. Hoare fought a long and vigorous battle (chiefly at the expense of the War Office's other plans) to provide more modern equipment, but his promises tended to be more heavily optimistic than the numbers of guns warranted.* In March 1939 he announced the increase of TA anti-aircraft divisions from five to eight, at a time when the five themselves were nowhere near complete. Although the programme then totalled 1264 heavy guns and 4728 search-lights, only 570 guns and 1950 search-lights actually existed.

Whatever the political urgency of the orders, factors of production and financial restrictions would have involved delay. It is interesting that, soon after Munich, Warren Fisher made a vituperative attack on the Air Ministry in which he accused them for the previous five years of handing out 'soothing syrup and incompetence in equal measure' and recommended a fresh DRC review in order to create 'the maximum concentration possible of the resources available for all purposes in the creation of an air force calculated in type and strength to make the Germans think it too much of a gamble either to ignore us or to try conclusions with us'.† But this reversion to the idea of an air deterrent – the only common ground between Baldwin and the Treasury in 1934 – was rebutted. Hopkins wrote to Kingsley Wood shortly before the air estimates speech of November 1938, to warn him against giving an over-optimistic figure for 1939–40: 'there are a good many people about who have lost all sense of money questions and all regard for the preservation of our economic resources [and] soberer minds are bound to be gravely perturbed by speculations of this character which I should expect to have serious reactions on the inter-

---

* The forecast he gave the House of Commons on 3 November, that all guns in service would be 3.7 inch, with some 4.5 inch, by mid-1939, was wildly inaccurate.
† 'The events of the past few months,' he wrote (1 October 1938, PREM 1/252) 'may well prove for civilisation the writing on the wall unless we, and likewise the French, put such time as may still be allowed to us to much more effective use than has been done since 1933. The French have a good army, we have a good navy, but these weapons have failed to deter the Germans or to provide a sense of security in France or Belgium. The explanation is simple: the Germans have from the start recognised the significance of the air and in consequence possess a striking force which is much more than a match for the combined air forces of Britain and France.'

national exchange, on credit and on trade.'[24a] And in a letter to Chamberlain, Horace Wilson added: 'Some very large figures are in mind at the War Office and at the Air Ministry and it would be well to get on record that we must hesitate before departing too far from the aggregate sums approved, reluctantly, by the Cabinet earlier in the year.'[24b]

The most serious charge of failure to rearm relates to the Army. The isolationist strategy of 1937–8 was not modified in any way in spite of the promise of support to Daladier and in spite of the guarantee to Czechoslovakia, which the Government was even less capable of fulfilling than they had been six months before. This attitude was defined even more precisely in December, when the War Office claim that Munich had made a fully equipped field force inevitable was swept under the carpet by the Cabinet bureaucracy.

The War Office argument was that France was weakening in relation to Germany, and would therefore require British aid to make up for the lost Czech divisions; and that Munich had brought much closer the likelihood of a German attack on the West and of occupation of the Low Countries. They held it essential to strengthen the entente with France by staff talks and to create a fully equipped, highly trained, mobile expeditionary force intended specifically for use in Europe.

French demands were received by the British Government with a mixture of hostility and incomprehension.* Chamberlain's promise to Daladier, on 26 September, that 'France and this country stood together', was the last warm breath of the entente for several months. The staff talks, begun before Munich, languished and this state of affairs only changed when the rumour of a German attack against Holland at the end of January 1939 induced the British to embark on 'specific joint plans which would constitute a far more binding commitment than has hitherto been contemplated'.[25]

The French were usually rebutted with the reply that they should first complete the Maginot Line to the sea – an argument they bitterly resented, because completion was the most

---

* The Foreign Office was so conscious of the Cabinet's attitude that in mid-October a debate took place as to whether France might refuse to help Britain if Germany attacked Belgium or Holland. Sargent was seriously worried, and made French isolationism one of the reasons for urging a visit by British ministers to Paris in November 1938 (C 12144/11169/18).

likely way to let Britain off her obligations altogether. Yet, so long as the European situation did not change, they had no weapon sufficient to compel the British to change their minds. Nor did the War Office, although the story of their failures and eventual success makes an instructive case history in decision-making after Munich.

As early as 3 October, the War Office Staff had concluded that 'the first and main lesson is that we must expect to have to send troops to help the French...now is the time to raise the whole question again.'[26] During the next fortnight a paper was prepared for the Cabinet, outlining the main deficiencies of the Army, concentrating on the Field Force and its Territorial Army reserves, and thus opening up the whole question of the role of the Army which had apparently been settled in 1937. These proposals were put in a General Staff paper 'Role of the Army in the light of the Czechoslovak crisis',* in order to get them past Hore-Belisha, who reluctantly† accepted some and forwarded them to the Cabinet Committee on Defence Preparations and Acceleration which was set up on 26 October.

This Committee decided that the paper raised such wide issues that it should be passed to the CID instead.[27] Thereafter, deliberate delay seems to have been imposed, partly at Treasury instigation but chiefly at the wish of the Prime Minister and Foreign Secretary, for whom such a clear formulation of discord in foreign policy could have been a major domestic and international embarrassment. As Chamberlain told the House of Commons on 1 November: 'We are not now contemplating the equipment of an army on a continental basis.'[28]

Realising that they had come up against an immovable force, the War Office began to play down the proposed change of

---

* The War Office recommended the formation of two mobile divisions for the Field Force, in addition to four infantry divisions, all to be ready for service in fourteen days. This would cost £5 million, plus £13 million to equip the whole at Continental standard. Two more divisions were to follow (for overseas garrisons) in one month (£11 million); the first TA contingent of four divisions in four months (£30 million); the second, of two motorised and two infantry in six months; and the third TA contingent of one motorised division, one mobile division and three infantry divisions in eight months. £11 million was allotted for colonial forces and Palestine. Total cost £200 million; of which Hore-Belisha actually recommended only the first three items and the last, costing £70 million (COS 809 (CAB 53/43)).

† 'I am compelled to ask for the following modifications to the programme,' he wrote, in the note covering COS 809 (CAB 53/43).

role and resorted to pressure on individual members of the Committee, Hoare and Brown and some of the discontented junior ministers. In mid-December R. H. Hudson, head of the Department of Overseas Trade, Lord Strathcona, Under-Secretary for War, and Lord Dufferin, Under-Secretary for the Colonies, joined in a damaging attack on Hore-Belisha and Inskip; they were supported by sections of the Press.[29] In November, before Chamberlain's visit to Paris, some of the Staff briefed Colonel Fraser, Military Attaché in Paris, to ginger up his French colleagues to demand more of an expeditionary force;* nothing came of the manoeuvre then, but on 22 December Fraser wrote officially to say that if France had to face Germany and Italy on her own, 'the disproportion of numbers would be too great. . . . From this it becomes apparent that all French strategy must depend finally not only on friendship with Great Britain but on a knowledge of what Britain is prepared to do to help her on land.'[30]

Chamberlain refused to take advice on the subject of the Field Force from the CID or Chiefs of Staff before the Paris visit, and he did not mention their views during the discussions with the French. The War Office were forced to rely on occasional rumours from central Europe: 'on these waves of fear, we get propelled a little further each time, sinking into the lazy hollows of the waves in between . . .'.[31] The CID referred the War Office paper back to the Chiefs of Staff for a strategic appreciation, later in December. Chamberlain had already complained in the Cabinet that 'This scheme of Hore-Belisha's did not tally with his impression of Hitler's next move, which would be eastwards, in which case we might well not be involved at all.'[32]

In January 1939, support for the War Office grew steadily among the Naval and Air Staffs.[33] The decisive change, however, occurred as a result of secret information, provided by the Foreign Office, that Germany intended to make a surprise attack on Holland. At a Cabinet meeting on 25 January, Hore-Belisha, now supported by Halifax, Kingsley Wood, Stanley and Brown, won a preliminary round for the TA. The main debate occurred on 2 February when the principal Army

* According to Pownall, General Denz of the French General Staff agreed to tell Chamberlain and Halifax that 'effort financier' was not enough; 'il faut effort de sang' (Diary, 5 November).

demands, totalling £81 million, were considered. Even then, Chamberlain saw the Field Force as 'a rather new conception' and Simon prophesied gloomily about the impact of the budget on future borrowing.[34] Both questioned the priority of the Army over the home air defence or the ARP. Sixty-four million pounds was eventually granted, but the momentum of the change slackened again when the attack on Holland proved to be an illusion. Only on 22 February, after private talks between Chamberlain, Simon, Inskip and Hore-Belisha, did the Cabinet accept a Field Force of one mobile division, four regular and four TA divisions. They postponed the two new colonial divisions, and the Continental scale of training equipment for the rest of the TA. Moreover, the principle of rationing was retained and Simon confessed himself 'gravely disturbed' at what had been allowed to pass.[35]

For the first time, Chamberlain admitted that the situation had changed since Munich, but it was only after the invasion of Czechoslovakia that the Army was embodied on a scale of thirty-two divisions – the total for which France had been asking for six months. These decisions owed nothing to the lessons of Munich. The programme was still sketchy and incomplete. The training and equipment of the first thirteen TA divisions was established on a lower scale than the Regular Army. TA strength was doubled in early April as an alternative to conscription, but when conscription did come, training and equipment lagged far behind manpower. As Major-General Pownall wrote in May, it would be eighteen months or two years 'before this paper army is an army in the flesh'.[36] The cold fact was that when war did break out only four divisions were actually sent to France; and their guns and tanks were wholly out-classed by the German panzer divisions in 1940. As Colonel Martel, then Assistant Deputy Director of Mechanisation, wrote: 'They had started equipping their formations at least five years before us, and in mechanical engineering it takes a long time to catch up a start of five years.'[37]

In spite of the protests of the experts, the defensive strategy, based on the concept that in a war with Germany France would sustain the land defence of the whole western frontier, was adhered to for six months after Munich. If, instead, a formidable military programme had been ordered as an immediate consequence of Munich, it could have been under way by September

1939. If the decision had been taken earlier to equip the Army for a European war, development of medium and heavy tanks could have gone ahead at a speed which might have left the Army better fitted for the campaigns of 1940 in France and 1940–2 in north Africa. A more substantial deterrent to German aggression would have existed and French morale might have gained from the knowledge. No doubt German policy would have altered; but not necessarily in an unfavourable way.* On a wider scale, mobilisation of the economy and the machinery of government, with conscription and rearmament, might have provided the outlet in peacetime for the national effort which came in 1940. These things were deliberately sacrificed by the British Cabinet in order to gather the fruits of the Munich settlement – their third justification for what had been done. Did those fruits exist?

Advice given to the Cabinet by the Foreign Office and other Government agencies, though never entirely consistent, was at first strongly in favour of a revision of foreign policy after Munich, and was almost unanimous in its insistence on the need for drastic rearmament to back up whatever new policy was adopted. On 14 October, Cadogan sent a memorandum[38] to Halifax which was intended to be the precursor of a more general Foreign Office summary. Basing his argument on the need for immediate stocktaking, he advocated rapid rearmament – to include Dominion aid in the defence of India and the Far East – and the widening of the scope of Britain's alliances by strengthening the entente with France and making overtures to Portugal, Turkey and Greece. He wanted to try to resume friendly relations with Italy and to wean Germany away from her autarkic leanings, towards participation in international trade. The public had to be educated – 'the people who are ignorant are the people of this country' – and a new principle had to be found to replace the League of Nations. This, Cadogan found in the concept of Western European and Mediterranean security, 'cutting our losses' in central and Eastern Europe, and

* There is little evidence of British determination to alter German policy by propaganda. In the middle of December 1938, Halifax produced a scheme for broadcasting into Germany and using the personal contacts of British businessmen (14 and 21 December, CAB 23/96). In the end, it boiled down to a few transmissions from Radio Luxemburg and neutral Leichtenstein. Neither of the obvious agencies, the BBC and the Federation of British Industries, was asked to co-operate.

in fostering good relations with the Dominions and the United States.

In many ways, the first Foreign Office reaction to Munich represented a return to the policy of deterrence and Anglo-German détente pursued until 1937, and Cadogan can be seen as lineal heir of the Vansittart of 1936. But the opinions of his juniors were more conflicting than they had been two years previously. On 9 November various memoranda[39] were sent to Halifax, not as a combined assessment, but as individual views. In each case it proved easier to define the British predicament than to suggest solutions, although none of four, Strang, Collier, Ashton-Gwatkin and Nichols, claimed that Munich had been a success.

Strang blamed the Munich débâcle on Britain's military weakness, and concluded 'the first essential is rearmament'. Compulsory military service and Dominion participation were essential. But, while he saw the need for national unity, he could find no means to achieve it: the League was dead, democracy 'was no longer a fighting creed', Imperialism and Christianity had lost their power as rallying-cries. Japan might be exhausting herself in the struggle against China, and Italy in Spain, but Britain's real problem remained her relationship with Germany. In the end, Strang came out as a defeatist, leaning towards appeasement. He wanted France to break her treaty with Poland, leaving Germany free in central and Eastern Europe; and to contain Germany only on the Western frontier* and the Mediterranean. His exposition is one of the clearest indications of the fear that commitment to Russia could lead to a communist regime in Germany.

Against him and the wholly appeasement-minded Nichols, Collier, of the Northern Department, advocated a *modus vivendi* with Russia, a continued fight against Fascism in Spain, an admission that to detach Mussolini from Hitler was hopeless, and resistance to German colonial claims. On this tough line, he would promote national unity and dispel the suspicions of the Opposition and the working-class. Ashton-Gwatkin, though less outspoken, saw hope in the 'reasonable opposition' inside Germany, and insisted that the security of Poland was the only

---

* Strang assumed that if Britain regained air parity with Germany, Hitler would be 'in no position to provoke a war by taking the offensive in Western Europe' (C14471/41/18 (FO 371/21659)).

barrier left against a mid-European German confederation. In this sense, Munich had been a decisive historical event: 'the one risk [for Hitler] had been world war, which would almost certainly have resulted in a revolution in Germany and the overthrow of the Nazi party'.

In preparing the combined document, Strang took the leading part, and he and Cadogan drafted the main assumptions which Halifax was to put before the Foreign Policy Committee. They were substantially less firm than Cadogan's original draft of 14 October, because Halifax had already indicated what way the wind was blowing. (It is, after all, the duty of the Office to make ministerial policy work, and the Foreign Secretary's intervention seems a more conclusive explanation of what happened than that Cadogan simply gave way to Strang.)

These final recommendations emphasised the positive danger of a link with Russia, and the need for Britain to accept that she could no longer 'police Europe'. The positive policies were seen to be perilous: alliance with Germany would mean 'abdicating the position we have held in the world since the end of the Napoleonic wars'; a Western alliance would mean France repudiating her pact with Russia, which, they wrote, 'is reminiscent of Machiavelli, but should not be dismissed for that reason alone. . . . It could lead to a lasting balance of power.' Too timorous to choose either, they recommended a modified version of the Western Europe–Mediterranean ring of security, with the vague philosophic justification of a 'Christian Europe', and heavy dependence on France and the United States. In practice, they asked for implementation of the Anglo-Italian agreement; for Chamberlain to visit France; for an increase in *defensive* armaments and a Ministry of National Service; for Anglo-German discussions on trade, and a combined scheme with France and Portugal for colonial appeasement; for France to denounce her pact with Russia, and for Britain to denounce the idea of encircling Germany; to suspend or strictly limit Jewish immigration into Palestine,* and for the League to withdraw from Danzig.

* The Cabinet showed itself quite unsympathetic to the problem of Jews escaping from Germany. Even after the horrifying pogrom of 9 November, the Foreign Policy Committee was not prepared to envisage finding place in Britain for more than a fraction of the number expected to flee. They debated, inconclusively, settling some Jews in British Guiana or Western Australia, and blamed the United States for not increasing the American quota (14 November, CAB 27/624).

In its tacit encouragement of German expansion in eastern and south-eastern Europe, there is evidence here to justify the Soviet charge that Britain planned to set Germany at war with Russia, in the hope that the result would be 'the lasting balance of power'. Appeasement, as defined in 1937–8, was to continue. As Cadogan wrote, at the end of the document, 'if we show that we are willing to remedy 80 per cent of Germany's remaining grievances, will Hitler get his people to fight for the remaining 20 per cent?' It is true that rearmament and national unity still formed part of the Foreign Office submission; but in all other respects it underwrote the Chamberlain line. So, in October, did the Chiefs of Staff. The War Office counter-attack had scarcely begun when on 27 October the Chiefs of Naval and Air Staff recommended that the Anglo-French staff talks be allowed to die.[40]

There were other opinions, but they were not given prominence. Foreign Office information from Germany indicated the surprise of the Nazi leaders at the ease of the Munich victory and their consequent optimism about future gains.[41] In a paper dated 18 September[42] the Secret Service asked for an 'unremitting build-up of our armaments' – although in other respects they supported what became the policy of defence of Western Europe and the Mediterranean. Vansittart warned that the German moderates' case against war in the West had been gravely weakened, but he played Cassandra, even when he wrote

It is quite certain that the active elements in the Nazi Party, and they have become far more influential since Munich, are entirely opposed to any genuine 'settlement' with this country and France. They are not in any real mood to bargain even about colonies. The cry will be kept alive to cover the impending further German drive to the east, but the view of all the active and extreme Nazis now is that there is no hurry about the colonies for when they have firmly established their hold in the east (by this is meant the Polish Corridor and the Ukraine) they will then be in a position to turn west and not to bargain about colonies but simply to dictate to us what we shall have to hand over.[43]

Perhaps the most damning post mortem on Munich was actually given to the Foreign Policy Committee by Halifax on 14 November. In the first meeting to be held since June, he reviewed the situation in the light of Munich and his forthcoming visit with Chamberlain to Paris. Halifax read out a series of Intelligence reports: the first, reflecting the thinking of the conservative opposition in Germany, suggested that Germany's economic strength was being destroyed by the armaments programme. Hitler was caught between the warlike Ribbentrop and the restraint of Goering, while the extremists were looking to a Nazi millennium in which 'blackmail and every form of murder and crime is not only allowed, but the supreme duty of its statesmen'.[44]

The next two reports – one from Theodore Kordt – explained why Hitler's speeches had become increasingly anti-British. The German leaders, it appeared, thought that they had Britain in their pocket. England was decadent and they need not fear her rearmament – she was 'so completely unprepared that only the most super-human efforts on her part could make any impression and save the British Empire'. The fourth report stated that Hitler believed England's collapse was 'only a matter of time' and that if conscription was not introduced by spring 1939 the Empire would be lost. 'It is astounding', Hitler was reported to have said, 'how easily the democracies make it for us to reach our goal. I would adopt the same tactics in regard to the colonial question, as I did in Czechoslovakia. The more they offer, the more blusteringly will I make demands on them.'

Finally, an informant whom Halifax clearly trusted quoted Ribbentrop as saying that Hitler had gone back on his *Mein Kampf* plans and had decided to attack the British Empire, after cultivating France in order to break the entente, after bringing pressure to bear through Japan and Italy, and by creating trouble in the Palestine Mandate. There would be no demand for colonies since these would fall to Germany in due course. Meanwhile, Germany would rearm at top speed and consolidate her gains in south-eastern Europe.

No more damning evaluation of British policy during the previous eighteen months could have been imagined. On such evidence, even the Foreign Office plans had little chance of success. Yet although these sources were the same as had been proved correct in August, only two months before, their conclusions were rejected. Halifax spoke of the 'great success' at Munich, and the fund of goodwill towards Britain shown by the German people. Chamberlain averred that 'The Germans were now much stronger and more arrogant than they had been and anything in the nature of threats would only result in our hand being called. In the present circumstances we were not in a position to frighten Germany.'[45]

Chamberlain put forward a three-point policy, almost identical with that of 1937: first, to play on Italy's weakness and to take up Mussolini's invitation to visit Rome; second, to capitalise on the 'widespread feeling in Germany of gratitude to Britain' for sparing them from war; finally, to rearm, though not in conflict with existing trends, and not to the extent of a National Service register. The defensive side of policy supervened, in defiance of the work of the Government's Intelligence services, and in flat contradiction to the conclusion to be drawn from the dismemberment of Czechoslovakia in the weeks following the Munich Settlement.*

The meeting on 14 November settled the main issues of policy down to the end of January 1939. Whatever the Foreign Office had advised, the result would probably have been the same. On 1 November, Halifax had outlined his future plans in a letter to Phipps, in which he took it for granted that Britain and France had to accept, 'for obvious geographical economic reasons', German predominance in central Europe. 'In these conditions it seems to me that Britain and France have to uphold their predominant position in Western Europe by the maintenance of such armed strength as would render any attack upon them hazardous. They should also firmly maintain their hold on the Mediterranean and the Near East. They should also keep a tight hold on their Colonial Empire and maintain the closest possible ties with the United States.'[46]

Halifax went on: if France broke her alliance with Poland, then Poland would fall into the German orbit and Eastern

* The immediate sequel to Munich was pitiful but was barely allowed to affect its policy by the British Government. The International Commission proved almost wholly ineffectual to restrain Germany and Italy in their dictation of the terms of partition of Czechoslovakia. On 1 October Teschen was handed over to Poland at twenty-four hours' notice. Despite the provocative nature of Hitler's speeches in October, Chamberlain told the House of Commons on 1 November that to attack Munich was 'to foul one's own nest'. Then came the so-called 'Vienna award'. Ribbentrop and Ciano met at the Belvedere Palace in Vienna on 2 November and carved out of the Southern boundary of Czechoslovakia an area to satisfy Hungarian claims, without even referring to Chamberlain or Daladier. It was a total breach of the Munich terms yet the British failed to act: the Cabinet, on 16 November, postponed any decision, pending consultation with the other signatories, and referred the matter to the Foreign Policy Committee who did not consider it until 6 December.

Europe could balance the West: and Mussolini would be either induced or cajoled into playing what Halifax called 'the classic Italian role of balancing between Germany and the Western Powers'.

Likewise, Chamberlain looked far beyond the projected visit to Paris. Writing shortly before the Foreign Policy Committee meeting, he spoke of a visit to Rome in January 1939.

I feel that Rome at the moment is the end of the axis on which it is easiest to make an impression. I don't believe that Spain is a menace to European peace any longer—all the same I should immensely like to stop the conflict there and although Musso wasn't very forthcoming on the subject at Munich, I got the idea that it would be worthwhile now to take it up with him again, after our own Agreement had come into force. But of course I want a lot more than that. An hour or two tete-a-tete with Musso might be extraordinarily valuable in making plans for talks with Germany and if I had explored the subject first with France, we might see some way of getting a move on. In the past I have often felt a sense of helpless exasperation at the way things have been allowed to drift in foreign affairs, and now I am in a position to keep them on the move and while I am P.M. I don't mean to go to sleep.[47]

There is no need to describe in detail the attempt of the British Government to ride once again the two horses of the Anglo-Italian agreement and the appeasement of Germany, between November 1938 and March 1939. In spite of German intransigence and the advice from inside and outside Whitehall, the policy was not changed until European events or rumours forced reconsideration on an unwilling Cabinet.

There was no shortage of evidence of anti-British sentiment. In the first week of November, as if Hitler had never signed the Joint Declaration, he attacked Britain for rearming after Munich and stigmatised both sides of the parliamentary opposition (Churchill and Greenwood) as 'war-mongers'. In the anti-semitic fury which raged after the murder of vom Rath, a German diplomat in Paris on 9 November, by a Polish Jew, much of the blame for the pogroms was ascribed by the German Press to the instigation of British politicians.* In mid-

* Vansittart wrote on 13 December—'One of the merits of the Jewish persecution in Hitler's eyes is that it enables him to confuse democracy and Jewry in the eyes of the ignorant. Moreover the persecution being bound to excite overt horror furnishes the means to keep alive, by counter press campaigns, German feeling

November, *The Times* correspondent in Berlin reported an interview, given to German journalists, in which Hitler announced that he no longer placed any value on British friendship. Rearmament, he said, had destroyed British claims to consideration by Germany. 'Britain could not at the same time run with the United States and Nazi Germany, as American policy was under the influence of Wall Street and International Jewry.'[48]

Quite apart from the aggressive overtones of the naval programme, Germany intervened to foment discontent in Palestine during the autumn;[49] and the British assumption that the next step would be to attack Poland received a jolt early in January 1939 when the Polish Premier, Colonel Beck, visited Berchtesgaden, and when Ribbentrop went to Warsaw and reaffirmed the validity of the German–Polish Agreement of 1934.[50]

There were also attempts by the German opposition to awaken a response in London. In November, the Foreign Office was told of a plot to make Goerdeler Chancellor in Hitler's place.[51] But Cadogan mistrusted it: 'we cannot ally ourselves with these plotters. . . . Our only concern is a peaceful Germany.'[52] Chamberlain refused utterly to have anything to do with the plot; Halifax concurred, and by December even Vansittart admitted that it was impossible to give them any encouragement.

In spite of this evidence, Chamberlain regarded fulfilment of the Anglo-Italian agreement as the necessary preliminary to the longed-for détente with Germany.[53] Already, on 9 October, Ciano had warned that, unless it was shortly brought into effect, Italy would conclude a military alliance with Germany. When, later in October, Italy proposed to withdraw 10,000 troops (nearly half the total) from Spain, apparently to fulfil Mussolini's pledge to Chamberlain at Munich,[54] the British were let off the hook of *de jure* recognition of Abyssinia, and Italian rule was recognised by a vote of 345 to 138 in the Commons on 2 November. The road to Rome lay open.

The French agreed to a visit without enthusiasm, perhaps because their Cabinet had just been severely shaken by the dis-

against the democracies and against this country in particular. It is worth noting that the German press campaigns are directed rather against us than against France. All this is part of a plan and it needs constantly to be remembered.' (C15689/95/62 (FO 371/21627)).

covery that Bonnet had been negotiating directly with Ribbentrop, who was prepared to visit Paris in order to sign a joint declaration, similar to that made between Chamberlain and Hitler, but also embodying a pledge of mutual respect of frontiers. Mistrust that the remaining fragments of the entente were being driven apart by German policy does not seem to have disturbed the British Cabinet, although the claims for the visit to Rome diminished as the date approached.[55]

The visit took place on 11 January 1939. So barren was the outcome that the two British Ministers were reduced to telling the Cabinet that 'the atmosphere was most friendly and easy' and that it had 'done good' with the Italian public, whom they judged to dislike Mussolini's association with Hitler.[56] Even allowing the assumption about that volatile material, the visit was pointless. In response to Chamberlain's request for reassurances about Hitler's aims, Mussolini merely gave the opaque answer that Hitler desired peace 'to fuse together the component parts of the expanded Reich' and denied categorically that Hitler intended an attack on the West. 'This loyalty,' Chamberlain said, 'reflected credit on Signor Mussolini's character.'[57]

The overtures to Germany were no better rewarded. In December, Chamberlain showed himself deeply worried by the continued attacks of the German Press;

and the failure of Hitler to make the slightest gesture of friend-liness. Unless this strong and virile people can be induced in partnership with others to improve the general lot, there will be neither peace nor progress in Europe in the things that make life worth living. [Nevertheless] it takes two to make an agreement. . . . I am still waiting for a sign from those who speak for the German people . . . it would be a tragic blunder to mistake our love of peace and our faculty for compromise, for weakness.[58]

Nothing came of it, nor of the renewed schemes for an offer of colonies and economic appeasement which led to the abortive mission to Germany of Stanley and Leith-Ross, cancelled in the aftermath of the German invasion of Czechoslovakia in March 1939.[59] Instead, as in the military sphere, the persistent rumours of a planned German invasion of Holland forced the Foreign Policy Committee on 23 and 26 January into two

important debates – the first sign of the end of the whole foreign
policy of 1937–8.

The Foreign Office defined a German attack on Holland as
an immediate *casus belli*, just as Baldwin had laid down in
1934.[60] Yet at first the politicians tried to evade the issue;
Halifax declared: 'all things are both possible and impossible
and there are no rational guiding rules'. Chamberlain pointed
to the lack of a Continental army. Sir Horace Wilson wished to
issue a guarded statement referring merely to Britain's 'interest'
in the Low Countries. At the next meeting, however, three days
later, the Chiefs of Staff defined the threat to Holland as 'more
serious than the Empire has ever faced before'.[61] Whatever
France, Belgium and the United States might do, Britain had
'no choice but to regard [it] as a direct challenge to our security'.
Because the danger had shifted from Eastern Europe to the
West, the military advisers were at last restored to their former
position; Halifax and Chamberlain agreed that if Britain failed
to defend Holland, 'at some later stage we should have to face
the same struggle with Germany, with fewer friends and in
far worse circumstances'. Now, they had no doubts that the
Empire would fight. Full staff talks with France were approved,
covering not only war against Germany and Italy, but also the
Middle and Far East, and the tricky questions of supply.

The German attack on Holland turned out to be an illusion
yet it began the slow change which the tangible threats to Austria
and Czechoslovakia had failed to accomplish. In the event,
France replied with a fresh list of complaints and requests[62] and
Belgium and Holland showed no desire to participate, fearing
to trigger off the attack.[63] The transformation occurred in
London, not among the Locarno partners; and it was followed
by a period of quiescence and second thoughts which was not
entirely shattered by the invasion of Czechoslovakia. Although
the role of the Army was rewritten, and although Chamberlain
suspected 'We are getting near to a critical point when the
whole future direction of European politics will be decided',[64]
the Cabinet minutes in February suggest a relaxing of tension.
This, in spite of the public declaration of support for France
which Chamberlain made to the Commons on 6 February.[65]
Lindsay in Washington thought the British were being incredibly
over-optimistic.[66] Warnings from Paris that Hitler was looking
towards *rapprochement* with Russia were ignored.[67] Cor-

roboration from Sir William Seeds, the new British Ambassador in Moscow, being less acceptable to the Cabinet than Chilston's views, made no impact. Relations with Russia were not debated by either Cabinet or Foreign Policy Committee until 18 March. One reason for the relapse was that, in mid-February, Nevile Henderson returned to Berlin after a prolonged holiday and assiduously fostered the belief that Hitler intended no more adventures.[68] But a breach had been made in the monolithic confidence of the British Government; its leaders had acknowledged that Munich had borne no fruits and that war might have to be faced. They had taken the step which was a precondition to the far greater commitment of March.

When the German coup against Czechoslovakia took place on 15 March, following the Slovak secessionist crisis, the Cabinet's first reaction was to play down its significance. To all intents and purposes, Germany already had control over Czechoslovakia's destiny. Halifax returned only a mild rebuke to von Dirksen, the German Ambassador, and told his colleagues blandly that 'our guarantee was not a guarantee against the exercise of moral pressure'.[69] But Chamberlain's 'cool and objective' – almost tepid – account in the emergency debate in the Commons raised a storm of protest from the Conservative opposition, from Eden as well as the Churchill group. At the same time, the remaining small nations of Eastern Europe clamoured for security and Tilea, Rumanian Minister in London, raised a scare that Germany had demanded his country's total economic dependence in return for a non-aggression pact.

Under this dual pressure, and prepared in part at least by the activity over Holland, Halifax sent a much tougher note for Henderson to deliver in Berlin. Chamberlain made his speech at Birmingham on 17 March, in which he asked: 'is this . . . a step in the direction of an attempt to dominate the world by force?'[70] An emergency Cabinet met the next day. Already it was suspected that Tilea had committed an indiscretion; but the discussion proceeded on the basis of what would happen if, at some future date, Germany attacked Russia, and seized the oil wells around Ploesti.

Could Britain prevent Germany's further aggression? Lord Chatfield, now Minister for Co-ordination of Defence, gave almost exactly the answer which the Chiefs of Staff had provided, in the case of Czechoslovakia, in March 1938. 'If, however,

P

the support of Poland and Russia could be secured, the position would be entirely changed.'[71] This set the tone; and thereafter the debate was concerned with the support of both, or either, of the eastern powers. Chamberlain indicated that he felt deeply the pressure from within his own party, and the other ministers gave him 'warm approval' when he said 'no reliance could be placed on any of the assurances given by the Nazi leaders'. He stated categorically that Britain must take up a challenge to Rumania's independence, and must therefore 'ascertain what friends we had who would join us'. Poland, he thought, was the key, thus overriding Chatfield's advice to seek support from Russia.* Halifax put the likely allies in descending order: France, Poland, Turkey – Russia last.

For this Eastern European crisis, the reaction was the same as for the scare in January. That had been the first stage of a new policy; the muddled, diplomatically inept approaches in March and April 1939 to Paris, Warsaw, Moscow, Ankara, Athens and Bucharest in search of friends, were the second. The *diktat* to Rumania turned out, like the threat to Holland, to have been an illusion, but the alteration of view behind British foreign policy was clear enough. On 20 March, Chamberlain announced that the particular *casus belli* was not important: if Germany took the offensive again, 'we must take steps to stop her by attacking her on all points . . . in order to pull down the bully . . . not just to save a particular victim'.[72] A week later, to the Foreign Policy Committee: 'our object [is] to check and defeat Germany's attempt at world domination'. Likewise Halifax: 'If we have to choose between two great evils he favoured going to war.'[73]

The attempts to win support from Russia and Poland belong, properly, to the history of the diplomatic prelude to the 1939 war. After a week of disagreement between Chatfield, who was asking for co-ordinated military planning with Russia, and Chamberlain who spoke in terms of a 'bold declaration' and independent guarantee to Poland,[74] Poland was chosen. To appease the clamour of the Opposition in Britain, something was provided for Rumania because her oil was vital to Germany

* It is interesting that the Foreign Office had, earlier, ruled out support for Poland in the event of a German attack – although it had been suggested that they could encourage Poland to attack Germany in the rear (C12277/2166/55 (FO 371/21808) 5 Oct 1938).

in a European war.[75] The Chiefs of Staff had declared it a British interest.[76] Under the stimulus of the German acquisition of Memel from Lithuania, and parallel treaties with Rumania and Slovakia, the Cabinet decided to make the guarantee to Poland unilateral and public. On 13 April, at the request of France, a separate guarantee was given to Rumania.

This apparent revolution in British foreign policy was, essentially, a return to the Eden–Baldwin line of 1936. Chamberlain's earlier policy was abandoned, in the recognition that appeasement had failed and that the dictators were no longer to be trusted. Rearmament and the new diplomacy represented a conscious revival of the policy of deterrence and containment. But war was not yet seen as inevitable: Germany might yet respond. And during the succeeding months, the British Government showed itself ready to take every chance, as the Wilson-Wohlthat talks indicate. As Halifax told the Cabinet on 29 March, Britain must gain time – to rearm and to exploit Germany's difficulties. Britain was not anxious to attack. The search for unity and support from France, the Dominions, and the United States would go on.*

Two years had passed since that position had been abandoned. The inept diplomacy and hasty unco-ordinated activities of late March and early April – the ingrown habits of the private conduct of foreign affairs – could equally well have been undertaken in October 1938. There was far less chance of Germany giving way six months later, and the effect of the intervening events on Britain's standing with her potential allies had been disastrous. The Cabinet's final justification of Munich was that it had set a limit, in world opinion, to Hitler's drive to *Weltmacht*. This is scarcely true.

Britain's conduct towards Czechoslovakia after Munich was utterly humiliating in the eyes of any nation mindful of the balance of power. The Cabinet conclusion that 'Czechoslovakia had conceded everything and gained nothing. ... The result was to be deplored but there was nothing we could do'[77] was spelt out by the inordinate delay in formulating specific proposals with the French to Germany about guaranteeing Czechoslovakia,

* Sir Horace Wilson still hoped for something also from Italy: on 19 March he suggested giving Mussolini the impression 'if he wants to take it, of getting closer to us and drawing away from Hitler' (PREM 1/327).

until February 1939, and then by acceptance of Hitler's evasive reply. The failure to ensure even the shadow of equity (as defined at Munich) was blatantly revealed by the awards made to Poland and Hungary; and the logic of Nevile Henderson – 'there will never be peace in Central Europe until the Czechoslovak state is reduced to Czechs and Slovaks and does not govern completely alien and hostile races'[78] – had its long term effect in the profound mistrust of Britain shown by both Poland and Rumania, even after guarantees had been given to them in 1939.

On Britain's putative allies, the failure to recover the ground lost at Munich was more serious. In September 1939, Halifax claimed Dominion support for the war as the consequence of the proof of Germany's evil ambitions in March 1939.[79] In fact only Australia actually approved of the guarantee to Poland[80] and the Dominions generally opposed any involvement beyond the strict scope of Locarno. No attempt was made by the Cabinet to educate them for the new role Britain would play in Europe. At the end of May 1939 MacDonald reported that the High Commissioners believed that if Britain could make an agreement with Russia, there might be 'a renewal of the search for appeasement'.[81] This was little enough with which to face European war. As late as 23 August, on the very eve of war, there was still evidence of hesitancy. According to Inskip, the High Commissioners were afraid that if Britain reaffirmed the guarantee to Poland it would encourage Beck to stand out against the Germans.[82] In this sense at least, they were preparing for another Munich. On 26 August, Inskip wrote: 'the High Commissioners came at noon. Except Jordan [New Zealand], they all want to meet Hitler halfway: to put the most favourable interpretation on his words and to offer to discuss everything.'[83] The mood soon changed; messages of support came directly from Menzies, in Australia, and MacKenzie King in Canada, but the circumstances hardly justify Halifax's claim.

United States policy scarcely altered as a result of Munich. Roosevelt had, indeed, said 'good man' when he heard that Chamberlain would go to the Conference.[84] Later, some of Cordell Hull's advisers feared that the break-up of Czechoslovakia presaged further German adventures,[85] and American relations with Germany worsened. After the anti-Semitic outrages of November 1938, Ambassador Wilson was recalled from

Berlin. Yet Roosevelt continued to hope that German aggression could be contained peacefully. Rather than encourage resistance by the Western powers, after Hitler's seizure of Czechoslovakia and Mussolini's invasion of Albania, he appealed to the dictators on 14 April 1939 not to attack the nations of Europe or the Near East for ten years.[86] The replies were humiliating but the United States scarcely reacted; and Roosevelt's message, on 24 August, begging Germany and Poland to refrain from hostilities, was barely stronger than the appeal he had made before Munich.

Britain did nothing during that time to win over American opinion, and although there was probably little that would not have excited a charge of meddling, Munich must be held partly responsible for the state described by a recent historian of American foreign policy:

American diplomats did not see that the stake was more than commitment to a nation's life; it was the entire system of French, if not European, security and the opening of Eastern Europe to German economic and political domination.... Americans, whatever misgivings they may have had at the time, only later condemned the British and French for doing what they would have done in their place.[87]

As early as 19 October, Phipps had warned that France 'would adopt a more defeatist position and would tend to rely more upon this country'.[88] The French Government had already been shaken by the British refusal to extend military co-operation, or adopt conscription. Suffused with domestic discontent, France presented a very different face to Chamberlain and Halifax, when they visited Paris on 23 November, from the reception forecast by Phipps in the ecstatic aftermath of Munich. The two British Ministers listened to cries of 'Vive Eden' and 'A bas Munich' from the crowd and to steadily escalating demands for military support from Daladier's Cabinet. They gave nothing for French comfort but an equally unwelcome request that France should remedy her desperate weakness in air defence – 'to strengthen Daladier and encourage him to do something at last to put his country's defences in order and to pull his people into greater unity'.*

* Chamberlain letters, 26 November. In his request for more motorised divisions for the British Field Force, Daladier had said that he 'wished to emphasise the

P*

The British Cabinet, with their tradition of contempt for the vagaries of French political life, do not seem to have realised how fast French morale was ebbing during the autumn of 1938. They were aware of the worsening ratio between French armed strength and that of Germany, but they allowed themselves to be optimistic about promised purchases from the United States, and reported increases in air production after February 1939.* The most serious factors were less evident. France's production base was seriously weakened in 1938–9 by massive strikes, and shortages of raw materials and industrial capacity. The tank force was dissipated over the whole infantry formation and the completion rate of capital ships was exceedingly slow. (The two battleships launched in 1938–9 had been laid down in 1932 and 1934.)

The almost imperceptible progress of the staff talks may explain British ignorance, but not the lack of response to what Inskip described as:

a growing feeling in France that the loss of Czechoslovakia makes it essential to demand a larger effort from Britain, in the nature of a continental army. The French General Staff ... want after 3 months from Britain an army of a size to do something to reverse the balance between France and Germany ... they suspect Britain of wanting to fight her wars on the Continent with French soldiers. . . .[89]

After Munich, General Weygand had told Hankey that France might survive if she rearmed in time.[90] Instead, beset by working-class discontent, upper-class sympathy for Germany, and political ineptitude, the Third Republic seemed about to founder. The violent and irrational response to a transparently

need for greater support from Britain. . . . It was not enough to send two divisions after three weeks' (C 14652/13/17 (FO 371/21592)). See also CAB 23/96, for 16 November, 22 November and CAB 23/97, 1 February, when Chamberlain said that if France went to war with Italy, Britain should avoid being committed in case Germany joined in.

* According to La Chambre, the Minister of Air, giving evidence at the Riom trial in 1942, the monthly production rate of all types in the summer of 1938 was only 39. Concentration on fighter defence, for similar reasons to the British, began to produce an up to date screen during 1939 but of 390 bombers in the Air Force on the outbreak of war, every one was obsolete or obsolescent. The rate rose from 100 a month in February 1939, to between two and three hundred by September, but in spite of purchases from the United States, France only put up 500 frontline fighters during the battle of 1940.

factious claim by Italy to Nice, Tunis and Corsica should have alerted Britain; that Daladier felt it necessary to make a military tour of Tunisia and Corsica was a plain indication of the erosion of his popular support. Yet, until the scare over Holland in January 1939, Britain failed to show enough imaginative sympathy to make even a slight gesture to secure the future of her only assured European ally. The change of policy in 1939 came too late in terms of French morale or military readiness.

Enough has been said earlier to show the reasons for the British fear of any entente with Russia which would be stronger than mere words. In spite of the pressure exerted by some members of the Foreign Office such as Lawrence Collier, Russia was implicitly excluded from Cabinet debates until March 1939. Lord Chilston continued to exude gloom: 'It is impossible to obtain even an inkling of what is discussed within [the Kremlin] walls,' he wrote in October 1938'[*] and a post mortem on the Czech crisis dismissed as untrue reports that Russia had seriously intended to intervene on behalf of Czechoslovakia.[91] The Chiefs of Staff continued to emphasise Russian weaknesses, and the deficiencies in direction and supply of the Red Army. At the end of April 1939, they were still talking of the effect of the purges, and they refused to accept as significant, figures based on army manpower. They regarded the Soviet air force as an obsolete weapon, and pointed up the ideological objections within the Communist Party to involvement in the preservation of bourgeois regimes.[92] The experience of the Finnish campaign suggests that they were correct in military judgement; but the question of political will remains uncertain. The evidence of Seeds early in 1939 is that Churchill was right to think that prolonged British hostility had by then made co-operation virtually impossible: 'The Soviet Government and people see no sign whatever that France and Great Britain could do anything but continue to capitulate; the Soviet Union would therefore keep aloof all the more readily as their interests are not directly threatened.'[93]

In the Far East, where Britain played the old game, for want of strength to do otherwise, the six months' course of appeasement after Munich weakened the credibility of what had always been an exercise in bluff. A £10 million guarantee was given to

* N5764/97/38 (FO 371/22289). This was a handicap from which his successor, Sir William Seeds, did not suffer.

aid the Chinese export trade in December 1938 – coinciding with a similar credit from the United States – and Craigie reported that it made an impression in Tokyo.[94] On the other hand, the Chinese had no difficulty in seeing through British policy – 'that we are entirely self-seeking, and have been merely keeping them in play with fair words, throwing them a bone now and again, hoping that they would fight long enough to exhaust Japan, and so remove a potential danger to ourselves'[95] – a contention amply justified by the evidence.[96]

Japan's 'New Order' for East Asia was not something to which Britain could accommodate herself, as the Japanese Foreign Minister, Arita, pointed out in December 1938.[97] Lacking American co-operation, Britain could not bring economic pressure to bear on Japan without jeopardising the commercial interests in China which she was striving to protect. The full extent of the dilemma was revealed by the ignominious blockade of the Tientsin concessions which began in the summer of 1939. The only recourse might have been to have played a high hand in Europe. Japanese leaders, after all, showed how sensitive they were to European events when the Craigie–Arita agreement was signed in June 1940, in the aftermath of the Nazi–Soviet Pact.

Leaving aside all other considerations, it is worth asking whether British policy after Munich had *any* chance of success with Germany. Continued appeasement had the effect of reinforcing the German belief that Britain and France were far gone in the slough of bourgeois decadence. The time was well past when Hitler desired anything that Britain could offer. He had been prepared in May and September 1938 to accept compromise on a temporary basis as part of his transition to a programme of expansion, but he was not prepared to offer any form of permanent concession in return. After Munich, the field of British manoeuvre was narrowed to one where only acknowledgement of German hegemony in Europe could form the basis for a détente. The directive ordering the encouragement of separatist movements and the eventual liquidation of Czechoslovakia was issued three weeks after Munich[98] and the subsequent military plans were given to Keitel on 17 December.[99] Hitler showed himself quite uninterested in talk of colonial restitution and replied blandly to the final offer in March 1939 by saying that he would 'write a letter', in due course. None came. The evidence suggests that he was preparing, as he told General Engel, for a series of 'little Silesian wars', directed first against Poland.[100] He foresaw the need to neutralise Russia if he was to attack the West. The rest may have been improvisation, but there is no reason to doubt the validity of the information which Halifax gave to the Foreign Policy Committee on 14 November, which damned conclusively a policy of Anglo-German reconciliation.

British policy did not change as a result of Munich. The style of Cabinet decision-making remained the same, with Chamberlain at the apex of the pyramid. For him, Munich was always right. During the 'phoney war' in December 1939, he wrote – prematurely – 'I stick to the view that I have always held, that Hitler missed the bus in September 1938. He could have dealt France and ourselves a terrible blow, perhaps a mortal blow, then. The opportunity will not recur.'[101]

In almost his last letter, he was still defiant: 'Never for one single instant have I doubted the rightness of what I did at Munich, nor can I believe that it was possible for me to do more than I did to prepare the country for war after Munich, given the violent and persistent opposition I had to fight against all the time. . . .'[102]

There is as much truth after Munich as before, in depicting decision-making from 1937–8 as Chamberlain's personal province, a rigid satrapy closed against the light of opposition and informed only by the servants of appeasement, Henderson, Wilson and the rest. Yet this case must not be overstated: as in the earlier period, Chamberlain's freedom of action was demarcated by the assent of his colleagues. He had given way to the weight of logic before: to Swinton by granting the Air Force increases of April 1938, and, most spectacularly, twice to Halifax in the dismal days after Godesberg. If he was permitted to run the Foreign Office over the Foreign Secretary's head, or to select the advice he wished the Cabinet to hear, or to work with a pliable and sycophantic inner group, the fault was not wholly his. The power of the Prime Minister is not so great that his colleagues cannot restrict it: if loyally or weakly they acquiesced, then they abdicated their own responsibility.

More than most governments, however, Chamberlain's reflected the single-mindedness of the Premier. Given his early experience of international affairs, his desire to subordinate foreign policy to an over-all set of priorities drawn up in the light of 'the national interest', on financial criteria, is scarcely surprising. He was not the first to believe that the introduction of a new discipline could solve the intractable problems of a different sphere. Moreover, his long impatience with Eden and the relics of the Baldwin Government, evident from the frequent frustrations of his diaries, spurred him to act even beyond his usual capacity. In Lord Randolph Churchill's mordant phrase about Gladstone, Chamberlain was 'an old man in a hurry'.

His own personal composition led him to assume, even after Munich, that other heads of state acknowledged the same wider interests in peace and economic tranquillity. He could not understand that Germany should wish to make barter agreements in Eastern Europe instead of taking advantage of the greater opportunities of international markets; nor could he accept that Hitler would use world war, not merely as a weapon of diplomacy but as an actual means of action. His failure of insight was intensified by his belief that problems could be solved and neatly disposed of. He was ill-attuned to the style of European diplomacy, where the tidy briskness of his mind was mocked for its old-maidish quality. Hitler and Mussolini were infinitely less able politicians – in the sense that they chose to subordinate to foreign adventure their capacity to govern and to harmonise social and economic policy – but Hitler at least possessed an intuitive appreciation of strategic realities; and he was prepared to use his armoury in a way which Chamberlain did not comprehend.

In his failure to come to terms with the ideological motivation of German foreign policy, Chamberlain was no more culpable than Baldwin, Eden or the other British politicians who dealt with Hitler in the 1930s. But he became Prime Minister at a critical moment, when Hitler's own assessment of Britain's role in relation to Germany was changing. Having once been prepared to accept a reconciliation of interests, Hitler moved, during 1937, towards a far more hostile attitude. Through his belief that he personally could deal with this situation, Chamberlain lost the limited freedom of action which Baldwin, through profound mistrust, had held. The last accusation which should be made against Chamberlain is that of cowardice; but the fact that

Munich did not alter his calculations raises a different charge.

Most political leaders are vain, some justifiably so, and it serves no useful purpose to discuss this failing in personal terms unless it influences public policy. Chamberlain's single-minded assurance comes nearer to the theological sin of pride, the first of the deadly sins. There is no lack of evidence: witness his estimate of the work of others, as well as his disparagement of the French and Czechoslovak leaders. Unchecked by his colleagues or his allies, he professed to arbitrate on foreign questions, submitting intricate ethnic and geographic problems to a higher criticism. No wonder that a policy designed to preserve Europe from war in the name of humanity should appear inhuman when the prizes of partition were awarded according to a subjective standard, projected outwards on the world. 'I am completely convinced that the course I am taking is right and therefore cannot be influenced by the attacks of my critics.'[103]

His wholly admirable horror of war cannot outweigh the fact that in the last resort Chamberlain avoided the full responsibility of choice by referring to personal standards of morality, which were not universal qualities. Because he believed that it was the ultimate sin to create war, Chamberlain regarded the sufferings of individuals and minorities as worth while if they served to prevent it. But to exclude as unthinkable the deliberate launching of war creates strategic blindness and led directly to blackmail by leaders who did not acknowledge Chamberlain's standards and used them as weapons against him when they could.

Halifax's stance after Munich is less easy to explain. After his revolt against the Prime Minister, he cannot have been unaware of his power to alter policy. Yet, apart from the tentative suggestion that an election was desirable in the autumn of 1938, there is no evidence that he attempted to influence Chamberlain's conduct of foreign affairs before March 1939. How he could destroy his own Foreign Office argument that Munich had been a failure, on 14 November, and follow his leader, apparently plastic in Chamberlain's hands, and yet remain an alternative Prime Minister acceptable to the Labour Party and many Conservatives in May 1940, remains an enigma.[103a] Perhaps a pointer can be found in a conversation with Ambassador Kennedy on 12 October, when Halifax denied that Hitler wanted war with Britain and appeared ready to accept a separate non-European sphere of influence: 'unless there is direct interference with England's dominions . . . the future of England . . . is to mind her own business'.[104]

Strang, no firm defender of Europe, thought that Halifax was resigned to following wherever Chamberlain led.[105] There was no issue of conscience, where he might have been stirred up, except the purge of the Jews which, on the evidence of the Cabinet minutes, only angered a minority of ministers. The most curious thing was the detachment of a man whose private morality was unquestioned. After the Second World War, talking to a friend, he described his interview with Mussolini in January 1939. Outside, the Roman crowd was roaring 'Duce! Duce!' At a touch of a bell on the dictator's desk, the noise ceased. Halifax was fascinated, not with the nature of such power, but the mechanics of it.[105a] As he had said once, when Czechoslovakia was still free, he 'would fight for the great moralities that transcend frontiers' – but not for the realities which sustained them.

In all the Cabinet meetings and especially the Foreign Policy Committee meeting of 14 November, Chamberlain had only to speak for Halifax to fall loyally into step.* In these six months Chamberlain dominated his Government and decided its foreign policy more than he had done at any time before. For individual ministers there was no recourse, except resignation; but so long as Chamberlain remained Prime Minister there was no way back into political life for a rebel, since the Tory opposition seemed permanently excluded. Even if Churchill or Eden had replaced Chamberlain, they would have been unlikely to look with favour on the men of Munich. Some Ministers were frightened of the Prime Minister, others merely acquiesced in his trenchant use of the prerogative. No one should deny Chamberlain's sincerity, nor his genuine conviction that he was irreplaceable, but like other delusions this cult of personality was dangerous unchecked. The creative function of opposition within the Cabinet was lost. Those colleagues who disagreed with him had cried 'Wolf' too often to affect his convictions.† Even on 2 September 1939, when Stanley, Elliott, Burgin and Brown were

* Particularly 26 October (CAB 23/95) when Halifax asked for a compulsory National Service Register.
† Inskip diary, 26 August 1939: 'There are some people in the Cabinet . . . who see ghosts of Munich in every sentence that comes from Germany.'

in what Inskip called 'a state of semi-revolt',[106] it was enough for Chamberlain to summon them for a talk for them to withdraw their objection.

The cumulative effect of the lack of genuine tension and argument in the Cabinet was to create an attitude of mind which spread outwards by contagion to the departments and advisers. Stasis prevailed at the centre, and since none of the external factors altered no new policy could grow out of the Government's bankruptcy of ideas. Hence the euphoria of ministers' public statements, culminating in Hoare's ineffable 'Golden Age' speech at Chelsea Town Hall only five days before Prague fell.

The disunity of the Foreign Office helped to destroy the impact of what had been in October a firm demand for revaluation of the Munich policy. The advice of the Service experts, likewise, made no impact on the carapace of the inner group, until events in Europe in 1939 compelled them to accede to both. The machinery of government which had been evolved during 1937 continued to function in the same way until it was modified by the force of external affairs.

French demands proved insufficient for such a change, even though it had been a cardinal assumption of British policy, up to Munich, that the security of France herself was a British interest. In this sense, the British became more, not less, prone to appeasement after Munich.* There was no strong current of public opinion, partly because the public face maintained by the Government indicated a greater degree of rearmament and awareness than was in fact the case. The Labour opposition, with its strenuous, unrealistic and irresponsible opposition to conscription after the fall of Prague – which involved the Government in imposing the 'guillotine' to get the Bill through the House of Commons – reinforced all Chamberlain's arguments about their inability to participate in foreign policy.

However, the statement that the change of March 1939 was brought about by events in Europe may need some qualification. The Conservative opposition reacted violently against Munich. Churchill called it 'a disaster of the first magnitude'; Amery 'a triumph of sheer naked force exercised in the most blatant and brutal fashion'; and Lord Cranborne 'one of the most humiliat-

---

* viz. Chamberlain's congratulations to Bonnet on the Franco-German agreement, November 1938 (C 14652/13/17 (FO 371/21592)), 'which constituted another step towards appeasement in Europe'.

ing episodes in our history'.[107] Thirty Conservatives, including Eden, abstained in the vote which followed the Munich debate – a decisive split within the party, whose chief significance was that it brought to an end the period in which none of the separate groups had offered an alternative foreign policy. Thereafter, Churchill, Eden, Duff Cooper, Cranborne, Amery, Boothby, Macmillan, and J. P. L. Thomas were ranged, identifiably, against the Government – in complete contrast to the position in France where only two deputies (other than the seventy-three Communists) voted against Daladier.[108]

As Macmillan wrote, much later: 'everyone knew that so great was the strength of the Government in the country that nothing could seriously shake them in Parliament. At our almost daily conferences with our friends, we had the gloomiest forebodings. The tide was, at present, too strong and it was flowing against us.'[109]

The wave of unpopularity flowed over them all and Churchill was nearly disowned by his own constituency. Chamberlain evinced extreme hostility.[110] But they had a cause and a rallying-cry; the national emergency was being ignored. Abstention from voting gave way to tougher tactics: on 18 November, Churchill, Macmillan and Bracken voted against the Government on the motion to establish a Ministry of Supply; and in December came the threat of the five junior ministers, Hudson, Crookshank, Lindsay, Strathcona and Dufferin, to resign.

There is no evidence that the discontent of the minority was echoed by Conservative Central Office or by the constituency organisations, in spite of the adverse opinion-polls and the by-election swing of autumn 1938. Harvey thought, in December, that 'a spontaneous movement has begun in the City for more resolute and more "national" Government'[111] but somewhat earlier he had seen how 'A. E[den] and all his friends are having difficulty with their local executives. The party organisation is being screwed up.'[112] On the other hand, while looking to 'a renewal of power for several years during which the policy of appeasement can be effectively tried out',[113] Hoare complained also of Chamberlain's 'negativeness', and on 15 March 1939 Halifax spoke for the Tory opposition when he told Chamberlain to denounce the invasion of Czechoslovakia.[114] What precise weight may be put on party feeling cannot accurately be assessed here, but at the least it was a formative factor in the change of attitude in 1939.

Since 1918, Britain had been continuously in search of a foreign policy where her obligations and resources would balance. Only at certain moments, in the four years after Locarno, and perhaps in the brief glow after Stresa in 1935, did she manage to discover one. But an attempt was made, in 1937–9, to bring commitments and power into alignment, and Chamberlain's Government may be commended for its realistic acceptance of Britain's diminished estate in relation to the rest of the world. As a recent historian of British foreign policy says:

It has been axiomatic in post-1945 British ideas about the country's pre-war foreign policy that it was conducted by naive and gullible men supported and sustained by a timid, comfort-loving public opinion. Naive the Chamberlainites of the 1930s might have been, and timid public opinion certainly was. But few who take this stereotype for granted seem to have seriously considered how it would have been possible for Britain and France in 1938, with Soviet Russia's intentions uncertain, Italy and Japan sympathetic towards the Third Reich, and the United States if anything even more isolationist than in 1914, to take on Germany whom they were barely able to defeat in the first World War when all those four Powers were on their side. The assumption that Hitler's bluff could have been easily called by a stout refusal to do business with him stems from the uncritical premise that Britain was then still at the top of the league table of Powers.[115]

Nevertheless, the criticisms made here of British foreign policy are valid. If the Chamberlain Government regarded the security of France as an essential interest – as it showed in January and March 1939 – then the previous lack of liaison and their high-handed treatment of their ally was unwise and probably deeply harmful. Britain bears a heavy share of responsibility for undermining the will of France to resist. Secondly, a charge which can be explained but not excused, the British deliberately refused to envisage Russia as an ally, rebuffed what, on the evidence available, appear to have been genuine overtures and alienated the Soviet government so far that the negotiations of 1939 were crippled before they began. A country in Britain's position cannot afford to choose only those allies with whom it is in sympathy. Thirdly, the extreme degree of isolationism ceased to make sense when reduced to strategic terms. The building-up of a fighter and radar defence screen and a navy capable of preventing a German invasion indicated a policy of with-drawal from Europe, yet the British patently relied on France to hold the Western front on land and to provide reinforcements for Britain in the air. Without offering a field force in return, the expectation of French altruism was remarkable. The counter argument, that the fighter screen enabled Britain to defeat the German attack in 1940, ignores the possibility that, if a proper Field Force had been provided at the beginning, the Battle of Britain might not have occurred. The saddest comment on the reordering of defence priorities in 1937 is the lamentable state of ARP and home air defence at the time of Munich. Even the strategy of withdrawal was handled ineptly.

Finally, the Government may be condemned for the way in which the Foreign Office and military experts were overridden or sidetracked – not because this is wrong in itself but because the results were poor and the principle behind it was unsound. A profit-and-loss account of any political project is hard enough to draw up a generation later, with the benefit of more sophistic-ated techniques of accounting. To attempt to cost the national interest in 1938 was undesirable and probably impossible.* The foreign policy of a nation depends on commercial, industrial, military and manpower strength. Without these it carries weight only so long as it is not challenged. In 1938, by throwing too much light, Chamberlain helped to reveal how thin British pretensions were.

The wider question, whether these two years were wholly retro-grade or not, is hard to answer since it depends on judgements about alternatives and the historical inevitability of the war. The Eden–Baldwin policy, if it had been continued after 1936, might have advanced through deterrence the sort of stalemate created since the 1950s by nuclear stockpiles. It might also have led to tacit acknowledgement of spheres of influence. Alterna-tively, after 1936, the British Government *could* have with-drawn into total isolation, by allowing Hitler to dominate the Continent, defeat France, overrun south-eastern Europe and,

* The attempt was also based on a view of economic capacity which the 1939–45 war proved to have been a gross underestimate.

perhaps, Russia. It might have been possible then to come to a settlement without having to defend the Empire against another German onslaught and to have maintained British trade by skilled negotiation, like the seventeenth-century diplomacy of the Venetian republic when the Doges' real power had gone. To do so would have involved a break with traditions at least 400 years old and, if the example of Venice is taken, a steady reduction in status and final extinction at the hands of the un-sentimental. The choice was impossible so long as Britain aspired to great-power status and so long as her Government recognised an interest in the survival of France.

Preventive war was not an option available in the context of British public opinion, but after the crisis of May 1938 the Government could have emphasised, rather than undermined its firmness and warned the British public as well as Germany. As Churchill said, in answer to the question, would he have gone to meet Hitler? 'Yes, but I would have invited Hitler to come and meet me in the North Sea on board a British battleship.'[116] Creation of a 'grand alliance', encouragement of the German resistance to Hitler, and accelerated rearmament after May 1938 might have induced Hitler to abandon the plan to invade Czechoslovakia. To postulate a détente would to be to go too far, given the evidence of Hitler's long-term plans, but the limited success suggested by the May crisis might have provided the occasion for a fundamental reappraisal of British policy towards dictators.

Yet this still evades the question about the inevitability of war. If Britain had prepared to mobilise and promised full support to France in August 1938, Hitler might have backed down. On the evidence of his intentions given here, Germany was more likely to fight. Debates about what might have happened usually ignore the likelihood that Germany would have acted otherwise in other contingencies, and there is much to be said for the point put by Chamberlain and Nevile Henderson that warnings repeated too often would ultimately be seen as bluff. In 1938, Britain came near to fulfilling the role Hitler had cast for her, without success. The alternative – that war was preferable then, rather than in 1939 – was a difficult if not impossible choice, for in that case the Government would have had to make in peacetime all the decisions normal in time of war. They would have had to win consent for full rearma-

ment, subordination of the economy to war priorities, the introduction of national service and conscription, war budgets and cuts
in welfare services, the conversion of industry, the raising of
taxation and foreign loans, the sale of overseas investments.
By the skilful use of propaganda they might have succeeded,
but such mobilisation had never been done in peacetime and
during the First World War it had taken nearly two years from
August 1914 to convert Britain into an armed camp. Not even
Lord Beaverbrook, later the most sanguine exponent of the use
of indoctrination, would have found it easy to convert the public,
Press and Parliament in 1938.

Is democracy then the scapegoat? Must Britain have been, as
Baldwin used to say, two years behind the dictators? (As
Cadogan minuted, in November 1938, 'national disunity *is*
democracy'.[117]) Was it possible by 1938, as Churchill had
pleaded earlier, that 'there need be no talk of working up public
opinion. You must not go and ask the public what they think
about this'?[118] There was no demand. Churchill himself was in
broad agreement with the Government over its policy towards
Czechoslovakia until the summer of 1938. None of the political
'rebels' disagreed. Even the Labour Party leaders showed themselves more worried about Spain. Czechoslovakia was a question
which aroused something as near to a national consensus of
opinion as any issue in the 1930s – until Munich.

The six months after Munich are the real test. Until then, a
better case can be made out for Chamberlain and his Cabinet
than is usually done. It is hard to see that Eden's alternative
policy would have accomplished more; and Chamberlain's might
conceivably have achieved the Anglo-German détente, if put
into effect early in 1937 rather than a year later. Taken at its
original, pre-Munich level, Chamberlain's intention may be expressed as coexistence on the basis of separate spheres of influence,
a conception as modern as the deterrent-based foreign policy of
the Baldwin Government. He might well have succeeded with
Mussolini or Stalin, or Goering if he had come to power on the
shoulders of the German opposition. To say this, however, is
not to excuse the failure to take stock after Munich, nor the
inability to educate the British public.

Politicians do not need to accept the limits imposed by their
own definitions of public opinion nor make them the excuse for
inaction. They do not need to look for simple total solutions

which may be easy blind alleys. They do not need to work on unquestioned assumptions, lulled by the stifling wind of approval around them. There is a category of spiritual strength which is not accounted for in statistics. The public, too, have their responsibility, so long as they are informed. If the choice is between guns and butter, they must accept that it is a choice, and make it if the chance is given. But Chamberlain ignored advice to call an election after Munich from colleagues who wanted 'national unity' as well as mere party advantage. This, with the admission that Munich was a bare escape from the pit, followed by the preparations eventually made in March 1939, might have saved more than that Government's reputation.

Unwillingly, half-heartedly, the British Government eventually admitted that it could not relinquish interest in the balance of power in Europe. In the long parabolic movements between involvement in European affairs and service to the concept of an Atlantic island with a seaborne empire, Britain was nearer to isolationism in 1937–9 than at any time since the start of the twentieth century. Preoccupation with the domestic boom, abandonment of the gold standard, imposition of tariffs and the attempt to create a closer imperial trading link, had given an economic aspect to withdrawal from Europe earlier in the 1930s. The entente with France, the guarantee to Poland, ended both. The Cabinet cared just as little for Poland as for the Sudeten areas, but they put British freedom of action into the hands of an ally, giving Poland what they had denied France for twenty years. As Halifax and Chamberlain told the Cabinet on 30 March 1939: 'If the Poles regarded the Danzig issue as constituting a threat to their independence and were prepared to resist by force, then we should have to come to their help.' The Czechoslovak experience had been assimilated – six months late, and at a price which, by postponing war to 1939, ensured that the Europe Britain finally fought for would never be restored.

Notes

INTRODUCTION

1 R. K. Middlemas and A. J. L. Barnes, *Baldwin* (London 1969) chs 27 and 28.
2 22 Dec 1937, CAB 23/90A.
3 For a discussion of the British historiography see D. C. Watt, 'Appeasement: The Rise of a Revisionist School?', *Political Quarterly* (Apr-June 1965).

CHAPTER 1: *Britain and Germany in the 1930s*

1 *Hansard*, 5th series, vol. 144, col. 2937. 16 Apr 1919.
2 C7752/55/18 (FO 371/18851). 21 Nov 1935.
3 F. S. Northedge, *The Troubled Giant* (London 1966) p. 619.
4 *Hansard*, 5th series, vol. 302, col. 373. 22 May 1935.
5 22 Mar, 1938 CAB 23/93.
6 Notably by E. Mantoux, *The Carthaginian Peace* (London 1946).
7 *The Times*, 31 Oct 1935.
8 *DBFP*, series 1A, vol. 1, app. X, p. 846.
9 6 Dec 1938, CAB 27/624.
10 CID 1385-B Chiefs of Staff Sub-committee, Strategic Review 1937.
11 CAB 50/37, 'Note on the situation of Germany vis-a-vis the other European Powers', 13 Mar 1938.
12 *Hansard*, 5th series, vol. 188, col. 429. 18 Nov 1925.
13 CAB 32/130.
14 cf. D. C. Watt, *Personalities and Policies* (London 1965) p. 150.
15 CAB 32/130.
16 Watt, *Personalities and Policies*, pp. 139-74; also N. Mansergh, *Survey of British Commonwealth Affairs, Problems of External Policy 1931-39* (Oxford 1952).
17 Chamberlain letters, 14 Feb 1934.
18 Middlemas and Barnes, *Baldwin*, pp. 919-20.
19 Royal Institute of International Affairs, *Survey for 1938*, III 460, 510-21.
20 Vansittart Papers, 19 Nov. 1937.
21 Evidence given before the Riom Tribunal, 18 Mar 1942; Pierre Cot, *Le Procès de la République* (Chicago 1944), vol. 2, pp. 63-4.
22 *DGFP*, series C, vol. 5, no. 42, p. 67.

23 Arnold Offner, *American Appeasement; United States Foreign Policy and Germany, 1933–38* (Cambridge, Mass., 1969) pp. 146–53.
24 Cordell Hull: *Memoirs*, 2 vols (New York 1948) vol. 1, p. 243.
25 *F.D.R.: His Personal Letters 1928–45*, ed. Elliot Roosevelt, 2 vols (New York 1950) vol. 1, p. 475.
26 Watt, *Personalities and Policies*, pp. 39–40 and 42n.
27 Lord Templewood, *Nine Troubled Years* (London 1954) p. 263.
28 *DBFP*, series 2, vol. 9, p. 282.
29 W. N. Medlicott, *British Foreign Policy since Versailles*, 2nd ed. (London 1968) p. 16.
30 C14 256/42/18 (FO 371/21658).
31 *Hansard*, 5th series, vol. 286, col. 2078. 8 Mar 1934.
32 CAB 50/21.
33 Middlemas and Barnes, *Baldwin*, ch. 27.
34 Cmd. 5107, p. 14.
35 Middlemas and Barnes, *Baldwin*, p. 771.
36 Cmd. 5107, p. 16.
37 6 Feb 1937, CAB 23/87.
38 A particularly useful account of this policy before 1937 is to be found in W. N. Medlicott, *Britain and Germany, the Search for Agreement 1930–37* (London 1969).
39 H. A. Jacobsen, *National-socialistische Aussenpolitik 1933–38* (Frankfurt 1968) p. 391.
40 Cmd. 5143, pp. 63–4.
41 *Paris-Midi*, 28 Feb 1936. Hitler's interview with Bertrand de Jouvenal.
42 Dawson to Baldwin, 4 Apr 1936; Baldwin Papers.
43 Earl of Avon, *Facing the Dictators* (London 1962) pp. 477–8.
44 FO minutes on C3621/270/18, 10 May 1937.
45 13 Jan 1937, CAB 23/87.
46 *The Diplomatic Diaries of Oliver Harvey 1937–40*, ed. John Harvey (London 1970) p. 404.

CHAPTER 2: *Chamberlain's Way*

1 For the background to this letter see J. M. Blum, *From the Morgenthau Diaries* (Boston 1959) pp. 458–67. According to Lord Avon (*Facing the Dictators*, p. 527) the reply was drafted in the Foreign Office. I. Colvin, *Vansittart in Office* (London 1965) p. 141, wrongly claims the authorship for Vansittart.
2 Middlemas and Barnes, *Baldwin*, p. 1018.
3 Chamberlain letters, 8 Dec 1935.
4 *Hansard*, 5th series, vol. 261, col. 296. 4 Feb 1932.
5 Chamberlain's son, writing in *The Times*, 26 Nov 1962.
6 Sir Keith Feiling, *Life of Neville Chamberlain* (London 1946) p. 293.

7   Feiling, *Neville Chamberlain*, p. 306.
8   Feiling, *Neville Chamberlain*, p. 311.
9   Feiling, *Neville Chamberlain*, p. 287.
10 Feiling, *Neville Chamberlain*, p. 320.
11 Chamberlain letters, 18 May 1935.
12 *The Times*, 15 Apr 1938.
13 Chamberlain diary, 13 Jan 1934.
14 Chamberlain letters, 9 Dec 1934.
15 Diary, 11 Dec 1934.
16 See Iain Macleod, *Neville Chamberlain* (London 1961) pp. 192–3, and Middlemas and Barnes, *Baldwin*, pp. 909–17 *passim*.
17 Diary, 26 June 1932.
18 Chamberlain letters, 4 Mar 1933.
19 Chamberlain letters, 18 Nov 1933.
20 Diary, 18 Jan 1934.
21 Diary, 24 Mar 1934.
22 Chamberlain letters, 12 May 1934.
23 Diary, 1 July 1934.
24 Chamberlain letters, 12 Dec 1934.
25 Feiling, *Neville Chamberlain*, pp. 255–6.
26 Chamberlain letters, 23 Mar 1935.
27 Chamberlain letters, 6 Apr 1935.
28 Chamberlain letters, 14 July 1935.
29 Chamberlain letters, 25 Aug 1935.
30 Chamberlain letters, 21 Mar 1936.
31 Diary, 27 Apr 1936.
32 Letters, 4 Apr 1936.
33 *The Times*, 11 June 1936.
34 Diary, 17 June 1936.
35 Letters, 28 July 1934.
36 Diary, 21 Mar 1935.
37 Wilson Memorandum. See also Sir Nevile Henderson, *Failure of a Mission* (London 1940) p. 17.
38 Maisky broadcast, quoted in Martin Gilbert and Richard Gott, *The Appeasers* (London 1963) p. 52.
39 Chamberlain letters, 13 Apr 1936.
40 Maisky broadcast, quoted in Gilbert and Gott, *The Appeasers*, p. 51.
41 Chamberlain letters, 22 Nov 1936.
42 Diary, Apr 1936.
43 Diary, July 1933.
44 Chamberlain letters, 29 Aug 1937.
45 Feiling, *Neville Chamberlain*, p. 323 (16 Jan 1938).
46 Chamberlain letters, 13 Oct 1934.
47 Feiling, *Neville Chamberlain*, p. 292.

48 Chamberlain letters, 26 May 1935.
49 Letters, 14 Nov 1936.
50 Chamberlain letters, 8 Dec 1935.
51 Feiling, *Neville Chamberlain*, pp. 314–15.
52 Diary, 25 Oct 1936.
53 Chamberlain letters, 6 Feb 1937.
54 Thomas Jones, *Diary with Letters* (London 1954), p. 350 (30 May 1937).
55 Jones, *Diary with Letters*.
56 *Diaries of Oliver Harvey*, p. 27.
57 Avon, *Facing the Dictators*, p. 445.
58 Chamberlain letters, 1 Aug 1937.

CHAPTER 3: *Power and Influence*

1 Feiling, *Neville Chamberlain*, p. 303.
2 Feiling, *Neville Chamberlain*, p. 311.
3 Templewood, *Nine Troubled Years*, p. 257.
4 e.g. *Diaries of Oliver Harvey*, pp. 117–18.
5 Chamberlain Diary, 11 Dec 1934.
6 For Macmillan's view of the proper state of affairs, see *Tides of Fortune* (London 1969) pp. 464–5.
7 Avon, *Facing the Dictators*, p. 445.
8 Chamberlain letters, 1 Aug 1937.
9 Diary, May 1937.
10 Templewood, *Nine Troubled Years*, p. 280.
11 *Diaries of Oliver Harvey*, p. 100.
12 Halifax, *Fullness of Days*, p. 191.
13 *Diaries of Oliver Harvey*, p. 124.
14 Chamberlain diary, 16 Mar 1937.
15 Diary, Mar 1937.
16 Chamberlain diary, Jan 1934.
17 Diary, 11 May 1937.
18 Chamberlain letters, 22 May 1937; Duff Cooper, *Old Men Forget*, p. 209. Leslie Hore-Belisha was made Secretary for War.
19 Middlemas and Barnes, *Baldwin*, pp. 872–3.
20 *Diaries of Oliver Harvey*, p. 51.
21 Captain Stephen Roskill, *Hankey, Man of Secrets*, vol. 1 (London 1970), covering the years 1908–22, has already appeared. For Hankey's relationship with Baldwin see Middlemas and Barnes *Baldwin, passim*. There is no biography of Fisher, but Watt, *Personalities and Policies* pp. 100–17, gives a preliminary study of his influence on rearmament in the 1930s. I am much indebted to Captain Roskill for informing me of Hankey's views during 1937–8.
22 Middlemas and Barnes, *Baldwin*, p. 318.

23 Hankey papers: letter to his son, 1 Mar 1938.
24 Major-General H. R. Pownall, Diary, Apr-May 1938. (Shortly to be published by Pall Mall Press, edited by Brian Bond.)
25 Royal Archives, K2506/8.
26 CP104/34, 7 Apr 1934; *DBFP*, series 2, vol. 6, pp. 975–90.
27 Medlicott, *Britain and Germany*, p. 3.
28 *Diaries of Oliver Harvey*, p. 44.
29 *Diaries of Oliver Harvey*, p. 57.
30 *Diaries of Oliver Harvey*, p. 86.
31 FP 36/36, July 1937.
32 C7932 (FO 371/20736), 10 May 1937.
33 C7932 (FO 371/20736), 10 May 1937.
34 Minutes on C3621/270/18. For the memorandum itself see J. R. M. Butler, *Lord Lothian* (London 1960) app. 4, pp. 354-62.
35 Watt, *Personalities and Policies*, pp. 96–9.
36 For a full account of his mission, see Gerhard Ritter, *The German Resistance* (London 1958). The balance of power in Germany and the significance of the visit is discussed in Chapter 5.
37 Colvin, *Vansittart in Office*, pp. 149–56.
38 Colvin, *Vansittart in Office*, p. 154.
39 *Diaries of Oliver Harvey*, p. 44.
40 Avon, *Facing the Dictators*, pp. 447–8.
41 Colvin, *Vansittart in Office*, pp. 147–9.
42 Chamberlain letters, 14 Nov 1937.
43 Chamberlain letters, 12 Dec 1937.
44 A. C. Johnson, *Eden* (London 1955) p. 146.
45 *DGFP*, series D, vol. 1, p. 177 (14 Jan 1938).
46 Chamberlain letters, 6 Nov 1937.
47 *DGFP*, series D, vol. 1, p. 224.
48 P. J. Grigg, *Prejudice and Judgment* (London 1948) p. 53.
49 Feiling, *Neville Chamberlain*, p. 255; Middlemas and Barnes, *Baldwin*, p. 796.
50 Pownall diary, 19 Feb 1934.
51 Watt, *Personalities and Policies*, p. 116.
51a See particularly the Hopkins papers (T/175/28, 47, 96) and the correspondence between Fisher and Chamberlain (PREM 1/252).
52 'Cato', *Guilty Men* (London 1940) pp. 62–4.
53 Chamberlain diary, May 1937.
54 Lord Avon, *The Reckoning*, (London 1965) p. 21.
55 Wilson Memorandum
56 Halifax, *Fullness of Days*, p. 231.
57 Lord Woolton, *Memoirs* (London 1959) p. 140.
58 As is argued, by implication, in Watt, *Personalities and Policies*, pp. 115–16.

59   F. A. Johnson, *Defence by Committee* (London 1960) p. 268.
60   Middlemas and Barnes, *Baldwin*, pp. 1027–8.
61   *Royal United Services Institute*, Feb 1966, p. 61.
62   Admiral W. S. Chalmers, *Life and Letters of Earl Beatty* (London 1951) p. 318.
63   B. H. Liddell Hart, *Memoirs*, 2 vols (London 1965) *passim*.
64   Pownall diary, 30 July 1934. I am indebted to the publishers, Pall Mall Press, who are about to publish the work, edited by Dr Brian Bond, for permission to quote this and other extracts.
65   Pownall diary, 27 Jan 1936.
66   Chamberlain letters, 25 Apr 1937.
67   K. G. Robbins, 'Konrad Henlein, the Sudeten Question and British Foreign Policy', *Historical Journal* XII 4 (1969).
68   13 July 1938, CAB 32/38.
69   Major-General Sir Kenneth Stronge, *Intelligence at the Top* (London 1968), gives a useful account of the work of Service attachés and of the contacts maintained with France.
70   F. W. Winterbottom, *Secret and Personal* (London 1969); see also Christopher Felix, *The Spy and his Masters* (London 1963).
71   COS 698 (CAB 50/37).
72   cf. the bewilderment expressed by both Vansittart and Cadogan in May 1937, in their minutes on C3621/270/18.
73   *Diaries of Oliver Harvey*, p. 91.
74   Middlemas and Barnes, *Baldwin*, pp. 748–50, 951.
75   Butler, *Lord Lothian*, p. 202.
76   Gilbert and Gott, *The Appeasers*, ch. 2.
77   Air Marshal Sir John Slessor, *The Central Blue* (London 1956) p. 222.
78   For this, see Dr Brigitte Granzow, *A Mirror of Nazism* (London 1964); and A. J. B. Marwick, 'Middle Opinion in the Thirties', *English Historical Review* (Apr 1964).
79   Middlemas and Barnes, *Baldwin*, pp. 946–8.
80   Cecil additional MSS. 51073 quoted in Keith Robbins, *Munich 1938* (London 1968) pp. 124–5.
81   Quoted in Martin Gilbert, *Britain and Germany between the Wars* (London 1964) pp. 34–5.
82   Murray MS., 6 Apr 1936; quoted in Robbins, *Munich, 1938*, p. 123.
83   *Diaries of Oliver Harvey*, pp. 109–55, *passim*, p. 221 and p. 256.
84   *The Next Five Years: An Essay in Political Agreement* (London 1935) p. 222.
85   Quoted in Martin Gilbert, *Plough My Own Furrow* (London 1965) pp. 375–6.
86   Murray Papers. Letter to H. M. Swanwick, 22 Dec 1934, quoted in Keith Robbins, *Munich 1938*, p. 95.

87 Cecil Additional MSS., 51073. Letter to Churchill 1 Dec 1936, quoted in Robbins, *Munich 1938*, p. 125.

88 Chamberlain letters, 28 July 1934.

89 See Watt, *Personalities and Policies*, ch. 6. 'German Influence on British Opinion in 1933–38 and the Attempts to Counter it'.

90 Gilbert and Gott, *The Appeasers*, pp. 137–8. *History of the Times*, vol. 4, pp. 745–6.

91 See Watt, *Personalities and Policies*, p. 134. Spier blamed *The Times* and the Beaverbrook-Rothermere press empires. But the *Daily Telegraph, Manchester Guardian, News Chronicle* and *Daily Herald* also failed to report the campaign.

92 Hugh Cudlipp, *Publish and Be Damned* (London 1953) pp 221–5.

93 C. Madge and T. Harrisson, *Britain by Mass Observation* (London 1939) p. 24.

94 Avon, *Facing the Dictators*, p. 508.

95 *Diaries of Oliver Harvey*, p. 102. See also Middlemas and Barnes, *Baldwin*, pp. 412–13, for similar restrictions imposed during the General Strike.

96 Labour Party Annual Report, 1933, p. 186.

97 *Hansard*, 5th Series, vol. 292, col. 2432, 30 July 1934.

98 *Hansard*, 5th series, vol. 292, col. 2432, 30 July 1934.

99 *Daily Herald*, 4 Apr 1935.

100 Middlemas and Barnes, *Baldwin*, p. 946.

101 *The Times*, 15 Nov 1936.

102 Chamberlain letters, 25 Aug 1937.

103 Labour Party Annual Report, 1936, p. 182.

104 Labour Party Annual Report 1936, p. 205.

CHAPTER 4: *Positive Thinking*

1 Chamberlain diary, 19 Feb 1938.

2 C7752/55/18 (FO 371/18851).

3 Vansittart Papers, 7 Nov 1935; cf. also his views in C997/4/18 (FO 371/19885).

4 Vansittart Papers, June 1936.

5 C8524/55/18 (FO 371/18852); see above, p. 41.

6 Avon, *Facing the Dictators*, pp. 137 and 142.

7 FP36/41 CAB 27/626.

8 *Hansard*, vol. 102, cols 274–5, 27 July 1936.

9 C7626/5740/18 (FO 371/19948).

10 3 Feb 1937 CAB 23/87.

11 FP 36/18. 4 Mar 1937 CAB 27/622.

12 6 Apr, CAB 27/622.

13 FP 36/26 (CAB 27/626).

13a Henderson, *Failure of a Mission*, pp. 67–9. Sir Horace Wilson confirmed that this was the reason accepted by Chamberlain (Wilson Memorandum).
14   21 June, CAB 27/622.
15   Chamberlain letters, 4 July 1937.
16   CID minutes, CAB 2/6 passim.
17   Cmd. 5107 (Defence White Paper 1936).
18   CP 41/37.
19   CP 42/37.
19a This review was originally undertaken by Inskip at Eden's request in December 1936 (Middlemas and Barnes, *Baldwin*, p. 1022) to show Britain's readiness for war as at 1 May 1937. See Appendix 1 to CAB 23/87, 24 February.
20   28 Apr, CAB 23/88.
21   5 May, CAB 23/88.
22   30 June 1937, CAB 23/88.
23   29 July, CAB 23/89.
24   CP 257/37.
25   27 Oct, CAB 23/90A.
26   CID No. 1366B, embodied by Inskip in CP 295/37.
27   CID No. 1366B, para. 42.
28   8 Dec, CAB 23/90A.
29   8 Dec, CAB 23/90A.
30   CP 316/37.
31   CP 316/37, para. 44.
32   CP 316/37, paras 69–71.
33   CP 313/37, para. 37.
34   *Hansard*, 5th series, vol. 277, cols. 60–1, 25 Apr 1933.
35   PREM 1/250 22 Oct 1937.
35a T/175/28 minutes on CP 226 (32).
35b T/175/96 4 Feb 1937 (Hopkins to Chamberlain).
36   22 Dec, CAB 23/90A.
37   Chamberlain letters, 9 July 1937.
38   FP 36/36. CAB 27/626.
39   Chamberlain diary, 19 Feb 1938.
40   Chamberlain letters, 8 Aug 1937.
41   Chamberlain letters, 29 Aug.
42   Chamberlain diary, 18 Feb 1938.
43   8 September 1937, CAB 23/89.
44   Avon, *Facing the Dictators*, p. 464.
45   Chamberlain letters, 12 Sept 1937.
46   *Diaries of Oliver Harvey*, p. 57.
47   CP 202/37.
48   Lord Birkenhead, *Halifax* (London 1965) p. 365.
49   *Diaries of Oliver Harvey*, p. 61.

50   Chamberlain letters, 24 Oct 1937.
51   Chamberlain letters, 6 Nov; see also Avon, *Facing the Dictators*, pp. 506–7.
52   Chamberlain letters, 14 Nov.
53   Chamberlain letters, 14 Nov.
54   Hickleton papers, quoted in Birkenhead, *Halifax*, p. 366.
55   Schmidt's transcript, *DGFP*, series D, vol. I, pp. 62–3.
56   R7783/1/22 (FO 371/21162).
57   24 Nov, CAB 23/90A.
58   Hickleton papers, 21 Nov. Quoted in Birkenhead, *Halifax*, p. 374.
59   24 Nov, CAB 23/90A.
60   e.g. his views in R3127 (FO 371/21117) and R2320/989/3 (FO 371/21119).
61   Avon, *Facing the Dictators*, p. 503.
61a For the general view of the Foreign Office, see FP 36/36, July 1937 (CAB 27/626).
62   Chamberlain letters, 21 Nov.
63   Chamberlain letters, 26 Nov.
64   Avon, *Facing the Dictators*, p. 506.
65   Phipps to Eden, 23 Nov. CAB 23/90A, also Chamberlain letters, 26 Nov.
66   1 Dec, CAB 23/90A.
67   R2320/989/3 (FO 371/21119), and Vansittart papers.
68   *Diaries of Oliver Harvey*, p. 63.
69   *Diaries of Oliver Harvey*, p. 56.
70   Chamberlain letters, 5 Dec.
71   Diary, 18 Feb 1938.
72   Diary, 18 Feb 1938.
73   Chamberlain letters, 9 Jan.
74   Diary, 18 Feb.
75   24 Jan, CAB 27/623.
76   Avon, *Facing the Dictators*, p. 518.
77   *Diaries of Oliver Harvey*, p. 70.
78   *FRUS* 1937, vol. 1. pp. 132–5.
79   Chamberlain letters, 9 Oct.
80   Chamberlain letters, 21 Nov.
81   Hull, *Memoirs*, vol. 1, pp. 561–2.
82   W. L. Langer and S. E. Gleason, *The Challenge to Isolation 1937–40*, 2 vols (New York 1964), vol. I, pp. 22–6.
83   Secret Addendum to CAB 23/92, 24 Jan.
83a For the best account of these meetings, see Avon, *Facing the Dictators*, p. 560–5. The minutes are not among the official archives but Lord Avon's copy is held by the Cabinet Office.
84   Langer and Gleason, *Challenge to Isolation*, p. 32.

85 Offner, *American Appeasement*, pp. 191–4.
86 Secret addendum to Cabinet, 24 Jan, CAB 23/92.
87 CAB 27/623.
88 FP 36/46–48.
89 Chamberlain letters, 30 Jan.
90 Avon, *Facing the Dictators*, p. 571.
91 Avon, *Facing the Dictators*, p. 575.
92 10 Feb, CAB 23/92.
93 Diary, 18 Feb.
94 Avon, *Facing the Dictators*, p. 577.
95 Chamberlain letters, 13 Feb.
96 Chamberlain diary, 18 Feb.
97 19 Feb, CAB 23/92.
98 1 Mar, CAB 23/92.
99 *Diaries of Oliver Harvey*, p. 122.
100 CP 58/38.
101 9 Mar, CAB 23/92.
102 1 Mar, CAB 27/623.
103 Henderson, *Failure of a Mission*, pp. 115–18.
104 *Diaries of Oliver Harvey*, p. 109.

CHAPTER 5: *The German Negative*

1 This chapter is based primarily on the accounts given in Hans Adolf Jacobsen, *Nationalsocialistische Aussenpolitik, 1933–38* (Frankfurt 1968); E. N. Petersen, *The Limits of Hitler's Power* (Princeton 1969) and Klaus Hildebrand, *Vom Reich zum Weltreich, Hitler NSDAP und Kolonial Frage 1919–45* (Munich 1967) and *Deutsche Aussenpolitik Kalkül oder Dogma* (Stuttgart 1970); also Arthur Schweitzer, *Big Business in the Third Reich* (Bloomington, Ind., 1964); E. M. Robertson, *Hitler's Pre-War Policy and Military Plans, 1933–39* (London 1963); A. Hillgruber, *Hitlers Strategie 1940–41* (Frankfurt 1965) and Albert Speer, *Inside the Third Reich* (London 1970).
2 For the conflicting literature up to 1965, see D. C. Watt, 'Appeasement: The Rise of a Revisionist School' *Political Quarterly* (April-June 1965).
3 A. J. P. Taylor, *The Origins of the Second World War* (London 1961) p. 68.
4 Petersen, *Limits of Hitler's Power*, p. 431.
5 Speer, *Inside the Third Reich*, p. 131.
6 Otto Dietrich, *Zwölf Jahre mit Hitler* (Munich 1955).
7 Speer, *Inside the Third Reich*, p. 71.
8 *Hitler's Second Book* (New York 1962) pp. 146–58.
9 CP73/36, Cabinet 9 Mar 1936.

10 P. S. Schmidt, *Hitler's Interpreter* (London 1951) p. 41; and Speer, *Inside the Third Reich*, p. 72.
11 Jacobsen, *Nationalsocialistische Aussenpolitik*, p. 391.
12 H. Mau and H. Krausnick, *German History 1933–45* (London 1964) p. 66.
13 *Ciano's Diplomatic Papers* (London 1948) pp. 52–61.
14 Speer, *Inside the Third Reich*, p. 72.
15 *DGFP*, series C, vol. 5, p. 853A.
16 *DGFP*, series C, vol. 5, pp. 853–82.
17 *DGFP*, series C, vol. 5, p. 855.
18 Schweitzer, *Big Business*, pp. 504–39; also R. J. O'Neill, *The German Army and the Nazi Party 1933–39* (London 1966) *passim*.
19 Petersen, *Limits of Hitler's Power*, p. 75.
20 Page 394 below. Henderson, *Failure of a Mission*, p. 161.
21 Gerhard Ritter: *The German Resistance*, pp. 83–4.
22 Jacobsen, *Nationalsocialistische Aussenpolitik*, pp. 421–5.
23 Nuremberg Documents C/175.
24 Hildebrand, *Vom Reich zum Weltreich*, p. 235.
25 *DGFP*, series D, vol. 1, no. 19, p. 32.
26 *DGFP*, series D, vol. 1, no. 31, p. 62.
27 Jacobsen, *Nationalsocialistische Aussenpolitik*, p. 481.
28 E. Kordt, *Wahn und Wirklichkeit* (Stuttgart 1948) p. 142.
29 Speer, *Inside the Third Reich*, p. 121.
30 A. Hillgruber, 'Der Faktor Amerika in Hitlers Strategie 1938–41', *Das Parlament* (May 1966).
31 F. Hossbach, *Zwischen Wehrmacht und Hitler 1934–38* (Hanover 1949) p. 218.
32 *DGFP*, series D, vol. 1, no. 19, pp. 29–39.
33 For the latter view, see A. J. P. Taylor, *Origins of the Second World War*, pp. 131–5.
34 Jacobsen, *Nationalsocialistische Aussenpolitik*, p. 435.
35 Watt, in *Political Quarterly* (1965), p. 202.
36 Jacobsen, *Nationalsocialistische Aussenpolitik*, p. 435.
37 *DGFP*, series D, vol. 1, pp. 635–8.
38 Vansittart papers.
39 Watt, in *Political Quarterly* (1965) p. 242.
40 Jodl's Diary, quoted in Mau and Krausnick, *German History*, p. 76.
41 *DGFP*, series D, vol. 1, no. 19, p. 32.
42 *DGFP*, series D, vol. 1, no. 19, p. 33.
43 Speer, *Inside the Third Reich*, p. 72.
44 *DGFP*, series D, vol. 1, p. 36.
45 Petersen, *Limits of Hitler's Power*, p. 62.
46 *DGFP*, series D, vol. 1, pp. 162–8.
47 *DGFP*, series D, vol. 1, p. 3.

48 *DGFP*, series D, vol. 1, p. 5.
49 *DGFP*, series D, vol. 1, p. 1.
50 *Ciano's Diary 1937–38*, p. 73.
51 *Hitler's Table Talk*, ed. N. Cameron and R. Steven (London 1953) p. 403.
52 K. G. Robbins, 'Konrad Henlein, the Sudeten Question and British Foreign Policy', *Historical Journal*, XII 4 (1969).
53 Jacobsen, *Nationalsocialistische Aussenpolitik*, p. 443.
54 *DGFP*, series D, vol. 2, p. 123.
55 *DGFP*, series D, vol. 2, pp. 197–9.
56 *DGFP*, series D, vol. 2, pp. 239–40. Jacobsen, *Nationalsocialistische Aussenpolitik*, pp. 443–4.
57 A viewpoint held by Speer, *Inside the Third Reich*, p. 107.

CHAPTER 6: *March 1938*

1   12 Mar 1938, CAB 23/93.
2   12 Mar 1938, CAB 23/93.
3   19 Feb 1938, CAB 23/93.
4   Memorandum by Halifax, 18 Mar, CAB 27/623.
5   15 Mar, CAB 27/623.
6   *DBFP*, series 3, vol. 1, p. 50.
7   FP 36/56.
8   *DBFP*, series 3, vol. 1, p. 488.
9   Chamberlain letters, 20 Mar 1938.
10 FP 36/57 (COS 698, CAB 50/37).
11 FP 36/56.
12 21 Mar 1938, CAB 27/623.
13 21 Mar 1938, CAB 27/623.
13a Ibid.
14 FP 36/57, para. 87 (COS 698).
15 Duff Cooper, *Old Men Forget*, p. 218.
16 22 Mar, CAB 23/93.

CHAPTER 7: *The Public Face*

1   Royal Institute of International Affairs, *Documents on International Affairs* (1938), vol. 1, pp. 314–5.
2   COS 698, p. 192 above.
3   C1866/132/18 (FO 371/21674).
4   C1935/95/62 (FO 371/21626).
5   C1935/95/62 (FO 371/21626).
6   Chamberlain letters, 20 Mar.
7   C1865/132/18 (FO 371/21674).
8   *DBFP*, series 3, vol. 1, p. 89.
9   *DBFP*, series 3, vol. 1, pp. 83–5.

10 *DBFP*, series 3, vol. 1, pp. 86–8.
11 *DBFP*, series 3, vol. 1, p. 91.
12 22 Mar, CAB 23/93.
12a Sir Harold Nicolson, *Diaries and Letters 1930–39*, ed. Nigel Nicolson (London 1966) p. 332. Attlee later denied that these talks had taken place.
13 *Hansard*, 5th series, vol. 333, col. 1399, 24 Mar.
14 *Hansard*, 5th series, vol. 333, col. 1400.
15 *Hansard*, 5th series, vol. 333, col. 71, 14 Mar.
16 *Hansard*, 5th series, vol. 333, col. 1437, 24 Mar.
17 *Hansard*, 5th series, vol. 333, col. 1437.
18 Virginia Cowles, *Winston Churchill: The Era and the Man* (London 1953) p. 308.
19 L. Amery, *My Political Life*, III 239.
20 Duff Cooper, *Old Men Forget*, p. 218.
21 Harold Macmillan, *Winds of Change* (London 1966) p. 541.
22 *The Times*, 25 Mar.
23 *Daily Herald*, 25 Mar.
24 *New Statesman*, vol. 15, no. 370, p. 510. 26 Mar 1938.
25 Chamberlain letters, 20 Mar 1938.
26 Chamberlain letters, 27 Mar.
27 *The Private Papers of Hore-Belisha*, ed. R. J. Minney (London 1960) p. 106.
28 Chamberlain letters, 27 Mar 1938.
29 Chamberlain letters, 27 Mar 1938.
30 'Since I am at this moment the head of the French Government'. 26 Mar, CAB 23/93.
31 *DBFP*, series 3, vol. 1, p. 94.
32 *DBFP*, series 3, vol. 1, p. 95.
33 *DBFP*, series 3, vol. 1, p. 102.
34 *DGFP*, series D, vol. 2, pp. 192–3.
35 Reported in *DBFP*, series 3, vol. 1, p. 103.
36 Chamberlain letters, 13 Mar 1938.
37 Offner, *American Appeasement*, p. 246.
38 6 Apr, CAB 23/93.

CHAPTER 8: *The Conversion of France*

1 29 Mar, CAB 27/623.
2 29 Apr, CAB 23/93.
3 Chamberlain letters, 16 Apr 1938.
4 *DGFP*, series D, vol. 1, pp. 1082–3. See also *Ciano's Diary 1937–38*, p. 96, 3 Apr 1938.
5 *Ciano's Diary 1937–38*, p. 96.
6 18 May, CAB 23/94.

7 Chamberlain letters, 16 Apr 1938.
8 7 Apr, CAB 27/623.
9 13 Apr 1938, CAB 27/623.
10 *DGFP*, series D, vol. 1, pp. 1092–3.
11 COS 727 (CAB 50/38).
12 6 Apr, CAB 23/93.
13 Pownall diary, 12 Mar 1938.
14 6 Apr 1938, CAB 23/93.
15 13 Apr, CAB 23/93.
16 13 Apr, CAB 23/93.
17 13 Apr, CAB 23/93.
18 Quoted in G. M. Young, *Stanley Baldwin* (London 1952) p. 36.
19 *DBFP*, series 3, vol. 1, pp. 140–3.
20 Chamberlain diary, 26 June 1932.
21 Halifax to Joseph Kennedy, American Ambassador in London, 16 May, *FRUS* 1938 vol. 1, p. 504.
22 J. Paul Boncour, *Entre deux Guerres, Souvenirs de la 3e République* (Paris 1946) vol. 3, pp. 100–1.
23 *FRUS* (1938), vol. 1, p. 647.
24 *DBFP*, series 3, vol. 1, p. 197.
25 27 Apr CAB 23/93.
26 *DBFP*, series 3, vol. 1, pp. 198–233. CP 103/38.
27 Chamberlain letters, 1 May 1938.
28 *DBFP*, series 3, vol. 1, p. 202.
29 Chamberlain letters, 1 May.
30 *DBFP*, series 3, vol. 1, pp. 243–5.
31 *DBFP*, series 3, vol. 1, p. 246.
32 4 May, CAB 23/93.
33 4 May, CAB 23/93.
34 *DBFP*, series 3, vol. 1, p. 270.
35 *DBFP*, series 3, vol. 1, pp. 277–80.
36 *DBFP*, series 3, vol. 1, pp. 257–8.
37 Chamberlain letters, 8 and 15 May.
38 *DBFP*, series 3, vol. 1, pp. 281–2.
39 Northedge, *The Troubled Giant*, p. 507.
40 *DBFP*, series 3, vol. 1, pp. 284–7.
41 *DGFP*, series D, vol. 2, pp. 255–6.
42 K. G. Robbins, 'Konrad Henlein, the Sudeten Question, and British Foreign Policy', *Historical Journal*, XII 4 (1969) pp. 692–3.
43 C5490/1941/18 (FO 371/21723).
44 18 May, CAB 23/93.
45 Lord Birkenhead, *The Prof in Two Worlds* (London 1961) p. 173; Winston S. Churchill, *The Gathering Storm* (London 1948) p. 223.
46 *DBFP*, series 3, vol. 1, pp. 630–3.
47 *DBFP*, series 3, vol. 1, p. 298.

48 Robbins, *Munich, 1938*, p. 222.
49 *DBFP*, series 3, vol. 1, p. 270.
50 *DBFP*, series 3, vol. 1, p. 320.
51 *DBFP*, series 3, vol. 1, pp. 309–10.
52 11 May, CAB 23/93.
53 18 May, CAB 23/93.
54 *DBFP*, series 3, vol. 1, p. 317.
55 For a discussion of the crisis, see Robbins *Munich, 1938*, pp. 219–71; also W. V.Wallace, 'The Making of the May Crisis of 1938', *Slavonic and East European Review*, vol. 41 (June 1963) pp. 368–90.
56 e.g. *DGFP*, series D, vol. 2, p. 310n.
57 *DGFP*, series D, vol. 2, p. 276.
58 *DGFP*, series D, vol. 2, p. 277.
59 18 May, *DBFP*, series 3, vol. 1, p. 310.
60 22 May, CAB 23/93.
61 *DBFP*, series 3, vol. 1, p. 318.
62 *DBFP*, series 3, vol. 1, pp. 329–30.
63 C4851/1441/18 (FO 371/21721).
64 *DBFP*, series 3, vol. 1, pp. 231–2.
65 *FRUS* (1938), vol. 1, p. 572.
66 *Diaries of Oliver Harvey*, p. 143.
67 22 May, CAB 23/93.
68 *DGFP*, series D, vol. 2, p. 327.
69 22 May, CAB 23/93.
70 Chamberlain letters, 22 May 1938.
71 Chamberlain letters, 28 May.
72 *DGFP*, series D, vol. 2, p. 358.
73 Quoted in J. Wheeler-Bennett, *Munich, Prologue to Tragedy* (London 1948) p. 51.

CHAPTER 9: *The Hunting of the Snark*

1 25 May, CAB 23/93.
2 25 May, CAB 23/93.
3 R. Luza, *The Transfer of the Sudeten Germans* (New York, 1964) p. 163.
4 cf. 22 Mar, CAB 27/623.
5 *DGFP*, series D, vol. 4, pp. 129–32.
6 *Diaries of Oliver Harvey*, p. 142.
7 C6786/1941/18 (FO 371/21726).
8 See Elizabeth Wiskemann, *Czechs and Germans*, 2nd ed. (London 1967) pp. 274–82.
9 12 Sept, CAB 23/95.
10 *DBFP*, series 3, vol. 1, pp. 271–2; 27 Sept, CAB 27/646 (below, p. 391).
11 COS 698.

12 *FRUS* (1938), vol. 1, pp. 493–4.
13 25 May, CAB 23/93.
14 25 May, CAB 23/93.
15 *DBFP*, series 3, vol. 1, pp. 369–71.
16 *DBFP*, series 3, vol. 1, p. 418.
17 Chamberlain letters, 17 May 1938.
18 *The Times*, 19 May 1938.
19 *Ironside Diaries*, p. 58.
20 6 July, CAB 23/94.
21 13 July, CAB 23/94.
22 Duff Cooper, *Old Men Forget*, p. 219.
23 CP 170/38.
24 Duff Cooper, *Old Men Forget*, p. 222.
25 1 June, CAB 23/93. Also C5440/1941/18 (FO 371/21723).
26 C5440/1941/18 (FO 371/21723); also *Diaries of Oliver Harvey*, p. 146.
27 *Diaries of Oliver Harvey*, p. 146.
27a *DBFP*, series 3, vol. 1, pp. 495–6. Bonnet told this to Osusky, the Czech Minister in Paris.
28 *DBFP*, series 3, vol. 1, pp. 496–7.
29 *DBFP*, series 3, vol. 1, p. 503.
30 *DBFP*, series 3, vol. 1, app. 4, pp. 647–52.
31 FP 36/63.
32 FP 36/63.
33 Chamberlain letters, 18 June.
34 Chamberlain letters, 18 June.
35 Chamberlain letters, 18 June.
36 Chamberlain letters, 28 May.
37 Chamberlain letters, 18 June.
38 13 July, CAB 23/94.
39 CP 127/38.
40 2 June, CAB 27/623.
41 cf. W. N. Medlicott, *History of the Second World War; United Kingdom Civil Series; the Economic Blockade* (London 1952) vol. 1, p. 14.
42 Chamberlain letters, 20 June.
43 Chamberlain letters, 9 July.
44 7 July, CAB 23/94.
45 22 June, CAB 23/94.
46 *DBFP*, series 3, vol. 1, pp. 510–11.
47 *DBFP*, series 3, vol. 1, pp. 581–3.
48 C7009 and 7315/1941/18 (FO 371/21721 and 21728).
49 C7007/1941/18 (FO 371/21721).
50 *Diaries of Oliver Harvey*, p. 161.
51 Chamberlain letters, 16 July.

52 Chamberlain letters, 16 July.
53 *DBFP*, series 3, vol. 1, pp. 584–9.
54 Chamberlain letters, 20 July.
55 7 July, CAB 23/93.
56 *DBFP*, series 3, vol. 1, pp. 600–1.
57 *Hansard*, 5th series, vol. 338, cols 2957–8. 26 July.
58 *DBFP*, series 3, vol. 2, pp. 3–4.
59 *DBFP*, series 3, vol. 2, pp. 10–12.
60 *Hansard*, 5th series, vol. 110, col. 1284.
61 27 July, CAB 23/93.
62 *DBFP*, series 3, vol. 2, p. 13.
63 Luza, *Transfer of the Sudeten Germans*, p. 135; see also, Robbins, 'Konrad Henlein, the Sudeten Question and British Foreign Policy', *Historical Journal*, vol. XII 4 (1969) p. 697.
64 *DBFP*, series 3, vol. 2, p. 100.
65 *DBFP*, series 3, vol. 2, p. 142.
66 Sir H. Wilson to Chamberlain, 25 Aug (PREM 1/265).
67 *DBFP*, series 3, vol. 2, p. 143.
68 *DBFP*, series 3, vol. 2, pp. 42–5.
69 *DBFP*, series 3, vol. 2, pp. 46–7.
70 *DBFP*, series 3, vol. 2, p. 46 (Nos 576 and 577).
71 *DBFP*, series 3, vol. 2, pp. 58–60.
72 *DBFP*, series 3, vol. 2, pp. 58–60.
73 Pownall diary, 8 Aug.
74 Pownall diary, 8 Aug.
75 Chamberlain letters, 13 Aug.
76 *DBFP*, series 3, vol. 2, pp. 54–6.
77 *DBFP*, series 3, vol. 2, p. 78.
78 *DBFP*, series 3, vol. 2, pp. 127–9; *DGFP*, series D, vol. 2, pp. 599–601.
79 *DGFP*, series D, vol. 2, pp. 599–601.
80 *DBFP*, series 3, vol. 2, pp. 125–6.
81 *DBFP*, series 3, vol. 2, p. 159.
82 *DBFP*, series 3, vol. 2, pp. 159–60.
83 *DBFP*, series 3, vol. 1, pp. 357 and 577–8.
84 *DBFP*, series 3, vol. 2, p. 160.
85 C8520/1941/18 (FO 371/21732); also Vansittart papers, VNST 1.
86 Vansittart papers.
87 *DBFP*, series 3, vol. 2, app. 4, pp. 686–7.
88 C8520/1941/18 (FO 371/21732).
89 *DGFP*, series D, vol. 2, pp. 608–9.
90 Northedge, *Troubled Giant*, p. 520.
91 The file PREM 1/265 contains Wilson's correspondence with Chamberlain during the period of the Runciman mission.

92   *DBFP*, series 3, vol. 2, pp. 188–9.
93   *DBFP*, series 3, vol. 2, pp. 101–3.
94   *DBFP*, series 3, vol. 2, pp. 190–1.

CHAPTER 10: *Revaluations*

1   PREM 1/260.
2   Watt, *Personalities and Policies*, p. 169.
3   30 June, CAB 23/94.
4   Watt, *Personalities and Policies*, p. 169.
5   13 July, CAB 23/94.
6   22 Mar, CAB 23/93.
7   CAB 53/41, COS 764.
8   30 Aug, CAB 23/94.
9   CAB 53/37, COS 698.
10   FRUS 1938, vol. 1, p. 526.
10a   *DBFP*, series 3, vol. 2, pp. 162–5. 30 May. To be fair to the
      staff of the Moscow Embassy, this view was corroborated
      from other sources: information from Ciano (R4474/3815/22),
      Japan (C9525/1941/18) and MacFarlane's informant at
      German GHQ (C6923/1180/18).
11   CAB 53/38, COS 716. 26 Apr 1938.
12   PREM 1/265.
13   N4317/954/38 (FO 371/22299).
14   *DBFP*, series 3, vol. 2, pp. 255–6.
15   Chamberlain letters, 9 July.
16   20 July, CAB 23/94.
17   Offner, *American Appeasement*, pp. 251–3.
18   DGFP, series D, vol. 1, p. 723 n.
19   *Public Papers of F. D. Roosevelt* (New York 1938–50) VII pp.
      491–4.
20   Offner, *American Appeasement*, p. 256.
21   *FRUS* (1938), vol. 1, p. 551.
22   *DBFP*, series 3, vol. 2, pp. 212–13.
23   *FRUS* (1938), vol. 1, pp. 560–1.
24   *DBFP*, series 3, vol. 7, p. 36.
25   C10114/1941/18 (FO 371/21739). 19 Sept.
26   Madge and Harrisson, *Britain by Mass Observation*, p. 20.
27   A. Christiansen, *Headlines All My Life* (London 1961) p. 143.
28   PREM 1/249, *passim*.
29   Colvin, *Vansittart in Office*, pp. 221–2.
30   *New Statesman*, vol. 16, 27 Aug 1938.
31   *DBFP*, series 3, vol. 2, p. 257. 6 Sept.
32   *The Times*, 7 Sept 1938.
33   Duff Cooper, *Old Men Forget*, p. 227.
34   *Hansard*, 5th series, vol. 338, col. 2943. 26 July.

35 *Hansard*, 5th series, vol. 338, col. 2994.
36 *Hansard*, 5th series, vol. 338, col. 3029–32.
37 Lady Asquith in the *Daily Telegraph*, 12 Mar 1965.
38 PREM 1/238.
39 Chamberlain letters, 25 June 1938.
40 Liddell Hart, *Memoirs* vol. 2, pp. 210–11.
41 Rhodes James, *Churchill*, p. 335.
42 *Diaries of Oliver Harvey*, pp. 256–7.
43 Rhodes James, *Churchill*, p. 332.
44 W. S. Churchill, *Step by Step* (collected articles 1936–9) (London 1968) pp. 255–8. (Article first printed in June 1938.)
45 Chamberlain letters, 4 July.
46 PREM 1/237, 1/323, 1/345.
47 PREM 1/265, 31 Aug.
48 Inskip diary, 12 Sept.
49 PREM 1/249.
50 PREM 1/249, and *Gilbert Murray, an unfinished autobiography*, (ed. Jean Smith and A. Toynbee) p. 183.
51 PREM 1/249.
52 PREM 1/249.
53 CAB 53/38, COS 716.
54 CAB 53/38–41, *passim*.
55 CAB 53/40, COS 755.
56 Pownall Diary, July.
57 Liddell Hart, *Memoirs*, vol. 2, pp. 145–6.
58 PREM 1/241.
59 Memorandum of 23 Apr 1938. Vansittart papers.
60 *DBFP*, series 3, vol. 1, app. 2, p. 633.
61 Vansittart papers, 25 July.
62 Vansittart papers, 30 Aug 1938 (C9004/1941/18 (FO 371/22345)).
63 Wilson Memorandum (Thomas Jones papers).
64 Wilson Memorandum. A reference to Vansittart's 'act of faith' in regard to Germany in December 1936 (above, p. 111).
65 PREM 1/265.
66 Vansittart papers, 9 Aug 1938.
67 Wilson Memorandum.
68. *DGFP*, series D, vol. 2, pp. 299–303.
69 *DGFP*, series D, vol. 2, p. 358 (30 May).
70 Taylor, *Origins of the Second World War*, p. 167.
71 Viz. Hillgruber, *Hitlers Strategie, passim*.
72 *DGFP*, series D, vol. 2, pp. 239–40.
73 *DGFP*, series D, vol. 2, pp. 357–62.
74 cf. Jodl's diary, 10 Aug, quoted in Alan Bullock, *Hitler: A Study in Tyranny* (London 1959) p. 451.

75 Robertson, *Hitler's Pre-War Policy*, p. 134.
76 *DGFP*, series D, vol. 2, p. 504.
77 J. Hencke, 'Hitler und England, 1937–39' (Mannheim University, unpublished thesis).
78 Erich Raeder, *Struggle for the Sea* (London 1959) p. 123.
79 *DGFP*, series D, vol. 7, app. 3 K, pp. 640–3.
80 *DGFP*, series D, vol. 2, pp. 686–7.
81 H. von Dirksen, *Moscow-Tokyo-London* (London 1951) p. 218.
82 *DGFP*, series D, vol. 2, p. 587.
83 *DGFP*, series D, vol. 2, p. 700.
84 Schmidt, *Hitler's Interpreter*, p. 106.
85 Details of the conspiracy are to be found in Terence Prittie, *Germans against Hitler* (London 1964) pp. 61–4.
86 P. Seabury, *The Wilhelmstrasse* (Berkeley 1954) p. 93ff. Below, p. 321.
87 Ritter, *The German Resistance*, p. 103.
88 Speer, *Inside the Third Reich*, p. 96.
89 C7315/1941/18 (FO 371/22261).

CHAPTER 11: *Narrow Choices*

1 Chamberlain letters, 27 July.
2 30 Aug, CAB 23/94.
3 30 Aug, CAB 23/94.
4 30 Aug, CAB 23/94.
5 PREM 1/265 includes this letter.
6 Chamberlain letters, 3 Sept.
7 Inskip diary, 30 Aug.
8 Inskip diary, 9 Sept.
9 Inskip diary, 30 Aug.
10 Chamberlain letters.
11 Sir Alec Douglas-Home, letter to the author, 4 Nov 1969.
12 Chamberlain letters, 3 Sept.
13 *DBFP*, series 3, vol. 2, pp. 195–6.
14 *DBFP*, series 3, vol. 2, pp. 226–9.
15 *DBFP*, series 3, vol. 2, pp. 258–9.
16 *DBFP*, series 3, vol. 2, p. 295.
17 *DBFP*, series 3, vol. 2, pp. 196–8.
18 *DBFP*, series 3, vol. 2, p. 216.
19 *DBFP*, series 3, vol. 2, p. 246.
20 *DBFP*, series 3, vol. 2, p. 262.
21 *DBFP*, series 3, vol. 2, p. 262.
22 *DBFP*, series 3, vol. 2, p. 270.
23 Vansittart papers.
24 Inskip diary, 12 Sept.

25 *DBFP*, series 3, vol. 2, pp. 216–17.
26 Colvin, *Vansittart in Office*, pp. 234–7.
27 Theodore Kordt, *Nicht aus der Akten* (Stuttgart, 1950) pp. 279–81.
28 *Diaries of Oliver Harvey*, p. 171.
29 Colvin, *Vansittart in Office*, p. 237.
30 Inskip diary, 9 Sept.
31 Inskip diary, 9 Sept.
32 *DBFP*, series 3, vol. 2, p. 277.
33 *DBFP*, series 3, vol. 2, p. 303 n.
34 *DBFP*, series 3, vol. 2, p. 303.
35 Wrench, *Geoffrey Dawson and Our Times*, pp. 370–2.
36 Wrench, *Geoffrey Dawson and Our Times*, p. 371.
37 *DGFP*, series D, vol. 2, p. 734.
38 *Diaries of Oliver Harvey*, p. 171.
39 *Diaries of Oliver Harvey*, p. 170.
40 Wheeler-Bennett, *Munich*, p. 97.
41 *DBFP*, series 3, vol. 2, pp. 277–8.
42 12 Sept, CAB 23/95.
43 *DBFP*, series 3, vol. 2, p. 280; also pp. 283–4.
44 Templewood, *Nine Troubled Years*, p. 301.
45 Colvin, *Vansittart in Office*, p. 240.
46 PREM 1/226A.
47 Hoare Papers, X5.
48 Chamberlain letters, 11 Sept.
49 Inskip diary, 12 Sept.
50 *DBFP*, series 3, vol. 2, pp. 293–4.
51 Chamberlain letters, 11 Sept.
52 Inskip diary, 12 Sept.
53 Chamberlain letters, 11 Sept.
54 Templewood Papers, X5.
55 12 Sept, CAB 23/95.
56 12 Sept, CAB 23/95. See also PREM 1/242 for interviews between MacDonald and the High Commissioners, 12–24 Sept.
57 12 Sept, CAB 23/95, app. 2.
58 12 Sept, CAB 23/95, app. 2.
59 12 Sept, CAB 23/95, app. 2.
60 *DBFP*, series 3, vol. 2, p. 303.
61 Inskip diary, 12 Sept.
62 Inskip diary, 12 Sept.
63 Templewood Papers, X5.
64 *DBFP*, series 3, vol. 2, pp. 305–6.
65 *DBFP*, series 3, vol. 2, pp. 311.
66 *DBFP*, series 3, vol. 2, p. 309.
67 *DBFP*, series 3, vol. 2, p. 312.

68 *DBFP,* series 3, vol. 2, p. 323.
69 *DBFP,* series 3, vol. 2, p. 314.
70 *DBFP,* series 3, vol. 2, p. 306.
71 See also 14 Sept, CAB 23/95.
72 Inskip diary, 12 Sept.
73 Inskip diary, 14 Sept.
74 13 Sept, CAB 27/646.
75 13 Sept, CAB 27/646.
76 Templewood Papers, X5.
77 Inskip diary, 14 Sept.
78 14 Sept, CAB 23/95.
79 14 Sept, CAB 23/95.
80 Inskip diary, 14 Sept.
81 14 Sept, CAB 23/95.
82 14 Sept, CAB 23/95.
83 14 Sept, CAB 23/95.
84 14 Sept, CAB 23/95. But see below, p. 360.
85 14 Sept, CAB 23/95.
86 Inskip diary, 14 Sept; CAB 53/41, COS 770 and 771.

CHAPTER 12: *The Lobster and the Pot*

1 *The Times* 16 Sept. The stock-market headline was 'General Recovery'.
2 Chamberlain letters, 19 Sept.
3 Inskip diary, 16 Sept.
4 Templewood papers, X5.
5 16 Sept, CAB 27/646.
6 C10219/9572/18 (FO 371/21782).
7 Wilson notes.
8 16 Sept, CAB 27/646.
9 Inskip diary, 17 Sept.
10 Inskip diary, 17 Sept.
11 CAB 53/41, COS 773. 24 Sept.
12 CAB 53/41, COS 770. 23 Sept.
13 CAB 53/41, COS 772. 24 Sept.
14 CAB 27/646. 15 Sept.
15 CAB 27/646, 15 Sept (see below, p. 361).
16 *Diaries of Oliver Harvey,* pp. 180–1.
17 Chamberlain, Simon, Hoare, Halifax, with Lord Runciman, Vansittart, Cadogan and Wilson in attendance.
18 CAB 27/646, 16 Sept.
19 16 Sept, CAB 27/646.
20 16 Sept, CAB 27/646.

Q

21   Inskip diary, 17 Sept.
22   Inskip diary, 17 Sept.
23   17 Sept, CAB 23/95.
24   *Diaries of Oliver Harvey*, p. 181.
25   *Diaries of Oliver Harvey*, p. 188.
26   9 Sept, CAB 53/41, COS 764 *et seq.*
27   *DBFP*, series 3, vol. 2, p. 453. 21 Sept.
28   *Diaries of Oliver Harvey*, p. 180.
29   Chamberlain's report to the Cabinet, 19 Sept. CAB 23/95.
30   *DBFP*, series 3, vol. 2, p. 369.
31   19 Sept, CAB 23/95.
32   Templewood papers, X5.
33   Northedge, *The Troubled Giant*, p. 529.
34   Vansittart papers, 17 Sept.
35   Max Beloff, *The Foreign Policy of Soviet Russia*, 2 vols (London 1947–49) vol. 2, p. 156.
36   *DBFP*, series 3, vol. 2, pp. 404–6.
37   Duff Cooper, *Old Men Forget*, p. 231.
38   Inskip diary, 19 Sept.
39   19 Sept, CAB 23/95.
40   19 Sept, CAB 23/95.
41   19 Sept, CAB 23/95.
42   19 Sept, CAB 23/95.
43   Inskip diary, 19 Sept.
44   19 Sept, CAB 23/95.
45   19 Sept, CAB 23/95.
46   *DBFP*, series 3, vol. 2, p. 336.
47   C7512/1941/18.
48   C8118 and 8872/1941/18.
49   See Luza, *Transfer of the Sudeten Germans*, pp. 141–2, and Robbins, *Munich, 1938*, p. 264.
50   *DGFP*, series D, vol. 2, pp. 801–2.
51   *DGFP*, series D, vol. 2, p. 826.
52   *DBFP*, series 3, vol. 2, p. 332.
53   Royal Institute of International Affairs, *Survey 1938*, vol. 2, p. 315.
54   *DBFP*, series 3, vol. 2, p. 358.
55   Files C4851 to 9818/1941/18.
56   *DBFP*, series 3, vol. 2, p. 425.
57   *DBFP*, series 3, vol. 2, p. 425 (20 Sept).
58   *DBFP*, series 3, vol. 2, pp. 437–8.
59   PREM 1/242.
59a   PREM 1/266A and Wilson Memorandum confirm that he was mainly responsible for drawing up the document.
60   PREM 1/266A.

61 CAB 53/42, COS 766.
62 CAB 27/646.
63 CAB 27/646.
64 CAB 23/95.
65 *Diaries of Oliver Harvey*, p. 192.
66 CAB 23/95.
67 C10114/1941/18 (19 Sept).
68 CAB 23/95.
69 Wilson Memorandum.
70 Schmidt, *Hitler's Interpreter*, p. 96.
71 *DGFP*, series D, vol. 2, p. 875.
72 Wilson Memorandum.
73 Wilson Memorandum—'P.M. much disturbed.'
74 Wilson Memorandum.
75 Speer, *Inside the Third Reich*, p. 100.
76 Luza, *Transfer of the Sudeten Germans*, p. 144.
77 *DGFP*, series D, vol. 2, p. 806.
78 *Diaries of Oliver Harvey*, p. 181.
79 *DGFP*, series D, vol. 2, p. 901.
80 Wilson Memorandum.
81 Kirkpatrick, *Inner Circle*, p. 122.
82 CAB 27/646. 16 Sept.

CHAPTER 13: *The Price of Peace*

1 Madge and Harrisson, *Mass Observation*, pp. 4–5.
2 22 Sept 1938
3 21 Sept 1938.
4 *DGFP*, series D, vol. 2, p. 886.
5 22 Sept, CAB 27/646.
6 *DBFP*, series 3, vol. 2, pp. 457–8.
7 CAB 53/41, COS 765.
8 CAB 27/646.
9 22 Sept, CAB 27/646.
10 22 Sept, CAB 27/646.
11 23 Sept, CAB 27/646.
12 CAB 27/646.
13 *DBFP*, series 3, vol. 2, nos 1022 and 1023, p. 459, and telegram 284 unprinted.
14 *DBFP*, series 3, vol. 2, p. 461.
15 23 Sept, CAB 27/646.
16 23 Sept, CAB 27/646.
17 23 Sept, CAB 27/646.
18 *DBFP*, series 3, vol. 2, p. 490.
19 *DBFP*, series 3, vol. 2, p. 462.

20 24 Sept, CAB 27/646.
21 24 Sept, CAB 27/646.
22 24 Sept, CAB 27/646.
23 24 Sept, CAB 27/646.
24 Templewood papers, X5.
25 Birkenhead, *Halifax*, p. 399.
26 24 Sept, CAB 23/95.
27 24 Sept, CAB 23/95.
28 Templewood papers, X5.
29 Duff Cooper, *Old Men Forget*, p. 235.
30 Amery, *My Political Life*, vol. III, pp. 268–9.
31 PREM 1/266A.
32 James, *Churchill, A Study in Failure*, p. 336; Lady Asquith in the *Daily Telegraph*, 12 Mar 1965.
33 Birkenhead, *Halifax*, p. 400.
34 CAB 23/95.
35 Birkenhead, *Halifax*, p. 401.
36 *DBFP*, series 3, vol. 2, p. 510.
37 *DBFP*, series 3, vol. 2, pp. 497–9.
38 *DBFP*, series 3, vol. 2, p. 498.
39 CAB 27/646. 23 Sept.
40 cf. Northedge, *The Troubled Giant*, p. 534.
41 *New Documents on the History of Munich* (Prague 1958), vol. 2, no. 29.
42 Luza, *Transfer of the Sudeten Germans*, p. 146.
43 *DBFP*, series 3, vol. 2, p. 301.
44 *FRUS* (1938), vol. 1, pp. 595–6, 600–1.
45 H. L. Ickes, *Secret Diary* (New York 1955), vol. 2, pp. 467–9.
46 Lindsay to Halifax. *DBFP*, series 3, vol. 7, pp. 627–9.
47 *DBFP*, series 3, vol. 7, p. 630.
48 *FRUS* (1938), vol. 1, pp. 657–8.
49 Templewood Papers, XIX6.
50 PREM 1/242.
51 23 Sept, CAB 27/646.
52 25 Sept, CAB 23/95.
53 26 Sept, CAB 23/95.
54 Noguères, *Munich*, p. 179.
55 Templewood papers, X5.
56 Wilson Memorandum.
57 26 Sept, CAB 23/95.
58 25 Sept, CAB 23/95.
59 25 Sept, CAB 23/95.
59a An idea for which Hoare claimed credit (Templewood papers, X5).
60 28 Sept, CAB 23/95. Author's italics.

61 *Royal Institute of International Affairs, Documents 1938*, vol. 2, p. 261.
62 Templewood papers, X5.
63 Duff Cooper, *Old Men Forget*, pp. 237-8.
63a Hankey papers.
64 *The Private Papers of Hore-Belisha*, ed. R. J. Minney, p. 148.
64a 27 Sept, CAB 27/646. Wilson's decision was approved by Henderson and Kirkpatrick (Wilson Memorandum).
65 *The Speeches of Adolf Hitler 1922-39*, ed. N. H. Baynes (London 1942) vol. 2, pp. 1508-27.
66 Wilson Memorandum. Also 27 Sept, CAB 23/95.
67 Wilson Memorandum. Also 27 Sept, CAB 23/95.
68 27 Sept, CAB 23/95.
69 27 Sept, CAB 23/95.
70 27 Sept, CAB 27/646.
71 *DBFP*, series 3, vol. 2, p. 558.
72 CAB 27/646.
73 CAB 27/646.
74 CAB 27/646. The actual telegrams are given in *DBFP*, series 3, vol. 2, p. 570.
75 CAB 53/41, COS 765, 24 Sept.
76 CAB 53/41, COS 773.
77 CAB 53/41, COS 772.
78 *DBFP*, series 3, vol. 2, pp. 512-13.
79 Henderson, *Failure of a Mission*, p. 161.
80 *DBFP*, series 3, vol. 2, p. 578; also FO 408/68, pp. 198-9.
81 CAB 23/95.
82 CAB 23/95.
83 27 Sept, CAB 23/95, Appendix.
84 *FRUS* (1938), vol. 1, pp. 679-80.
85 *DBFP*, series 3, vol. 2, pp. 618-20.
86 *FRUS* (1938), vol. 1, pp. 680-1.
87 *DBFP*, series 3, vol. 2, pp. 582-3.
88 Offner, *American Appeasement*, p. 267.
89 *DGFP*, series D, vol. 2, pp. 981-2.
90 21 Sept, CAB 23/95.
91 C10114/1941/18 (FO 371/21739). 19 Sept.
92 *DBFP*, series 3, vol. 2, p. 561.
93 Wilson Memorandum.
94 *DBFP*, series 3, vol. 2, p. 603.
95 Schmidt, *Hitler's Interpreter*, p. 106.
96 *DBFP*, series 3, vol. 2, p. 587.
97 See General Jodl's diary, quoted in Robertson, *Hitler's Pre-War Policy*, p. 148.
97a *DBFP*, series 3, vol. 2, p. 578.

98 *DBFP*, series 3, vol. 2, p. 599.
99 *DBFP*, series 3, vol. 2, p. 601.
100 30 Sept, CAB 23/95.
101 Wilson Memorandum.
102 *Memoirs of Ernst von Weizsäcker*, trans. J. Andrews (London 1951) p. 154.
103 30 Sept, CAB 23/95.
104 Strang, *Home and Abroad*, pp. 146–7.
105 Chamberlain letters, 30 Sept.
106 Lord Swinton, *Sixty Years of Power* (London 1966), p. 120.
107 Feiling, *Neville Chamberlain*, p. 456.
108 30 Sept, CAB 23/95.
109 Vansittart papers.
110 30 Sept, CAB 23/95.
111 *Manchester Guardian* 1 Oct. See also Robbins, *Munich, 1938*, p. 327.
112 Templewood papers, XIX6, 30 Sept.
113 Templewood papers, XIX6, 30 Sept.
114 *The Roosevelt Letters*, ed. E. Roosevelt, 2 vols (London 1952), vol. 2, pp. 243 and 244.
115 *FRUS* (1938), vol. 1, p. 688.
116 Offner, *American Appeasement*, p. 269.
117 Chamberlain papers, 30 Sept 1938.

CHAPTER 14: *Reckoning*

1 Northedge, *The Troubled Giant*, p. 548.
2 Watt, 'Appeasement: the Rise of a Revisionist School?', *Political Quarterly* (April–June 1965) p. 212.
3 Feiling, *Neville Chamberlain*, p. 453.
4 Chamberlain letters, 22 Oct. 1938.
5 P1259/4/150 (FO 395/561).
6 Wheeler-Bennett, *Munich*, p. 433.
7 Templewood papers, X5, 5 Oct 1938.
8 Feiling, *Neville Chamberlain*, p. 385.
9 *The Times*, 28 Oct 1938.
10 Birkenhead, *Halifax*, p. 407.
11 Birkenhead, *Halifax*, pp. 453–5.
12 Chamberlain letters, 16 Oct 1938.
13 Murray to Lady Asquith, 7 Mar 1939. Quoted in Gilbert and Gott, *The Appeasers*, p. 227.
14 Ismay, *Memoirs* (London 1960) p. 92.
15 16 Dec, COS 809 (CAB 53/43).
16 19 Oct, CAB 23/96 (CP219/38).
17 3 Oct, CAB 23/95.

18 31 Oct, CAB 23/96.
19 *Hansard,* 5th series, vol. 340, col. 87.
20 *Hansard,* 5th series, vol. 344, cols 234–5.
21 Sir John Wheeler-Bennett, *King George VI* (London 1958) pp. 357–8.
22 7 Nov, CAB 23/96.
23 *Hansard,* 5th series, vol. 341, col. 353. 10 Nov.
24 14 Dec, CAB 23/96.
24a T/175/101 8 Nov 1938.
24b PREM 1/252 25 Oct 1938.
25 25 Jan, CAB 23/97.
26 Pownall diary, 3 Oct.
27 CP 247/38.
28 *Hansard,* 5th series, vol. 340, col. 86.
29 *Private Papers of Hore-Belisha,* ed. R. J. Minney, p. 164.
30 COS 825 (CAB 53/43).
31 Pownall diary, 14 Dec.
32 14 Dec, CAB 23/96.
33 COS 827–830 (CAB 53/43).
34 2 Feb, CAB 23/97.
35 22 Feb, CAB 23/97.
36 Pownall diary, 6 May.
37 General Sir Gifford Martel, *An Outspoken Soldier* (London 1949), pp. 134–5.
38 C14471/41/18 (FO 371/21659).
39 C14471/41/18 (FO 371/21659).
40 COS 789 (CAB 53/42).
41 C12747/1941/18.
42 C14471/41/18 (FO 371/21659).
43 C15689/95/62 (FO 371/21627).
44 14 Nov, CAB 27/624.
45 14 Nov, CAB 27/624.
46 *DBFP,* series 3, vol. 3, pp. 251–3.
47 Chamberlain letters, 6 Nov 1938.
48 *DBFP,* series 3, vol. 3, pp. 278–9.
49 C14256/42/18 (FO 371/21658), 10 Nov.
50 *DBFP,* series 3, vol. 3, pp. 589–90.
51 C14809/62/18 (FO 371/21665).
52 C14809/62/18 (FO 371/21665).
53 16 Nov, CAB 23/96.
54 26 Oct, CAB 23/96.
55 21 Dec, CAB 23/96.
56 18 Jan, CAB 23/97.
57 18 Jan, CAB 23/97.
58 Chamberlain letters, 11 Dec 1938.

59 Gilbert and Gott, *The Appeasers,* pp. 193–208.
60 23 Jan, CAB 27/624.
61 CP20/39. 26 Jan, CAB 27/624.
62 *DBFP,* series 3, vol. 4, p. 50.
63 *DBFP,* series 3, vol. 4, pp. 52 and 66.
64 Chamberlain letters, 12 Feb 1939.
65 *Hansard,* 5th series, vol. 343, col. 623.
66 *FRUS* (1939), vol. 1, p. 18.
67 *DBFP,* series 3, vol. 4, pp. 70–1.
68 *DBFP,* series 3, vol. 4, pp. 120–2, 163–5.
69 15 Mar, CAB 23/98.
70 *The Times,* 18 Mar 1939.
71 18 Mar, CAB 23/98.
72 20 Mar, CAB 23/98.
73 27 Mar, CAB 27/624.
74 20 Mar, CAB 23/98.
75 27 Mar, CAB 27/624.
76 27 Mar, CAB 27/624.
77 22 Nov 1938, CAB 23/96.
78 *DBFP,* series 3, vol. 2, p. 599 (28 Sept 1938).
79 Birkenhead, *Halifax,* p. 437.
80 30 Mar, CAB 23/98.
81 24 May, CAB 23/99.
82 Inskip diary, 23 Aug.
83 Inskip diary, 26 Aug.
84 *FRUS* (1938), vol. 1, p. 688.
85 *FRUS* (1938), vol. 1, pp. 704–7.
86 *FRUS* (1939), vol. 1, pp. 130–3.
87 Offner, *American Appeasement,* p. 279.
88 19 Oct, CAB 23/96.
89 Inskip diary, 11 Jan 1939.
90 Hankey papers.
91 C13414/5302/18 (FO 371/21778).
92 COS 887 (FP 36/82), 24 Apr 1939.
93 *DBFP,* series 3, vol. 4, pp. 123–4.
94 *DBFP,* series 3, vol. 8, pp. 343–4.
95 *DBFP,* series 3, vol. 8, pp. 137–8.
96 e.g. C14471/42/18 (FO 371/21659).
97 *DBFP,* series 3, vol. 8, pp. 355–8.
98 *DGFP,* series D, vol. 4, p. 99.
99 *DGFP,* series D, vol. 4, pp. 185–6.
100 A. S. Milward, *The German Economy at War* (London 1965), pp. 8–12.
101 Chamberlain diary, Dec 1939.
102 Feiling, *Neville Chamberlain,* p. 456.

103 Chamberlain letters, 25 June 1938.
103a Beaverbrook dubbed Halifax 'the holy fox'. (R. Young, *Churchill and Beaverbrook*, p. 174).
104 *FRUS* (1938), vol. 2, p. 85.
105 Birkenhead, *Halifax*, p. 421.
105a I am indebted to Captain Stephen Roskill for this account.
106 Inskip diary, 2 Sept 1939.
107 *Hansard*, 5th series, vol. 339, debate of 3 Oct.
108 Noguères, *Munich*, p. 321.
109 Macmillan, *Tides of Fortune*, p. 567.
110 Chamberlain letters, 9 Oct 1938.
111 *Diaries of Oliver Harvey*, p. 226 (11 Dec).
112 *Diaries of Oliver Harvey*, p. 212 (10 Oct).
113 Templewood papers, X5.
114 Wheeler-Bennett, *Munich*, pp. 354–5.
115 F. S. Northedge, in *International Affairs*, Jan 1970, p. 38.
116 Colvin, *Vansittart in Office*, p. 286.
117 9 Nov, C14471/42/18 (FO 371/21659).
118 *Hansard*, vol. 286, col. 2074 (3rd series) 8 Mar 1934.

Bibliography

Unpublished Documents

British Government Archives, available in the Public Record Office, London, in various categories, especially:
Cabinet:
Minutes and conclusions (CAB 23)
Cabinet Committees (CAB 27)
Committee of Imperial Defence:
Minutes and reports (CAB 2 *et seq*)
Reports of Chiefs of Staff and other sub-committees (CAB 50 *et seq*)
Prime Minister:
Various files (PREM)
Foreign Office:
General correspondence and minutes, in particular FO 371
Green papers
Confidential prints
Treasury:
Sir Richard Hopkins papers.

PRIVATE COLLECTIONS
Neville Chamberlain papers; especially his manuscript diaries and letters to his sisters (to be available at Birmingham University Library).
Thomas Jones (National Library of Wales, Aberystwyth).
Sir Thomas Inskip, diary (Churchill College, Cambridge).
Major-General Pownall, diary (J. W. Pownall-Grey Esq.)
Lord Templewood (Sir Samuel Hoare) (Cambridge University Library).
Lord Vansittart, miscellaneous papers (Churchill College, Cambridge).

Published Documents

Czechoslovak Republic and the Union of Soviet Socialist Republics, *New Documents on the History of Munich* (Prague, Orbis, 1958).
Documents on British Foreign Policy 1919–1939 (HMSO).
Documents on German Foreign Policy 1918–45, series D, vols I and II (HMSO).

Foreign Relations of the United States (Washington DC, US Government Printing Office).

International Military Tribunal, *Trial of the Major War Criminals before the International Military Tribunal, 14 November 1945 to 1 October 1946,* 42 volumes (Nuremburg, IMT, 1947–9).

Parliamentary Debates (House of Commons).

Royal Institute of International Affairs, *Documents on International Affairs 1938,* vols. I and II (London, 1942–3).

Soviet Documents on Foreign Policy, vol. II (London 1953).

Various newspapers and periodicals, notably *The Times, Manchester Guardian, Daily Herald, New Statesman and Nation* and *Daily Telegraph.*

Other Published Works

MEMOIRS

Amery, L. S., *My Political Life,* vol. III (London 1955).

Avon, Earl of (Anthony Eden), *Facing the Dictators* (London 1962).

—, *The Reckoning* (London 1965).

Beneš, Eduard, *Memoirs: From Munich to New War and New Victory* (Boston 1954).

Bonnet, Georges, *Défense de la Paix: de Washington au Quai D'Orsay* (Geneva 1946).

Boothby, R., *I Fight to Live* (London 1947).

Churchill, Winston S., *The Gathering Storm* (London 1948).

Ciano, Count Galeazzo, *Ciano's Diary 1937–38,* ed. M. Muggeridge (London 1952).

Cooper, Alfred Duff, *Old Men Forget* (London 1953).

Cot, Pierre, *Triumph of Treason* (Chicago 1944).

Dalton, Hugh, *The Fateful Years* (London 1957).

Gamelin, General Maurice, *Servir,* vol. II (Paris 1946).

Halifax, Earl of, *Fullness of Days* (London 1957).

Harvey, Oliver, *Diplomatic Diaries, 1937–40* (London 1970).

Henderson, Sir Nevile, *Failure of a Mission* (London 1940).

Hitler, Adolf, *Mein Kampf* (London 1939).

—, *Second Book* (New York 1962).

Hore-Belisha, L., *The Private Papers of Hore-Belisha,* ed. R. J. Minney (London 1960).

Hossbach, Friedrich, *Zwischen Wehrmacht und Hitler* (Hanover 1949).

Hull, C., *Memoirs,* 2 vols (New York 1948).

Ickes, H. L., *Secret Diary* (London 1955).

The Ironside Diaries 1937–40, ed. R. Macleod and Denis Kelly (London 1962).

Ismay, Lord, *Memoirs* (London 1960).

Jones, Thomas, *A Diary with Letters* (London 1954).

Keitel, Field-Marshal, *The Memoirs of Field-Marshal Keitel*, ed.
   Walter Görlitz (New York 1966).
Kirkpatrick, Sir I., *The Inner Circle* (London 1959).
Kordt, Erich, *Wahn und Wirklichkeit* (Stuttgart 1948).
Liddell Hart, B. H., *Memoirs*, 2 vols (London 1965).
Macmillan, Harold, *Winds of Change* (London 1966).
Maisky, Ivan, *Who Helped Hitler?* (London 1964).
Nicolson, Sir Harold, *Diaries and Letters, 1930–1939*, ed. Nigel
   Nicolson (London 1966).
—, *Diaries and Letters, 1939–1945*, ed. Nigel Nicolson (London 1966).
Raeder, Grand Admiral Erich, *My Life* (Annapolis 1960).
Ribbentrop, Joachim von, *The Ribbentrop Memoirs* (London 1954).
Schellenberg, W., *Memoirs* (London 1956).
Schmidt, Dr Paul, *Hitler's Interpreter* (London 1951).
Selby, Sir Walford, *Diplomatic Twilight* (London 1953).
Simon, Viscount (Sir John Simon), *Retrospect* (London 1952).
Slessor, Sir John, *The Central Blue* (London 1956).
Speer, Albert, *Inside the Third Reich* (London 1970).
Strang, Lord, *Home and Abroad* (London 1956).
Swinton, Earl of, *Sixty Years of Power* (London 1966).
Templewood, Viscount (Sir Samuel Hoare), *Nine Troubled Years*
   (London 1954).
Vansittart, Lord, *The Mist Procession* (London 1958).
Weizsäcker, Ernst von, *Memoirs of Ernst von Weizsäcker*, trans. John
   Andrews (London 1951).
Zetland, Marquis of, *Memoirs* (London 1956).

BIOGRAPHIES
Abshagen, K. H., *Canaris* (London 1956).
Birkenhead, Earl of, *Halifax* (London 1965).
Blum, J. M., *From the Morgenthau Diaries* (Boston 1959).
Bowle, John, *Viscount Samuel* (London 1957).
Bullock, Alan, *Hitler: A Study in Tyranny* (London 1959).
Butler, J. R. M., *Lord Lothian* (London 1960).
Clark, R. W., *Tizard* (London 1965).
Colvin, Ian, *Vansittart in Office* (London 1965).
Feiling, Sir Keith, *Life of Neville Chamberlain* (London 1946).
Gilbert, Martin, *Plough My Own Furrow* (London 1965).
Heuston, R. F. V., *Lives of the Lord Chancellors 1885–1940* (Oxford
   1964).
Macleod, Iain, *Neville Chamberlain* (London 1961).
Middlemas, R. K. and Barnes, A. J. L., *Baldwin* (London 1969).
Whelan, R. J., *The Founding Father: John Kennedy* (New York 1964).
Wrench, J. E., *Geoffrey Dawson and Our Times* (London 1955).

SECONDARY SOURCES

Air Ministry, *The Rise and Fall of the German Air Force, 1933–1945* (London 1948).

Beloff, Max, *The Foreign Policy of Soviet Russia 1929–1941*, 2 vols (London 1947).

Bonnet, Georges, *Quai D'Orsay* (London 1965).

Brueghel, J. W., *Tschechen und Deutsche* (Munich 1967).

Butler, J. R. M., *History of the Second World War: U.K. Military Series: Grand Strategy*, vol. II (London 1957).

Carr, E. H., *German-Soviet Relations Between the Two World Wars, 1919–39* (London 1952).

Cato (pseud.), *Guilty Men* (London 1940).

Celovsky, B., *Das Münchener Abkommen von 1938* (Stuttgart 1958).

Chapman, Guy, *Why France Collapsed* (London 1968).

Churchill, Winston S., *Step by Step* (collected articles, 1936–9) (London 1968).

Cienciala, Anna M., *Poland and the Western Powers 1938–39* (London 1968).

Davidson, Eugene, *The Trial of the Germans* (New York 1966).

Deutsch, Harold C., *The Conspiracy against Hitler in the Twilight War* (Minneapolis 1968).

Divine, David, *The Broken Wing: A Study in the British Exercise of Air Power* (London 1966).

Eubank, Keith, *Munich* (Oklahoma 1963).

Flandin, P. E., *Politique Française 1919–40* (Paris 1947).

Furnia, Arthur H., *The Diplomacy of Appeasement* (Washington D.C. 1960).

Gedye, G. E. R., *Fallen Bastions* (London 1939).

George, Margaret, *The Warped Vision: British Foreign Policy 1933–39* (Pittsburgh 1965).

Gilbert, Martin, *Britain and Germany between the Wars* (London 1964).

—, *The Roots of Appeasement* (London 1966).

Gilbert, Martin, and Gott, Richard, *The Appeasers* (London 1963).

Görlitz, Walter, *The German General Staff* (London 1953).

Granzow, B., *A Mirror of Nazism: British Opinion and the Emergence of Hitler 1929–33* (London 1964).

Higham, Robin, *Armed Forces in Peacetime 1918–1939* (London 1962).

Hildebrand, Klaus, *Vom Reich Zum Weltreich, Hitler NSDAP und Kolonial Frage 1919–45* (Munich 1969).

—, *Deutsche Aussenpolitik, Kalkül oder Dogma* (Stuttgart 1970).

Hillgruber, A., *Hitlers Strategie 1940–41* (Frankfurt 1965).

Hinsley, F. H., *Hitler's Strategy* (Cambridge 1951).

Hitler, Adolf, *The Speeches of Adolf Hitler 1922–39*, ed. N. H. Baynes, 2 vols (London 1942).

Hitler, Adolf, *Hitler's Table Talk,* trans. N. Cameron and R. Steven (London 1953).

Jacobsen, H. A., *Nationalsocialistische Aussenpolitik 1933-38* (Frankfurt 1968).

Johnson, J. F., *Defence by Committee* (London 1960).

Kennan, George, *Russia and the West* (Boston 1960).

Kennedy, John F., *Why England Slept* (London 1940).

Kimche, John, *The Unfought Battle* (London 1968).

Klein, B., *Germany's Economic Preparations for War* (Cambridge, Mass., 1959).

La Gorce, Paul-Marie de, *The French Army* (London 1963).

Langer, W. L., and Gleason, S. E., *The Challenge to Isolation 1937-40,* 2 vols (New York 1964).

Liddell Hart, B. H., *The Defence of Britain* (London 1939).

—, *The German Generals Talk* (New York 1948).

— (ed.), *The Soviet Army* (London 1956).

Luza, Radomir, *The Transfer of the Sudeten Germans* (New York 1964).

Madge, C., and Harrisson, T., *Britain by Mass Observation* (London 1939).

Maisky, Ivan, *Who Helped Hitler?* (London 1964).

Medlicott, W. N., *From Metternich to Hitler* (London 1963).

—, *History of the Second World War: United Kingdom, Civil Series: The Economic Blockade,* vol. 1 (London 1952).

Mendelssohn, Peter de, *The Nuremburg Documents* (London 1946).

Milward, A. S., *The German Economy at War* (London 1965).

Namier, Sir Lewis B., *Europe in Decay* (London 1950).

—, *Diplomatic Prelude 1938-39* (London 1948).

—, *In the Nazi Era* (London 1952).

Noguères, Henri, *Munich* (New York 1965).

Northedge, F. S., *The Troubled Giant: Britain among the Great Powers 1916-39* (London 1966).

Offner, Arnold, *American Appeasement: United States Foreign Policy and Germany 1933-38* (Cambridge, Mass., 1969).

O'Neill, R. J., *The German Army and the Nazi Party 1933-39* (London 1966).

'Pertinax' (Géraud André), *The Grave-Diggers of France* (New York 1944).

Peterson, E. N., *The Limits of Hitler's Power* (Princeton 1969).

Postan, M. M., *History of the Second World War: United Kingdom, Civil Series: British War Production* (London 1952).

Prittie, Terence, *Germans Against Hitler* (London 1964).

Pyper, C. B., *Chamberlain and His Critics* (London 1962).

Rhodes James, R. V., *Churchill, a Study in Failure* (London 1970)

Ritter, Gerhard, *The German Resistance* (London 1958).

Robbins, Keith, *Munich, 1938* (London 1968).

Robertson, E. M., *Hitler's Pre-War Policy and Military Plans, 1933–39* (London 1963).
Rock, William R., *Appeasement on Trial* (New York 1966).
Roosevelt, Franklin D., *F. D. R.: His Personal Letters 1928–45*, ed. Elliot Roosevelt, 2 vols (New York 1950).
Roskill, Captain S. W., *Naval Policy between the Wars* (London 1968).
Rothfels, Hans, *The German Opposition to Hitler, an Appraisal* (Hinsdale, Ill., 1948).
Rothstein, Andrew, *The Munich Conspiracy* (London 1958).
—, *British Foreign Policy and its Critics 1830–1950* (London 1969).
Rowse, A. L., *Appeasement—A Study in Political Decline 1933–1939* (London 1961).
Royal Institute of International Affairs, *Survey of International Affairs, 1939* (London 1951).
Schweitzer, A., *Big Business in the Third Reich* (Bloomington, Ind., 1964).
Seabury, Paul, *The Wilhelmstrasse, German Diplomats under the Nazi Regime* (Berkeley 1954).
Shirer, William L., *The Collapse of the Third Republic* (New York 1969).
Spier, E., *Focus: A Footnote on the History of the Thirties* (London 1963).
Strong, Major-General Sir Kenneth, *Intelligence at the Top* (London 1968).
Taylor, A. J. P., *The Origins of the Second World War* (London 1961).
Taylor, Telford, *Sword and Swastika* (New York 1952).
—, *The Breaking Wave* (London 1967).
Thorne, Christopher, *The Approach to War, 1938–9* (London 1967).
Tissier, Pierre, *The Riom Trial* (London 1942).
Watt, D. C., *Personalities and Policies* (London 1965).
Webster, Sir Charles, and Frankland, Noble, *The Strategic Air Offensive Against Germany, 1939–45*, vol. 1 (London 1961).
Wendt, B. J., *Appeasement 1938* (Frankfurt/M 1966).
Wheeler-Bennett, Sir John, *Munich, Prologue to Tragedy* (London 1948).
—, *The Nemesis of Power: The German Army in Politics 1918–1945* (London 1954).
Wiskemann, Elizabeth, *The Rome–Berlin Axis* (London 1966).
—, *Europe of the Dictators* (London 1966).
—, *Czechs and Germans* (London 1967).
—, *Germany's Eastern Neighbours* (London 1956).

ARTICLES

Adams, D. B., 'Munich: British Cabinet Papers', *History of the 20th Century*, LIX (March 1969).

Bakurin, Martin, 'The United States and Munich', *International Affairs* (Moscow) v (April 1959).

Beaumont, Maurice, 'French Critics and Apologists Debate Munich', *Foreign Affairs*, xxv (July 1947).

Brueghel, J. W., 'German Diplomacy and the Sudeten Question before 1938', *International Affairs*, vol. 37 (1961).

Fergusson, Gilbert, 'Munich: The British and French Roles', *International Affairs*, xliv (October 1968).

Haight, John McVickar, Jr, 'France, the United States and the Munich Crisis,' *Journal of Modern History*, xxxii (December 1960).

Robbins, K. G., 'Konrad Henlein, the Sudeten Question and British Foreign Policy', *Historical Journal*, xii, 4 (1969).

Schmitt, Bernadotte E., 'Munich', *Journal of Modern History*, xxv (June 1953).

Sontag, Raymond J., 'The Origins of the Second World War', *Review of Politics*, xxv (October 1963).

Stronge, Brigadier H. C. T., 'The Military Approach to Munich', *The Times*, September 1967.

Taborsky, Edward, 'The Triumph and Disaster of Edward Beneš', *Foreign Affairs*, xxxvi (July 1958).

Taylor, A. J. P., 'The Myths of Munich', *History of the 20th Century*, lix (March 1969).

Vital, David, 'Czechoslovakia and the Powers, September 1938', *Journal of Contemporary History*, i (November 1966).

Wallace, W. V., 'The Foreign Policy of President Beneš in the Approach to Munich', *Slavonic and East European Review*, xxxix (1960).

—, 'The Making of the May Crisis of 1938', *Slavonic and East European Review*, vol. 41 (June 1963).

Watt, D. C., 'Appeasement: The Rise of a Revisionist School?', *Political Quarterly* (April-June 1965).

—, 'The May Crisis 1938, A Rejoinder to Mr Wallace', *Slavonic and East European Review* (July 1966).

—, 'The Rome–Berlin Axis 1936–40: Myth and Reality', *Review of Politics* (October 1960).

Webster, Sir Charles, 'Munich Reconsidered: A Survey of British Policy', *International Affairs* (London) xxxvii (1961).

Index

National Defence Contribution, 56
National Defence Loan, 108n, 127
National Expenditure Committee, 415
National Industrial Conference, 1919, 82
National Voluntary Scheme, 415
Navy, Royal, 16, 19, 21–2, 30, 89n, 169n, 311, 328, 376, 453; Anglo-French staff talks, 218, 251; anti-submarine defence, 222n; expansion of, 33, 34, 35, 251–2, 423; fleet manoeuvres, 314; inter-service rivalries, 86, 116, 117, 118, 216, 250; mobilisation, 389, 391; New Standard, 119, 120, 123, 124, 251, 252; Two-Power Standard, 423; see also defence
Nazi-Soviet Pact, 446
Nehru, Pandit, 282
Neurath, Konstantin Freiherr von, 40, 43, 49, 115, 116, 135, 137, 148, 165, 169 & n, 171, 173, 306, 402
New Deal (USA), 24, 127
'New Imperialists', 98–9
New Statesman, 101, 206, 288
New Zealand, 21, 22, 23, 31, 68, 131, 190, 196, 211–12, 282, 442
News Chronicle, 101, 102n, 288, 407
Newall, Air Marshal Sir Cyril, 87, 283
Newton, Basil (British Minister in Prague), 71, 113n, 137, 187, 189, 203, 208, 224, 229–30, 231, 233, 234, 236, 237, 245, 248, 253 & n, 254 & n, 262, 263, 264, 270n, 278, 317, 318, 320, 354, 356, 358, 359, 360, 371, 372, 382, 401
Nicolson, Harold, 291
Nine-Power Treaty (1922), 30; 1937 conference, 78, 133, 144
Next Five Years Group, 99
Noel-Baker, Philip, 290
Nuremberg Rally (of Nazi Party), 1937: 133, 164; 1938: 264, 271, 272, 275, 278, 288, 293, 298, 303n, 304, 305, 313, 321, 323, 325, 326n; Hitler's speech at (1938), 330–1, 357
Nuremberg Trial, 171, 303, 306
Nyon Conference (1937), 130–1, 176, 282

Observer, 98, 101, 323–4
Ormsby-Gore, W., (later: Lord Harlech), 65, 66, 113, 114n, 142n, 146, 153n, 155, 183n, 191, 201, 249, 316
Osusky, Stefan, 359

Ottawa Conference (1932), 12, 49
Overseas Defence Committee *see* CID

Pacific Security Pact, 23
Palestine, 32, 212, 431, 433, 436
Papen, Franz von, 49 & n, 167, 177
Parliamentary Labour Party *see* Labour Party
Perth, Lord, 71, 130, 150, 152, 154, 156, 234, 398, 399
Phillips, US Ambassador (in Rome), 398n, 408
Phipps, Sir Eric (British Ambassador in Paris), 40, 71, 72 & n, 113n, 115, 160n, 193, 202–3, 207, 223, 225, 228, 248, 253, 275, 283, 319, 320, 323, 331, 350, 359, 380–1, 391, 397 & n, 398, 401n, 407, 434, 443
Pirow, Oswald (South African Defence Minister), 86n, 281, 282
Plymouth, Lord, 111
Poland, 15, 71, 260n; British policy, 3, 184n, 200, 414, 419, 439–40, 442, 443, 446, 457; East European security, 28, 38, 39; French Pact with, 20, 430, 434; German Agreement (1934), 162, 436; minority claims in Czechoslovakia, 244, 337, 347, 354, 355, 358, 360, 362, 364–5, 367, 375, 401, 403, 405, 435n, 441; Russia and, 39, 200, 238, 319 & n, 354, 381–2
Popular Front (in France), 24
Portugal, 139, 142, 429, 431
Potemkin, N. A., 319n
Pownall, Major-General, 88–9 & n, 295, 427n, 428
press, British, Czech crisis and, 206, 210, 288–9, 323–4, 339, 347, 355, 370, 374, 388, 406; influence on policy-makers of, 95, 101–4, 108; post-Munich, 414, 415, 427
Price, Ward, 245n
Principal Supply Officers Committee, 82, 85
public opinion, British, 15, 95–101, 105 & n, 108–9, 247, 286–7, 318, 323–4, 370, 374, 401, 407, 412, 451, 452; Gallup Polls, 417 & n, 419 & n; Mass Observation Surveys, 370, 416, 417 & n; national unity after Munich, 413, 414–19

Raeder, Admiral, 171, 172, 302, 400
Rath, Baron Ernst von, murder of, 435
Reading, Lord, 70